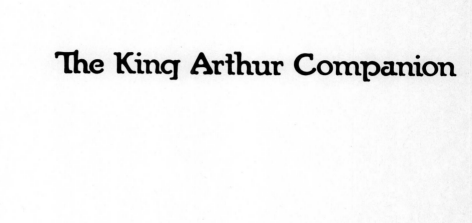

The King Arthur Companion

The
King Arthur
Companion

The Legendary World of Camelot and the Round Table as Revealed by the Tales Themselves,
Discussed and Related by the Authoress with Warm Concern,
The Greatest and the Humblest in the Realm, Interpreted in Hundreds of Entries
Arranged Alphabetically for Convenient, Secure Reference and Pleasure.

by

Phyllis Ann Karr

ISBN 0-8359-3698-8

Special thanks are extended to the following individuals and institutions for permission of quote from or to otherwise employ materials owned by them: to Carnegie Institution of Washington (D.C.), for *The Vulgate Version of the Arthurian Romances* (8 vols.), ed. by H. Oskar Sommer, 1909-1916; to Charles Scribner's Sons, for *The Realms of Arthur,* by Helen Hill Miller, 1969; to The University of Chicago Press, for *The Complete Works of the Gawain Poet,* by John Gardner, 1965; to The Council of the Early English Text Society, for *Arthurian Localities,* by J. S. Stuart Glennie, 1869; to Mr. Frank Graham, for *A Topographical and Historical Description of Cornwall,* by John Norden, 1728, reprinted 1966; to Harper & Row, Publishers, Inc., for *Reader's Handbook of Famous Names* (2 vols.), by E. Cobham Brewer, 1899, reprinted 1966; to Lyle Stuart, Inc., for *LE MORTE DARTHUR,* in an edition by A. W. Pollard, 1920, 1961. Drawings by Aubrey Beardsley are from *Beardsley's Illustrations for LE MORTE DARTHUR,* as arranged by Edmund V. Gillon, Jr., and published by Dover Publications, Inc., 1972.

First Edition 9 8 7 6 5 4 3 2 1

Cover illustration by Jody Lee.
Editorial and layout by Lynn Willis.
Maps by Yurek Chodak.

Contents

Foreword

Arthurian enthusiasm takes two forms — research and storification — and divides into two schools — the realistic and the romantic. This volume is based primarily on the romantic storifications of Malory and the French prose authors who appear to have supplied Malory much of his material. It is not a work for those who are searching for "The Real Arthur," nor is its emphasis on Arthur as the unifier of Britain and the holder back for a generation of the Saxon tide.

The realistic school seems to have been easily the most popular for at least a generation or two. Most of the serious new Arthurian novels coming out concern themselves more or less with recreating "how it might really have been." This school has produced some masterpieces, like Sutcliff's **Sword at Sunset**; but why does there seem to be rather less uniformity in the realistic school than in the romantic? If Arthur existed, why is it so hard to figure out whether he was a Roman, a Briton, a Romano-Briton, an Iron Age youth, or whatever? From what I have read so far, I find the arguments of those who say there probably was no single historical original of Arthur considerably more convincing than the arguments of those who say there must have been. Whether Arthur and those closest to him had historical originals or not, however, is supremely indifferent to me; if anything, I rather hope they did not. The Arthurian legend has a different significance for us in the Twentieth Century than it seems to have had for Malory, for the authors of the versions called the French Vulgate, for Chrétien de Troyes ... No doubt it had a different significance again for those who told the old Welsh and other Celtic tales to which certain Arthurian characters and elements can still be traced (and which I have here taken little account of); no doubt it will have a different significance to the Twenty-Fifth Century. As long as we can find no identifiable, indisputable Arthur, the legend has almost complete freedom to grow, to change, to spread and contract, to be many things to many ages, many readers, many romancers. If it is ever crystallized, captured in one definite span of years and pinned to one historical original, by so much will it lose its fluidity, its universality. At present, it has a mythic, psychological, perhaps racial truth; I, for one, would not like to see that dwindled to a historical truth. In this volume, I have more or less treated Malory and the Vulgate as if they were quasi-historical documents; but I have tried to do so in consciousness that the legend has room for countless other versions and interpretations.

This book grew from research originally commissioned by Greg Stafford for his very enjoyable game **King Arthur's Knights**. To this origin may be traced some of the book's idiosyncracies, especially in the geographical sections. I do not put forward my identifications of various sites and subkingdoms with the authority of those who have done actual work in the field — I suspect there is enough argument among them without that! I do not intend my identification of Winchester with Camelot, for instance, as a serious entry into the debate of whether the real Camelot was at Camelford, Cadbury, Camlan, or somewhere else substantiated by archaeological evidence — I merely say that Malory says it was Winchester, and that is good enough for my purposes. I tried in every case to find plausible identifications; but there was ever the consideration that the finished game board would take in as much of Britain as possible and it would be best to spread out the important sites as much as possible over that playing field. The game would be set after Arthur had driven out the Saxons and settled his kingdom; partly for this reason, and partly because I was not looking for the historical Arthur, you will find little if any attempt in these pages to fix the sites of Arthur's dozen great battles against the Saxons.

This should be a more complete book. But the body of Arthurian literature, both medieval and modern, fictional and nonfictional, is far vaster than the time available, and even while doing the final revision of this volume, I was constantly finding more material that should have been fitted in somewhere.

One of Greg's original questions, for example, had been whether there were any female knights in Arthurian literature; I could only find one more or less probable example of a female knight. Had I begun reading Spenser's **Faerie Queen** in time, I could have increased the list by two undoubted lady knights — Britomart, who plays a major role in the action, and Palladine, who is only mentioned in Book III, Canto VII, but who may have been meant for the "hero" of one of Spenser's unwritten books.

In references to Malory, I have followed the book and chapter divisions called Caxton's. The Roman numeral refers to the book, the Arabic to the chapter. This, of course, can only be helpful to readers who have access to an edition of Malory that is likewise divided according to Caxton; still, some help is better than no help, and the size of the number will at least tell readers about how far into Malory's narrative the incident cited may be found.

Where the words King and Queen stand alone and are capitalized, they refer to Arthur and Guenever. In most cases, I have tried to keep the spelling of names more or less standardized but, in some cases like those of Morgan/Morgana and Guenever/Guenevere, I gave up the attempt and spelled as a medieval author might have in the days before dictionaries. The name of Tristram's love is spelled Isoud in my copy of Malory, so it somehow crept into this volume under that spelling, though I think Isolde is much more graceful. The word "court," as in a monarch's court, should be understood as referring to Arthur's court unless otherwise specified or otherwise obviously attached to another ruler.

Compiling this book has been an education experience for me (and for my mother, who proofread these pages and bore with my oral expoundings); I hope it may add a bit to other readers' appreciation of Arthurian literature.

Rice Lake, Wisconsin
August 3, 1979 / August, 1982

Chief Incidents in the Morte d'Arthur

ABOUT THE TEXT

In general, internal references will be of two kinds. If the reference was only to the last preceding sentence, then the citation will be inside the period concluding that sentence. If the reference is to the last two or more sentences, then the citation will be found outside the last pertinent period.

Scattered throughout the body text of 'People,' 'Places,' and 'Things' are a number of short essays in smaller type. While not major jewels, they are yet too precious not to be included. The only locational criterion used in placing them was that they be arranged in alphabetical order. Their titles occupy the greater portion of the Contents page.

The King Arthur Companion

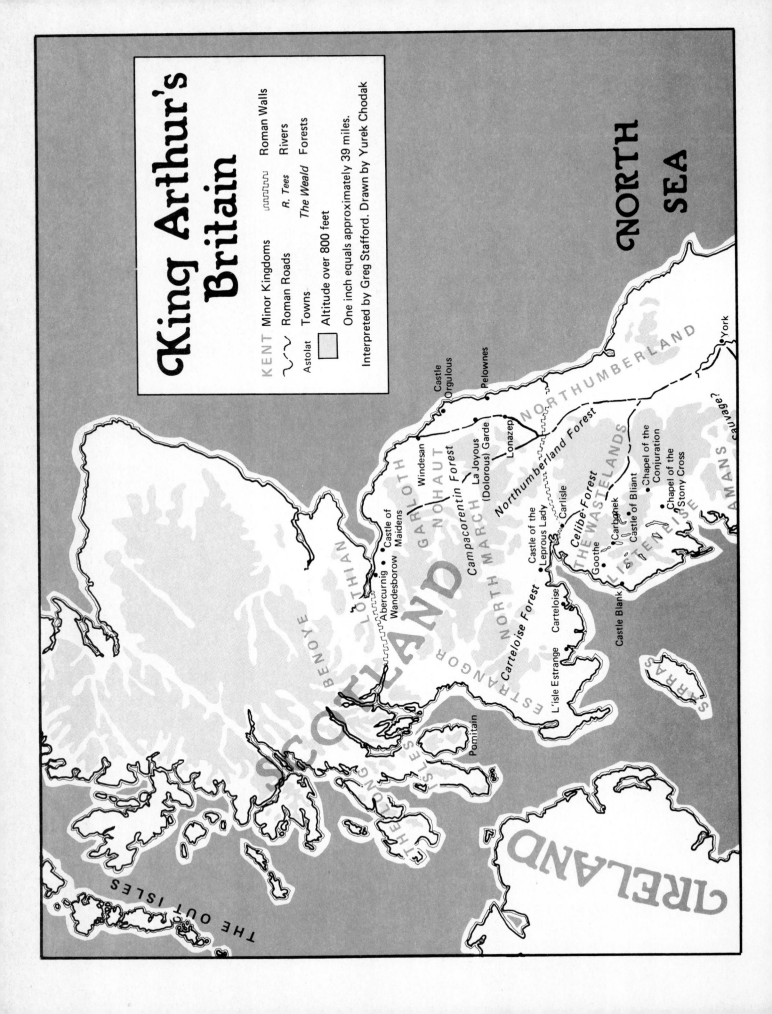

King Arthur's Britain

KENT Minor Kingdoms

Astolat Towns

〰 Roman Roads

ᴗᴗᴗᴗ Roman Walls

R. Tees Rivers

The Weald Forests

▢ Altitude over 800 feet

One inch equals approximately 39 miles.

Interpreted by Greg Stafford. Drawn by Yurek Chodak.

NORTH SEA

York

NORTHUMBERLAND

Castle Orgulous

Pelownes

Lonazep

Northumberland Forest

Windesan

NOHAUT

Campacorentin Forest

La Joyous (Dolorous) Garde

GARLOTH

Castle of the Maidens

Abercurnig

Wandesborow

LOTHIAN

BENOYE

SCOTLAND

NORTH MARCH

ESTRANGOR

Carteloise Forest

Castle of the Leprous Lady

Carlisle

Celibe Forest

THE WASTELANDS

Goothe

Carbonek

Castle of Bliant

Chapel of the Conjuration

Chapel of the Stony Cross

LISTENEISE

SARRAS

AMANS

sauvage?

Castle Blank

Carteloise

L'isle Estrange

Pomitain

THE LONG ISLES

THE OUT ISLES

IRELAND

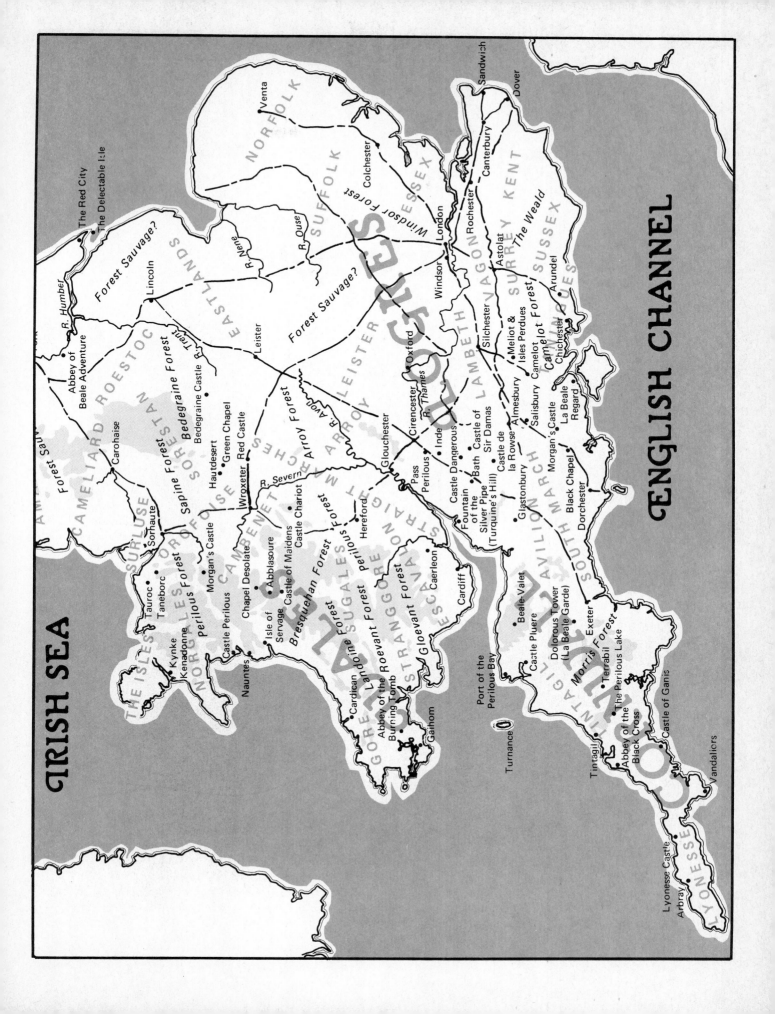

I. People

Introduction

At first I meant to group the character notes into different categories — Knights, Ladies, Kings, Religious, and so on. I quickly noticed, however, that numerous characters fall into more than one likely category. A king, for instance, may well be also a knight of the Round Table, like Uriens or Bagdemagus; indeed, almost all kings are also knights and may be titled "Sir" instead of "King." A knight may retire and become a holy hermit, like Sir Baudwin of Britain. And what of such a woman as Lynette, who, though primarily remembered today as a damsel and the wife either of Gareth or Gaheris, yet displayed enough magical ability to be classified, perhaps, among the enchantresses?

To handle the situation, I decided to divide the People section into two parts. One part, "Groupings," consists, to be blunt, of lists (awful word!): groupings of Knights (Round Table and otherwise), Holy Folk, Kings, Magicians, Ladies, Villains, Giants, and so on. These you will find as an appendix.

The other part makes up the body of the People section — it is sort of a Who's Who in Arthur's World. This section is selective rather than exhaustive, at that; for instance, of at least six Ywaines, I include only two. I discuss minor characters rather more generously if they were females, kings and dukes, villains, giants, retainers or relatives of major figures, and so on than if they simply were knights, even Round Table knights, of whom there is no shortage.

These notes do not pretend to perfect objectivity.

THE ARRANGEMENT

A dagger (†) beside or within a boldface entry indicates that the character is not found in Malory.

A reference to "Malory XIX, 11" means that the man is listed among those who tried unsuccessfully to heal Sir Urre, and is, therefore, presumably a member of the Round Table. I use the terms "knight of the Round Table," "companion of the Round Table," "member of the Round Table," and any other variant you might find completely interchangeably.

I have tried to keep the character notes in alphabetical order. Arthur himself takes his alphabetical place in the A's. The giants, too, are mixed in the other folk; only in the case of the animals have I kept a group separate — the half-dozen named animals of the romances are given their own short bestiary at the end of 'People.' Where spelling is so unstandardized and variants so rife, however, any alphabetical order is tricky. For most of the characters named in Malory, I have tried to use the spelling, or one of the alternate spellings, from Pollard's edition, that being the version I had most readily to hand while assembling this work. In some half-dozen cases I have preferred a variant from Sommer's version of the Vulgate or even from Tennyson, as sounding to me less confusing, more mellifluous, or possibly better-known; in such cases, and elsewhere as they seemed needed, I have tried to provide sufficient cross-references. I have not always adhered consistently to one spelling of a given name; for instance, I have used Morgan and Morgana interchangeably. My own inconsistencies rarely affect the alphabetization.

Titles such as King, Queen, and so on are disregarded in alphabetization, and appellations like "Lady of the Lake" and "Queen of the Out Isles" will be found under the first distinctive word. Examples: Lady of the *L*ake, Queen of the *O*ut Isles, King *A*grippe's Daughter, Damsel des *M*ares, Giant of the *M*ount of Araby. The italicized letter indicates the word under which the entry will be found. I have listed all the Elaines together, regardless of how I found the name spelled (Eleine, Helayne, etc.), but I have not attempted to standardize the masculine version of this popular name. The title "Sir" has been omitted from before the names of most knights, unless used to show that a hermit is a retired knight.

In most cases, a cross-reference like **Mungo†** – **see KENTIGERN** means that this is one character with two different names, while a reference like **Bellagere of Magouns** – **see under ANGLIDES** means that the first-named character has no separate note, but that information about him or her may be found under the second-named character. Some cross-references will send you to the second or third sections of this book, 'Places' or 'Things.'

In a very few cases, a "see under" note means that a character is entered under a different set of alphabetizing rules that those to which I generally adhered: for instance, **La Beale Isoud** – **see under ISOUD.** (One might with reason have expected to find La Beale Isoud among the B's.)

Some very minor characters in the following pages have neither notes nor even cross-references of their own, but are mentioned only in the notes for other characters with whom then are somehow connected.

A few saints, poets, and scholars, and one Saxon war-leader, come from historical or quasi-historical references. The rest come from romance, chiefly Malory and Vulgate Arthurian cycle. Information indicated as coming from Vulgate VII is to be accepted with extreme caution, due to peculiar research conditions affecting that volume only.

Numerous characters, especially damsels and ladies, are left nameless in the romances. This does not necessarily mean that they are minor figures, only that some literary conventions have changed between medieval days and our own. Where such characters were identified, or where I could identify them simply (by the name of a castle, a relative, etc.), I did so as, for instance, the Damsel of La Beale Regard and King Agrippe's Daughter. I did not particularly like to identify a woman only by the name of a male relative, but it seemed the most convenient course, and readers are left free to gives these ladies names to their own taste. Where I could not readily use such a simple tag, I chose a name arbitrarily from a short list of feminine names drawn from the romances. This seemed handier than giving a lump sub-section of "Unnamed Damsels," and the names can always be changed to taste. Such names are enclosed in double quotation marks: **"ORNAGRINE."** In a few cases, like that of the king 'Premier Conquis,' the quotation marks were bestowed by Sommer, not by me. These names I enclose in single quotation marks, rather than double ones.

LISTS OF FAMILIES AND RETAINERS

Occasionally in this section you will find appended to a character's entry a list of known family members and retainers for that character. I was prompted to attempt such lists by the prominence of blood feuds. While seemingly not "court cases" except in the event of treachery, such feuds appear to be recognized unofficially. Malory, for instance, has Gawaine and his brothers indulging in several of them with no reprisals from their royal uncle. If someone slays one of your kinsmen, even in battle or tournament, the code apparently permits you to hunt him down and slay him in turn, preferably in honest battle. This may make the difficult tangle of inter-linking family relations rather interesting. Such lists are doubtless incomplete, and are starting-points at best. They do not include enemies, they do not reflect animosities within the family, and so on. The allegiances of retainers frequently shift.

Despite the importance of family, medieval folk seem to have had fewer exact words than we do for pin-pointing relations. "Cousin" covers almost anything outside of father, mother, brother, sister, son, and daughter. "Cousin" sometimes seems interchangeable with "nephew." In Malory VI, 1, for instance, Lionel, Lancelot's cousin, is called his nephew (though this may be the result of a different tradition). When in doubt, "kinsman" or "kinswoman covers the relationship. For convenience in all of this book, I have tried to use our familiar modern terms where available.

MISCELLANEOUS GLEANINGS

The short boxed notes scattered in alphabetical order throughout this and the following sections are not offered as notes to actual cultural history. Some of the material may reflect historical fact, but I have long felt it a mistake to strongly base notions of what life was really like in any age on the fiction or the fiction-equivalent of that age. Although the old romancers may have lacked our sense of historical accuracy in fiction and nonfiction — although they may, perhaps, have seen nothing incongruous in picturing Herod and Pilate in the costumes of their own medieval magistrates — they do make it clear by numerous references that they are setting their tales in an earlier time, that things in that earlier time are not always as things are "today." Frequently such references have a "good old days" quality — the setting of the romances has been to some degree idealized, in contrast with the supposed degeneracy of the writer's own time. The result is an era that never was, built up of anachronisms, semi-utopian fancies, and the evil and violence necessary for the plot — a setting comparable with the "Old West" of our twentieth-century Westerns: an era of psychological and spiritual, rather than of historical truth.

I · PEOPLE

ACCOLON OF GAUL

A lover of Morgan le Fay's, and a knight of Arthur's court, Accolon conspired with Morgan to kill kings Arthur and Urien and make themselves king and queen of England. When the actual fight came about through Morgan's plots, Accolon did not realize who his opponent was until after Arthur had given him his death wound. Upon recognizing Arthur, the dying Accolon confessed all and begged forgiveness. Arthur forgave him, but sent his dead body to Morgan as "a present." [Malory IV, 6-12] See also the Magical Acts portion of the appendices.

ADRAGAIN†

A former knight, he became a black friar in Gaul. After kings Ban and Bors were defeated by King Claudas, Adragain visited Britain, where he reproached Arthur for not coming to the aid of Ban and Bors as he had promised earlier, when they had crossed the Channel to help him against the rebel kings. King Urien honored Adragain for the sake of his brother Mador [de la Porte?]. On his way to Britain, Adragain visited Elaine of Benwick and Evaine in the Royal Minster, telling Elaine that her son Lancelot was safe, happy among friends. Adragain was in a position to know, being an uncle of Seraide, a damsel of the French Lady of the Lake. [Vulgate III]

AGLOVALE

King Pellinore's "first son begotten in wedlock" [Malory X, 23]. Malory mentions him only about half a dozen times, once as one of the knights killed by Lancelot and his men during the rescue of Guenever from the stake. One could have expected Aglovale to be a more important figure than this indcates. He was, of course, a member of the Round Table, and is named in Malory XIX, 11.

AGRAVADAIN DES VAUS DES GALOIRE† ([A]Gravadain Du Chastel Fort?)

Castellan of the castle Des Mares. Merlin caused King Ban to sleep with Agravadain's daughter, the Damsel des Mares, while on a visit. This coupling resulted in Sir Ector de Maris. After Agravadain's death, his son became castellan of Des Mares.

AGRAVAINE

The second and probably the most unpleasant son of King Lot and Queen Margawse of Orkney. The romances seem agreed that, although a good knight of arms, he was not a likable character. Vulgate IV characterizes him as envious and evil-disposed, without love or pity; he was very handsome, but his beauty was the best part of him. (Sounds to me as if he may have been spoiled in childhood, perhaps because of his beauty.) At the same time, he was a member of the Round Table, and got around quite a bit on adventures.

There seems some dispute as to whether Agravaine or Mordred was the more culpable in the conspiracy against Lancelot and Guenever. In Malory, Mordred seems to emerge as the chief force, especially since — in Malory — Agravaine is killed during Lancelot's escape from the Queen's chamber. In the Vulgate, where Lancelot's escape is not so bloody, Agravaine, not Mordred, seems the chief villain until he is killed when Lancelot rescues the Queen from the stake. Agravain is motivated chiefly, however, by a desire to hurt Lancelot, while Mordred is motivated by a desire for the throne.

KING AGRIPPE†

A minor monarch of—my guess—somewhere in Wales. [Vulgate IV]

KING AGRIPPE'S DAUGHTER†

King Vadalon was besieging King Agrippe. (If my personal translation is correct, Vadalon claimed Agrippe had killed Vadalon's brother, the King of Norgales.) Food ran short and all the wells except one supplying the besiegers were dried up. King Agrippe's daughter poured strong poison into this last well, killing 5000 besiegers and forcing the others to return to their own country. Vadalon had the princess tracked and seized. Thinking death too lenient, he had two iron bands fixed so tightly round her body that they cut the skin in several places. She defied Vadalon, telling him she would find a deliverer, but would let no one remove the bands unless he also swore to avenge her. Vadalon, she said, would recognize her avenger because he would carry the shield of Vadalon's brother whom Agrippe was said to have killed. The princess, who could travel only in easy stages, was on her way with a few companions to Arthur's court to find a champion when Sir Bors found her resting in her pavilion. Swearing to bear the shield in question for a year and a day and to punish Vadalon, Bors gently broke her bands with his bare hands. [Vulgate IV]

KING AGWISANCE (Anguish) OF IRELAND

Agwisance was one of the rebel kings at the beginning of Arthur's reign, but later apparently became a companion of the Round Table, being listed in Malory XIX, 11. I believe Agwisance to be identical with King Anguish of Ireland, the father of La Beale Isoud. Anguish used to exact tribute from King Mark. When Mark finally refused tribute, Anguish chose his wife's brother, Sir Marhaus, as champion. Mark's champion was Tristram, who killed Marhaus and freed Cornwall from Anguish's truage, but got a poisoned wound from Marhaus's sword and finally had to come to Anguish's court in disguise to be healed. Anguish became Tristram's friend, and, when Tristram's disguise was uncovered and the Irish queen tried to kill him, Anguish himself excused his brother-in-law's death and sent Tristram away with kind words. Later, when Bleoberis and Blamore de Ganis summoned Anguish to Arthur's court on a charge of treacherously murdering their cousin, Tristram came along by chance in time to fight as Anguish's champion and win his acquittal. This expedited Tristram's errand of seeking La Beale Isoud to be Mark's bride; Anguish only regretted that Tristram did not ask her for himself instead. [Malory VIII]

I also much suspect that King Anguish of Ireland is to be identified with King Anguish of Scotland.

Daughter: La Beale Isoud	**KING AGWISANCE'S**
Son? Nephew?: Lanceor	**FAMILY**
Father-in-Law: King Marhalt	
Brother-in-Law: Marhaus	
Cousin: Lady of the Launds	

KING ALAIN OF ESCAVALON†

The father of Floree, Gawaine's love, and possibly the father also of Sir Galeshin. In addition, we know the name of one of Alain's nephews, Arguais. [Vulgate IV]

ALICE LA BEALE PILGRIM

Alice was called "La Beale Pilgrim" after her father, Duke Ansirus the Pilgrim, "of the kin of Sir Lancelot." When Alice heard of the way in which Sir Alisander le Orphelin was defending the remains of the castle La Beale Regard against all comers, she went to Arthur's court and announced that whatever knight could defeat Alisander would gain her hand and land. She then set up her pavilion beside the ruins of La Beale Regard. Seeing Alisander defeat Sagramore le Desirous, Alice

> leapt out of her pavilion, and took Sir Alisander by the bridle, and...said: Fair knight, I require thee of thy knighthood show me thy visage.

He did, and she immediately fell in love with him. At his request, she unwimpled and showed him her face, which had a similar effect on him. They wed, and when his year of defending the ruins was up, they "went into their country of Benoye, and lived there in great joy" until King Mark contrived to murder Alisander [Malory X, 38-39]. Presumably Alice charged their son, Sir Bellengerus le Beuse, to avenge his father's death, as Alisander's mother had charged Alisander to avenge the murder of his father, Prince Boudwin.

ALIPHANSIN†

A leader of the Sesnes. He was involved in the attack on Vandaliors, the castle of the rebel kings. [Vulgate II]

ALISANDER LE ORPHELIN

After King Mark murdered his brother Prince Boudwin, Boudwin's wife Anglides escaped from Cornwall with her infant son Alisander. She reached Magouns castle, where she raised Alisander. On the day he was made knight, she gave him his father's bloody doublet and shirt, charging him to avenge Boudwin's death. Sir Alisander bore his father's shirt "with him always till his death day, in tokening to think of his father's death." [Unlike La Cote Male Taile, however, Alisander seems not to have actually worn it.] Riding to London by Tristram's advice, to seek Lancelot, Alisander took a wrong turning and ended up at a tournament of King Carados', where he did so well that Morgana heard of him and determined to meet him. After the tournament, Alisander fought and killed Sir Malgrin for the sake of a damsel whom Malgrin was persecuting. Morgan arrived in time to watch at least part of this battle, and then spirited Alisander, who "had sixteen great wounds, and in especial one of them was like to be his death," away in a horse litter. She searched his wounds, first aggravating them further and then healing them, apparently to increase his gratitude. Next, putting him to sleep for three days, she took him to the castle La Beale Regard, where she tried to make him her lover. But he maintained, "I had liefer cut away my hangers than I would do her such pleasure."

The damsel who was rightful owner of La Beale Regard helped Alisander by summoning her uncle to burn down the castle, thus driving Morgan away. Having escaped before the holocaust by a privy postern, Alisander and the Damsel of La Beale Regard returned to the site. Alisander had promised Morgana not to leave the castle for a year and a day, so he now announced he would defend what once had been his chamber against all comers for that period of time. Alice La Beale Pilgrim heard of this, came, and fell in love with him, marrying him and giving him a son, Sir Bellengerus le Beuse. After his year at the ruins, Alisander returned with her to Benoye. He never managed to avenge his father, being murdered in his turn by Mark first. Nor did Alisander ever reach Arthur's court:

> And it happed so that Alisander had never grace nor fortune to come to King Arthur's court. For an he had come to Sir Lancelot, all knights said that knew him, he was one of the strongest knights that was in Arthur's days, and great dole was made for him. [Malory X, 32-40]

AMABLE†

Malory seems to know nothing of her, unless she can be identified with a nameless damsel who meets Lancelot on the road and guides him to both Sir Turquine and Sir Peris de Forest Savage to stop their evil practices by exterminating them. Before parting with him, this damsel remarks it is a shame he has no lady but Guenever, whereon he gives her an exposition on the joys and virtues of celibate bachelorhood [Malory VI, 7-10]. It is also possible she appears elsewhere in Malory, but anonymously.

Indeed, she apparently has a name in only one of the manuscripts that Sommer collated. Even nameless, however, she plays a major role throughout the Vulgate **Lancelot**. One day, when he had just met Amable and her brother beside a fountain, Lancelot drank from the fountain and fell deathly sick—the water had been poisoned by venomous serpents in it. Amable used a combination of medicines and sweating therapy to cure him. In the process, she fell sick herself for love of him. On his recovery, he explained to her that he could not return her love because he already had a highborn lady. Amable found a way out, a way which modern society might find risible, but which accorded very well with the traditions of chivalric romance. "All I ask is that you always and everwhere stand my friend," she told Lancelot. "As for myself, I will vow never to love any other man and always to remain a virgin. Thus you may love your other lady as a woman and me as a maiden, without wronging either of us." Lancelot agreed, and Amable thus became the lady he loved best after Guenevere. Even the Queen, learning the situation, accepted Amable without the jealousy she displayed toward the Elaines.

No stay-at-home, Amable frequently appears throughout the rest of the Vulgate **Lancelot**, enjoying various rescues at the hands of Lancelot and others, entertaining her rescuers at her castle, and so on. Amable may have been a friend or cousin of King Brandegoris' daughter, for Lancelot once found Amable in a pavilion, and they were visited there by Brandegoris' daughter, with her son by Bors. [Vulgate V]

KING AMANS (Aniause)

Amans seems to have been a contender for the kingship of Carmelide (Cameliard), which he fought to reconquer while Arthur, King Ryons, and the Sesnes were busy with each other. King Bors killed Amans in battle. [Vulgate II]

Amans of the Vulgate is apparently identical with Malory's King Aniause. [Malory XVI, 7, 13, and see next below]

KING AMANS' (Aniause') DAUGHTERS

Vulgate VI makes them the king's daughters, and Amans in the Vulgate is probably Aniause in Malory, but Malory makes the relationship less clear [Malory XVI, 7-9, 13]. I recap the Vulgate version, which is more coherent.

Amans entrusted all his land and men to the elder of his daughters, but she proved a bad ruler. So Amans expelled her and put the younger daughter in charge. As soon as Amans died, the elder daughter went to war against the younger, and succeeded in gaining most of the property. When Sir Bors, on the Grail Quest, came to the younger sister's last remaining castle, he found the lady, although young and beautiful, poorly dressed. She prepared an elaborate meal for him; he ate only bread and water. She gave him the best chamber and a fine bed; he slept on the floor—but rumpled the bed to appear as if he had slept in it, out of regard for her feelings. In her castle, he had symbolic dreams which indicated the choices he should make the following day in Grail tests. He listened to the debate of the two sisters, declared that the younger seemed to be in the right, championed her cause against the older sister's champion, Priadan (Pridam) le Noir, and won.

In the context of the spiritual allegory of the Grail Quest, King Amans symbolized Christ, the elder sister the Old Covenant, the younger sister Holy Church, dressed in mourning for the sins of evil-doers. Amans and his daughters seem also to have had their own flesh-and-blood existence, independently of the allegory.

AMANT

A knight of King Mark's. Mark killed Bersules, another of his knights, in a rage for praising Tristram. Amant, witnessing this, threatened to appeach Mark of treason before Arthur. Since Mark could not just then defeat Amant and the two squires (Amant's and Bersules'), Mark said, "An thou appeach me of treason I shall thereof defend me afore King Arthur; but I require thee that thou tell not my name." Sir Amant agreed and allowed Mark to depart for the nonce, while he and the

squires buried Bersules. When the trial by combat came, "by misadventure Mark smote Amant through the body. And yet was Amant in the righteous quarrel." Mark got away from there in a hurry.

> Then were there maidens that La Beale Isoud had sent to Sir Tristram, that knew Sir Amant well. Then by the license of King Arthur they went to him and spake with him; for while the truncheon of the spear stuck in his body he spake: Ah, fair damosels, said Amant, recommend me unto La Beale Isoud, and tell her that I am slain for the love of her and of Sir Tristram...and all was because Sir Bersules and I would not consent by treason to slay the noble knight, Sir Tristram.... [And] when Sir Tristram knew all the matter he made great dole and sorrow out of measure, and wept for sorrow for the loss of the noble knights, Sir Bersules and Sir Amant. [Malory X, 7, 14-15]

AMIDE

She was Sir Percivale's sister and Sir Galahad's lady, the latter relationship being platonic. I found the name in one place only, a footnote of Sommer's in Vulgate IV, p.343. In fact, I am far from certain that "Amide" is really the original name of Percivale's sister. Another reference suggests she was yet another Elaine. Usually she is left nameless, as in Malory. But the romances are overfull of Elaines, and if any nameless damsel needs a name, she is Percivale's sister.

Amide came and found Sir Galahad at the hermitage of Sir Ulfin:

> Galahad, said she, I will that ye arm you, and mount upon your horse and follow me, for I shall show you within these three days the highest adventure that ever any knight saw.

After stopping for a short rest at a castle near Collibe, she led him on to the seaside, where they found a ship with Sirs Bors and Percivale waiting. All being aboard, "the wind arose, and drove them through the sea in a marvellous pace." Eventually their ship encountered King Solomon's Ship (see *Things* section). Amide was able to tell the knights part, if not all, of the history of King David's Sword, and to assure Galahad, who was somewhat reluctant to attempt drawing the sword, that he was the one knight to whom the warnings did not apply. When Galahad needed a new belt to gird on the sword, Amide produced one:

> Lo, Lords, said she, here is a girdle that ought to be set about the sword. And wit ye well the greatest part of this girdle was made of my hair, which I loved well while that I was a woman of the world. But as soon as I wist that this adventure was ordained me I clipped off my hair, and made this girdle in the name of God. Ye be well found, said Sir Bors, for certes ye have put us out of great pain, wherein we should have entered ne had your tidings been.

Girding Galahad with the sword, she exclaimed,

> Now reck I not though I die, for now I hold me one of the blessed maidens of the world, which hath made the worthiest knight of the world. Damosel, said Galahad, ye have done so much that I shall be your knight all the days of my life.

Amide and the knights returned to land. She was with them when they destroyed the evil brothers of Carteloise castle and when they saw the white hart with four lions and the marvels of the chapel in the forest. At the castle of the Leprous Lady, though her companions could have defended her, Amide willingly submitted to the custom and gave her blood to heal the Leprous Lady.

> So one came forth and let her blood, and she bled so much that the dish was full. Then she lift up her hand and blessed her; and then she said to the lady: Madam, I am come to the death for to make you whole, for God's love pray for me.

Before dying, she directed her knights to put her body into a boat, and promised they would find her again at Sarras, where they must bury her. Ironically, the night after Amide's blood healed the Leprous Lady, the castle was destroyed by tempest and lightning, and all within killed, in Heaven's vengeance for the death of Amide and the maidens who had died giving their blood before her.

Lancelot found and boarded the ship bearing Amide.

> And as soon as he was within the ship there [Lancelot] felt the most sweetness that ever he felt, and he was fulfilled with all thing that he thought on or desired. Then he said: Fair sweet Father, Jesu Christ, I wot not in what joy I am, for this joy passeth all earthly joys that ever I was in. ... So with this gentlewoman Sir Launcelot was a month and more. If ye would ask how he lived, He that fed the people of Israel with manna in the desert, so was he fed.

Next Galahad found the ship and joined his father. They spent half a year together in the ship, sometimes landing for awhile to find "many strange adventures and perilous." After Galahad left the ship, it brought Lancelot to Carbonek, where he half-achieved the Grail. True to Amide's prediction, when Galahad and his companions Bors and Percivale arrived at Sarras, they found the ship with her body already there, and had time to bury her richly before King Estorause clapped them into prison. [Malory XVII, 1-14, 21]

The warning connected with the girdle of King David's Sword was that if ever the maid who replaced the original hempen girdle should break her virginity she would "die the most villainous death that ever died any woman." It is possible that Amide's death at the castle of the Leprous Lady hints at some irregularity in her life; but the facts that the castle was destroyed by the wrath of God, and that Amide's body, saint-like, apparently stayed fresh and sweet, and even seems to have filled the ship with an atmosphere of spiritual joy, belies the idea. Besides, Amide's death seems preferable to that of other ladies in the tales.

AMUSTANS†

Once Arthur's chaplain, and later a hermit, Amustans knew Guenever in her childhood and was instrumental, by scolding Arthur and helping get deathbed confessions from Genievre and Bertholai, in reconciling Arthur with Guenever after Genievre's last attempt to supplant her half-sister. [Vulgate IV]

Amyr — see BORRE

ANDRED

Sir Tristram's cousin and nemesis, Andred seems to have filled more or less the role at Mark's court that Mordred filled at Arthur's, as a general rotter, spying on and ambushing Tristram [Malory VIII, 32-34] and spreading, through his paramour, false news of Tristram's death in order to get the land of Tristram [Malory IX, 20]. In Book XIX, 11, Malory mentions that "all that were with King Mark that were consenting to the death of Sir Tristram were slain, as Sir Andred and many other" (apparently by Sir Bellangere le Beuse). Edward Arlington Robinson, in his generally excellent **Tristram**, makes Andred a half-wit and transfers Tristram's murder from Mark to Andred. Malory's Andred, however, must have had some competence as a fighter, for, when the Saxons attacked under Elias, Andred led one of Mark's three divisions in the battles of defense [Malory X, 28].

ANEURIN†

Glennie lists Aneurin, along with Merlin, Llywarch Hen, and Taliessin, as one of the four great bards of the Arthurian age.

ANGIS†

When Lancelot left court because of Guenever's anger over the Elaine of Astolat incident, Angis was his squire and only companion [Vulgate VI]. Malory does not mention Lancelot's return to court between the tournament of Winchester and his last interview with Elaine [Malory XVIII]. The Vulgate says it was a very brief return; its very brevity convinced Arthur that Morgan's accusation of Lancelot's and Guenevere's guilt was false.

ANGLIDES

When King Mark killed her husband, Prince Boudwin, Anglides escaped to Magouns castle in Sussex with her young son, Alisander le Orphelin. The Constable of Magouns, Sir Bellangere, who was married to Anglides' cousin, told Anglides that the castle was hers by inheritance. Anglides raised Alisander there. When he was knighted, she gave him his father's bloody doublet and shirt, told him how Mark had stabbed Boudwin before her eyes, and charged her son to avenge the deed. [Malory X, 32-34]

King Anguish — see KING AGWISANCE

King Aniause — see KING AMANS

King Aniause's Daughters — see KING AMANS' DAUGHTERS

ANNOWRE

A sorceress who loved Arthur and enticed him to her tower in the Forest Perilous. When she could not get him to make love to her, she plotted his death.

> Then every day she would make him ride into that forest [where his own knights were looking for him], to the intent to have King Arthur slain. For when this Lady Annowre saw that she might not have him at her will, then she laboured by false means to have destroyed King Arthur.

Nimue learned of the situation and came into the same forest, seeking Lancelot or Tristram to help the King. She found Tristram and brought him to the tower in time to see two strange knights defeating Arthur and unlacing his helm. "And the Lady Annowre gat King Arthur's sword in her hand to have stricken off his head." Tristram rushed up shouting, "Traitress, traitress, leave that," and killed the two knights. Meanwhile, Nimue shouted to Arthur not to let Annowre escape, so the King chased Annowre and smote off her head, which Nimue hung up by the hair to her saddlebow. [Malory IX, 16]

DUKE ANSIRUS THE PILGRIM

He was called "the Pilgrim" because of his passion for going on pilgrimage, "for every third year he would be at Jerusalem." He passed his nickname on to his daughter, Alice la Beale Pilgrim. Ansirus was of Lancelot's kin, apparently in the British branch of the family. His daughter and her knight, Alisander le Orphelin, settled in "their country of Benoye," which presumably was Ansirus's dukedom.

Antor — see ECTOR

ARCAUS†

Son of the King of Saxony, and the leader of Mordred's first division, apparently the Saxon division, in the last battle. [Vulgate VI]

ARGIUS

This knight "of the blood of King Mark" led a third of Mark's army in battle against Elias and the invading Sessoins. Dinas the Seneschal and Andred were Mark's other two commanders. [Malory X, 28]

ARGUSTUS

While on the Grail Quest, Lancelot "rode into a forest, and held no highway. And...he saw a fair plain, and beside that a fair castle." A tournament was in progress between the castle knights, in black, and other knights, in white. Lancelot entered on the side of the castle and was defeated and shamed. In sorrow he rode on through a deep valley, past a mountain, and to a chapel where a recluse lived. She explained to him that the tournament had a spiritual meaning. Although the combatants "were earthly knights," the

> tournament was a token to see who should have most knights, either Eliazar, the son of King Pelles, or Argustus, the son of King Harlon. But Eliazar was all clothed in white, and Argustus ...in black, the which were [over]come.

The knights in black symbolized sinners, those in white virgins and good men. [Malory XV, 5-6]

Finding nothing more about King Harlon and his son Argustus, I hypothesize that their country was in northern Logres or southern Scotland, so that Harlon's son and Pellam's could conveniently arrange their tournament. The last specific site Lancelot appears to have visited was the place I have called "Chapel of the Demon" (see *Places* section). At least two, perhaps three, days of travel seem to have passed between the time Lancelot left the chapel and the time he came to the tournament; it was hardly, however, uninterrupted travel. The similarity of the names suggests that possibly Harlon's son Argustus was also Aguarus. the nephew of the dead man whom Lancelot found in the chapel.

ARIES

A cowherd, reputed father of Sir Tor, and actual father of twelve sons besides. At the time of Arthur's marriage, Aries reluctantly yielded to Tor's desire and brought him to Arthur's court at London to request knighthood for the boy. After comparing Tor with his twelve supposed younger brothers, and finding him unlike any of them, Arthur dubbed the boy. Merlin then explained that King Pellinore had begotten Tor on the housewife Vayshoure when he took her maidenhead. Being assured both by Merlin and by the woman that Tor had been begotten before ever she was wedded, Aries remarked, "It is the less grief unto me." [Malory III, 3]

ARNOLD LE BREUSE

He and his brother, Sir Gherard le Breuse, were a murderous pair who "guarded" a passage of the water of Mortaise as an excuse to kill passing knights. Gareth slew them both on his way with Lynette to Castle Dangerous. This was Gareth's first conquest, not counting Sir Kay. [Malory VII, 6]

COUNT AROUZ (Arans, Aranz)†

Count of Flanders, he was killed when he came out to resist Arthur's army on its way to fight King Claudas in the war on behalf of Guenevere's cousin Elyzabel. [Vulgate V]

KING ARRANT OF DENMARK

This king of Denmark, who was a brother of one of the kings of Ireland, was killed in battle beside the Humber, along with his four allies, the kings of Ireland, Vale, Soleise, and the Isle of Longtains, when they tried to invade Arthur's realm [Malory IV, 2]. I got the name Arrant from Vulgate VII.

ARTHUR

Arthur was no chessboard king. The point is made frequently in the romances that he was a good knight in his own right, capable of fighting in field or tournament, of slaying terrific giants, and so on. His men loved him because he would jeopard his life like any of them, even riding incognito to seek adventure. Once he jousted down Lamorak, who, according to Malory, was the third best knight of the world [Malory IX, 14]. Another time, to demonstrate his strength, Arthur seized Gawaine at a tournament, lifted him out of the saddle, and carried him along, armor and all, on his horse's neck [Vulgate V]. (Gawaine already had won the tournament, and Arthur forewarned him to go along with whatever he did.) And although on at least one occasion Arthur had a clerk read a letter from Elaine of Astolat aloud to the court, Arthur was literate, like many of his knights and ladies, but unlike King Claudas. [Malory XVIII, 20; cf. Vulgate VI, 238]

Tennyson's Arthur can do no wrong. The Arthur of T. H. White is an idealistic and faithful man who has to be enchanted into going to bed with Morgawse, as well as a gentle, forgiving husband who is trapped into sentencing Guenever to the stake and rejoices at her rescue. It is this version of Arthur that seems to have colored almost all modern treatments. The Arthur of the Vulgate, Malory, and other medieval works, however, is a lusty and jealous man, who does not need to be enchanted before hopping into bed with at least two other lovely ladies (and probably more) besides Morgawse, who would have sentenced Guenever to death or to horrible maiming before her exile, if Lancelot had not saved her in trial by combat during the affair of Genievre, and who goes into a jealous rage and cries for the blood of both Guenever and Lancelot when their guilt is made clear to him.

He is also something of a practical joker. When Sir Baudwin of Britain made a vow never to be jealous of his wife, Arthur arranged for Baudwin to be out hunting one night. Then Arthur brought a young knight of his own to the chamber of Baudwin's wife, commanded admittance, and forced the young man into bed with the lady—though he did put a sword between them, threaten the knight with death if he touched the lady, and sat playing chess with one of her damsels at the bed's foot for the rest of the night. In the morning, Arthur showed Baudwin his wife apparently caught with a lover in her bed, thus testing Baudwin's vow of non-jealousy. Wonder of wonders, Baudwin passed. remaining truly non-jealous, whereupon Arthur explained the situation and praised the lady. [The Avowynge of King Arthur]

Also among Arthur's faults according to the medieval versions   and surely more serious faults than lust and jealousy   are pride and greed. By medieval thought, Arthur's final

−9−

ARTHUR AND THE ORKNEY KIN

⸗ *Indicates a known marriage.*
≠ *Indicates a union either known to be illicit or a union not proven to be a marriage.*

Numbers indicate the sequence of a character's relationships;
they should not imply that only those relationships occurred.

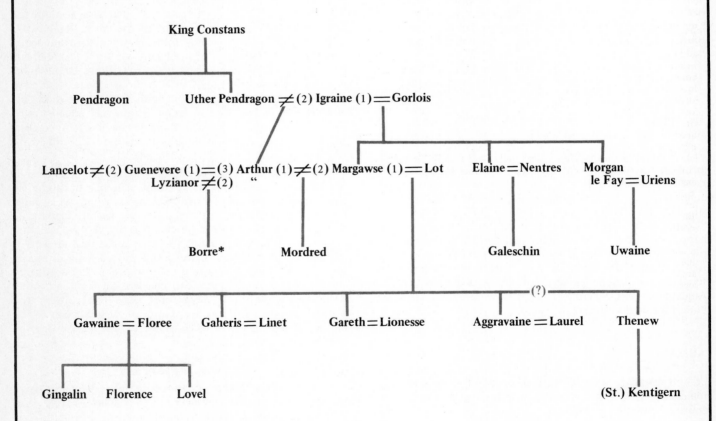

- *Gawaine's amours and wives are not well-known, and may vary from version to version.*
- *Thenew may have been Lot's daughter by Margawse, by an earlier wife, or by an amour. Thenew claimed an immaculate conception for her own son, Kentigern.*
- *King Lot is descended from Peter, one of the companions of Josephe, son of Joseph of Arimathea. King Uriens is descended from Josephe's brother Galaad.*

* *Sir Borre was the son of Lyzianor and Arthur.*

by Greg Stafford from sketches by Phyllis Ann Karr; notes by P.A.K.

downfall was brought less by the love of Lancelot and Guenever than by Arthur's own greed in wishing to conquer the world. Early versions give Mordred his chance at usurpation while Arthur is on the Continent to fight the Romans. Malory moves the war with Rome to fairly early in Arthur's career and gives it a triumphant ending, but the older version appears to survive in the Vulgate, which has the Romans attacking Arthur while he and Gawain are besieging Lancelot's castle in France.

High among Arthur's genuine virtues, by both medieval and modern standards, was loyalty to his word. After Lancelot had rescued Guenever from the stake, while he was protecting her in Joyous Garde, the Bishop of Rochester came to arrange the peace commanded by the Pope between Arthur and Lancelot. Lancelot naturally wanted to be sure it was safe to deliver Guenever up to her husband.

> And then [the Bishop] shewed Sir Launcelot all his writing, both from the Pope and from King Arthur. This is sure enough, said Sir Launcelot, for full well I dare trust my lord's own writing and his seal, for he was never shamed of his promise. [Malory XX, 14]

Grandfather (paternal): King Constans of England
Father: Uther Pendragon
Mother: Igraine
Uncles (paternal): Maines, Pandragon (both killed before Arthur's conception)
Uncle (maternal?): Duke Elise
Foster-father: Ector (not de Maris)
Foster-brother: Kay
Wife: Guenevere
Paramours: Margawse, Lyzianor, Countess of Orofoise's Sister
Sons: Borre (by Lyzianor), Mordred (by Margawse)
Half-sisters (by Igraine): Margawse, Elaine of Tintagil, Morgan le Fay
Brothers-in-law: King Lot (m. Margawse), King Nentres (m. Elaine), King Uriens (m. Morgan)
Nephews (by Lot and Margawse): Gawaine (favorite), Agravaine, Gaheris, Gareth Beaumains
Other Nephews: Ywaine (by Uriens and Morgan), Galeshin (by Nentres and Elaine)
Mentor: Merlin
Cousin: Hoel of Brittany (also an ally)
Allies (sampling): Kings Ban and Bors, Carbarecotins, Archbishop of Canterbury
Lieges (sampling): Damsel of the Marches, Lady of Nohaut
Would-be paramours: Annowre, Camille
No effort has been made to include all of Arthur's allies and liege subjects on this list.

KING ARTHUR'S FAMILY AND RETAINERS

ASELAPHES†

In the time of Joseph of Arimathea, the devil Aselaphes killed the pagan King Tholomer to keep him from being converted by Josephe. [Vulgate I]

KING ASTLABOR

The father of Sirs Palomides, Safere, and Segwarides [Malory X, 82-83]. Since they are Saracens, Astlabor's kingdom would be somewhere in Moorish lands.

"ASTRIGIS"†

This treacherous lady tried to trick Gawaine, through her lies, into killing her husband. Gawaine fought the husband; but when the husband told his side, Gawaine did not know whom to believe. He tried to take them both to find someone who could tell him which was in the right. On the way, the woman gave him the slip. Her husband remarked,

You knights of the Round Table are compelled by your oath to help any woman without knowing whether she deserves it or not. Would it not be more reasonable and honorable to inquire before you act if you are espousing a good cause?

The lord of the castle La Tour Quarree, where they repaired, agreed with the husband. [Vulgate V, appendix]

Both the wife and the husband are unnamed in the account. I have given her a minor place name.

Avarlon — see PINEL

"Automne" — see under "PRINTEMPS, ETE, & AUTOMNE"

AVENABLE (Grisandoles)†

Avenable, the daughter of Duke Mathem, disguised herself as a squire, took the name Grisandoles, and went to the court of the Emperor of Rome. Here she worked her way up to seneschal, presumably being knighted on the way.

One night the Emperor dreamed of a sow with a gold circle on her head and of twelve "loueaus." (I could not find an exact definition of "loueau," but the context explains it as well as need be.)

At that time Merlin was in the forest of Romenie. He took the semblance of a stag, ran through the palace, and told the Emperor that only "the wild man" could explain the dream. Merlin also played this same wild man. The Emperor promised his daughter to whoever found either the stag or the wild man. Eventually Grisandoles, instructed by the stag, found the wild man. The wild man laughed thrice on the way back: when he looked at Grisandoles, when he saw many poor people before an abbey, and when he saw a squire strike his master three times during Mass at a chapel. Brought before the Emperor, the wild man explained that he was a Christian and that he had laughed the first time because a good and beautiful woman had found both stag and wild man where many men had failed, the second time because the beggars at the abbey had a rich treasure buried under their feet, and the third time because a great treasure was hidden at the place where the squire struck his master. The Emperor's dream, which Merlin, as the wild man, related before expounding, to prove his knowledge, meant that the Empress's twelve handmaidens were twelve young men in disguise. The Empress and her twelve lovers were burned at the stake. Merlin advised the Emperor to marry Avenable and not act contrary to her will when they were married. Merlin also assured the Emperor that his daughter was really his and would not resemble the late Empress, her mother. Letters appearing over the door now revealed that the stag and the wild man were both Merlin. The Emperor sent for Avenable's parents and brother Patrices, married Avenable, married his daughter to Patrices, and lived long and happily with his new wife. [Vulgate II]

This seems to be a tale of Merlin's youth, and the Emperor in question may have been a predecessor of the Lucius whom Arthur conquered and killed. Even if the Emperor is identified with Lucius, a romancer might be justified in having the widowed Avenable-Grisandoles come back to Britain with other Continental knights, like Sir Priamus.

AXILLES†

He was Sir Bors's squire. Bors eventually knighted him and invested him with the castle of Le Terte Deuee [Vulgate V].

AGDEMAGUS (Baudemagus), KING OF GORE

Although Bagdemagus seems pretty well forgotten in our day, he was one of the more important companions of the Round Table.

King Uriens of Gore gave his country to his nephew Bagdemagus (see Gore, *Places*). At the time Arthur interred the second group of rebel kings with all honors, Merlin revealed to him that Bagdemagus was Arthur's cousin as well as Urien's kinsman (Malory II, 11; the name is here spelled Basdemegus, but there is no reason to doubt the identity). Bagdemagus later left Arthur's court in anger because Sir Tor had been chosen instead of himself to fill a vacant seat at the Round Table. Riding into the forest, Bagdemagus and his squire came to a cross where Bagdemagus stopped to say his prayers. The squire noticed a prediction written on the cross, saying that Bagdemagus would not return to court until he had won a knight of the Round Table, fighting body to body.

> So, sir, said the squire, here I find writing of you, therefore I rede you return again to the court. That shall I never, said Bagdemagus, till men speak of me great worship, and that I be worthy to be a knight of the Round Table. And so he rode forth, and there by the way he found a branch of an holy herb that was the sign of the Sangreal, and no knight found such tokens but he were a good liver.

Bagdemagus also found the rock under which Merlin was imprisoned, and spoke with Merlin, but could not lift the rock.

> And so Bagdemagus departed and did many adventures, and proved after a full good knight, and came again to the court and was made knight of the Round Table. [Malory IV, 5]

Strangely enough, after the incident of the holy herb (that was a sign of the Sangreal), Bagdemagus did not achieve the Holy Grail. Indeed, when he started out on the Quest, he attempted to take the Adventurous Shield reserved for Galahad, and as punishment was stricken down by an apparently angelic knight in white armor outside the abbey [Malory XIII, 9]. Malory XVII, 17, and Vulgate VI agree that sometime on the Grail Quest Bagdemagus was killed by Gawaine; neither account, however, describes the actual death scene, and Malory brings Bagdemagus back as one of Lancelot's advisors in XX, 19. This last reference is likely an error. When Bagdemagus was killed on the Grail Quest, Arthur mourned his loss more than that of any other three together of those killed [Vulgate VI].

Once, at a tournament, Bagdemagus requested a knight named Sauseise to strike down his son Meliagrant, "for I would he were well beaten of thy hands, that he might depart out of this field." Sauseise would have succeeded "had there not come rescues." (Malory X, 41: Meliagrant seems to have survived the tournament in good shape, despite the failure of his father's tender ruse to get him out of danger.) Later, Lancelot was very nervous about how to tell Bagdemagus he had killed Meliagrant to defend the Queen; Bagdemagus, being a fair and just man, forgave him [Vulgate IV]. Besides his son Meliagrant, Bagdemagus had at least one and possibly two daughters.

In her delightful modern romance **The King's Damosel**, Vera Chapman uses Bagdemagus as the name of her villain. He is so dissimilar to the Bagdemagus of Malory and the Vulgate, however, that I must assume them mere coincidental namesakes.

Son: Meliagrance One or more Daughters Uncle: King Uriens Aunt: Morgan le Fay Squire: Melias de Lile	**KING BAGDEMAGUS' FAMILY AND RETAINER**

KING BAGDEMAGUS' DAUGHTER(S)

An unnamed daughter of King Bagdemagus helped deliver Lancelot from Castle Chariot where he was being held by Morgan and other queens. The damsel's condition for helping Lancelot escape was that he help her father in a tournament against the King of Northgalis. [Malory IV, 4]

Vulgate IV mentions a stepsister of Sir Meliagrant. She hated him because he had calumniated her, causing her father to cut her off, so that she retained only a poor inheritance from her mother. This damsel was benefactress to the wife of a serf named Roliax, whom Meliagrant made Lancelot's jailor. Thus the stepsister was able to help Lancelot escape. This damsel may be identical with Malory's daughter of King Bagdemagus, or she may be a separate character; she may even be a daughter of Bagdemagus's wife, perhaps by a former marriage, and not of Bagdemagus himself.

Lancelot later learned, as he rode through the wood of Sapine, that Meliagrant's stepsister was to be burned at Florega the next day for the death of Meliagrant. Lancelot saved her in the nick of time and threw her accuser into the fire instead. [Vulgate IV]

BALAN

Born in Northumberland, Sir Balan was a good and unfortunate knight. Although never apparently, in Malory's version, a knight of the Round Table, he helped his brother Balin le Savage capture King Ryons for Arthur and win Arthur's war against Lot, Ryons, Nero, and the other kings of the second rebellion. He and his brother Balin, who is the more famous of the two, finally killed each other in a tragic battle, neither knowing the other's identity until too late. [Malory, II]

(Tennyson's idyll, "Balin and Balan," though an excellent tale in its own right, could hardly be called a retelling of Malory's book of Balin.)

Baldwin — see BAUDWIN

BISHOP BAUDWIN†

The bishop who sits on the dais beside Sir Ywaine in **Sir Gawaine and the Green Knight** also plays a major, if rather unclerical, role in "Sir Gawaine and the Carl of Carlisle." Very likely this notable churchman of Arthur's in pre-Malory romances is to be identified with Sir Baudwin of Britain.

BALIN LE SAVAGE (The Knight with the Two Swords)

Born in Northumberland, Balin somehow slew a cousin of Arthur's, for which Arthur imprisoned him for half a year. Balin was out of prison, but impoverished and still remaining at Arthur's court, when a damsel to whom I have arbitrarily assigned the name "Malvis" came to Camelot girded with the sword referred to as Balin's Sword in the *Things* section. When Balin, alone of the knights at court, had drawn the sword, the first English Lady of the Lake (not Nimue, but the one I have styled "Nineve") came to Arthur to demand either Balin's head or that of Malvis in return for Excalibur. The Lady of the Lake claimed that Balin had slain her brother. As Arthur tried to put her off, Balin saw her, heard she was asking for his head, and swapped off hers instead, explaining that she had caused his mother to be burnt. Arthur, annoyed, dismissed Balin from court. Sir Lanceor of Ireland rode out after Balin, challenged him, and died of Balin's spear when they jousted; Lanceor's lady Colombe, finding him dead, slew herself before Balin could stop her. Balin's brother Balan found him here, and shortly thereafter King Mark happened by. When Mark asked their names, Balan told him, "Sir...ye may see he beareth two swords, thereby ye may call him the Knight with the Two Swords."

Balin and Balan next got back Arthur's favor by capturing his enemy King Ryons in ambush and then joining the battle before Castle Terrabil on Arthur's side; Lamorak de Galis was to claim, years later, that Balin had been the one who had killed King Lot in that battle.

> Oh, where is Balin and Balan and Pellinore? said King Arthur [after the battle]. As for Pellinore, said Merlin, he will meet with you soon; and as for Balin he will not be long from you; but the other brother will depart, ye shall see him no more. By my faith, said Arthur, they are two marvellous knights, and namely Balin passeth of prowess of any knight that ever I found, for much beholden am I unto him; would God he would abide with me.

(Lancelot had not yet come to Britain, and Gawaine was still young and scarcely tried.)

Balin did return to Arthur, but only very briefly. Seeing Sir Herlews le Berbeus and his lady ride by his pavilion toward the castle of Meliot, Arthur sent Balin after them, and on the way back Herlews was slain by Sir Garlon, who rode invisible. Balin thereupon rode with Sir Herlews' lady in pursuit of Garlon, whom they traced by his other murders and depredations. They stopped one night at the castle of the Leprous Lady. Eventually tracking Garlon to King Pellam's castle, Balin succeeded in exterminating the villainous knight. He and the lady lingered, however, to collect some of Garlon's blood in order to heal a youth Garlon had left wounded. This gave Garlon's brother Pellam time to call for his weapon and go after Balin. Balin's sword breaking at the first stroke, he fled from Pellam until he found Longinus' Spear and dealt Pellam the Dolorous Stroke. The castle collapsed about them, killing Sir Herlews' lady. In three days Merlin released Balin from the wreckage.

After one or two other adventures, Balin came to the castle I have described under Meliot (*Places*). Here, to fulfill the customs of the place, Balin fought his brother Balan; Balan (having conquered the previous defender of the island) wore that knight's red armor, while Balin borrowed a shield offered to him for the occasion by one of the castle's knights. Thus neither recognized the other until after both were mortally wounded. Merlin later refurbished Balin's sword for Galahad. (The sword that Pellam had broken may have been the one Balin had, even before he drew that of Malvis; he wore only one of his two swords into the hall where he found and slew Garlon.) [Malory II; X, 24]

Although apparently never a companion of the Round Table, and seemingly doomed to do unfortunate deeds, Balin seems to have been a very sincere and well-meaning knight as well as a capable and valorous one.

Balin's Lady — see HERLEWS' LADY

KING BAN OF BENWICK

The French kings Ban and his brother Bors, who were wedded to the sisters Elaine and Evaine, were two of Arthur's major allies in his wars against the rebel kings at the beginning of his reign. It was largely through their assistance that Arthur won the battle of Bedegraine against the first rebel alliance. Ban and Bors returned to their own kingdoms, however, (Ban fathering Ector de Maris along the way) before the second alliance of rebel kings reared its head. Arthur failed to pay back the favor and come to France in time to help Ban and Bors against King Claudas. Escaping with his queen, Elaine, and their small son Lancelot, Ban looked back, saw his castle in flames and died, probably of heart seizure. Elaine, hurrying to her husband, left young Lancelot unattended for a few moments, and Viviane, the French Damsel of the Lake, appropriated him. [Vulgate II, III]

KING BAN'S FAMILY AND RETAINER
Brothers: King Bors, Gwenbaus Wife: Queen Elaine of Benwick Paramour: Damsel des Mares Sons: Lancelot (by Elaine), Ector de Maris (by the Damsel des Mares) Sister-in-law: Queen Evaine Nephews: Sir Bors de Ganis, Lionel Retainer: Phariance

KING BANDES

His daughter was loved by a Saracen knight, Sir Corsabrin, who would not suffer her to marry anyone else, and who spread the story that she was out of her mind. The princess enlisted the aid of Sir Palomides, who fought and killed Corsabrin during Duke Galeholt's tournament in Surluse. "And therewithal came a stink out of [Corsabrin's] body when the soul departed, that there might nobody abide the savour." [Malory X, 46-47]

BATTLE STRATEGY

Being no student of military art, I have little to say about the major battles of Arthur's reign or the strategy of his time. It would surely be much the same as in other medieval warfare. I did, however, find the following notes of possible interest:

Planning war on Claudas of France, Arthur decided to send a small company of good men rather than a larger number of indifferent ones. Arthur's army trounced that of Claudas. Of course, Arthur's "small company" was 54,000. [Vulgate V]

When the battle of Bedegraine was going against the rebel kings,

> All the eleven kings drew them together, and then said King Lot, Lords, ye must other ways than ye do ... ye may see what people we have lost, and what good men we lose, because we wait always on these foot-men, and ever in saving of one of the foot-men we lose ten horsemen for him; therefore this is mine advice, let us put our foot-men from us, for the noble Arthur will not tarry on the foot-men, for they may save themselves, the wood is near hand. And when we horsemen be together, look every each of you kings let make such ordinances that none break upon pain of death. And who that seeth any man dress him to flee, lightly that he be slain, for it is better that we slay a coward, than through a coward all we to be slain.

The other kings agreed, and the strategy must have been successful, for the battle finally had to be stopped by Merlin, who told Arthur that, though "of three score thousand this day hast thou left alive but fifteen thousand," yet "yonder eleven kings at this time will not be overthrown, but an thou tarry on them any longer, thy fortune will turn and they shall increase." [Malory I, 16-17]

Barant le Apres — see KING OF THE HUNDRED KNIGHTS

BAUDWIN OF BRITAIN

One of the most important of the less-remembered knights, Baudwin seems to have been a major figure in various pre-Malory romances. In "The Avowynge of King Arthur" we learn that he made three interesting vows prompted by early experiences campaigning in Spain: never to deny anyone meat and drink, never to fear death, and never to be jealous of his wife or any other woman. It is possible that Sir Baudwin should be identified with Bishop Baudwin.

The little Malory gives about him is telling. On Arthur's accession, he made Sir Baudwin constable of the kingdom at the same time he made Kay seneschal. When Arthur left for his war against the Emperor of Rome, he made Baudwin joint governor of England in his absence, along with the Sir Constantine who later succeeded to the throne of Britain. Later, apparently after the death of his wife, Baudwin became a holy hermit and a "full noble surgeon and a good leech," forsaking his lands to settle in "wilful poverty" with at least two servants somewhere in the neighborhood of Camelot and Astolat. His hermitage was "under a wood, and a great cliff on the other side, and a fair water running under it" some two or three miles from Camelot. Here, after the tournament at Winchester, Baudwin healed the gravely wounded Lancelot, whom he recognized by a scar on the latter's neck. [Malory I, 7; V, 3; XVIII, 12-13]

La Beale Isoud — see ISOUD

DAMSEL OF LA BEALE REGARD

This unnamed damsel, rightful heir to the castle La Beale Regard, was cousin to both Morgan le Fay and the Earl of Pase. Morgan appropriated La Beale Regard and brought Alisander le Orphelin there with intent to seduce him. To foil Morgan, the damsel sent a request to the Earl of Pase, who hated Morgan, to come and destroy the castle with wild-fire, which he did, while the damsel helped Alisander to escape by a privy postern, where she had his horse and harness ready for him. Since Alisander had promised Morgan to stay there a year, he waited in the garden while the castle was destroyed and then returned to defend his former bedroom against all comers. Alice la Beale Pilgrim came to the place and fell in love with him. The damsel of La Beale Regard, who might be considered as having a prior claim on Alisander, appears to have taken this in good humor and even, possibly, to have helped the romance along; at least, she did not hinder it.

One day Alisander went into a fit of being assotted on his lady, a sort of occupational hazard of being both knight and lover. While Alisander was in this helpless state, Mordred came along and started to mock him by leading his horse away. When the damsel of La Beale Regard saw this,

anon she let arm her, and set a shield upon her shoulder, and therewith she mounted upon her horse, and gat a naked sword in her hand, and she thrust unto Alisander with all her might, and she gave him such a buffet that he thought the fire flew out of his eyen.

This brought him out of his trance and enabled him to rout Mordred. One pictures him saying, "Thanks—I needed that."

But then Sir Alisander and Alice had good game at the damosel, how sadly she hit him upon the helm. [Malory X, 37-39]

The damsel of La Beale Regard's knowledge and skill in arming herself and using a sword to such good advantage suggest her as a possible female warrior.

BEAUVIVANTE (Maledisant, Bienpensant)

The history of Sir La Cote Male Taile and his damsel as recorded in Malory IX parallels, or perhaps parodies, the history of Gareth and Lynette in his Book VII. La Cote Male Taile's damsel is first called Maledisant ("Evil-speaking") for her raillery against her champion. Later, when she reveals to Lancelot that she had rebuked La Cote Male Taile not for hate but for love, fearing him too young and tender to risk his life questing, Lancelot names her Bienpensant ("Well-thinking"). Finally, after her marriage with La Cote Male Taile, she is called Beauvivante ("Well-living"). With so many unnamed damsels in the tales, it seems hardly fair that a single maiden should be given three distinctive, personality-tailored names. Her story suggests, however, that anyone with some knowledge of French can coin similar names for otherwise nameless characters. See also Maledisant's Shield, *Things*.

BEDIVERE (Bedevere, Bedwyr)

One of Arthur's first knights, and the last one left alive with him after the battle with Mordred on Salisbury Plain, Bedivere was the knight who had to throw Excalibur back to the Lady of the Lake.

Malory mentions Bedivere first as one of Arthur's two companions (the other was Kay) in the adventure of the giant of St. Michael's Mount on the way to the Continental campaign against the Emperor Lucius. Soon after the slaying of the giant, Bedivere, Gawaine, Lionel, and Bors were selected to carry Arthur's warlike message to Lucius. We do not, apparently, meet Bedivere again in Malory's account until he shows up at the tournament of Winchester and at the attempt to heal Sir Urre, which last marks him, if such evidence is needed, as a member of the Round Table. Bedivere, his brother Lucan the Butler, and a pair of bishops served as Arthur's messengers to Mordred to try and arrange a treaty. After the last battle, Bedivere obeyed, with famous reluctance, Arthur's command about Excalibur and then saw Arthur borne away in the boat with Morgan and her companions. Bedivere later found Arthur's grave at the hermitage of the former Archbishop of Canterbury. Bedivere became a hermit with the bishop. [Malory V, 5-6; XVIII, 11; XIX, 11; XXI, 3; XXI, 5-6]

This seems to be all Malory tells us of Bedivere. Nevertheless, I class him among the major knights. Along with Sir Kay, he seems to have been one of the earliest companions of Arthur to have remained in the romances through the centuries, although by the time Malory got hold of the material other knights had crowded him from prominence. Sutcliff, in **Sword at Sunset**, makes Bedivere (under the earlier version of his name) the Queen's lover, Lancelot having come too late into the body of Arthurian literature to fit Sutcliff's pseudo-historical retelling. In **The Hollow Hills**, Stewart seems to follow Sutcliff's lead in assigning the Queen's-lover role to Bedwyr. White identifies Bedivere with Pedivere in **The Once and Future King**, but in this instance I think he distorts Malory. Chapman includes Bedivere in his character as hermit in the cast of **King Arthur's Daughter**.

Lady of Beloc (Beloe, etc.)† — see under BELOE, *Places*

Belias — see FONTAINE DES DEUX SYCAMORS, *Places*

KING BELINANS OF SORGALES (Sugales?)†

This chap got a mention in Vulgate VII.

Bellangere of Magouns — see under ANGLIDES

BELLENGERUS LE BEUSE (Bellangere le Beuse)

> And by Alice he [Sir Alisander le Orphelin] gat ... Bellengerus le Beuse. And by good fortune he came to the court of King Arthur, and proved a passing good knight; and he revenged his father's death [apparently by killing King Mark]. [Malory X, 40]

Bellengerus became a knight of the Round Table, being listed in Malory XIX, 11. He accompanied Lancelot into exile and was made Earl of the Launds [XX, 18] Very likely he was named for Sir Bellangere, the constable of Magouns castle, who had taken in Bellengerus' grandmother, Anglides, when she fled from King Mark.

BELLEUS

A "passing good man of arms, and a mighty lord of lands of many out isles," Belleus was one of the victims of what was probably Sir Lancelot's worst habit: making free with other people's pavilions. One night Lancelot found a pavilion of red sendal, went in, and went to bed. After a while Sir Belleus came, it being his own pavilion, got into bed, and began to hug Lancelot, innocently and naturally believing the person who already lay in bed to be his leman. Up jumps Lancelot and, before anyone stops to ask questions, Belleus is wounded nigh unto death, to the horror of his lady, who arrives on the scene while Lancelot is staunching the wound he has given Belleus. Belleus shows himself to be of an understanding nature:

> Peace, my lady and my love, said Belleus, for this knight is a good man, and a knight adventurous, and there he told her all the cause how he was wounded; And when that I yielded me unto him, he left me goodly and hath staunched my blood.

The lady, who is left unnamed, demands to know Lancelot's name. On learning it she requires Lancelot to see to it, for the harm he has done her lord and herself, that Belleus be made a knight of the Round Table. This Lancelot does. [Malory VI, 5, 8] Malory seems not to mention Belleus again. Presumably, if he survived until the time of the rift between Arthur and Lancelot, he clove to Lancelot's party.

BELLIANCE LE ORGULUS

Sir Lamorak saved Sir Frol of the Out Isles from four knights who were fighting Frol all at once. Shortly thereafter Lamorak and Frol had a tiff and separated. Three or four days later Lamorak came along again and saw Frol give Gawaine a fall when Gawaine tried to take Frol's lady. Lamorak jousted with Frol to avenge Gawaine, and by mischance smote Frol fatally.

Frol's brother, Sir Belliance le Orgulus, came to avenge Frol. Learning Lamorak's identity, Belliance said,

> Ah, thou art the man in the world that I most hate, for I slew my sons for thy sake, where I saved thy life, and now thou hast slain my brother Sir Frol.

Lamorak tried to beg Belliance's pardon, but Belliance insisted on fighting. Lamorak fought him down, but refused to kill him, thereby winning his friendship so that they swore never again to fight each other [Malory VIII, 40-41].

Belliance is probably the "Sir Bellangere le Orgulous, that the good knight Sir Lamorak won in plain battle," who is listed as a knight of the Round Table [Malory XIX, 11]. He should not be confused with Bellengerus le Beuse, who is also sometimes called "Bellangere," as in XIX,11.

Belliance was among those killed during Lancelot's rescue of Guenevere from the stake [Malory XX, 8].

Bellicent — see MARGAWSE

BELLINOR†

When Lancelot and his followers left Arthur, Sir Bors' seat at the Round Table was given to Bellinor. Sir Bellinor was a king's son, but I know not of which king. [Vulgate VI]

Lady of Beloe† — see BELOE, *Places*

BENIGNE (Blevine, Blenined)†

She was the Damsel of Glocedon castle, and a cousin of the Damsel of Hongrefort. At Galdon castle, Sir Bors saved Benigne from being drowned by knights who had already slain her lover. Shortly thereafter, she joined her cousin of Hongrefort, who was searching for Sir Bors. [Vulgate IV]

BERCILAK (Bertilak) DE HAUTDESERT and WIFE†

Sir Bercilak was the Green Knight of **Sir Gawaine and the Green Knight**. It is uncertain whether Bercilak himself was magical; I am of the opinion that he was an ordinary mortal — albeit a prime specimen — who cooperated with Morgan, and that the transformation and all other magic involved was her work. Here is the way Gardner translated lines from the poem describing Bercilak in his human appearance:

> An immense man, indeed, mature in years;
> A beard broad and bright, and beaver-hued;
> His stance was proud and staunch, on stalwart shanks;
> His face flashed like fire; his speech was free;
> Surely a man well-suited . . .
> To lead as lord in a land of gallant men.

BERLUSE

The lieutenant of the castle of Sir Tor le Fise Aries. King Mark had killed Berluse's father before Berluse's eyes, and would have killed the son had he not escaped into the woods. Nevertheless, when Mark turned up at Sir Tor's castle, Berluse, motivated by love of Tor and of Lamorak, who was also a guest there, gave Mark truce and hospitality for the duration of his stay. Berluse warned Mark, however, to beware if ever they met outside the castle. [Malory X, 9]

From the similarity of the names, I suspect some connection between Berluse and the Sir Bersules whose story is given along with Amant's.

Berrant Le Apres — see KING OF THE HUNDRED KNIGHTS

Bersules — see under AMANT

BERTELOT

Bertelot was the brother of Breuse Sans Pitie. Sir Bliant, defending Lancelot from the brothers while Lancelot was mad, struck off Bertelot's hand [Malory XII, 2]. It is possible, but unlikely, that Bertelot could be identified with Sir Bertholai of the Vulgate.

BERTHOLAI†

Despite his advanced age, Bertholai was called the "best knight of Carmelide." Apparently this meant the best in arms, because he was not an endearing character. He was banished for the malevolent murder of another of King Leodegran's knights. Finding Genievre, who was also living in exile after the attempt by Cleodalis' relatives to substitute her for Guenever, Bertholai instigated a second attempt to substitute her for her more famous look-alike. They captured Arthur by luring him into the woods on a boar hunt and separating him from his companions. Then, with drugs and flattery, Genievre won his love and convinced him that she was Guenever, the true-born. Arthur had Genievre acknowledged Queen and renounced Guenever. Genievre wanted her rival's death, but eventually Guenevere was merely(?) condemned to lose the skin of her head (scalp?), cheeks, and palms, and be exiled forever.

This split the court. Lancelot renounced allegiance to Arthur, insisting on defending Guenever against three knights. (This caused a curious rivalry between Lancelot and Kay, who also wanted to serve as Guenever's champion.) Gawaine lent Excalibur to Lancelot for the battle. Thus Lancelot saved Guenever's skin, and Arthur gave her into Duke Galeholt's keeping. Galeholt set her up comfortably with Lancelot in Surluse. At Gawaine's urging, Arthur tried to win back Lancelot, but failed.

In his infatuation with Genievre, Arthur let his duties slip. When the Pope learned what had happened, he ordered Arthur to take back Guenevere and, when Arthur refused, interdicted Britain for twenty-one months. In the tenth month of interdiction, Genievre and Bertholai had paralytic strokes, losing the use of their limbs and all their senses except sight and hearing. They began to decay while still alive. The hermit Amustans upbraided Arthur and helped get deathbed confessions from Genievre and Bertholai, who confessed to save their souls. Gawaine took the news to Surluse, and finally Guenever and Lancelot were persuaded to return to Arthur. By the time she arrived, after spending more than two and a half years in Surluse, Bertholai and Genievre were dead. [Vulgate IV]

It is possible (though unlikely) that Bertholai could be identified with Malory's Sir Bertelot, the brother of Breuse Sans Pitie.

Bertilak de Hautdesert† — see BERCILAK DE HAUTDESERT

Bienpensant — see BEAUVIVANTE

BLAISE (Bleise)

Blaise was Merlin's master. After teaching him, Blaise retired to the forest of Northumberland to write down his pupil's deeds. Although so greatly eclipsed by his former pupil, Blaise must have had some skill in his time. Merlin frequently visited him in Northumberland. [Malory I, 17; other sources]

BLAMORE DE GANIS

Blamore was brother to Sir Bleoberis de Ganis, cousin to Lancelot, and a knight of the Round Table. Of the two brothers, Blamore was accounted the better man of his arms.

Blamore and Bleoberis once arraigned King Anguish of Ireland for the death of a cousin of theirs. Blamore was the one who fought the actual trial by combat against Anguish's champion, Sir Tristram. Defeated, Blamore tried to insist on death rather than surrender. Bleoberis seconded his brother's request, but Tristram and the judges refused to allow it.

> And then, by all their advices...the two brethren were accorded with King Anguish, and kissed and made friends for ever. And

then Sir Blamore and Sir Tristram kissed together, and there they made their oaths that they would never none of them two brethren fight with Sir Tristram, and Sir Tristram made the same oath. And for that gentle battle all the blood of Sir Launcelot loved Sir Tristram for ever.

Malory mentions Blamore several more times, fighting at the tournament of the Castle of Maidens, joining a quest to find Tristram, taking a fall from Sir Palomides at Duke Galeholt's tournament in Surluse. Blamore and Bleoberis were two of the guests at Guenever's small dinner party when Sir Patrise was poisoned. Later, they followed Lancelot into exile, and Blamore was made Duke of Limosin in Guienne. After the passing of Arthur, Blamore and Bleoberis eventually joined Lancelot, the former Archbishop of Canterbury, and others in their hermitage at Arthur's tomb. After Lancelot's death, Blamore and Bleoberis, along with Bors and Ector, went into the Holy Land to die warring against the Turks. [Malory VIII, 21-23; IX, 31, 36; X, 44; XVIII, 3; XX, 18; XXI, 10, 13]

DAMOISELLE DE LA BLANCHE LANDE†

Sir Gaheris' sweetheart, according to Vulgate V. I do not know where the "White Land" (Blanche Lande) was. See also under Clarisin, this section.

Bleise — see BLAISE

BLEOBERIS DE GANIS

Godson of King Bors, brother to Sir Blamore de Ganis, and cousin to Lancelot; as Bleoberis explains the relationship, he and Blamore "be sister's children unto my lord Sir Lancelot du Lake."

Malory first mentions Bleoberis as standardbearer for his godfather in the battle of Bedegraine during the first rebellion of British kings against Arthur. Like his brother, Bleoberis became a knight of the Round Table.

One time, before King Mark's marriage with La Beale Isoud, Bleoberis rode into Mark's court, demanded a gift, and, on being granted it for the sake of his renown and his place as a knight of the Round Table, he helped himself to Sir Segwarides's wife as the fairest lady at court and rode off with her. Segwarides came to rescue his wife, and Bleoberis defeated him. Next Tristram, who was at that time her lover, came on the same errand and defeated Bleoberis. The lady, however, was miffed at Tristram for letting her husband attempt her rescue first, and refused to return with Tristram, insisting instead that Bleoberis take her to the abbey where Segwarides lay wounded. Bleoberis complied. Another time, Lancelot and Bleoberis came upon Lamorak and Meliagrant in the midst of a battle over which queen was lovelier, Morgawse or Guenevere. Seeing Lancelot about to enter the fray on Meliagrant's side in defense of Guenevere's beauty, Bleoberis quelled the quarrel with some very sensible words:

> My lord Sir Launcelot, I wist you never so misadvised as ye are now...for I warn you I have a lady, and methinketh that she is the fairest lady of the world. Were this a great reason that ye should be wroth with me for such language?

BATTLEFIELD PILLAGERS

As in all eras, the aftermath of battle included pillagers. Following the last battle with Mordred, Arthur's two remaining knights bore him to a little chapel near the seaside.

> Then heard they people cry in the field. Now go thou, Sir Lucan, said the king, and do me to wit what betokens that noise in the field. So Sir Lucan departed ... [and] saw and hearkened in the moonlight, how that pillers and robbers

were come into the field, to pill and to rob many a full noble knight of brooches, and beads, of many a good ring, and of many a rich jewel; and who that were not dead all out, there they slew them for their harness and their riches. When Sir Lucan understood this work, he came to the king as soon as he might, and told him ... it is best that we bring you to some town. I would it were so, said the king. [Malory XXI, 4]

Presumably the lady Bleoberis mentions here is distinct from Segwarides' wife, but we never learn more about her.

Bleoberis and his brother arraigned King Anguish of Ireland, as described under Blamore. Bleoberis was castellan of Ganis castle, probably in Cornwall and probably named after the kingdom of his godfather. Active in tournaments and in jousting adventures in the books of Tristram, and one of Guenevere's guests at the intimate dinner party when Sir Patrise was poisoned, Bleoberis later followed Lancelot into exile and was made Duke of Poictiers. Later still, he became one of the hermits at the grave of Arthur. At last, after Lancelot's death, Bleoberis joined his brother Blamore and their cousins Ector and Bors as crusaders in the Holy Land, thus becoming one of the last of Arthurs's former knights of the Round Table to perish. [Malory I, 15; VIII, 15-18, 21-23; IX, 13-14, 37; XXI, 10, 13]

"BLEVINE"†

An unnamed female recluse who lived near enough the (commonest?) haunts of Breuse Sans Pitie to warn travelers against him. Unless Breuse's home territory was near the priory of the Queen of the Waste Lands, this likely was a different reclusive lady. [Vulgate III]

Bohort – see BORS

BORRE (Lohot, Loholz, Amyr?)

Arthur's son by his pre-Guenever leman, Lyzianor (Lionors), Sir Borre became "a good knight" and a companion of the Round Table [Malory I, 17]. Borre is probably identical with "Sir Bohart le Cure Hardy that was King Arthur's son," listed by Malory in XIX, 11. (Another knight with the surname "le Cure [Coeur] Hardy" — "the strong heart" — was Sir Ozanna, who seems to have been no relation to Borre.) That Borre should be identified with Lohot, or Loholz, who appears in the Vulgate and is mentioned at least once by Chrétien de Troyes, is reasonably evident from the mother's name. According to the Vulgate, Lohot killed the giant Logrin, but was killed in turn by Kay, who wished credit for the giant's death.

Julian Harris, in his introduction to Chrétien's **Yvain**, recaps old, pre-Chrétien rumors of Arthur's son Amyr, or Anir, and his marvellous tomb. Amyr is apparently unknown to the later romancers, at least by that name, but one of the old legends mentioned has it that he was killed by Arthur himself.

In her novel **Lionors**, Barbara Ferry Johnson transmogrifies Lionors' child by Arthur into a daughter, Elise (not to be confused with the heroine of Chapman's book, **King Arthur's Daughter**).

BORS (Bohort) DE GANIS

One of the major knights of the Round Table, Bors was the younger brother of Sir Lionel and a favorite cousin of Lancelot.

According to the Vulgate, after the death of King Bors, his sons Lionel and Bors the younger were taken by their father's conqueror, King Claudas. Seraide rescued the two children from Claudas and brought them to her mistress Viviane, the French Damsel of the Lake, to join their cousin Lancelot under Viviane's care.

Malory's first mention of Bors appears to be when Arthur sends him, with Lionel, Gawaine, and Bedivere, to carry a message of war to the Emperor Lucius. The four get the continental campaign against Rome off to a flying start. In battle with the Romans, Bors is named to Arthur's personal guard.

Sir Bors begat a child, Helin le Blank, on the daughter of King Brandegoris. Aside from this one lapse, Bors was celibate.

After Duke Galeholt's death, Seraide brought Galeholt's sword to Sir Bors, according to Vulgate IV.

Bors's prominence in Malory really begins in the Grail adventures. While on this quest, Bors championed the younger daughter of King Amans (Aniause). At the time, he was practicing ultra-austerity, eating only bread and water and sleeping on the floor. Vulgate VI tells us that when the lady gave him the best room in her castle and a splendid bed, he rumpled the bed to make it appear he had slept in it. Possibly he remembered that his hostess had seemed hurt when he ate only bread and water instead of the fine dinner she had prepared. In her castle, he had two dreams or visions, pointing out the choices he should make next day after winning the battle of his hostess and leaving her. The choices were whether to save his own brother Lionel from a captor who was beating him with thorns or to save a virgin from deflowerment (Bors saved the virgin) and, afterwards, whether to sleep with a temptress or allow her to jump from her tower and make her gentlewomen jump with her (he let them jump—they all turned out to be demons who disappeared on the way down).

Lionel later met Bors and attacked him in a towering rage for having been abandoned; Bors refused to defend himself against his brother until after an old holy man and a fellow companion of the Round Table had both been slaughtered trying to stop Lionel—then, when Bors at last took up weapon, a column of fire from Heaven intervened to stop the fight. None of Bors's decisions on this quest were made without much soul-searching, and he had also to undergo at least his share of false counsel by tempters in the guise of holy folk. Eventually joining Galahad, Percival, and Amide, Bors became the third of the three Round Table Knights to fully achieve the Holy Grail, and the only one of the three to return alive to Arthur's court.

Curiously, after the Grail Quest, we find Bors advising Lancelot in the latter's affair with Guenever, and even acting as go-between and peacemaker for the pair of adulterers. Accompanying Lancelot into exile, he was made king of all of Claudas' lands. Bors appears to have acted as Lancelot's executive officer during the fighting with Arthur, and later when Lancelot returned after the deaths of Arthur and Mordred to put down the remnants of Mordred's rebellion. Bors was the first, according to Malory, to find and join Lancelot as another hermit in the retreat of the former Archbishop of Canterbury. After Lancelot's death, Bors returned to settle affairs in his own country, and from thence he went, with Ector, Blamore, and Bleoberis, to die in crusade in the Holy Land.

By the time of the Winchester tournament and the affair of Elaine of Astolat, Bors could be recognized by a distinctive scar on his forehead. [Malory V, 6; XI, 4; XII, 9; XVI, 7-17; XVII-XXI; for the scar see XVIII, 15]

Father: King Bors	**SIR BORS' FAMILY**
Mother: Queen Evaine	**AND RETAINER**
Brother: Lionel	
Uncle: King Ban of Benwick	
Aunt: Queen Elaine of Benwick	
Cousins: Lancelot, Ector de Maris	
Mentors: Lionses, Phariance, Viviane, Seraide	
Paramour (one-night): King Brandegoris' Daughter	
Son: Helin le Blank	
Squire: Axilles	
Would-be lover?: Damsel of Hongrefort	

KING BORS (Bohort) OF GAUL (Gannes)

With his brother, King Ban of Benwick, King Bors was one of Arthur's major allies during Arthur's wars of accession. Ban and Bors were instrumental in helping Arthur win the battle of Bedegraine against the first rebel alliance, but perished when Arthur failed to return the favor and aid them against their enemy, King Claudas.

King Bors married Evaine, the sister of his brother's wife Helayne (Elaine of Benwick). The sons of Bors and Evaine were Lionel and Sir Bors de Ganis. [Vulgate II-IV; Malory I, 10-15]

> Brothers: King Ban, Gwenbaus
> Wife: Queen Evaine (Elaine of Benwick's sister)
> Sons: Lionel, Sir Bors de Ganis
> Sister-in-law: Queen Elaine of Benwick
> Godson: Bleoberis de Ganis
> Nephews: Lancelot, Ector de Maris **KING BORS' FAMILY**
> Retainers: Lionses?, Phariance **AND RETAINERS**

PRINCE BOUDWIN

The good Prince Boudwin, well-beloved by all the people of Cornwall, was King Mark's brother. Once, when the Saracens landed in Cornwall shortly after the Sessoins had gone, Boudwin "raised the country privily and hastily," put wildfire in three of his own ships, caused them to be driven among the ships of the Saracens, and so burned their entire navy. Then Boudwin and his men set on the Saracens and slew them all, to the number of forty thousand. Mark went wild with jealousy and murdered Boudwin. Boudwin's wife, Anglides, escaped with their young son, Alisander le Orphelin, to Magouns castle. [Malory X, 32]

BRAGWAINE

She was the chief gentlewoman of La Beale Isoud, and accompanied her to Cornwall from Ireland. The Irish queen, Isoud's mother, entrusted Bragwaine and Gouvernail with a love potion to give Isoud on the day of her marriage with Mark to ensure their wedded love. I believe that in some versions Bragwaine's carelessness is blamed for Tristram's accidentally drinking the love potion with Isoud on shipboard, but Malory is careful not to fix blame on anyone for the mischance.

Bragwaine seems to have been an herbwoman in her own right, as well as Isoud's well-loved favorite. Once two other handwomen of Isoud's conspired to kill Bragwaine out of envy - she was sent into the forest near Mark's court to gather herbs and there waylaid and bound to a tree for three days until Sir Palomides fortunately came by and rescued her.

When La Beale Isoud heard of Tristram's marriage to Isoud la Blanche Mains, she sent Bragwaine to Brittany with letters to Tristram. Bragwaine returned to Cornwall with Tristram, Gouvernail, and Kehydius. On a later occasion, also carrying letters from La Beale Isoud to Tristram, Bragwaine found him on his way to the tournament at the Castle of Maidens. At his invitation, she went with him, and was given a place near Guenever during the tourney. Not long thereafter, Lancelot met Bragwaine fleeing as fast as her palfrey could go from Breuse Sans Pitie. Lancelot, of course, rescued her. [Malory VIII, 24, 29; IX, 10, 27, 32, 36]

Bragwaine appears to have been an interesting, capable, and discreet dame, as well as an adventurous one, or, at least, one who attracted adventure.

BRANDAN†

A sixth-century saint who sailed west from Ireland into the Atlantic in search of the "Islands of Paradise."

KING BRANDEGORIS (Brangoire) OF STRANGGORE

One of the rebel kings at the beginning of Arthur's reign, he pledged to bring 5000 mounted men to the battle of Bedegraine. In that battle Brandegoris, King Idres, and King Agwisance unhorsed Sirs Griflet and Lucas. [Malory I, 12-15]

Surviving the battle, Brandegoris seems not to have joined the second coalition of rebel kings, for he is almost certainly to be identified with King Brandegore, on whose daughter Sir Bors begat a son, Helin le Blank. Bors revisited Brandegore when Helin was fifteen years old, and with Brandegore's consent, brought the boy to Arthur's court. King Brandegoris-Brandegore himself, however, seems never to have officially joined Arthur's court. [Malory XII, 9]

Brangoire also fathered a son, Evadeam [Vulgate II].

KING BRANDEGORIS' DAUGHTER

She was to be the prize of a tournament at the Castel de la Marche, held for the purpose of getting her a good husband. Sir Bors won the tournament, but, having sworn to remain chaste all his life, cried off by pleading that he was not ready to take a wife until his current quest, to avenge King Agrippe's daughter, was done. But Brandegoris's daughter fancied Bors. With the connivance of her old nurse, who gave Bors a ring to make him love the princess, the damsel spent that night with Bors, and Sir Helin le Blank was the result. The spell was broken in the morning when the ring fell off.

The twelve best knights of this tournament, after Bors, gave the princess "gifts" of varying silliness or bloodthirstiness. One, for instance, promised to cut off the heads of all the knights he conquered and send them to the princess.

The details given above come from Vulgate IV, but the princess is mentioned three or four times by Malory, once as the daughter of King Brandegore [XII, 9] and always as the mother of Helin le Blank.

BRANDELIS (Brandeharz, Brandeban, Brandelz)†

He was the Duke of Taningues [Vulgate IV].

BRANDILES

Malory mentions this knight of the Round Table perhaps half a dozen times. He was one of the knights invited to Guenever's small, select dinner party [XVIII, 3], one of the party who were a-Maying with Guenever when Meliagrant ambushed them [XIX, 1], and one of those killed during Lancelot's rescue of the Queen from the stake [XX, 8]. Sir Brandiles' sister was Gawaine's lady and the mother of Gawaine's sons Florence and Lovel [XIX, 11].

In the Vulgate, Floree, daughter of King Alain of Escavalon, is named as the mother of Gawaine's oldest son Guinglain. Assuming Guinglain to be Malory's Gingalin, Floree might be identified with Sir Brandiles' sister, making Brandiles the son of King Alain. See Floree, this section.

In the metrical romance "The Wedding of Sir Gawain and Dame Ragnell," Ragnell is made the mother of Guinglain. (It would seem from the names, however, that Floree must have been the mother of at least one of Gawaine's sons, Sir Florence.) In another, fragmentary romance collected by Hall, one Sir Brandles appears as the son of Sir Gilbert and brother of Sirs Gyamoure and Terry. This Brandles fights Gawaine for deflowering his chance-met sister (who clearly enjoyed it), proves Gawaine's equal, and parts from him at nightfall with the mutual promise to finish the fight another time; Brandles then beats his sister and abandons her. Sir Brandelys is one of Arthur's knights in "Sir Gawain and the Carl of Carlisle." See Louis B. Hall, **The Knightly Tales of Sir Gawain.**

SIR BRANDILES' SISTER

Either one of Gawaine's wives or one of his favorite paramours, since according to Malory she bore Gawaine two sons, Sirs Florence and Lovel [Malory XIX, 11]. Probably she should be identified with Floree; see also Brandiles.

BRANDUS DES ILLES†

The lord of La Doloreuse Garde before Lancelot conquered it. Brandus fled before Lancelot, tried to attack Arthur, and shortly thereafter, disguised as a vavasour, invited Gawaine, Ywaine, and their companions to La Dolorous Chartre, where they met some of their companions alive whose names they had read on false graves at Dolorous Garde. What Brandus had not told Gawaine and Ywaine was that he intended to imprison them, too, in Dolorous Chartre. Lancelot rescued them. [Vulgate III]

Brandus may perhaps be identified with Malory's Sir Brian of the Isles.

SIR BRASIAS

A hermit living near Windsor, he hosted Lancelot when the latter left Arthur's court in London after a quarrel with Guenever. (It was this quarrel that led to the dinner at which Sir Patrise was poisoned, for Guenever gave the dinner "to show outward that she had as great joy in all other knights of the Round Table as she had in Sir Lancelot.") [Malory XVIII, 2-5, 21].

Brasias probably is to be identified with Sir Brastias.

BRASTIAS

Brastias originally was a knight of Duke Gorlois. Merlin disguised Sir Ulfius as Sir Brastias on the night Uther begat Arthur. Later, on his accession to the throne, Arthur made Brastias "warden to wait upon the north from Trent forwards, for it was that time the most party the king's enemies." Brastias served Arthur well in the first wave of rebellion. With Ulfius, Brastias travelled across the Channel to summon Kings Ban and Bors to Arthur's aid. On the way, the two of them had to joust down eight of King Claudas's knights who tried to stop them. Brastias fought in the battle of Bedegraine, but afterwards seems to drop out of Malory's account, with no mention

that he remained with Arthur long enough to serve at the Round Table. [Malory I, 2, 7, 10-14] Brastias must already have been at least approaching middle age by the time of Arthur's coronation, and he may have retired early into a hermitage. He probably is to be identified with the hermit Brasias of Malory's Book XVIII.

BREUNOR

He was the wicked lord of Castle Pluere and, according to Malory, Duke Galeholt's father. Do not confuse this Sir Breunor with Sir Breunor le Noir, who is La Cote Male Taile.

Breunor le Noir — see LA COTE MALE TAILE

BREUSE SANS PITIE (Bruns Saunce Pité)

The "most mischievoust knight living" in Arthur's day, Sir Breuse, while not without skill and prowess at arms, regularly practiced every dirty trick available to force or guile. He even enlisted the aid of other knights by claiming that he was an innocent victim and that the knight chasing him was Breuse Sans Pitie (the unreliability of shields as identifying devices enabled him to get away with this one for a while). Among his favorite tricks was riding over an unhorsed knight; on one occasion, for instance, Breuse outjousted Gawaine and then rode over him twenty times in an effort to kill him.

Although he had at least one castle somewhere, Breuse seems likely to turn up almost anywhere, attack, kidnap, murder, and rape anyone, child or adult, for the sheer deviltry of it, and then disappear again, often pursued but never brought finally to justice. Unlike almost all other villains in Malory, Breuse seems never to be captured, utterly defeated, and either slain or converted to Arthur's side and the company of the Round Table. (Of course, Breuse was not afraid to turn tail and run when occasion demanded — but see the Brown Knight Without Pity, this section.)

In one passage, Malory gives Breuse a brother, Bertelot, but Bertelot is not nearly so prominent. Another time, King Mark writes to Morgan le Fay and the Queen of Northgalis begging them to rouse up Breuse Sans Pitie, among others, in a general manhunt for Alisander le Orphelin. [Malory IX, 26; X, 1, 35, 53; XII, 2; etc.]

In Vulgate VII I found what seemed to be a hint that Breuse was allied with the Saxons, but of this I am even less sure than of most data I took from the text of that volume.

Brewnor le Noir — see LA COTE MALE TAILE

BRIADES† — see under FONTAINE DES DEUX SYCAMORS, *Places*

BLOOD FEUDS

Side by side with the more official legal processes, the right of men to avenge their kinsfolk's deaths seems to have been more or less recognized and approved, at least by custom. Thus, Dame Anglides can give her son Alisander his father's bloody doublet and charge him as a duty to avenge the murder on his uncle Mark, La Cote Male Taile can appear at Arthur's court wearing his father's bloody coat and proclaiming his intention to wear it until his father is avenged, and Alisander's son Bellangere can at last avenge the deaths of both Alisander and Boudwin, all without a word of either legal or moral censure — indeed, with more than a hint of praise. [Malory X, 34; IX, 1; XIX, 11]

The important requirement seems to have been that such killings for revenge be done in the manner of fair and honorable

combat; a revenge killing done from ambush, or perpetrated by a number of men acting against one, were spoken of with outrage and contempt. It must also have helped if the person slain out of revenge was generally disliked; Mark's eventual death at Bellangere's hands seems to merit praise, while Pellinore's death at the hands of Lot's sons merits censure, even though both are merely mentioned, not described, in Malory's text [XIX, 11; XI, 10]. Mark was a recognized scoundrel, Pellinore was famed as a noble knight. Mark was also killed in revenge for treasons that would be considered murders today as well as in Arthur's time; Pellinore in revenge for a killing done in plain battle. This suggests that personal revenge may have been an accepted way of getting at your enemy when legal means failed or were unavailable for any reason.

BRIAN OF THE ISLES

Lord of the castle of Pendragon, Sir Brian was "a noble man and a great enemy unto King Arthur." He collected knights and ladies as his prisoners, among them La Cote Male Taile. Lancelot delivered the prisoners, fighting Brian until the latter yielded rather than be killed. Learning who it was that had defeated him, "Sir Brian [was] full glad, and so was his lady, and all his knights, that such a man should win them." Lancelot departed with La Cote Male Taile and his damsel on other adventures. Possibly Sir Brian made show of changing his ways and was left for a time in charge of his castle. However,

> as Sir Lancelot came by the Castle of Pendragon [on his return to Arthur's court] there he put Sir Brian de les Isles from his lands, for cause he would never be withhold with King Arthur; and all that Castle of Pendragon and all the lands thereof he gave to Sir La Cote Male Taile [Malory IX, 6, 9].

This may be the same Sir Brian of the Isles whom Malory introduces, much earlier, as sworn brother to Nimue's cousin Sir Meliot de Logres, and who appears again at the tournament at Dame Lyonors' Castle Dangerous, fighting against Arthur's side [Malory III, 13; VII, 28]. There are, however, many minor knights named Brian or Briant in Malory. I suspect that Brian of the Isles may be identified with the Vulgate's Sir Brandus des Illes, the former lord of La Dolorous Garde and Dolorous Chartre.

LADY OF BRIESTOC†

Apparently a sovereign lady, she lost all her knights while attempting to rescue Gawaine from Carados of the Dolorous Tower [Vulgate IV]. See also Briestoc, *Places.*

BRISEN (Brisane)

Dame Brisen, "one of the greatest enchantresses that was at that time in the world living," came to King Pellam and offered to arrange matters so that his daughter Elaine could lie with Lancelot. Pellam setting them up in his nearby Castle of Case for the trick, Brisen had a message brought to Lancelot by a man in the likeness of one he knew well, who brought him a ring that looked like one of Guenever's and told him that his lady awaited him in Case castle. When he arrived, Brisen gave Lancelot a cup of wine, which may have been drugged, before sending him upstairs to Elaine, who was already abed. Some time later, Brisen accompanied Elaine as handmaiden to Arthur's court for the festivities celebrating the victory over Claudas of France. Again Brisen helped her mistress enjoy Lancelot's love, this time, apparently, through simple intrigue. Elaine's chamber was next to the Queen's, Lancelot and Guenever planned to sleep together, and Brisen simply beat Guenever's messenger to Lancelot and guided him to Elaine's room instead. Lancelot went mad after that night's work, and turned up, a few years later, at Carbonek, where

eventually Dame Brisen recognized him and tactfully cast him into an enchanted sleep for an hour until he could be carried before the Sangreal, which healed him. [Malory XI, 2, 7-8; XII, 4]

BROMEL LA PLECHE (Brunout, Brinos de Plessie, Bruiol de Plessie)

After Galahad's birth, Sir Bromel, "a great lord" who had long loved Elaine of Carbonek, came to ask her to marry him. At last, trying to be rid of him, she told him she loved Lancelot. Bromel threatened to slay Lancelot. When Elaine exhorted him to do the great knight no treason, he vowed, "this twelvemonth I shall keep the pont [bridge] of Corbin for Sir Lancelot's sake, that he shall neither come nor go unto you, but I shall meet with him." Sir Bors happened to come first, however, defeated Bromel, and charged him to go the following Whitsunday to Lancelot and yield to him as knight miscreant. [Malory XI, 3-4] But according to the Vulgate, in which his name is Brunout or variants thereof, Elaine tells him she will love him instead of Lancelot if he proves himself better. When Brunout arrives in Camelot on Whitsunday, he comes in time to join Arthur's troops in the war against King Claudas. [Vulgate V]

THE BROWN KNIGHT WITHOUT PITY

The Brown Knight had a castle somewhere in the vicinity of the Duke de la Rowse, and his hobby was slaying other knights and imprisoning their ladies. He had collected thirty ladies when Gareth came by and slew him. [Malory VII, 32] If he had not been slain, I would have identified him with Breuse Sans Pitie.

BRUMANT L'ORGUILLEUS†

He was a nephew of King Claudas. One Eastertime, the knights of Claudas' court were discussing who was the best knight of the world. Everyone said it was Lancelot except Brumant, who said it was not Lancelot because Lancelot had never dared sit in the Siege Perilous. Although Claudas tried to dissuade him, Brumant swore to sit in the Siege Perilous on Whitsunday. By the time Brumant arrived at Camelot, he was weeping. (Perhaps he had sobered up and realized what kind of vow he had sworn.) He gave Lancelot a letter, telling him to read it in the event of Brumant's death. Then, saying, "I shall die for doing what you never ventured to do," Brumant sat in the Siege Perilous. A fire fell on him, from whence no one knew. It gave him just time to say, "By pride one gets but shame. I die by God's vengeance," before it consumed him to ashes. An evil smell filled the hall, but passed quickly. All the knights moved away from the holocaust except Lancelot, who, refusing to move from his own chair beside the Siege Perilous,

---

Probably the most notable blood feuds were the one between the sons of Lot and the family of Pellinore, which started early in Arthur's reign when Pellinore killed Lot in battle and which eventually resulted in the deaths of Pellinore, Margawse, Lamorak, possibly Dornar, and Patrise (who died of poison which a kinsman of Lamorak's meant for Gawaine); and the one between Gawaine and Lancelot, which rose in the very twilight of Arthur's reign, when Lancelot killed Gareth and Gaheris by accident in rescuing Guenever from the stake. It may have been such feuds as this that gave rise to the old saw,

> [T]here is hard battle thereas kin and friends do battle either against another, there may be no mercy but mortal war,

even though Lancelot cites the proverb, not in reference to blood feuds, but in reference to the wounds his kinsmen have inflicted on him in the Winchester tournament, through failing to recognize him as Lancelot. [Malory XVIII, 16]

We can understand murder and violent death giving rise to such vendettas; it is more surprising to find that mere jealousy almost started at least one such bloodletting.

> Sir Tristram achieved many great battles, wherethrough all the noise fell to Sir Tristram, and it ceased of Sir Launcelot; and therefore Sir Launcelot's brethren and his kinsmen would have slain Sir Tristram because of his fame. But when

remained unharmed. The letter Brumant had given Lancelot told the whole story of the rash vow. When Brumant's three brothers got the news from England, they took comfort in the thought that Brumant's was an honorable death. [Vulgate V]

Brunout — see BROMEL LA PLECHE

BYANNE†

The daughter of King Clamadon, Byanne may or may not have been responsible for the magic in her tale. She first appeared at Arthur's court with her lover Evadeam, son of King Brangoire (Brandegoris), Evadeam being in the form of an ugly dwarf. Byanne insisted, despite Kay's chaffing, that Arthur dub her dwarf knight. She herself fixed his left spur, while the King fixed his right. They did not give their names, but Merlin said the dwarf was highly born. After leaving court, Evadeam defeated at least one knight, Tradelmant, the grandson of the King of Norgales, and sent him back to Arthur's court. Later, while searching for Merlin, Ywaine and his companions met Byanne, who begged them to succor her dwarf. When they arrived, however, Evadeam had defeated five attacking knights all by himself.

Later, while Gawaine was riding around the woods in a reverie, he passed Byanne without saluting her. As a punishment, she told him he would for a time resemble the next person he met. That person was Evadeam, still in dwarf form. Wandering in the shape of the dwarf, Gawaine came near the place of Merlin's imprisonment. Merlin sent greetings to the King and Queen, and said that no one would ever hear his voice again. Later still, Gawaine met a damsel (I presume Byanne again) beset by two knights, and succored her. She had set it up to test him, enchanting the knights so that they could not be hurt. After swearing to help every damsel and never to forget to bow to any woman, Gawaine regained his true form. [Vulgate II]

I listed Byanne among the possible potential female knights on the grounds that she served her knighted dwarf in the capacity of a squire. She may also, of course, be considered an enchantress.

ADOR OF CORNWALL

The father of that Sir Constantine who was king after Arthur, Cador appears in Malory V as a knight of the Round Table, one of Arthur's counsellors, and a trusty officer in the war against Emperor Lucius. The name may be a variant of "Carados" — in Malory XIX, 11, Constantine is called 'Sir Carados' son of Cornwall.' Do not confuse Cador of Cornwall with Carados of Scotland or with Carados of the Dolorous Tower.

DUKE CALLES†

Duke Calles wanted to settle half his land on his daughter upon her marriage. When his three sons opposed the idea, he disinherited them in favor of the daughter. They surprised her husband in a wood and murdered him, then seized many of the Duke's castles. Gareth, Gaheris, and Agravaine arrived at the castle in which the Duke's sons were besieging their own father, and entered on the side of Calles. The first day they fought, Gareth killed one of the sons. Lancelot and Lionel arrived in company with "Ornagrine." These two knights, hearing a false account of the war, entered on the side of the rebellious sons and killed the Duke. [Vulgate V]

Calogrenant — see COLGREVANCE

Duke of Cambenet (Cambines?) — see EUSTACE

CAMILLE†

An enchantress of Saxon descent, she held the castle of La Roche and helped her people against Arthur. At the same time she loved Arthur—which did not prevent her having a lover, Gadrasolain, in the castle.

After a battle with the Saxons, Arthur accepted an invitation to visit Camille in La Roche. He had a good time with her, but afterwards he and Gaheris were captured with the help of Hargodabran and forty knights. A damsel of Camille's went to Lancelot, Duke Galeholt, Gawaine, and Ector, telling them that Camille meant to convey Arthur to Ireland. These four knights came into La Roche to save Arthur. The damsel's tale had been a ruse which enabled Camille to capture them also. She released Lancelot, however, who was demented with grief at being captured. Lancelot, wearing Arthur's arms and using Arthur's sword Sequence, grievously wounded Hargodabran in battle and then penetrated into La Roche, where he killed Gadrasolain and many others, and freed Arthur with his companions. Threatening to kill Camille unless she surrendered the castle, Arthur left Gawaine, whom she feared more than any other knight, in charge of La Roche. Kay found a former sweetheart of Gadrasolain's. This damsel, whom Camille had kept imprisoned for three years, warned Kay that if Camille escaped with her books and boxes all was lost. Kay burned the books and boxes. Camille, to Arthur's grief, threw herself from the rocks and perished.

It was after this episode that Lancelot, Galeholt, and Ector became members of Arthur's court (and of the Round Table at once?). [Vulgate III]

ARCHBISHOP (or Bishop) OF CANTERBURY

This churchman blessed the seats of the Round Table at the ordination of Arthur's first knights of the Table. Years later he resisted Mordred's attempt to usurp the throne, for which he was forced into religious retirement at Glastonbury.

Sir Launcelot wist how his kinsmen were set, he said to them openly: Wit you well, that an the envy of you all be so hardy to wait upon my lord Sir Tristram, with any hurt, shame, or villainy, as I am true knight I shall slay the best of you with mine own hands. Alas, fie for shame, should ye for his noble deeds await upon him to slay him. [Malory X, 88]

Considering the magnitude of the personalities involved, we breathe a sigh of relief that Lancelot nipped this affair in the bud.

As kinship and friendship was at the heart of these feuds, so, conversely, the parties involved might be protected from

further reprisal by other kinships and friendships. Thus the position of Gawaine and his brothers as favorite nephews of Arthur enabled them for years to carry on their feud with Pellinore's family with no more than moral interference from other noble knights who disapproved of the way they were handling it. For instance, Tristram once met Agravaine and Gaheris, told them "ye be called the greatest destroyers and murderers of good knights that be now in this realm," but refrained from chastizing them bodily for the death of Sir Lamorak: "Well ... for King Arthur's sake I shall let you pass as at this time." [Malory X, 55]

A political power as bishop, he seems also to have been a holy man, as evidenced by his life as a hermit. After burying the body of Arthur when the queens brought it to him, he became the nucleus of a group that finally included Bedivere, Bors, Lancelot, and others who embraced the religious life at Arthur's grave. When Lancelot died, the former Archbishop saw a vision of angels heaving up Lancelot's soul into Heaven. [Malory III, 2; XXI, 1, 6-12] The Archbishop might perhaps be identified with Dubric.

KING CARADOS OF SCOTLAND

This Carados seems to be the one who joined the first wave of rebellion against Arthur, pledging 5000 mounted men to the effort and fighting in the battle of Bedegraine. Carados of Scotland must have been reconciled with Arthur and avoided the second rebellion, for he later appears as a knight of the Round Table during the attempt to heal Sir Urre. Chances are he also was the Carados involved in the trial of Anguish of Ireland: "King Arthur assigned King Carados and the King of Scots to be there that day as judges" when Sirs Bleoberis and Blamore arraigned King Anguish for murder. [Malory I, 12-16; VIII, 20-23; XIX, 11]

Vulgate V has a King Karados Brief Bras [Short Arm] who was a nephew of Arthur and joined Arthur's war against King Claudas to free Elyzabel. In Vulgate VI, Carados appears as one of Arthur's advisors in Arthur's war against Lancelot.

Carados seems to have been a common name, and it is sometimes tricky to sort out various Caradoses and Cadors. I do not think, however, that King Carados of Scotland should be confused with Sir Carados of the Dolorous Tower.

SIR CARADOS OF THE DOLOROUS TOWER

This Carados, who was "made like a giant" and whom Lancelot later called "a full noble knight and a passing strong man," enjoyed capturing and imprisoning other knights. Sir Lancelot arrived on the scene when Carados was carrying Gawaine away on his saddlebow. Lancelot killed Carados and freed Gawaine and the other prisoners. Carados' brother, Sir Turquine, died in the attempt to avenge Carados' death on Lancelot.

Carados and Turquine illustrate the problem of Malory's chronology. Lancelot fights and kills Turquine in Book VI, 7-9. Turquine reappears, along with Carados, at the tournament at Castle Dangerous in VII, 26-29, where they do not appear to be villainous. The rescue of Gawaine and the slaying of Carados, for which Turquine seeks revenge, is not described until VIII, 28. Nor is the problem alleviated by the presence of at least one other Carados in Malory's account. Shall we blame it all on Caxton? Although in VIII, 28, Malory calls Carados of the Dolorous Tower "the mighty king," I am reasonably sure this Carados is not to be confused with King Carados of Scotland.

KING CARBARECOTINS (Kabbaranturs, Carbarentins) OF CORNOAILLE†

I believe that his territory was the French Cornoaille in Brittany, not the Cornwall in Great Britain. Carbarecotins was an ally of Arthur, whom he joined in the war against Claudas to free Elyzabel. [Vulgate V]

THE SUFFRAGAN OF CARLISLE

A suffragan is a bishop serving as assistant to the bishop of a diocese. It was the Suffragan of Carlisle who finally baptized Sir Palomides at Tristram's behest. [Malory XII, 14]

CASTOR

Lancelot was at Carbonek in one of his mad fits, subdued but unknown, at the time King Pellam's nephew Castor was grooming for knighthood.

> ...so [Castor] desired of [Pellam] to be made knight, and so... the king made him knight at the feast of Candlemas. And when Sir Castor was made knight, that same day he gave many gowns. And then Sir Castor sent for the fool—that was Sir Lancelot. And when he was come afore Sir Castor, he gave Sir Lancelot a robe of scarlet and all that longed unto him.

Now well-groomed, Lancelot fell asleep in the garden, where Elaine and Brisen found and recognized him at last and cured his madness by exposing him to the Holy Grail. Under the name of Le Chevaler Mal Fet, Lancelot planned to live with Elaine in Pellam's Joyous Isle.

> Sir, said Sir Castor...ever meseemeth your name should be Sir Lancelot du Lake, for or now I have seen you. Sir, said Lancelot, ye are not as a gentle knight: I put case my name were Sir Lancelot, and that it list me not to discover my name, what should it grieve you here to keep my counsel, and ye be not hurt thereby? but wit thou well an ever it lie in my power I shall grieve you, and that I promise you truly. Then Sir Castor kneeled down and besought Sir Lancelot of mercy: For I shall never utter what ye be, while that ye be in these parts. Then Sir Lancelot pardoned him. [Malory XII, 4, 6]

Cei — see **KAY**

DUKE CHALEINS OF CLARANCE

Chaleins appears at Duke Galeholt's tournament in Surluse, where he did "great deeds of arms, and of so late as he came in the third day there was no man did so well except King Bagdemagus and Sir Palomides." To this tourney he brings along a knight called Elis la Noire. Chaleins appears again at a tournament given by Arthur on Candlemas Day following the death of Elaine of Astolat; to this tourney he brings a hundred knights. [Malory X, 44, 48; XVIII, 22] Apparently Chaleins became a companion of the Round Table, being listed in Malory XIX, 11.

I suggest he be identified with the Vulgate's Galeshin.

CHANART†

King Claudas made his nephew Chanart co-commander-in-chief (with Claudin) of his army for the war with Arthur over Elyzabel. A good knight, Chanart succeeded in unhorsing Gawaine—though Gawaine later unhorsed him during the same battle. After Claudas' departure, Chanart helped welcome Arthur into Gannes. [Vulgate V]

CLAELLUS†

The seneschal of King Pellam of Listenois, according to Vulgate VII (which, however, also seems to give Minadoras as Pellam's senschal).

KING CLAMADON†

The father of Byanne.

Duke of Clarance — see **CHALEINS**; also **GALESHIN**

KING CLARIANCE (Clarence, Clarion) OF NORTHUMBERLAND

One of the kings in the first wave of rebellion against Arthur, Clariance pledged 3000 men of arms to the cause and fought in the battle of Bedegraine. Apparently he became a companion of the Round Table, for he is listed among those at the attempted healing of Sir Urre. Probably he is to be identified with the "King of Northumberland" who appears, for instance, at Arthur's Candlemas tournament after Elaine of Astolat's death, to which he brings a hundred good knights and where he gives Hoel of Brittany a fall, and with the King of Northumberland who is father to Sir Epinegris.

Vulgate VII tells of a king or ally of the Sesnes named Clarions. He is probably distinct from Clariance of Northumberland.

CLARIONS†

This Saxon king was involved in the attack on Vandaliors, a castle of the rebel kings early in Arthur's reign. It was from Clarions that Gawaine won his warhorse Gringolet.

"CLARISIN"†

After rescuing the unnamed damsel I have called Clarisin, Sir Gaheris tried to get her to go to bed with him. She argued him down, pointing out that he already had a sweetheart, the Damoiselle de la Blanche Lande, in that country; that "women are easily conquered, and therefore the wrong is all the greater to deceive them, and will bring you more shame than honour"; and that she already loved another knight and wished to remain true. At last Gaheris admitted she was right and stopped trying to seduce her. [Vulgate V]

I have borrowed the name from Malory V, 12. Arthur is besieging a stubborn city in Tuscany.

> Then came out a duchess, and Clarisin the countess, with many ladies and damosels, and kneeling before King Arthur, required him for the love of God to receive the city, and not take it by assault, for then should many guiltless be slain.

Arthur promised the ladies safety, "but the duke shall abide my judgment." Thus the town was surrendered without further bloodshed, but Arthur sent the duke of the Tuscan city to Dover as a life prisoner.

KING CLAUDAS OF GAUL

Malory mentions this important villain about a dozen times, always as an offstage menace or defeated enemy. The most significant thing Malory tells us of his character comes from Merlin's counsel to Arthur during the first wave of rebellion after the accession:

> And on these two kings [Ban and Bors] warreth a mighty man of men, the King Claudas, and striveth with them for a castle, and great war is betwixt them. But this Claudas is so mighty of goods whereof he getteth good knights, that he putteth these two kings most part to the worse.... [Malory I, 10]

The Vulgate gives much fuller information, calling him "brave but treacherous" and saying that his "character was a strange mixture of good and bad qualities." His original territory was "la terre deserte" in Gaul, so called because Uther Pendragon and Hoel had devastated it, sparing only Bourges. This alone would be enough to explain Claudas' antipathy to Uther's son Arthur, as well as his attempts to gain other lands. I also suspect that Claudas may have been trying to do in France what Arthur did in Britain: consolidate the petty kingdoms into one. Possibly the difference was that after conquering the petty kings, Arthur was willing to incorporate those who were still alive into his own government, leaving them as rulers of their old territories with him as their liege lord, and even making them companions of the Round Table. Claudas appears to have aimed simply at annihilating the opposition.

Claudas succeeded in defeating and bringing about the deaths of Ban and Bors after they had returned from helping Arthur. Claudas loved the wife of Pharien (Phariance) and for her sake made Pharien seneschal of Gannes after driving out

King Bors. [Malory brings Phariance to Britain with Ban and Bors to help Arthur in I, 10.] Claudas also took in King Bors' sons Lionel and Bors the younger, but surely regretted it when they killed Claudas' own son Dorin (who had already become quite dislikable by his death at age 15). Seraide rescued Lionel and Bors from Claudas.

Besides sending spies from time to time to Arthur's court (the spies were quite likely to decide to stay in Logres), Claudas himself went at least once, in disguise, to spy out Arthur's land. He was very impressed by Arthur's good qualities.

Eventually Arthur and Guenever declared all-out war on Claudas in the affair of Guenever's cousin Elyzabel. Despite the facts that Claudas accepted excellent advice, enlisted Rome as an ally, allowed those of his people who so wished to leave the country before the war started and gave great largess to win the hearts of those who stayed, despite his excellent commanders-in-chief Claudin (his son or stepson) and Chanart, he was at last utterly routed. In one battle near Gannes, he refused, with tears in his eyes, to leave his people in their danger on the battlefield. He might have ended the war by freeing Elyzabel after the first battle, but he refused—perhaps because it was Lionel, who had long ago killed Dorin, who asked for her release. Claudas did arrange an exchange of prisoners taken in battle; Claudas gave each of his prisoners a meal and a good horse, while Gawaine on the other side was giving the freed prisoners a rich garment apiece and lavish entertainment. Finally, forced to decamp, Claudas told his barons they should now do whatever seemed to them best, but he himself had no hope of personally making peace with Arthur and with Lancelot, whose father's lands he had taken so long before. Claudas then slipped out of Gannes to take refuge in Rome. [Vulgate III-V]

Claudas could not read, needing his clerks to read to him [Vulgate V].

Malory mentions Claudas' final defeat: "King Arthur had been in France, and had made war upon the mighty King Claudas, and had won much of his lands" [Malory XI, 6].

Son: Dorin Son or stepson: Claudin Lover: Phariance's Wife Nephews: Brumant l'Orguilleus, Chanart Kinsman (otherwise unspecified): Bertolle Seneschal: Phariance Knight of Gaul: Esclamor	**KING CLAUDAS' FAMILY AND RETAINERS**

CLAUDIN (Claudine)

According to Malory XVII, 21, he was King Claudas' son; according to Vulgate V, he was the king's stepson. Claudas made Claudin co-commander-in-chief (with Chanart) of his army for the war with Arthur. Gawaine admired Claudin's prowess in battle; Bors and Gawaine agreed that, after Lancelot and Gawaine himself, Claudin was the best knight. With Chanart and another good Gaulish knight, Esclamor (probably distinct from King Esclamor), Claudin welcomed Arthur into Gannes after Claudas escaped. [Vulgate V]

Claudin was one of three Gaulish knights who arrived at Carbonek to meet Galahad, Percivale, Bors, three Irish knights, and three Danish knights at the climax of the Grail Quest. Together, these twelve knights represented the twelve apostles at the Last Supper. At Carbonek they witnessed the mysteries of the Grail as performed by Joseph of Arimathea (or perhaps by his son Josephe). From the Vulgate we learn that all but one of the knights were to die on the Quest. After leaving Carbonek, the twelve knights went on their separate ways, apparently in small groups, as the Apostles were sent forth in all directions. Since Sir Bors was the survivor, Claudine presumably died before reaching home.

Claudin would seem to be the French equivalent to Galahad, or at least to Percivale.

CLEODALIS†

He was King Leodegran's seneschal, and the supposed father of Genievre. [Vulgate II]

Clochides† -- see under LE TERTRE DEUEE, *Places*

COLGREVANCE (Calogrenant, Galogrinans) OF GORE

Malory mentions "Sir Colgrevaunce de Gorre" as early as the battle of Bedegraine against the rebel kings, where he fights on Arthur's side [I, 17]. In IX, 24, Malory notes that Bors, Lancelot, and others "had made promise to lodge with Sir Colgrevance" for a night.

This knight of the Round Table had at least two deaths, both of them spectacular. During the Grail Quest, Colgrevance happened to find Sir Lionel ready to slay his own brother Bors, who had earlier left him a suffering captive in order to go rescue a virgin. Colgrevance loved Bors and tried to stop Lionel. They fought long, but Lionel got the upper hand. Colgrevance cried out to Bors for help; Bors, however, was busy doing the Right Thing by refusing to raise a hand against his brother. So Lionel, who had already cut down a hermit for coming between him and Bors, slew Colgrevance. Colgrevance died with a prayer on his lips, and then, at last, with tears, Bors dressed to defend himself. [Malory XVI, 14-16]

You can't keep a good man down, though. Colgrevance shows up again among the knights who try to heal Sir Urre, in Malory XIX, 11. Colgrevance of Gore was among the knights who went with Mordred and Agravaine to surprise Lancelot and Guenever together. Lancelot was unarmed, and Colgrevance was the first to go into the Queen's chamber.

> [Lancelot] unbarred the door, and with his left hand he held it open a little, so that but one man could come in at once; and so there came striding a good knight, a much man and large, and his name was Colgrevance of Gore.

Lancelot deflected his blow, killed him, and took his arms and armor. Colgrevance thus became the evening's first casualty. [Malory XX, 2-4] He might have been better off staying dead the first time; it was a more pious death and in a worthier cause.

It is, of course, possible that the Colgrevance slain by Lionel was different from the Colgrevance of Gore slain by Lancelot—in which case there were two companions of the Round Table by that name.

COLOMBE

When Sir Lanceor rode out after Sir Balin, Lanceor's lady Colombe came after him.

> And when she espied that Lanceor was slain, she made sorrow out of measure, and said, O Balin, two bodies thou hast slain and one heart, and two hearts in one body, and two souls thou hast lost. And therewith she took the sword from her love that lay dead, and fell in a swoon. And when she arose she made great dole out of measure, the which sorrow grieved Balin passingly sore, and he went unto her for to have taken the sword out of her hand, but she held it so fast he might not take it out of her hand unless he should have hurt her, and suddenly she set the pommel to the ground, and rove herself through the body. [Malory II, 6]

COLUMBA† (Columkill)

A sixth-century Irish saint of the family of the kings of Ulster. With twelve followers, he left Ireland and evangelized Scotland, founding 300 religious houses there. The first, that on the island of Iona, was founded in 563 A.D. According to Glennie, Columba was supposed to possess prophetic power. Phyllis McGinley, who calls him "Ireland's most typical saint," gives a physical description from old chronicles: tall, fair-skinned, dark-haired, gray-eyed, and with a melodious, far-sounding voice. She also retells the tale of why he left Ireland — in self-banishment for the horror of having started a war over his right to copy a book. [**Saint-Watching**, Viking, 1969]

KING CONSTANS OF ENGLAND†

He was Arthur's grandfather. Constans' three sons were Maines, Pandragon, and Uther (later Utherpendragon). Constans died a natural death. [Vulgate II] Malory seems not to mention Constans, unless he is to be identified with "Constantine the son of Heleine," whose holding the empire is cited as precedent for Arthur's refusal to pay truage to Rome [Malory V, 1].

CONSTANTINE

Almost all that Malory tells us of Sir Constantine is that he was the son of Cador (sometimes called Carados) of Cornwall, that Arthur left him and Sir Baudwin of Britain as joint governors of the realm during his continental war with Emperor Lucius of Rome, that he was a knight of the Round Table, that he became King after Arthur, and that he tried unsuccessfully to keep Sirs Bors, Ector de Maris, Blamore, Bleoberis, and other former companions of the Table with him in England after Lacelot's death [Malory V, 3; XIX, 11; XXI, 13]. Still, even allowing for the fact that the flower of Arthur's knighthood was either slaughtered or moved to Gaul and/or hermitages during and after the wars with Lancelot and Mordred, it does seem that the man who eventually succeeded Arthur must have been a person of some importance. Arthur would have done better to have reappointed Constantine governor, instead of Mordred, when he went to fight Lancelot in France. I suspect that Constantine may have tried to keep up the Round Table.

DUKE CORNEUS

The father of Sir Lucan the Butler [Malory I, 10].

CORSABRIN

A paynim, and "a passing felonious knight" [Malory X, 47]. See under King Bandes.

LA COTE MALE TAILE (Sir Breunor, Brewnor, or Bruin le Noire)

The tale of Sir Breunor in Malory IX parallels or — I think — parodies the tale of Sir Gareth in VII. Again, we have the young man arriving at court and being given a nickname by Sir Kay in mockery. Breunor is called La Cote Male Taile ("the evil-shaped coat") because he wears his father's coat with the marks of his father's death-wounds, being determined to avenge his father's murder.

Breunor gets off to a more visibly promising start than Gareth. At his request, Arthur knights him the day after his arrival, and almost immediately afterwards, when a lion breaks loose from its tower and comes hurtling at the Queen and her knights, only Breunor stands his ground to slay the beast. That same day the damsel first called Maledisant and finally Beauvivante comes into court looking for a knight to achieve the quest of a "great black shield, with a white hand in the midst holding a sword," which she carries with her. Breunor takes the quest, and, like Lynette, Maledisant promptly and continuously mocks him. Unlike Lynette, however, Maledisant later confesses that she has been prompted all along by love for Breunor, wanting to get him off the dangerous quest because he seems too young and likely to be killed on it. Also, in Malory's version of Gareth and Lynette, Gareth finally weds not Lynette but her sister; the romancer corrects this in the later tale and matches Breunor with Maledisant-Beauvivante.

I confess I lose the train of Breunor's quest with Maledisant and cannot quite figure out what it was all about; Breunor, however, unlike Gareth, is sometimes realistically allowed to be defeated on his first quest. Eventually Lancelot makes him lord of the castle of Pendragon in place of Sir Brian de les Isles. A little after this, La Cote is made knight of the Round Table. He does finally succeed in avenging his father, though Malory does not give the details. The last we seem to hear of La Cote Male Taile, aside from his appearance at the attempt to heal Sir Urre, is as one of the guests at Guenever's small dinner party when Sir Patrise is poisoned. La Cote Male Taile was brother to Sir Dinadan. [Malory IX, 1-9; XVIII, 3; XIX, 11]

Although placed later in Malory's work, the tale of Sir Breunor is meant to precede that of Beaumains chronologically, for when Kay mocks Beaumains, Lancelot reminds him of how well La Cote Male Taile turned out [Malory VII, 2].

KING CRADELMAS

One of the rebels at the beginning of Arthur's reign, Cradelmas pledged 5000 mounted men to the cause and fought in the battle of Bedegraine [Malory I, 12, 15]. Possibly he should be identified with Tradelmans.

AGONET, SIR

The King's fool, or court jester, Arthur "loved him passing well, and made him knight with his own hands." Sir Griflet called him "the best fellow and the merriest in the world." Kay sent him after La Cote Male Taile on the latter's first quest; although La Cote bested him, the clash lent Maledisant ammunition for further raillery: "Fie for shame! now art thou shamed in Arthur's court, when they send a fool to have ado with thee, and specially at thy first jousts." Dagonet appears adventuring about the countryside in the long rambling books of Tristram. Once, riding alone with two squires, Dagonet meets Tristram in a fit of madness. The madman ducks Dagonet and the squires in a nearby well, to the merriment of nearby shepherds who have been feeding Tristram. Dagonet and the squires, thinking the shepherds put Tristram up to it, begin to beat them, whereupon Tristram kills one of the squires. Escaping to King Mark, Dagonet warns him against going near "the well in the forest, for there is a fool naked, and that fool and I fool met together, and he had almost slain me." Later, joining a party of some half-dozen knights of

the Round Table, Dagonet takes the suggestion of the wounded Mordred, dons Mordred's armor, and rides after Mark with such a fierce show that he makes Mark ride for dear life. Palomides happens along in time to rescue Mark. [Malory IX, 3, 19; X, 12-13]

Tennyson makes exquisite use of Dagonet in the idyll, **The Last Tournament**.

DAMAS

Sir Damas, a villainous knight, was unjustly keeping a manor from his good younger brother Sir Ontzlake, and imprisoning all good knights so that they would not champion Ontzlake. Morgana used the situation to get Arthur and her lover Accolon into a fight as the brothers' champions. Arthur, ironically enough, was championing the wicked brother, Damas, while Accolon, who was actually meant to kill Arthur, was officially representing the good brother, Ontzlake. After Arthur, through Nimue's help, had won, he commanded that Ontzlake should hold the manor from Damas for the yearly fee of a palfrey, "for that will become [Sir Damas] better to ride on than upon a courser" — Damas has no business riding into battle on a warhorse, like an honorable knight. [Malory IV, 6-12]

A knight named Damas was killed during Lancelot's rescue of Guenever from the stake. It might have been a different Damas, or it might be that Ontzlake's brother reformed and joined Arthur's court. Malory also mentions at least one and possibly two knights named Darras — an old knight with five sons who gives Tristram lodging after the tournament at the Castle of Maidens, and a knight of the Round Table who appears at the attempt to heal Sir Urre — and the names Damas and Darras may have been easy to confuse. [Malory IX, 34-37; XIX, 11; XX, 8]

Dareca† — see MONENNA

SAINT DAVID (Dewi)†

Born c. 496 to Prince Xantus of Cereticu (Cardiganshire) and a nun named Malearia, Saint David was an uncle of Arthur. After entering religious life on the Isle of Wight, the ascetic David moved to Menevia, Pembrokeshire, where he founded 12 convents. In 577 the archbishop of Caerleon resigned his see to David, who moved the seat of the diocese to Menevia, which became the metropolis of Wales under the name St. David's. According to Drayton, he lived in the valley of Ewias between the Hatterill hills, Monmouthshire. The waters of Bath were said to owe their qualities to the blessing of David. He reportedly died in 642, aged 146.

DE ( ) — see the word following 'De' or 'De la', etc.

Count Del Parc† — see TURQUINE'S HILL, *Places*

DINADAN

A good knight with a sense of humor and, what seems even rarer among the companions of the Round Table, a sense of practicality, Dinadan was never willing to rush into a fight for the sake of wounds and glory. He wanted to know first that he had some chance of success and that he was going in on the right side.

Dinadan had more than a little satirical talent. Malory characterizes his lampoon against Mark of Cornwall as "the worst lay that ever harper sang," probably in the sense of hardest hitting. Dinadan was equally able, however, to laugh at himself. One of Malory's best episodes for Dinadan-watching is Duke Galeholt's tournament in Surluse, to which Dinadan first came in disguise, and did great deeds of arms. He was unmasked by the fifth day, if not earlier—Galeholt sent Lancelot to unhorse him, apparently with a bit of clowning on both sides. On the evening of the sixth day, seeing Galeholt in a dark mood at being served fish, which he hated, Dinadan got "a fish with a great head" and served it up elaborately to Galeholt with the quip, "Well may I liken you to a wolf, for he will never eat fish, but flesh." This snapped Galeholt out of his bad humor. Dinadan then asked Lancelot, "What devil do ye in this country, for here may no mean knights win no worship for thee." Lancelot, entering into the spirit, replied by praying to be delivered from Dinadan's great spear: "God forbid that ever we meet but if it be at a dish of meat." Next day Lancelot entered the lists with a maiden's gown over his armor, unhorsed Dinadan before the latter recovered from his surprise, and then, with a group of co-pranksters, carried Dinadan into the forest and clothed him in the damsel's dress. A good time was had by all, and the Queen was vastly amused.

(In his excellent edition of Malory, John W. Donaldson interprets the tournament of Surluse as an attempt by Duke Galeholt and a co-conspirator to get Lancelot killed, and finds evidence in Dinadan's actions, especially the serving of the fish, that the shrewd, joking knight saw through the plot and meant to warn or protect Lancelot. This is an ingenious interpretation, but I have not yet been able to locate in the full edition of Malory the lines describing Galeholt's murderous intent, nor is it consistent with what we know from the Vulgate of the great friendship between Galeholt and Lancelot. It seems to me more likely that Dinadan's part in the Surluse tournament reflects pure high spirits.)

Dinadan, one knight who claimed to have no lady love, was the brother of La Cote Male Taile. Dinadan was "gentle, wise, and courteous," "a good knight on horseback," "a scoffer and a japer, and the merriest knight among fellowship that was that time living. And he...loved every good knight, and every good knight loved him again." Tristram in particular loved him above all other knights except Lancelot. Alas, Mordred and Agravaine took a dislike to him, apparently because of something he said to them about the matter of Lamorak's death, and, although he had once rescued them from Breuse Sans Pitie, "cowardly and feloniously" they killed him during the Grail Quest, though Malory does not give fuller details. [Malory VII, 2; X, 10, 20, 25, 27, 40-49, 55]

DINAS

Originally King Mark's seneschal of Cornwall, Dinas renounced his allegiance to Mark in anger at Mark's treatment of Tristram, gave up all the lands that he held of Mark, and became Tristram's trusty friend and ally, helping Sir Sadok and others garrison Lyonesse on Tristram's behalf. Eventually, probably after Tristram's death, Dinas came to Arthur's court where he became a knight of the Round Table. He followed Lancelot into exile and was made Duke of Anjou. From what we are told of Dinas, he seems an honorable and capable man.

He did not, however, have the most enviable love life, if the following is a fair example:

... hunting she slipped down by a towel, and took with her two

brachets, and so she yede to the knight that she loved, and he her again. And when Sir Dinas came home and missed his paramour and his brachets, then was he the more wrother for his brachets than for the lady.

He caught up with them, smote down his rival, and then the lady asked to come back to Dinas.

Nay, said Sir Dinas, I shall never trust them that once betrayed me, and therefore, as ye have begun, so end, for I will never meddle with you. And so Sir Dinas departed, and took his brachets with him, and so rode to his castle. [Malory IX, 40; X, 50; etc.]

DODINAS (Dodynel) LE SAVAGE

Son of Belinans, the brother of King Tradelmans of Norgales [Vulgate II]. Dodinas was a knight of the Round Table, and one of those who seem to be much in evidence, but upon whose personality I can get no grip. In **Erec et Enide**, Chrétien de Troyes lists him as one of the "ten most important knights" of Arthur's court, but Harris (introduction to **Yvain**) remarks that Chrétien "included among the ten . . . some who were of no importance whatever," being interested really in catchy names. Dodinas also is listed among Arthur's knights in **Sir Gawaine and the Green Knight**. He may have been prominent in certain pre-Malory romances, and the prominence echoed wanly through into Malory, but the major adventures did not. Dodinas may well have been a friend of Sagramore's, for they ride together three times in the books of Tristram; on the third occasion, Gawaine and Ywaine are also with them. Dodinas may have been one of the Queen's most immediate circle, for he was in her party when they went a-Maying and Meliagraunt ambushed them. [Malory VIII, 16; X, 4, 66; etc]

DORIN†

Son of King Claudas — see under Claudas.

DORNAR (Durnore, Dornard)

A son of King Pellinore, apparently his third in wedlock, and a knight of the Round Table, Dornar is greatly eclipsed by his brothers Lamorak, Percivale, and even Aglovale and the bastard half-brother Tor. Dornar appears at Duke Galeholt's tournament in Surluse and at the attempt to heal Sir Urre. He seems to have met his death before or during Lancelot's sojourn with Elaine of Carbonek in the Joyous Isle, for while Aglovale and Percivale are searching for Lancelot they visit their mother, who mourns the death of her husband Pellinore and two of her four sons. [Malory X, 23, 48; XI, 10; XIX, 1]

KING 'DOUTRE LES MARCHES'†

He was an ally of Duke Galeholt [Vulgate III].

DRUAS†

Brother to Sir Sornehan. See under Druas' Hill, *Places*.

ST. DUBRIC (Dubricus)†

The Archbishop of Caerleon who crowned Arthur king. According to Geoffrey of Monmouth, Dubric was primate of Britain and so eminent for piety that he could cure any sick person by his prayers. He abdicated later, to become a hermit.

Malory seems to know nothing of him, unless St. Dubric is to be identified with the Archbishop of Canterbury. To Tennyson, however, Dubric is the "high saint," who not only crowned Arthur but officiated at his marriage, and who is as eminent in the spiritual realm as Merlin in the magical.

Durnore — see DORNAR

ASTLAND (Sorestan?), QUEEN OF

In Malory VI, 3-4, the Queen of Eastland, Morgana, and the Queens of Northgalis and the Out Isles kidnap Lancelot and take him to Castle Chariot, wishing him to choose one of them for his paramour. The Vulgate version of this episode has only three kidnapers: Morgan, the Queen of Sorestan, and Sebile the enchantress [Vulgate V]. From this and other evidence, I suspect Eastland to be identical with Sorestan; thus the Queen of Eastland is to be identified with the Queen of Sorestan. Incidentally, the reputations of the Queens of Eastland, Northgalis, and the Out Isles as dames of magic seem to rest — as far as Malory is concerned — on their association with Morgan and on Lancelot's assertion that they are all four "false enchantresses."

ECTOR (Antor)

Merlin selected this "lord of fair livelihood in many parts in England and Wales," whom he called "a passing true man and a faithful" to Uther, to be Arthur's foster-father. Accepting the task at Uther's behest, for which Uther granted him great rewards ahead of time, Ector followed Merlin's directions and gave Arthur to his wife for suckling, entrusting his own son, Kay, to a wetnurse. Some years later, when Kay tried to claim credit for drawing the Sword from the Stone, Ector saw through the claim and made his son "swear upon a book how he came to that sword."

Modern romancers have presented us with the tale that Arthur was always aware he was not Ector's true son and that he grew up believing himself a bastard and destined to a humbler lot in life than Kay. According to Malory, however, Arthur was completely surprised and dismayed when the incident of the Sword in the Stone prompted Sir Ector to reveal as much of the truth as he knew. (Apparently Ector himself did not know the full story of Arthur's birth and parentage.)

> Alas, said Arthur, my own dear father and brother, why kneel ye to me? ...
>
> Then Arthur made great dole when he understood that Sir Ector was not his father. Sir, said Ector unto Arthur, will ye be my good and gracious lord when ye are king? Else were I to blame, said Arthur, for ye are the man in the world that I am most beholden to, and my good lady and mother your wife, that as well as her own hath fostered me and kept. ...God forbid I should fail you.

Ector asked of Arthur only that Kay be made seneschal of all Arthur's lands, which the young King eagerly promised. I see no reason to believe from all this that Arthur occupied a lesser position in Ector's household during his formative years than did Kay, except for a slight age difference, or to assume that Arthur did not fully expect to be made knight in his turn. Ector was clearly an ideal foster-father.

This Sir Ector must not be confused with Sir Ector de Maris, Lancelot's brother. Vulgate II names Arthur's foster-father Antor. Tennyson gives him the name Anton (**The Coming of Arthur**).

ECTOR DE MARIS (Hector des Mares)

This major knight of the Round Table was Lancelot's English-born half-brother. Through Merlin's unsolicited contrivance, King Ban of Benwick fathered Ector on the Damsel des Mares (Vulgate).

Malory seems first to mention Ector de Maris in Book VI. Lancelot left court with his cousin Lionel to seek adventure. Lancelot was napping under a tree when Lionel saw Sir Turquine ride by, pursued him without waking Lancelot, and was captured by Turquine, while Morgana and her cohorts chanced along from another direction and kidnapped the slumbering Lancelot. Ector, meanwhile, learning how Lancelot had left court, "was wroth with himself" and went out to find and join him. Coming to Turquine's stronghold, and being informed of the danger by a local forester, Ector challenged Turquine and was defeated in his turn, stripped, beaten with thorns, and imprisoned along with Lionel and others until Lancelot could come to rescue them. A little later Ector, Sagramore, Gawaine, and Ywaine saw Lancelot riding in Kay's arms, thought it was indeed Kay, and tried—unsuccessfully, of course, to joust him down. When Mark sent Tristram to Ireland for La Beale Isoud, a storm drove him ashore "fast by Camelot." Ector de Maris and another knight of Arthur's, Morganore, welcomed Tristram with a joust.

> Alas, said Sir Ector [on being defeated], now I am ashamed that ever any Cornish knight should overcome me. And then for despite Sir Ector put off his armour from him, and went on foot, and would not ride.

When Tristram later dropped out of sight after the Castle of Maidens tournament, however, Ector was one of nine knights who joined Lancelot in a vow to search for him.

Despite the defeats mentioned above, Ector was a good man of arms, showing up well at tourneys. At least once during Duke Galeholt's Surluse tournament, Ector got the better of the formidable Palomides.

Chancing to meet during a search for Lancelot, Ector and Percivale took time out for a friendly little fight that ended with both wounded nigh unto death and lying helpless on the ground. At Percivale's prayer, the Sangreal came and healed them. Travelling on together, Ector and Percivale found Lancelot living with Elaine of Carbonek at Joyous Isle and persuaded him to return to Arthur's court.

While on the Grail Quest, Ector met and rode for awhile with Gawaine. One night each had a vision. In Ector's vision, he saw Lancelot humbled and himself turned away from a rich man's wedding feast. Later, when Ector came knocking at Carbonek (his brother Lancelot being already within), King Pellam denied him admittance, saying that he was "one of them which hath served the fiend, and hast left the service of Our Lord." This may reflect the high standards of the Grail rather than Ector's depravity, for Ector seems no worse than most "worldly" knights and a good deal better-living than many.

Naturally rallying at once to Lancelot's side when the break came with Arthur, Ector helped rescue Guenevere from the stake. He afterwards accompanied Lancelot into exile and was crowned King of Benwick. Later, he was one of the last to refind Lancelot at the hermitage of the former Archbishop of Canterbury. Ector did not arrive until Lancelot was dead.

> ... and then Sir Ector threw his shield, sword, and helm from him. And when he beheld Sir Launcelot's visage, he fell down in a swoon. And when he waked it were hard for any tongue to tell the doleful complaints that he made for his brother. Ah Launcelot, he said, thou were head of all Christian knights, and now I dare say...that thou were never matched of earthly knight's hand.

After returning to settle affairs in Benwick, Ector went with Bors, Blamore, and Bleoberis to die fighting the Turks in the Holy Land. [Malory VI, 1-2, 7-9, 13; VIII, 19; IX, 36; X, 79; XI, 13-14; XII, 7-10; XVI, 1-2; XVII, 16; XX, 5-8, 18, etc.]

Ector's first love was Perse. Later he took a niece of the Lady of Roestoc's dwarf and cousin of the Lady of Roestoc. She died, and he was eventually reunited with Perse. [Vulgate V, appendix]

Do not confuse Ector de Maris with the older Ector who was Arthur's foster-father.

EDWARD OF ORKNEY

Brother to Sir Sadok, cousin to Gawaine, and a knight of the Round Table. [Malory X, 68; XIX, 11]

EDWARD OF THE RED CASTLE

He and his brother, Hue of the Red Castle, extorted a barony from the Lady of the Rock. Sir Marhaus, winning it back for her, killed Edward in combat. [Malory IV, 26-27]

ELAINE OF ASTOLAT (Elaine le Blank)

For his own excellent artistic purposes, T. H. White combines Elaine of Astolat and Elaine of Carbonek into one character and identifies them both with the damsel in the scalding bath (**The Once and Future King**, Book III, especially chapters 11 and 40). In Malory, Elaine of Astolat is definitely distinct from her namesake of Carbonek. Elaine of Carbonek may have been the damsel in the scalding bath (though I am far from convinced of it), but there is no way to combine the two Elaines.

The younger Elaine, Tennyson's "lily maid of Astolat" **(Lancelot and Elaine)**, was the daughter of Sir Bernard of Astolat and the sister of Sirs Lavaine and Tirre. Lancelot, traveling secretly to the tournament at Winchester, lodged with Sir Bernard and borrowed the shield of the recently wounded Sir Tirre, leaving his own shield with Elaine for safekeeping. He also did for her what he had never done for any other woman, including Guenevere: with a view to heightening his incognito, he accepted Elaine's token to wear in the lists. Elaine fell deeply in love with him. When she learned he was wounded and lodged with Sir Baudwin the hermit, she insisted on going herself to nurse him. She asked to be his paramour if he would not marry her; and even Sir Bors counselled him to love Elaine if he could; but Lancelot remained true to Guenevere. After Lancelot left her, Elaine died for love of him. According to her dying instructions, her body was put in a barget and steered down to Westminster, where King, Queen, Lancelot, and the rest of the court grieved to see the body and read the explanatory letter in its hand, which requested Lancelot to give the Mass-penny for her soul. [Malory XVIII, 9-20]

QUEEN ELAINE OF BENWICK

Wife of King Ban and mother of Sir Lancelot. After the death of her husband and the appropriation of her young son by Viviane, Queen Elaine founded a religious house, the Royal Minster, on the scene of her losses in Benwick and lived there for many years as a saintly woman. This we find in the Vulgate. Malory only records that Merlin, visiting her, assured her she would live long enough to witness her son's fame and glory. [Malory IV, 1]

She visited her nephews Bors and Lionel when they were in Gaul during Arthur's war against King Claudas. From her nephews she got news of her son. Later, when the war was won, she visited Lancelot himself in Gannes, afterwards returning to her minster. [Vulgate V]

Her sister was Evaine, who married Ban's brother Bors.

ELAINE OF CARBONEK

Do not confuse her with Elaine of Astolat.

Vulgate II calls Elaine of Carbonek, King Pellam's daughter, the wisest woman who ever lived. "The best of the world" seems to be a figure of speech with the old romancers, and I am not sure the statement is meant to be taken as literal fact.

When Lancelot first came to Carbonek, rescued the damsel in the scalding bath, and killed a troublesome dragon, Elaine fell in love with him. At that time, she seems to have been acting as the "damosel passing fair and young" who bore the Holy Grail at dinnertime in the castle. With the help of Dame Brisen and the connivance of King Pellam, Elaine managed to sleep one night with Lancelot by tricking him into thinking she was Guenever. Thus was Galahad begotten, who was by his holy life to expiate the fornication of his father and mother and to heal his grandfather Pellam and Pellam's kingdom of the effects of the Dolorous Stroke. When Lancelot woke up in the morning and saw how he had been tricked, he came near smiting Elaine down with his sword.

> Then ... Elaine skipped out of her bed all naked, and kneeled down afore Sir Launcelot, and said: Fair courteous knight ... I require you have mercy upon me, and as thou art renowned the most noble knight of the world, slay me not, for I have in my womb him by thee that shall be the most noblest knight of the world. ... Well, said Sir Launcelot, I will forgive you this deed; and therewith he took her up in his arms, and kissed her, for she was as fair a lady, and thereto lusty and young, and as wise, as any was that time living.

He threatened, however, to slay Dame Brisen if ever he saw her; but nothing ever came of the threat.

After Galahad's birth, Elaine and Brisen came to Arthur's court to help celebrate Arthur's victory over Claudas. Again they tricked Lancelot into Elaine's bed by pretending she was Guenever. This time Guenever herself, whose room was next door and who had been expecting Lancelot in her own bed, heard them. She came into Elaine's room, found them together, and jealously accused Lancelot, setting off a fit of his madness. After wandering a long time insane and unknown, he came again to Carbonek, where he was eventually recognized and cured by exposure to the Grail. Pellam now set him up with Elaine in the Joyous Isle. Lancelot agreed to this arrangement because he thought he could never again return to Arthur's court after his disgrace. As Le Chevaler Mal Fet, he lived with Elaine in the Castle of Bliant and kept the Joyous Isle against all comers for perhaps two years. Then, to Elaine's grief, Ector de Maris and Percivale came to the Joyous Isle and persuaded Lancelot to return to court. By this time Galahad, who had been growing up at his grandfather's castle Carbonek on the mainland, was fifteen years old; and Elaine promised that he could come to Arthur's court to be made knight that same feast of Pentecost.

When Lancelot came once again to Carbonek during the Grail Quest, he learned to his sorrow that Elaine had died in the interim. [Malory XI, 1-3, 7-9; XII, 1-9; XVII, 16]

It is possible, as T. H. White has it, that Elaine of Carbonek was herself the damsel Lancelot rescued from the scalding bath (**The Once and Future King**). But I doubt this. According to the Vulgate, the damsel in the bath was being punished for sin, and as Grail-bearer Elaine must have been free of fleshly sin before her night with Lancelot. (After that night, of course, they had to find a new damsel to carry the Grail. Amide may have fulfilled this office for a time.)

ELAINE OF TINTAGIL, QUEEN OF GARLOTH

The second daughter of Gorlois and Igraine, she was married to King Nentres of Garlot at about the same time her mother was married to Uther Pendragon and her sister Morgawse to King Lot (Malory I, 2). Elaine became the mother of Galescin. She is greatly eclipsed by her sisters Morgana and Morgawse. Chapman identifies her with "Vivian called Nimue" and makes her the youngest of Igraine's "witchy" daughters (**The Green Knight**, Part 1). This is ingenious and symmetrical, but I found nothing in Malory or the Vulgate to substantiate it, or even to suggest that the other two sisters shared Morgan's talent for necromancy.

Helaine the Peerless† — see under PERSIDES OF GAZEWILT

ELEINE

The beautiful, golden-haired daughter of King Pellinore and the Lady of the Rule, Eleine killed herself with the sword of her lover Sir Miles after he was treacherously slain by Loraine le Savage. The tragedy was compounded in that Pellinore himself passed by before Miles' actual death, and Eleine appealed to him, but he was in eager pursuit of another quest — the rescue of Nimue — and did not stop to help them. Only after finding them both dead on his return, and all of the lady eaten by lions except for the head, did Pellinore learn that she was his own daughter. [Malory III, 12-15]

ELIAS

A captain of the Sessoins and "a good man of arms," Elias commanded an invading Saxon host against King Mark. Elias led his men nobly in battle before Tintagil. But, after many of them were killed and the rest became loathe to do battle again, he offered to settle the invasion in single combat. Mark's champion was Tristram. Elias put up a good fight. Tristram remarked at the end, "Sir Elias, I am right sorry for thee, for thou art a passing good knight as ever I met withal, except Sir Lancelot." With Elias dead, Mark took prisoners and sent the rest of the Sessoins back to their own country, [Malory X, 28-30]

ELIAZAR

He was a holy knight, the son of King Pellam, living at Carbonek. Eliazar brought back from Mategant's castle to Carbonek the broken sword with which Joseph had been wounded. [Vulgate IV; see also Swords, *Things*] Eliazar fought a tournament with symbolic overtones; see under Argustus.

Curiously, Eliazar is not among the twelve knights who represented the twelve apostles at the Mass celebrated by Joseph in Carbonek during the climax of the Grail adventures. Indeed, Pellam, Eliazar, and "a maid which was [Pellam's] niece" must specifically be sent out of the room before the Mysteries can begin. [Malory XVII, 19]

ELIEZER†

Gawaine's squire. He is a fairly important character in Vulgate VII.

In Vulgate VI, p. 329, Gawaine's squire balks at taking Gawaine's challenge to Lancelot in the war of vengeance for the deaths of Gareth and Gaheris. The squire tells him that "A wrong cause often makes a good knight blunder, while a right one transforms an indifferent knight into a hero." Either this is a case of squire rebellion, or a suggestion that squires are not the subservient ciphers they sometimes seem to be considered, or an indication that Gawaine's squire, like Tristram's Gouvernail, may be a special case. The squire in Vulgate VI is left unnamed, but for the sake of convenience I would identify him with Eliezer.

Like Gouvernail, Eliezer seems to be a "career squire," one with little or no intention of becoming a knight.

ELIOT

Dinadan taught his satirical lay against King Mark to a minstrel and harper named Eliot, who in turn taught it to many other harpers. After singing it to Tristram, Eliot asked if he dared sing it before Mark. Tristram said yes, promising to be his warrant—although Tristram himself does not seem to have attended dinner in Mark's hall on the occasion. When Mark spoke angrily at the song's end, Eliot excused himself by explaining that Dinadan had made him sing it and a minstrel had to obey the lord whose arms he bore. Told by Mark to leave quickly, Eliot escaped to Tristram, who wrote to Lancelot and Dinadan and "let conduct the harper out of the country" (probably the country of Cornwall). [Malory X, 27, 31]

DUKE ELISE

This "worshipful duke," seemingly named Elise, is apparently mentioned only once by Malory, at Duke Galeholt's tournament in Surluse. The duke is mentioned, however, as "uncle unto King Arthur." He had a son, also, it seems, named Sir Elise. [Malory X, 46]

QUEEN ELIZABETH OF LYONESSE

The sister of King Mark was "a full meek lady, and well she loved her lord," King Meliodas of Cornwall. But while she was pregnant with Tristram, Meliodas was waylaid on a hunt and imprisoned by an enchantress who loved him.

> When Elizabeth ... missed her lord, and she was nigh out of her wit, and also as great with child as she was, she took a gentlewoman with her, and ran into the forest to seek her lord.

Here she gave birth to her son.

> But she had taken such cold for the default of help that deep draughts of death took her ... Now let me see my little child, for whom I have had all this sorrow. And when she saw him she said thus: Ah, my little son, thou hast murdered thy mother, and therefore I suppose, thou that art a murderer so young, thou art full likely to be a manly man in thine age.

With this wry humor, and charging her gentlewoman to ask the king to name his son Tristram, "that is as much to say as a sorrowful birth," she gave up the ghost and died. [Malory VIII, 1]

ELYZABEL†

Guenever's cousin and, seemingly, her most intimate confidante, Elyzabel was a brave and resourceful woman as well as a discreet one. On one occasion, when Lancelot, Bors, and Lionel were all from court and Guenever had no one else to confide in about Lancelot, she took to her bed with no attendant but Elyzabel. Once the Queen sleepwalked in a nightmare. Elyzabel, awaking, sprinkled her with holy water and said, "Go quickly to bed—the King is coming," thus bringing her to her senses.

In her efforts to find the missing Lancelot, Guenever once sent Elyzabel to the Royal Minster in Gaul to bring back the French Damsel of the Lake, Viviane. King Claudas, who was at that time popular and residing in Gannes, welcomed and feasted Elyzabel at first, but then suspected she was a spy for Lancelot and his cousins. He had her, her squire, and her dwarf seized and searched. The dwarf threw Guenever's box containing the message to Viviane into the river, but Claudas' seneschal saw him do it. Claudas imprisoned them all and sent two squires to Britain as spies. The spies were so impressed by Arthur's court that one of them stayed on, entering Guenever's service. When, a year later, Guenever asked him where he came from, he told her all. Thus she learned that her cousin was a prisoner. She wrote an indignant letter to Claudas, sealed it with her seal, and sent it by the squire. Claudas forced the squire to return it with an insulting answer. This led to the war in which Arthur defeated Claudas for once and all and freed Elyzabel. [Vulgate V]

Enid (Enide)† – see under GERAINT

EPINEGRIS (Epinogrus)

> Well, said Sir Tristram, I know that knight well with the covered shield of azure, he is the king's son of Northumberland, his name is Epinegris; and he is as great a lover as I know, and he loveth the king's daughter of Wales, a full fair lady.

Epinegris seems to make his first appearance in Malory at the Castle Dangerous tournament in the book of Gareth Beaumains. Later, Tristram and Dinadan encounter him while they are in the midst of a discussion about whether or not knights in love make the better fighters. With the words quoted above, among others, Tristram eggs Dinadan on to make the test, Dinadan having boasted about his lack of a lady. After asking, "Sir ... is that the rule of you errant knights for to make a knight to joust, will he or nill?" Epinegris, the lover, unhorses Dinadan. He appears a little after this in unsuccessful pursuit of Breuse Sans Pitie.

Later still, Palomides finds Epinegris wounded. They tell each other their woes. Palomides complains of his love for La Beale Isoud. Epinegris says his case is much worse, for in the tournament of Lonazep he had won his lady (here, the daughter of an earl) by killing her father and one of his two knights. But the next day, as they reposed by a well, Sir Helior le Preuse came, challenged, and fought Epinegris, defeating him and winning away the lady. Palomides brings Epinegris safe to a hermitage, then finds Helior, wins back the lady, defends her against yet another challenger (who turns out to be Palomides' brother Safere), and returns her to Epinegris.

Epinegris is mentioned again at the tournament of Winchester and as one of the knights of the Round Table who attempt to heal Sir Urre. [Malory VII, 26; X, 55, 65, 82-84; XVIII, 10; XIX, 11]

Erec – see GERAINT

Erminide – see HERMIND

Duke Escan – see EUSTACE

KING ESCLAMOR†

A sub-king probably contemporary at least with Arthur's early days, if not with his later ones. Esclamor's territory seems to have been in the neighborhood of the "Forest of the Boiling Well." See Le Tertre Deuee in *Places*.

KING ESTORAUSE (Escorant, Escarans, etc.) OF SARRAS

He "was a tyrant, and was come of the line of paynims, and took them [Galahad and his companions] and put them in prison in a deep hole." On his deathbed, however, he sent for them and begged forgiveness. By divine guidance, Galahad was chosen king of Sarras after Estorause's death, thus bringing the Grail Quest to its conclusion. [Malory XVII, 22]

Damsel of Estroite Marche – see LESTROITE MARCHE

"Été" – see under PRINTEMPS, ÉTÉ, and AUTOMNE"

ETTARD (Ettarre)

See under Peleas, and remember that Ettard had not asked Pelleas to love her and pester her with his unsolicited devotion.

BISHOP EUGENE†

According to Vulgate IV, he was the man who crowned Guenever and officiated at her marriage. See also Archbishop of Canterbury, and Dubric.

DUKE EUSTACE OF CAMBENET (Escan of Cambenic)

He pledged 5000 mounted men to the first rebellion of subkings against Arthur, and fought in the battle of Bedegraine. That is all I can find of him in Malory unless he is to be identified with the "Duke Cambines" who appears at Duke Galeholt's tournament in Surluse. [Malory I, 12-17; X, 49] According to Vulgate II, this duke's name was Escan, and Cambenic was a rich and prosperous city.

EVADEAM†

The son of King Brangoire (Brandegoris), Evadeam was 22 years old when he appeared, in the form of an ugly dwarf, with his lady Byanne at Arthur's court. See Byanne.

EVAINE†

Sister of Queen Elaine of Benwick, Queen Evaine was the wife of King Bors and the mother of Lionel and Bors de Ganis. After the death of her husband and the seizure of her young sons, she joined her sister at the Royal Minster, but died there much sooner than did Elaine. [Vulgate III-IV]

Evelake – see MORDRAINS

Ewaine – see YWAINE

alse Guenevere, The'† – see GENIEVRE

KING FARAMON OF FRANCE and DAUGHTER

Malory mentions this monarch only in VIII, 5, where the daughter of King Faramon of France, being in love with Tristram, sends him letters and "a little brachet that was passing fair." Receiving no regard from the knight, the princess dies for love of him. (Tristram keeps the brachet.)

Faramon may have been a kind of high king of France in Uther Pendragon's time, for in Vulgate V, when Frolle of Alemaigne tries to seize Gaul, Arthur maintains that his own claim is stronger than Frolle's, since his father Uther was suzerain of Faramon in King Ban's day.

FELELOLIE

The sister of Sir Urre of Hungary, Felelolie accompanied her mother and brother throughout Europe searching for the best knight of the world, who alone could heal Urre's wounds. When they had found Lancelot in Logres, and Urre was healed, "Sir Lavaine cast his love unto Dame Felelolie ... and then they were wedded together with great joy." [Malory XIX, 10, 13]

EARL FERGUS

A Cornish knight, Fergus "was but a young man, and late come into his lands" when Sir Marhaus came along to kill his troublesome neighbor, the giant Taulurd. When next we meet Fergus in Malory, he is one of Tristram's knights and acts as messenger for Tristram. Later we learn that he has become a fellow of the Round Table. With Tristram, Dinas, and others, Fergus grieves for Prince Boudwin and refuses to raise hand against Sir Sadok for helping Boudwin's wife Anglides escape with her son. His last appearance seems to be at the attempt to heal Sir Urre. [Malory IV, 25; IX, 18; X, 26, 32, 35; XIX, 11]

The Vulgate has at least one Fergus, but I am not sure he can be identified with Malory's character.

Fisher King—see PELLAM

FLOEMUS†

Apparently King Lot's seneschal. [Vulgate VII]

FLOREE

According to the Vulgate, she was the daughter of King Alain of Escavalon and the mother of Gawaine's oldest son, Guinglain. Vulgate VII seems to describe the encounter: after Gawaine rescued her, Floree came to his bed somewhat in the manner of Sir Bercilak's lady in **Sir Gawaine and the Green Knight**. But, since Floree meant it, it went farther, and Guinglain apparently resulted from this adventure. I do not know for sure whether Gawaine married Floree or not, but according to **The Wedding of Sir Gawaine and Dame Ragnell** he was married several times.

Malory does not name Floree, but in XIX, 11, he calls Sir Brandiles' sister the mother of Gawaine's sons Florence and Lovel. Although Malory does not name Brandiles' sister as the mother of Gawaine's son Gingalin, who surely is identical with the Vulgate's Guinglain, the name of the second son, Florence, is so similar to the name Floree that it strongly suggests a mother-son connection. Floree, then, might be identified with Sir Brandiles' sister. But see under Brandiles and Ragnell.

FLORENCE

The elder, apparently, of Gawaine's two (?) sons by Sir Brandiles' sister, Florence became a knight of the Round Table. With his brother Lovel, he joined the party that helped Mordred and Agravaine try to trap Lancelot with the Queen. All but Mordred were killed by the escaping Lancelot. [Malory XIX, 11; XX, 2-4]

Malory also mentions a Sir Florence in Arthur's Continental campaign against the Emperor of Rome.

> Then ... the king called Sir Florence, a knight, and said to him they lacked victual, And not far from hence be great forests and woods, wherein be many of mine enemies with much bestial: I will that thou ... go thither in foraying, and take with thee Sir Gawaine my nephew [and others] ...

The foragers run afoul of a force of Spanish knights, defeat them, and win plenty of rich spoils. [Malory V, 9-11] Although Malory's internal chronology is confusing, he puts the war against Emperor Lucius much too early in the work to make me feel comfortable identifying this Florence with Gawaine's second son; moreover, it seems unlikely that Arthur would put Gawaine's son, rather than Gawaine himself, in charge of an expedition which included Gawaine.

The Foul Ladye†—see RAGNELL

Frol of the Out Isles—see under BELLIANCE LE ORGULUS

KING (?) FROLLE OF ALEMAIGNE †

Frolle, who was a head taller than most men, tried to take advantage of Arthur's war with Claudas to invade Gaul himself. But Arthur, arriving in Gaul, said that his own claim was older than Frolle's, since Uther Pendragon had been suzerain of Faramon, King of Gaul, in King Ban's day. Arthur substantiated his claim by killing Frolle in single combat. [Vulgate V]

 ## AHERES†

A nephew of the King of Norgales, Gaheres received Gareth's seat at the Round Table after Gareth was killed during Lancelot's rescue of Guenever from the stake. [Vulgate VI] Do not confuse Gaheres with Gareth's brother Gaheris, who was killed with Gareth during the rescue of Guenever.

GAHERIS (Guerrehes)

The third son of Lot and Morgawse. Vulgate IV remarks that Gaheris was a good knight, and that his right arm was longer than his left.

He first came to court in youth with his mother and brothers Gawaine, Agravaine and Gareth (who must have been very young indeed) when Morgawse visited Arthur between the two early waves of rebellion. Morgawse and her sons returned to Arthur's court after the second rebellion, at the burial of Lot; Morgawse clearly returned home afterwards with Gareth, but the three older boys apparently stayed. Before his own dubbing, Gaheris served as squire to his oldest brother Gawaine, towards whom he acted, at the same time, as a sort of advisor and second conscience. During the celebration of Arthur's marriage, when Gawaine said he would kill Pellinore in revenge for King Lot's death, Gaheris held him back, "for at this time I am but a squire, and when I am made knight I will be avenged on him," and besides, if they killed Pellinore now they would trouble the feast. Pellinore's eventual death is not described in detail, but his widow later complains that Gawaine and Gaheris "slew him not manly but by treason." When Gawaine was sent on the quest of the White Hart, Gaheris, still his squire, accompanied him. On this adventure Gawaine defeated Sir Ablamar and was about to ignore his plea for mercy when Ablamar's lady came between them and took Gawaine's stroke. As she fell headless, Gaheris rebuked his older brother:

> Alas, said Gaheris, that is foully and shamefully done, that shame shall never from you; also ye should give mercy unto them that ask mercy, for a knight without mercy is without worship.

Retiring into Ablamar's castle for the night, Gaheris shrewdly warned Gawaine not to unarm: "Ye may think ye have many enemies here." Almost at once four knights angrily attacked Gawaine, and Gaheris fought very capably at his brother's side.

Like all his brothers, Gaheris became a knight of the Round Table. While Gareth was out on his first series of knightly adventures, Morgawse visited Arthur's court at Pentecost. Gawaine, Agravaine, and Gaheris, not having seen her for fifteen years, "saluted her upon their knees, and asked her blessing." Later, however, Gaheris slew his mother in anger at her taking Pellinore's son Lamorak for a lover. The two had an assignation at Gawaine's castle near Camelot, where Morgawse was staying on another visit, at her sons' invitation. Gaheris watched and waited as Lamorak went to the queen's bedroom.

> So when the knight, Sir Gaheris, saw his time, he came to their bedside all armed, with his sword naked, and suddenly gat his mother by the hair and struck off her head.
> When Sir Lamorak saw the blood dash upon him all hot, the which he loved passing well ... [he] leapt out of the bed in his shirt as a knight dismayed, saying thus: ... Alas, why have ye slain your mother that bare you? with more right ye should have slain me.. The offence hast thou done, said Gaheris, notwithstanding a man is born to offer his service; but yet shouldst thou beware with whom thou meddlest, for thou hast put me and my brethren to a shame, and thy father slew our father; and thou to lie by our mother is too much shame for us to suffer. And as for thy father, King Pellinore, my brother Sir Gawaine and I slew him. Ye did him the more wrong, said Sir Lamorak, for my father slew not your father, it was Balin le Savage: and as yet my father's death is not revenged. Leave those words, said Sir Gaheris, for an thou speak feloniously I will slay thee. But because thou art naked I am ashamed to slay thee. But wit thou well, in what place I may get thee I shall slay thee; and now my mother is quit of thee; and withdraw thee and take thine armour, that thou were gone.

(T. H. White, who makes Gaheris something of a nonentity, transfers the matricide to Agravaine: **The Once and Future King** III, 26.)

After Duke Galeholt's tournament in Surluse, Gaheris joined with his brothers (except Gareth) to ambush and kill Lamorak. As with other killings, Malory has his characters allude to the incident rather than describe it himself: Finding that Gaheris and Agravaine have just killed a knight for saying that Lancelot was better than Gawaine, Tristram rebukes the two brothers both for this and for Lamorak's death, of which he has just learned from Palomides. Tristram jousts them down and says he is leaving it at that only for the sake of their relationship to Arthur. Remounting, they chase him in anger, and he unhorses them again.

Among other adventures, Gaheris fought the Cornish knight Matto le Breune and took away his lady, whose loss drove Matto out of his mind. Malory weds Gaheris to Lynette. Vulgate V gives him the Damoiselle de la Blanche Lande as a sweetheart. The accounts are not mutually exclusive. Gaheris, like other knights, demonstrates considerable taste for sampling various damsels. See also "Clarisin."

On at least one occasion Gaheris visited King Mark, bringing him and Isoud news of the Castle of Maidens tournament. Mark and Gaheris seem to have enjoyed each other's company well enough. Gaheris was among the guests at Guenever's intimate dinner party when Sir Patrise was poisoned; Agravaine, Gaheris, and Mordred may have been present, however, largely because Gawaine and Gareth were invited. Gaheris took no part with Agravaine and Mordred when they tried to trap Guenever with Lancelot. After Guenever's trial, Arthur asked Gawaine to help lead the Queen to the stake. Gawaine refused.

> Then said the king to Sir Gawaine: Suffer your brothers Sir Gaheris and Sir Gareth to be there. My lord, said Sir Gawaine, wit you well they will be loath ... but they are young and full unable to say you nay. Then spake Sir Gaheris, and the good knight Sir Gareth, unto Sir Arthur: Sir, ye may well command us to be there, but wit you

well it shall be sore against our will; but an we be there by your strait commandment ye shall plainly hold us there excused: we will be there in peaceable wise, and bear none harness of war upon us.

According to the Vulgate, however, they were armed and fought back when Lancelot and his men attacked the guard to save the Queen. It is also hard to believe that Gawaine's statement of Gaheris' youth is to be taken literally. The result was the same in any case: Gaheris and Gareth were both killed. [Malory I, 19; II, 11; III, 4-8; VII, 25, 35; IX, 19, 38; X, 24, 54-56; XVIII, 3; XIX, 11; XX, 2, 8; etc.]

To Gaheris' further discredit, the Vulgate records how he widowed Lancelot's cousin "Iblis." Vulgate V, however, also depicts him showing a concern for common folk which other knights might also have shown, but examples of which are rarely recorded. While involved in settling a quarrel among the knightly class, Gaheris accidentally frightened a poor man. The poor man fled, leaving his donkey alone in the woods. Returning, he found it devoured by wolves. As the donkey had been essential to his livelihood, he would now be forced to beg. Gaheris, having inadvertently caused the trouble, requested his host—whose life he had just saved, and who thus owed him a favor—to give the poor man a horse. The host obliged, and the peasant's livelihood was saved.

In Sommer's edition of the Vulgate, the name Gaheries is given to the brother we know as Gareth, Malory's Gaheris being called Guerrehes in the Vulgate.

Gaheris de Kareheu†—see under PINEL LE SAVAGE

GAIDON DE GALVOIE†

I have found him only in Sommer's appendix to Vulgate V. He married the Lady of Galvoie.

Galagars—see under GRIFLET

GALAHAD

On a tomb near Carbonek was written a prophecy: "Here shall come a leopard of king's blood, and he ... shall engender a lion ... the which lion shall pass all other knights." When Lancelot came to Carbonek, King Pellam, recognizing him as the leopard, and, apparently aware that the lion of the prophecy would heal himself and his land, helped arrange for Lancelot to beget Galahad on Elaine. Lancelot's own baptized name had been Galahad, before it was changed by Viviane, and this is no doubt where Elaine got the name for her son. Sir Bors visited Carbonek while Galahad was a babe in arms, and remarked on his likeness to Lancelot.

> Truly, said Elaine, wit ye well this child he gat on me. Then Sir Bors wept for joy, and he prayed to God it might prove as good a knight as his father was.

There is some confusion as to Galahad's upbringing. According to the Vulgate, Galahad lived at Carbonek with his grandfather during the time Lancelot lived with Elaine at Joyous Isle, and, when Lancelot departed, Galahad, wanting to remain near his father, travelled to the convent where Pellam's sister was abbess and lived there until he was about eighteen. When Lancelot leaves Joyous Isle, Malory has Elaine tell him that "at this same feast of Pentecost shall ... Galahad be made knight, for he is fully now fifteen winter old." A few chapters later, however, when an unnamed gentlewoman brings Lancelot to the convent to visit his son, the nuns present Galahad as "this child the which we have nourished." It appears to me that Malory cut out three years Galahad spent at the convent, but failed to make his account fully consistent in so doing.

Lancelot's visit to the convent came on the eve of Pentecost. At this time Lancelot dubbed Galahad knight, but Galahad did not return at once to Arthur's court with his father. Next day the sword which had once been Sir Balin's floated down the river to Camelot. After Gawaine and Percivale, at the King's behest, had attempted without success to draw the sword, "a good old man, and an ancient" (Nascien?) brought Galahad to court "on foot, in red arms, without sword or shield, save a scabbard hanging by his side." The old man led Galahad to the Siege Perilous, which was now found to bear his name, and sat him in it. After dinner, Arthur took Galahad to the river, where the young knight drew the sword from its floating marble. Now a gentlewoman rode to them to tell Lancelot he was no longer the greatest knight in the world and to predict the Grail Quest. Disturbed by the thought that he would never see all his knights together again after the Quest, and wanting to prove Galahad, Arthur held one last tournament before the Quest. At this tourney Galahad "defouled many good knights of the Table save twain, that was Sir Launcelot and Sir Percivale." When Guenevere looked at Galahad's face after the tourney, she said:

> Soothly I dare well say that Sir Launcelot begat him, for never two men resembled more in likeness, therefore it nis no marvel though he be of great prowess. ... he is of all parties come of the best knights of the world and of the highest lineage; for Sir Launcelot is come but of the eighth degree from our Lord Jesu Christ, and Sir Galahad is of the ninth degree from our Lord Jesu Christ ...

That evening the Holy Grail, veiled in white samite, appeared in Arthur's hall to feed the knights at supper, and Gawaine was first to vow to quest for a clear look at the vessel. Later the Queen questioned Galahad about his father and place of birth. He told her readily of his country, but would neither affirm nor deny his relationship to Lancelot. When Guenevere assured him he need not be ashamed of his father, whom he so much resembled,

> Then Sir Galahad was a little ashamed and said: Madam, sith ye know in certain, wherefore do ye ask it me? for he that is my father shall be known openly and all betimes.

Embarking on the Quest, Galahad rode four days, apparently alone, without adventure before coming to the "Abbey of the Adventurous Shield" where he met Ywaine and Bagdemagus. Galahad agreed to let Bagdemagus try to take the Adventurous Shield first. The White Knight who waited outside struck down Bagdemagus. Then, when Galahad came with the shield, the knight saluted him courteously and told him the shield's history. Bagdemagus' former squire Melias de Lile, who had begged to accompany Galahad, now begged to be made knight, and Galahad obliged. The two returned briefly to the abbey and Galahad cleared the churchyard of an unquiet soul, who cried, when Galahad blessed it, "Galahad, I see there environ about thee so many angels that my power may not dere [harm] thee." Melias and Galahad left again, and parted at a crossroads, but Melias soon got into trouble and Galahad had to rescue him. Leaving the wounded Melias with an old monk, Galahad went on to Abblasoure and thence to "Chapel Desolate" where a voice directed him to destroy the wicked customs at the Castle of Maidens. Galahad went at once and drove out the seven wicked brothers, who swore to avenge themselves by killing all of Arthur's knights they could overcome — which was none, since the first three they met were

Gawaine, Gareth, and Ywaine, who soon exterminated them all seven. For this deed Gawaine later was rebuked by a hermit who said: "Sir Galahad himself alone beat them all seven the day to-fore, but his living is such he shall slay no man lightly."

Meanwhile, meeting Lancelot and Percivale by chance, Galahad unhorsed both, but then fled, "adread to be known," when a nearby recluse began praising him. Galahad's next recorded adventure came as he passed a rather bloody tournament and entered on the side that was being literally slaughtered. Gawaine and Ector de Maris got into the melee, and Galahad wounded Gawaine with the stroke which had been predicted as punishment for an unworthy attempt to draw Balin's sword.

From here Galahad rode to Ulfin's hermitage, where Percivale's sister Amide came to lead him to a ship in which Bors and Percivale, tested and purified by their own adventures, were waiting. Sailing in this vessel, the four came to King Solomon's Ship where Galahad drew King David's Sword from its scabbard and was girded with it by Amide. Returning to their own ship, the party came ashore at Carteloise castle, where they slew the murderous and incestuous brothers who had thrown their own father, Earl Hernox, in prison and raped and murdered their sister. Hernox counted himself blessed to die in Galahad's arms, counselling the young knight to go to the Maimed King as soon as possible. Leaving Carteloise, Galahad and his companions followed the mystical white hart and four lions through the forest to a chapel where they experienced a Eucharistic vision during Mass.

Next the knights came to the "Castle of the Leprous Lady," defending Amide till she agreed to give blood willingly, which caused her death. After putting her body into a ship and setting it adrift, the three knights separated for a time. Lancelot found the ship with Amide's body and embarked in it. After about a month, Galahad joined him; they journeyed together in the ship for half a year, serving God and sometimes going ashore for strange adventures on beast-infested islands. Finally a "knight armed all in white" appeared on shore, leading a white horse, and summoned Galahad to his own further adventures. Lancelot had already been at Carbonek and gone away again by the time Galahad arrived there, so that father and son never saw each other again. Galahad went first to the "Abbey of King Mordrains," where he healed and saw released from mortal coil that long-lived sufferer.

Next Galahad entered the "Forest of the Boiling Well," where he stopped the water from boiling, and came to the burning tomb of Simeon, an ancestor of his, who was enduring a kind of purgatory for a sin against Joseph of Arimathea. After releasing Simeon's soul, Galahad met Bors and Percival again, and they came at last to Carbonek, where Galahad mended the broken sword wherewith Joseph had been striken through the thigh. The three British knights met nine other knights of various countries and all experienced the climactic Mysteries of the Grail, celebrated by Joseph of Arimathea. Instructed by Joseph, Galahad healed the Maimed King by anointing him with blood from Longinus' Spear. Then Galahad, Bors, and Percivale embarked in a ship with the Sangreal (miraculously preceding them aboard). They were carried to Sarras, where they

---

ARTHURIAN CLASSES AND ROLES
  In footnotes on successive pages follow alphabetized entries and extracts about certain categories of people found in Arthurian tales: Children, Clerks, Hermits, Messengers, Minstrels, Sorcerers, Squires, Surgeons, Varlets, and Vavasours.

found and buried Amide's body. The Pagan king of Sarras, Estorause, threw them into prison for a time, but freed them when on his deathbed, begging for and receiving their forgiveness. A voice now directed the city council to make Galahad their king. He reigned there for one year, at the end of which Joseph of Arimathea came again to accompany his soul, borne up by a great company of angels along with the Grail and the Spear, into Heaven. (According to the Vulgate, Galahad had been given the grace to die at an hour of his own choosing.)

I have recapped Galahad's whole earthly career according to Malory partly to show the sequence of the various miracles which only Galahad could accomplish and partly because, of all the knights whose reputations have suffered with the changing times, Galahad's has perhaps suffered the most. Gawaine's reputation probably comes in second, but his was on the decline much earlier, and our century seems able to understand more easily the frivolous ladykiller Gawaine has become than it can understand Galahad's high ideals and purity.

Therefore, in modern versions, Galahad tends to become a prissy, a hypocrite, a fool, somebody else's half-witted pawn, or all of these together. Tennyson's Sir Galahad — "My good blade carves the casques of men . . ." — has hadly helped matters, of course, nor has John Erskine's **Galahad**, though the latter gives a more sympathetic picture than might have been expected. Fraser's Harry Flashman even believes that Galahad was lustier in bed than his father Lancelot ever was [**Flashman in the Great Game**, chapter 4].

Malory's Galahad, however, far from going around quipping about the purity of his heart, gave Bagdemagus first chance at the Adventurous Shield and later, aboard King Solomon's Ship, allowed Bors and Percivale the first attempts to draw King David's Sword and said, on their failure, "I would draw this sword out of the sheath, but the offending is so great that I shall not set my hand thereto," and had to be reassured by Amide. If this was not humility, it was at least courtesy toward his companions. Galahad's reluctance to slay any man lightly also contrasts favorably with the almost casual killings so many of the other knights, including his own father Lancelot, committed in battles or comedies of errors. On the one occasion when the battle rage that regularly seized Lancelot descended on Galahad and his companions, at Carteloise castle, it was Bors, not Galahad, who rationalized the slaughter.

Then when they beheld the great multitude of people that they had slain, they held themself great sinners. Certes, said Bors, I

ween an God had loved them that we should not have had power to have slain them thus. But they have done so much against Our Lord that He would not suffer them to reign no longer. Say ye not so, said Galahad, for if they misdid against God, the vengeance is not ours, but to Him which hath power thereof.

Galahad does not seem to have been reassured that he and his friends had served as Heaven's tools until a local priest seconded Bors' opinion. Galahad's wishing to accompany his father from Carbonek and their sojourn together in the ship also points to a better father-son relationship than is sometimes supposed. Nor do I find any evidence to support Harry Flashman's belief about Galahad's sex life, any reason to suppose that his regard for Amide, though deep, was not platonic, nor any reason to imagine that Galahad's purity made less a man of him. It may also be remarked, in this age of cult leaders, that Galahad seems not to have abused his power as king of Sarras, nor to have clung to it. Indeed, remembering the legend that he had been granted to name the time of his own death, one may speculate that perhaps he chose to leave such power before it could corrupt him. [Malory XI, 1, 3; XII, 1-17; XVII, 1-14; Vulgate, chiefly vol. VI]

GALAPAS

A giant who fought with the Romans against Arthur.

[Galapas] was a man of an huge quantity and height, [Arthur] shorted him and smote off both his legs by the knees, saying, Now art thou better of a size to deal with than thou were, and after smote off his head. [Malory V, 8]

Galehodin — see GALIHODIN

DUKE GALEHOLT OF THE LONG ISLES AND OF SURLUSE (Galahalt the Haut Prince; Galahad; Galehot; etc.)

Do not confuse him with Sir Galahad, Lancelot's son. Malory, in Pollard's edition at least, spells their names identically or almost identically, and, to keep matters simple, sometimes even calls Lancelot's son "the high prince," although that title seems more commonly to belong to the older Galahalt. To try to avoid confusion, I have followed a spelling Sommer uses in the Vulgate and also tried to use Galeholt's title of Duke consistently rather than sporadically.

Malory makes Duke Galeholt the son of the evil Sir Breunor of Castle Pluere; but perhaps we can take this with a grain of salt. At least, Galeholt does not condone Breunor's evil customs, nor start a feud to avenge his death. Vulgate IV calls Galeholt "the son of the beautiful giantess."

In the Vulgate, Duke Galeholt is prominent for a longer time than Sir Galahad. Although called "Duke," he had con-

Children

Guenever was once reduced to using a child of her chamber as a messenger. The child, probably a page, was in her Maying party when it was ambushed and captured by Meliagrant and his men. Guenever called the child, who was "swiftly horsed," and slipped him her ring and a message for Lancelot. Escaping from the group even while Meliagrant was getting it back to his castle, the child proved himself a very reliable and competent messenger. [Malory XIX, 3]

This is about the only thing I have found relative to children in general, at least older than infancy. There is, of course, the episode of the May babies [Malory I, 27], the tale of Arthur's own birth, and incidents in the childhood years of certain characters, like Bors and Lionel, who came to prominence as adults. And there is the evidence that a number of characters — Merlin,

Percivale, Galahad, Viviane, Elaine of Astolet, Arthur himself — became prominent in their early teens, only a few years removed from the age we consider childhood. It may be worth noting that our sentimental emphasis on Childhood as a semi-sacred state of being and Children as innocent little angels to be coddled and envied seems to be a much later development, perhaps largely a product of this and the last century. Arthurian children may well have been treated with more practical regard for their capabilities, given responsibility earlier and less carefully shielded from "sex and violence" — and this may have led to their seeming invisibility in the romances.

At the same time, some careers seem to have lasted much longer in the romances than we might think likely, with our common idea that medieval people were considered aged by fifty. For instance, think of the Vulgate's testimony that Mador de

quered thirty kingdoms, of which Surluse (Sorelois) was his favorite. Malory's mentioning the Long Isles specifically, along with Surluse, suggests that Galeholt considered them his second best kingdom. Some of the kingdoms, of course, were probably little more than city-castles, and the majority of them may not have been too far-flung; still, Duke Galeholt was one of the strongest as well as one of the most lovable of Arthur's early foes. Arthur's own knight Galegantis, the only member of Arthur's court who had yet seen him, described him as "a young bachelor, most gentle, kind-hearted, and generous." [Vulgate III, 202]

Galeholt attempted to win Arthur's allegiance. Instead, Lancelot won Galeholt's allegiance for Arthur. Galeholt then became Lancelot's close friend and confidant in the latter's affair with Guenevere. The Lady of Malohaut, who had been in love with Lancelot, became Guenevere's confidante and Galeholt's paramour. During the affair of "the false Guenevere" (Genievre), Galeholt gave Lancelot and Guenevere shelter in Surluse. Is it possible that Lancelot's son was named as much in honor of Lancelot's friend as because Lancelot's own baptismal name had been Galahad?

Duke Galeholt was one of the wisest of princes. In order to make himself a still worthier knight, he went to mix with Arthur's court, first deputizing King Bagdemagus of Gore to administer his territories and turn them over to Galeholt's nephew Galihodin in the event of Galeholt's death. The only hard evidence I can produce that Galeholt became a companion of the Round Table is that Malory lists him, perhaps posthumously, among the would-be healers of Sir Urre; but it would be surprising if the illustrious Haut Prince had been kept out of that company.

Galeholt's clerks, especially Helyes of Thoulouse, determined by study that he had only a few more years to live, but could prolong his life by keeping his friend Lancelot with him. Despite this, Galeholt unprotestingly let Lancelot return to Arthur's court. Later, while Lancelot was wandering in a fit of madness, Galeholt came to believe that Lancelot had been killed and he himself not there to help. Galeholt went into a slump of melancholy which so weakened him that a wound breaking open and a strange illness attacking him simultaneously killed him. Lancelot found his body buried in a religious house and carried it to Joyous Garde for reburial.

Galeholt hated to eat fish. [Vulgate III-IV; Malory VIII, 24-27; X, 48; XIX, 11; etc.]

At one point [X, 50], Malory has King Mark learning that Galeholt and Bagdemagus have arranged the Surluse tournament with intent to slay or shame Lancelot for jealousy. This is very difficult to reconcile with the Vulgate's insistence on the friendship between Galeholt and Lancelot and with Malory's own depiction of Bagdemagus' character. Possibly Mark misunderstood the situation, or possibly Malory just needed an occasion for Mark to exercise his malice, and trumped up a peculiarly flimsy and inconsistent one.

See also Ossa Cylellaur.

Father: Breunor of Castle Pleure	**DUKE GALEHOLT'S**
Mother: "a beautiful giantess"	**FAMILY AND RETAINERS**
Nephew: Galehodin	
Lover: Lady of Malohaut	
Ward: King Gloier's Daughter	
Clerk: Helyes of Thoulouse	
Knights and nobles of Surluse: Ossaise, Earl Ulbawes	
Protege: King Marsil	
Allies: King 'Doutre les Marches,' King 'Premier Conquis,'	
King of the Hundred Knights	
Special friend: Lancelot	

GALESHIN†

A knight of the Round Table. Sommer in a footnote makes him the son of King Nentres of Garlot (and thus the son of Elaine of Tintagil and a nephew of Arthur), but points out that the Vulgate in other places makes him the son of King Alain of Escavalon (and thus the brother of Floree) or the son of the King of Norgales and thus the brother of Dodinal le Savage. [Vulgate IV, p. 90] Further on, Sommer explains that Galeshin and Dodinal are cousins, not brothers. [Vulgate IV, p. 229] Also in the Vulgate, Galeshin is identified as the Duke of Clarence, a title he was given by Arthur; "Galeshin" certainly could be a variant of the name Malory uses for the Duke of Clarence, "Chaleins." Take your choice. Galeshin would seem to be a most flexible character.

GALIHODIN (Galehodin)

Nephew of Duke Galeholt and lord of Peningue Castle. Galihodin may have become ruler of Norgales after Ryons.

Once Sir Aglovale killed a relative of Galehodin in battle. The dead man's brother (not Galehodin) later found Aglovale and attacked him. Aglovale, being unarmed at the moment, fled. A large party of knights pursued him past the house of a wealthy burgher who lived on a hill. Gawaine and some of his companions were staying with this burgher. They piled out and rescued Aglovale, killing sixty knights. The burgher was horrified: "You have ruined me! Galehodin will kill me and mine. You will go away and I shall have to bear the consequences." Gawaine, confident that Galehodin would pardon them even if they had killed half his men, because three of them were of high lineage, promised to make the burgher's peace with his lord.

---

la Porte had served Arthur forty-five years and was still hale and hearty enough to give Lancelot a good fight in Guenever's trial by combat. Contrary to the popular modern picture, the testimony of Malory and the Vulgate indicates that Guenever must have been somewhat older than Lancelot — sort of an Elizabeth-Essex love, in a way; Margawse must have been considerably older than her lover Lamorak. Literary convention may have expanded these great character's ages and youths, of course. Also, I have long believed that we commonly misinterpret the statistics of "average life expectancy" in other centuries — I suspect that life expectancy was short because of high mortality among infants, children, and youths, not because a person was "old" at age thirty — that a member of the upper classes, with a reasonably good diet and a reasonably good balance of work, exercise, and rest, could look forward to as strong and sound a "three-

Clerks

I confess I do not know whether to classify clerks as holy folk, magicians, neither, or both. Clerks were very likely clerics or clergy, but this does not necessarily imply personal holiness. In historical times, a man's entering the lower orders of the clergy did not preclude his later taking a wife. Possibly Arthurian clerks included persons who were not officially clergy but who specialized in reading and writing. Notice, however, that the knights and ladies of Arthurian romance are frequently, perhaps score and ten" or longer as can we moderns, barring plague and accident. Whatever the historical truth, however, the impression I draw from the medieval Arthurian romances is of a society in which age differences and generation gaps were not nearly so important as we have made them today.

Sure enough, Galehodin was so impressed by manly explanation that he not only pardoned Gawaine's party and scolded his own people, but invested the burgher with the castle of Peningue and promised to dub him knight on Whitsunday. [Vulgate V]

Malory has Galihodin a "nigh cousin" to Galeholt and "a king within the country of Surluse." Galihodin helps Lancelot play a practical joke on Dinadan at the tournament in Surluse. Later Galihodin shows up with twenty knights and tries to win La Beale Isoud by jousting, but Palomides, with Tristram's permission, jousts him and his knights down. Galihodin became a knight of the Round Table; he was among the guests at Guenever's small dinner party and among the knights who tried to heal Sir Urre. Following Lancelot into exile, Galihodin was made Duke of Sentonge. He later joined Lancelot and others in the hermitage of the former Archbishop of Canterbury, but returned to his own country after Lancelot's death. [Malory X, 49, 56, 65-66; XVIII, 3; XIX, 11; XX, 18; XXI, 10, 13]

GALLERON OF GALWAY

This knight of the Round Table became Sir Palomides' godfather. Palomides had just struck Galleron down in single combat when Tristram came along, entered conversation with the Saracen knight, and asked why he was still postponing his baptism. Palomides replied that he had still one battle to do in the name of Christ before being baptized, in fulfillment of a vow he had made years before. Tristram borrowed the armor of the wounded Galleron and gave Palomides his battle. This formality over, Palomides was baptized by the Suffragan of Carlisle, with Tristram and Galleron as godfathers.

Malory also mentions Galleron, very briefly, as one of the attempted healers of Sir Urre and as one of the knights who was killed trying to help Mordred and Agravaine trap Lancelot with the Queen. [Malory XII, 12-14; XIX, 11; XX, 2]

Galogrinans—see COLGREVANCE

Lady of Galvoie† — see under GALVOIE, *Places*

GANIEDA† (Gwendydd)

According to the Red Book of Hergest, she was the twin sister of Merlin. Glennie, from whom I gleaned this tantalizing scrap, does not make it clear whether she, also, was a necromancer. I only wish I could tell you more!

Ganora—see GUENEVERE

GARAUNT

A knight of Cameliard, mentioned once, in passing, by Malory. His only apparent claim to interest is that he was a cou-

sin of Guenevere. [Malory X, 36] The similarity of names makes it conceivable that he could be identified with Sir Geraint, the name Tennyson uses for Erec.

GARETH OF ORKNEY (Beaumains)

The youngest true-born son of Lot and Morgawse, Gareth was one of the best knights of his arms of the world and probably remains today the best-loved of the Orkney brothers, as well as one of the best-loved members of Arthur's Round Table. His story is quite familiar. The last of the brothers (except, presumably, Mordred) to come to court, he appeared anonymously and asked Arthur for three gifts. The first was to be fed for a twelvemonth, at the end of which time he would ask the other two. Kay took charge of feeding him, nicknamed him Beaumains ("Fair-hands") in mockery, and put him in the kitchen. Both Lancelot and Gawaine befriended him, the latter not recognizing him as brother, and even Kay seems to have taken pride in Beaumains' strength in the sports of casting bars or stones. At the end of the year, Lynette came to court requesting a champion for her sister Lyonors against Sir Ironside, alias "The Red Knight of the Red Launds," who was besieging their castle. Beaumains made his remaining requests: that he be given Lynette's adventure, and that Lancelot be sent after them to dub him knight on command.

To Lynette's chagrin, Arthur granted both gifts. Kay rode after them to give the kitchen boy his first test, and Beaumains promptly jousted him down; Lancelot came shortly thereafter and gave Beaumains a fall, but when they fought with swords, Gareth fought so well that Lancelot "dreaded himself to be shamed" and called a truce and knighted the young man. Despite Lynette's continued mockery, Gareth completed the adventure, conquering and either converting or slaying numerous knights on the way—Gherard and Arnold le Breusse, the four brothers Percard, Pertelope, Perimones, and Persant, and finally Ironside himself. (Tennyson, who changes and simplifies the tale somewhat in one of his best idylls, **Gareth and Lynette**, ends it with Gareth's victory at Lyonors' castle and marries Gareth to the livelier sister, Lynette.)

Malory continues the story quite a bit further: Gareth begs to see the lady he has just saved from Ironside, but Lyonors tells him he must first labor for a year to win greater fame and her love. Already in love with him, however, she enlists her brother Sir Gringamore to bring him to her with a mock kidnapping of Gareth's dwarf. Biding together in the castle after this practical joke, Gareth and Lyonors decide to consummate their love in advance of the wedding ceremony, but Lynette uses a bit of magical art to keep her sister an honest woman. Meanwhile, Pertelope, Perimones, Persant, and Ironside arrive

---

generally literate; it comes as a shock to learn that King Claudas cannot read [Vulgate V]. Nevertheless, several different manuscript styles had developed, each with specified official uses — writers and polished calligraphers being different entities, clerks therefore would fill important roles at even generally literate courts in the days before printing.

As well as keeping written records, clerks seem to have made sure that etiquette was upheld. They also conducted investigations into the future, by searching dreams and visions [Vulgate V].

Hermits, Monks, Nuns

We read of "white monks," "black monks," and so on. Since no Rome-authorized orders were yet established, the older British Christianity must have had its own traditions and garb.

As terms, "friar" and "monk" are not interchangeable. Monks settle down in a monastic community — geographical stability is a condition of his "contemplative" vocation. Friars travel about imparting the Gospel — they have "active" vocations. Friars, like the Crusades, are an Arthurian anachronism, for the preaching orders of friars developed much later than the earlier monastic orders. A "convent" applies to houses of monks or of nuns.

Hermits are distinct from friars and monks. The image of hermits, living alone and in poverty, does not seem incompatible with Arthurian tradition, but Malory states a different picture:

For in those days it was not the guise of hermits as is nowadays, for there were none hermits [then] but that they had been men of worship and of prowess; and those hermits held great household, and refreshed people ...in distress [XVIII, 3].

at Arthur's court to describe their young conqueror's exploits. Queen Morgawse also comes to visit her brother Arthur, and her older sons learn of their relationship with Beaumains.

At Gareth's advice, Lyonors holds a great tournament at her castle on the feast of Assumption. Lyonors gives her lover a ring which enables him to fight in the tournament incognito (see Lyonors' Ring, *Things*), but he is recognized when his dwarf cunningly gets possession of the ring. Then Gareth slips away from the tournament and obtains lodging at the castle of the Duke de la Rowse by promising the Duchess to yield to the absent Duke whenever he meets him. Continuing, he kills a knight named Bendelaine in battle and defends himself successfully against twenty of Bendelaine's men who attack him seeking revenge. He then defeats and slays the Brown Knight without Pity, rescuing thirty ladies from his castle. He next meets the Duke de la Rowse and offers to yield to him as per his promise, but the Duke insists on having a fight instead, is defeated, and swears fealty to Gareth and Arthur. At last Gareth and Gawaine meet, neither knowing the other, and battle for two hours before Lynette arrives to stop the fight by shouting to Gawaine that his opponent is his brother. Lynette heals their wounds with her craft, and so Gareth is finally restored to Arthur's court and wed to Dame Lyonors. [Malory, Book VII]

Vulgate IV tells us that Gareth had a splendid physique and a fine head, was a favorite with ladies and liked their company, was generous and charitable, and was Gawaine's favorite brother. Vulgate V tells us that on one occasion Arthur offered Gareth the crown of Orkney, but Gareth declined until the Grail should be achieved.

Malory, who does not seem to like Gawaine, is always careful, whenever the other Orkney brothers do evil (as when they bring about the deaths of their mother Morgawse and her lover Sir Lamorak) to make it clear that Gareth had no part in the villainy. According to Malory, Gawaine's vengefulness caused a rift between him and the unvengeful Gareth, so that the younger brother preferred Lancelot's company. [Malory VII, 34; X, 58; etc.]

Against his will, Gareth obeyed Arthur's command to join the group of knights taking Guenevere to the stake. According to Malory, Gareth and his brother Gaheris went unarmed and were cut down by mischance in the confusion, Lancelot not recognizing them. (The Vulgate has Gareth and Gaheris wearing arms during this scene and giving a good account of themselves before their deaths.) It was for Gareth's death that Gawaine turned against Lancelot and pressed the war, to the ultimate destruction of Arthur's Round Table. [Malory, XX, 8; Vulgate VI]

GARETH'S DWARF

When Gareth first came to Arthur's court, he was accompanied by two men, mounted on horseback like himself, and a dwarf on foot, who held all three horses while the men escorted Gareth into the hall. Once Gareth was established at court, the two men and dwarf seem to have left, all without saying a word. Presumably they were servants or retainers from home and returned to Orkney. At the end of Gareth's year in the kitchen, when he obtained Lynette's adventure, the dwarf, apparently the same one, showed up again with his young master's horse and armor. After conquering Kay, Gareth mounted the dwarf on Kay's horse. Little is said of the dwarf's opinions or services during the journey to Castle Dangerous; after Gareth had conquered the last knight on the way, the dwarf was sent on ahead to the castle, where he sang his master's praises to Lyonors, describing all his victories and telling the lady that her champion was the king of Orkney's son, nicknamed Beaumains by Sir Kay and dubbed knight by Sir Lancelot—he declined, however, to give Gareth's real name. Lyonors had the dwarf carry ample provisions to a hermitage in her territory and then guide Beaumains and her sister to the hermitage from Sir Persant's city to spend the night, all which instructions the dwarf capably fulfilled. Returning alone to Castle Dangerous, the dwarf met Sir Ironside and boldly defied him on Gareth's behalf, again praising his master and telling Ironside, "... it is marvel that ye make such shameful war upon noble knights."

Later, when Ironside was conquered and Lyonors had sent Gareth away, supposedly to prove his worth for a year, she made the dwarf the nub of a lover's prank. Her brother Sir Gringamore, acting on her instructions, came stalking up from behind and kidnapped the dwarf while Gareth slept. Awakened by the dwarf's cries, Gareth promptly got up and rode in pursuit. Meanwhile, Gringamore got the dwarf to his own castle, where Lyonors and Lynette were waiting to question the dwarf as to Beaumains' birth and lineage, playfully threatening him with lifelong imprisonment unless he told all. Probably recognizing the farcical nature of the affair, he replied that he "feared not greatly" to reveal his master's name and family (in effect, this entailed only adding Gareth's true name to what he had already told Lyonors) and met her threat with another in kind, mentioning all the damage Gareth would do in the country if he were angered. Gareth arrived, still thinking the matter was in earnest, and no doubt really would have done great slaughter in order to save his dwarf, whom he had had considerable trouble in tracking, had any slaughter proven necessary.

In the tournament at Castle Dangerous, Gareth fought wearing Dame Lyonors' ring, which concealed his identity by continually changing the color of his armor. When he rode off

---

Maybe anyone could become a hermit without even leaving home, by devoting himself or herself to prayers, piety, and hospitality. An old, retired knight might be both a vavasour and a hermit at once; many anchorites might not have bothered to obtain special authorization from the British Church.

"I will take me to penance," says Lancelot at the end of his knightly career, "and pray while my life lasteth, if I may find any hermit, either gray or white, that will receive me" [Malory XXI, 10]. There was and is a type of religious settlement in which the members, instead of living the common life of a monastery, come together for Mass and some of their prayers, and otherwise live alone in their separate little dwellings. I would guess that the hermitage of the former Archbishop of Canterbury, where Lancelot and so many of his former brothers of the Round Table ended up, became a settlement of this type.

Messengers and Pursuivants

And ... Tristram met with pursuivants, and they told him that there was made a great cry of tournament between King Carados of Scotland and the King of North Wales, and either should joust against other at the Castle of Maidens; and these pursuivants sought all the country after the good knights, and in especial King Carados let make seeking for Sir Launcelot du Lake, and the King of Northgalis let seek after Sir Tristram de Liones. [Malory IX, 25]

For less official messengers, almost anyone can be used — damsels, dwarves, clerks, squires, minstrels, even, at need, children. Hermits and monks, of course, would have been exempt from being pressed into messenger-service except in the very gravest emergency. I do not recall one knight ever using another

the field to "amend his helm" and take a drink of water, however, the dwarf took charge of the ring, ostensibly to prevent Gareth's losing it while he drank. Whether Gareth's returning to the field without the ring was due to his own eager haste and forgetfulness or to the dwarf's cunning is unclear, but certainly the dwarf was well pleased to keep the ring, for he wished his master to be recognized. After the tournament, the dwarf followed Gareth into the woods, returned briefly to the castle to deliver Lyonors her ring and her lover's au revoir, and then rejoined Gareth. Presumably, although the dwarf now fades from attention, he continued to accompany and serve his master. [Malory, Book VII]

Malory gives much more information about Gareth's dwarf than about any other, but Gareth's may perhaps be considered an example of dwarf-knight relationships and of the duties of dwarfs to knights, which seem to closely resemble the duties of squires, except that squires would be expected to fight at need.

GARLON

Although brother to Pellam, the guardian of the Grail, Garlon was a real rotter. He must have had some knowledge of magic, or else a working arrangement with a magician, because he went around invisible, slaying knights at will. When he showed up visible at his brother's banquet in Listeneise, he is described as having a "black face," which here probably means dour. Balin killed him, very sensibly, considering that any man as dangerous and treacherous as Garlon should be put out of action definitely and permanently. The act, however, angered Pellam, who chased Balin through the castle (probably Carbonek) until Balin found Longinus' Spear and struck Pellam with it in self-defense. Thus Garlon became the immediate occasion of the Dolorous Stroke. [Malory II, 12-15]

GAWAINE

Oldest son of King Lot and Queen Morgawse, chief of the Orkney clan (which included his brothers Agravaine, Gaheris, Gareth, and Mordred), Arthur's favorite nephew, and one of the most famous knights of the Round Table.

These are some highlights of his career according to Malory: He first came to court with his mother and three full brothers between the two early rebellions of the petty British kings against Arthur. He seems to have returned about the time of Arthur's marriage and the establishment of the Round Table, when he asked and received Arthur's promise to make him knight — they had now learned of their uncle-nephew relationship. At Arthur's wedding feast, Gawaine was sent, by Merlin's advice, on the quest of the white hart. On this quest, he accidentally

slew a lady who rushed between him and her lord, whom he had just defeated in battle and was about to behead; for this his brother Gaheris, then acting as his squire, rebuked him severely, and Guenevere ordained that Gawaine should "for ever while he lived ... be with all ladies, and ... fight for their quarrels."

When the five kings of Denmark, Ireland, the Vale, Soleise, and Longtains invaded Britain, Gawaine, Griflet, and Arthur followed Kay's example to strike them down and save the battle. After this campaign, Gawaine was elevated to the Round Table on King Pellinore's advice. Nevertheless, Gawaine later slew Pellinore in revenge for Lot's death (though Malory only alludes to the incident without describing the scene). When Arthur banished Gawaine's favorite cousin, Ywaine, on suspicion of conspiracy with his mother, Morgan le Fay, Gawaine chose to accompany Ywaine. They met Sir Marhaus, and later the three knights met the damsels "Printemps, Été, & Automne" in the forest of Arroy. Leaving his companions to make the first choice of damsels, Gawaine ended with the youngest (who, however, left him and went with another knight). It was on this adventure that Gawaine became involved in the affair of Pelleas and Ettard, playing Pelleas false by sleeping with Ettard, for which cause "Pelleas loved never after Sir Gawaine."

These adventures lasted about a year, by the end of which time Arthur was sending out messengers to recall his nephews. In Arthur's continental campaign against the Roman emperor Lucius, Gawaine and Bors de Ganis carried Arthur's message to Lucius, to leave the land or else do battle; when Lucius defied Arthur's message, hot words passed on either side, culminating when Gawaine beheaded Lucius' cousin Sir Gainus in a rage, which forced Gawaine and Bors to take rather a bloody and hasty leave. Malory seems to insinuate that Gawaine was accessory to Gaheris' murder of their mother, though "Sir Gawaine was wroth that Gaheris had slain his mother and let Sir Lamorak escape." Certainly Gawaine was with his brothers Agravaine, Gaheris, and Mordred when they later ambushed and killed Morgawse's lover, Lamorak, for which Gawaine seems to have lost Tristram's goodwill. Despite Gawaine's vengefulness, however, Lancelot, who had once rescued him from Carados of the Dolorous Tower, remained his friend until the end.

At the time of Galahad's arrival in Camelot, Gawaine reluctantly, and at Arthur's command, was the first to attempt to draw Balin's Sword from the floating marble; shortly afterwards, it was Gawaine who first proposed the Quest of the Holy Grail, in the midst of the fervor which followed the Grail's miraculous visit to court. Gawaine rather quickly tired of the Quest, however, and had very bad fortune on it besides; in addition to being seriously wounded himself by Galahad, in divine retribution for having attempted to draw Balin's Sword,

knight for the mere and sole purpose of a messenger, but knights did give each other messages and news to take back to court. Kings could surely have used knights for messengers; likely, however, a non-combatant would have had a certain ambassadorial immunity as messenger which a knight would not want to have.

Ambassadorial immunity did not always work. At the advice of Nimue, Arthur made Morgan's damsel wear a cloak that Morgan had sent as a gift to Arthur; the cloak burned the messenger to coals — Nimue must have suspected some such outcome when she made her suggestion [Malory IV, 16]. When Guenever sent her cousin Dame Elyzabel to France to summon Viviane, Claudas held Elyzabel, her squire, and her dwarf in prison until Guenever realized the errand was taking far too long; eventually, Arthur had to go to war against Claudas to gain Elyzabel's release.

Minstrels

When the harper [Eliot] had sung his song [Dinadan's lay against Mark] to the end King Mark was wonderly wroth, and said: Thou harper, how durst thou be so bold on thy head to sing this song afore me. Sir, said Eliot, wit you well I am a minstrel, and I must do as I am commanded of these lords that I bear the arms of. And sir, wit you well that Sir Dinadan, a knight of the Table Round, made this song, and made me to sing it afore you. Thou sayest well, said King Mark, and because thou art a minstrel thou shalt go quit, but I charge thee hie thee fast out of my sight. [Malory X, 31]

Sorcerers, Necromancers, Enchantresses

Probably people who simply knew the natural properties of various herbs were considered sorcerors and sorceresses, as well as folk who knew the more "supernatural" branches of necro-

he slew both King Bagdemagus and Yvonet li Avoutres—the latter and apparently the former also by mischance in friendly joust.

> Sir Gawaine had a custom that he used daily at dinner and at supper, that he loved well all manner of fruit, and in especial apples and pears. And therefore whosomever dined or feasted Sir Gawaine would commonly purvey for good fruit for him ...

Sir Pinel le Savage, a cousin of Lamorak's, once tried to use this taste to avenge Lamorak, by poisoning the fruit at a small dinner-party of the Queen's.

Gawaine had "three sons, Sir Gingalin, Sir Florence, and Sir Lovel, these two were begotten upon Sir Brandiles' sister."

Gawaine was not party to Agravaine's and Mordred's plotting against Lancelot and the Queen; indeed, Gawaine even warned his brothers and sons against what they were doing. When Lancelot killed Agravaine and all three of Gawaine's sons in escaping from Guenevere's chamber, Gawaine was ready to forgive all their deaths, and pleaded earnestly with Arthur to allow Lancelot to defend Guenevere and prove their innocence in trial by combat. Not until Lancelot slew the unarmed Gareth and Gaheris in rescuing Guenevere from the stake did Gawaine feel bound to take vengeance, in pursuit of which vengeance he stirred Arthur to besiege Lancelot first in Joyous Garde and later, after the Pope had enjoined peace in Britain, in Lancelot's lands in France. Gawaine would continually challenge Lancelot to single combat; Lancelot would defeat but refuse to kill Gawaine, who would challenge him again as soon as his wounds were healed.

Learning of Mordred's usurpation, Arthur returned to England, to meet Mordred's resistance at Dover; in this battle, the wounds Gawaine had received from Lancelot broke open fatally. Between making his last Confession and dying, Gawaine wrote a letter to Lancelot, asking his prayers and forgiveness and begging him to hurry back to England to Arthur's assistance. His death took place at noon, the tenth of May, and

> then the king let inter him in a chapel within Dover Castle; and there yet all men may see the skull of him ...

His ghost appeared to Arthur in a dream the night of Trinity Sunday, accompanied by the ladies whose battles he had fought in life. In the dream Gawaine warned Arthur to avoid battle with Mordred until after Lancelot had arrived. [Malory I, 19; II, 10, 13; III, 2, 6-8; IV, 4, 16-23, 28; V, 6; VIII, 28; X, 55; XIII, 3, 7; XVI, 1-2; XVII, 17; XVIII, 3; XIX, 11; XX, 2; XXI, 3; etc.]

These are not all of Gawaine's adventures even according to Malory, and a recapitualtion according to earlier sources would be far more favorable to the famous knight. Malory did not seem to like him, making him a rather unpleasant personality and not even all that impressive a fighter, when compared with other great champions, being defeated by Lancelot, Tristram, Bors de Ganis, Percivale, Pelleas, Marhaus, Galahad, Carados of the Dolorous Tower, and Breuse Sans Pitie. [Malory IV, 18; VII, 1; VIII, 28; IX, 26] Presumably Lamorak, Gareth, and others could also have defeated him, had he finished a fair fight with them. (Once, indeed, he did fight Gareth unknowingly, but left off at once when Lynette revealed Gareth's identity. VII, 33)

Modern treatments are based largely on Malory. By the time we reach Tennyson, Gawaine's courtesy had degenerated into smooth-talk and his chivalry into casual love affairs. William Morris turned him from one of Guenevere's most ardent defenders into one of her chief accusers. Edward Arlington Robinson retained the superficiality of Tennyson's character. John Erskine seems simply to have accepted this version of Gawaine as a matter of course. Hal Foster, while making him a major and generally likable character in **Prince Valiant**, tends to emphasize his lightness and lady-killing qualities. T. H. White, while generally not unsympathetic, turned him into a rather brusque personality and even gave the adventure of the Green Knight to Gareth instead. [**Once and Future King**, Book IV, ch. 9] It remained for **Monty Python and the Holy Grail** to sink Gawaine to his lowest point yet: in a line that goes by so fast you're likely to miss it, Gawaine is named as one of the knights slain by the vicious white rabbit! Vera Chapman created a second Gawaine, nephew and namesake of the more famous, rather than attempt to rehabilitate Malory's character. One of the few exceptions to the modern picture of Gawaine is Sutcliff's, in **Sword at Sunset**, and her Gwalchmai seems to owe as little to the pre-Malory Gawaine as to the post-Malory one.

Once, however, before his place was usurped by Lancelot, Gawaine was considered the greatest of all the knights, the epitome both of prowess and courtesy. As I recall, in **Gawaine at the Grail Castle** Jessie Weston suggests that in now-lost versions of the story, Gawaine may have achieved the Grail. The Gawaine of **Sir Gawaine and the Green Knight** is certainly an idealistic young knight very nearly as worthy, pure, and polite as mortal can be—though I must add, in fairness, that critical opinion is divided as to whether the sexual mores of the Gawaine in this poem reflect the general character of the Gawaine of other early romances, are a conscious deviation from the tradition on the part of an individual author, or even have anything to do with his behaviour toward Sir Bercilak's wife, whom he refuses, by this theory, through refusal to betray his host's hospitality. For an excellent study of Gawaine's pre-Malory character, at least in the English romances, see **The Knightly Tales of Sir Gawaine**, with introductions and translations by Louis B. Hall.

---

mancy. The Latin *veneficium* means both "poisoning" and "sorcery."

Any woman, or at least any beautiful woman, like Guenever or Isoud la Blanche Mains, might have a touch of the enchantress about her. Possibly the twelve damsels of the tower, who had such mutual animosity for Sir Marhaus and whom he characterized as "sorceresses and enchanters many of them," come under this classification — though Marhaus claimed that they could make a knight, be he never so good of body and full of prowess, "a stark coward to have the better of him," they certainly are not shown doing anything to justify this supposed power; Marhaus' distinction between them and "good ladies and gentlewomen" may be merely the distinction between amorous temptresses and modest dames. [Malory IV, 17-18]

Squires

We notice two types of squires: young men completing their education, for whom squirehood is a step to knighthood, and older men who have apparently made squiring their lifetime career. One example of an older squire who seems to have had no intention of ever advancing to knighthood is Tristram's gentleman tutor and servant Gouvernail. Sir Gawaine's Eliezer seems to me another example. Beric, Prince Valiant's squire in the early years of Hal Foster's strip, appears to be a faithful modern interpretation of this type of squire. Such squires were much more than servants to their knights — they were also friends, battle companions at need, sometimes even mentors.

Generally, in the Arthurian romances, squires accompany their knights or ladies; we seldom see squires striking out on

Even as late as the Vulgate, Gawaine is definitely second only to his close friend Lancelot as the greatest knight of the world (excluding spiritual knights like Galahad). In this version Gawaine comes across as much steadier and more dependable than Lancelot, much less prone than Lancelot to fits of madness, to berserk lust in battle, to going off on incognito adventures for the hell of it without telling the court in advance, or to settling down uninvited in somebody else's pavilion and killing the owner on his return. The Vulgate tells us that Arthur made Gawaine constable of his household and gave him the sword Excalibur for use throughout his life. For a time, as Arthur's next of kin and favorite nephew, Gawaine was named to be his successor. Gawaine was well-formed, of medium height, loved the poor, was loyal to his uncle, never spoke evil of anyone, and was a favorite with the ladies. Many of his companions, however, would have surpassed him in endurance if his strength had not doubled at noon. [Vulgate IV] In the Vulgate, when Gawaine appears in Arthur's dream, he comes not with ladies and damsels exclusively, but with a great number of poor people whom he succored in life. [Vol. VI, p. 360]

The romancers seem agreed on the fact of Gawaine's strength always doubling, or, at least, being renewed at noon.

> Then had Sir Gawaine such a grace and gift that an holy man had given to him, that every day in the year, from underne [9:00 a.m.] till high noon, his might increased those three hours as much as thrice his strength ... And for his sake King Arthur made an ordinance, that all manner of battles for any quarrels that should be done afore King Arthur should begin at underne ... [Malory XX, 21]

Modern scholars seem satisfied that this is because Gawaine was originally a solar god. The Vulgate gives a more Christian explanation, alluded to by Malory: the hermit who baptized Gawaine and for whom the child was named prayed for a special grace as a gift to the infant, and was granted that Gawaine's strength and vigor would always be fully restored at noon. For this reason many knights would not fight him until afternoon, when his strength returned to normal. [cf. Vulgate VI, p. 340-341] Sometimes the reason for Gawaine's noon strength is described as being kept a secret; the fact, however, must have become obvious early in Gawaine's career. Nor was Gawaine the only knight to enjoy such an advantage; Ironside's strength also increased daily until noon, while Marhaus' appears to have increased in the evening.

Among numerous ladies whose names are coupled with that of Gawaine are Floree, who may be identical with Sir Brandiles' sister, and Dame Ragnell, his favorite wife and the mother of his son Guinglain (surely identical with Gingalin) according to **The Wedding of Sir Gawaine and Dame Ragnell**,

which mentions that Gawaine was often married (and, presumably, often widowed)—which is one way to reconcile the various tales of his loves and romances. (See the list "Love—Marital & Otherwise")

I have heard his name pronounced both Gah-WANE (rhymes with Elaine) and GAH-w'n. The first seems by far the most popular today, but I prefer the second; I have no scholarly opinion to back me up, but GAH-w'n seems the preferred pronunciation in the dictionaries I have checked, it seems to match the pronunciation of the modern derivative name Gavin, and emphasizing the first syllable seems a better safeguard against aural confusion with such names as Bragwaine and Ywaine.

SIR GAWAINE'S FAMILY AND RETAINER
Father: King Lot
Mother: Margawse
Brothers: Agravaine, Gaheris, Gareth
Half-brother: Mordred
Sister?: Thenew
Wives and paramours: Floree, Sir Brandiles' Sister (Floree and Sir Brandiles' Sister are probably the same), Ragnell, Helain de Taningues' Sister, Hellawes, Helaes, Lore de Branlant, the King of Norgales' Daughter, the Lady of Roestoc?, the Lady of Beloe
Sons: Gingalin, Florence, Lovel
Uncle: Arthur
Aunts: Elaine of Tintagil, Morgan le Fay
Baptizer (godfather): Hermit Gawaine
Father-in-law?: King Alain of Escavalon
Brother-in-law?: Brandiles
Brother-in-law (by the marriages of Gaheris and Gareth): Gringamore
Sisters-in-law: Laurel (m. Agravaine), Lynette (m. Gaheris), Lyonors (m. Gareth)
Nephew: Melehan
Nephews?: St. Kentigern, Ider
Cousins: Ywaine (by Morgan), Galeshin (by Elaine), Edward of Orkney, Sadok
Squire: Eliezer
Ally: Lady of Briestoc

GAWAINE†

The more famous Sir Gawaine was baptized by and named for this saintly hermit. When begged to give the infant a gift, the hermit Gawaine prayed to Heaven, obtaining the grace that Sir Gawaine, however exhausted before noon, would always grow fresh and vigorous again at midday. [Vulgate VI, p. 340-341]

Genievre — see GUENEVERE

GENIEVRE†

King Leodegran was a busy man. On the same night he engendered Guenevere on his wife, he engendered a second daughter on the wife of Cleodalis, his seneschal. The two child-

---

their own until after they are dubbed knight. The dubbing, however, can be performed by a squire's own knight or any other knight on very short notice and anywhere, even the battlefield.

Vulgate III says that "a squire must not strike a knight" [I, 372]. Nevertheless, "gentlemen and yeomen" could help knights attack other knights [cf Malory X, 84]. Intermediary ground appears between temporary squires and lifelong squires — men who, for some reason, delayed being knighted. Quite possibly whether or not a squire was allowed to strike a knight depended on the squire's birth and degree of nobility and also on the circumstances of the fight. At least one squire, Helain de Taningues, became lord of a castle before being dubbed. True, his folk did not much like it, but he had promised his mother not to let anyone dub him except Sir Gawaine. [Vulgate III]

Venturing outside the Arthurian romances for further examples, in Charles Kingsley's novel **Hereward the Wake,** Hereward, a contemporary of William the Conqueror, remained a squire for a long while, but attached himself to no knight and fought as freely, in tournament and elsewhere, as a knight — he remarked that he wanted to show the world that an English squire was as good as a Norman knight. Suffolk, the English commander at Orleans when Joan of Arc raised the seige of that city, is said to have dubbed the French squire Guillaume Regnault a knight before surrendering to him, refusing to be captured by anyone under the rank of knight. (Mark Twain, transferring the tradition to a lesser English officer, gives a short and effective dramatization of the incident in his **Personal Recollections of Joan of Arc.**)

ren were born on the same day, looked exactly alike (despite having different mothers), and, just to keep things simple, Leodegran gave them both the same name. (Sommer distinguishes the bastard daughter as "the false Guenevere," but this seems to me unfair—it was not her fault she was born with Guenevere's looks, and she had just as much right as the true-born daughter to the name she was given. Therefore, I have used an alternate spelling for the name Guenevere—the spelling Sommer gives both Gueneveres in Vulgate II—for this second one.)

Genievre was raised as the supposed daughter of Cleodalis, which must have been either a good trick or a courteous pretense, considering her looks and name. Rich relatives of Cleodalis, hating Leodegran, tried to substitute Genievre for Guenevere on Arthur's wedding night, but the attempt to kidnap Guenevere was foiled by Ulfius and Brastias. At Leodegran's order, Cleodalis took Genievre away from Carohaise; he also disowned her. On the same night as the attempted abduction, Bertholai, one of Leodegran's knights, murdered another knight out of hatred, and was disinherited and banished for the deed. Some time afterwards, Bertholai came to the place where Genievre was living. [Vulgate II] See Bertholai for the rest of the story.

GERAINT (Erec)†

Malory does not mention Geraint, unless he is to be identified with Sir Garaunt. Possibly this companion of the Round Table is best known today from Tennyson's Idylls **The Marriage of Geraint** and **Geraint and Enid**. According to Tennyson, Geraint was a "tributary prince of Devon" and knight of the Round Table, who met and married Enid, only child of Earl Yniol, in a romatic adventure that involved Geraint's defeating Yniol's enemy and nephew Edyrn son of Nudd ("The Sparrow-Hawk") and restoring Yniol to his earldom. (Edyrn reformed and became a knight of the Round Table himself.) Geraint proudly presented his wife as a handmaid to Guenevere; but later, growing nervous at the rumors of Guenevere's guilt with Lancelot, the prince used the proximity of his own land in Devon to "a territory,/Wherein were bandit earls and caitiff knights" as a pretext to leave court and take Enid home to his own castle, away from courtly corruption. Here Geraint became so enmeshed in loving domesticity as to forget all calls of knightly honor, duty, and glory. Enid, more mindful than her husband of his rusting reputation, and fearing the cause to be herself, murmured in soliloquy one morning: "I fear that I am no true wife." He was just waking up, heard this sentence, misconstrued it, and took her out on a long test of faithfulness. They rode alone, without even a squire, and he commanded her to ride some distance before him and never dare speak to him. They

kept coming to groups of thieving knights and other robbers. Enid would see them and hear their plans, disobey her husband's orders about silence in order to warn him, and he would scold her, slay his attackers, appropriate their gear and horses (which he made Enid drive on ahead of her), and thus make more than enough to pay their expenses on the road. After numerous adventures of increasing peril, including a couple of other men who tried to make Enid marry them, Geraint was at last convinced of her worth and they were reconciled.

Were Tennyson the only source, I would probably forget about Geraint; but Tennyson appears to have taken his story directly from **Erec et Enide** by Chrétien de Troyes. Chrétien's is obviously the more authoritative work and the one to be summarized here; unfortunately the works of Chrétien are not easy to obtain, and my **Erec et Enide** is in an incomplete and maladroit translation. Chrétien makes Erec the son and heir of one King Lac, who is still alive and begs his son not to undertake the adventure with Enide. Otherwise, the story is clearly the same and, as nearly as I can judge, Tennyson seems to have followed Chrétien more closely than he tends to follow Malory.

Gherard le Breuse — see under ARNOLD LE BREUSE

Gifflet — see GRIFLET

GILDAS†

An actual person, an historian and probably a monk, who flourished ca. 560 A.D. Brewer gives his dates as 493-570 and calls his work "utterly worthless as history, extremely dull, meagre, and obscure." I am sure that I encountered Gildas some years ago as a rather unpleasant character in a competent but undistinguished modern Arthurian novel which I had borrowed and returned, and the author of which I have forgotten. Poor Gildas almost has to be better than the above sentences suggest!

GINGALIN (Guinglain)

Sir Gawaine's son, apparently the oldest. According to **The Wedding of Sir Gawain and Dame Ragnell**, Ragnell was Guinglain's mother.

In Malory IX, 18, we find Gingalin jousting with Tristram at Tintagil, apparently for the sport of it, and being defeated, his horse killed under him. King Mark witnesses the fight. Mark does not learn Tristram's identity, for Tristram rides off into the woods; but Mark does send a squire out to Gingalin, and, on learning who the defeated knight is, welcomes him and gives him a horse. It sounds as if Gingalin was on rather close

---

Surgeons and Leeches

There do seem to have been males who made a definite profession and livelihood of the healing arts. Women and hermits could be and frequently were surgeons and healers also, sometimes notable ones, like both the Isouds and the Lady Leech of Cornwall. I doubt, however, that a woman, unless she was a village herbwoman or wise woman of the peasantry, could have made a profession of it in the sense of earning her livelihood thereby; and a hermit should not have needed to heal for material payment. The opinion of a good female healer seems nevertheless to have been considered as good as the opinion of a professional male medic. Doubtless it would have been, if not necessary, at least very, very handy for women — indeed, for anyone — to have some knowledge of healing and nursing, as well

as of first aid. One never knew when the need might arise. For instance, Lancelot fell sick one time of drinking from a fountain that had been infected by poisonous serpents; Amable used a combination of medicine and sweating therapy to cure him [Vulgate V].

And them that were hurt [Arthur] let the surgeons do search their hurts and wounds and commanded to spare no salves nor medicines till they were whole. [Malory V, 8]

And when [Marhaus'] head was searched a piece of Sir Tristram's sword was found therein, and might never be had out of his head for no surgeons, and so he died of Sir Tristram's sword; and that piece of the sword the queen, his sister, kept it for ever with her, for she thought to be revenged an she might. [Malory VIII, 8]

terms with Mark; but Mark may, for once, have simply been showing the hospitality of the times.

Gingalin became a knight of the Round Table, being listed, with his brothers Florence and Lovel, among those who attempted to heal Sir Urre. Gingalin, Florence, and Lovel were among the knights who tried to trap Lancelot with the Queen and were slain when he escaped; in this episode, however, Arthur later tells Gawaine, "remember ye he slew two sons of yours, Sir Florence and Sir Lovel," without adding Gingalin, so it is conceivable there may have been two Gingalins. [Malory XIX, 11; XX, 2-4, 7]

KING GLOIER'S DAUGHTER

Gloier was king of Soreloise (Surluse). When Duke Galehot conquered the country, he cared for his dead enemy's orphaned daughter. [Vulgate III]

GONDEFLE†

A leader of the Sesnes, involved in the attack on Vandaliors castle early in Arthur's reign. [Vulgate II]

DUKE GORLOÏS

Duke of Tintagil, Igraine's husband, and the father of Morgawse, Elaine, and Morgana, Gorloïs long warred against Uther Pendragon. Eventually Uther summoned Gorloïs to make peace, but Uther's motive seems to have been to see Igraine, whom he charged the Duke to bring along. When Uther tried to seduce her, she told her husband at once and they returned home to Cornwall, where Gorloïs prepared his strong castles Tintagil and Terrabil, putting Igraine in charge of the first and himself in the second. On the same night that Uther, given Gorloïs' appearance by means of Merlin's magic, begot Arthur on Igraine, the real Gorloïs was killed in a sally at Terrabil. [Malory I, 1-2]

My edition of Malory does not give Igraine's husband the name Gorloïs (or any other name), but Tennyson uses it, and Brewer credits to Malory a quotation in which it appears.

GOUVERNAIL

Tristram's tutor and squire.

And then [King Meliodas, Tristram's father] let ordain a gentleman that was well learned and taught, his name was Gouvernail; and then he sent young Tristram with Gouvernail into France to learn the language, and nurture, and deeds of arms.

Gouvernail apparently chose a permanent career as squire in preference to becoming a knight himself. After seven years of teaching Tristram in France, he returned as Tristram's servant. When Tristram commanded Gouvernail to leave him alone on

the island where he would fight Sir Marhaus to the uttermost, "either departed from other sore weeping." Gouvernail is usually found at Tristram's side, serving him faithfully and well and advising him prudently. On at least one occasion, Gouvernail was instrumental in saving his master's life, when he, with Sirs Lambegus and Sentraille, pulled Tristram up from the sea cliffs of Cornwall; when, immediately after this, Tristram escaped into the woods with La Beale Isoud, Gouvernail was the only man he kept with him.

It is tempting to pair Gouvernail with Isoud's favorite handmaiden, Bragwaine. The only grounds for such a match that I find in Malory, however, are that Gouvernail is entrusted, along with Bragwaine, with the love potion intended for Isoud and Mark, and when Tristram and Isoud find it by mischance, Tristram jokingly remarks that Bragwaine and Gouvernail have kept what he supposes is merely good wine for themselves. Also, when Tristram, Sir Kehydius, Bragwaine and Gouvernail are blown ashore near Castle Perilous, North Wales, Tristram takes Kehydius adventuring in the forest, saying, apparently to Bragwaine, "Here shall ye abide me these ten days, and Gouvernail, my squire, with you."

I have not discovered what happened to Gouvernail after Tristram's death.

[Malory VIII, 3, 6, 16, 21, 24, 31, 35; IX, 10; X, 4]

Gravadain du Chastel Fort† — see under AGRAVAINE DES VAUS DE GALOIRE

Green Knight† — see BERCILAK DE HAUTDESERT

GRIFLET LE FISE DE DIEU (Gifflet)

At the beginning of Arthur's reign,

on All Hallowmass at the great feast, sat in the hall the three kings [Arthur, Ban, and Bors], and Sir Kay seneschal served in the hall, and Sir Lucas the butler ... and Sir Griflet, that was the son of Cardol, these three knights had the rule of all the service that served the kings. [Malory I, 10]

Shortly after this feast, Sir Griflet proved a good man in the battle of Bedegraine [Malory I, 14-17]

A few chapters farther on, however, we find Griflet still a squire.

Then on a day there came in the court a squire on horseback, leading a knight before him wounded to the death, and told ... how there was a knight in the forest had reared up a pavilion by a well, and hath slain my master, a good knight, his name was Miles; wherefore I beseech you that my master may be buried, and that some knight may revenge my master's death. ... Then came Griflet that was but a squire, and he was but young, of the age of the king Arthur, so he besought the king for all his service that he had done him to give the order of knighthood. Thou art

---

Then the king for great favour made Tramtrist to be put in his daughter's [La Beale Isoud's] ward and keeping, because she was a noble surgeon. And when she had searched him she found in the bottom of his wound that therein was poison, and so she healed him within a while. [Malory VIII, 9]

So upon a day, by the assent of Sir Launcelot, Sir Bors, and Sir Lavaine, they made the hermit to seek in woods for divers herbs, and so Sir Launcelot made fair Elaine to gather herbs for him to make him a bain [bath]. In the meanwhile Sir Launcelot made him to arm him at all pieces ... and ... strained himself so straitly ... that the button of his wound brast both within and without; and therewithal the blood came out so fiercely that ... he fell down on the one side [of his horse] to the earth like a dead corpse ...

With this came the holy hermit, Sir Baudwin of Brittany, and when he found Sir Launcelot in that plight he said but

little, but wit ye well he was wroth; and then he bade them: Let us have him in. And so they all bare him unto the hermitage, and unarmed him, and laid him in his bed; and evermore his wound bled piteously, but he stirred no limb of him. Then the knight-hermit put a thing in his nose and a little deal of water in his mouth. And then Sir Launcelot waked of his swoon, and then the hermit staunched his bleeding. [Malory XVIII, 17]

There came to be a difference between doctors and surgeons; in *Gil Blas,* Le Sage displays mistrust, not to say contempt, for doctors, but respect for surgeons. I do not sense such a clear distinction in the Arthurian romances; but possibly the beginnings of the division may be visible in the two types of treatment: cleaning and bandaging, and using herbs and other medicinal preparations. The latter type of treatment would have

full young and tender of age, said Arthur, for to take so high an order on thee. ... Sir, said Merlin, it were great pity to lose Griflet, for he will be a passing good man when he is of age, abiding with you the term of his life. And if he adventure his body with yonder knight at the fountain, it is in great peril if ever he come again ...

Nevertheless, Arthur dubs Griflet, who goes out to joust with the knight at the fountain. The knight at the fountain is King Pellinore, who leaves Griflet badly wounded; Arthur then has a go at Pellinore, and Merlin finally stops the fighting by casting Pellinore into sleep. (See Magical Acts 3) [Malory I, 21-24]

During the battle with the five invading kings on the bank of the Humber, when things looked bad for Arthur's side, Griflet joined Arthur, Kay, and Gawaine in trying to get Guenevere to safety; and, the invading kings catching up with them, Griflet did his part and slew one of the enemy monarchs. It was after this battle that Griflet, along with King Uriens, Sir Hervise de Revel, a couple of older knights called the King of the Lake and Sir Galagars (whom Malory mentions only this once), Gawaine, Kay, and Tor, was made a companion of the Round Table. [Malory IV, 4-5]

Griflet's epithet "le Fise de Dieu" ("the son of God") seems to suggest religious leanings. It is therefore surprising that we do not hear more of him during the Grail Adventures.

According to Malory, Griflet was one of those slain by Lancelot's party during Lancelot's rescue of Guenevere from the stake. [Malory XX, 8] In the Vulgate, however, Griflet, not Bedivere, is the last knight left alive with Arthur and the one who must throw Excalibur into the lake. [Vulgate VI] I cannot make up my mind whether Griflet is one of the more minor of the "major" knights or one of the more major of the "minor" ones.

Grim Baron of Castle Hewin† — see GROMER SOMER JOURE

GRINGAMORE

The brother of Dames Lyonors and Lynette, Sir Gringamore lived in the Isle of Avilion and is described as carrying all black arms, though this could have been for anonymity. Do not confuse him with Gringolet, Sir Gawaine's horse, nor with "The Black Knight" of Gareth's earlier adventure, Sir Percard.

After Gareth had defeated Sir Ironside, Dame Lyonors sent Gringamore to kidnap Gareth's dwarf, so that they could learn who and what the champion "Beaumains" was who had freed Castle Dangerous from Ironside's siege. When brought to Gringamore's castle, the dwarf used the occasion to boast of his master; on Gareth's arrival, Gringamore and his sisters welcomed them both as guests. Without revealing herself as the lady of Castle Dangerous, Lyonors attracted Gareth's love with

passionate flirtation. Observing the looks that passed between them, Gringamore called her aside into a chamber to tell her how much he approved the match, and then went to Gareth to assure him of the lady's love. [Malory VII, 19-20]

EARL GRIP

He warred on King Howel in Brittany, and was killed by Tristram. [Malory VIII, 36]

Grisandoles† — see AVENABLE

GROMER SOMER JOURE

While hunting alone in Inglewood, Scotland, Arthur once fell into the power of Sir Gromer Somer Joure, who threatened to take vengeance because, Gromer claimed, Arthur had wrongfully given some of his lands to Gawaine. Gromer finally agreed to let Arthur go for a year, on Arthur's parole to return at the end of that time prepared to meet his death if he could not answer the question, "What is it women most desire?" Arthur got the answer from Dame Ragnell, who turned out to be Gromer's sister; as soon as Gromer heard it, he cursed Ragnell as the only one who could have taught it to the King.

The Wedding of Sir Gawaine and Dame Ragnell, the source of the above information, leaves the impression that Arthur and Gromer parted enemies, the King vowing never to fall into Gromer's power again. Malory, however, mentions Gromore Somir Joure as one of the knights who accompanied Mordred and Agravaine in their attempt to trap Lancelot with the Queen, and who were killed during Lancelot's escape. All these knights "were of Scotland, outher of Sir Gawaine's kin, either wellwillers to his brethren." [Malory XX, 2-5] This suggests that somewhere along the line Gromer became reconciled with Arthur and Gawaine and joined Arthur's court, possibly as a companion of the Round Table.

Glennie refers to the basic story, calling Gromer only "The Grim Baron of Castle Hewin" and Ragnell only "The Foul Ladye," and pinpointing Arthur's meeting with the Grim Baron at Tarn Wadling in Inglewood.

GRUMMORE GRUMMURSUM

A "good knight of Scotland" who became a companion of the Round Table, being listed among the would-be healers of Sire Urre. [Malory VII, 26; XIX, 11] This is about all Malory tells us of him, and in the second reference his name is given as "Sir Gromere Grummer's son." I do not think he should be identified with Gromer Somer Joure. Grummore Grummursum is a minor knight — but with a name like that, I simply could not resist the temptation to include him here.

---

required the same type of knowledge as that needed by a poisoner, so that healing may have been considered akin to sorcery when practiced by anyone other than surgeons and holy hermits.

Varlets

A varlet was a man or boy acting as a servant, a groom, or as other attendant to a military leader. By extension the word came to mean anyone of a knavish or rascally disposition. Though varlet seems a popular insult word in today's pseudo-archaic dialogue, the first definition is the one we want in reading such passages as this:

So Sir Tristram had three squires, and La Beale Isoud had three gentlewomen, and both the queen and they were richly apparelled; and other people had they none ... but varlets to bear their shields and their spears [Malory X, 65].

Vavasours

A feudal tenant ranking immediately below a baron, according to the Oxford English Dictionary. The modern equivalent, after 1611 A.D., might be "baronet." (A baronetcy, however, is hereditary, and I do not know whether a vavasourship was. Since the rank of baronet was officially instituted after the days of feudalism, the approximate equivalence of rank must lack economic and other strictly feudal overtones.) Vavasours turn up frequently in the romances, usually being older, respectable knights with beautiful daughters, eager and ambitious sons, or both. One gets the impression that the two most popular roles for knights who survived to a ripe old retirement age were that of hermit and that of vavasour.

GUENEVERE (Guenever, Genievre, Ganora, Vanora, Wander, Guenhumara, etc.)

Arthur first saw Guenevere when he went, with his allies Kings Ban and Bors, to rescue her father King Leodegrance of Cameliard from King Ryons. When Arthur's barons insisted he take a wife, he told Merlin:

> ... I love Guenever the king's daughter Leodegrance of the land of Cameliard, the which holdeth in his house the Table Round that ye told he had of my father Uther. And this damosel is the most valiant and fairest lady that I know living ...

And he insisted on marrying her, despite Merlin's warning that she would have Lancelot for a lover. Leodegrance sent Arthur the Round Table, along with a hundred knights, as a wedding gift.

When Arthur prepared to go and meet the five invading kings of Denmark, Ireland, the Vale, Soleise, and the Isle of Longtains, he took Guenevere along on the campaign, saying that she would cause him "to be the more hardy" and promising to keep her safe. While they were camped beside the Humber, the invading kings attacked by night. Arthur, Kay, Gawaine, and Griflet tried to get the Queen over the Humber River to safety, but

> the water was so rough that they were afraid to pass over. Now may ye choose, said King Arthur, whether ye will abide and take the adventure on this side, for an ye be taken they will slay you. It were me liefer, said the queen, to die in the water than to fall in your enemies' hands and there be slain.

At Kay's urging and example, the four men slew the five invading kings who were bearing down on them, for which Guenevere praised Kay greatly and promised to bear his fame among the ladies.

Malory records that Guenevere "made great sorrow ... and swooned" at the departure of her husband and his men for their continental war with the Emperor Lucius, and that she came to meet him at Sandwich on his return.

As Arthur had his Knights of the Round Table, Guenevere had her own company, the Queen's Knights, who carried white shields; at first, the Queen's Knights were apparently made up of youthful aspirants to the Table, but eventually there seems to have been considerable overlapping in the membership of the two companies. Malory is unclear on when and how Guenevere and Lancelot became more to each other than she was to all of her knights, but by the time Lancelot slew Turquine and Peris de Forest Savage, gossip was already hot enough that the damsel who guided the great knight to Peris could mention it to his face, while by the time Tristram and La Beale Isoud gave in to their passion, the relationship was sufficiently established and known that Isoud could send Palomides to Arthur's court charging him

> there recommend me unto Queen Guenever, and tell her that I send her word that there be within this land but four lovers, that is, Sir Launcelot du Lake and Queen Guenever, and Sir Tristram de Liones and Queen Isoud.

Perhaps Guenevere shows to her worst advantage in this long, stormy love affair. Lancelot called forth her jealousy in a way that Arthur seems never to have done (although, ironically, Arthur probably deserved her jealousy more, Lancelot being drawn into side affairs and appearances of affairs through trickery and misfortune). She accepted Lancelot's explanation of the engendering of Galahad and forgave him, but later, when Elaine of Carbonek tricked Lancelot into her bed at Arthur's court itself, within earshot of Guenevere's own room, the Queen's rather

understandable fury drove Lancelot mad. While he wandered out of his wits she spared no expense to find him, financing the knights who went out searching, so that when Percivale and Ector de Maris finally found him at Joyous Isle, Percivale could say that "I was sent by the queen for to seek you." The affair seems to have become even more tempestuous after the Grail Quest. Lancelot quickly forgot the vow he had made during the holy adventures to break it off with Guenevere—Malory's wording seems to put the responsibility for the resumption of the affair more on Lancelot than on the Queen—but he also became more careless about secrecy. Then, when he realized the scandal they were causing and began championing as many ladies and damsels as possible to throw the gossips off the scent, Guenevere waxed angry and jealous again, speaking to him so hotly that he followed his cousin Bors' advice and left court again, hiding with the hermit Sir Brasias at Windsor until the Queen should repent her words and want him back.

It was at this time that Guenevere held a "privy dinner" for 24 other knights of the Round Table, to show that she took joy in all of them — at which dinner Sir Patrise of Ireland died of a poisoned apple meant for Gawaine.

Guenevere was accused of the crime, reproached by Arthur himself for being unable to keep Lancelot at hand when she needed him, and driven to beg Sir Bors to champion her in Lancelot's place; Lancelot, meanwhile, secretly informed of the situation by Bors, laid low and let Guenevere stew, not showing up until the very last minute. Shortly after this incident, Lancelot tried to stay in London with the Queen while the rest of the court went to Winchester for a great tournament. This time Guenevere told Lancelot to leave her and attend the tournament, lest their enemies use the occasion for further scandal. "Madam," said Sir Lancelot, "I allow your wit, it is of late come since ye were wise." Somewhat illogically, after accepting Guenevere's reasoning, he went to Winchester in disguise, and his wearing the favor of Elaine of Astolat in the lists led to another jealous rift, which was not quite healed until Elaine's death bore testimony to Lancelot's avoidance of sexual entanglement with her. In justice, Guenevere seems genuinely to have pitied the dead Elaine. She also prudently insisted that from now on Lancelot wear her favor in tournament, to avoid such injury as he sustained at Winchester when his kinsmen, not knowing him, ganged up on him.

Guenevere shows to better advantage in the adventure of Sir Meliagrant, which Malory (or his first editor, Caxton) places after the last-mentioned incidents, but which probably occurred earlier. When Meliagrant and his men ambushed Guenevere and her party while they were out a-Maying, she kept her head; seeing her ten unarmored knights outnumbered, defeated, and wounded, she surrendered rather than let them be slain, even calling on the four who were still on their feet to leave off fighting, since it was hopeless. She managed, however, to slip her ring to a child of her chamber and send him back to Lancelot. When Lancelot arrived and cowed Meliagrant, Guenevere seems to have promoted the cause of peace and truce, though she prudently insisted that, as long as they remained in Meliagrant's castle, her wounded knights should be put in her own chamber so that she could be sure they received the best treatment. Lancelot came to her at the garden window that night, injured his hands in pulling out the window bars to get in, and so left blood in her bed, giving Meliagrant the chance to accuse her of lying with the injured knights. Again Lancelot had to fight her trial by combat to save her from burning, and this time she "wagged her head ... as though she would say: Slay [Meliagrant]," which may have been more prudence than bloodthirstiness and was certainly understandable, all things considered.

When cornered at last together in the Castle of Carlisle by Mordred, Agravaine, and their dozen knights, Lancelot offered, after slaying thirteen of the attackers and driving Mordred away wounded, to take Guenevere with him at once to safety. She, however, refused to go, probably hoping that the good of the court might yet be salvaged, telling him only that if he saw they would burn her, then he might rescue her as he thought best. Most modern versions depict Arthur as being forced with a heavy heart to bow to the righteousness of the Law in sentencing Guenevere, but a close reading of Malory and the Vulgate version gives the impression of what might be called a kangaroo court, save that the King himself was presiding, with Arthur seeming to rejoice in the law (though it is just possible his rage was less for Guenevere's inconstancy than for the deaths of his thirteen knights) and hotly refusing Gawaine's plea to allow Lancelot to fight a trial by combat yet again and prove their innocence—which would, of course, have averted the final catastrophe. Indeed, Arthur apparently forbade any trial by combat at all and, far from hoping that Lancelot would come to the rescue, as in T. H. White's version, seems to have tried to burn her at once, before Lancelot got his chance. Guenevere probably never knew that even Lancelot had seemed to falter a little in his resolve to save her: talking the matter over with his kinsmen, he said

> ... and this night because my lady the queen sent for me ... I suppose it was made by treason, howbeit I dare largely excuse her person, notwithstanding I was there by a forecast near slain ...

Despite Arthur's attempt to burn her, she returned to him and showed herself a loyal wife and prudent queen while he was overseas besieging Lancelot. She was not taken in by Mordred's forged letters purporting that Arthur was dead, but she pretended to agree to marry Mordred, thus getting him to let her go to London, supposedly to buy what whe wanted for the wedding, actually to barricade herself well in the Tower of London, with men and provisions; and when Mordred laid siege to the Tower she answered him "that she had liefer slay herself than to be married with him." Learning at last of Arthur's actual death (or "passing"), Guenevere "stole away" with five of her ladies to Almesbury, where she became a "nun in white clothes and black," and lived in great penance, "fasting, prayers, and alms-deeds," "and never creature could make her merry," which last must have been especially severe, as Malory elsewhere shows her possessed of a keen sense of humor and fun. She became Abbess. She had one more meeting with Lancelot; he sought her out, with thoughts of taking her back with him to his kingdom in France, but, couselling him to keep his realm in peace, take a wife, and pray for his old lover, she refused to leave her sanctuary and penance. "And therefore, lady," said Lancelot, remembering his broken resolutions of the Grail Adventures, "sithen ye have taken you to perfection, I must needs take me to perfection, of right." He did not see her again until, learning of her death in a vision, he and eight companions went on foot from Glastonbury to Almesbury to bring back her body for burial. [Malory I, 18; III, 1, 5; IV, 2-3; V, 3, 12; VI, 10; VIII, 31; X, 49; XI, 6-9; XVIII, 1-21; XIX, 1-9; XX, 3-17; XXI, 1, 7-11, etc.]

Malory does not show, except perhaps between the lines, as in the number of cases of conquered knights being sent to

her and in her presiding at Duke Galeholt's tournament in Surluse when Arthur himself was unable to attend [X, 40-49], how good a queen Guenevere was, that part of her character being overshadowed by her affair with Lancelot. The Vulgate, which calls her, after Elaine of Carbonek, the wisest woman who ever lived [vol. II], throws more light on this and other points. That she was an excellent day-to-day administratress is evidenced by how greatly the affairs of the kingdom slipped while Arthur banished her for two and a half years to live in infatuation with her look-alike, Genievre, giving knights, court, and common people much cause to yearn for their wise and generous true Queen. Guenevere was understandably reluctant to return to Arthur after Genievre's death, for, as she said, he had in effect dissolved her marriage by condemning her to death in this case, and she was well content in Surluse with a man who would make her a much better husband. Except for Elaine of Carbonek (whom she made some attempt to accept—cf. Malory XI, 7) and Elaine of Astolat, whom she did not meet alive and grieved for dead, she seems to have befriended all women, even accepting Amable as Lancelot's platonic lady love. She seems to have inspired more than common devotion in Gawaine, who lent Lancelot Excalibur when he fought to save her from Arthur's sentence in the Genievre episode, and in Kay, who openly envied Lancelot his position as her champion.

In Malory Book VI, chapter 10, an unnamed damsel remarks to Lancelot: "It is noised that ye love Queen Guenevere, and that she hath ordained by enchantment that ye shall never love none other but her." This is the only hint I remember reading that Guenevere may have dabbled in magic; and I think this evidence either comes under the heading of gossip and metaphor, or that it reflects some confusion with Lancelot's mentor Viviane, the French Damsel of the Lake, who according to the Vulgate largely engineered the affair (with a bit of intriguing assistance from Duke Galeholt and the Lady of Malohaut).

A Middle English romance, **The Adventures at Tarn Wadling**, currently available in Louis Hall's **Knightly Tales of Sir Gawaine**, describes an interesting meeting of Guenevere with her mother's ghost. The ghost describes her penitential suffering, the sins—especially pride—that led to it and the virtues that would have helped her avoid it, asks Masses for her salvation, and warns against Arthur's greed as the cause of his future downfall. The description of the ghost's appearance would stir professional jealousy in the heart of any monster-movie makeup artist; nevertheless, Guenevere has Gawaine at her side, and, after her initial fright, questions the spirit bravely and compassionately, afterwards ordering a million Masses for her.

Guenevere had gray eyes (cf. **Sir Gawaine and the Green Knight**) and more than one commentator has remarked that the root of her name means "white," suggesting a pale complexion and very fair blond hair. According to the Vulgate, she was also the best chess player of Arthur's court.

Father: King Leodegrance Husband: King Arthur Half-sister: Genievre Lover: Lancelot Would-be Lover: Meliagrance Cousins: Elyzabel, Garaunt, Guiomar, Guy, Labor	**QUEEN GUENEVERE'S FAMILY AND RELATIONS**

'Guenever,' the False — see GENIEVRE

GUINAS† — see under GUINAS' CASTLE, *Places*

Guinebas — see GWENBAUS

GUINEMANS†

Apparently either a leader of the Sesnes or one of their allies in the attack on Vandaliors castle, early in Arthur's reign. [Vulgate II]

Guinglain — see GINGALIN

GUIOMAR†

A cousin of Guenevere, he was one of Morgana's earliest lovers. Guenevere's anger over Morgan's affair with Guiomar led to the rift between the two women, Guenevere banishing Guiomar from court and Morgan leaving to learn witchcraft from Merlin. I found Guiomar's name in Vulgate VII, the story in Vulgate IV.

GUY

A knight of Cameliard, mentioned once by Malory, in passing, along with Sir Garaunt. [X, 36] Guy's and Garaunt's claim to fame is that they were cousins of Guenevere.

GWENBAUS (Guinebas)

The brother of Kings Ban and Bors, Gwenbaus accompained them to England when they came as Arthur's allies during the early war against the rebel kings. Malory characterizes Gwenbaus simply as "a wise clerk." From the Vulgate we learn that he was a clerk of necromancy and did a bit of hobnobbing with Merlin. Gwenbaus met, loved, and remained with a king's daughter in the Forest Perilous in England until his and her deaths (apparently natural). See Forest Perilous, *Places.*

Gwendydd† — see GANIEDA

ARGODABRANS†

A leader of the Sesnes, involved in the attack on Vandaliors, Hargodabrans was 15 feet tall. He worked with the sorceress Camille against Arthur at La Roche; but, grievously wounded and taken prisoner by Lancelot, he stabbed himself when carried to the tents. [Vulgate II, III]

King Harlon—see under ARGUSTUS

DAMOISELE À LA HARPE†

She took Oriolz the Dane to heal him. She was either a sister or a cousin of Helaes de la Forest Perilleuse. [Vulgate VII] The name suggests she may have been castellaine of the Castel de la Harpe.

HARRY LE FISE LAKE

A companion of the Round Table, "a good knight and an hardy." His biggest moment in Malory comes during a scuffle with Breuse Sans Pitie in Book I, chapter 53. He is also listed in XIX, 11. In XX, 5, he appears as one of the knights who sided with Lancelot after Mordred surprised the great knight with Guenevere. Sir Harry's epithet, "le Fise Lake" ("fise" = fils = son) suggests a close relationship (adoptive? friendly?)

with Lancelot du Lake. Perhaps, however, Harry is the son of the extremely minor King of the Lake; see under Griflet.

HEBES LE RENOUMES

A squire of Tristram's, sent to Tristram first by King Faramon's daughter, with a love letter and a gift brachet. After Faramon's daughter had died of love, Hebes returned to the great knight. He remained in Britain when Mark sent Tristram to Ireland to be cured of the wound from Marhaus' spear. Hebes accompanied Gawaine, however, to Ireland for the tournament for the Lady of the Launds, hoping "to be made knight," and there recognized Tristram, promised not to reveal his true identity, and asked to receive his knighthood from Tristram's hands. Tristram obliged, after which Hebes "did right well that day" at the tournament and afterwards held with Tristram. When the Irish queen, Isoud's mother, discovered Tristram was the man who had killed her brother Marhaus, it was Sir Hebes who bodily prevented her from slaying Tristram in his bath.

After Tristram's death, Hebes remained in Arthur's court as a companion of the Round Table, being listed among those who tried to heal Sir Urre. He accompanied the exiled Lancelot into France, where Lancelot made him Earl of Comange. [Malory VIII, 5, 9-11; XIX, 11; XX, 18]

Hector des Mares—see ECTOR DE MARIS

HELAES DE LA FOREST PERILLEUSE (Helaes the Beautiful)

Helaes was an orphan, the Countess of Limos, the sister of one Clapor le Riche and the niece of one Meleager le Rous, a sister or cousin of the Damoisele à la Harpe, and also unmarried and a determined lover of Sir Gawaine. Enlisting the aid of Oriolz the Dane, she won a place in Gawaine's bed. [Vulgate VII]

It is likely that Helaes should be identified with Malory's sorceress Hellawes of the Castle Nigramous.

Helaine (as a woman's name)—see ELAINE

HELAIN DE TANINGUES†

This squire was castellan of a castle in the neighborhood of Taningues. Gawaine visited him anonymously. Helain confided to the knight that "My people have often blamed me for delaying my entry into the order of chivalry," but, after a dream twelve years before, his mother had made him promise not to request anyone but Sir Gawaine to dub him. Gawaine revealed himself and dubbed Helain next day, also promising Helain's beautiful sister to be her true knight. [Vulgate III]

HELAIN DE TANINGUES' SISTER†

After dubbing her brother, Gawaine promised this unnamed damsel to be her true knight, giving her a girdle and a locket which the Lady of Roestoc had given him. [Vulgate III]

Helaine the Peerless†—see under PERSIDES OF GAZEWILT

HELIADES†

A very late king in our period, Heliades was given Scotland by Mordred during the latter's rebellion. [Vulgate VI] If he fought with Mordred in the last battle, he was, of course, killed there.

HELIAP†

As nearly as I can make out the text of Vulgate VII, Heliap was Sir Sagramor's lady love.

HELIN LE BLANK (Hellaine, Helain, Elian)

Like Percivale and Galahad, Helin, the son of Sir Bors and King Brandegoris' daughter, appears to have been knighted at the age of 15, and at about the same time as Galahad. He became a knight of the Round Table and "proved a good knight and an adventurous." [Malory XII, 9; XIX, 11] He was eventually to become emperor of Constantinople [Vulgate IV]. "Le Blank" signifies "the white" and is also an appellation of Elaine of Astolat; I find the resemblance in the names of two such different characters very interesting.

HELLAWES

The lady of Castle Nigramous and the Chapel Perilous, she tried to kill Lancelot with a kiss, so that she could keep his dead body always to cherish and serve. Failing in her attempt, she died of love for him. She had a similar passion, though not so deadly, for Gawaine. [Malory VI, 15]

Very likely Malory's Hellawes should be identified with the Vulgate's Helaes de la Forest Perilleuse.

HELYAN OF IRELAND†

When Arthur refilled the seats of the Round Table after Lancelot and his followers had left, Lancelot's seat was given to Sir Helyan. This alone suggests that Helyan was an excellent knight, at least "of his hands." He was a king's son, but of which Irish king I do not know. [Vulgate VI] Presumably he perished with Arthur in the last battle.

HELYES OF THOULOUSE†

Duke Galeholt's chief clerk, Helyes had nine other clerks under him, including Petroines and a clerk of Cologne. Galeholt said of Helyes that he surpassed all other clerks as gold all other metals. Helyes had enough knowledge and power to call up at least one wonder, and might have performed miracles had he chosen to study along those lines. See also Helyes' Book, *Things* and Magical Act 33 in that appendix.

HEMISON

Sir Hemison was a lover of Morgan le Fay, living with her at one of her castles. One time Morgan gave a Cornish knight lodging, but next morning informed him that he was her prisoner until he told her who he was. She gave him, however, the place of honor at her side, which aroused Hemison's jealousy until he almost attacked the stranger, but "left it for shame." When the stranger privately told Morgan his identity, she regretted her promise to let him go so easily, but made him promise to carry a shield of her design at the next tournament (see Morgan's Shield, *Things*). As the Cornish knight departed, the jealous Hemison prepared to follow him, and Morgan's strenuous objections only resulted in a quarrel and sent Hemison away the more "wood wroth."

> Fair friend, said Morgan, ride not after that knight, for ye shall not win no worship of him. Fie on him, coward, said Sir Hemison, for I wist never good knight come out of Cornwall but if it were Sir Tristram de Liones. What an that be he? said she. Nay, nay, said he, he is with La Beale Isoud, and this is but a daffish knight. ... For your sake, said Sir Hemison, I shall slay him. ...

Well, Hemison was wrong. It was Tristram. After the fight, Hemison begged his varlet to bring him back to Morgan's castle,

for deep draughts of death draw to my heart that I may not live, for I would fain speak with her or I died: for else my soul will be in great peril an I die.

His varlet got him to the castle, "and there Sir Hemison fell down dead. When Morgan le Fay saw him dead she made great sorrow out of reason" and buried him with honor. [Malory IX, 41-43]

Herlews le Berbeus—see under BALIN LE SAVAGE

SIR HERLEWS' LADY

When Herlews was mortally wounded by the invisible Garlon, he told Balin le Savage to take his horse and follow his lady in "the quest that I was in as she will lead you, and revenge my death when you may." She seems to have been a capable, loyal, and hardy damsel, surviving the ordeal—which killed at least three score other maidens—of giving a dish of her blood to the Leprous Lady, and carrying with her the truncheon with which Garlon had slain Herlews until Balin called for it to stick into Garlon's body and complete the revenge. She was killed when Balin dealt King Pellam the Dolorous Stroke and the castle fell down upon them. [Malory II, 12-16] One would have said she deserved a better fate; one would have said that Balin deserved a better fate, too. See also under Balin le Savage.

KING HERMANCE OF THE DELECTABLE ISLE AND THE RED CITY

Tristram and Palomides found the body of King Hermance in a rich vessel covered with red silk, which grounded on the bank of the Humber River. In the dead king's hand was a letter telling how he had been traitorously slain by two poorly-born brethren whom he had brought up, and pleading for some knight to avenge him. Palomides took the quest, journeyed to the Red City, met Sir Ebel, a faithful old retainer who had written the letter for his dead king, and Sir Hermind, the king's brother. Palomides fought and slew the wicked brothers, Sirs Helius and Helake, and freed Hermance's kingdom. [Malory X, 59-64] King Hermance may well have been alive and ruling, but keeping to himself, during the first part of Arthur's reign.

HERMIND (ERMINIDE)

The brother of King Hermance of the Red City, Hermind fought Sir Palomides for the right of avenging Hermance's death, but yielded to Palomides as the better warrior. Hermind may have become king after his brother, though there is no evidence for this; Palomides apparently left Hermance's territory in the hands of the people. [Malory X, 62-64] Hermind did become a knight of the Round Table, being listed among those who tried to heal Sir Urre. He was one of the men killed during Lancelot's rescue of the Queen from the stake. [Malory XIX, 11; XX, 8]

EARL HERNOX

The lord of Carteloise Castle, Earl Hernox was good but unfortunate. His three sons raped and murdered their sister and imprisoned their father. After Galahad and his companions Bors and Percivale had killed the sons in righteous battle, Hernox died, counting himself blessed, at least, that he died in Galahad's arms. [Malory XVII, 7-9]

HERTANT†

A Saxon warrior, involved in the attack on Vandaliors castle early in Arthur's reign, Hertant was the nephew of the Saxon king or leader Minadus. [Vulgate II]

HERVISE (Hervi) DE REVEL

An excellent knight who, Vulgate III tells us, was already of a "great age" at the beginning of Arthur's reign. Malory mentions him twice, the first time as doing "marvellous deeds with King Arthur" in the battle against the rebel kings at Terrabil, the second time as being chosen, on Pellinore's advice, to fill one of the empty seats at the Round Table after the battle with the five invading kings (of Denmark, etc.) at the Humber. [II, 10; IV, 4] Hervise de Revel may be a character with a rich history of his own, who was either incorporated into the Arthurian cycle or whose original importance was crowded into the background by more recently-added characters.

Robert Browning's poem **Hervé Riel** is about a Breton sailor and hero of the late seventeenth century.

Hoel   see HOWELL

Damsel of Hongrefort — see HONGREFORT, *Places*

HONTZLAKE

In Malory Book III, chapters 5 and 12, Sir Hontzlake of Wentland comes into Arthur's court and forcibly abducts Nimue, who has not yet become an enchantress and who has ridden into court to claim a stolen brachet. King Pellinore pursues them, kills Hontzlake, and rescues Nimue.

In Malory Book IV, chapters 7 and 8, the name Ontzlake reappears, this time attached to the good brother of the evil Sir Damas. Here Sir Ontzlake keeps a fair manor through "prowess of his hands ... and dwelleth [therein] worshipfully, and is well beloved of all people." (See also **Damas**)

HOWELL (Hoel) OF BRITTANY (Little Britain)

Sometimes called King, sometimes called Duke, Hoel was Arthur's cousin and ally. Lady Hoel, his wife, was killed by the Giant of St. Michael's Mount, Brittany, who in turn was slain by Arthur, Kay, and Bedivere.

Hoel was the father both of the second wife of King Meliodas of Cornwall and of Isolt le Blanche Mains. Tristram's stepmother became his sister-in-law! Hoel's son was Sir Kehydius, who became enamoured of La Beale Isolt. [Malory V, 5; VIII, 2; etc.]

Cousin: Arthur	**HOEL'S FAMILY**
Son: Kehydius	
Daughters: King Meliodas' Second Wife (Tristram's stepmother), Isoud la Blanche Mains	
Sons-in-law: King Meliodas, Tristram	

HUE OF THE RED CASTLE

Hue and his brother, Sir Edward of the Red Castle, extorted a barony from the Lady of the Rock. Sir Marhaus defeated them, killed Edward, and sent Hue to Arthur's court. [Malory IV, 26-27] Malory seems to say nothing more about Hue, but if he followed the usual pattern he probably reformed and became a companion of the Round Table.

THE KING OF [with] THE HUNDRED KNIGHTS (Barant, Berrant le Apres

One of the rebel kings at the beginning of Arthur's reign, he was a "passing good man and young." Malory gives his name once as Berrant le Apres and once as Barant le Apres (the alternate spellings may be the result of editor's work), but he is far more commonly known as "The King of (or, with) the Hundred Knights." He pledged 4,000 mounted men of arms to the rebellion. Two nights before the battle of Bedegraine, this monarch

met a wonder dream ... that there blew a great wind, and blew down their castles and their towns, and after that came a water and bare it all away. All that heard of the sweven [dream] said it was a token of great battle.

He acquitted himself well in the battle, and did not join Lot's later rebellion, going over to Arthur's side instead and becoming a member of the Round Table. [Malory I, 8-17; X, 60; XIX, 11]

Vulgate II gives his country, or perhaps his city, as Malahaut, suggesting the Lady of Malohaut may have been his viceregent or vassal. He had a son named Marant and a daughter named Landoine, and was an ally of Duke Galeholt, one of the two allies Galeholt loved and trusted most. [Vulgate III] He seems to be one of the more important minor characters.

Pondering on his title and on the fact that he must have had many more than a hundred knights at his command, I wonder if this monarch might not have kept a Table something like Arthur's, perhaps even round, which seated a hundred. Since Arthur had got the Round Table from King Leodegrance, who had got it from Uther Pendragon, the King of the Hundred Knights would have had Uther's or Leodegrance's example for such a Table.

HUNTRESS OF WINDSOR

This unnamed lady lived in Windsor Forest, hunted daily with women only, and one day accidentally shot Lancelot in the buttock with an arrow as he lay beside a well near Brasias' hermitage. [Malory XVIII, 21]

Curiously, in the Vulgate it is a male hunter who shoots Lancelot by mistake.

BLIS"†

One night Gaheris came to four pavilions. He helped himself to food in the first, and in the fourth lay down in bed with a sleeping lady, not noticing that her husband was also asleep in the same bed. In the middle of the night the husband awoke, found Gaheris, thought his wife was playing him false, and dragged her out of bed by her hair. Gaheris woke, saw him mistreating the lady, and cleft him to the shoulders with no further questions, to the lady's additional grief. In the morning, Gaheris insisted she go with him, even extracting a promise from her that she would never love any other knight after him. Her four brothers tried to rescue her, and Gaheris defeated them, leaving one seriously wounded in charge of a physician who promised to heal him in eight weeks. Gaheris and the lady spent the night in a convent of white nuns. Here she craftily took the veil, thus escaping from Gaheris without breaking her word. She afterwards did much for the convent, and led a saintly life. [Vulgate V]

I borrowed the name Iblis for this lady from that of Lanzelet's wife according to the German **Lanzelet** of Ulrich von Zatzikhoven (about which work I know nothing further). It seemed a not unfitting name in that the lady of the Vulgate is a cousin-german of Lancelot, Bors, and Lionel.

IDER

Malory mentions this knight at the beginning of the war against the Emperor Lucius, calling him Ywaine's son. A few chapters earlier, Ywaine himself appears quite young. This indicates either that Malory did not arrange his material in strict chronology or that Ider was the son of some other Ywaine, not Ywain son of Urien and Morgana. Malory seems not to mention Ider again, unless he is identical with "Sir Idrus the good knight," who seems likewise to be mentioned but once. Ider and Idrus were on Arthur's side, but I find no firm evidence that he or they were members of the Round Table. [Malory V, 2, 6; cf IV, 19]

KING IDRES OF CORNWALL

One of the rebel kings at the beginning of Arthur's reign. When the Saracens attacked Wandesborow Castle, forcing the rebel kings to suspend their war against Arthur, King Idres with four thousand men of arms was put into the city of Nauntes in Britain "to watch both the water and the land." [Malory 1, 12, 14, 15, 18]

IGRAINE (Igerne, Ygraine etc.), DUCHESS OF TINTAGIL and later QUEEN OF ENGLAND

Arthur's mother, she "was called a fair lady, and a passing wise." The first part of her story is basic, how she repulsed Uther Pendragon's advances, telling her husband Duke Gorlois, "I suppose that we were sent for that I should be dishonoured; wherefore, husband, I counsel you, that we depart from hence suddenly, that we may ride all night unto our own castle"; how on the night of her husband's death at Castle Terrabil Merlin introduced Uther into her bed at Tintagil disguised as the Duke, how that night Arthur was engendered, and how afterwards Uther married Igraine, urged thereto by Sir Ulfius and others as well as by his own desire. Uther did not tell her who had lain with her on the night of her husband's death, however, until half a year after the marriage, when at last, as she waxed larger,

> he asked her, by the faith she owed to him, whose was the child within her body, then [was] she sore abashed to give answer. Dismay you not said the king, but tell me the truth, and I shall love you the better by the faith of my body.

After making her tell her story, he told her his. "Then the queen made great joy when she knew who was the father of her child." Malory does not record Igraine's sentiments when Uther took away her son to give him over to Merlin; nor is it clear from this account why Merlin demanded secrecy in the matter, when one might have expected that Uther's barons had wished him to marry precisely in order to produce an heir—although later interpretations have made the spiriting away of the child seem a political necessity.

Igraine's children by Duke Gorlois were Morgawse, Elaine, and Morgan le Fay; the first two daughters were married to King Lot and King Nentres respectively, and the last put into a nunnery, at the time of Igraine's marriage to Uther.

What seems often overlooked is that Igraine was still around during at least the first part of Arthur's reign. After Uther's death she would presumably have been Queen Dowager, and later she would have been recognized as Queen Mother, though Merlin appears to have arranged a sort of practical joke in bringing about this recognition. Arthur had Merlin send for Igraine so that he could talk to her himself and learn the truth of his birth.

In all haste, the queen was sent for, and she came and brought with her Morgan le Fay, her daughter, that was as fair a lady as any might be, and the king welcomed Igraine in the best manner.

But Sir Ulfius came in and appeached Igraine of treason,

> For an she would have uttered it in the life of King Uther Pendragon, of the birth of you ... ye had never had the mortal wars that ye have had; for the most part of your barons ... knew never whose son ye were ... and she that bare you of her body should have made it known openly in excusing of her worship and yours, and in like wise to all the realm, wherefore I prove her false to God and to you and to all your realm, and who will say the contrary I will prove it on his body.
>
> Then spake Igraine and said, I am a woman and I may not fight, but rather than I should be dishonoured, there would some good man take my quarrel. More, she said, Merlin knoweth well, and ye Sir Ulfius, how King Uther came to me in the Castle of Tintagil in the likeness of my lord, that was dead three hours to-fore, and ... after the thirteenth day King Uther wedded me, and by his commandment when the child was born it was delivered unto Merlin and nourished by him, and so I saw the child never after, nor wot not what is his name, for I knew him never yet. And there, Ulfius said to the queen, Merlin is more to blame than ye. Well I wot, said the queen, I bare a child ... but I wot not where he is become. Then Merlin took the king by the hand, saying, This is your mother. And therewith Sir Ector bare witness how he nourished him by Uther's commandment. And therewith King Arthur took his mother, Queen Igraine, in his arms and kissed her, and either wept upon other. And then the king let make a feast that lasted eight days.

Nothing more was said about trial by combat or treason; Ulfius' accusation seems to have been staged to make the revelation more dramatic. [Malory I, 1-3, 21]

IRONSIDE (The Red Knight of the Red Launds)

This is the knight who was besieging Lyonors in Castle Dangerous when Lynette came to Arthur's court for a champion and was given Gareth Beaumains. After defeating Ironside, Gareth sent him to Arthur. Ironside had hanged nearly forty armed knights by the neck from trees, perhaps the most shameful death that could be inflicted on a knight, but this was forgiven because he had done it to fulfill a promise to a lady, his former love. Her brother had been slain, either by Lancelot or by Gawaine as she thought, and she had made Ironside swear "to labour daily in arms unto [sic] I met with one of them; and all that I might overcome I should put them unto a villainous death." The lady who exacted this promise seems never mentioned again, but Ironside became a knight of the Round Table. Malory mentions him at least twice more, as one of the guests at Guenevere's small dinner party and as one of ten knights to ride a-Maying with the Queen when Meliagrant ambushed her. He also appears among the would-be healers of Sir Urre.

While he besieged Castle Dangerous, Ironside's shield, arms, and harness were all blood red. This may create some confusion, but Ironside does not seem to have been related to the brothers Percard, Pertolepe, Perimones, and Persant, whom Gareth defeated on his way to Castle Perilous, even though Perimones also wore all red arms and armor.

Ironside's strength, like Gawaine's, increased daily until noon, until he had the strength of seven men. [Malory VII, 2-18, 35; XVIII, 3; XIX, 1, 11]

In **Sir Gawaine and the Carl of Carlisle**, Ironside is called the father of Sir Raynbrown, "the knight with the green shield," by the fair damsel of Blanche Land. He was armed both in the winter and the hot summer, in constant combat with giants, and his horse was named Sorrel-Hand.

LA BEALE ISOUD (Isolt, Iseult Ysolde, etc.)

The daughter of King Anguish of Ireland and the niece, on her mother's side, of Sir Marhaus, La Beale Isoud was already "a noble surgeon" when Tristram came to Ireland, disguised under the name Tramtrist, to seek a cure for the wound Marhaus had given him with a venomed spear. Isoud healed Tristram, who fell in love with her during the process and taught her to play the harp, "and she began to have a great fantasy unto him." About this time Palomides also visited Ireland and began to court Isoud. She sponsored Tristram in a tournament against Palomides—curiously, the winner of the tournament was to receive the Lady of the Launds in marriage, but Tristram clearly declined this prize, contenting himself, as the winner, with forbidding Palomides to wear armor for a year. Chased from Ireland by the anger of Isoud's mother, who finally realized he was Marhaus' killer, Tristram had a rivalry with King Mark for the love of Sir Segwarides' wife, but this affair was ended by the time Mark sent his nephew back to Ireland to fetch Isoud to be the king's wife. (Mark had heard of her beauty and goodness from Tristram himself, but Mark's true purpose in sending for her was to get Tristram slain on the mission.)

On his way, Tristram had the fortune to represent King Anguish in a trial by combat, which made Tristram welcome again at the Irish monarch's court despite the death of Marhaus. Isoud's mother gave the princess' favorite handwoman, Bragwaine, a love potion meant for Isoud and Mark to drink on their marriage night, but on the ship Tristram and Isoud happened to find it and drink it under the impression it was innocent wine, thus cementing a love which had already been burgeoning. On the way back to Cornwall they halted at Castle Pluere where, in defense of Isoud and himself, Tristram killed Sir Breunor and his lady and ended their evil customs; Breunor's son Duke Galeholt came to avenge his father, with the King of the Hundred Knights for his ally, but after a fight both became Tristram's friends.

Isoud married King Mark as arranged, but if by that time she had not already consummated her love for Tristram, she must have wasted little time in proceeding to do so. Some little while later, Tristram met Sir Lamorak when the latter was weary with jousting down 30 knights. Lamorak, feeling slighted because Tristram refused to give him a good fight under such unequal circumstances, waylaid a knight who was taking Morgan le Fay's magical drinking horn, designed to test the loyalty of wives, to Arthur's court, and made him take it to Mark's court instead. See Morgan's Drinking Horn, *Things*.

Thus Mark learned that Isoud, along with 96 out of 100 other court dames, was an unfaithful wife, and would have

burned them all had not his barons sensibly opposed the mass execution and saved their ladies. Tristram's cousin Andred, however, played the spy until he caught Tristram with Isoud. Tristram was taken bound to "a chapel that stood on the sea rocks" and there condemned to death, but he broke his bonds, fought off his captors, and at last jumped down and fell upon the crags.

Isoud, meanwhile, was sent to a "lazar-cote," or house of lepers. Gouvernail, Sir Lambegus, and Sir Sentraille de Lushon pulled Tristram from the rocks, he rescued Isoud, and they spent a loving interlude in a fair manor in the forest, until Mark learned where they were, came one day when Tristram was out, and fetched Isoud home again. She sent her lover a message, by way of a cousin of Bragwaine's, that he should seek help in healing his latest wound — an arrow-wound in the shoulder, given him by a man whose brother he had killed — from Isoud la Blanche Mains, Howell's daughter. Traveling to Brittany, Tristram not only gave Howell some welcome help in Howell's war against Earl Grip, but also fell in love with and married his new surgeon; conscience-smitten on the marriage night, however, he refrained from taking her maidenhead, and she was too innocent and untaught in the ways of love to recognize the omission.

Lancelot, learning of Tristram's marriage, denounced him as untrue to his first lady; while La Beale Isoud sent a letter of complaint to Guenevere, who returned her a letter of comfort. La Beale Isoud then sent Bragwaine to Brittany with letters in which she begged Tristram to return, bringing his wife, "and they should be kept as well as she herself." Tristram at once headed back for Cornwall, bringing his brother-in-law Sir Kehydius, along with Bragwaine and Gouvernail, but leaving La Blanche Mains in Brittany. After various valorous adventures, the party arrived at Mark's court, where the affair gained a new dimension when Kehydius fell in love with La Beale Isoud and began writing her poems and letters. Though not returning his love, she pitied him and tried to comfort him in another letter, which Tristram found and misinterpreted. In the rage of accusations that followed, Isoud was driven into a swoon, while Kehydius jumped from an upper window to escape Tristram's sword, and land, much to Mark's astonishment, in the middle of Mark's game of chess. Fearing repercussions, Tristram fled to the forest, where he brooded until he went mad, so that even Palomides, who had all this while been his rival for the love of La Beale Isoud, pitied him.

With an eye to Tristram's lands, Andred fomented a rumor that Tristram was dead. This drove La Beale Isoud almost mad, so that she propped a sword up breast-high in a plum tree in her garden and tried to run against it. The attempt was stopped by Mark, who "bare her away with him into a tower; and there he made her to be kept, and watched her surely, and after that she lay long sick, nigh at the point of death." Mark now found but did not recognize Tristram, who was naked and wild but had recently slain the giant Tauleas. Admiring this deed, Mark had the naked madman carried to his castle, where eventually La Beale Isoud and Bragwaine recognized him by means of their pet brachet, the gift of King Faramon's daughter to Tristram. Isoud's love restored Tristram to his wits. Unfortunately, Mark and Andred recognized Tristram the same way, and Mark would have sentenced him to death but, on the insistence of his barons, banished him from Cornwall for ten years instead.

Isoud sent Bragwaine after Tristram with letters. After a long search, Bragwaine found Tristram and attended the tournament at the Castle of Maidens with him, expecting to return from there with his answering letters to his lady. Tristram, Palomides, and Dinadan left the tournament early and privately, however, Tristram with a wound from a joust with Lancelot, leaving Lancelot, nine other knights, and Bragwaine to search for Tristram, while Isoud learned how well her lover had done at the tournament from Gaheris and others of Arthur's knights who visited Cornwall and who got into a free-for-all of battle and treachery with Mark and Andred. Meanwhile Tristram, Palomides and Dinadan fell into the hands of one Sir Darras, who threw them into his prison because Tristram had killed three of his sons in the tournament. Eventually Bragwaine headed back for Cornwall, and Sir Darras repented when Tristram fell deathly sick, and released his captives. Tristram and Palomides began appointing days to do battle with each other, one or other of them consistently missing the appointment due to wounds or imprisonment.

After various adventures, Lancelot brought Tristram to Arthur's court, where he was welcomed into the company of the Round Table. Both Mark and La Beale Isoud had their spies to report on Tristram's fame, he for hate and she for love and pride in her paramour. Finally Mark took Sirs Amant and Bersules and went disguised into Logris with intent to slay Tristram. Amant and Bersules revolted and ended up dead, while Mark only got into plenty of trouble, but finally Arthur made truce between Mark and Tristram and they returned to Cornwall together. Arthur, Lancelot, and Guenever kept up a correspondence with Tristram and Isoud, Lancelot warning them to beware of Mark; the damsel who carried the letters was also in Mark's confidence and shared them with him, causing him to return letters of such a nature as to call down a satiric lay of Dinadan's upon his head.

Tristram saved Mark from a Saxon invasion led by Elias. For thanks, when Mark learned of a plot afoot to slay Lancelot at the Surluse tournament, the Cornish king planned to send Tristram in disguise, hoping he would be mistaken for Lancelot. Tristram was badly hurt, and Mark, pretending great love, spirited him away secretly to prison. Isoud appealed to Sir Sadok to learn where Tristram was; the upshot of this move was that Sadok, joined by Mark's former seneschal Sir Dinas, raised the country of Lyonesee for war with Mark, while Percivale came and made Mark free Tristram and promise his safety. Mark forged letters to make it appear that the Pope was ordering him to go on crusade, and thus, arguing "this is a fairer war than thus to arise the people against your king," tricked Dinas and Sadok into disbanding their rebellion. Mark then threw Tristram back into prison.

Now Tristram sent La Beale Isoud a letter requesting her to ready a ship for their escape. She reacted promptly and capably, preparing the ship and enlisting Dinas and Sadok to put Mark himself into prison until she and Tristram were safely in England. Lancelot gave them a home in Joyous Garde. Here "they made great joy daily together with all manner of mirths that they could devise, and every day Sir Tristram would go ride a-hunting," but even here Isoud prudently insisted he ride armed, in case of "perilous knights" or further efforts on Mark's part. Malory records other episodes, such as how Tristram and Isoud left Joyous Garde for a time to attend the tournament at Lonazep. The pair remained in Joyous Garde and Isoud continued in at least occasional correspondence with Guenever, during the period when Guenever's jealousy of Elaine of Carbonek drove Lancelot to madness.

Lancelot being found, Tristram proposed they go to court to help celebrate. Isoud's answer seems to be a model of lady's love for knight; she would not go herself, "for through me ye be marked of many good knights, and that caused you to have much more labour for my sake than needeth you," but she insisted he go, to prevent the accusation that she was keeping him in idle dalliance to the rusting of his honor. (Compare with the tale of Enid.) She also sent four knights with him, but within a half mile he sent them back. On this journey he met Palomides and they finally had their battle, ending in their reconciliation and Palomides' baptism. The feast they attended at Camelot saw the beginning of the Grail Quest, but Tristram returned to Joyous Garde and Isoud rather than seek the holy vessel.

Here Malory, or his early editor, simply drops the tale of Tristram and Isoud, remarking, "Here endeth the second book of Sir Tristram that was drawn out of French into English. But

than the Greeks). Seeing an artist paint the history of Aeneas gave Lancelot, while a prisoner in Morgana's castle, the inspiration for muralizing his own exploits [Vulgate V]. Very occasionally, as in the tale of Viviane's birth, we see a hint that the deities of classical and other non-Christian mythology may have been considered real, whether or not diabolic [Vulgate II]. Closer to Arthur's time were the heroes of early British history.

> I have understood that Belinus and Brenius, kings of Britain, have had the empire in their hands many days, and also Constantine the son of Heleine, which is an open evidence that we owe no tribute to Rome. [Malory V, 1; Arthur speaking]

The Heleine of this passage would be the same Saint Helena credited with finding the True Cross. A chronicle of early British history may be found in Spenser's **Faerie Queen**, Book II, Canto X — Spenser's version of Arthurian adventure is pro-

bably irreconcilable with Malory's, but, in a well-annotated edition (like that edited by Thomas P. Roche, Jr., Penguin Books, 1978) his list of British rulers from Brute to Uther may be helpful to those who wish to go more deeply into the subject. There are other accounts.

Palomides, his brothers, and Priamus might have brought Eastern lore and legends to Arthur's England, if they still wanted to talk about such "pagan" things when they had determined to be Christened. Similarly, Urre of Hungary could have brought bits of Eastern European lore; and so on. As Arthur's Round Table drew knights from distant lands and became a symbol of the world, so Arthur's court may well have enjoyed a much wider range of culture and literature than we usually associate with the period.

here is no rehersal of the third book." Much later, Malory remarks that Mark finally slew Tristram as he sat harping before Isoud, but does not go into further particulars, not even to tell us where it happened. Presumably Isoud did not long survive Tristram.

La Beale Isoud was not without a sense of humor; once she invited Dinadan into Joyous Garde and chid him gently for his stand against love. At his quipping refusal to fight against three knights for her, despite her beauty, "Isoud laughed, and had good game at him," not neglecting hospitality, however. Bleoberis and Extor de Maris once described Isoud to Guenever in the following terms:

> ... she is peerless of all ladies; for to speak of her beauty, bounte, and mirth, and of her goodness, we saw never her match as far as we have ridden and gone. O mercy Jesu, said Queen Guenever, so saith all the people that have seen her and spoken with her. God would that I had part of her conditions ....

It is worth remarking that these two women, who would seem to have had every cause for jealousy of each other except a man, never displayed such jealousy, but remained friends and admirers of one another. [Malory VIII-XII; XIX, 11]

I have recapped Malory's version of Isoud's story at length because the books of Tristram are notoriously the most rambling portion of **Le Morte D'Arthur**, capable of bogging down the most interested reader, and the thread of narrative often becomes difficult to follow. I have found no other early version so conscientiously dovetailing Tristram's story with Arthur's.

Father: King Anguish (Agwisance) of Ireland	
Husband: King Mark	
Lover: Tristram	
Uncle (maternal): Marhaus	
Gentlewoman: Bragwaine	**LA BEALE ISOUD'S**
Mentor: Brother Ogrins	**FAMILY AND RELATIONS**

ISOUD LA BLANCHE MAINS (Iseult, Yseult, Isolt, etc., of the White Hands)

She was the daughter — apparently the younger daughter — of Howell of Brittany, presumably by that wife who was so brutally slain by the Giant of St. Michael's Mount, which would have cast a tragic shadow on her childhood and on that of her brother Kehydius.

As La Beale Isoud had cured Tristram of the wound of Marhaus' envenomed spear, so Isoud of the White Hands met him when Bragwaine and Gouvernail had conveyed to Brittany expressly so that she, also a good surgeon, could heal him of the wound of a poisonous arrow. Tristram became infatuated with his newest nurse and married her as much, it appears, because her name was the same as that of his real love as for any other reason. It was a virginal marriage.

> And so when they were abed both Sir Tristram remembered him of his old lady La Beale Isoud. And then he took such a thought suddenly that he was all dismayed, and other cheer made he none but with clipping [hugging] and kissing; as for other fleshly lusts Sir Tristram never thought nor had ado with her ... the lady weened there had been no pleasure but kissing and clipping.

La Blanche Mains sailed with Tristram on at least one occasion, when their barget was blown ashore on the coast of Wales, where La Beale Isoud learned of Tristram's marriage and invited both him and his wife to Cornwall, Tristram left La Blanche Mains behind. Apparently he never saw her again. In Cornwall, he spoke of his denying his wife her conjugal rights as a praiseworthy deed:

> But as for thee, Sir Kehydius ... I wedded they sister Isoud la Blanche Mains for the goodness she did unto me. And yet, as I am true knight, she is a clean maiden for me ....

Malory is silent on the later life of Isoud La Blanche Mains of Brittany. Robinson gives a sympathetic picure of her in his **Tristram**. [Malory VIII, 35-38; IX 10, 17]

OSPEH OF ARIMATHEA and JOSEPHE

Joseph of Arimathea was the disciple of Jesus. Josephe was Joseph's son, first bishop of Britain, miraculously consecrated by Christ Himself. According to a tradition which I encountered orally and not in connection with the Arthurian cycle, Joseph first visited Britain with Jesus during the latter's hidden years before His public preaching; they came ashore in Cornwall. After Christ's resurrection, Joseph and Josephe converted Nascien and Mordrains and their families and returned to Britain, bringing Christianity, the Holy Grail, the flowering thorn which Joseph planted at Glastonbury, and a number of followers, as described in detail in Volume I, **Lestoire del Saint Graal,** of the Vulgate.

Unlike Nascien and Mordrains, Joseph and Josephe did not miraculously survive into Arthur's times. Either Joseph or Josephe did, however, return to Carbonek Castle to celebrate the climactic mysteries of the Grail at a Mass attended by Galahad and his companions. Galahad himself is called a direct descendant of Joseph; since both Pellam and Lancelot were descended from Joseph's convert Nascien, the relation would seem either to be spiritual, like that of a godparent and godchild, or to have come through intermarriage between Nascien's male and Joseph's female descendants. Josephe's cousin (Joseph's nephew?) Lucans first was appointed guardian of the ark containing the Grail, before Josephe reassigned the keepership of the holy vessel to Nascien's descendant Alain (or Helias) le Gros. Joseph's younger son Galaad, born after the arrival in Britain, becomes the direct ancestor of King Urien.

Only in the case of Joseph and Josephe is it important in this handbook that a single letter differentiate two characters. Or, rather, it would be important, but centuries less spelling-conscious than ours have hopelessly confused the issue. Malory, or his editors, seem to know nothing of Josephe, ascribing some of his deeds (such as marking the Adventurous Shield) to Joseph. [Malory II, 16; IX, 2; XIII, 3, 11; XVII, 18-20, 22]

AINUS LE STRANGE (Kay De Stranges, Kay the Stranger

A knight of the Round Table. Malory mentions him appearing at the tournament of Lonazep (where he was jousted down by Palomides), as being among the would-be healers of Sir Urre, and as being among those killed during Lancelot's rescue of Guenevere from the stake [X, 79; XIX, 11; XX, 8]. He should not be confused with Arthur's foster-brother, Kay.

KANAHINS (Kadin, Canains)†

When Lancelot was preparing to depart from Britain in exile, he sent the squire Kanahins to Camelot with his shield so that it could be hung in St. Stephen's cathedral [Vulgate VI]

KING KARADOS OF ESTRANGOR†

Although apparently one of the rebels against Arthur, Karados had been a companion of the Round Table (during the time of Uther Pendragon?). He did not occupy his seat during the rebellion. [Vulgate II]

I am not sure whether or not he should be identified with either King Carados of Scotland, Sir Carados of the Dolorous Tower, or Cador of Cornwall, father of the Constantine who became King after Arthur.

KAY (Cei, Kai, Kex)

Arthur's foster-brother, Seneschal of England, knight of the Round Table, and my own personal favorite of all the male characters in the Arthurian cycle.

Throughout most of the medieval romances I have examined, Kay can be depended upon to speak rudely, boast a lot, bully young hopefuls like Gareth, Percival, and La Cote Male Taile, and usually be unhorsed in every joust. This characterization seems to have been first given him by Chrétien de Troyes (cf. Harris, **Yvain**) and it stuck with amazing consistency for centuries, although several recent versions have painted a much more sympathetic picture. His pre-Chrétien reputation, as in Geoffrey of Monmouth, Wace, and the old Welsh myths (where he figures as Cei) was heroic. Both his heroic and his churlish aspects appear in Malory.

On Merlin's instruction, Kay's father, Sir Ector, gave the infant Arthur to his wife for nourishing and put Kay out to a wetnurse; this indicates an age difference of no more than a few years in the boys. There is no evidence in Malory that either Kay or Arthur realized they were not born siblings; there are, however, indications of real brotherly affection between the two.

To help find the man who would prove himself King by pulling the marvellous sword from the stone and anvil, Merlin and the Archbishop of Canterbury called a great tournament in London on New Year's Day. Sir Ector brought Kay, who had been knighted on All Hallowmass two months before, and Arthur, who appears to have been serving as Kay's squire. On the way to the tournament, Kay discovered he had left his sword at the house where they were lodging and sent Arthur back to get it. But when Arthur arrived,

the lady and all were out to see the jousting. Then was Arthur wroth, and said to himself, I will ride to the churchyard, and take the sword with me that sticketh in the stone, for my brother Sir Kay shall not be without a sword this day. ... And as soon as Sir Kay saw the sword, he wist well it was the sword of the stone and so he rode to his father Sir Ector, and said: Sir, lo here is the sword of the stone, wherefore I must be king of this land.

Sir Ector saw through Kay's claim and insisted on taking both young men back to the churchyard (which had providentially been abandoned by the men who were supposed to have been guarding it) and repeating the experiment. Curiously, the closest thing to a rebuke Kay seems to have received was that Ector made him "swear upon a book how he came to that sword," after which he requested as his only favor from his foster-son, who was having some trauma accepting the situation, that Arthur make Kay his seneschal. Promising "that

never man shall have that office but he, while he and I live," Arthur carried this out at his coronation.

The first serious threat of rebellion was made at Pentecost, and, on Merlin's advice, Arthur sent for Kings Ban and Bors as allies. At the feast celebrating their arrival, on All Hallowmass, Kay served in the hall, assisted by Sirs Lucan and Griflet—which seems to be noted as an honor for all parties. At the tournament following this feast Kay "did that day marvellous deeds of arms, that there was none did so well as he that day," but was finally unhorsed by one Sir Placidas, at which Griflet and other knights in Kay's party angrily avenged his fall. The kings awarded the prize of this tournament to Kay, Griflet, and Lucan. Kay proved his worth in practical warfare during the bloody battle of Bedegraine against the rebel kings, and again in the battle against Nero and King Lot before Castle Terrabil.

Kay's greatest moment of glory came during the invasion of the five kings of Denmark, Ireland, the Vale, Soleise, and the Isle of Longtains. While Arthur, his wife, and his army were camped by the Humber River, the enemy army surprised them with a night attack. Trying to get the Queen to safety, Arthur, Kay, Gawaine, and Griflet were trapped on the edge of the rough water.

And as they stood so talking, Sir Kay saw the five kings coming on horseback by themselves alone, with their spears in their hands. ... Lo, said Sir Kay, yonder be the five kings; let us go to them and match them. That were folly, said Sir Gawaine, for we are but three [maybe Gawaine is not counting the King] and they be five. That is truth, said Sir Griflet. No force, said Sir Kay, I will undertake for two of them, and then may ye three undertake for the other three. And therewithal, Sir Kay let his horse run as fast as he might, and struck one of them through the shield and the body a fathom, that the king fell to the earth stark dead.

Inspired by this example, Gawaine, Arthur, and Griflet each struck down another of the five invaders.

Anon Sir Kay ran unto the fifth king, and smote him so hard on the helm that the stroke clave the helm and the head to the earth. That was well stricken, said King Arthur, and worshipfully hast thou holden thy promise, therefore I shall honour thee while that I live ... [and] always Queen Guenever praised Sir Kay for his deeds, and said, What lady that ye love, and she love you not again she were greatly to blame; and among ladies, said the Queen, I shall bear your noble fame, for ye spake a great word, and fulfilled it worshipfully.

It was after this battle that Kay became a companion of the Round Table, on the advice of Pellinor, who pointed out,

for many times he hath done full worshipfully, and now at your last battle he did full honourably for to undertake to slay two kings. By my head, said Arthur, he is best worth to be a knight of the Round Table of any that ye have rehearsed ...

When, on his way to fight the Emperor Lucius on the Continent, Arthur stopped to exterminate the giant of Saint Michael's Mount, Brittany, Kay and Bedivere were the two companions he chose to take on the secret expedition. Having slain the giant, Arthur assigned Kay the task of cutting off the head and bearing it to Howell. In the battle with Lucius, Kay was among Arthur's personal bodyguard.

From about this point Malory's Kay slides downhill. He turns up among the knights rescued from Sir Turquine, and when Lancelot departs suddenly after vanquishing Turquine, Kay takes an oath with Lionel and Ector de Maris to find him again. Kay's next action on being released from prison may be typically stewardly: he sees to supper.

> ... there came a forester with four horses laden with fat venison. Anon, Sir Kay said, Here is good meat for us for one meal, for we had not many a day no good repast.

In an often-retold incident, Kay, having become separated from Ector and Lionel, is set on by three knights at once beneath the window which happens to be of Lancelot's bedchamber. Lancelot descends by a sheet, rescues Kay, and in the morning, before Kay is awake, leaves with Kay's horse and armor, whether accidentally or on purpose. Lancelot thus gets the chance to strike down several knights who mistake him for "the proud Kay; [who] weeneth no knight so good as he, and the contrary is ofttime proved." Lancelot's reputation, on the other hand, is already such that Kay, disguised perforce as Lancelot, makes it back to court without being challenged.

Kay's treatment of Gareth, whom he nicknamed Beaumains, is one of the most widely-known and typical tales of the seneschal, though it is usually glossed over that, despite his bullying, Kay seems to have taken a certain pride in Beaumains: When Gareth displayed his strength in courtyard sports, "[t]hen would Sir Kay say, How liketh you my boy of the kitchen?" Kay's mockery of La Cote Male Taile and of Percivale is in similar vein, though neither of them came under his authority as Beaumains did, and for most of Percivale's story we must go outside Malory, to tales stemming from Chretien's **Perceval**.

During the rambling adventures of Malory's books of Tristram, in which Kay occasionally appears, Tristram, meeting him by chance, pretty well sums up his reputation:

> ... now wit ye well that ye are named the shamefullest knight of your tongue that now is living; howbeit ye are called a good knight, but ye are called unfortunate, and passing overthwart of your tongue.

In fairness to Tristram, this is said in response to Kay's repetition of the old saw about no good knights ever coming out of Cornwall. On the other hand, some chapters later, when Kay finds Ywaine treacherously and gravely wounded by Mark, the seneschal makes sure of getting Ywaine safely to the Abbey of the Black Cross for healing.

Kay plays no part in the Grail Adventures except to remind Arthur, shortly before Galahad's arrival on Pentecost, of the King's old custom of never sitting down to dinner on the feast day until they have seen some adventure. Malory mentions him as one of the guests at Guenever's small dinner (where Sir Patrise was poisoned), as the chief of three knights whom Arthur sends to bring in the barge bearing the body of Elaine of Astolat, as one of the small party of unarmed knights who ride a-Maying with Guenever and are ambushed and kidnapped by Meliagrant, and as one of those who attempt to heal Sir Urre. This is the last we hear of Sir Kay in Malory's pages; perhaps he becomes confused with Sir Kainus le Strange, who is killed by Lancelot and his party during their rescue of Guenever from the stake. [Malory I, 3, 5-17; II, 10; IV, 3-4; V, 5, 8; VI, 9, 11-12, 18; VII, 1-4; IX, 1-3, 15, 38; X, 6, 79; XI, 12; XIII, 2; XVIII, 3, 20; XIX, 1-9, 11]

The Vulgate fills in furthur details. Kay got his sharp tongue from his nurse, apparently the one who took charge of him when his own mother took over Arthur's nursing. On more than one occasion he bore Arthur's standard into battle.

He was deeply devoted to Guenever, although in a more platonic way (in practice if not in desire) than Lancelot, and rivalry arose between the two, as in the affairs of "the false Guenever" Genievre and of Meliagrant, as to which should defend her in trial by combat. (Lancelot always won the honor.) Kay is said to have murdered Arthur's bastard son Borre in order to get credit for killing a giant Borre had exterminated; the Vulgate "Merlin" adds that this was the only treacherous deed Kay ever committed.

In the Vulgate version, Kay plays a more prominent part in the Meliagrant affair, beginning when he comes into court armed and announces he is leaving because his services are not appreciated; Arthur and Guenever beg him to stay, which he does on condition he be allowed to defend the Queen against Meliagrant, who has offered to free the exiles in Gorre's Terre Foraine in return for the chance to attempt Guenever's capture (this differs from Malory's version, in which Meliagrant ambushes Guenever's party a-Maying). Meliagrant defeats Kay and later accuses Kay in particular of sleeping with the Queen (in Malory, it is a general accusation against the ten wounded knights).

Kay met his death during Arthur's and Gawaine's siege of Lancelot's city in France—the Emperor of Rome took advantage of Arthur's presence on the continent to invade Burgundy and advance on the British. In the resulting battle, Gawaine killed the Emperor's nephew and the Emperor, seeking revenge, mortally wounded Kay, whereon Arthur slew the Emperor.

According to Wace, Kay was given the title of Duke of Anjou. In **Sir Gawain and the Carl of Carlisle**, the Carl presents Kay with a blood-red horse swifter than any other the knight has ever seen. I do not remember ever finding a lady for Kay in the old romances; perhaps his courtly devotion to Guenever precluded a more mundane relationship with another woman.

Despite Kay's reputation as braggart, when he comes back to court in Lancelot's armor, he frankly gives Lancelot all the credit for the conquests made by the knight in Kay's armor. [Malory VI, 18] In the Vulgate version of the episode, vol. V, near the end of the Livre de Lancelot del Lac, on top of incident after incident of frequently senseless and avoidable bloodshed committed by such "good" knights as Lancelot and Bors, Kay's statement that he has not overcome any knight since leaving court strikes me as not only honest, but downright commendable.

Perhaps the contrast between Kay's early prowess at arms and the frequent defeats of his middle and later years is explained by the performance of his duties as Seneschal occupying too much of his time to allow him to keep in fighting trim. It is not hard, by reading between the lines, to see that he must have been conscientious and competent in his official capacity. As for his reputation as braggart and churl, I suspect that, just as later kings needed scapegoats for popular dislike of various mistakes and policies, so did Arthur. The seneschal, largely responsible for the practical, day-to-day functioning of the court, would have been a logical candidate for the role of scapegoat. If Arthur's bastard son Borre, or Lohot, is to be identified with Arthur's son Anir, or Amyr, of shadowy early legends, it is interesting that, while Borre's death is charged to Kay, Anir's is charged to Arthur himself.

I also theorize that Kay's mockery of and jousts with young hopefuls like Beaumains and Perceval may have been part of a program to weed out country lads who came to court with no qualifications for knighthood beyond their own aspirations; there may well have been a great many of these, especially after the easy knighting of Sir Tor, but only the tales of those who really were of noble birth and valorous worth have been preserved for us.

A popular device of old romancers was to contrast Kay's churlish behavior with Gawaine's courtesy, always, of course, to Gawaine's advantage. **The Knightly Tales of Sir Gawain**, with introductions and translations by Louis B. Hall, in addition to being a gold mine about Gawaine, has also a rich vein of information about Kay.

KEHYDIUS

Howell's son, and the brother of Isoud la Blanche Mains. Kehydius was with Tristram and La Blanche Mains when they blew ashore near the Isle of Servage and Tristram slew Sir Nabon le Noire. Kehydius later accompanied Tristram, Gouvernail, and Bragwaine back to Cornwall; this time they were blown ashore near Castle Perilous, North Wales, where Tristram took Kehydius into the forest with him for a few days of adventure, leaving Gouvernail with Bragwaine at the boat. Kehydius begged for and obtained first chance to joust with the first knight they encountered. He promptly got a fall and a severe wound — the knight was Lamorak, who proceeded to give Tristram himself a fall, though Tristram redeemed his honor with sword, and they ended by agreeing never to fight each other again.

When Tristram and his party finally got to Mark's court, Kehydius fell in love with La Beale Isoud and wrote love letters to her. She felt sorry for him and wrote a letter in return. Malory does not say what, exactly, was in her letter; but when Tristram found both sides of the correspondence, he misconstrued the situation, charged Isoud with falseness, and rounded on Kehydius with drawn sword. While Isoud swooned, Kehydius jumped out the window and landed in the middle of Mark's chess game, much to Mark's astonishment. Kehydius, thinking quickly, covered up by saying he had fallen asleep at the window and so tumbled out. This incident reads like domestic comedy; the outcome of the whole affair, however, was tragic for Kehydius, who at last died of his love, as her other unrequited lover, Palomides, remarks to Tristram later at Joyous Garde: "...well I wot it shall befall me as for her love as befell to the noble knight Sir Kehydius, that died for the love of La Beale Isoud." [Malory VIII, 36-38; IX, 10-11, 17; X, 86]

ST. KENTIGERN (St. Mungo)†

The royal virgin Thenew, daughter of the Scots King Lothus, had the misfortune to give birth to Kentigern in 518, Glennie reports. Her story of an immaculate conception notwithstanding, she was placed in a boat and cast adrift from Aberlady Bay. Kentigern was put into Culross monastery under the discipline of St. Servanus. If King Lothus was the Arthurian King Lot, then his daughter must have been Gawaine's sister, and Kentigern was Gawaine's nephew!

Kex† — standard version of 'Kay' used in the Vulgate

The King of the Hundred Knights — see HUNDRED KNIGHTS, THE KING OF

The Knight with the Two Swords — see BALIN LE SAVAGE

ABOR†

This trusty and valiant knight was Guenever's cousin and helped her escape when the barons who had taken Mordred's part were trying to force her to marry Mordred. [Vulgate V]

Duke Ladinas — see DUKE DE LA ROWSE

King of the Lake — see under GRIFLET

Lady Leech of Cornwall — see LEECH

LADY (Damsel) OF THE LAKE

There are two distinct Ladies of the Lake in Malory; there seem to be three in all, taking the Vulgate into account: one who raised Lancelot in France, one who gave Arthur his sword, and Nimue. Likely all started as one character but, in the present state of the legends, I see nothing for it but to split them.

The French Lady seems to be basically good. So does Nimue; although she imprisons Merlin, she thereafter acts beneficently to Arthur and his court. However, the one who gave Arthur his sword, even in that instance cooperating with Merlin, appears to have been evil. [Malory I, 25; II, 1-4]

Tennyson makes the Lady of the Lake a good, mysterious, almost angelic benefactress of Arthur, but Vivien a villainess who seduces and imprisons Merlin as part of her design to bring back Paganism.

For convenience I distinguish them as follows: Viviane (the French Damsel of the Lake, who raised Lancelot), "Nineve" (Malory's first English Lady of the Lake, who gave Arthur his sword), and Nimue (the second English Lady of the Lake, who gained the position after "Nineve's" death and became benefactress to Arthur's court). Though "Nineve" is never actually named, Nineve is a variant of both the names Nimue and Viviane, and it is a handy one for my purpose.

Both Nimue and Viviane are credited with imprisoning Merlin; but, whereas Viviane must be in France to raise Lancelot, Malory definitely puts Nimue in Britain. Take your choice as to which one actually did away with the great necromancer. Viviane definitely, and Nimue apparently, had other damsels of the lake under them. The Vulgate says the Damsels of the Lake owed their knowledge of magic to Merlin, and Malory corroborates this as far as Nimue is concerned, but not as far as "Nineve" is portrayed.

LAMBEGUS

One of Tristram's knights, he boldly pursued Sir Palomides once when Palomides had succeeded by ruse in getting La Beale Isoud for a short while. Palomides defeated Lambegus easily. On a later occasion, however, Lambegus was useful enough, helping Gouvernail and Sir Sentraille de Lushon rescue Tristram from the rocks by pulling him up with towels.

After Tristram's death Lambegus remained in Arthur's court as a knight of the Round Table. He was among those killed during Lancelot's rescue of Guenever from the stake. [Malory VIII, 30, 35; XIX, 11; XX, 8]

LAMORAK DE GALIS (Lamerake of Wales)

He was King Pellinore's son, apparently the second born in wedlock. His brothers were Aglovale, Dornar, Percivale, and Tor; his known sisters, Eleine and Amide. A companion of the Round Table, Lamorak was "the most noblest knight [but] one that ever was in Arthur's days as for a worldly knight."

> ... so all the world saith, that betwixt three knights is departed clearly knighthood, that is Launcelot du Lake, Sir Tristram de Liones, and Sir Lamorak de Galis: these bear now the renown.

So Sir Persant of Inde tells Gareth Beaumains, adding that if Gareth conquers Ironside he "shall be called the fourth of the world." At the Michaelmas jousts marking Gareth's marriage, Lamorak overthrew 30 knights, to Tristram's 40 and Lancelot's 50. At the end of these jousts, both Lamorak and Tristram "departed suddenly, and would not be known, for the which King Arthur and all the court were sore displeased." It may have been before this tournament, though it is described later in the **Morte D'Arthur**, that Lamorak, traveling with one Sir Driant, gave another 30 knights their falls within sight of King Mark's pavillion. Mark sent Tristram to match Lamorak, sorely against Tristram's will, for, as the Cornish knight pointed out, he himself was fresh, while Lamorak would be spent with his 30 conquests. Nevertheless, Tristram obeyed Mark far enough to give Lamorak a fall (Lamorak's horse, also, being tired and going down before Tristram's spear). But he then refused to fight Lamorak with the sword, "for I have [already] done to thee over much unto my dishonour and to thy worship." Lamorak did not appreciate Tristram's courtesy. While still in a pique over Tristram's refusal to fight, he met the messenger bearing Morgana's magic drinking horn to Arthur's court and made him bear it to Mark's court instead, which almost resulted in the execution of La Beale Isoud and more than 90 other ladies. This angered Tristram.

While Tristram was in Brittany, Lamorak was shipwrecked near the Isle of Servage and nursed back to health (apparently having caught a chill in the water) by fishermen. Here Tristram and Isoud la Blanche Mains, also shipwrecked, met him, and the two knights buried their differences to plot how to exterminate the evil Sir Nabon le Noire, whom Lamorak especially hated for having shamefully drawn a cousin of his, Sir Nanowne le Petite, limb from limb. Nabon holding a tournament about this time, both Tristram and Lamorak attended; Lamorak, having borrowed horse and armor from Nabon himself, gave him such a good fight that, when he "was so sore bruised and short breathed, that he traced and traversed somewhat aback," Nabon spared him: to Tristram fell the honor of killing Nabon. On his way back to Arthur's court, Lamorak encountered Sir Frol of the Out Isles, Sir Belliance le Orgulus, had a friendly encounter with Lancelot, and a not-so-friendly one with Gawaine.

Lamorak next encountered Tristram when the latter's party was blown ashore near Castle Perilous, North Wales. Here Tristram remembered his annoyance at the drinking-horn incident and Lamorak remembered the friendship they had pledged each other in the Isle of Servage; they fought longtime, Tristram at first promising it would be to the death, but ended by yielding to each other and swearing eternal friendship in honor of one another's prowess. Not long thereafter, Lamorak got into a battle with Meliagrant over which queen was the more beautiful, Morgawse or Guenever. See under Bleoberis de Ganis for the incident.

Lamorak's love for Margawse was his undoing, for Lamorak was the son of the man who had killed King Lot in battle, and Lot's sons felt it an insult that the son of their father's killer should become their mother's lover and potential husband. They therefore first killed Morgawse, as described under Gaheris, while she was in bed with her lover. Gaheris refusing to fight Lamorak at that time, Lamorak left the place, but "for the shame and dolour he would not ride to King Arthur's court, but rode another way." He surfaced again at Duke Galeholt's tournament in Surluse, where he did great deeds of battle and complained to Arthur of the wrongs done him by Lot's sons. Arthur expressed his grief at his sister's death, wished that she had been married to Lamorak instead, and promised to protect Lamorak from Lot's sons and arrange a truce if Lamorak would stay with him. Lamorak, however, refused to remain with Arthur and Lancelot, and departed alone. Palomides later describes, first to Ector de Maris, Bleoberis, and Percivale, and later to Tristram, Gareth, and Dinadan, what happened then:

> ...[of] his age he was the best that ever I found; for an he might have lived till he had been an hardier man there liveth no knight now such ... And at his departing [from the Surluse tournament] there met him Sir Gawaine and his brethren, and with great pain they slew him feloniously...would I had been there, and yet had I never the degree at no jousts nor tournament thereas he was, but he put me to the worse, or on foot or on horseback; and that day that he was slain he did the most deeds of arms that ever I saw knight do in all my life days. And when him was given the degree by my lord Arthur, Sir Gawaine and his three brethren, Agravaine, Gaheris, and Sir Mordred, set upon Sir Lamorak in a privy place, and there they slew his horse. And so they fought with him on foot more than three hours, both before him and behind him; and Sir Mordred gave him his death wound behind him at his back, and all to-hew him for one of his squires told me that saw it.

[Malory I, 24; VII, 13, 35; VIII, 33-41; IX, 10-14; X, 17-24, 40-49, 54, 58, etc.]

LANCELOT OF THE LAKE (Launcelot du Lake, du Lac)

Lancelot, probably the most famous of all Arthur's Knights of the Round Table, was the most illustrious of an illustrious family which included King Ban his father, King Bors his uncle, Sirs Lionel and Bors de Ganis his cousins, and Sir Ector de Maris his bastard British-born half-brother.

Lancelot, then called by his christened name of Galahad, was an infant when his parents, Ban and Elaine of Benwick, fled their city with a few retainers. When King Ban looked back and saw his castle burning, he suffered a seizure of some kind, possibly a heart attack. Queen Elaine, hurrying to him, left her son alone for a few moments. It was then that Viviane, the French Damsel of the Lake, took him, brought him to her rich city in the illusory magical Lake at Bois en val, and raised him, renaming him Lancelot. The widowed Elaine remained nearby, building the Royal Minster on the hill where Ban had died. Lancelot's cousins Lionel and Bors, with their mentors, were eventually welcomed into Viviane's Lake with Lancelot to finish their knightly education.

When Lancelot reached 18 years of age and was itching to become a knight, Viviane gave him a last lecture on the history and duties of that state of life, provided him with a sword of proven worth, a snow-white horse, and the rest of his outfit, all in white and silver, and brought him, accompanied by Lionel, Bors, Seraide, and others, to Arthur's court, where the King dubbed him on St. John's Day. He may have become a member of the Queen's Knights at this time; before officially settling down at Arthur's court, however, he spent some time wandering in knight errantry, beginning when he left to succor the Lady of Nohaut — his first rivalry with Kay seems to have been over which of them would serve as her champion.

During this period Lancelot won La Dolorous Garde, which became his own castle of Joyous Garde. Here the court joined him for a time, and Dagonet found him one day allowing his horse to wander wherever it would while he gazed in a fond trance at Guenever. Leaving Joyous Garde, he became the prisoner of the Lady of Malohaut, who held him for the death of her seneschal's son, but allowed him to leave on parole to fight in tournament, and fell in love with him when he returned. During this period he also conquered Duke Galeholt, winning the Duke's allegiance for Arthur and his friendship for Lancelot himself. Meanwhile, Viviane had been softening Guenever, and when next Lancelot joined the court for a time, he and Guenever declared their love, with Galeholt and the Lady of Malohaut for go-betweens. This time, when Lancelot left again, he inspired perhaps the first of what was to become a standard activity—a party of Arthur's knights, including Gawaine and Kay, went out searching for him. Lancelot next joined Arthur at the siege of Camille's fortress of La Roche, where he fought in one battle wearing Arthur's arms and carrying Arthur's sword Sequence.

The love of Lancelot and Guenever is more fully described under Guenever. Genievre's second, and temporarily successful, attempt to supplant Guenever followed sometime after the defeat of Camille, and after literally saving Guenever's skin, Lancelot retired with her to Galeholt's kingdom of Surluse. They only returned to their places at court — Guenever to her throne, Lancelot to his seat at the Round Table — after Genievre's death, while Galeholt let them go despite a prophecy that he could prolong his own life by keeping Lancelot with him.

Immediately following the celebrations of Guenever's return, Carados of the Dolorous Tower abducted Gawaine. Setting out to rescue him, Galeshin and Lancelot came to Morgan's Val sans retour; see under *Places*. As a true lover, Lancelot was able to free Morgan's prisoners here, but she succeeded in kidnapping him in return. She let him go long enough to kill Carados and free Gawaine, but then, by a ruse, sent Lancelot's ring (a gift from Guenever) back to court with a pretended message from the knight that he would never return. This drove Lancelot mad until the Damsel of the Lake found him wandering in Cornwall and cured him. Meanwhile, however, Duke Galeholt had gotten a false report of Lancelot's death, which caused his own. Before Lancelot's return to court, Meliagrant succeeded in abducting Guenever, also taking Kay prisoner; Lancelot pursued them to Gorre, freeing not only Guenever and Kay but also the occupants of Gorre's "Terre Foraine." Lancelot made up his differences with the Queen in her bed and eventually killed Meliagrant in trial by combat before Arthur.

Some time later, traveling on other adventures, Lancelot found Duke Galeholt's grave and almost killed himself in grief, but was prevented by Seraide, at whose direction he had his friend's body taken to Joyous Garde for reburial. Lancelot was gone so long on his adventures that Gawaine and other knights went out searching for him again, while Guenever, distraught, sent Elyzabel to France to summon Viviane. After her departure, a damsel whom Lancelot had succored arrived at court with the news that he was still alive, which was so welcome that Arthur gave the messenger her choice of castles (she chose Leverzep).

Lancelot, meanwhile, met his virgin love, Amable. Lancelot was found at last by his cousin Lionel, only to be separated again when Lionel went off to pursue and be captured by Sir Terican (Turquine) while Lancelot was napping. Lancelot was captured while asleep by Morgana and her cohorts, but escaped through the help of Duke Rochedon's daughter, succored Meliagrant's sister (see King Bagdemagus' Daughter), and visited Carbonek, where he engendered Galahad on Pellam's daughter Elaine. After this he visited the Forest Perilous, *Places*, repaid Duke Rochedon's daughter by saving her from an unwanted marriage and forcing Morgan's friend the Queen of Sorestan to restore her inheritance, and finally rejoined the court at a tournament in Camelot, which Amable also attended and where Guenever accepted her platonic relationship with Lancelot. After the tournament, Lancelot, Bors, Gareth, and Bagdemagus went out looking for Lionel and Ector de Maris, saved Mordred from Maten's men at the Castel de la Blanche Espine, *Places*, and Lancelot eventually killed Terican and freed Lionel and the other prisoners.

After a few other adventures, Lancelot fell again into Morgana's hands, who tricked him into her castle, drugged him with wine and a powder blown into his nose, and held him for two winters and a summer; during this time, Lancelot painted his own history, including his love for Guenever, on his bedroom walls. Inspired by a spring rose that reminded him of the Queen, he finally broke the iron bars of his window and escaped. He then rescued Lionel again, this time from a trumped-up charge of treason in King Vagor's country, fought Bors at Le Tertre Deuee, *Places*, visited the site of his grandfather's death in the Forest of the Boiling Well, killed Merlan le Dyable, and rescued Mordred at the castle of the Fontaine des Deux Sycamors. Mordred at this time was still a promising young knight, who won Lancelot's praise as they traveled together and who saw with him the mystic stag and four lions in the forest moonlight. Lancelot witnessed the revelation in the woods near Peningues that marked the turning point in Mordred's life, and parted company with him after the tournament of Peningues. Lancelot had been included in the priest's prophetic greeting of them as "the two most unfortunate knights who ever lived," and he was much shaken when Mordred slew the prophet before the latter had time to predict his — Lancelot's — fate. It was after the Peningues tournament that Lancelot rescued Kay from attacking knights and then left in the morning with Kay's horse and armor.

Lancleot returned to court in time to witness the attempt of Sir Brumant l'Orguilleus to sit in the Siege Perilous. By now it had been learned that Dame Elyzabel was being held prisoner by King Claudas, and Arthur and Guenever went to war, finally defeating Claudas and driving him into exile. After Claudas' defeat, Queen Elaine of Benwick came to visit her son and other male relatives at Gannes.

After Arthur's return from the Continent, Elaine of Carbonek visited the victory celebration, tricked Lancelot into her bed again, and so aroused Guenever's jealousy that Lancelot went mad again. He wandered for up to two years and finally ended at Carbonek, where he was recognized, restored to

by Greg Stafford from sketches by Phyllis Ann Karr; notes by P.A.K.

LANCELOT'S KIN

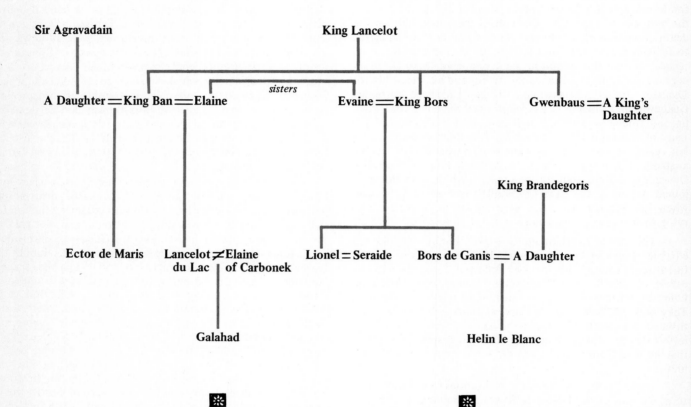

═ *Indicates a known marriage.*
≠ *Indicates a union either known to be illicit or a union not proven to be a marriage.*

- *Evelake, Seraphe, and Flegentine were converted to Christianity by Joseph of Arimathea. Both Mordrains and Nacien remained alive until the time of Lancelot du Lac's son, Galahad. Nacien, as a hermit and holy man, perhaps remained alive even longer. I do not know the wives of Nappus, Nacien (The Younger), Helias, or Lisias.*

- *Apparently because Joseph, Jesus' contemporary, converted Nacien, Sir Galahad is said to be "of the ninth degree from our Lord Jesu Christ," Sir Lancelot of the eighth.*

- *The affair between Lancelot and Elaine would have been a one-night stand (and he was enchanted into that) if he had not been tricked again.*

SIR LANCELOT'S FAMILY AND RETAINERS

Father: King Ban of Benwick
Mother: Queen Elaine of Benwick
Mentor-guardian (self-appointed): Viviane
Half-brother: Ector de Maris
Cousins: Lionel, Bors de Ganis, Iblis, Oruale de Guindoel
Lover: Guenevere
Virgin lady: Amable
Paramour: Elaine of Carbonek
Would-be paramours: Elaine of Astolat, Hellawes, Lady of Malohaut
Son (by Elaine of Carbonek): Galahad
Grandfather of son: King Pellam
Squires: Angis, Kanahins
Protégés: Lavaine, Nerovens de Lile, Urre of Hungary
Especial friend: Duke Galeholt
Dearest foe?: Morgan le Fay
Insistent guide: Ornagrine

sanity by exposure to the Grail, and given Joyous Isle to live in with Elaine. Under the self-imposed impression that he could never again return to Arthur's court, he called himself "Le Chevaler Mal Fet" and guarded the island against all challengers. Eventually Ector de Maris and Percivale found him here and persuaded him to return.

During the Grail Adventures, Lancelot suffered unaccustomed defeats and humiliation at arms, as well as experiencing a few visions and semi-visions of his own. After meeting and adventuring for a time with his son Galahad in the vessel with Amide's body, he arrived at Carbonek. Here, having resolved to amend his life of his adulterous love for Guenever, he had a Grail vision of his own—not the full experience of Galahad and his companions, but one which put Lancelot into a swoon for nearly a month, from which he awakened filled with the ineffable marvels he had seen.

Returning from the Grail Quest, however, Lancelot soon relapsed into his old love, but became more careless about secrecy. Then followed more stormy episodes between the lovers, including the incidents of the poisoning of Sir Patrice of Ireland and the passion and death of Elaine of Astolat. Eventually trapped alone with Guenever by Agravaine and Mordred, Lancelot fought his way free, leaving the Queen behind with reluctance and returning to rescue her from the stake, with great slaughter of Arthur's men, including Lancelot's old favorite Gareth. Arthur and Gawaine, who had always until now been counted one of Lancelot's dearest friends, first besieged Lancelot, his kinsmen and supporters, and Guenever in Joyous Garde. At the Pope's intervention, Lancelot restored Guenever to Arthur, who took her back and pardoned her, but exiled her lover. Lancelot returned to his lands in France, where he parcelled out the territories and titles among his kinsmen and followers. Arthur and Gawaine pursued Lancelot across the Channel and besieged him in Gannes. Lancelot met Gawaine in single combat, but with the utmost reluctance, and always, when Lancelot won, he refused to kill Gawaine. At news of Mordred's rebellion, Arthur and his men returned to Britain without making up their differences with Lancelot. Gawaine, dying at Dover, wrote a plea to Lancelot to return and aid Arthur, but, thanks to the famous premature battle at Salisbury, Lancelot and his men arrived too late; Mordred and virtually all the men of both armies were dead, and Arthur had passed. Lancelot was able, however to mop up the last of the rebellion, which was being kept alive by Mordred's two sons. Both of these lads exterminated, Lancelot found the chapel where Arthur's grave was marked and joined the former Archbishop of Canterbury and others, including many of his kinsmen, as a hermit. Here the great knight died, in Tennyson's words, "a holy man." His body was taken to Joyous Garde and buried beside that of Duke Galeholt.

I have recapped Lancelot's career, with many, many omissions, as given in the Vulgate, Volumes III-VI. After a few forecasts [II, 8, 19; III, 1], Malory brings him onstage in V, 2, in time for Arthur's campaign against Emperor Lucius. Malory gives the episode of Lancelot's abduction by Morgana and her cohorts, his escape and slaying of Sir Turquine, and the incident of returning to court in Kay's armor in Book VI; the begetting of Galahad and Lancelot's madness and subsequent sojourn with Elaine of Carbonek in Joyous Isle in Books XI and XII; Lancelot's Grail adventures in Books XIII, XV, and XVII; the poisoning of Sir Patrise and the Elaine of Astolat affair in Book XVIII, Meliagrant's kidnapping of Guenever in Book XIX, and the last, tragic adventures in Books XX and XXI, including Lancelot's last interview with Guenever in her convent [XXI, 9] and his bringing her body to Glastonbury, having learned of her death in a vision [XXI, 10-11]. Most of these episodes, especially the Meliagrant affair, are given somewhat differently in Malory, but the outlines are recognizable. Malory also describes Lancelot's mentorship of La Cote Male Taile (IX), his friendship with Tristram (IX, X), and his miraculous healing of Sir Urre of Hungary [XIX, 10-12] following the Meliagrant affair.

According to Malory, the only "worldly" knight who could conceivably have beaten Lancelot in single combat (except during the Grail Adventures or perhaps in Lancelot's first few years of knighthood) was Tristram; their big battle, however, ended in a draw, each surrendering to the other on learning one another's identity. [Malory X, 5] Coupled with this strength, skill, and prowess was an unfortunate tendency to blood-lust in battle; the film **Monty Python and the Holy Grail**, while hardly a reliable general picture of Arthur's court and reign, seems to me to have caught this facet of Lancelot's character to near perfection. One of his unluckiest habits was that of going to sleep in somebody else's pavilion without the owner's knowledge, which usually led to bloodshed and not infrequently to somebody's death. (See Belleus and "Iblis" — Iblis was widowed by Gaheris, but my impression is that Lancelot was the knight most frequently involved in this sort of incident.) Another of his habits was that of taking off secretly on unannounced adventures:

> And when Sir Lancelot was thus missed they marvelled where he was become; and then the queen and many of them deemed that he was departed as he was wont to do, suddenly. [Malory XIX, 7]

This, coupled with his absences on fits of madness, must have kept him very much away from court. Nevertheless, he attained great political influence; his "will was law throughout the kingdom of Logres." [Vulgate V]

Eventually jealousy of Lancelot grew among the other knights of the Round Table, caused in part by Arthur's praise [Vulgate V].

When Morgana and her cohorts kidnapped Lancelot, Morgana did not recognize him because he had short hair, his hair and nails having fallen out during the sickness from which Amable cured him, and his hair not having fully grown back [Vulgate V]. At some point in his career, he acquired a wound on his cheek; it was by this scar that the hermit Baudwin recognized him after the Winchester tournament at which he carried Elaine of Astolat's token. [Malory XVIII, 13]. Lancelot had an inconvenient habit of talking in his sleep of his love for Guenever [Malory XI, 8].

His relationship with his son Galahad seems to have been very good, friendly and loving on both sides. With Morgana he seems to have had a curious relationship—she varied between hating him and trying to seduce him.

LANCEOR

Son of one of the kings of Ireland (Malory does not specify which), Lanceor was "an orgulous [haughty] knight" of Arthur's court, but not, apparently, of the Round Table, early in Arthur's reign. Jealous of Balin's success in drawing the sword worn by "Malvis," Lanceor pursued Balin, jousted with him, and was killed. Lanceor is mainly memorable for being one of the comparatively few knights with a lady who is named—

Colombe—and because their tomb (erected over them, curiously enough, by King Mark) became a kind of landmark when Merlin accurately predicted that Lancelot and Tristram would someday fight each other there [Malory XI, 4-8].

LANDOINE (Landoigne)†

Daughter of the King of the Hundred Knights [Vulgate V].

THE LADY OF THE LAUNDS

Her "nigh cousin," King Anguish of Ireland, held a tournament to find her a husband.

> And what man won her, three days after he should wed her and have all her lands. This cry was made in England, Wales, Scotland, and also in France and Brittany.

Both Palomides and Tristram fought in this tournament; Palomides at first was winning, but Tristram (rather surprisingly urged thereto by La Beale Isoud) bested the Saracen and made him swear not to bear arms for a year. Everybody seems to have forgotten completely that the original purpose of the tournament was to find the Lady of the Launds a mate. [Malory VIII, 9-10]

Laudine† — see under YWAINE

LAUREL

The niece of Lyonors and Lynette, Dame Laurel was "a fair lady" who was wedded to Agravaine at the same time Lyonores was married to Gareth and Lynette to Gaheris [Malory VII, 35].

LAVAINE

Sirs Tirre and Lavaine were the sons of Sir Bernard of Astolat and the brothers of Elaine, the Lily Maid. They had recently been knighted when Lancelot stopped at Astolat on his way to the Winchester tournament. The main importance of the older brother, Tirre, seems to be that he had been wounded the same day he was made knight and was still lying abed with his wounds, so that his shield was available for Lancelot to borrow. Lavaine, the younger son, went with Lancelot to the tournament, made a good showing, and helped the gravely wounded Lancelot away to the hermit Baudwin. Returning to Winchester — apparently sent by Lancelot to seek Bors or some other kinsman — Lavaine first encountered his sister Elaine and later located Bors, bringing them both to the wounded Lancelot. Lavaine remained at court after Elaine's death, "and ever in all places Sir Lavaine gat great worship so that he was renowned among many knights of the Table Round". In Arthur's Christmas tournament, Lavaine encountered Arthur himself in the lists and they smote each other down. Made a companion of the Round Table at the same time as Sir Urre of Hungary, Lavaine married Urre's sister Felelolie. Remaining in Lancelot's faction during the break with Arthur, Lavaine accompanied Lancelot into exile and was made Earl of Arminak. [Malory XVIII, 9-23; XIX, 13; XX, 5, 18]

A LADY LEECH OF CORNWALL

> Then the king [Mark] let send after all manner of leeches and surgeons, both unto men and women, and there was none that would behote [Tristram] the life. Then came there a lady that was a right wise lady, and she said plainly unto King Mark, and

to Sir Tristram ... that he should never be whole but if Sir Tristram went in the same country that the venom [of Marhaus' spearhead] came from ... [Malory VIII, 8]

I assume from the context that she was a leech or surgeon; she may, of course, have been an herb-woman or even one who simply knew how to speak out with authority. Mark and Tristram took her advice seriously and followed it, to Tristram's healing.

KING LEODEGRANCE (Leodegance, Leodegran) OF CAMELIARD (Carmelide)

The father of Guenever and Genievre, Leodegrance held in his house the Round Table, which he received from Uther Pendragon. He was not involved in the rebellion of the kings at Arthur's accession, possibly because he already had his hands full with King Ryons. Leodegrance appealed for Arthur's help against Ryons; Arthur came, bringing with him his allies Ban and Bors, and succored Cameliard. At this time Arthur first saw Guenever. When Arthur later requested her hand in marriage, Leodegrance was honored and delighted. Casting about in his mind for a gift that would please his new son-in-law, Leodegrance reasoned that "he hath lands enow, him needeth none; but I shall send him a gift shall please him much more, for I shall give him the Table Round," together with a hundred knights [Malory I, 18; III, 1; Vulgate].

	KING LEODEGRANCE'S
Daughter: Guenevere	
Daughter (by wife of seneschal): Genievre	FAMILY
Son-in-law: Arthur	AND RETAINERS
Seneschal: Cleodalis	
Knights: Bertholai, Garaunt, Guy, Guenever's cousins (q.v.)	

Leonce — see LIONSES

"Leprous Lady" — see same, *Places*

DAMSEL OF LESTROITE MARCHE†

For some reason, although other damsels and ladies acted as apparently independent chatelaines, this damsel could not hold her father's castle in her own right after his death. The lord of Lestroite Marche therefore tried to find her a good husband by insisting that each of his knightly guests spend half a day defending the castle. The damsel fell in love with Ector de Maris, who defeated Sir Marganor during his half-day's service; but Ector hedged by telling her he already had a lady. Then the damsel gave his a ring with a stone that had the power to make the man who received it love with ever-increasing force the woman who gave it. [Vulgate III]

DAMSEL OF LEVERZEP†

She was rescued by Lancelot on one of his long adventures away from court. He sent her back to let the court know he was still alive, and Arthur was so delighted with the news that he rewarded her with the castle of her choice. She chose Leverzep, where she had been born. [Vulgate V]

DUKE LIANOUR

Duke of the Castle of Maidens, Lianour and his eldest son were slain by seven evil brothers who then raped the Duke's elder daughter, appropriated his property and treasure, and set about oppressing the common folk and taking all passing knights and damsels prisoner. After seven years of this, the seven brothers were routed by Galahad and his companions. Lianour's elder daughter had died, so the castle was restored to her younger sister. [Malory XIII, 15]

LILE OF AVELION
Called "the great lady Lile of Avelion," this enigmatic person may have been an enchantress. Avelion is almost certainly Avilion or Avalon, suggesting religion, mysticism, magic, and benevolence; yet Lady Lile helped the damsel "Malvis," whom Merlin characterized as wicked. Perhaps in this case Lile, although good, mistakenly helped the wrong side — the Round Table heroes were often enough guilty of helping the wrong side, through siding with the first party who appealed to them, or unquestioningly taking the part of any woman against any man. [Malory II, 1-4]

Lile would not have been a Lady of the Lake, for Lancelot's Lady of the Lake, Viviane, was in France. The first English Lady of the Lake came to demand the heads of Balin and the very damsel whom Lile had helped, and the second English Lady of the Lake was Nimue.

I have treated Lile in the above notes as a person because in Malory she does seem definitely a person, not a personification, even though she remains an offstage figure. My opinion, however, is that this mysterious dame came into being when some scribe or translator mistook the French for "the island of Avalon" (*l'ile d'Avilion*) for a personal name.

Linet – see LYNETTE

LIONEL
The first son of King Bors, the older brother of Sir Bors de Ganis and the cousin of Lancelot, Lionel owed his name to a birthmark shaped like a lion. At the death of King Bors, one of his former retainers, Sir Pharien, appropriated Lionel and Bors, aged 21 and 9 months, and took over their training. The growing boys occupied what must have been a rather uneasy place in the court of King Claudas, and finally gave Claudas' son Dorin his death wound during a fray at dinner. Seraide, who had been sent by Viviane, rescued Lionel and Bors by giving them the shape of greyhounds for a while. They, along with their tutors Pharien, Lambegues, and Leonce, were welcomed into Viviane's Lake, where they finished their education at the side of their cousin Lancelot, and where Lionel took Seraide to be his lady. Lionel and Bors accompanied Lancelot to England, where they were to become knights of the Round Table. [Vulgate III]

As early as V, 6 Malory has Arthur sending Lionel, with Bors, Gawaine, and Bedivere, on an embassy to Lucius during the war with Rome. Soon after their return from the Continent, Lionel accepted Lancelot's invitation to seek adventures, they two alone. While Lancelot was asleep, Lionel saw three knights fleeing from a single adversary. Lionel got up without waking his cousin and took off after them. The single knight was Turquine, who defeated them all, took them prisoner, threw them into his dungeon, stripped them naked, and beat them with thorns. Meanwhile, Lancelot was captured by Morgana and her companions, so that Lionel had a longish wait before his cousin arrived to rescue him.

At least once during the middle years of Arthur's reign Lionel joined a search, headed by Lancelot, for Tristram. Lionel, Bors, and Ector de Maris were the first to leave court,

sent and supplied by Guenever, to find Lancelot when he disappeared in a fit of madness caused by Guenever's jealousy of Elaine of Carbonek; Lionel spent at least two years on this search. It is possible, though no specific names are named, that Lionel was among those kinsmen of Lancelot's who once sought Tristram's death out of envy because his fame was overshadowing Lancelot's — a murderous effort which Lancelot himself stopped when it came to his attention.

As T.H. White noticed in the **Once and Future King**, Lionel was unlucky about getting beaten with thorns. On the Grail Quest,

> [Sir Bors] met at the departing of the two ways two knights that led Lionel, his brother all naked, bounden upon a strong hackney, and his hands bounden to-fore his breast. And everych of them held in his hands thorns wherewith they went beating him so sore that the blood trailed down more than in an hundred places of his body ... but he said never a word; as he which was great of heart he suffered all that ever they did to him, as though he had felt none anguish.

Bors was about to rescue him, when he saw a knight about to rape a virgin on the other side of the road. So, with a prayer to Jesu to keep Lionel, Bors went to help the maiden instead. This, rather understandably, irked Lionel; and, no matter how nobly he bore suffering, he was also capable of bearing a strong grudge. When next the brothers met, Lionel threatened to kill Bors for his unbrotherly action. Bors made no defense, but a good old hermit ran out to put himself between the brothers. Lionel hewed the old holy man down. Then Sir Colgrevance, a fellow companion of the Round Table, came along and tried to save Bors. Lionel killed Colgravance, too. It took a fiery cloud from Heaven to stop Lionel. On the Heavenly voice instructing Bors to go and join Percivale, Bors, relieved to find that Lionel had not been struck dead by God's vengeance, prepared to go.

> Then he said to his brother: Fair sweet brother, forgive me for God's love all that I have trespassed unto you. Then he answered: God forgive it thee and I do gladly.

Lionel, of course, sided with Lancelot when the break with Arthur came. Accompanying Lancelot into exile, Lionel was crowned King of France. After all, though, he died in England — he was slain apparently during the last of Mordred's rebellion, when he took 15 other lords from Dover to London to seek Lancelot, who may already have found Arthur's grave (see Melehan). [Malory V, 6; VI, 1-9; IX, 36; X, 88; XI, 10; XII, 9; XVI, 9-17; XX, 5, 18; XXI, 10]

Lionesse – see LYONORS

Lionors – see LYZIANOR

LLYWARCH HEN (Llywarch, The Aged)†
Glennie lists him as one of the four great bards of the Arthurian age; see under Taliessin.

Lohot – see BORRE

LORAINE LE SAVAGE
"A false knight and a coward," he came up from behind and slew Sir Miles of the Launds with a spear [Malory III, 15]. I cannot find that he was ever overtaken and made to answer for the deed; presumably that task would have fallen to King Pellinore, who had learned that Miles was the lover of Pellinore's daughter Eleine. Loraine's modus operandi suggests that of Garlon or of Breuse Sans Pitie.

LORE DE BRANLANT†

She was a cousin of a knight named Sir Drians li Gaiz of Gais castle. Branlant seems to have been the name of Lore's own castle; her seneschal was called Bruns de Branlant. Lore was among the many ladies who loved Gawaine. [Vulgate VII]

LORE OF CARDUEL (Lore de Kardoil, Lorete, Lore la Fille Doon)†

Carduel is surely Cardoile, or Carlisle. Dame Lore of Carduel served as the King's cupbearer. At a lovers' rendevous between the two couples Lancelot and Guenever, and Duke Galeholt and the Lady of Malohaut, Lore of Carduel and Duke Galeholt's seneschal were also present. [Vulgate III]

In Vulgate VII Lore is a sister or—more likely—a cousin of Guenever, and either the sister or the lover of Sir Giflez (Griflet?). In some extremely tricky (at least to me) passages, Lore and the Queen appear to help Giflez cross a lake. Four knights seem to have captured Gareth; Kay, after killing one of them, gives his destrier to Lorete (Lore), who then proceeds with the Queen to rescue, mount, and arm Gareth. Once he is armed, the women apparently stand back and watch; however, there is at least a hint that Lorete might do a bit of fighting.

KING LOT (Loth) OF LOTHIAN AND ORKNEY

Lot married Morgawse, daughter of Igraine and Gorlois, at the same time Uther Pendragon married Igraine. The father of Gawaine, Agravaine, Gaheris, and Gareth, Lot was one of the rebel kings at the beginning of Arthur's reign. He showed himself a good strategist during the battle of Bedegraine:

> Then all the eleven [rebel] kings drew them together, and then said King Lot, Lords, ye must other ways than ye do ... ye may see what people we have lost, and what good men we lose, because we wait always on these foot-men, and ever in saving of one of the foot-men we lose ten horsemen for him; therefore this is mine advice, let us put our foot-men from us, for it is near night, for the noble Arthur will not tarry on the foot-men, for they may save themselves, the wood is near hand. And when we horsemen be together, look every each of you kings ... that none break upon pain of death. And who that seeth any man dress him to flee, lightly that he be slain, for it is better that we slay a coward, than through a coward all we to be slain.

Acting upon Lot's advice, the kings at least saved themselves, though not the battle.

After Bedegraine, Lot's wife Morgawse came to Arthur's court, "in manner of a message, but she was sent thither to espy the court." Although we know from the Vulgate account that Morgawse did not share Lot's enmity against Arthur, from Malory's account it appears that at this point Lot was sounding Arthur out, leaving himself free to opt for either peace or fur-

ther rebellion according to Arthur's strength and disposition. Unfortunately, Arthur begat Mordred on Morgawse, and later, learning that a boy born on May-day would destroy him, had Mordred, along with all the other lords' sons born about that time, put on a ship and sent out to sea to die. Whether Lot knew that Arthur had cuckolded him, or whether he believed Mordred — apparently killed with the other babies — to have been his own son, his enmity against Arthur was now cemented, and he joined Ryence and Nero as ringleaders of the second rebellion of twelve kings. This time the crucial battle was fought before Terrabil castle. During the first part of the battle, Merlin cunningly "came to King Lot...and held him with a tale of prophecy, till Nero and his people were destroyed." Learning too late of their destruction, Lot cried,

> Alas ... I am ashamed, for by my default there is many a worshipful man slain ... Now what is best to do? ... whether is me better to treat with King Arthur or to fight, for the greater part of our people are slain and destroyed? Sir, said a knight, set on Arthur for they are weary and forfoughten and we be fresh. As for me said King Lot, I would every knight do his part as I would do mine.

So he went into battle and was killed by King Pellinore (though there must have been some confusion, for Pellinore's son Lamorak later claimed it had been Balin who dealt the fatal stroke).

There is an almost Grecian fate about Lot's death. Merlin had known that either Arthur or Lot must die at Terrabil that day, and preferred it be Lot; yet even Merlin regretted the necessity. "Alas he might not endure," says Malory, "the which was great pity, that so worthy a knight as [Lot] was should be overmatched..." All the rebel kings died in the battle, and Arthur buried them all with full honors in Saint Stephen's Church in Camelot. "But of all these twelve kings King Arthur let make the tomb of King Lot passing richly, and made his tomb by his own ..." [Malory I, 2, 18-19, 27; II, 10-11; X, 24]

Lot may also have been the father of Thenew, and thus the grandfather of St. Kentigern.

LOVEL

One of Gawaine's three sons, apparently the youngest, "begotten upon Sir Brandiles' sister," Lovel became a companion of the Round Table. Joining his uncles Agravaine and Mordred in their attempt to trap Lancelot with the Queen, Lovel was killed by the escaping Lancelot. [Malory XIX 11; XX 2-4]

LUCAN THE BUTLER (Lucas; Lucanere de Buttelere)

Son of Duke Corneus and possibly brother of Bedivere, Sir Lucan appears to have been a good knight and sensible, and gentle in the best sense of the word. One of Arthur's earliest knights, he may have been appointed butler at the same time

---

DATING THE ERA AND CHARACTERS

The era of Arthur, according to the Vulgate and Malory, is the first half of the Fifth Century after Christ. Galahad arrived at Arthur's court in the year 454 A.D. [Vulgate VI; Malory XIII, 2]. A more complete, though highly tentative, chronology may be found in the appendices.

By long usage, characters of the Sixth Century, especially saints and poets, may be incorporated into Arthurian adventure. Certain personages from earlier centuries may also appear: Nascien the hermit and King Mordrains, contemporaries of Joseph of Arimathea, both miraculously survived into Arthur's time, and Joseph himself appears in visions. Other saints and angels could surely appear in visions as well. I have never yet encountered the Wandering Jew in Arthurian legend, but see no reason why he should not appear in Arthur's world.

Christ himself appears in the form of an old holy man; Vulgate VI strongly suggests that the old man who arrives by boat to explain Percivale's visions on the island during the Grail Quest is "the bread of life from heaven," i.e., Christ. [Vulgate VI, p. 82; cf. Malory XIV, 7]

The Devil likewise appears in person. He may take the form of a venerable holy man to interpret falsely someone's vision or experiences, a beautiful woman to tempt a knight's chastity, or even a horse to try to drown its rider. According to Nascien, it was the Devil who entered into Guenever and made her desire Lancelot, because that was the only way the evil one could get a hold on the great knight [Vulgate VI]. I also found one named demon, Aselaphes, who killed King Tholomer lest Josephe convert him [Vulgate I, p. 76]. This was long before Arthur's time, but devils are immortal. Nearer home, a devil is credited with fathering Merlin.

Kay was named seneschal; at least, he appears in that post, serving with Kay and Griflet, at the feast given by Arthur in honor of his newly-arrived allies Kings Ban and Bors. Lucan fought valiantly in the battle of Bedegraine; we can probably assume that he also fought at Terrabil and on Humber bank. Through most of Malory's work Lucan remains in the background, presumably carrying out his duties as butler. He does appear half a dozen times in the books of Tristram and those immediately following the Grail Adventures, chiefly jousting at tournaments. At least once during the books of Tristram Lucan shows up riding by and for adventure; he has now attained Round Table status. Outjousted and injured by Tristram, he is brought safely to the abbey of Ganis by Ywaine.

Lucan remained with Arthur when the split came between the King and Lancelot. When Arthur was encamped before Benwick, it was Lucan who met Lancelot's messengers, a damsel and her dwarf.

> And when she came to the pavilion of King Arthur, there she alighted; and there met her a gentle knight, Sir Lucan the Butler, and said: Fair damosel, come ye from Sir Launcelot du Lake? Yea sir, she said, therefore I come hither to speak with my lord the king. Alas, said Sir Lucan, my lord Arthur would love Launcelot, but Sir Gawaine will not suffer him. ... I pray to God, damosel, ye may speed well, for all we that be about the king would Sir Launcelot did best of any knight living.

As one of the last two knights left alive with Arthur after the last battle at Salisbury, Lucan tried to prevent the King from attacking Mordred.

> Now give me my spear, said Arthur unto Sir Lucan, for yonder I have espied the traitor that all this woe hath wrought. Sir, let him be, said Sir Lucan, for he is unhappy; and if ye pass this unhappy day ye shall be right well revenged upon him. Good lord, remember ye of your night's dream, and what the spirit of Sir Gawaine told you this night, yet God of his great goodness hath preserved you hitherto. Therefore, for God's sake, my lord, leave off by this, for blessed be God ye have won the field, for here we be three alive, and with Sir Mordred is none alive; and if ye leave off now this wicked day of destiny is past.

But Arthur insisted on attacking Mordred, killing him but getting his own death wound in the process. Lucan and Bedivere got Arthur to a little chapel. Hearing people cry in the battlefield, the King sent Lucan to see what was going on. Lucan found robbers and pillagers stealing from the corpses.

> When Sir Lucan understood this work, he came to the king as soon as he might, and told him all what he had heard and seen. Therefore by my rede, said Sir Lucan, it is best that we bring you to some town.

But when Lucan tried to help Bedivere lift Arthur, a wound opened and part of Lucan's bowels burst out, and so he died. [Malory I, 10-14; IX, 37; X, 74; XVIII, 11, 23; XIX, 11; XX, 19; XXI, 4-5]

In Malory, Bedivere, the other survivor of the last battle, is called Lucan's brother. I am not sure whether this means blood relationship, or brother in the sense that both were of the Round Table. In Vulgate VI, where Griflet and not Bedivere is the last knight left alive with Arthur, Lucan is nevertheless the next-to-the-last, and dies when Arthur embraces him.

LUCIUS, EMPEROR OF ROME

"Emperor Lucius, which was called at that time, Dictator or Procuror of the Public Weal of Rome," sent twelve ancient, venerable ambassadors to Arthur's court to command from him the traditional obeisance and truage paid by the kings of Britain to Rome, and threatening dire war against Arthur if he refused to pay. Arthur refused to pay, citing the examples of "Belinus and Brenius, kings of Britain, [who] have had the empire in their hands many days, and also Constantine the son of Heleine." Arthur then crossed the Channel to meet Lucius on the Continent, perhaps reasoning that thus he could keep the destruction of warfare out of Britain. Lucius summoned Rome's allies to his aid, gathered his army and his personal bodyguard of "fifty giants which had been engendered of fiends," and set out to meet Arthur in France. Arthur sent Gawaine, Bors, Lionel, and Bedivere in embassy to command Lucius to return to Rome. Haughty words passed on both sides, Lucius showing himself as proud as Arthur, and finally Gawaine fell into a rage and slew Lucius' cousin Sir Gainus in the Emperor's presence. The ensuing skirmish turned into a battle, with much bloodshed and taking of Roman prisoners. Lucius arranged an ambush to rescue the Roman prisoners as they were being sent to Paris. The attempt was foiled by Lancelot and Cador. A senator who escaped from the fray reached Lucius with this counsel:

> Sir emperor, I advise thee for to withdraw thee; what dost thou here? ... for this day one of Arthur's knights was worth in the battle an hundred of ours. Fie on thee, said Lucius, thou speakest cowardly; for thy words grieve me more than all the loss that I had this day.

Lucius proceeded to the crucial battle with Arthur, and met death from Arthur's own sword, following which Arthur marched on Rome, took it, and was crowned Emperor of Rome by the Pope himself. [Malory V]

It seems that Arthur was not able to maintain himself as both King of Britain and Emperor of Rome, for the Romans attacked him again when he was besieging Lancelot in France toward the end of his reign [Vulgate VI]. We may perhaps surmise that there was originally but one campaign against Rome (in some medieval versions, Mordred makes his bid for the throne while Arthur is absent on the Roman campaign rather than while Arthur is in France for the specific purpose of fighting Lancelot). It also makes sense, however, to accept a successful British war against Rome, as described by Malory, during the early or middle years of Arthur's reign, followed by a revolt of Rome against Arthur in the last, troubled years of his reign, as described in Vulgate VI.

I am not sure whether it was Lucius or his predecessor who married Avenable.

Lucius' Bodyguard — see under LUCIUS

LUNETE†

A cousin germaine of Niniane (Nimue and/or Viviane) [Vulgate VII]. I assume that, like her cousin of the Lake, Lunete is a magician, but she may be simply a damsel. There is the possibility that Lunete should be identified with Malory's Dame Linet, the Damsel Savage (see Lynette).

A Lunette appears in Chretien's **Yvain** as Dame Laudine's chief handmaid and advisor. Here Lunette, though not actually a sorceress, has a magic ring which provides the wearer invisibility. She also has a good store of sense and wit which enable her, after befriending Ywaine, to matchmake for him and Laudine.

LYNETTE (Linet, The Damosel Savage)

When Sir Ironside laid siege to Lynette's sister Lyonors in Castle Dangerous, Lynette came to Arthur's court to find a champion. At first reluctant for some reason to tell her sister's name, she seemed about to reveal it in order to gain a worthy knight when Beaumains, hot from his year in the kitchen and not yet knighted, asked for the adventure. Since this was serious business — Gawaine himself had just called the Red Knight "one of the perilloust knights of the world" — we may understand Lynette's annoyance at being given an unproved kitchen page for her sister's champion, especially when Lancelot and Gawaine, the two knights Ironside most sought to fight, were both at court. She industriously rebuked Gareth all the way from Arthur's court to the city of Sir Persant of Inde. It is possible that, like Beauvivante, she hoped to discourage her youthful knight from risking his life, but during his battle with Perimones, it was Perimones whom she cheered on. The triumphant Gareth threatened to kill Pertelope, Perimones, and Persant, each in turn, unless "his lady" told him to spare them; she always did, though couching the instruction in scornful terms the first few times. By the time they came to Persant's city, though, she had relented, begged Gareth's pardon, and warned him sincerely against taking on Persant and later Ironside. In Ironside's case, she also craftily counselled Gareth to wait until after noon, when Ironside's strength would be on the decline, before issuing his challenge. (He scorned the suggestion, of course.) At one point in the battle with Ironside, when Gareth was temporarily on the bottom, Lynette cheered on her former kitchen knave, reminding him that Lyonors was looking on and thus stirring him to victory. Like the Isouds and other ladies, Lynette had surgical skill, tending the wounds of both Gareth and Ironside after the fight.

Not long thereafter, when Gareth and Lyonors "were accorded to abate their lusts secretly," Lynette used her craft and a magic salve to keep them honest before marriage. Although this is Malory's only instance of Lynette in the apparent role of sorceress, and although she could simply have gotten hold of Sir Priamus' restorative balm or some similar unguent, the evidence suggests some sorcerous, rather than merely surgical, knowledge on her part. For instance, when the leeches examined the wounds Lynette's knight inflicted on Gareth, they "said that there was no man . . . should heal him throughout of his wound but if they healed him that caused that stroke by enchantment." Then Lynette "laid an ointment and a salve to him as it pleased to her, that he was never so fresh nor so lusty."

Lynette's brother was Sir Gringamore, her niece was Dame Laurel. When Lyonors was wedded to Gareth, the quick-tongued, crafty, and lively though somewhat puritanical Lynette was wedded to Gaheris. [Malory VII]

Perhaps she is best remembered today for Tennyson's graceful version in **Gareth and Lynette**, one of the most enjoyable of his Idylls. Tennyson has Gareth fall in love with and marry Lynette rather than Lyonors, which perhaps seems more satisfying to the modern mind. Because of Tennyson's Idyll, because the Tennysonian names seem to me more musical than the Malorian, and because Malory names the other sister Lionesse, which sounds confusingly like the country of Lyonesse, I have used Tennyson's names instead of Malory's in this work.

The King's Damosel, a charming modern romance by Vera Chapman, which catches the medieval spirit with a good admixture of modern taste, uses Lynette for its heroine. Chapman (who does take considerable liberties with Malory) has Lynette leaving Gaheris almost at once to become a carrier of messages for Arthur. In Chapman's version, Lynette, although not a virgin, achieves the Grail. She reappears in Chapman's other romances, **The Green Knight** and **King Arthur's Daughter,** which show her surviving the downfall of Arthur's kingdom to help plant the seeds of Arthur's spirit in future generations.

LYONORS (Lionesse)

Sister of Lynette, chatelaine of Castle Dangerous (also called Castle Perilous), lady and wife of Sir Gareth, Dame Lyonors also had a brother, Sir Gringamore, and a niece, Dame Laurel. I have preferred Tennyson's version of her name.

Though rather outshadowed by her sister, Lyonors does show considerable character of her own. Hers must have been a wealthy castle, for she was able to host a tournament there for Arthur's knights and others, and she seems to have been a competent chatelaine, to judge by her foresight when Gareth's dwarf brought her word that his master and her sister were nearing the castle. She sent the dwarf to a hermitage appertaining to Castle Dangerous, taking the hermit

> wine in two flagons of silver, they are of two gallons, and also two cast of bread with fat venison baked, and dainty fowls; and a cup of gold ... And go thou unto my sister and greet her well, and commend me unto that gentle knight, and pray him to eat and to drink and make him strong ...

She was coy, for even after Gareth defeated Ironside for her, she declared she would not love her champion until he was "called one of the number of the worthy knights. And therefore go labour in worship this twelvemonth, and then thou shalt hear new tidings." In this she may only have acted according to the postures of her milieu. Apparently endowed, however, with a sense of humor, she enlisted her brother's aid for an elaborate practical joke involving the kidnapping of Gareth's dwarf and encompassing Lyonors' own flirtation, under an assumed identity, with Gareth (who had not until then seen the lady of Castle Dangerous close up). No prude, she was ready enough to go to bed with Gareth now, before marriage, though Lynette prevented it. On the whole, we may hope that Lyonors and her husband enjoyed a happy wedded life. [Malory VII]

LYZIANOR (Lionors, Lisanor)

The daughter of Earl Sanam, Dame Lionors "came thither [to Arthur] for to do homage, as other lords did after the great battle" of Bedegraine. She pleased Arthur so well that he begat on her Sir Borre, "that was after a good knight, and of the Round Table" [Malory I, 17]. This was, of course, before Arthur met Guenever. Lyzianor seems to have been chatelaine of Karadigan castle. [Vulgate VII. p. 206]

In Vulgate II, Sommer uses Lisanor for her name, and her son by Arthur is called Lohot. To try to avoid confusion with Lyonors of Castle Dangerous, I have here preferred the variant name for Arthur's early paramour as given in Vulgate VII.

Barbara Ferry Johnson's competent novel **Lionors** is based on this character. Johnson's portrayal is along totally different lines from those I have etched in, making Lionors Arthur's secret, lifelong lover and also, for some reason, transforming her son into a daughter called Elise.

AAGLANT†

A leader of the Sesnes, involved in the attack on Vandaliors castle early in Arthur's reign. [Vulgate II]

MADOR DE LA PORTE

This companion of the Round Table must have been one of Arthur's first knights. Malory mentions him fighting, along with Sirs Mordred and Galahantine, on the side of the King of Northgalis in a tournament between him and King Bagdemagus, and "against them three [Bagdemagus] nor [his] knights might bear no strength." Lancelot, fulfilling a promise to Bagdemagus' daughter, entered the tournamant and defeated all three, Mador first. Lancelot defeated Mador again some time later at the Surluse tournament.

When — according to the Vulgate account, which here varies considerably in detail from Malory's — Mador had served Arthur for 45 years, Guenever invited him as one of two dozen guests at a small dinner party she gave to show the world she delighted in all the knights of the Round Table, not only in Lancelot, who was absent at the time. At this dinner Mador's cousin Sir Patrise (in the Vulgate, his brother Sir Gaheris de Kareheu) fell accidental victim to poison which Sir Pinel le Savage (in the Vulgate, Sir Avarlon) meant for Gawaine. Suspicion naturally fell on the Queen.

> [Then Gawaine said,] madam, I dread me lest ye will be shamed, ... This shall not so be ended, said Sir Mador de la Porte, for here have I lost a full noble knight of my blood; and therefore upon this shame and despite I will be revenged to the utterance. And there openly Sir Mador appealed the queen of the death of his cousin, Sir Patrise.

Arthur arrived, regretting that his duty to act as judge prevented him from fighting for Guenever himself and promising Mador that she would find a champion. "My gracious lord, said Sir Mador ... though ye be our king in that degree, ye are but a knight as we are, and ye are sworn unto knighthood as well as we." According to the Vulgate, Mador resigned his allegiance to Arthur in order to fight this trial by combat. Lancelot arrived in time to champion the Queen and, for the third time in Malory's book, defeated Mador, who then asked for mercy, "released the queen of his quarrel," and was welcomed back to his place among the knights of the Round Table. The fight, however, had lasted "nigh an hour, for this Sir Mador was a strong knight, and mightily proved in many strong battles." Perhaps Mador continued to mistrust the Queen, for he joined the group that helped Mordred and Agravaine corner Lancelot with Guenever, and was killed when Lancelot made his escape. [Malory VI, 6, 7, 18; X, 45; XVIII, 3-7; XX, 2-4; Vulgate VI]

References to Mador de la Porte in **Sir Gawaine and the Green Knight** and elsewhere suggest that in earlier romances he was much more important than we would assume from Malory alone.

Brothers: Adragain, Gaheris de Kareheu	**FAMILY TO**
Cousin: Patrise of Ireland	**SIR MADOR DE LA PORTE**

Maimed King — see PELLAM

MAIMED KNIGHT†

In one hand the Maimed Knight involuntarily grasped a sword which had penetrated his other hand. Only the best knight in the world could remove the sword. The Maimed Knight was understandably annoyed when Bors and Agravaine, meeting him, entered into an argument about whether Lancelot or Gawaine was the best knight. Naturally, it was Lancelot who finally relieved him of the sword. [Vulgate IV]

I am not sure whether this knight travelled in a litter or remained in his castle or manor; if the latter he probably was located near the marches of Stranggore.

MAINES†

Maines was one of the three sons, apparently the oldest, of King Constans of England, Arthur's grandfather. Thus, he would have been Arthur's uncle, but he was killed early, murdered by a dozen barons who wanted Vortigern for their king. Maines was survived and avenged by his brothers Uther and Pandragon. [Vulgate III]

Maledisant — see BEAUVIVANTE

MALGRIN

A dangerous, probably villainous knight located in the general neighborhood of the castle La Beale Regard, Sir Malgrin is mentioned in the same breath with Breuse Sans Pitie:

> Then [Mark] sent unto Queen Morgan le Fay, and to the Queen of Northgalis, praying them in his letters that they two sorceresses would set all the country in fire with ladies that were enchantresses, and by such that were dangerous knights, as Malgrin, Breuse Saunce Pité, that by no means Alisander le Orphelin should escape [Malory X, 35]

In the next chapter, Alisander meets a chatelaine who asks him to joust for her sake with her neighbor, Sir Malgrin, who "will not suffer me to be married in no manner wise for all that I can do, or any knight for my sake." Alisander and Malgrin jousted and fought on foot for

> three hours, [and] never man could say which was the better knight. ... But this Malgrin was an old roted [practiced] knight, and he was called one of the most dangerous knights of the world to do battle on foot, but on horseback there were many better.

During a lull in the fight, the felonious Malgrin told Alisander,

> Wit thou well ... for this maiden's love, of this castle, I have slain ten good knights by mishap; and by outrage and orgulité [pride] of myself I have slain ten other knights.

Alisander at last ended Malgrin's career by smiting off his head. As for the chatelaine, she asked Alisander to give her in marriage to her old sweetheart, Sir Gerine le Grose, who lived in that area. Alisander obliged. [Malory X, 36-37]

LADY OF MALOHAUT†

She ruled a town called Le Puis de Malohaut, apparently in the territory of Malahaut. Since Vulgate II assigns this country to the King of the Hundred Knights, the Lady may have been his viceregent. She was a good governor, loved by the people, and a widow.

She imprisoned Lancelot for killing the son of her seneschal, but released him on his parole so that he could attend an assembly or tournament. Probably she did not really expect him to return, but he came back without fanfare and quietly went to sleep in his cell. When the Lady found his weapons and armor battered, his horse wounded, himself wounded and asleep in his cell, she fell in love with him.

Later, however, witnessing a lovers' meeting between Lancelot and the Queen, the Lady of Malohaut set aside her own feelings and offered herself as Guenever's confidante. Lancelot could confide in Duke Galeholt, and the Lady told Guenever, "I believe that four can keep a secret better than three." Guenever then tried a little matchmaking between the Lady of Malohaut and Duke Galeholt. She went about it in direct style, counselling each of them frankly to love one another, and succeeded in bringing them together so well that after Galeholt's death, the Lady of Malohaut died for love of him. [Vulgate III-IV]

Vulgate VII mentions a *Senayns li chastelains du Puj de Malohaut.* I would guess that Senayns was the widowed Lady's dead husband; the name might be transferred to the Lady herself.

"MALVIS"

This damsel arrived at Arthur's court "on message from the great lady Lile of Avelion," girded with a cumbersome, uncomfortable sword. She said she was looking for a knight who could draw the sword from its scabbard and thus relieve her of it, "but he must be a passing good man of his hands and of his deeds . . . a clean knight without villainy, and of a gentle strain of father side and mother side." Not finding such a knight at King Ryon's court, she had come on to Arthur's. Here only the impoverished prisoner Sir Balin Le Savage could draw the sword.

> Certes, said the damosel, this is a passing good knight, and the best that ever I found, and most of worship without treason, treachery, or villainy, and many marvels shall he do. Now gentle and courteous knight, give me the sword again. Nay, said Balin ... Well, said the damosel, ye are not wise to keep the sword from me, for ye shall slay with the sword the best friend that ye have, and the man that ye most love in the world, and the sword shall be your destruction. I shall take the adventure, said Balin ... but the sword ye shall not have ... Ye shall repent it within short time, said the damosel, for I would have the sword more for your avail than for mine, for I am passing heavy for your sake; for ye will not believe that sword shall be your destruction, and that is great pity. With that the damosel departed, making great sorrow.

Meanwhile, the first English Lady of the Lake, Nineve, arrived to claim the gift Arthur had promised her when she gave him Excalibur. She asked the head either of Balin or of Malvis: "I take no force though I have both their heads, for he slew my brother, a good knight and a true, and that gentlewoman was causer of my father's death." Arthur refused Nineve's request, but Balin, learning of it, came and swapped off Nineve's head to the King's chagrin. Balin explained that he had been seeking her for three years for having caused the death of his mother, that "this same lady [of the Lake] was the untruest lady living, and by enchantment and sorcery she hath been the destroyer of many good knights"

After Balin's departure, Merlin arrived. Being told all that had happened, the Mage explained:

> [T]his same damosel that here standeth [did stand?], that brought the sword unto your court, I shall tell you the cause of her coming: she was the falsest damosel that liveth. Say not so, said they. She hath a brother, [said Merlin] a passing good knight of prowess and a full true man; and this damosel loved another knight that held her to paramour, and this good knight her brother met with the knight that held her to paramour, and slew him by force of his hands. When this false damosel understood this, she went unto the Lady Lile of Avelion, and besought her of help, to be avenged on her own brother. And so this Lady Lile of Avelion took her this sword that she brought with her, and told there should no man pull it out of the sheath but if he be one of the best knights of this realm, and he should be hard and full of prowess, and with that sword he should slay her brother. ... Would God she had not come into this court, but she came never in fellowship of worship to do good, but always great harm.

If, in this welter of accusation and counter-accusation, we take Merlin's tale as sooth, then Malvis was a wicked woman. Personally, I hold Merlin's testimony suspect. By Balin's own account, which seems reliable — Merlin himself calls Balin a good knight — and by Nineve's own vengeful request, the dead Lady of the Lake had been wicked; but Nineve appears to have been a friend of Merlin himself, and a long tale of the other damsel's wickedness may have been Merlin's sagest way of taking attention off Nineve's wickedness and his own possible guilt by association with her. Moreover, when we look for the fulfillment of Merlin's prophecy that Balin would slay the damsel's brother with the sword, we find as about the only named candidates for her brother to be Sir Garlon and Sir Balan.

It is possible that Malvis was indeed the sister of both Balin and Balan; the fact that they did not recognize each other as siblings does not negate that chance, for the romances are full of such cases — one sibling leaves home while the other is still an infant, and so on (compare with Lancelot and Ector de

DISTANCES AND TRAVEL TIME

Thirty English miles could be covered in four days — see Vulgate VI, p. 262, where Lancelot and Ector, four days before Lancelot must be at Camelot to fight for the Queen, pass the night at Alphin castle, thirty English miles from Camelot. (I suspect, however, that at need, thirty English miles could be covered in a much shorter time than four days.)

Also according to the Vulgate [VI, p. 264], Arthur and his army reached Joyous Garde on the second day after leaving Camelot, after one overnight stop. The Vulgate, however, makes Camelot distinct from Winchester (in flat contradiction to Malory) and puts Joyous Garde on the Humber river (also in contradiction to Malory). Nevertheless, Camelot appears reasonably near Winchester even in the Vulgate. Thus, from the vicinity of Winchester to the Humber, the distance could be covered in less than two days. Even allowing for the fact that this may have been a forced march, such speed makes identification of one site by its distance according to days' travel from another exceedingly chancy.

Sir Persant's city was seven miles from Castle Dangerous. Gareth offered to be finished with Persant "within two hours after noon ... And then shall we come to the siege [of Castle Dangerous] by daylight." Gareth presumably meant that he would also have time to fight the besieging champion by daylight. The season was late spring or early summer — a few days after Whitsuntide so that the days would have been fairly long. As it turned out, Gareth and Lynette stopped for the night with Persant, but Gareth's statement may help indicate normal travelling time on horseback.

Six miles was considered a reasonable distance to travel to hear Mass. Presumably, travelling six miles for this purpose was permissible on a Saturday or Sunday, even though other travel was frowned upon on the Sabbath; Gawaine was once admonished by a friar for riding late on Saturday; the knight swore not to do so again unless it was unavoidable. [Vulgate IV, p. 148]

> Then ... on foot they yede [travelled] from Glastonbury to Almesbury, the which is little more than thirty mile. And thither they came within two days, for they were weak and feeble to go [Malory XXI, 11].

Normal travelling time on horseback from Georgia to

Maris, Gawaine and Gareth). It is also possible that the damsel's brother was one of the knights killed in battle against Ryons, Nero, and Lot, or that Malory omitted the death in question completely. It is even conceivable that Sir Lanceor was Malvis' brother, although Balin slew him with lance rather than sword. Garlon, however, seems the likeliest knight for the brother of Merlin's tale, and Garlon's patent villainy hardly tallies with Merlin's praise of the damsel's brother. Moreover, although the damsel's praise of Balin may have been a ruse to tickle his vanity and ensure that he would keep the sword, Malvis' subsequent efforts to get it back from him and prevent the coming tragedy sound sincere to me. Since I can find nothing more about this damsel, unless she is to be identified with one of Malory's other ladies, the question of her guilt or innocence may perhaps be considered open. [Malory II, 1-5]

MANASSEN

While escaping from Arthur after her attempt to destroy him and Uriens, Morgan le Fay found Sir Manassen bound and about to be drowned by another knight. Manassen was of Arthur's court, but he was also the cousin of Sir Accolon, Morgana's recently-killed paramour. For Accolon's sake, Morgana freed Manassen, let him drown his enemy, and directed him to tell Arthur how she had escaped him by turning herself and her knights into the likenesses of boulders, which errand Manassen carried out. [Malory IV, 15]

MARANT (Maranz, Martans)†

Son of the King of the Hundred Knights [Vulgate V].

KING MARBOAR (Marboac, Marboart, Narboat, etc.)

His territory was apparently on the way to Estrangor. One of his fortresses seems to have been the Castel del Molin. [Vulgate IV]

THE DAMSEL OF THE MARCHES†

Apparently a sovereign in her own right, this lady was a liege of Arthur's, who came to her aid when Duke Galeholt invaded her territory. [Vulgate III]

THE DAMSEL DES MARES†

The daughter of Sir Agravadain des Vaus de Galoire, she was the victim of what seems to have been either a practical joke or a venture by Merlin into planned genetics.

Five days after the visit of Ban and Merlin, a rich knight of the neighborhood asked for the Damsel's hand in marriage. She meekly but firmly refused, confessing at last that she was with child by King Ban. Sir Agravadain requested the young lover, whose name seems to have been Leriador, to wait for two years and then try again. Instead, Leriador besieged the castle and Agravadain had to beat him off. The Damsel seems to have remained unmarried after giving birth to her son, Sir Ector de Maris, who resembled his father, King Ban.

After Sir Agravadain's death, the castle was held by his son, Ector's uncle and the Damsel's brother. The Damsel seems never to have forgot her lover, for she always kept a sapphire ring he had given her. This ring had been given him by his wife, Elaine of Benwick, who kept another one like it. Years afterwards, the Damsel des Mares was able to prove to Lancelot that her son was his half-brother by means of this ring.

The damsel left her family's castle at least once, to travel to the Royal Minster in Gaul and meet Lancelot's mother, Queen Elaine. [Vulgate III]

MARGANOR†

The seneschal of the King of the Hundred Knights, Sir Marganor was vanquished by Sir Ector de Maris before the castle Lestroite Marche. [Vulgate III]

MARGAWSE, QUEEN OF LOTHIAN AND ORKNEY (Morawse, Bellicent)

One of the three daughters — seemingly the oldest — of Igraine and Gorlois, Margawse was wedded to King Lot at the same time that her mother was wedded to Uther Pendragon, her sister Elaine to King Nentres, and her other sister, Morgana, was put to school in a nunnery. By her husband, King Lot, Margawse became the mother of Gawaine, Agravaine, Gaheris, and Gareth, and by her half-brother Arthur she became the mother of Mordred.

Although her own husband was one of the chief rebels against Arthur, the Vulgate tells us that Margawse was a staunch supporter of the young High King, encouraging those of her sons who were old enough, especially Gawaine, to join Arthur's side. She herself rode down through dangerous territory to join Arthur's side in person, having several adventures on the way. Malory, however, insinuates that Lot sent his wife to Arthur's court as a spy.

New Orleans (550 miles) was 13½ days in the middle of the nineteenth century. A horse named Paddy, ridden by Sam Dale with a vital message, is cited for covering the distance in 7½ days, cutting six days from the normal travel time. On the other hand, in a feature article printed in the **Chicago Sun-Times**, April 12, 1978, Dennis Waite describes trying to hike from Llanberis, Wales, to the summit of Mount Snowden, three and a half miles on a dirt road. Waite's landlady claimed the walk was "two hours up and one hour back," but an English couple Waite's party met as the Americans finally turned back in discouragement said the walk, round-trip, took a full day. Obviously, time spent in travelling from place to place in the Arthurian landscape depends on type of terrain — forested, mountainous, and so on — as well as on type of locomotion (horse, mule, wagon, foot) and availability of roads (many of the old Roman roads, like the famous Watling Street, would naturally have been available to Arthurian travellers).

When it was necessary or desired, messengers and pursuivants could carry news quite rapidly — as we think of news as spreading in those days. Gareth defeated Ironside and raised the siege of Castle Dangerous shortly after Pentecost. There followed a

few extra adventures which must have taken up to a week. Arthur and Lyonors then decided to have a tournament at Castle Dangerous at Assumption, in mid-August.

> And so the cry was made in England, Wales, and Scotland, Ireland, Cornwall, and in all the Out Isles, and in Brittany and in many countries; that at the feast of our Lady the Assumption next coming, men should come to the Castle [Dangerous] beside the Isle of Avilion; ... And two months was to the day that the tournament should be.

Two months for the messengers to cover all that area and still leave the interested knights time to see to their preparations (though they seem to have kept ready for knightly adventure throughout the warm seasons) and travel to Lyonors' castle from those distant countries!

One further note: romance accounts of time spent in travel need not always be taken literally or seriously. Harris, commenting on a passage in Chrétien's **Yvain**, theorizes that Chrétien may have been poking fun at the speed of characters' travel in old romances. [Dell ed. of **Yvain**, New York, 1963, p. 151]

And thither came to [Arthur], King Lot's wife, of Orkney, in manner of a message, but she was sent thither to espy the court of King Arthur; and she came richly beseen, with her four sons, Gawaine, Gaheris, Agravaine, and Gareth [who must still have been a babe in arms], with many other knights and ladies. For she was a passing fair lady, therefore the king cast great love unto her, and desired to lie by her; so they were agreed ... So there she rested her a month, and at the last departed.

At this time, at least in Malory's account, she did not know Arthur was her half-brother. How she reacted to Arthur's seizure of her youngest born, Mordred, along with other lords' sons that were born at the same time, in order to destroy them, Malory does not record, though he does note it as Lot's motive for the second rebellion.

Her husband killed in this second rebellion, Margawse apparently remained north, governing Orkney and raising her youngest sons. When Gareth was old enough, she sent or allowed him to go to Arthur. After something more than a year, she followed him, arriving at Arthur's court while Gareth was absent on his first round of knightly adventures.

And as they sat at the meat, there came in the Queen of Orkney, with ladies and knights a great number. And then Sir Gawaine, Sir Agravaine, and Gaheris arose, and went to her and saluted her upon their knees, and asked her blessing; for in fifteen year they had not seen her.

She had somehow learned how Gareth had spent his first year at court.

Ah, brother, said the Queen unto King Arthur, and unto Sir Gawaine, and to all her sons, he did yourself great shame when ye amongst you kept my son in the kitchen and fed him like a poor hog. Fair sister, said King Arthur, ye shall right well wit I knew him not ... meseemeth ye might have done me to wit of his coming, and then an I had not done well to him ye might have blamed me. ... Sir, said the Queen of Orkney ... wit ye well that I sent him unto you right well armed and horsed, and worshipfully beseen of his body, and gold and silver plenty to spend. It may be, said the King, but thereof saw we none.

Margawse's relations with her brother and his court seem to have been cordial. Although by now middle-aged, she was still beautiful enough that Sir Lamorak, who became her paramour, was ready to defend her beauty against that of Guenever. Lamorak being the son of Pellinore, the man who had dealt King Lot his death wound, Margawse's new affair did not please her sons. She accepted their invitation to a castle near Camelot, and there she and her lover arranged a tryst. Her son Gaheris, watching his chance, came to their bedside and struck off her head. Learning it, "the king was passing wroth, and commanded him to go out of his court." [Malory I, 2, 19; VII. 25; IX, 13; X, 24; Vulgate II]

T. H. White (who transfers her murder to Agravaine) gives her at least enough grasp of sorcery to conjure Arthur into bed with her by enchantment. I do not recall finding any indication in Malory or in the Vulgate that Margawse was an enchantress; it has been suggested, however, that, although definitely two individual characters in the sources on which I have concentrated, Morgana and Margawse originally were the same character, and became split when some scribe got confused with the case endings of a language not his own (what we would do without clumsy scribes as handy explanations I do not know). Most modern romancers put the blame for Mordred's conception entirely upon Margawse, whom they usually make aware of the incest at the time — Stewart's popular version, which for some reason changes Margawse's own parentage to make her not a legitimate daughter of Igraine and Gorlois but a bastard of Uther, is particularly hard on her, stripping away even the shadow of self-justification for the act that other romancers allow her.

In my opinion, all this is part of the modern whitewashing of Arthur. (Notice that there is more suggestion of underlying affection than of smoldering hatred and resentment when brother and sister bicker about Gareth, as Malory records the scene.) Tennyson, unable to charge his Arthur with incest, or even adultery, on any pretext whatever, named the wife of Lot and the mother of Gawaine, Gareth, and Mordred Bellicent, perhaps to avoid any identification of her with the lusty and accidentally incestuous (but also spirited and generous) Margawse.

MARGONDES†

A leader of the Sesnes, involved in the attack on Vandaliors castle early in Arthur's reign. [Vulgate II]

KING MARHALT OF IRELAND

Malory gives four names for Irish kings. Two, Agwisance and Anguish, I believe to be variants of a single name and to refer to the same man. The third Irish king is Ryons (Rience), also king of Norgales, etc. The fourth is Marhalt.

Marhalt was the father of Sir Marhaus, and thus the father-in-law of King Anguish, who married Marhaus' sister. The king is mentioned in Malory X, 66, fighting in the Lonazep tournament, but most of the time he remains in the background, perhaps busily governing his territory.

MARHAUS (Morolt, etc.)

This Irish knight, the son of King Marhalt, brother-in-law of King Anguish and uncle of La Beale Isoud, was one of the most promising of the first generation of Arthur's knights, playing a substantial role in the early part of Malory's book. Gawaine and Ywaine, having left court after Morgana's attack on Arthur and Uriens, found a white shield which Marhaus had left hung to a tree, and twelve damsels defiling it on the grounds that its owner "hateth all ladies and gentlewomen." Marhaus returned, driving the damsels back into their tower and slaying the two knights of that tower in joust; he then recovered the muddied shield, telling it, "... for her love that gave me this white shield I shall wear thee." He now jousted in friendly adventure with Gawaine. Whereas Gawaine's strength increased at noon and then gradually declined until evening, Marhaus became stronger and stronger as evening drew on; thus, Marhaus defeated Gawaine. He explained that the twelve damsels who had defiled his shield were false enchantresses, but "to all good ladies and gentlewomen I owe my service as a knight ought to do." Marhaus swore friendship with Gawaine and Ywaine and the three traveled together until, in Arroy, they met the damsels Printemps, Été, and Automne. Marhaus chose Ete and went adventuring with her for a year.

Coming to the castle of the Duke of the South Marches, Marhaus introduced himself — perhaps a little prematurely — as a knight of King Arthur's and member of the Table Round. The Duke had sworn vengeance on that company because of Gawaine's slaying seven of his sons in battle, so he regretfully insisted that Marhaus encounter him and his remaining six sons. Marhaus defeated them all and converted them to Arthur's party. The damsel brought him next to a tournament cried by the Lady de Vawse, where he "had sometime down forty knights," and so won the prize, a gold circlet worth a thousand besants. Within a week, his damsel brought him to the territory of young Earl Fergus, where Marhaus slew the troublesome giant Taulurd. On his way back to his year's-end rendezvous with Gawaine and Ywaine, he met and smote down four other knights of Arthur's court, Sagramore le Desirous, Osanna, Dodinas le Savage, and Felot of Listinoise. Rejoining Gawaine and Ywaine, he returned with them to Arthur's court, where he "was named one of the best knights living" and enrolled in the Round Table at the same time as Sir Pelleas. During Arthur's war with Lucius, Marhaus joined Lancelot, Bors, Kay, and Marrok as one of the King's personal bodyguard. He was among the knights rescued by Lancelot from Sir Turquine.

Unfortunately, when King Mark decided to stop paying truage to King Anguish of Ireland, Marhaus fought as his brother-in-law's champion. Mark's champion was the newly-knighted, untried Tristram. Marhaus suggested, in kindly fashion, that the young knight abandon a battle he had no apparent hope of winning, but Tristram insisted on fighting.

> Thus they fought still more than half a day, and ... Sir Tristram ... [at the last] smote Sir Marhaus upon the helm such a buffet that it went through his helm, and through the coif of steel, and through the brain-pan, and the sword stuck so fast in the helm and in his brain-pan that Sir Tristram pulled thrice at his sword or ever he might pull it out from his head; and there Marhaus fell down on his knees, and the edge of Tristram's sword left in his brain-pan. And suddenly Sir Marhaus rose grovelling, and threw his sword and his shield from him, and so ran to his ships and fled his way ... [to Tristram's shouts of] Ah! Sir Knight of the Round Table, why withdrawest thou thee? ... rather than I should withdraw me from thee, I had rather be hewn in an hundred pieces. Sir Marhaus answered no word but yede his way sore groaning.

Leaving his sword and shield for Tristram to appropriate, Marhaus regained his ship and was taken back to Ireland, where he died, despite all the efforts of Anguish's servants, of the piece of Tristram's sword stuck in his skull. It argues in favor of his great strength that he was able to run away at all and survive as long as he did. He almost had a Pyrrhic victory, however, for he had wounded Tristram with a poisoned spear. In a final twist of irony, when Tristram became a knight of the Round Table, his name appeared on the chair formerly occupied by Marhaus.

Marhaus' behavior in his final battle seems strange — why should such a noble champion have poisoned his spearhead? In other versions of **Tristram**, the Irish king's champion is presented as a rather less sympathetic figure from the outset, and my guess is that Malory either identified two originally distinct characters or created a nobler early history for Marhaus, but needed the poisoned spear-wound to get Tristram to Ireland, so carried it over from other versions. Or perhaps Marhaus' defeat by Sir Turquine had made him over-cautious. In any case, it is a sign of Malory's storytelling skill and lasting power that he so arranged Tristram's maiden battle as to extend the reader's sympathy to both champions. [Malory IV, 17-19, 24-25, 28; V, 8; VI, 9; VIII, 4-8; X, 6]

Mariales† – see under GALVOIE, *Places*

Mariagart (Mangars li Rois, Margarit le Roux, Marigart le Rox)† – see under GUINDOEL, *Places*

KING MARK OF CORNWALL

In Malory, the husband of La Beale Isoud and the uncle of Sir Tristram is generally painted as a scoundrel, capable of almost any ruse or treachery, both by violence — when he had the strength and advantage — and by craft, even to forging letters purportedly from the Pope, ostensibly commanding Mark himself to go on crusade, this being a ploy to put down rebellion in his own neighborhood and get Tristram away to the Holy Land. Mark's behavior toward his nephew Tristram, the son of his sister Elizabeth, is notorious — he alternately begged Tristram's help against enemies and tried to get Tristram killed or out of the country. (Shades of Saul and David! Of course, Mark did have some grounds for complaint against Tristram because of La Beale Isoud.)

Mark was "a fair speaker, and false thereunder." Lancelot called him King Fox, and it was a long time before he was compelled to swear fealty to Arthur. The knights Mark killed, both Arthur's men and his own (in rage, etc.) and presumably knights-errant and knights of other courts as well, may equal or outnumber the victims of Breuse Sans Pitie. Among Mark's victim's was his own brother, Prince Boudwin, whose popularity and success in battle Mark envied. By the murder of Boudwin, he gained the enmity of his nephew, Alisander le Orphelin; Mark eventually managed to get Alisander killed, but Alisander's son Bellangere le Beuse finally avenged Boudwin and Alisander (and, incidentally, Mark's most famous victim, Tristram), presumably by dealing Mark his well-deserved death.

Like Arthur, Mark on occasion sallied forth dressed as an ordinary knight, keeping his true identity secret — especially if he heard his companions-for-the-nonce talking against Mark of Cornwall. Faced with combat, Mark often turned poltroon — though at least once he defended himself competently in trial by combat, winning even though he was in the wrong. (Malory comments that Mark won by chance, but at least Mark had sufficient honor to show up at the battleground, having given his word to do so. See Amant.) For all his villainy, Mark fails to become a commanding figure, frequently seeming more of a butt and buffoon.

Very curiously, it was Mark who, finding Sir Lanceor and Lady Colombe dead, stopped to bury them and erect a rich tomb above them, apparently for no other motivation than kindliness and pity. In other versions of **Tristram**, earlier as well as later, Mark is shown as a more sympathetic, or at least less malicious character. Perhaps Malory put so much emphasis on Tristram and integrated his saga so thoroughly with Arthur's in order to play up the parallel between the

KING MARK'S FAMILY AND RETAINERS
Wife: La Beale Isoud
Brother: Prince Boudwin
Sister: Queen Elizabeth of Lyonesse
Brother-in-Law: King Meliodas
Sister-in-Law: Anglides
Bastard son: Meraugis de Porlesquez
Nephews: Tristram (by Elizabeth, Alisander le Orphelin (by Boudwin)
Grand-Nephew (by Alisander): Bellengerus le Beuse
Kinsman (unspecified): Dinas
Seneschal: Dinas
Retainers: Andred (also Mark's nephew?), Amant, Bersules, Sadok, Lady Leech?
Ally?: Morgan le Fay

two great love triangles: Arthur-Guenever-Lancelot and Mark-Isold-Tristram. And, having done so, Malory might have been constrained to make Mark as bad as possible in order to present a contrast with the comparatively good Arthur. [Malory II, 7-8; VIII, 1, 4-32; IX, 19; X, 8-15, 22, 26, 32-35, 50-51; XIX, 11]

MARROK

I find Sir Marrok mentioned only twice in Malory, once as one of Arthur's personal bodyguard (along with the notable knights Lancelot, Bors, Kay, and Marhaus) in the war with Emperor Lucius. The second reference, however, where Marrok appears among the Round Table knights who try to heal Sir Urre, is the interesting one: "Sir Marrok, the good knight that was betrayed with his wife, for she made him seven year a wer-wolf." [Malory V, 8; XIX, 11]

I believe Marrok must be a werewolf knight whom I encountered years ago, in the retelling of an old tale which I later learned was apparently one of Marie de France's.

This knight's wife pestered him to know where he went when he left her for several days and nights of every week. At last he confessed that, through no fault of his own, he was a werewolf — here, simply a man who turns into a wolf of normal appearance and, in this form, is identical in body to natural wolves and no more dangerous — probably less dangerous — to humans than they. He had to leave his clothes in a special hiding-place when he became a wolf, for if he did not have them to put on again when his wolf-time was up, he would not be able to change back into a man. This pleased his wife, who loved another knight better. She stole her husband's clothes, and he had to remain a wolf full-time for seven years. Then one day the King came hunting. The wolf seemed to appeal to him for clemency, acting like a dog or, almost, like a human. Struck with the animal's behavior, the King forbade it to be killed and had it taken back to court instead. The wolf was gentle to all humans, except two: whenever he saw his wife or her lover, he went for them savagely. This aroused the King's suspicions, and he questioned wife and lover until he had a full confession of what the woman had done and where she had hidden her husband's clothes. (I believe the wife and the lover were then executed, but cannot remember for sure.) The King and his barons recovered the clothes and laid them out on a bed in front of the wolf, but the wolf only looked at them. "He's been a wolf too long," said some of the barons, "He can no longer change back." But the King realized that the wolf would naturally be reticent about changing back in full view of a sizeable audience, so he took all the men out of the chamber and had the door closed. When, about an hour later, they ventured in again, they found the knight, fully dressed, lying asleep on the bed.

KING MARSIL OF POMITAIN

"King Marsil, that had in gift an island of Sir Galahalt [Galeholt] the haut prince; and this island had the name Pomitain." This, apparently Malory's only reference to King Marsil, comes when he is defeated by King Bagdemagus during Duke Galeholt's tournament in Surluse. [Malory X, 44]

Maten† — see under BLANCHE ESPINE, *Places*

MATTO LE BREUNE

Ah, said King Mark, that is Sir Matto le Breune, that fell out of his wit because he lost his lady; for when Sir Gaheris smote down Sir Matto and won his lady of him, never since was he in his mind, and that was pity, for he was a good knight. [Malory IX, 19]

As it happens, King Mark has here mistaken Dagonet's account of a crazed Tristram for Sir Matto; but from this tantalizing reference, which seems to be Malory's only mention of Sir Matto, we can at least infer that he was probably a Cornish knight and running around wild in the forests in that part of the country.

MAUDUIT†

One country, possibly in or near Cornwall (that part of the island being noted for them) was infested with giants. Arthur killed them all except a giantess and her baby son, whom he gave, along with the land, to a knight who asked for them. The baby giant was Mauduit. At fourteen, he was larger than a grown man. At fifteen, he was knighted by his foster-father. Later, he killed his parents in a fit of rage and began terrorizing the countryside. Finally he fell in love, but the lady accepted him only on condition that he swear to amend and not to leave his castle. He hung his arms in a pavilion, hoping some knight would take them and thus give him an excuse to leave his castle. The people charged twelve damsels to guard Mauduit's arms.

Ywaine came along and found an old woman beating a dwarf. At first she said she would stop if Ywaine kissed her, but then she amended the condition and made him take down Mauduit's helmet, sword, and shield. She tied the helmet and sword to the tail of her horse and made Ywaine carry the shield. Then she rode away, while the dwarf and the twelve damsels grieved. Ywaine had innocently given Mauduit the excuse to leave his castle.

Ywaine only learned the story later, from a hermit of the country. Ywaine fought and conquered a knight named Triadan and told him to go to the giant with the message that Ywaine alone was responsible and the people of the country should be spared. Mauduit's answer was to cut off Triadan's hand and go on a spree of indiscriminate slaughter. Some of the people captured Ywaine and imprisoned him in the Castel del Trespas to await Mauduit's coming. Here Lancelot, Bors, Gareth and Bagdemagus found their comrade. Bors insisted on carrying Mauduit's shield and fighting the giant. Bors, of course, won and killed Mauduit. [Vulgate V]

MEDELANT†

Apparently either a leader of the Sesnes or a king allied with them, involved in the attack on Vandaliors castle early in Arthur's reign [Vulgate II].

Medraut — see MORDRED

MELEHAN†

One of Mordred's two sons, probably the oldest. After Mordred's death, Melehan and his unnamed brother seized England. In a battle with Lancelot's men on the plain of Winchester, Melehan killed Lionel but was then killed by Bors, while Lancelot slew Mordred's other son. [Vulgate VI]

MELIAGRANT (Meliaganus, Meliagance, Meliagraunce, Meleagant, etc.)

Vulgate IV characterizes him as a proud and evil-disposed man who considered himself Lancelot's equal. Despite his faults, Meliagrant became a member of the Round Table, perhaps by virtue of being King Bagdemagus' son. He was among the knights who came with Arthur to Dame Lyonors' tournament at Castle Dangerous, where he "brake a spear upon Sir Gareth mightily and knightly." He is also recorded as fighting in Duke Galeholt's Surluse tournament, where his father Bagdemagus enlisted one Sir Sauseise to try to beat him so as to get him off the field in comparative safety.

Meliagrant's downfall was his love for Guenever. Once, during the high days of Tristram's career, Meliagrant entered a battle with his brother of the Round Table, Lamorak, over which was the lovelier queen, Guenever or Margawse. The quarrel was happily ended by the cool reasoning of Sir Bleoberis, who happened upon the scene with Lancelot; but Meliagrant "was a good man and of great might," and put up a fairly good defence against Lamorak while it lasted.

Finally his passion led Meliagrant into outright villainy. He ambushed the Queen and a small party of ladies, unarmed knights, squires, and yeomen while they were out a-Maying. After wounding several of Guenever's knights, Meliagrant and his men took the Queen and all their other prisoners to Meliagrant's castle, but one child, at the Queen's behest, managed to escape and tell Lancelot. When Lancelot started after the abductor, some of Meliagrant's archers waited in hiding and shot the great knight's horse out from under him, so that he had to finish his journey in a cart. (This is one origin of the "Knight in the Cart" appellation.) Meliagrant yielded to the Queen, begging mercy, rather than fight Lancelot on the latter's arrival, and the whole group remained overnight in the castle. Lancelot, deciding to spend the night with the Queen, wounded his hands tearing out the window bars to reach her bed. In the morning, Meliagrant rather rudely opened the Queen's bedcurtains to find out why she was sleeping so late, and found blood on the sheet and pillow. On this evidence, he accused her of adultery with one or more of the wounded knights. To prevent Lancelot from defending her in the trial by combat, Meliagrant set another trap.

> Then Sir Meliagrance said to Sir Launcelot: Pleaseth it you to see the estures of this castle? ... And then they went together from chamber to chamber ... So it befell upon Sir Launcelot that no peril dread, as he went with Sir Meliagraunce he trod on a trap and the board rolled, and there Sir Launcelot fell down more than ten fathom into a cave full of straw

The damsel who acted as Lancelot's gaoler freed him in return for a kiss on the scheduled day of combat. When the fight went against Meliagrant, he tried to yield. Lancelot, seeing that the Queen wished her enemy slain, insisted on fighting to the utterance; but Meliagrant refused to rise and fight again until Lancelot offered to fight with his head and the left quarter of his body unarmed and his left hand bound behind him. Even this handicap did not help Meliagrant — Lancelot lost no time cleaving his head in two. [Malory VII, 27-28; IX, 12-13; X, 41; XIX, 1-9]

Malory puts the story of how Meliagrant abducted the Queen near the end of his work. The Vulgate puts it earlier, stretches it out and makes more of it, and differs in many details, as in the role played by Kay; but the outlines are pretty much the same. In the Vulgate, Lancelot dreads the duty of telling Bagdemagus of his son's death, but his fear is needless, for Bagdemagus, being a just man, takes it well.

See also King Bagdemagus' Daughters.

Meliagrant's Stepsister – see KING BAGDEMAGUS' DAUGHTERS

MELIAS DE LILE

Son of the King of Denmark, Melias entered the Grail Quest as squire to King Bagdemagus, but left him at the White Abbey and went with Galahad instead. After requesting and receiving knighthood at Galahad's hands, Melias said,

> ... sithen ye have made me a knight ye must of right grant me my first desire that is reasonable ... suffer me to ride with you in this quest of the Sangreal, till that some adventure depart us.

The adventure came in about a week, when they arrived at a crossroads where was a sign warning any but good men and worthy knights from taking the road to the left, because "if thou go on the left hand thou shalt not lightly there win prowess, for thou shalt in this way be soon assayed." Melias begged of Galahad to let him take the left road. He failed the test, for when he came to a " lodge of boughs ... wherein was a crown of gold," he appropriated the crown. At once another knight came and smote him down, took back the crown, and left him there until Galahad came and rescued him. Galahad brought the grievously wounded Melias to an old monk and waited three days until it became apparent that Melias would survive. The monk explained to Melias that in following the left-hand road he had acted in pride and presumption, and by taking the crown he had sinned "in covetise and in theft."

Purged, we may hope, of his excess pride, Melias became a knight of the Round Table. He went with Lancelot into exile and was made Earl of Tursaud. [Malory XIII, 9-14; XIX, 11; XX, 18]

KING MELIODAS OF LYONESSE

Tristram's father (according to Malory) was brother-in-law to both Mark of Cornwall and Howell of Brittany. Meliodas' imprisonment by an amorous enchantress caused the death of his first wife, Mark's sister Elizabeth, who gave birth suddenly to Tristram while searching the woods for her husband and then died of cold and exposure. Merlin released Meliodas from the enchantress on the morning after Elizabeth's death. "But the sorrow that the king made for his queen that might no tongue tell." After seven years of widowerhood, Meliodas married a daughter of Howell of Brittany — presumably an older sister of Isoud la Blanche Mains — who gave him more children. This second queen decided to get rid of Tristram so that her own offspring would inherit Lyonesse. Her first attempt to poison Tristram ended in the death of her own son, who drank the poison by mistake. She tried again, and this time Meliodas himself almost drank the poison. When she snatched it from him, he grew suspicious and, by threatening her at sword point, made her confess all. He would have burned her, but Tristram himself pleaded for her life and "made the king and her accorded. But then the king would not suffer young Tristram to abide no longer in his court," and sent him into France (perhaps to Howell's court?) under the tutorship of Gouvernail. After seven years, Tristram came home again, already well accomplished, and stayed until the age of eighteen years.

And then the King Meliodas had great joy of Sir Tristram, and so had the queen, his wife. For ever after ... because Sir Tristram saved her from the fire, she did never hate him more after, but loved him ever after, and gave Tristram many great gifts

When Meliodas' court received news of Sir Marhaus' impending battle with Mark's champion — providing Mark could find one — to settle the truage question with the Irish king. Tristram begged his father to let him go to his uncle, be made knight at Mark's hands, and fight as his champion. After cautioning his son of Marhaus' might, Meliodas agreed. "I will well, said King Meliodas, that ye be ruled as your courage will rule you." These would seem to be Meliodas' last words to his famous son; presumably he died a natural death while Tristram was on his adventures. [Malory VIII, 1-5]

MELIOT DE LOGRES

After rescuing Nimue from Hontzlake, King Pellinore met her cousin, Sir Meliot of Logurs, and his "sworn brother," Sir Brian of the Isles. Meliot was happy to see his cousin in such good hands as Pellinore's. At this time, Meliot does not seem to have been a knight of Arthur's court, but he later became a companion of the Round Table. He had earned this distinction by the time he fought and killed Sir Gilbert the Bastard, being grievously wounded himself in the process, so that Lancelot had to brave the Chapel Perilous to get the cloth needed to heal him. Meliot is named as having fought in the Winchester tournament and as trying to heal Sir Urre. He was among those knights who went with Mordred and Agravaine to trap Lancelot with the Queen, and were thus killed by the escaping Lancelot. [Malory III, 13; VI, 14-15; XVIII, 11; XIX, 11; XX, 2-4]

MERAUGIS DE PORLESQUEZ†

A natural son of King Mark [Vulgate VII].

MERLAN LE DYABLE†

In earlier life called Merlan le Simple, he acquired the sobriquet "le dyable" ("the devil") after his coronation because he turned out to be a real rotter, cruel and treacherous. He hanged his own father on an oak in the forest. (Apparently it was Carteloise, the forest of the stag and four lions; Merlan's kingdom seems to have been somewhere in southern Scotland or northern Logres.) He was eventually killed when he insisted on fighting Lancelot before granting him hospitality in his pavilion. Although Lancelot only learned it after killing the petty monarch, he had done the country a good turn. [Vulgate V]

MERLIN

T. H. White loves him. So do Mary Stewart and Vera Chapman. Tennyson seems to admire him greatly. E. Marshall, B. F. Johnson, John Gloag, the makers of "Mr. Magoo's" version of King Arthur, and, indeed, almost all modern roman-

cers, except Mark Twain, seem to regard the old mage with varying degrees of affection, liking, and sometimes awe; and most of them are able to communicate their devotion to their readers. While reading White or Chapman, I love Merlin too. But the more I read of the medieval versions — Malory and the Vulgate — the less I understand where all these modern writers found a mage to inspire their devotion. My own personal dislike for Merlin, which probably exceeds even Mark Twain's — and which applies only to the Malorian mage, not to the Myrddin of older lore, should be taken into account by readers of these notes.

According to a tradition not found in Malory, but very likely familiar to Malory's readers, Merlin was engendered, despite all precautions, by a fiend on a woman who had been trying to remain pure. At her trial, the infant Merlin himself revealed who was his father and made a few other prophecies and revelations, at least one of them rather embarrassing to the judges. [Vulgate II] Even in Malory's account, Merlin is occasionally called a devil's son, and now and then a medieval romancer throws in a comment to the effect that, although usually regarded as beneficent, Merlin is really evil. (To use a modern and not, perhaps, strictly applicable parallel, would you trust Rosemary's baby as chief advisor to the President?) In all fairness, however, I must point out a remark in Vulgate II that, while Merlin owed his knowledge of the past to the Devil, he owed his knowledge of the future to the Lord. Again, Vulgate II tells us that Merlin never laid his hands upon anyone, though with his power, he hardly needed to be physical! Vulgate II contains a statement that he was "treacherous and disloyal by nature" and mentions a stone at which he slew two other enchanters.

During Merlin's childhood, King Vortigern arrested him, planning to cement a new tower with his blood. Young Merlin coolly saved himself by his accurate revelations (see Vertiger's Tower, *Places*). Merlin then left to study magic from Blaise, while Vortigern went on to be killed by the sons of Constans, as per Merlin's prophecy.

Outstripping his master in necromantic learning, Merlin swore never to do Blaise harm and asked him to write a book. Blaise retired into the forest of Northumberland to write down the doings of his former student. Here Merlin used to visit him from time to time.

When Constans' son, King Pandragon, was killed by the Sesnes, Merlin brought the stones of Stonehenge from Ireland to serve as his tomb. Merlin then became advisor to the new king, Pandragon's brother Uther, now surnamed Pendragon in honor of the late king. To Uther Merlin revealed the mysteries of the two holy tables — the one Christ and His disciples used at the Last Supper and the one Joseph of Arimathea and his followers set up when they came to Britain. Merlin erected the third great table, the Round Table, for Uther at Cardoel in Wales (from where it passed into the keeping of Leodegrance and thence to Arthur).

HOLDING COURT

When Uther Pendragon held court, the clerks would not allow any knight to take his seat unless he had a face wound. This custom was discontinued in Arthur's time, when Lancelot, Duke Galeholt, and Ector de Maris became companions of the Round Table; but it was replaced by the custom that no companion could take his seat on high festivals unless he had conquered a knight the week before. Ywaine, at least, found the custom irksome. [Vulgate V] So, most likely, did Kay and other knights.

Also, at the first court Arthur held after his marriage, on the fifteenth of August (Assumption), he made his famous vow never to sit down to dinner until some adventure was reported to him. [Vulgate II, p. 319-320]

Arthur held five courts annually at which he wore his crown: at the feasts of Easter, Ascension, Whitsuntide (Pentecost), All Saints, and Christmas. Easter was the highest festival, Whitsuntide — the renewal of Easter joy — the most joyful. [Vulgate III, p. 107-108]

Uter conceiving a lust for the duchess Igraine of Tintagil, Merlin played his pander, magically giving Uter the appearance of the lady's husband Gorloïs, so that she lay with him unsuspecting. After the apparently coincidental death of Gorloïs, Uter married Igraine.

> Soon came Merlin unto the king, and said, Sir, ye must purvey you for the nourishing of your child. As thou wilt, said the king, be it. Well, said Merlin, I know a lord of yours in this land ... and he shall have the nourishing of your child, and his name is Sir Ector ... let him be sent for, for to come and speak with you ... And when the child is born let it be delivered to me at yonder privy postern unchristened ... Then when the lady was delivered, the king commanded two knights and two ladies to take the child, bound in a cloth of gold, and that ye deliver him to what poor man ye meet at the postern gate of the castle. So the child was delivered unto Merlin.

Those modern romancers who stick to some recognizable variant of this episode have exercised considerable ingenuity to explain Merlin's motives for taking Arthur and giving him to Ector with so much secrecy — not even Igraine was told where her child was taken. Tennyson came up with the most plausible explanation I've yet encountered, but he had to kill off Uter on the same night of Arthur's birth to do it.

Returning to Malory, I cannot help but wonder why and how it should have been for the good of Arthur and the kingdom to raise the heir in such secrecy. Uter married Igraine so soon after Gorloïs' death that by the rules of the milieu Arthur should have been recognized easily as Uter's legal son and heir; at any rate, the whole explanation was accepted by enough of the kingdom to give Arthur a following when Merlin finally gave it years later; why should it not have been equally well accepted at once? Malory's Uter survived for at least two years after Arthur's birth, and after his death his widow seems to have been left unmolested, even though the realm was thrown into confusion for lack of a visible heir. If there had been a visible heir, a son known to be of Uter's marriage, would the child really have run a great risk of assassination, surrounded as he would have been by barons? Would not Igraine or some strong baron simply have been named regent until his majority? Merlin arranged the famous test of the Sword in the Stone and had Arthur crowned king on the strength of this test alone, and the sentiment of the "commons ... both rich and poor."

Under such circumstances, how blameworthy were those rebel kings and barons who refused to yield their allegiance at once to an unknown, unproven youth, the protégé of a devil's son? True, when the rebels gave Arthur their challenge, Merlin made them a bald statement, with no supporting evidence, of Arthur's birth; it seems hardly surprising that "some of them laughed him to scorn, as King Lot; and more other called him a witch." Nor had Merlin yet told Arthur himself of his parentage, which omission resulted in the incestuous begetting of Mordred on Margawse. Not until after the battle of Bedegraine — a slaughter so bloody it seems to have disgusted Merlin him-

self, who had helped engineer Arthur's victory by bringing the army of Ban and Bors swiftly and secretly to the place — did Merlin reveal Arthur's parentage, with some supporting evidence, to Arthur and the assembled court, in a scene that suggests a practical joke played by Merlin on Igraine to give her an additional moment of grief before restoring her to her son. In this scene Sir Ulfius, a former knight of Uter's and his companion in the abduction of Igraine at Tintagil, as well as Merlin's seeming accomplice (though perhaps unaware) in the "joke" on Igraine, himself stated that "Merlin is more to blame than" Igraine for the wars of rebellion. Perhaps the key to why Merlin wished to arrange Arthur's upbringing lies in the word "unchristened." Was Arthur ever christened, or did Ector, on receiving him, assume that Uter had seen to that point? It seems heretical to suggest it, but did Merlin wish to make of Arthur his own pawn and tool?

Merlin did considerable traveling on the Continent, most of it, one supposes, during the years when Sir Ector was raising Arthur (although some of it may also have been in the years between Vortigern's death and Pandragon's). One of his continental adventures may be found under Avenable. Surprisingly, Merlin also dabbled in Christian missionary work, converting King Flualis of Jerusalem and his wife; this royal couple had four daughters, who in turn had 55 sons, all good knights, and these went forth to convert the heathen; some of them reached Arthur's court. It may also have been during this period that Merlin met Viviane, fell in love with her and taught her his crafts in return for the promise of her love.

It would be difficult and tedious to list every deed and prophecy of Merlin's; one does not envy Blaise his task. The Great Necromancer could prophesy anything — though fairly early in his career, before Arthur's birth, he decided to phrase his prophecies in obscure terms. He could apparently do anything within the scope of necromancy, except break the spell that was his own downfall. He must have made rather a pest of himself with his disguises, popping up as toddler, beggar, blind minstrel, stag, and so on, and so on, usually for no apparent reason. Indeed he seems to have had the temperament of a practical joker. Some of his prophecies may well have been more mischievous than useful. He entered the battlefield with Arthur and his armies, and does seem to have given them invaluable help, but one of Merlin's pastimes in battle was moving around the field and telling the King and his knights, every time they took a short break from doing really tremendous deeds of arms and valor, what cowards they were and how disgracefully they were carrying on. (Maybe that was Merlin's style of cheerleading.)

Merlin may not have counselled Arthur to destroy the May babies, Herod-like, but he certainly sowed the seed of that sin by telling Arthur that one of these babies would be the King's destruction, and he appears not to have lifted his voice against the mass slaughter. In all fairness, we must remember that he did warn Arthur against marrying Guen-

---

At the Pentecost court of Galahad's arrival, the Queen and her ladies appear to be dining apart from the King and his men. Other scenes, however, show men and women as dining together, those of highest rank taking the highest seats on the dais. (See, for instance, **Sir Gawaine and the Green Knight**.) Serving at table seems to have been an honor — sometimes, at least, for the servers as well as those served. Clearly, the higher-ranking were those who served you, the more were you honored — on the Pentecost of the Grail, Malory records that young knights (probably as opposed to squires or pages) served at table [XIII,

3]; when Arthur feasted Kings Ban and Bors at All Hallowmass, near the beginning of his reign, Sir Kay the seneschal, Sir Lucas the butler, and Sir Griflet served, or at least "had the rule of all the service that served the kings" [I, 10]; according to Vulgate IV, four kings and other high barons served at Arthur's table on the Pentecost of Galahad's arrival (perhaps Malory's serving knights served at the lesser tables). In the tale of Gareth Beaumains, the various knights he has conquered during his adventures show up and as honors beg to serve as his chief butler, sewer-chief, wine-server, and so on at the feast.

ever, foretelling her affair with Lancelot, and Arthur ignored his advice in that instance. (But did Merlin thus implant the suspicion that finally irrupted in Arthur's vengeful rage?) Merlin engineered Arthur's acquisition of Excalibur, sword and sheath, but in this the mage apparently acted in unison with Malory's first British Lady of the Lake, who was later revealed, by the sincere though unfortunate Balin le Savage, to have been very wicked; it is noticeable that Merlin, when he learned of Balin's accusation, did not defend his slain cohort by denying the charge, nor rail against Balin for killing her, but only replied with a countercharge against the damsel Malvis.

For all his foresight, Merlin had a habit of arriving just a little too late to do the most good. We know he was capable of very rapid travel, yet he let Balin lie beneath the ruins of Pellam's castle for three days before coming to rescue him, by which time Balin's damsel (Sir Herlews' lady) was dead. Later he showed up the morning after the deaths of Balin and Balan, just in time to write their names on their tomb. He delivered King Meliodas of Lyonesse from the enchantress' prison the morning after the death of Meliodas' wife — had Merlin arrived a few days earlier, the brave and devoted Elizabeth would not have died.

Although from the above Merlin would appear something of a misogynist, he could hardly have been insensitive to a beautiful face. He did not spend all his time at Arthur's court, and during one of his absences he taught Morgan le Fay necromancy in Bedingran. He later instructed Nimue in the art, when she came to court, and it was she who finally rid the world of him. (In my opinion, Nimue did the world a favor.) At various times, Bagdemagus and Gawaine passed near his tomb and spoke with him; perhaps others did as well. Gawaine seems to have been the last to hear his voice (this incident is recorded under Byanne).

Malory puts the place of Merlin's imprisonment under a stone in Cornwall. I continue to find it unconvincing that the mighty Merlin could not free himself from a spell woven by one of his own students. Other, older versions of the tale have Nimue (or Viviane) retiring Merlin through affection, giving him a retreat of comfort and cheer. It is interesting that White, who loves Merlin and makes him endearing, puts him in cozy retirement in a tumulus on Bodmin Moor, Cornwall, although Nimue is not in evidence to share his society (**The Book of Merlyn**). Perhaps Merlin requested Nimue to take over the mentorship of Arthur's court for him; she does appear from time to time in this role throughout much of Malory's work. [Vulgate, chiefly vols. II & III; Malory I, 1-3, 8-25; II, 4, 8-10, 16, 19; III, 1-2; IV, 1, 5; VIII, 2; XIV, 2]

In Vulgate VII, I found what appeared to be a prophecy that either Perceval or Galahad was to rescue Merlin after achieving the Grail, but nowhere else did I uncover a hint of any such deed.

Glennie calls Merlin, with Taliessin, Llywarch Hen, and Aneurin, one of the four great bards of the Arthurian Age. I have no reason to doubt this is any other Merlin than the necromancer. It was also in Glennie's book that I found the tantalizing reference to Merlin's twin sister, Ganieda.

MILES OF THE LAUNDS

This promising young knight was treacherously slain by Sir Loraine le Savage while on his way to Arthur's court with his lady, Eleine, King Pellinore's daughter. When her lover died, Eleine slew herself with his sword. [Malory III, 12, 15]

DUKE MINADORAS†

He was King Pellam's seneschal. The name is from Vulgate VII, which also, however, gives Sir Claellus as Pellam's seneschal.

MINADUS†

A Sesnes leader, involved in the Vandaliors castle attack. He fathered Oriels, and had a nephew, Herlant. [Vulgate II]

Modred — see MORDRED

SAINT MONENNA (Dareca)†

Saint Monenna, or Dareca, of Kilslleibeculean, Ulster, founded a church and nunnery on Dunpeledur (Edinburgh, Scotland). Glennie suggests a connection with the Castle of Maidens at Edinburgh. The saint died in 518. I assume Monenna was a woman; the "a" ending is not infallible (cf. Columba), but it was a nunnery that Monenna founded.

KING MORDRAINS (Evelake)

King Evelake, or Evelac, was a pagan contemporary of Joseph of Arimathea. Joseph converted him and his brother-in-law Nascien, with their families. Evelake, now bearing the baptismal name of Mordrains, came with Joseph to Britain. Despite a warning voice, Mordrains tried to see the Grail, and, not being quite good enough, was blinded and paralyzed for the attempt. Meekly accepting his punishment, he prayed to be allowed to live to see Galahad. A voice, heard only by Mordrains, Nascien, Joseph, and Josephe, promised him this favor, adding that he would be healed when Galahad visited him. He waited several centuries, praying in a monastery, for Galahad to come. Upon being healed at last by Galahad, Mordrains enjoyed a holy death. [Vulgate, chiefly I & VI; Malory XIII, 10; XIV, 4; XVII, 4,18]

The fact that Evelake and Mordrains are the same man is not apparent in Malory, and there is one passage — XVII, 4 — in which I strongly suspect Malory or his editor confused the names of Nascien and Mordrains.

MORDRED (Modred, Mordret, Medraut, etc.)

At Carlion, shortly after the battle of Bedegraine and before his marriage with Guenever, Arthur engendered Mordred in conscious adultery and unconscious incest upon his visiting half-sister, King Lot's wife Margawse. That same night, Arthur dreamed of a serpent which came forth from his side, destroyed his land and people, and fought with him to their mutual destruction. The nightmare was so vivid that Arthur had it pictured in a painting in Camelot cathedral. Some little time later, probably shortly before or shortly after Mordred's birth in Orkney, Merlin told Arthur that the child who would destroy him would be born on May-day, thus inciting Arthur to send for all noblemen's sons born about that time, put them into a leaky ship, and send them out to sea. The infant Mordred was among these children, but when the ship went down, he was cast up on shore, where "a good man found him, and nourished him till he was fourteen year old, and then he brought him to the court ... toward the end of the Death of Arthur." Other evidence, however, suggests that the boy was somehow identified and returned to his mother to be raised and educated by her; certainly he was known to be the youngest brother of Gawaine, Agravaine, Gaheris, and Gareth. Possibly he was identified when the "good man" brought him to court at age fourteen, and returned to Margawse at that time for five or six years. Meanwhile, Arthur's Herod-like trick had inspired Lot and other nobles to fresh revolt, in which Lot was killed.

Vulgate IV tells us that Mordred was knighted at the age of twenty. He was tall, with fair curly hair, and would have been handsome but for a wicked expression. Only for the first two years of his knighthood did he do any good. He hated all good knights.

During those first two years, however, he seems to have been very promising. For a time he travelled adventuring with Lancelot. Together they saw the mystic stag and four lions in Carteloise forest, and Mordred won praise from the great Du Lac for his manly endeavors. All this time, Mordred believed himself the son of King Lot.

Unfortunately, after seeing the stag and lions, Lancelot and Mordred went on toward Peningues castle to attend a tournament. They stayed with a vavasor near the castle and went into the woods next morning to find a church or chapel at which to hear Mass. They came upon an old but vigorous priest praying at a magnificent tomb. This priest greeted Lancelot and Mordred as the two most unfortunate knights who ever lived. When they asked why, he began with Mordred. First he stripped away Mordred's belief about his parentage: Mordred was not Lot's son, but Arthur's, the serpent of Arthur's dream, who would destroy his father and do more harm in his lifetime than all his ancestors had done good, and so on, and so on.

It was rather extreme of Mordred to kill the priest, but then, all this must have been a very traumatic revelation for a young knight (no older than twenty-two) who had been winning praise until that morning. Other knights, like Lionel and Lancelot himself, did as much and more, often on less provocation, when the battle rage took them. The vavasor was greatly perturbed at the priest's death, but for Lancelot's sake said nothing. Lancelot would have found a pretext to kill Mordred, but refrained for the sake of Mordred's brother Gawaine. (Lancelot was in a shaky position to cast stones at Mordred — among the victims of Lancelot's battle rages were men whose only offense consisted in Lancelot's having made free with their pavilions without first apprising them of his presence — but this time Lancelot was annoyed because Mordred had killed the priest before he could get around to predicting Lancelot's own future. Lancelot should have been grateful for that.)

They went on to hear Mass and then to the tournament. Such was the temper of the times. That day Mordred was left in a pitiable state on the tournament field, for he would have preferred death to surrender.

The old priest's prophecy seems to me one of the most mischievous in all the cycle (tying only with Merlin's about the May baby). It formed the turning-point of Mordred's career, for after this episode his evil side took the upper hand. Lancelot, on returning to court, told Guenever of the prophecy, but did not add that Arthur was Mordred's father. Guenever did not believe the prophecy, and so did not mention it to Arthur, who might have banished Mordred had he known of the episode.

Whether on the strength of his early promise, or because of his family connections, or because he remained a competent fighter "of his hands," Mordred became a companion of the Round Table. He seems to have retained some sense of humor;

once he joined Sir Dinadan and others in playing a joke on a "Cornish knight" (King Mark): Mordred's shield was silver, with black bends. Dinadan told Mark it was Lancelot carrying this shield, after which Mordred, who was wounded, gave the shield and his armor to Dagonet, the jester, who then gave Mark a merry chase. (This same shield suggests that Mordred may have been allied, at least for a time, with Morgan le Fay.) Again, one time Mordred came upon Sir Alisander le Orphelin in a state of besottedness upon his lady love, and began leading him mockingly away, apparently for mere sport. When Percivale came to court, Mordred apparently joined Kay in mocking the young man.

More serious, he may well have been party to the scheme which culminated in Gaheris' murder of Margawse, and when the brothers tracked down Lamorak, it was Mordred who gave that knight his death wound, striking him from behind. Mordred and Agravaine also conceived a dislike for Dinadan because of the latter's friendship toward Lamorak, and during the Grail Adventures they found an opportunity to kill him.

At last Mordred and Agravaine conspired to corner Lancelot with the Queen. Mordred survived Lancelot's escape and must have played chief witness against the lovers, thus precipitating the break between Arthur and Lancelot. When Arthur went with Gawaine to attack Lancelot in France, he left Mordred as regent and "chief ruler of all England," with governance even over Guenever. Malory says Arthur did this because Mordred was his son, but this would seem to make Arthur surprisingly slow-witted about connecting Merlin's old prophecy and his own nightmare with Mordred, so it is my guess that Arthur may still have been unaware of the relationship and made Mordred his regent because Mordred was the last surviving brother of the King's favorite nephew Gawaine.

Left in charge, Mordred counterfeited letters telling of Arthur's death in battle. He then called a parliament to name him king, had himself crowned at Canterbury, and tried to marry Guenever, but she tricked him and barricaded herself in the Tower of London. Mordred drove the Archbishop of Canterbury into exile for opposing him and besieged Guenever, but withdrew on receiving word that Arthur was on his way back. Mordred tried to prevent Arthur's landing at Dover and then retreated to Canterbury. The last battle was fought on Salisbury plain; Mordred was the last man left alive of all his army and allies who fought there, and at the last he was killed by Arthur — though Mordred did not return Arthur a mortal blow until he felt that he himself had his death wound.

Among Mordred's allies were the Saxons or Sesnes, who hated Arthur and wanted revenge on him. Mordred also had Irish, Scotch, and Welsh divisions in his army. He left behind two grown sons, one named Melehan and one whose name is not given. They gradually seized England after Mordred's death; but, on Lancelot's return, Bors killed Melehan and Lancelot the other son. [Vulgate II-IV; Malory I, 27; VI, 7; IX, 3, 36; X, 12, 13, 18(?), 24-25, 39, 46, 54, 58; XI, 12; XVIII, 11, 23; XX-XXI]

Father: Arthur	**SIR MORDRED'S**
Mother: Margawse	**FAMILY AND ALLIES**
Half-brothers: Gawaine, Agravaine, Gaheris, Gareth	
Son: Melehan	
Allies: Arcaus, Heliades	
Mordred had also a second son, whose name I could not find.	

MORGAN (Morgana) LE FAY

Morgan was one of the three daughters, apparently the youngest, of Igraine and Gorlois, and thus an elder half-sister of Arthur's. When Igraine was wed to Uther and her daughters Margawse and Elaine to Kings Lot and Nentres, Morgan was put to school in a nunnery, where, as Malory tells us, "she learned so much that she was a great clerk of necromancy." Later she was married to King Uriens of Gore, to whom she bore Ywaine le Blanchemains.

After being an early rebel, Uriens came over to Arthur and was made a companion of the Round Table. He seems to have spent much time in Arthur's court, along with his wife and son. At first Morgan and Guenever were friends, and Guenever gave almost identical rings to Morgan and to Lancelot (not necessarily, one supposes, at the same time). But Morgan took Guiomar, a cousin of Guenever's, for a lover. Finding them together, the angry Guenever banished Guiomar. Morgan fled to Merlin, learned (or increased her earlier knowledge of) necromancy, and hated Guenever ever afterwards. This incident is recorded in Vulgate IV and may refer to the same period mentioned in Vulgate II, when Morgan met Merlin in Bedingran at the time of the knighting of Gawaine and his brothers.

Eventually returning to Arthur's court, Morgan took a new lover, Sir Accolon of Gaul, with whom she plotted the deaths of both Arthur and Uriens, planning to put Accolon and herself on the throne of Britain. The scheme was thwarted by Nimue. On learning of Accolon's death at Arthur's hands, some distance from court, Morgan attempted at least to murder her sleeping husband — surprisingly, by the natural means of a sword — but was prevented by their son Ywaine. Gaining Ywaine's promise of secrecy on her own pledge of future good behavior, she got Guenever's permission to leave court, pretending urgent business at home. She stopped at the nunnery where Arthur lay wounded and stole the scabbard of Excalibur; the sword she could not get since he was sleeping with it. Pursued by Arthur, she threw the scabbard into a deep lake and then changed herself and her men into stones to escape capture. Their danger past, she saved Sir Manassen, a cousin of Accolon's, from enemies and sent him back to Arthur to tell how cleverly she had eluded him. She returned to Gore and garrisoned her castles in preparation for attack, nor was the precaution groundless, for Malory mentions Arthur's attempts to win back at least one castle he himself had given her in friendlier times. Soon after this return to Gore, she sent him a poisoned mantle as a pretended peace-offering, but Nimue's advice saved him from death.

One conceives that she was eventually forced to vacate Gore rather than run afoul of her husband or his deputy King Bagdemagus. She owned, acquired, or usurped more than one castle outside Gore, from which she could operate. (See La Beale Regard, Castle Chariot, and Morgan's Castle, *Places*.) Her last known lover was Sir Hemison, whom she mourned deeply and buried richly when he was slain by Tristram. She also tried to make Alisander le Orphelin her paramour, and, more than once, Sir Lancelot. She seems, however, to have had her lovers one at a time, taking a new one only some while after the former one was slain or otherwise lost.

With Lancelot she seems to have had an especial love-hate relationship. Malory records one instance of her kidnapping him (acting in concert with her companions at the time, the queens of Northgalis, Eastland, and the Out Isles); the Vulgate records other occasions when she got him into her power.

She hated Lancelot because Guenever loved him, and also, we may suspect, because he loved Guenever and repulsed Morgan's own advances. Yet, whenever she captured him, she tried to get him into her own bed. As an example of one of their exchanges, after he had saved Duke Rochedon's Daughter, Morgan conjured him by what he loved best to doff his helmet. (This was probably not enchantment, but a rule of courtesy.) When he unhelmed, she said that if she had known his identity before, he would not have escaped so easily. He replied that if she were a man, he'd know how to deal with her; she responded that he would regret that comment.

For some time, probably many years, Morgana seems to have been or had the reputation of being at the heart of some network of enchantresses and villains. Once King Mark appealed to Morgan and the Queen of Northgalis to set the country "in fire" with enchantresses and wicked knights like Malgrin and Breuse Sans Pitie; this suggests that there was such a network, or at least that Morgan and the Queen of Northgalis wielded authority over other necromancers and wicked men. These same two are credited in Malory with putting a damsel into a scalding bath. Morgan's nephew Mordred may have served her at least for a time. Another instance of Morgan's mischief may be found under Val Sans Retour, *Places*.

After the episode of the poisoned mantle, however, Morgan's efforts against Arthur seem almost entirely directed at forcing him to recognize the love of Lancelot and Guenever. Sir Bertilak de Hautdesert remarked to Gawaine that the affair of the Green Knight's beheading game had been staged by Morgan to shock Guenever to death — an explanation which we may take figuratively, if not with a grain of salt; nevertheless, Morgan may well have continued to resent the fact that, after raising such a fuss about her friend's affair with Guiomar, Guenever proceeded to enjoy a long, adulterous liaison of her own. Efforts by Morgan to reveal the adultery of Lancelot and Guenever may be found under Morgan's Shield, Morgan's Ring, and Morgan's Drinking Horn, *Things*.

In **Sir Gawaine and the Green Knight,** Morgan appears as an extremely old woman. This is curious, for here, as in Malory, she is Gawaine's aunt, and Gawaine, like Arthur and the rest of his court, is still quite young. Igraine must be granted a remarkably long period of childbearing if Morgan has naturally attained her great age in this work. I think it much more likely that, as Morgan could give Bertilak the appearance of the Green Knight, so she could give herself the appearance of any age she wished.

Father: Duke Gorlois	**MORGAN LE FAY'S**
Mother: Igraine	**FAMILY AND ALLIES**

Father: Duke Gorlois
Mother: Igraine
Sisters: Margawse, Elaine of Tintagil
Half-brother: Arthur
Husband: King Uriens
Son: Ywaine
Husband's bastard son: Yvonet li Avoutres
Brothers-in-law: King Lot (m. Margawse), King Nentres (m. Elaine)
Nephews: Gawaine, Agravaine, Gaheris, Gareth, Mordred (all by Margawse); Galeshin (by Elaine
Grandson?: Ider
Lovers: Guiomar (Guenevere's cousin), Accolon of Gaul, Hemison
Lover's (Accolon's) cousin: Manassen
Allies: Queen of Eastland?, Queen of Northgalis, Queen of the Out Isles?, Queen of the Waste Lands?, Sebile, King Mark?, Breuse Sans Pitie?, Malgrin?
Protégé?: Oriolz the Dane

Eventually, Morgan retired to her castle near Tauroc, Wales, where she lived quietly for so long that Arthur and his court came to assume her dead. At last, however, Arthur chanced upon her castle while hunting, and she welcomed him warmly. On this occasion he spent a week visiting her, and the only attempt she made on his wellbeing was to show him the murals Lancelot had once painted while a prisoner in this castle, which murals revealed his relations with Guenever. Arthur refused to believe even this evidence, but invited his half-sister to Camelot. She replied that she would never leave her castle again until the time came for her to go to Avalon.

Despite her long role as antagonist to Arthur, Guenever, and their court, Morgan was the chief of the grieving ladies who came to bear Arthur away to Avilion after the last battle. [Vulgate II-VI; Malory I, 2; II, 11; IV, 1-14; VI, 3; VIII, 34; IX, 41-43; X, 35-38; XI, 1; XXI, 6]

MORGAN'S DAMSEL

When he met her in Sir Damas' castle, masquerading as Damas' daughter, Arthur thought he recognized her as a damsel he had seen around his own court [Malory IV, 7].

Perhaps she could be identified with the damsel who brought Arthur Morgan's gift of a poisoned cloak. On Nimue's counsel, Arthur forced the maiden messenger to try the cloak on herself, despite her reluctance, and it promptly burned her to death. [Malory IV, 16]

Morgawse — see MARGAWSE

Morolt — see MARHAUS

GIANT OF THE MOUNT OF ARABY

After conquering the Giant of Saint Michael's Mount, Brittany, Arthur reminisced about the one he conquered "in the mount of Araby," who was not quite so big and fierce [Malory V, 5]. Since there seems no record, at least in Malory, of Arthur's having been out of Britain before, the "Mount of Araby" may have been in Britain — perhaps Saint Michael's Mount in Cornwall.

St. Mungo† — see KENTIGERN

ABON LE NOIRE

The lord of the Isle of Servage, he was "a great mighty giant" who hated Arthur and destroyed all of Arthur's knights who came his way. In jousting, Nabon had a trick of killing his opponent's horse. In battle, Sir Tristram slew Nabon and made Sir Segwarides lord of the isle in his place. [Malory VIII, 37-39; see also Nanowne le Petite]

Nacien — see NASCIEN

NANOWNE LE PETITE

All that Malory seems to tell us of this unhappy knight of Arthur's is that he was the last victim of Nabon le Noire, who put him to a shameful death, "for he was drawn limb-meal" [Malory VIII, 37].

NASCIEN (Nacien, Seraphe)

Seraphe was the brother-in-law of King Evelake. Joseph of Arimathea converted them and their families to Christianity, giving Seraphe the baptismal name of Nascien and Evelake that of Mordrains. Nascien's wife was Flegentine, their son Celidoine, and among their descendants were the Fisher Kings, Lancelot and Galahad, Percivale and Amide.

Mordrains, Nascien, and their families came to Britain with Joseph and Josephe. Here, forty years after Christ's Passion, Nascien successfully endured temptation by a fiend in the Port of Perilous Rock. Mordrains, meanwhile, came to the Isle of Turnance, found King Solomon's Ship, and broke King David's Sword by drawing it unworthily to slay a giant that was chasing him. Somehow killing the giant without the use of the sacred weapon, Mordrains returned to Solomon's Ship and was carried to the Port of Perilous Rock, where Nascien, fresh from his testing, miraculously repaired the sword and returned it to its sheath. They were warned by a voice to leave Solomon's Ship, and, in so doing, Mordrains received a sword wound in the right foot as punishment for drawing the sword. [Malory XVII, 4: in this passage, Nascien is credited with drawing King David's Sword and Mordrains with its mending, but, convinced that the two names have been transposed here, I have recapped the tale accordingly.]

Surviving as a holy hermit until the reign of Arthur (or perhaps returning as an apparition), Nascien filled very approximately the role in the spiritual world of the Grail Adventures that Merlin had formerly played to Arthur and his knights in the secular world: Nascien was their more or less elusive prophet, mentor, guide, and confessor. I believe he is to be identified with Malory's unnamed hermit who came to the Round Table the Whitsunday before Galahad's birth and predicted that event within the year, also with the "good old man, and ... ancient, clothed all in white, and there was no knight knew from whence he came" who actually brought Galahad into Arthur's court. As Galahad succeeded in drawing Balin's sword from its floating rock, a damsel riding a white palfrey appeared on the river bank to tell Lancelot he was no longer the greatest knight of the world and to bring Arthur Nascien's message "that thee shall befall the greatest worship that ever befell king in Britain." Just before the departure of the Questers, "an old knight ... and in religious clothing" came into court to give them Nascien's warnings and instructions for the holy enterprise, among which was the injunction that no knight should be allowed to take along a woman. (Interesting, in light of Amide's importance to Galahad, Percivale, and Bors, and also in view of Nascien's own use of a damsel as one of his messengers.) When Galahad came to the Abbey of the Adventurous Shield, the angelic White Knight, telling the story of the shield, mentioned Nascien's death and burial in that same abbey. Nevertheless, while in the Grail Quest Gawaine and Ector, asking for a hermit to explain their dreams, were told:

Here is one in a little mountain, but it is so rough there may no horse go thither, and therefore ye must go upon foot; there shall ye find a poor house, and there is Nacien the hermit, which is the holiest man in this country.

Then [they] rode till that they came to the rough mountain, and there they tied their horses and went on foot to the hermitage. And when they were come up they saw a poor house, and beside the chapel a little courtelage [courtyard], where Nacien the hermit gathered worts, as he which had tasted none other meat of a great while.

He explained their dreams and, finding them unworthy, gave them some harsh counsel, which they rejected. It is not unlikely that Nascien should also be identified with some of the nameless holy men who counselled other knights on this Quest, nor does it seem unlikely that, if he had indeed spent several centuries of miraculously prolonged life in Britain, he might have had more than one hermitage scattered about the island. [Vulgate, chiefly I, V, & VI; Malory, XI, 1; XIII, 3-4, 5, 8, 11; XV, 4; XVI, 2-5; XVII, 4]

According to Vulgate VII, Nascien's mother was *la bele Damoisele de la Blanche Nue* (or *Nuage*) — the lovely maiden of the white cloud. I am not completely sure, however, that this is the same Nascien. Here he appears in the thick of battle, helping 16 other knights succor Agloval. I remember no other testimony that the hermit Nascien indulged in martial activities during Arthur's reign.

KING NENTRES (Nantres, Ventres) OF GARLOTH (Garlot)

Nentres married Elaine of Tintagil, by whom he sired Sir Galescin. Nentres joined the first rebellion against Arthur, pledging 5000 mounted men to the cause and fighting well in the battle of Bedegraine. When the kings had to suspend their rebellion because of the Saracen attack on Wandesborow castle, Nentres was put in charge of the city of Windesan. Apparently remaining aloof from the second rebellion, Nentres eventually became a companion of the Round Table. [Malory I, 2, 8, 12-18; XIX, 11; Vulgate II]

NERO

A "mighty man of men," Nero helped his brother King Ryons war against Leodegrance and others. Ryons captured by Balin and Balan, Nero joined battle with Arthur before Castle Terrabil. Meanwhile, Merlin came to Nero's ally, King Lot, "and held him with a tale of prophecy, till Nero and his people were destroyed." [Malory II, 9-10]

NEROVENS DE LILE

When La Cote Male Taile set out with the damsel Maledisant in her quest, Lancelot followed after, "and by the way upon a bridge there was a knight proffered Sir Launcelot to joust." After a noble sword battle, the strange knight yielded, and turned out to be Sir Nerovens de Lile, whom Lancelot himself had dubbed knight. Happily reunited, Nerovens warned Lancelot of Sir Brian de les Isles, lord of the Castle of Pendragon, who had just captured La Cote Male Taile the day before. After defeating Sir Brian, Lancelot gave Nerovens rule, under La Cote Male Taile, of Pendragon Castle and its surrounding country. Nerovens also became a companion of the Round Table. [Malory IX, 5-6, 9, 11]

Very likely Nerovens should be identified with Sir Neroneus, who accompanied Lancelot into exile and was made Earl of Pardiak [Malory XX, 18].

NIMUE

At Arthur's marriage feast, Merlin bade the knights sit still around the Table, telling them they would soon see a strange and marvellous adventure. As they sat, in ran a white hart, chased by a white brachet, with thirty couple of black hounds running after. The brachet bit the hart, which then leaped and knocked over a knight. This knight got up, caught the brachet, and left the hall to mount his horse and ride away. Immediately in rode a lady on a white palfrey and cried aloud to King Arthur, Sir, suffer me not to have this despite, for the brachet was mine ... with this there came a knight riding all armed on a great horse, and took the lady away with him with force, and ever she cried and made great dole. When she was gone the king was glad, for she made such a noise.

But Merlin insisted that the adventures could not be dismissed so lightly. So, on the mage's advice, Gawaine was sent after the white hart, the newly-knighted Tor after the knight who had stolen the brachet, and King Pellinore after the knight who had stolen the damsel. Tor came through the adventures with the most honor, for Gawaine had the mischance to slay a lady while aiming for her lord, Sir Ablamar of the Marsh, while Pellinore was so hot in his quest that he did not try to stop to help a lady with a wounded knight — only learning when he came back and found them dead that she had been his own daughter Eleine. Pellinore succeeded in the quest itself, however; he found and slew the abductor, Sir Hontzlake of Wentland, made the acquaintance of the damsel's cousin, Sir Meliot of Logurs, and his sworn brother Sir Brian of the Isles, and brought the damsel back to court. This damsel of the white brachet was Nimue.

Merlin now became besotted with Nimue, taught her magic, and took her with him on a visit to Benwick. She might already have been one of the minor damsels of the Lake; now, perhaps through Merlin's influence, she became the chief Lady of the Lake in place of the one Balin had slain (see Nineve). Troubled by Merlin's lecherous intentions, however, and "afeard of him because he was a devil's son," Nimue at last used the crafts he had taught her to imprison him under a great stone. (Other early versions, however, show her as putting him in comfortable retirement through genuine affection, perhaps sisterly, for him.)

Perhaps, having retired Merlin for whatever reason, Nimue felt obligated to take Arthur under her wing in Merlin's stead. Whereas Merlin's style seems to have been hovering around the court keeping more or less underfoot, Nimue apparently spent most of her time in her Lake, appearing only at need. For instance, she arrived just in time to foil Morgana's crafts and help Arthur win the fight against Sir Accolon, then quietly left again. She appeared in the Forest Perilous just in time to enlist Sir Tristram's aid and save Arthur from the sorceress Annowre. Sometimes she did not arrive as early as she might have, as in the affair of the poisoned apples; but neither had Merlin always been on time, and his tardiness had sometimes resulted in unnecessary deaths. At any rate, despite Arthur's annoyance with Nimue's noise at their first meeting, "ever she did great goodness unto King Arthur and to all his knights through her sorcery and enchantments." Despite her former opposition to Morgana, Nimue accompanied Morgana, the Queen of Northgalis, and the Queen of the Waste Lands when they came in their ship to bear away the mortally wounded Arthur.

Nimue found Sir Pelleas when he was bemoaning Gawaine's betrayal of him in the matter of Dame Ettard. Falling in love with Pelleas herself, Nimue caused him to love her instead of Ettard, and Ettard to love him as hopelessly as he had originally loved her. Although she brought him to Arthur's court and may well have sponsored him when he was made a companion of the Round Table, after their marriage Nimue kept Pelleas safe from harm, presumably even in the final battles between Arthur and Mordred. (Her union with Pelleas could be reconciled with the "loving retirement" theory of what she did to Merlin. Cf. Thomas Wentworth Higginson, **Tales of Atlantis and the Enchanted Isles**, chapter VII.)

[Malory III, 5-15; IV, 1, 10, 22-23, 28; IX, 16; XVIII, 8; XXI, 6; see also The Lake, *Places*]

"NINEVE" ("Niniane," "Nynyue")

The name Nimue is a clerical error for Nineve or Nynyue, and the character is named Viviane in the Old French **Merlin** (see Lady of the Lake). For the sake of convenience, I have adopted the name Nineve for Malory's first British Lady of the Lake, introduced and disposed of before Nimue's appearance.

After Arthur's sword broke in combat with King Pellinore,

> No force, said Merlin, hereby is a sword that shall be yours, an I may. So they rode till they came to a lake, the which was a fair water and broad, and in the midst of the lake ... an arm clothed in white samite, that held a fair sword in that hand. Lo! said Merlin, yonder is that sword that I spake of. With that they saw a damosel going upon the lake. What damosel is that? said Arthur. That is the Lady of the Lake, said Merlin; and within that lake is a rock, and therein is as fair a place as any on earth, and richly beseen; and this damosel will come to you anon, and then speak ye fair to her that she will give you that sword.

The damsel greeted Arthur and agreed to give him the sword Excalibur if he would give her a gift when she asked it. When he promised to do so, she pointed out a barge in which he could row over and take the sword and scabbard.

When, some little time afterwards, Balin drew the sword of the damsel I call Malvis, this Lady of the Lake

> came on horseback, richly beseen, and saluted King Arthur, and there asked him a gift that he promised her when she gave him the sword ... Well, said the lady, I ask the head of the knight that hath won the sword, or else the damosel's head that brought it; I take no force though I have both their heads, for he slew my brother, a good knight and a true, and that gentlewoman was causer of my father's death. Truly, said King Arthur, I may not grant neither of their heads with my worship, therefore ask what ye will else ... I will ask none other thing, said the lady. When Balin ... saw the Lady of the Lake, that by her means had slain Balin's mother, and he had sought her three years; and when it was told him that she asked his head of King Arthur, he went to her straight and said, Evil be you found; ye would have my head, and therefore you shall lose yours, and with his sword lightly he smote off her head before King Arthur.

Arthur was greatly displeasured and banished Balin from court, Balin still maintaining that

> this same lady was the untruest lady living, and by enchantment and sorcery she hath been the destroyer of many good knights, and she was causer that my mother was burnt, through her falsehood and treachery.

Arthur buried the lady richly, but we may probably accept Balin's accusation as accurate. This first British Lady of the Lake, if not one of Merlin's cohorts, was at least willing to work in concord with him; and yet when Merlin returned to court and learned of what had happened, Malory does not record that even he made any attempt to deny Balin's charges. [Malory I, 25; II, 3-4]

LADY OF NOHAUT†

She seems to have been a ruler in her own right, as well as a liege of Arthur's. When the King of Northumberland besieged her, she sent a messenger to Arthur, asking for a champion. The newly-dubbed Lancelot craved to act for her. He made a side trip to rescue a damsel from a big and apparently cruel knight; this, however, turned out to be a test arranged by the Lady of Nohaut — the big knight had wanted to champion and wed her, and she had consented on condition he defeat the champion Arthur sent. (He did not.) When Lancelot arrived at Nohaut, the Lady put him to bed for fifteen days to recover from his wounds. Meanwhile, hearing no news of Lancelot at court, Kay requested the errand and was sent to Nohaut in his turn. After a quarrel between Kay and Lancelot, the Lady settled the question of which was to act for her by requesting the King of Northumberland to allow her two champions. They fought two knights of Northumberland. Lancelot, after vanquishing his opponent, offered to help Kay; but Kay refused the offer and eventually succeeded in mastering his own adversary. Kay returned to court with the Lady's thanks, while Lancelot lingered awhile at Nohaut. [Vulgate III]

THE KING OF NORGALES' DAUGHTER†

Gawaine made love to her, and possibly considered himself married to her, according to Vulgate III, which makes her the only child of the King of Norgales. (I am not sure of which king of Norgales she was the daughter.)

THE KING OF NORGALES' DAUGHTER'S HANDMAID†

Sir Sagremor is matched with her in Vulgate III.

QUEEN OF NORTHGALIS (Norgales)

She was one of four queens who kidnapped Lancelot and held him in Castle Chariot. The others were the Queen of Eastland, the Queen of the Isles, and Morgan le Fay.

The Queen of Northgalis appears at least thrice more in association with Morgan le Fay. Trying to rouse the enchantresses and wicked knights against Alisander le Orphelin, King Mark wrote "unto Morgan le Fay, and to the Queen of Northgalis." The Queen of Northgalis is credited, along with Morgana, with putting the damsel into the scalding bath. Finally, the Queen of Northgalis appeared with Morgan, the Queen of the Waste Lands, and Nimue in the ship that carried Arthur away after the last battle. [Malory VI, 3-4; X, 35; XI, 1; XXI, 6]

From all of this, it seems likely that the Queen of Northgalis was both Morgan's friend and associate, and the second most powerful sorceress in Britain, excluding the Lady of the Lake.

GRINS, BROTHER†

In Bérouls, the earliest known version of Tristram, Brother Ogrins is a hermit who counsels the wandering Tristram and Yseut to repent of their sin. When they protest that they cannot because of having drunk the potion, he relaxes his holy rule in order to give them shelter for the night. In this version, the effects of the potion wear off after three years, and the lovers return in penitence to the hermit, who arranges a reconciliation for Yseut with Mark. Apparently a shrewd dealer for a "nonworldly" man, Ogrins buys and barters so well that Yseut can appear before Mark richly apparelled and mounted.

I have only a partial translation on hand, and do not know what happens afterwards, but there seem to be indications that Tristram and Yseut still love each other, love potion wearing off or not.

Onztlake – see under HONTZLAKE

ORIEL†

A Saxon warrior, involved in the attack on Vandaliors castle [Vulgate II].

ORIOLZ THE DANE (Ogier?)†

He was the son of King Aminaduf of Denmark. The Damoiselle à la Harpe took Oriolz to heal him, but her cousin, Helaes de la Forest Perilleuse, asked him as a favor to capture Gawaine, put him in her prison, and fight with him daily — all so that she could have Gawaine as her lover. [Vulgate VII]

Could Oriolz be identified with Ogier the Dane? Brewer says that Morgan once took Ogier to Avalon, gave him a ring of youth and a crown of forgetfulness, and introduced him to King Arthur. Two hundred years later, she sent Ogier to fight the Moors in France; there he routed them, and returned to Avalon. Ogier's swords were Curtana — the cutter — and Sauvagine; his horse was Papillon — butterfly.

"ORNAGRINE"†

This unnamed damsel first appeared to Lancelot with her hair loose and a wreath of roses round her head, and directed him after the knight he was then pursuing, in return for a promise that he would follow her at once whenever she required him to do so. When next she appeared, she looked seventy years old and gave Lancelot barely time to conquer a knight who was threatening to kidnap Guenever before requiring him to follow her. Lancelot followed Ornagrine with his opponent's lancehead still in his side.

Since this damsel's second appearance was in the vicinity of La Fontaine aux Fees, *Places*, she may have been a fairy. Certainly magic must be involved in her story somehow. She seemed to lead Lancelot, however, only into the type of adventures normally encountered by knights-errant, not into treachery or ambush. [Vulgate IV]

THE COUNTESS OF OROFOISE and HER SISTER†

The Countess seems to have been a sovereign lady. When she sent her beautiful sister to Arthur seeking help, Arthur took the opportunity to go to bed with the beautiful sister. He then fought a giant on behalf of the Countess. The giant wore armor of impervious serpent-hides, which must have caused Arthur a spot of trouble. [Vulgate VII]

ORUALE (Orvale) DE GUINDOEL†

She was a cousin of Lancelot, although she had last seen him, at the time of her rescue by Ector de Maris, when Lancelot was two months old. Oruale's mother had been a cousin of King Ban; both Oruale's parents died about two years after settling in Britain.

For Oruale's troubles at the hands of Sir Marigart, see Guindoel Castle, *Places*. After rescuing her, Ector offered to be her true knight always and everywhere for Lancelot's sake; this does not, however, necessarily imply a romantic relationship. [Vulgate IV]

OSSA CYLELLAUR†

He is my token "historical" military figure, a leader of the Saxons and Arthur's opponent at the battle of Badon Hill. Ossa does not appear, at least by this name, in Malory or the Vulgate, but Glennie seems to try to connect him with Gallehault (Duke Galeholt?) — a connection which need not concern us here, except as it may give grounds for making Duke Galeholt a Saxon.

OSSAISE

A knight of Surluse, he fought in Duke Galeholt's tournament and was unhorsed by Gaheris [Malory X, 48].

QUEEN OF THE OUT ISLES

With the Queen of Eastland, the Queen of Northgalis, and Morgan le Fay, she kidnapped Lancelot and held him prisoner in Castle Chariot [Malory VI, 3-4]. See under Queen of Eastland.

Owain – see YWAINE

OZANA (Osanna, Ozanna) LE CURE HARDY ("Ozana of the Hardy Heart")

Towards the beginning of Sir Marhaus' career, as he was returning from killing the giant Taulurd, he chanced to meet four knights of Arthur's court, Sirs Sagramore, Osanna, Dodinas le Savage, and Felot of Listenoise; Marhaus smote them down all four with one spear. Malory next mentions Sir Ozana travelling with the two Ywaines, Brandiles, Agravaine, and Mordred, all by now members of the Round Table. Dinadan meets them and cooks up with them a scheme to rout King Mark by dressing the jester Dagonet in Mordred's armor and telling Mark it is Lancelot; the scheme backfires when Mark, fleeing, meets Palomides, who refuses to be routed and instead unhorses Dagonet, Ozana, and the others. Ozana appears again at the Winchester tournament, where he is bested by Sir Lavaine.

INDIVIDUAL COMBATS AND COURTESY

By the way as [Sir Dinadan] rode he saw where stood an errant knight, and made him ready for to joust. Not so, said Dinadan, for I have no will to joust. With me shall ye joust, said the knight, or that ye pass this way. Whether ask ye jousts, [said Dinadan] by love or by hate? The knight answered: Wit ye well I ask it for love and not for hate. It may well be so, said Sir Dinadan, but ye proffer me hard love when ye will joust with me with a sharp spear. [Dinadan then proposed that they meet at Arthur's court and have the joust there.] ... Well, said the knight, sith ye will not joust with me, I pray you tell me your name.

Learning it, the strange knight said he knew Dinadan for a good knight and agreed to call off the joust entirely. [Malory X, 20]

A trial of arms seems to have been almost as common a method for two knights, meeting by chance, to greet each other as a hello and a handshake. The perplexing rule, which seems standard, of jousting first and asking names afterwards could lead to tragedy, especially when knights so often travelled with strange, blank, or covered shields rather than their own; nevertheless, it seems to be an outgrowth of a more general precept of etiquette that frowned on exchanging names too quickly. For instance, Sir Bercilak and his people welcomed Gawaine into their castle, unarmed him, offered him a choice of indoor apparel, assigned him a chamber and servants, and brought him to supper, all before asking him — by hints and subtle, delicate questions — his identity and court of origin; Gawaine did not ask his host's name until after the beheading contest, when host and Green

Despite all these bestings, Ozana may well have been a good knight, most of whose history did not get into Malory's epic; a good device to show off a new knight is listing how many fine knights of established standing he can defeat. Ozana was among the knights who rode a-Maying with Guenever when Meliagrant abducted her, and among the knights who attempted to heal Sir Urre. [Malory IV, 25; X, 11-13; XVIII, 11; XIX, 1, 11]

By his apparent choice of travelling companions, we may perhaps theorize that Ozana was more of Gawaine's faction than Lancelot's, and hence that he remained with Arthur during the split and perished in the last battle.

ALOMIDES (Palomides)

Sir Palomides the Saracen was the most notable of King Astlabor's three sons, the others being Sirs Safere and Segwarides, both of whom seem to have officialized their conversion to Christianity considerably before their brother.

Malory introduces Palomides in Ireland at the time when Tristram, disguised as Tramtrist, was there to be healed by La Beale Isoud. Palomides was already in love with Isoud, even "in will to be christened for her sake," and much in favor with her parents.

But Isoud favored Tristram, and persuaded him to fight in rivalry to Palomides at the tournament for the Lady of the Launds. A tried and proven Palomides rode with a black shield and unhorsed, among others, many Round Table knights, including Gawaine, Kay, Sagramore, and Griflet.

Palomides might well have won the tournament but for Tristram, who defeated him and rather ungraciously, as it seems, made him swear under threat of death to forsake Isoud and to refrain from wearing armor and bearing arms for a year and a day. "Then for despite and anger Sir Palamides cut off his harness, and threw [it] away."

After the wedding of Mark and Isoud, Palomides appeared in Cornwall. (His excuse may have been to visit his brother, if Segwarides, Astlabor's son, is to be identified with the Segwarides of Mark's court.) The year being up, Palomides was back in armor, and he came in time to rescue Dame Bragwaine from a tree where two envious ladies had bound her.

Isoud, delighted at the safe restoration of her favorite handmaid, promised to grant Palomides a boon, providing it was not evil. He asked that she ride away with him as if adventuring, and Mark, hearing the whole story, agreed, planning to send Tristram to rescue her. Tristram being out hunting and not immediately available, Mark's knight Lambegus went after Palomides, who gave him a fall. During the fray, Isoud escaped and found refuge in the tower of one Sir Adtherp. Tristram came and fought furiously with Palomides before the tower, until Isoud begged Tristram to spare Palomides, lest he die unbaptized. She sent Palomides, sorely chagrined, to the court of King Arthur, rubbing in Tristram's victory over her heart by charging his rival to deliver Guenever the message that "there be within this land but four lovers" — Lancelot and Guenever, Tristram and Isoud.

Perhaps it was during this sojourn at Arthur's court that Palomides became a companion of the Round Table. He appears briefly in the tale of La Cote Male Taile, whom he encountered by chance while both were out adventuring. La Cote considered his unhorsing at the hands of Palomides no disgrace. Palomides may have been in pursuit of the Questing Beast when he met La Cote; he appears in this quest only a few chapters later, when Tristram and Lamorak meet him (Tristram being en route back to Cornwall from Brittany, where he has left his wife Isoud la Blanche Mains to return to his first Isoud).

Palomides' adoption of the Questing Beast is curious in light of Pellinore's old statement that this beast could never be achieved except by himself or by his next of kin; it has led at least one commentator (Keith Baines to assume, on apparently no other grounds than this, that the Saracen Palomides was somehow next of kin to the Welsh descendant of Nascien, Pellinore. Some degree of distant cousinship is possible, dating back to some relative of Nascien's who refused to be converted by Joseph and Josephe, choosing to remain behind and father or mother a line of Saracens; but I think it more likely that Palomides took on an apparently impossible quest in the effort to prove himself worthy of baptism. (Might

Knight were revealed as one and the same. [**Sir Gawaine and the Green Knight**]

Sir Lamorak, adventuring anonymously, outjousted and unhorsed both Palomides and Dinadan, "but their horses he would not suffer his squires to meddle with ... because they were knights-errant" [Malory X, 18]. This, however, may have been more Lamorak's generosity than common practice. Strictly speaking, the arms and steeds of the defeated knights probably always belonged by right to the victorious opponent, but in friendly encounters the victors, especially when Round Table companions or otherwise notable for honor and courtesy, seem generally to have waived their claim. Strictly speaking, the defeated combatant also seemed to owe his service and allegiance to his conqueror; this rule seems always to have been applied when the victor was of Arthur's court and could thus gain his opponent's allegiance for the King.

At the castle of Sir Tor le Fise Aries, the lieutenant of the castle, Sir Berluse, recognized King Mark as the man who had killed his father and would have killed Berluse himself. But

> for the love of my lord [Tor] of this castle I will neither hurt you nor harm you, nor none of your fellowship [said Berluse]. But wit you well, when ye are past this lodging I shall hurt you an I may, for ye slew my father traitorly. But first for the love of my lord, Sir Tor, and for the love of Sir Lamorak, the honourable knight that here is lodged, ye shall have none ill lodging. [Malory X, 9]

It appears that castles and the rules of hospitality could serve as well as a church for sanctuary.

his failure to achieve the Questing Beast have led to the vow he made sometime between his sojourn in Ireland and the Surluse tournament, not to be baptized until he had done seven true battles for Jesu's sake?) At any rate, he was so hot in the quest of the beast that he unhorsed both Tristram and Lamorak with one spear without stopping to give them swordplay, whereat Tristram, much annoyed, told Lamorak to relay the message that he — Tristram — wanted a rematch at that same well where they had just encountered.

Tristram and Palomides next encountered each other at the tournament of the Castle of Maidens, where Palomides used a black horse and a black-covered shield. Between Tristram's participation in the tournament and Lancelot's, Palomides won less honor than he had hoped. At the end of the second day's fighting, Tristram found Palomides alone in the forest in a near-suicidal rage and forcibly prevented him from harming himself, without, however, letting him know who it was that held him.

> Alas, said Sir Palomides, I may never win worship where Sir Tristram is ... and if he be away for the most part I have the gree, unless that Sir Launcelot be there or Sir Lamorak ... I would fight with [Tristram], said Sir Palomides, and ease my heart upon him; and yet, to say thee sooth, Sir Tristram is the gentlest knight in this world living.

Still hiding his identity, Tristram persuaded Palomides to accept lodging in his pavilion that night. After the tournament, Palomides remained so angry with Tristram for doing him out of the honors that he followed him and lost his horse in a river. Tristram, learning of this, had his rival brought to the castle of Sir Darras, where he was staying with Sir Dinadan. Unfortunately, Sir Darras learned that Tristram was blamed for slaying three of his sons at the tournament, and put Tristram, Dinadan, and Palomides all three into prison, where Tristram fell sick. At first, still spurred by the old rivalry, Palomides spoke harshly to Tristram. "But when Sir Palomides saw the falling of sickness of Sir Tristram, then was he heavy for him, and comforted him in all the best wise he could." Finally, learning Tristram's identity, Darras set them free and nursed Tristram back to health.

After parting when they left Darras' castle, Tristram next met Palomides by chance in time to rescue him from Breuse Sans Pitie and nine of his knights. Palomides agreed to fight Tristram in a fortnight, when his wounds were healed, beside the tomb of Lanceor and Colombe in the meadow by Camelot. When the day came, however, Palomides was in some other lord's prison (we know little of the circumstances this time) and Tristram fought Lancelot instead, by mistake; the battle ended in a draw, after which Lancelot brought Tristram to court, where he was installed in Sir Marhaus' old seat at the Round Table.

Palomides, meanwhile, getting out of prison, returned to the pursuit of the Questing Beast. We know little of his adventures during this period, but once he rescued King Mark by striking down Brandiles, the two Ywaines, Ozana, Agravaine and Griflet in rapid succession (in this scene, asked his identity through a squire, Palomides claimed to be "a knight-errant as they [who ask] are . . . and no knight of King Arthur's court," but this may simply have been a ploy to preserve his anonymity; all the participants were being very coy with their names). Shortly thereafter, he passed his mother's manor and, too hot on the Beast's trail to stop, sent her greetings and a request for food and drink. (Perhaps the entire family, or at

least the [widowed?] mother and her three sons, had all come to Britain together, she settling somewhere in the southwest?) Palomides also met Lamorak outside Morgan's castle, bearing an anonymous red shield as he fought off her knights. Palomides courteously offered to help him, Lamorak took this as an insult and insisted on proving his lack of weariness by fighting Palomides, Palomides (who had a temper of his own) responded in kind, and at the end of the battle, when they learned each other's identity, they swore everlasting friendship, promising to love each other better than any other man except their respective brothers Saferë and Tor. (I find no hard evidence in this scene, however, for the theory that Palomides was closely related to Pellinore, for he does not seem to recognize Lamorak as a cousin.)

Palomides next appears at the Surluse tournament, where he won much more honor than at the Castle of Maidens. In addition to the regular tournament fighting, he championed two damsels. The first "loved Sir Palomides as paramour, but the book saith she was of his kin," and she appealed for justice against one Sir Goneries "that withheld her all her lands." She seems to have been responsible for actually getting Palomides to the site of the tournament, for he was resting in a hermitage from his pursuit of the Questing Beast, and she sought him out when no other knight present would take her quarrel. He made short work of Goneries. The second damsel was King Bandes' daughter, who "heard tell that Palomides did much for damosels' sake" and enlisted him to rid her of Sir Corsabrin's unwelcome attentions. The stink that rose from Corsabrin's unchristened body put Guenever and Duke Galeholt in mind that Palomides, still officially a Saracen, was in danger of a similarly unhallowed end, and they begged him to be baptized.

> Sir, said Palomides, I will that ye all know that into this land I came to be christened, and in my heart I am christened ... But I have made such an avow that I may not be christened till I have done seven true battles for Jesu's sake, ... and I trust God will take mine intent, for I mean truly.

Palomides also successfully defended himself against a charge of treason brought by Goneries' brother Sir Archade. The tournament lasted seven days, and Palomides won third place, after Lancelot and Lamorak.

Tristram and Palomides next met when Tristram and La Beale Isoud were living in Joyous Garde and the Questing Beast led the Saracen to the surrounding woods. As Palomides remarked, "I found never no knight in my questing of this glasting beast, but an he would joust I never refused him." But since Tristram neither identified himself nor requested a joust, and since several other knights of the Round Table and Breuse Sans Pitie also showed up in the area at this time for a general mix-and-match melee, Isoud's two lovers did not fight each other. They jousted shortly thereafter when they met by chance, without recognizing each other, on the way to the Lonazep tournament. This time Palomides, learning who had just given him a fall, appears to have made a sincere effort to bury his enmity:

> I pray you Sir Tristram, forgive me all mine evil will, and if I live I shall do you service above all other knights ... I wot not what aileth me, for meseemeth that ye are a good knight, and none other knight that named himself a good knight should not hate you

On the way to Lonazep, they found the body of King Hermance, and Palomides proved his worth by taking on himself the dead man's written request that he be avenged and his kingdom set again to rights; Tristram judged that his own primary obligation was to be at the tournament. Palomides cleared up the troubles at Hermance's Red City, so winning the people's love and gratitude that they offered him a third of their goods if he would stay with them; nevertheless, he departed and rejoined Tristram in time for the Lonazep tournament.

At first they escorted Isoud jointly and fought on the same side in the lists, but Palomides' old jealousy reasserted itself — on the first day, though he won the honors, it was not without a moment of shame when, in his overeagerness, he slew Lancelot's horse. On the second day he found Arthur ogling Isoud and (not recognizing the King) angrily struck him down; the Saracen then went over to the opposite party, Lancelot's, and changed his armor, all in an effort to fight Tristram down and perhaps do him serious mischief while feigning not to recognize him; rebuked that evening by Isoud (who had seen all) and Tristram, Arthur and Lancelot, he wept all night after the party had separated. On the last day, beaten out of the prize again by Tristram and Lancelot, Palomides raged in the woods until the kings of Wales and Scotland found him and brought him under some sort of control. Then he stood outside Tristram's tent in the dark taunting and threatening Tristram for a time before he departed with the kings, mourning his new rift with Isoud and Tristram.

Refusing to remain with the friendly kings, Palomides found Sir Epinogris wounded. After they exchanged complaints of love, Palomides rescued and restored Epinogris' lady. In the course of this adventure, he met his brother Safere. Travelling together, they were soon captured by the men of a lord whom Palomides had slain in the fighting at Lonazep. They tried the brothers, freed Safere, and condemned Palomides, who prepared himself to meet a shameful death nobly. But as he was led past Joyous Garde to Pelownes castle for execution, both Tristram and Lancelot came to his rescue, Lancelot getting there first.

Then Palomides lived awhile in Joyous Garde, secretly tormented by the daily sight of Isoud and her love for Tristram. At last one day he went into the woods alone and made a long poem of love for Isoud. Tristram happened by and was so angered at hearing his rival sing his lady's praises that he might have killed Palomides had the Saracen not been unarmed. Once again they set a day to fight — a fortnight thence in the meadow under Joyous Garde (Palomides needed the time to recover from his lovesick weakness), but this time Tristram was wounded in a hunting accident and failed to appear. Palomides departed with Tristram's promise to come seeking him when he was whole again. Tristram won great fame that summer seeking Palomides, but failed to find him.

The end of the long rivalry did not come until shortly before the adventures of the Grail. That year, riding to the great Pentecost feast at Camelot, Tristram, unarmed but for spear and sword, met Palomides in full armor and attacked him, to the Saracen's perplexity, who could neither leave the battle without shame nor return the blows of an unarmored man without shame. At length he calmed Tristram's rage with courteous words and they were about to part peaceably when Tristram decided to give Palomides the last of the seven great battles he had vowed to do in Jesu's name before being baptized. Tristram borrowed the armor of Sir Galleron of Galway, another Round Table knight whom Palomides had

jousted down just before meeting Tristram and whose response to his defeat was, "Alas ... pity that so good a knight ... should be unchristened." So Palomides and Tristram at last fought their long-postponed fight, hacking valiantly for more than two hours until Tristram struck Palomides' sword from his hand. They then were reconciled, and Tristram and Galleron rode with Palomides to the Suffragan of Carlisle, who baptized him while they stood his godfathers, after which all three knights rode on to Camelot.

Rather surprisingly, we hear nothing of Palomides during the Grail Adventures; Malory next mentions him as one of the guests as Guenever's small dinner party when Sir Patrise was poisoned. The former Saracen ended in Lancelot's faction, presumably helped rescue Guenever from the stake, and accompanied Lancelot into exile, where he was made Duke of the Provence. [Malory VIII, 9, 29-31; IX, 3, 12, 32-34, 40; X, 2, 13. 18-19, 41-88; XII, 12-14; XVIII, 3, 10, 23; XX, 5, 18]

Except in matters touching Isoud and Tristram, which were apt to drive him out of self-control, Palomides seems to have been one of the best and most courteous knights, honorable, a reliable champion, and an excellent fighter. T. H. White refers to him as "black," almost certainly using the British meaning, which includes all non-white races; I see no objection to a black Palomides in the U. S. sense.

John Erskine's novel **Tristram and Isolde, Restoring Palamede** (which probably should have been titled "Palamede and Brangain," but no doubt they thought that would sell fewer copies) gives a different but especially endearing picture of this knight.

PANDRAGON†

The second son of King Constans of England, Pandragon and his younger brother Uther burned Vortigern in his tower in revenge for Vortigern's barons' murder of their older brother Maines. Pandragon became King, but was killed by the Saxons in battle near Salisbury. Merlin erected Stonehenge as Pandragon's memorial, and Uther adopted his older brother's name in his honor. [Vulgate II]

PANTELION (Pantesileus)†

Pantelion was the master consul of Rome at the time of Arthur's war with Claudas [Vulgate V].

THE COUNT 'DEL PARC'†

He lived three leagues from Terican's (Turquine's) Hill. After Lancelot killed Turquine, the Count del Parc visited the tower and gave each former prisoner a horse. Arthur's knights returned his generosity by giving him Turquine's property. [Vulgate V]

Parzival — see PERCIVALE

EARL OF PASE

This earl was uncle of the Damsel of La Beale Regard. Morgana having usurped that castle, the Damsel sent a message to her uncle requesting him to come and burn La Beale Regard with wild-fire. Hating Morgana, he complied. [Malory X, 38]

His earldom would probably be within fairly easy reach of La Beale Regard.

SAINT PATRICK†

Saint Patrick's dates, 389?-461 A.D., make him a contemporary of Arthur according to the dates given by Malory and the Vulgate.

PATRIDES†

This knight of Arthur's was made Count of Flanders after Arouz was killed resisting Arthur's army on its way to battle Claudas and free Elyzabel. [Vulgate V]

Either this knight or another of the same name was rescued by Percivale from the castle of Garantan, where he had been imprisoned for trying to run away with the lady of the place. [Vulgate V; this appears, however, to be a variant of the tale of the Uncourteous Lady and Sir Persides in Malory XI, 12.]

PATRISE

A knight of Ireland, cousin of Mador de la Porte, and a companion of the Round Table. One of the guests at a small dinner-party of Guenever's, Patrise was accidentally poisoned and killed by eating an apple meant for Gawaine. (The poisoner was Sir Pinel.) [Malory XVIII, 3; cf. Gaheris de Kareheu]

PEDIVERE

Sir Pedivere was chasing his wife when Lancelot found them. "Knight, fie for shame, why wilt thou slay this lady?" said Lancelot. "What hast thou to do betwixt me and my wife?" replied Pedivere. "I will slay her maugre thy head." To prevent this, Lancelot rode between them.

> Sir Launcelot, said the knight, thou dost not thy part, for this lady hath betrayed me. It is not so, said the lady, truly he saith wrong on me. And for because I love and cherish my cousin germain, he is jealous betwixt him and me; and as I shall answer to God there was never sin betwixt us.

As they were riding and talking, Pedivere called Lancelot's attention to some pretended men of arms riding after them, and swapped off the lady's head when Lancelot's back was turned. Lancelot, understandably upset, made him carry the body to Guenever. She made him take the body to Rome and get his penance from the Pope.

> [The] Pope bade him go again unto Queen Guenever, and in Rome was his lady buried by the Pope's commandment. And after this Sir Pedivere fell to great goodness, and was an holy man and a hermit. [Malory VI, 17]

T. H. White identifies Pedivere with Bedivere. I find this identification only slightly less improbable than White's combination of Elaine of Carbonek and Elaine of Astolat — it is artistic, but I do not think it is Malory. On the other hand, there is a chance that this Pedivere could be identified with Pedivere of the Straight Marches, serving a time at the Grail Castle between his return from Rome and his retirement into a hermitage.

PEDIVERE OF THE STRAIGHT MARCHES

When Sir Bors passed the night in the Castle Adventurous at Carbonek, a spear with a head that seemed to burn like a taper came and wounded him in the shoulder. Then a knight came and bade him arise and fight. Sir Bors "bare him backward until that he came unto a chamber door." The strange knight ducked through the door and rested in that chamber for a long time before coming out to renew the battle. In order to win, Bors had to prevent him from going into the chamber again.

This knight was Pedivere of the Straight Marches. Bors charged him to go to Arthur's court that Whitsunday. The chamber in which Pedivere refreshed himself was very likely that in which the Grail was kept. [Malory X, 4-5]

This Pedivere might be identified with Pedivere the wife-slayer and hermit, described above.

KING PELLAM OF LISTENEISE (Pelles, The Fisher King, The Rich Fisher, King of the Waste Lands, King Pescheour, The Maimed King, etc.)

Accounts of the Fisher King are confused, perhaps hopelessly. Even Sommer seems to have had trouble getting on top of the situation. There are at least two versions in Malory alone of the Dolorous Stroke (though I do not consider them necessarily incompatible). Some versions have two or even three maimed kings, sometimes including Pellinore, contemporary with Arthur. To add to the fun, there may or may not have been an obscure connection or confusion somewhere along the line with Sir Pelleas — note the similarity of names. Reversing my technique of splitting the Lady of the Lake into three separate characters, I have attempted a simplified, but I hope acceptable version which rolls the maimed kings into a single man. (Even in Malory, I believe that Pellam, Pelles, and King Pescheour can be considered identical, "Peschour" being a pun on the French words for fisher and sinner. This king stays in his castle at Carbonek, guarding the Holy Grail and waiting to be healed. Malory does mention King Pellam as appearing at various tournaments, but this can be considered another Pellam, likely identical with Pellinore — who, according to Sommer, appears in some versions as an additional maimed king.)

When Joseph of Arimathea and his followers came to Britain, the Grail at first was in the keeping of Joseph's kinsman Lucans. It was given over, however, into the care of Nascien's great-great-grandson Alain (or Helias) li Gros. Alain had, at Joseph's bidding, caught a fish in a British pond. The fish was miraculously enlarged to feed all the sinners of the company (the Grail had fed those who were worthy). This incident gained for Alain and his successors the name Rich Fisher or Fisher King. While Alain's immediate descendants ended up in France to engender Lancelot du Lake, the keeping of the Grail passed over to the line of Alain's brother Josue, from whom Pellam, the last of the Fisher Kings, descended. Pellam had three known brothers: Pellinore, Alain (of Escavalon?), and Garlon (apparently the family black sheep).

In his hale days, Pellam held a feast to which no knight was admitted unless he brought his wife or his paramour. Balin le Sauvage traced Sir Garlon to this feast and there cut him down. Pellam rose, swearing that he and no man else should kill Balin in vengeance for his brother Garlon. He "caught in his hand a grim weapon," and broke Balin's sword with it, then chased Balin through the castle until they came to the chamber of the Grail, where Balin caught up the marvellous spear and smote Pellam with it, upon which both Pellam and a great part of his castle fell down, entrapping them for three days. This is Malory's first version of the Dolorous Stroke. [II, 14-15]

Later, during the Grail Quest, Dame Amide tells another version to Galahad, Percivale, and Bors: while Pellam "might ride[,] he supported much Christendom and Holy Church." But one day, while out hunting, he found King Solomon's Ship and had the temerity to pull David's Sword partially from its scabbard. "So therewith entered a spear wherewith he was smitten him through both the thighs, and never sith might he be healed," until Galahad's coming. [XVII, 5]

The hunting incident might be taken to precede Garlon's death by a longer or shorter period of time, and Balin interpreted as Heaven's unwitting instrument in dealing the Dolorous Stroke, though in this particular Amide abridges the account, perhaps out of delicacy toward Balin and Garlon.

Maimed, Pellam waited in his castle until Lancelot arrived and showed his worth by rescuing the damsel from the scalding bath and slaying a dangerous dragon. The Maimed King then connived with his sorceress Dame Brisen and his daughter Elaine to bring about Galahad's begetting through trickery, fornication, and supposed adultery. Perhaps Pellam acted through inspired foresight, or perhaps he merely wanted a grandson whom he could piously educate to work his cure; it is understandable if he wanted himself and his country (which had also suffered through the Dolorous Stroke) healed as soon as possible. Pellam appears to have had the immediate supervision of Galahad's upbringing until Galahad's early adolescence, or even his middle teens. For a part of this time, having had Lancelot cured, by exposure to the Grail, from a fit of madness, Pellam set up Lancelot and Elaine to live together, without benefit of clergy, in the Joyous Isle.

Lancelot appeared at Carbonek again during the Grail Adventures, brought there by the ship with Amide's body. He had a partial vision of the Grail and fell into a twenty-four-day coma. Pellam had him nursed through this period and, when he woke, told him the sad news of Elaine's death. After Lancelot's departure, Galahad, Percivale, and Bors joined nine holy knights of other nations at Carbonek for the climactic Grail Mysteries. Neither Pellam nor his son Eliazar were permitted to remain with these knights for the great vision (though "a maid which was [Pellam's] niece" appears to have been allowed to remain — probably the Grail Bearer, or perhaps Amide, miraculously resurrected for the hour). At these mysteries, Galahad received blood from the miraculous spear with which to anoint his grandfather and cure him at last.

Some of Pellam's actions seem, to say the least, surprising for a man holding such a sacred trust as his, and it may not appear strange that, after Pellam's cure, the Grail and its accompanying relics chose to leave Carbonek forever, going with Galahad, Percivale and Bors to Sarras and thence out of this world. Pellam, no longer guardian of the Grail, "yielded him to a place of religion of white monks, and was a full holy man." [Malory II, 14-16; XI, 2-4; XIII, 4-6; XVII, 5, 16-21]

Brothers: Pellinore, Alain of Escavalon, Garlon
Sister: King Pellam's Sister, Abbess of a convent not far from Camelot
Wife?: Queen of the Waste Lands
Daughter: Elaine of Carbonek
Son: Eliazar
Grandson (by Elaine and Lancelot): Galahad
Nephews: Castor, Pinel le Savage?
Daughter's handmaid: Dame Brisen
Daughter's suitor: Bromel la Pleche
Seneschals: Claellus?, Duke Minadoras?
Retainer?: Pedivere of the Straight Marches

KING PELLAM'S FAMILY AND RETAINERS

KING PELLAM'S SISTER†

She was abbess of the convent where Galahad's education was completed. [Vulgate V]

PELLEAS

Malory calls Sir Pelleas one of the six knights who could defeat Gawaine. When Gawaine first met him, during the adventure of the damsels Printemps, Été, & Automne, Pelleas was not yet a member of Arthur's court. Gawaine found him diligently pursuing his love for Ettard. At a three-day tournament in Ettard's part of the country, Pelleas had proved the best of 500 knights, winning the prize, a circlet of gold, and presenting it to Ettard as the fairest lady there (although in fact there were some fairer ones present).

> And so he chose her for his sovereign lady, and never to love other but her, but she was so proud that she had scorn of him, and said that she would never love him though he would die for her. ... And so this knight promised the Lady Ettard to follow her into this country, and never to leave her till she loved him.

He lodged by a priory, and every week she sent knights to fight him. He would defeat them all, then allow them to take him prisoner so that, when they brought him in disgrace before their lady, he would get a sight of her.

> And always she [did] him great despite, for sometime she [made] her knights to tie him to his horse's tail, and some to bind him under the horse's belly; thus in the most shamefullest ways

that she could devise (apparently desperate, poor lady, to be rid of him) was he brought to her.

Gawaine promised Pelleas to act as a go-between:

> I will have your horse and your armour, and so will I ride unto her castle and tell her that I have slain you, and so shall I come within her to cause her to cherish me, and then shall I do my true part that ye shall not fail to have the love of her.

Gawaine managed all this except the last part — he stopped before he got around to pleading Pelleas' case. The month was May, so they went outside to take their pleasure in a pavilion. Here Pelleas found Gawaine and Ettard sleeping together, and went well-nigh mad with grief. He considered killing them, but ended by laying his naked sword "overthwart both their throats." Then he rode back to his own pavilions and announced to his knights and squires that he was going to bed and would never get up until he was dead, and when he was dead they were to take his heart between two silver dishes to Ettard.

Apparently he changed his mind about dying in bed, because Nimue met him wandering around the woods on foot. She caused an enchantment whereby Ettard fell madly in love with Pelleas, while all his love for her turned into hate. Then Nimue got Pelleas' love for herself, by enchantment or perhaps simple seduction, and married him, while Ettard died of love.

When Pentecost came, Nimue brought Pelleas to Arthur's court, where he took the prize at jousting and was elected to the Round Table, at the same time as Sir Marhaus. Nimue did not keep Pelleas completely sequestered with her in her Lake; he appears fighting in at least one tournament, riding a-Maying with Guenevere, and trying to heal Sir Urre. But Nimue "saved him that he was never slain." Probably when the Round Table was destroyed by the feud between Lancelot and Gawaine and by Mordred's rebellion, Nimue simply took Pelleas permanently into the Lake, not letting him fight at Salisbury.

One of Caxton's chapter headings calls Pelleas "King." I suspect confusion with King Pelles/Pellam. Malory tells us, immediately after describing Pelleas' election to the Round Table, that he "was one of the four that achieved the Sangreal," but we never hear any more of this; again I suspect confusion with Pelles, or possibly Percivale. Being married to Nimue, Pelleas was hardly a virgin or, like Bors, a celibate; nor was Nimue one to have taken tamely the stricture against ladies accompanying their knights in that Quest! [Malory IV, 20-28; XVIII, 23; XIX, 1, 11]

King Pelles – see PELLAM

KING PELLINORE ('The Knight with the Strange Beast')

King Pellinore of the Isles earned his title, 'The Knight with the Strange Beast,' for his pursuit of the Questing Beast. He was engaged in a twelve-month quest of this creature, not unlikely one of many such yearlong stints, when he first met Arthur, then in the early flush of kinghood. Having just ridden his own horse to death, Pellinore insisted on taking Arthur's, and when the young man requested to follow the Beast in the other's place, Pellinore replied, "It is in vain thy desire, for it shall never be achieved but by me, or my next kin." (Since after Pellinore's death Palomides the Saracen picked up the quest of Galtisant, it is just possible that Pellinore lied to keep Arthur from interfering.)

Before Pellinore rode off, Arthur expressed a desire to see which of them would prove better in a fair joust, to which Pellinore replied, "Well ... seek me here when thou wilt, and here nigh this well thou shalt find me." Not long thereafter, Arthur got word that "one of the best knights of the world, and the strongest man of arms" had set up his pavilion by a well in the forest (possibly the same one where he had promised to give Arthur his joust) and was taking on all comers. After the young Sir Griflet begged the adventure and was defeated, Arthur himself went to fight the forest knight, who turned out to be Pellinore. After a terrific battle, Arthur's sword was broken. Rather than yield, he tried wrestling his opponent down. Adread at Arthur's strength, Pellinore managed to unhelm him and prepared to smite off his head. Merlin arrived and told Pellinore who his adversary was, which had an opposite effect to the one desired, for now Pellinore was even more adread and would have killed Arthur to avoid reprisals. Merlin had to cast Pellinore into an enchanted sleep, whereon Arthur, mistaking it for death, blamed Merlin for slaying so good a knight. Merlin replied by revealing Pellinore's name and future good service to the High King, predicting the births of his sons Lamorak and Percivale, and adding that "he shall tell you the name of your own son, begotten of your sister, that shall be the destruction of all this realm." Malory seems not to follow up or explain this last tantalizing morsel, but it may provide an additional reason for the later enmity between Margawse's sons and Pellinore's.

Merlin took Arthur on to the Lake to receive Excalibur from Nineve, and when Pellinore woke up, he may have sworn himself to another twelvemonth of pursuing Galtisant. Pellinore next turned up on Arthur's side during the battle with Nero, Lot, and the second rebel alliance before Castle Terrabil. In this battle Pellinore slew King Lot. He departed after the battle but soon rejoined Arthur, coming to court the day after the arrival of his own son Tor. At this time Merlin led him to the Siege Perilous and the neighboring seat (which would someday be Lancelot's) and told him, "This is your place and best ye are worthy to sit therein of any that is here." Gawaine

and Gaheris, already angered by the death of their father Lot, were stirred to even greater wrath at this.

When the marriage feast of Arthur and Guenevere was enlivened by the episode of the white hart, the white brachet, and Dame Nimue, Pellinore, on Merlin's advice, was given the task of rescuing Nimue, which he accomplished, bringing her back to court. His adventure was marred, however, when in his dogged haste to find Nimue he refused to stop and help a wounded knight and his lady; they died for lack of help, and Pellinore later learned that the young woman had been his own daughter Eleine (see Eleine and Nimue). Also on their way back, while camped for the night, Pellinore and Nimue overheard two passing knights plot the poisoning of King Arthur; presumably Pellinore and Nimue warned the King on their return, for nothing more is heard of this plot.

Arthur called Pellinore to his assistance against the five invading kings of Denmark, Ireland, the Vale, Soleise, and Longtains, but Pellinore and his army did not arrive in time for the action. Arthur joined them three miles from the Humber after the battle and asked Pellinore's advice on the best men to fill eight vacancies in the Round Table the battle had made. Pellinore suggested four older knights, Uriens, Hervise de Revel, the King of the Lake, and Galagars, and four young ones, Gawaine, Griflet, Kay, and for the last either Bagdemagus or Tor — "but because Sir Tor is my son I may not praise him, but else . . . I durst say that of his age there is not in this land a better knight." Arthur chose Tor, and presumably Bagdemagus' pique extended to Pellinore as well as to Arthur.

In the tenth year after he was knighted, Gawaine avenged his father King Lot by killing Pellinore with his own hands, and with the help of Gaheris. Malory does not describe the actual scene, mentioning it first as a thing to come and later as one that is past, but Pellinore's wife called it shameful treason.

Pellinore was the brother of Pellam the Fisher King, Alain, and Garlon. His sons in wedlock were Aglovale, Lamorak, Dornar, and Percivale. He had at least one bastard son, Tor, begotten on Vayshoure; since Tor was begotten "half by force," we may suspect that Pellinore had a degree of rash heat in his nature and may have fathered other bastards. He had two known daughters: Amide (who may have been legitimate, since her mother is unknown) and Eleine, begotten on the Lady of the Rule — apparently an extra-marital liason. Pellinore seems also to have been hasty-tempered and hard to turn from his purpose once it was fixed. Nevertheless, his suggestion of Gawaine for the Round Table argues either a generous nature or an ingenuous one. Pellinore's kingdom, "the Isles," probably was off the coast of Wales. [Malory I, 19-24; II, 10-11; III, 3-5, 12-15; IV, 2-5; XI, 10; see The Isles, *Places*]

Brothers: Pellam, Alain of Escavalon, Garlon
Wife?: La Veuve Dame de la Gaste Forest Soutaine
Paramours: Lady of the Rule, Vayshoure
Sons (in wedlock): Aglovale, Lamorak, Dornar, Percivale
Son (by Vayshoure): Tor
Daughter (by Lady of the Rule): Eleine
Daughter (by ?): Amide
Nephew?: Pinel le Savage

KING PELLINORE'S FAMILY AND RELATIONS

Pendragon – see PANDRAGON

by Greg Stafford from sketches by Phyllis Ann Karr; notes by P.A.K.

THE FISHER KINGS AND THE KIN OF PELLINORE

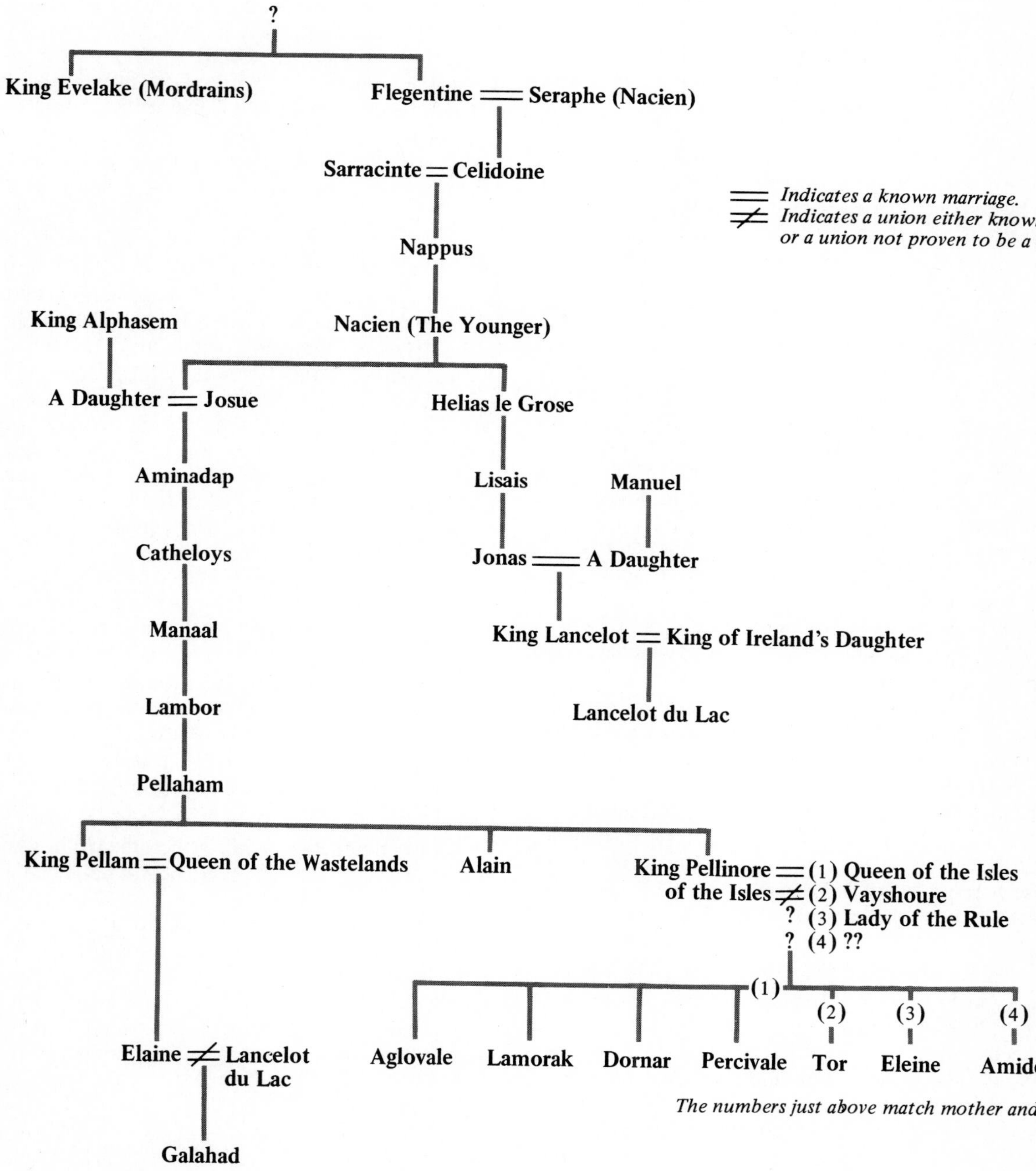

= Indicates a known marriage.
≠ Indicates a union either known to be illicit or a union not proven to be a marriage.

The numbers just above match mother and child.

After the death of Josephe (son of Joseph of Arimathea), Helias le Grose converted King Kalafes (baptised name Alphasem) and his people. Josue, Helias' brother, married Alphasem's daughter and inherited the kingdom, which was to become The Waste Lands. At Alphasem's request, the Grail was left in his country (the castle Carbonek being built for it), and Josue started the line of Grail guardians known as the "Fisher Kings or "Rich Fishers." ("King Petchere" is probably a play on the French words for "fisher" and "sinner," which are very similar.

PERCARD ('The Black Knight,' 'The Knight of the Black Laund')

Sir Percard was the first of four brothers who had "long time ... holden war against the knights of the Round Table" and whom Gareth encountered on his way to fight Sir Ironside at Castle Dangerous. Gareth slew Percard. The other brothers, Pertolepe, Perimones, and Persant, all became knights of the Round Table, as no doubt Percard also would have, had he survived, for on learning of his death Arthur and many knights of the court called it "great pity." Percard's shield and arms, of course, were entirely black. Although Ironside was called 'The Red Knight of the Red Launds,' Percard and the other brothers do not seem to have been related to him in any way, nor involved in his siege of Castle Dangerous. [Malory VII]

PERCIVALE OF WALES (Parzival, Perceval, Peredur, etc)

The following note on this famous knight takes into account only Malory, the Vulgate, and such parts of Chrétien de Troyes' **Perceval** as seem more or less implied in Malory's account, with no reference to the German or early Welsh versions.

Percivale was King Pellinore's youngest son in wedlock, his older brothers being Lamorak, Aglovale, and Dornar. Pellinore seems to have been killed when Percivale was still a child, and the mother, fearing to lose her youngest son as she had lost his father and older brothers to the call of chivalry, raised him in isolation and ignorance of knights and knighthood. One day, when nearing the age of fifteen, Percivale saw Ywaine and other knights riding through the forest, approached and began questioning them under the impression they were angels, and learned from them something of what his mother had kept from him. At once he decided to go to Arthur's court at Carlisle and become a knight himself. His mother swooned on hearing the news. While waiting for her to wake up, he chose the best horse available — a bony, piebald nag, and improvised saddle, trappings, and weapons of twigs and sticks.

When his mother woke up, she instructed him that on reaching court, he should tell them who he was and ask to be knighted at Arthur's hands; that he should say a paternoster in every church he passed; that he could take meat and drink if he saw and needed them; that whenever he heard an outcry he should help the distressed party, especially if it was a woman; that if he saw a fair jewel he should win it and thus acquire fame, but give it away freely and thereby win praise; and that if he saw a fair woman he should pay her court and thus obtain love.

It has been suggested that the good woman purposely gave her son advice calculated to make him appear a bumpkin and thus nip his knightly career at once and bring him back to her; and, indeed, his efforts to follow her counsel made him seem far from courtly at the first pavilion he found. Discovering a fair damsel alone in the pavilion, he greeted her and then promptly kissed her 20 times despite her struggles, took her emerald ring by force, helped himself to wine and venison pasties, and left the innocent and bewildered lady in serious trouble with her jealous lover, who refused to believe, when he returned and found the traces of Percivale's visit, that she had not been willingly seduced. (Meeting them later, by chance, Percivale had to fight him and rescue her.) Nevertheless, the advice in itself sounds like plausible knightly etiquette, and even Percivale's overdone behavior in the pavilion was no rougher nor more high-handed, and much less bloody, than such knights as Lancelot and Gaheris displayed on occasion.

When Percivale arrived at court, the King lightly agreed to dub him, and a maiden who had not laughed for six years greeted him as the future best knight of the world. This so angered Kay that he struck her with his palm. Meanwhile, Percivale rushed forth to punish a strange knight who had insulted the Queen a short time before and was now waiting outside to take on all comers. Though untrained in knightly weapons, Percivale could throw a javelin (his mother had not shielded him from the skills of the hunt) and quickly demolished his opponent with a javelin through the eye. He could not get the dead knight out of his armor, however, without the help of a friendly courtier. Percivale then rode away, swearing not to return to court until he had avenged the maiden Kay struck.

In his travels, Percivale was instructed by a castellan in the knightly weapons, found a lady love, and called at the Grail Castle. Arthur learned Percivale's whereabouts from the knight of the damsel Percivale kissed and unburdened of her ring on his way to court; finding this jealous knight mistreating the lady, Percivale had chastised him in battle and sent him to Arthur.

The season was now winter. One morning Percivale found in the snow the blood of a fowl that had been attacked by a falcon. The red blood and white snow reminded him of the complexion of his lady (very flattering!) and he fell into a reverie of love. It was thus that Arthur and his party found him. Percivale being lost in meditation, Sir Sagremor's summons went unanswered and, when that knight spoke roughly, Percivale jousted him to the ground and returned to his contemplation of the bloody snow. Next Kay tried his luck, greeting Percivale in a characteristically rude style. Percivale left him with a dislocated collarbone and a broken arm. Then Gawaine approached the young many and, being justly surnamed the Golden-Tongued for his great courtesy, managed to engage him in pleasant conversation and persuade him to come back to court, where he was received with general joy and delight.

The above comes mainly from Chrétien and from a substantially similar account, with omissions and some varying details, in Bulfinch's **The Age of Chivalry**, and genealogy from Malory. Chrétien was priming Percivale to achieve the Grail, but left the romance unfinished. I now switch to Malory.

Malory first mentions Percivale in Merlin's prophecy of his future greatness, made just before Arthur's acquisition of Excalibur. Percivale's arrival at court is described in the middle of the books of Tristram. Tristram has joined the Round Table, Arthur has supposedly reconciled his quarrel with King Mark, and the two have gone back to Cornwall together. Eight days later, Sir Algovale brings his younger brother Percivale, acting as his squire, to Arthur's court and requests that he be made knight. Arthur dubs him the next morning, and at dinner commands him to be seated "among mean knights."

> Then was there a maiden in the queen's court that was come of high blood, and she was dumb and never spake word. Right so she came straight into the hall, and went unto Sir Percivale, and took him by the had and said aloud ... Arise Sir Percivale, the noble knight and God's knight, and go with me ... And there she brought him to the right side of the Siege Perilous, and said, Fair knight, take here thy siege, for that siege appertaineth to thee and to none other. Right so she departed and asked a priest. And as she was confessed and houselled then she died. Then the king and all the court made great joy of Sir Percivale.

Chrétien's account has become much shorted and more ethereal — no mention is made of Kay's striking the prophetic damsel, but now she proceeds to a death probably symbolic in its holiness. Nevertheless, much later on, Percivale tells Persides, whom he has just rescued, to go to court and

> Also tell Sir Kay the Seneschal, and to Sir Mordred, that I trust to Jesu to be of as great worthiness as either of them, for tell them I shall not forget their mocks and scorns that they did to me that day that I was made knight; and tell them I will never see that court till men speak more worship of me than ever men did of any of them both.

Unless Malory's editor omitted a portion of the account of Percivale's arrival at court, this passage can best be explained as an accidental carry-over from some version of Chretien's material. In the next chapter after bringing Percivale to court, Malory describes the murder of Margawse and departure of Percivale's older brother Lamorak. This may not accurately reflect the chronology, but it provides a logical reason for Percivale to leave court — also to turn against Mordred and his brothers.

Percivale next appears in time to rescue Tristram from Mark's prison and to scold Mark. When Mark protests that Tristram is La Beale Isoud's lover, the pure and innocent Percivale refuses to believe it, gives Mark a further lecture on the shame of evil thoughts, makes him promise not to hurt Tristram (causing him to turn from overt to secret villainy) and then heads alone for his home country of Wales. A few chapters later, Percivale appears in the neighborhood of Joyous Garde, where Tristram and Isoud have taken refuge. Percivale seems to have joined Ector de Maris and Harry le Fise Lake as temporary companions in adventure; they meet Palomides, among others, and Percivale learns from the Saracen of Lamorak's death. After swooning for grief, the young knight mourns, "Alas my good and noble brother Sir Lamorak, now shall we never meet." Apparently Percivale rode off alone in his grief, for he is not named as fighting at the Lonazep tournament, whither the other knights turn up at about this point.

When Lancelot ran away mad after Guenever found him in bed with Elaine of Astolat, Percivale and his brother Aglovale were among the knights who joined the search for him. Aglovale and Percivale began their search by riding home to visit their mother, "that was a queen in those days." She besought them to remain with her lest she lose them as she had lost Pellinore, Lamorak, and Dornar. When they left despite her prayers, she sent a squire after them; the squire fell afoul of one Baron Goodewin, who slew him because Aglovale had slain Goodewin's brother Sir Gawdelin. Meeting the funeral party, Aglovale and Percivale went back and avenged the squire. Long time later, after much fruitless searching, the brothers lodged at Cardican castle, and there Percivale rather inexplicably woke Aglovale's squire at midnight and made him ride secretly away with him, leaving Aglovale behind. Percivale rescued Sir Persides from the Uncourteous Lady and bade him return to court with the message to Kay and Mordred quoted above, as well as the message to Aglovale not to come seeking him, for he would never return until he had found Lancelot. (Perhaps Aglovale had determined to give up the search and ride back to court.)

Percivale eventually met Ector de Maris and they almost killed one another in a knightly battle "to the uttermost," apparently for the excellent reason of proving their strength. But Percivale prayed to Jesu and, since he was "one of the best knights of the world ... in whom the very faith stood most in," and "a perfect clean maiden" (we must now forget the lusty experiments and lady love of Chrétien's Percivale), the Grail came

and healed both knights, and Percivale got an imperfect "glimmering of the vessel and of the maiden that bare it." Percivale and Ector continued on together and found Lancelot living with Elaine at Joyous Isle. Percivale had a good two hours of chivalrous battle with him before they learned his identity and persuaded him to return to court.

That Pentecost, Galahad came to court and the Grail Adventures began. Percivale and Lancelot were the only Round Table knights whom Galahad did not defeat and "defoul" at his one tournament before Arthur, the day before the Questers departed. Percivale apparently began the Quest in Lancelot's company, but they encountered Galahad again near the hermitage of a female recluse: this time Galahad jousted them both down. The recluse cheered the victor so eagerly that Galahad rode away for modesty, while Lancelot rode away for shame, leaving Percivale alone with the holy woman, who turned out to be his aunt. She gave him good counsel, advising him that to find Galahad, whose fellowship he wished, he should ride to Goothe castle and, if unsuccessful there, to Carbonek. Percivale visited King Mordrains in his abbey. He was saved from 20 attacking knights by Galahad, but Galahad rode off again before Percivale could catch up. He was given a black, demon horse that would have plunged him into the roiling water had he not made the sign of the cross in time. Fasting along on a rocky island, he was joined by the devil in the guise of a fair damsel, who tempted him almost to the point of making love, but again Percivale made the sign of the cross in time; the devil vanished and Percivale drove his own sword into his thigh as penance.

After these and other mystical adventures and visions, a divine or angelic messenger brought him a ship all covered in white samite to escape from the island of his temptation. When the ship came ashore on the mainland, Percivale was joined by Sir Bors de Ganis. The ship then brought them to their rendezvous with Galahad and Percivale's sister Amide. The four traveled together for a time, found King Solomon's Ship, purged the castle of Earl Hernox of its wicked occupants, and shared Eucharistic visions in Carteloise forest. At last they came to the Castle of the Leprous Lady, where Percivale lost his sister, promising her on her deathbed to see that her last wishes were carried out. After the destruction of the castle, the three knights separated again for a while, but met once more and proceeded together to Carbonek for the climactic mysteries of the Grail.

Percivale left Carbonek with Galahad and Bors; they found their ship (with the Grail miraculously aboard) and sailed to Sarras, where they found the vessel with Amide's body and buried her before being thrown into prison by King Estorause. When they were freed and Galahad made king for a year in Estorause's place, Percivale and Bors presumably acted as his chief counsellors. Immediately after Galahad, the Grail, and Longinus' Spear were taken to Heaven, Percivale "yielded him to an hermitage out of the city, and took a religious clothing," Bors remaining with him but not taking the habit.

> Thus a year and two months lived Sir Percivale in the hermitage a full holy life, and then passed out of this world; and Bors let bury him by his sister and by Galahad in the spiritualities.

Besides supplying Percivale's age at fifteen when he received knighthood, the Vulgate reaffirms that he led a pure and chaste life and was second in holiness only to Galahad, adding that he went to Confession weekly. [Malory I, 24; X, 23, 51, 53-54, 68; XI, 10-14; XII, 7-8; XIII, 3, 17; XIV, 1-10; XVI, 17; XVII, 2-12, 19-23; Vulgate V]

PERIMONES ('The Red Knight')

Perimones was the third of four brothers whom Gareth encountered on his way to fight Sir Ironside at Castle Dangerous. The other brothers were Percard, Persant, and Pertolepe. Perimones' shield and arms were entirely red, and care must be taken not to confuse him with Sir Ironside, who also was armed in red and called 'The Red Knight of the Red Launds.'

Perimones was lord of a white tower, "well matchecold all about, and double dyked," where he was preparing to host a tournament when Gareth passed by and he fought the young knight in an attempt to avenge his brother Percard. Perimones had at least fifty knights in his service, and on being defeated he yielded them all, as well as himself, to Gareth's command. He jousted in Lyonors' tournament at Castle Dangerous and made a creditable showing, and later came to court about the time of Gareth's wedding, obtained the favor of being made Gareth's butler at the high feast of Michaelmas, and was made a member of the Round Table. Perimones was one of the knights in Guenevere's guard at the stake, and was killed when Lancelot rescued her. [Malory VII, 10, 28, 35; XX, 8]

PERIS DE FOREST SAVAGE

This knight, who apparently operated near the vicinity of Sir Turquine's tower, was in the habit of haunting a fair highway in order to distress all ladies and gentlewomen, ravishing or at least robbing them.

> As Sir Turquine watched to destroy knights, so did this knight attend to destroy and distress ladies, damosels, and gentlewomen.

An unnamed damsel described his depredations to Lancelot, led the great knight to the vicinity, and then rode ahead as bait, bringing out Sir Peris so that Lancelot could kill him. [Malory VI, 10]

PERSANT OF INDE

Sir Persant earned his surname for his preference to "the colour of Inde," dark blue, which he used for his arms, armor, shield, the trappings of his horses, the livery of his male and female attendants, and his pavilion. A goodly knight and the lord of a fair city, he was the last of four brothers whom Gareth defeated on his way to fight Sir Ironside at Castle Dangerous; the other three were Percard, Perimones, and Pertolepe. After his defeat, Persant lodged Gareth and Lynette nobly for the night, and proved himself a more than hospitable host, at least by today's standards: he sent his eighteen-year-old virgin daughter to Gareth's bed with instructions to "make him no strange cheer, but good cheer,

and take him in thine arms and kiss him." Persant was much impressed with Gareth's nobility when the young knight sent her back undefoiled.

On Gareth's command, Persant, bringing a hundred knights, came with his surviving brothers to Arthur's court at Pentecost, where they were pardoned for the war they had long held against the knights of the Round Table. Persant fought in Lyonors' tournament at Castle Dangerous, and later came to court about the time of Gareth's wedding and obtained the favor of being Gareth's sewer-chief at the feast of Michaelmas. He was soon elected to the Round Table.

Persant appears as one of Guenevere's guests at the select dinner party where Sir Patrise was killed, and as one of ten knights to ride a-Maying with her and fall into Sir Meliagrant's ambush. He was also among the knights who tried to heal Sir Urre. He is not mentioned as being with his brothers Pertopele and Perimones when they were killed during Guenevere's rescue from the stake; Persant may have been the oldest — the age of his daughter at the time of his meeting with Gareth suggests his maturity — and have been already retired from active service. [Malory VII, 12, 23-24, 26-28, 35; XVIII, 3; XIX, 1; XX, 8] For the possible location of his city, see under Castle Dangerous, *Places*.

PERSE†

Dame Perse was an early love of Sir Ector de Maris. When Ector was late returning to her (since he was out searching for Lancelot), her dying father gave her, against her will, to Zelotes. Zelotes, however, neither married her nor permitted anyone else to marry her, but fought and killed all who approached his castle. At last Ector and his companions came by. Ector fought and killed Zelotes and was reunited with Perse. (He had found another love in the interval, but she was now dead.) Sir Lionel, seeing Perse with Ector, remarked that a woman's heart was a marvellous thing, since neither misfortune nor suffering could change its purpose. [Vulgate V, Appendix]

PERSIDES DE BLOISE

Going to the tournament at the Castle of Maidens, Tristram lodged with old Sir Pellounes, whose castle seems to have been within sight of the Castle of Maidens. At this same time Pellounes' son, Sir Persides, gladdened his father's heart by coming home after a two years' absence. Tristram remarked to Pellounes, "I know your son well enough for a good knight." Learning that Tristram was of Cornwall, but not his name, Persides described how he had once been in Cornwall, and jousted down ten knights before King Mark, but

---

then Sir Tristram "overthrew me, and took my lady away from me, and that shall I never forget." He may or may not have also told Tristram of a more recent adventure, only a few days before, when he had fought and wounded Sir Mordred and would have slain him "had it not been for the love of Sir Gawaine and his brother [probably Gareth]." As they stood talking at a bay-window they could watch "many knights riding to and fro toward the tournament," among whom was one whom Persides recognized with admiration as Palomides, then engaged in jousting down a baker's dozen of knights.

> Fair brother, said Sir Tristram unto Sir Persides, let us cast upon us cloaks, and let us go see the play. Not so, said Sir Persides, we will not go like knaves thither, but we will ride like men and good knights to withstand our enemies.

As a result of his honesty, Persides got a fall from Palomides. Later, in the tournament proper, he was "smitten down and almost slain" by a large party with Bleoberis and Gaheris at its head, but rescued by Tristram. Presumably Persides learned Tristram's identity and they were reconciled before the end of the tourney.

Later, Sir Percivale, searching for Lancelot, found Persides chained to a stone pillar outside the Castle of the Uncourteous Lady, rescued him, and sent him back to Arthur's court with various messages. (It is possible, however, that this was a different Persides from the one mentioned above; this Persides is identified as a knight of the Round Table, but not given the surname "de Bloise.")

Though Persides de Bloise is a minor character, his is one of the few shields that Malory describes: green with a lion of gold. [Malory IX, 27-28, 30, 32, 36; XI, 12; see "Castle of the Uncourteous Lady," *Places*]

PERSIDES [of Gazewilte]†

This Sir Persides was lord of Gazewilte Castle. His lovely wife, Helaine the peerless, claimed that her beauty was superior to his bravery, so he imprisoned her until the question could be settled. She spent five years in prison, until her sister, looking for Gawaine, found Ector de Maris and fetched him instead. Ector defeated Persides and sent him and Helaine to Guenever. [Vulgate III]

I rather doubt this knight could be identified with Malory's Persides.

PERTOLEPE ('The Green Knight')

Pertolepe was the second of four brothers whom Gareth encountered on his way to fight Sir Ironside at Castle Dangerous; the others were Percard, Perimones, and Persant. Pertolepe's trappings were "all in green, both his horse and his

harness." On seeing Gareth in the black armor of his brother Percard, and learning that Gareth had slain Percard,

> the Green Knight rode unto a horn that was green, and it hung upon a thorn, and there he blew three deadly notes, and there came two damosels and armed him lightly. And then he took a great horse, and a green shield and a green spear.

(Although each of the four brothers is connected with a color, and although Pertolepe should not be confused with the more famous Green Knight of Gawaine's adventure, Bercilak de Hautdesert, the above passage may suggest a common origin in the roots of legend for the two.)

After his defeat, Pertolepe pledged himself and thirty knights to be at Gareth's service, lodged Gareth and Lynette for the night, and, true to Gareth's command, showed up along with his surviving brothers at Arthur's court that Pentecost. He made a good showing in Dame Lyonors' tournament at Castle Dangerous, and returned to court about the time of Gareth's wedding, bringing his thirty knights and obtaining the favor of acting as Gareth's chamberlain at the high feast of Michaelmas. Soon thereafter he was elected to the Round Table. He was among the knights killed when Lancelot rescued Guenever from the stake. [Malory VII, 8-9, 23-28, 35; XX, 8]

PETROINES†

This clerk held the first school at Oxford, and there, also, wrote down Merlin's prophecies. From Oxford he came to Duke Galeholt's court, where he seems to have been the most prominent clerk after Helyes of Thoulouse. [Vulgate IV]

PHARIANCE (Pharien)

Malory calls Sir Phariance "a worshipful knight." When Ulfius and Brastias brought Arthur's call for support to Kings Ban and Bors, Phariance and Lionses were the two "knights of worship" sent to greet the Britons. Phariance and Lionses accompanied Ban and Bors to Britain, and fought nobly in the battle of Bedegraine.

The Vulgate picks up a somewhat less flattering sequel. While a retainer of King Bors, Pharien killed another knight, for which Bors banished him. Pharien changed sides and became a retainer of King Claudas. Claudas loved Pharien's wife and made Pharien seneschal of Gannes for her sake. After King Bors' death, Pharien confiscated Bors' two sons, Lionel (aged twenty-one months) and young Bors (aged nine months). Pharien and his nephew Lambegues thus became the tutors of Lionel and Bors. After Seraide's rescue of the two boys from Claudas' court, Claudas threw Pharien and Lambegues into prison, but Lionses used a ruse to accomplish their rescue. Pharien and his family were brought to the French Lake,

---

knight. A knight who fails to fulfil them disgraces himself in this world and loses his place in heaven.

As examples of worthy knights, the Damsel of the Lake then cited John the Hircanian, Judas Maccabeus and his brother Symon, and King David — all in the Old Testament time when the Israelites fought their enemies; and, after the Passion of Christ, Joseph of Arimathea, his son King Galahad, and their descendants King Pelles of Listenois and his brother Alain le Gros. [Vulgate III, p. 111-117]

Helin le Blank, Galahad, and Percivale were all dubbed knights at age fifteen. [Malory XII, 9; Vulgate V; Vulgate VI, however, says that Galahad was eighteen.] Lancelot, as appears above, was dubbed in his late teens. I believe that age twenty-one was usual in historical practice for a young man who had come up through the standard education of page, squire, and bachelor; I suspect that fifteen was unusually young even in romance and

legend, and is mentioned as showing that the youth was a prodigy.

Young knights were often put to the worse in jousting, for fighting on horseback required experience. But because of their youthful strength and agility, they were good on foot. Thus, older knights might seek to gain glory by jousting with younger, but then refuse to fight the younger knights on foot. Sir Mordred (probably still in his earlier promise, before his wickedness came to the surface) explains this to the damsel Maledisant:

> [La Cote Male Taile] is a good knight, and I doubt not but he shall prove a noble knight; but as yet he may not yet sit sure on horseback, for he that shall be a good horseman it must come of usage and exercise. But when he cometh to the strokes of his sword he is then noble and mighty, and that saw Sir Bleoberis and Sir Palomides, for wit ye well they are wily men of arms, and anon they know when they

where Pharien eventually died. His wife remained with Viviane, and his sons Anguins and Tatains went on to become gallant knights. [Malory I, 10, 15, 17; Vulgate III]

PHELOT

This villainous knight was a retainer of the king of Northgalis. Lancelot met Phelot's wife hurrying after her falcon, whose lunes had got entangled in a tree. She begged Lancelot to recover the bird, lest her husband slay her for its loss. Although protesting that he was "an ill climber," Lancelot stripped to his shirt and breeches, climbed the tree and threw down the hawk. Barely had the lady recovered it when Sir Phelot came charging out of ambush to reveal that his wife had acted on his orders in setting up a ruse to trap Lancelot up a tree without arms and armor and kill him. Lancelot killed Phelot instead, with the help of a tree branch, and left the lady in a swoon. [Malory VI, 16]

KING PIGNORES†

An ally of the Sesnes in their attack on Vandaliors castle. [Vulgate II]

PINEL LE SAVAGE (Avarlon)

Sir Pinel was a cousin to Sir Lamorak, and a knight of the Round Table. For "pure envy and hate," Pinel tried to poison Gawaine and avenge the death of Lamorak. The poison accidentally killed Sir Patrise of Ireland instead. After lying low while Mador de la Porte impeached the Queen for Patrise's death and Lancelot fought to save her life, Pinel "fled into his country" when Nimue uncovered the truth.

This may be the same Sir Pinel mentioned as "a good man of arms" who fought on Arthur's side in the battle of Bedegraine.

In Vulgate VI, the name of this mortal enemy of Gawaine's is Sir Avarlon. As Pinel in Malory, so Avarlon in the Vulgate tries to poison Gawaine with apples at a small dinner party given by the Queen. Here, Sir Gaheris de Kareheu falls accidental victim. (Do not confuse this Gaheris with Gawaine's brother.) [Malory I, 14; XVIII, 3-8; Vulgate VI]

Plaine de Force — see under PLENORIUS

PLENORIUS AND HIS BROTHERS

Sir Plenorius and his brothers, Sirs Plaine de Force, Plaine de Amours, Pillounes, Pellogris, and Pellandris kept a castle at the border of Surluse. They took La Cote Male Taile and King Carados of Scotland, among others, prisoner. Lancelot defeated them and rescued their prisoners, but refused to take their castle and lands.

Plenorius became a companion of the Round Table on the same Pentecost as La Cote Male Taile, "and Sir Plenorius' brethren were ever knights of King Arthur." Plaine de Force also made it to the Round Table. Eventually Plenorius followed Lancelot into exile and was made Earl of Foise, but Malory seems not to tell us what happened to the other brothers. [Malory IX, 7-9; XIX, 11; XX, 5, 18]

THE POPE

The reigning Pope took a hand (by messengers) in Arthur's affairs, as in the affairs of other kings, often enough that he must be recognized both as a force and as a character — or perhaps, since Pope follows Pope — as more than one character in the Arthurian saga. For instance, it was the Pope who ordered Arthur to be reconciled with Guenever in the matter of 'the false Guenever' (see Genievre, Bertholai). It was also the Pope who ordered Arthur to be reconciled with his wife after Lancelot rescued her from the stake, the Pope's command reaching them while Arthur besieged them in Joyous Garde.

Arthur met the current pontiff in person when he conquered Rome and "was crowned emperor by the pope's hand, with all the royalty that could be made, and sojourned [in Rome] a time." [Malory V, 12; XX, 13; Vulgate etc.]

KING 'PREMIER CONQUIS'†

He was one of the two allies whom Duke Galeholt loved and trusted most; the other was the King of the Hundred Knights. [Vulgate III]

PRIAMUS

A Saracen knight of Tuscany, descended from Alexander, Hector, Joshua, and Macabaeus, he was the "right inheritor of Alexandria and Africa, and all the out isles." In Arthur's war against Emperor Lucius, the Saracens were allies of Rome, and Gawaine encountered and fought Sir Priamus in Italy. They wounded each other almost to death, but luckily Priamus had a balm which healed their wounds within an hour; this same balm was the only thing that could cure a wound from Priamus' sword. Priamus eagerly converted to Christianity, became a companion of the Round Table, and was made Duke of Lorraine. He was among those killed when Lancelot rescued Guenever from the stake. [Malory V, 10-12; XX, 8; See Priamus' Sword, Priamus' Balm, *Things*]

"PRINTEMPS, ÉTÉ, & AUTOMNE"

One of these damsels was sixty years old or more and wore a golden garland about her white hair; the second was

---

see a young knight by his riding, how they are sure to give him a fall from his horse or a great buffet. But for the most part they will not light on foot with young knights, for they are wight and strongly armed. For in likewise Sir Launcelot du Lake, when he was first made knight, he was often put to the worse upon horseback, but ever upon foot he recovered his renown, and slew and defoiled many knights of the Round Table. And therefore the rebukes that Sir Launcelot did unto many knights causeth them that be men of prowess to beware; for often I have seen the old proved knights rebuked and slain by them that were but young beginners. [Malory IX, 4]

Malory also remarks that the knight "was never formed that all times might stand, but sometime he was put to the worse by mal-fortune; and at sometime the worse knight put the better knight to a rebuke" [IX, 12].

Sir Dinadan, after egging King Mark on to fight Lamorak,

be strictly a personal excuse rather than a widespread sentiment. As for the latter part of his statement, similar gratuitous expresrails at Mark for being bested:

Then Sir Dinadan mocked King Mark and said: Ye are not able to match a good knight. As for that, said King Mark, at the first time I jousted with this knight ye refused him. Think ye that it is a shame to me? said Sir Dinadan: nay, sir, it is ever worship to a knight to refuse that thing that he may not attain, therefore your worship had been much more to have refused him as I did; for I warn you plainly he is able to beat such five as ye and I be; for ye knights of Cornwall are no men of worship as other knights are. And because ye are no men of worship ye hate all men of worship, for never was bred in your country such a[nother] knight as is Sir Tristram. [Malory X, 8]

Dinadan was never a man to fight needlessly, and his opinion as to the glory of refusing single combat with a better knight may

thirty years old and wore a gold circlet about her head; the third was fifteen years old and wore a garland of flowers. They waited by a fountain in the forest of Arroy, and when Ywaine, Gawaine, and Marhaus came by, the damsels put themselves forward as guides for a year of adventuring. Ywaine chose the oldest, "for she hath seen much, and can best help me when I have need," Marhaus chose the thirty-year-old, and Gawaine thanked them for leaving him the youngest. Very likely these damsels were of supernatural origin in early versions of the tale or in the models from which Malory drew them, but in Malory's account they behave like ordinary women with no special powers aside from knowing their way around the territory.

These are the only characters to whom I gave names of my own invention: Printemps ("Spring") seems appropriate for the fifteen-year-old, Été ("Summer") for the thirty-year-old, and Automne ("Autumn") for the sixty-year-old.

Printemps soon grew disgruntled with Gawaine for not riding in to help Sir Pelleas right away, whether Pelleas wanted help or not, so she went off with another knight. Été brought Marhaus to the Duke of South Marches, whom he won for Arthur; to Lady de Vawse's tournament, where he won the prize circlet of gold; and to the lands of Earl Fergus, where he slew the giant Taulurd. Automne brought Ywaine to the Lady of the Rock, for whom he fought Sirs Edward and Hue of the Red Castle, so both the older damsels showed their knights good adventure. At the year's end all three knights and damsels returned to the fountain from whence they had set out, Printemps coming either with the knight for whom she had left Gawaine or perhaps by herself. Then the knights "departed from the damosels," who presumably settled down to await three more champions. [Malory IV, 18-28]

AGNELL†

Arthur had fallen into the power of the Grim Baron, Gromer Somir Joure, who made him swear to return in a year and a day and either bring the correct answer to the riddle "What is it women love best?" or meet his death. While searching for the answer, Arthur met in Inglewood Forest a lady carrying a lute and riding a beautiful, richly caparisoned palfrey — but the woman herself was incredibly ugly and hideous. This Foul Ladye was Dame Ragnell, Gromer's sister (though she did not tell Arthur that), and she gave Arthur the answer to the riddle in return for his and Gawaine's promise that Gawaine would wed her. (The answer to the riddle is generally given as 'Women most desire to have power over men,' or 'To have their own will in all things.' I suspect the answer might just as well be stated, 'Women most desire exactly the same thing that men most desire.') Gromer reluctantly sparing Arthur because of Ragnell's answer to the riddle, she came along to the King's court at Carlisle, insisting on her full rights.

Though Guenever begged her to be married secretly and privately, to spare Gawaine disgrace, Dame Ragnell calmly insisted on a full public ceremony with all the trimmings, and further set off her ugliness with a bridal dress worth three thousand gold pieces. At the marriage feast she enjoyed herself with hearty bad manners, gobbling down as much as any other six guests together. When, at last, she and Gawaine were alone in the bridal chamber, she demanded her marital rights, pointing out, "If I were beautiful, you wouldn't even have worried about whether we were married or not." When he turned to give her what she asked, he beheld one of the most beautiful women he could ever have imagined. She then explained that he could choose whether to have her beautiful at night for himself alone and ugly by day in the sight of the world, or beautiful by day and ugly by night. Stymied, or at least pretending to be, he gave the choice back to her. His generosity broke the enchantment completely — her stepmother had transformed her into an ugly hag until the best man in England married her and gave her control over his body and goods.

She remained beautiful by day and night both, and of all the wives and paramours he had in his lifetime, Gawaine loved her best. She became mother of Sir Guinglain (Gingalin), and obtained Arthur's promise of mercy for her brother. Alas, she lived only five years after her wedding. [**The Wedding of Sir Gawain and Dame Ragnell**, a Middle English metrical romance. A good prose translation and critical comments appear in Louis B. Hall's **The Knightly Tales of Sir Gawain**. Glennie mentions the Foul Ladye; Chaucer, John Gower, Howard Pyle, and no doubt many others have used the tale or a variant of it through the centuries.]

'The Red Knight of the Red Launds' — see IRONSIDE

For the other "color" knights in the story of Sir Gareth, see Percard (The Black Knight), Persant of Inde (The Blue Knight — "of the colour of Inde"), Pertolepe (The Green Knight — do not confuse with Gawaine's Green Knight, Bercilak de Hautdesert), and Perimones (The Red Knight).

The Rich Fisher — see PELLAM

sions occur so often in Malory's work (despite the fact that the Cornish knights who appear as characters seem no worse as a body than any other group of knights) that I believe "Cornish knight" jokes must have been to Malory's generation what "Polack" jokes are to ours; perhaps every generation has its butt for such jokes, whether it be the Cornish knight, the Irishman, the moron, the Pole, the Italian, or the mother-in-law.

Weapons might be poisoned. Sir Marhaus carried a venomed spear into battle with Tristram. It did not save Marhaus; but Tristram could not be healed of the wound until he went into Ireland, where the venom had come from, and was cared for by La Beale Isoud. (Does this suggest a bit of sorcery in the preparation of the venom?) Marhaus had been accounted a noble knight and had been a member of the Round Table, and I recall no censure of him for carrying a poisoned weapon, even though this trick might have been a holdover from an earlier version of the Tristram tale in which Marhaus lacked the noble history he has in Malory. [Malory VIII, 8, etc.]

Lancelot remarked, after Meliagrant's archers had shot his horse from ambush, "... it is an old saw, A good man is never in danger but when he is in the danger of a coward" [Malory XIX, 4]. Another point to remember is that "when men be hot in deeds of arms oft they hurt their friends as well as their foes." Again, Lancelot is talking, and he certainly ought to know! [Malory IX, 36]

Simply being wounded need not keep a good knight down. King Mark needed Tristram to fight the Saxon captain Elias, but Tristram was lying abed, sorely wounded from the previous day's battle. At Mark's plea, Tristram agreed to get up and fight again, "for as yet my wounds be green, and they will be sorer a seven night than they be now; and therefore ... I will do battle to-morn [against Elias]." Tristram won. [Malory X, 30]

King Rience — see RYONS

DUKE ROCHEDON'S DAUGHTER†

In Malory, Lancelot is released from Castle Chariot by King Bagdemagus' daughter [Malory VI, 4]. In Vulgate V, this role is taken by Duke Rochedon's daughter.

Rochedon once warred with the kingdom of Sorestan. When peace was made, Rochedon's daughter, aged five years, was betrothed to the King of Sorestan's grandson, aged six. Her parents died, and the Queen of Sorestan became her guardian. When the damsel's betrothed was killed, the queen refused to let her go, insisting instead that she marry her (the queen's) brother. The damsel freed Lancelot in return for his preventing this marriage.

When Lancelot returned to Castle Chariot as agreed with Rochedon's daughter, the queen's brother slipped away rather than fight. Lancelot forced the queen to free the damsel and restore her inheritance.

THE BISHOP OF ROCHESTER

This "noble clerk ... the French book saith, it was the Bishop of Rochester" was in Rome for some reason when the Pope charged him with carrying the threat of interdict to Britain if Arthur did not take Guenever back and make peace with Lancelot, whom he had been besieging in Joyous Garde. [Malory XX, 13]

THE LADY OF THE ROCK

The sixty-year-old damsel of Arroy brought Ywaine to visit this "much courteous" lady, who complained to him of Sirs Edward and Hue of the Red Castle. They had extorted a barony from her. Ywaine fought them and restored it. [Malory IV, 26-27; compare with "Printemps, Été, and Automne."]

THE LADY OF ROESTOC†

She seems to have been Roestoc's ruler. She fell in love with Gawaine and gave him a girdle and locket when he defeated Sir Segurades for her. Gawaine subsequently gave the girdle and locket to the sister of Helain de Taningues. [Vulgate III]

When Gareth conquered Sir Sornehan, it was to the Lady of Roestoc that he sent him [Vulgate V].

Vulgate VII names a *Helyes li chatelains de Roestoc*. The "li" is masculine, and Helyes appears to be one of the rebel kings, possibly killed in battle, which makes the Lady of Roestoc either his widow or his orphaned daughter.

ROLIAX†

Sir Meliagrant made his serf Roliax Lancelot's jailer when he locked the great knight in a solitary tower surrounded by morass. Roliax had to bring food by boat, and Lancelot had to draw up the provisions in a basket. Meliagrant's stepsister, who hated him for causing her disinheritance by King Bagdemagus, was a benefactress of Roliax's wife and thus was able to help Lancelot escape. [Vulgate IV]

"ROSSIGNOL"†

Viviane, the French Damsel of the Lake, sent two unnamed maidens to help Lancelot in Britain. Eventually, mistakenly believing Lancelot to have been killed, the maiden I call Rossignol took the veil and became a nun in England rather than return to the Lake. [Vulgate III]

DUKE AND DUCHESS DE LA ROWSE

When Gareth slipped away after the tournament at his love's Castle Dangerous, he came on a stormy night to another castle, where he identified himself as one of Arthur's knights and asked for lodging. The Duke de la Rowse was absent, but the duchess had the young man admitted, saying, "I will see that knight, and for King Arthur's sake he shall not be harbourless." She warned him, however, that her lord had "ever been against" Arthur, and so Gareth's condition for spending the night was "that wheresomever thou meet my lord, by stigh or by street, thou must yield thee to him as prisoner." Gareth agreed, with the counter-stipulation that the duke would not harm him on his surrender or, if the duke seemed about to offer injury, Gareth then retained the right to fight back. This agreement reached, the duchess and her people "made him passing good cheer." Just before he left in the morning, she asked him his name, and, when he gave it as Gareth, or Beaumains, she recognized it as the name of the knight who had fought for Dame Lyonors; apparently the De la Rowses were not only neighbors of Lynette and Lyonors, but managed to keep posted on the affairs of their neighborhood.

After a few intervening adventures, Gareth chanced to meet "a goodly knight" near or on a mountain. "Abide sir knight," said the stranger, "and joust with me." Asking his name, and learning that he was the Duke de la Rowse, Gareth tried to surrender as per his promise, but the duke replied, "... make thee ready, for I will have ado with you." At the end of an hour's sore fighting, the duke yielded to Gareth and promised to take a hundred knights and go to Arthur's court at the next feast to swear homage and fealty to the King. (De la Rowse appears to have been a true sportsman, more interested in playing the game than in accumulating prisoners or holding grudges.) The duke showed up, true to his word, at Michaelmas and obtained the favor of serving Gareth's wine at that feast. At the jousting held on that feast, "King Arthur made the Duke de la Rowse a Knight of the Round Table to his life's end, and gave him great lands to spend." [Malory VII, 31-32, 35]

One Sir Ladinas de la Rouse appears fighting on the side of Arthur, Ban, and Bors in the battle of Bedegraine. This may be the French knight Ladinas introduced a few chapters earlier at the tournament held by the three kings to celebrate their alliance. Sir Ladinas of the Forest Savage appears among the Round Table knights who go a-Maying with Guenever and fall into Meliagrant's ambush. It is tempting to identify these three Ladinases as the same knight, and to further identify them with Gareth's Duke de la Rowse, because of the surname "de la Rouse," even though we must then postulate that the French Sir Ladinas not only settled into a British dukedom after Bedegraine, but for some reason (perhaps because of the May babies?) shifted his alliance away from Arthur at an early period. [Malory I, 11, 17; XIX, 1]

THE LADY OF THE RULE

All I can find of her is that she was the mother of King Pellinore's daughter Eleine [Malory III, 15].

KING RYONS (Rience) of NORTHGALIS, IRELAND, and MANY ISLES

This charming monarch had a hobby of trimming, or "purfling," his cloak with the beards of the kings he conquered. He had already shown himself antagonistic to Arthur at the time of the first kings' rebellion, but he did not join the eleven rebelling kings, pursuing instead his "great war" on Leodegrance of Cameliard. One can well imagine that he was not popular with his fellow kings of Britain, whether they opposed Arthur or not. Not long after Bedegraine, and, as it seems, about the time Arthur acquired Excalibur, Ryons sent the young king notice that his cloak was now decorated with the beards of eleven kings who had shaved their chins as part of their homage to him, and he wanted Arthur's beard to make it an even dozen. Quipping that his beard was "full young yet to make a purfle of it," Arthur conquered Ryons instead, though not without the material assistance of Balin and Balan. Acting under the guidance of Merlin, these two knights waylaid Ryons when he took time out from besieging Castle Terrabil to ride to a tryst with the Lady de Vance. Balin and Balan smote down the king, slew more than 40 of his men, and routed the remnant. Ryons yielded rather than be slain, and the brothers delivered him prisoner to Arthur.

> King Arthur came then to King Rience, and said, Sir king, ye are welcome: by what adventure come ye hither? Sir, said King Rience, I came hither by an hard adventure.

This passage suggests that, with all his faults, Ryons had a streak of ironic humor and could apply it even to himself. Ryon's brother Sir Nero continued the war at Terrabil, leading ten battalions; King Lot, apparently with the rest of his royal allies of the second rebellion in his host, was on the way to join Nero, but Merlin delayed him with a ruse, so that both rebel armies were defeated and Nero, Lot, and the other kings killed in the battle. What happened to Ryons himself does not seem to be told. [Malory I, 17, 26; II, 6, 9-10]

The Vulgate, however, tells us that Ryons was a descendant of Hercules, and was killed by Arthur in single combat [Vulgate II]. The "King of Norgales" in later episodes would therefore be a different man — I think possibly Galehodin, nephew of Duke Galeholt, although I am not sufficiently confident of this to list Galehodin among the kings. Also according to the Vulgate, Tradelmant is the grandson of the King of Norgales.

Tennyson seems to identify Rience of Northgalis with Uriens of Gore, possibly as much for the similarity of names as for artistic purposes. Malory's Uriens of Gore, however, is listed in the first alliance of rebel kings, while Rience is off fighting Leodegrance. This is why I prefer the alternate spelling Ryons, which is a bit less like Uriens.

ADOK

Malory first mentions this Cornish knight as going with Sirs Tristram and Dinas to the tournament at Castle Dangerous.

Sadok was one of Mark's men, and when Mark murdered Prince Boudwin, he sent Sadok to bring back Boudwin's escaping wife Anglides and infant son Alisander. Sadok caught up with Anglides within ten miles, but let her go on condition she raise her son to avenge his father's death (which she may have intended to do anyway). Sadok returned to Mark and told him he had faithfully drowned Boudwin's son. Years later, hearing that Alisander had just been knighted, Mark realized that Sadok had betrayed his orders. Mark and some of his knights tried to kill Sadok at once, in the castle. Sadok fought and killed four knights in Mark's presence, then escaped, Tristram, Dinas, Fergus, and the other true-hearted knights about the place being in sympathy with him. Mark sent yet another "false knight" after Sadok, and Sadok slew this one, too. Then Mark sent messages to Morgana and the Queen of Northgalis, enlisting their aid against Alisander — and perhaps also against Sadok.

Sadok must have either remained at large in Cornwall or secretly returned to the vicinity, for when Mark put Tristram in prison, La Beale Isoud appealed to Sadok. Sadok and two of his cousins ambushed Mark's party near Tintagil. Sadok lost one of his cousins but slew Mark's four nephews and at least one "traitor of Magouns [castle]," then rode on to the castles of Lyonesse and Arbray, where he joined Sir Dinas and they roused the country to rebellion. Meanwhile, Percivale effected Tristram's release, and Mark tricked Dinas into disbanding the rebellion by pretending to be about to go on Crusade at the Pope's command. Mark put Tristram back in prison, Isoud appealed to Dinas and Sadok again, and this time Sadok presumably helped Dinas put Mark into prison long enough for Isoud to deliver and escape with Tristram. It is possible that Sadok and Dinas joined Tristram and Isoud at Joyous Garde.

Malory next mentions Sir Sadok and his cousin Sir Edward at the Lonazep tournament, where he calls them cousins of Sir Gawaine. (It is possible this is a different Sadok, but I think it was probably the same, for Gawaine's mother Margawse was of Cornish birth.) Sadok became a companion of the Round Table, accompanied Lancelot into exile, and was made Earl of Surlat. [Malory VII, 26-28; X, 33, 35, 50-51, 68; XIX, 11; XX, 18]

SAFERE

Sirs Safere and Segwarides, already christened, came with their still-unbaptized brother Palomides to the tournament at Castle Dangerous. Safere seems to appear next at a tournament given by King Carados, seemingly somewhere on the south coast, where he, Carados, and a score of other knights were struck down by young Sir Alisander le Orphelin. Safere put in another appearance at Duke Galeholt's tournament in Surluse. Between tournaments, he seems to have put in a good deal of time in errantry.

After the Lonazep tournament, somehow having acquired the shield used by Ector de Maris, Safere met, fought, and defeated one Sir Helior le Preuse and won the lady with him. Helior had just won this lady from Sir Epinogris, and Palomides arrived, to win her back for Epinogris, in time to see the fight between Helior and Safere. Palomides then fought Safere for more than an hour to win the lady, but at last, admiring each other's strength, they inquired and learned each other's identities and Safere knelt to beg Palomides' forgiveness, afterwards helping him escort the lady back to Epinogris. Safere then rode with Palomides for a time, but they were soon captured by men whose lord Sir Palomides had slain in the lists at Lonazep. Safere fought beside Palomides until they were defeated through weight of numbers, then spent three days in prison with him and was put on trial with him; but Safere was found not guilty, while Palomides was sentenced to die.

And when Sir Safere should be delivered there was great dole betwixt Sir Palomides and him, and many piteous complaints that Sir Safere made at his departing, there is no maker can rehearse the tenth part. ... So Sir Safere departed from his brother with the greatest dolour and sorrow that ever made knight.

He must have been equally delighted later to learn of Palomides' rescue by Lancelot.

Safere became a knight of the Round Table and continued to enjoy his tournaments, fighting at Winchester and elsewhere. He and Palomides were among Guenever's guests at the small dinner when Patrise was poisoned. They clove to Lancelot's party when the break came, and accompanied him into exile, where Safere was made Duke of Landok. [Malory VII, 26; X, 16, 36, 45, 83-84; XVIII, 3, 11, 23; XX, 17-18]

SAGRAMORE (Saigremor) LE DESIROUS

This was the name given to the knight William Bendix played to Bing Crosby's **Connecticut Yankee in King Arthur's Court**. (In Mark Twain's novel, however, it is Sir Kay and not Sir Sagramore who brings the Yankee to court.) The Sagramore of the romances is surely very unlike William Bendix's character!

True, Sagramore does not cut all that impressive a figure in Malory. He and three other knights of Arthur's court see Lancelot riding in Kay's armor, sally out against him, and are promptly unhorsed. He goes riding in the West Country with Sir Dodinas; they meet and defeat Sir Andred, but then encounter Tristram; Sagramore scornfully remarks, "it is seldom seen . . . that ye Cornish knights be valiant men of arms," rides against Tristram, and is again unhorsed, as is Dodinas in turn. Learning Tristram's name, they admiringly ask him to stay in their company, and bid him respectful Godspeed when he rides on to rescue Segwarides' wife from Bleoberis. Sagramore and Kay chance to meet Tristram before the Castle of Maidens tournament, get into a broil when Tristram, wishing to arrive at the tournament unbruised, tries to refuse a joust, and again Sagramore is unhorsed. Once again adventuring with Dodinas, Sagramore gets it yet a third time from Tristram; Sagramore and Dodinas remount and ride after him to demand a chance for revenge, but forbear on learning that he is on his way to fight Palomides at the tomb of Lanceor and Colombe.

When Alice la Beale Pilgrim announces her intention of marrying whoever can defeat Sir Alisander le Orphelin at the ruins of La Beale Regard, Sagramore is apparently the first challenger to present himself and be defeated, whereas Alice decides to love Alisander. Sagramore is one of twenty-three knights who set out searching for Lancelot when he has gone mad on being discovered by Guenever with Elaine of Carbonek. Lancelot unhorses Sagramore in the Winchester tournament. Sagramore is among the knights who ride a-Maying with Guenever and fall into Meliagrant's ambush. He is one of those who try unsuccessfully to heal Sir Urre. [Malory VII, 13; VIII, 15-16; IX, 25; X, 4, 38; XI, 10; XVIII, 11; XIX, 1, 11]

For all this, Sagramore seems to have been a knight of major stature among the Round Table companions, and I think it likely that Malory, unaware that his compilation/summarization/retelling would one day be the principal Arthurian sourcebook for the English-speaking world, used Sagramore's frequent unhorsings to emphasize the prowess of Lancelot, Tristram, and Alisander.

The Vulgate tells us that Sagramore was the nephew of the Emperor of Constantinople and came to Britain to join the flower of Arthur's chivalry in the first part of Arthur's reign.

Sagramore "knew no limits" in a fight; however, his blood had to be up if he were to be at his fighting best. When he cooled down, he usually had a headache and a ravenous hunger. He also had an illness (Epilepsy?) that manifested itself in sudden attacks, when he might think his end was near. Because of this illness, Kay gave him a second nickname besides "le Desirous": "Le mort jeune" ("The dead youth"). Sagramore was rash. He was killed at last by Mordred during the last battle. [Vulgate III, V, VI]

His nickname "le Desirous" may apply to battle-lust or some other trait than bed-lust (of which it would probably have taken a remarkable amount to be considered noteworthy), but Vulgate VII records the name of one of his paramours, Dame Senehauz, who gave him a daughter.

In the Idyll **Merlin and Vivien**, Tennyson applies to Sir Sagramore the story of a man who stumbles in the dark into the wrong bedroom and innocently sleeps the night through beside the woman whose room it really is, each one unaware of the other's presence until they wake in the morning. Gossip and public opinion then force them to marry, and they are happy. (Tennyson says it is a happy marriage because they are pure; a French author who retells the tale in a much later setting says they are happy because marriage is a lottery at best and they were lucky.) Arthur's court as Tennyson pictures it may have forced the parties to marry in such a situation, but I find it difficult to fit this tale of Sagramore's marriage to Arthur's court as depicted in the medieval romances.

THE GIANT OF SAINT MICHAEL'S MOUNT, FRANCE

One of the worst of the giants, and apparently one of the largest, he sat around naked by his fire forcing three young damsels to turn twelve babies, broached like birds on a spit, above the fire. He killed Duke Howell's wife by raping her, slitting her to the navel, which may be an indication of his size. Arthur, Kay, and Bedivere stopped to kill him and avenge the lady on their way to fight Emperor Lucius. [Malory V, 5]

According to the Vulgate, this giant wore a sword-proof serpent's skin.

EARL SANAM

Malory seems to mention him only once, as the father of Dame Lionors (see Lyzianor). He thus became the grandfather of Arthur's bastard son Borre. Sanam may already have died, since his daughter is mentioned as the one coming to do Arthur homage after the battle of Bedegraine. [Malory I, 17]

Saraide† — see SERAIDE

The Damosel Savage — see LYNETTE

SEBILE (Sebille?)†

According to Vulgate V, Sebile and Morgana were the two women most proficient in magic after the Damsel of the Lake. Instead of Malory's Queens of Gore (Morgan), Northgalis, Eastland, and the Out Isles, the Vulgate account of Lancelot's kidnapping has Morgan, Sebile, and the Queen of Sorestan as the abductresses. I believe the Queens of Eastland and Sorestan are probably identical; thus Sebile may be the Queen either of Northgalis or the Out Isles. Possibly, since Malory names Ryons as king of "Northgalis and Many Isles," the Queens of Northgalis and the "Out Isles" were originally one and the same character, and Malory or some scribe between him and the older versions mistakenly split her in two.

Vulgate VII has a Sebille who seems, as nearly as I can make it out, to be the pagan queen of Sarmenie, and who may have had an affair with Sagremor (Sagramore), who was her prisoner for a while and through whom she was converted and baptized. A knight called Le Noir Chevalier Fae appears as either her consort or her enemy — I suspect the former, but could not be quite sure from the text. Sebille seems to have journeyed to Britain with a company of knights armed in black, and she may possibly have been a warrior queen.

SEGWARIDES (Segurades?)

Vulgate III has a Sir Segurades whom Gawaine fought and defeated on behalf of the Lady of Roestoc. Malory may have two different Sirs Segwarides, but I am going on the theory that Palomides' brother Segwarides, who was already christened by the time of Dame Lyonors' tournament at Castle Dangerous, to which he came with his brothers, is the same Segwarides who appears in Cornwall, apparently having settled there in time to become embroiled with Tristram.

After first meeting La Beale Isoud in Ireland, Tristram returned to Cornwall. Before being sent back to Ireland to bring Isoud to Mark, and thus before drinking the love potion with her, the great knight had an affair with Sir Segwarides' wife. Mark also was in love with this lady, and ambushed Tristram on his way to her one night. Tristram left Mark and his two helpers in sorry state, but was wounded himself and left some of his blood in his paramour's bed. Finding it, Segwarides threatened his wife until she told him who her lover was. Segwarides pursued Tristram, was defeated (of course), and did not dare meddle with the great knight thereafter, "for he that hath a privy hurt is loath to have a shame outward."

After Segwarides' recovery, but still before Isoud's coming to Cornwall, Bleoberis de Ganis rode into Mark's court one day and asked a boon. When Mark granted it, Bleoberis rode off with Segwarides' wife. When Segwarides got wind of it, he set off after Bleoberis and was wounded severely in the fight. Then Tristram followed and fought Bleoberis until they decided to let the lady choose between them. She said that she would not return to Tristram, since he had not come to save her at once but had let her husband chase Bleoberis first. She begged Bleoberis to take her to the abbey where Segwarides lay wounded and Bleoberis obliged. So husband and wife were reconciled, at least outwardly, and the news of Tristram's battle with Bleoberis "pleased Sir Segwarides right well."

Much later, after Tristram's marriage, when he, Isoud la Blanche Mains, and Kehydius were blown ashore near the Isle of Servage, Segwarides turned up again, travelling in the forest with an unnamed damsel. Segwarides greeted Tristram with the words:

> I know you for Sir Tristram de Liones, the man in the world that I have most cause to hate, because ye departed the love between me and my wife; but as for that, I will never hate a noble knight for a light lady; and therefore, I pray you, be my friend, and I will be yours unto my power; for wit ye well ye are hard bestead in this valley, and we shall have enough to do either of us to succour other.

This is a masterpiece of reasoning. "And then Sir Segwarides brought Sir Tristram to a lady thereby that was born in Cornwall," possibly the same damsel mentioned earlier as riding with Segwarides, "and she told him all the perils of that valley." It was the valley of the wicked Sir Nabon le Noire, and after killing him Tristram made Segwarides lord of the Isle of Servage.

Sir Segwarides turned up yet again, in company with the King of the Hundred Knights, riding by Joyous Garde when Tristram was living there with Isoud. Tristram and his friends were preparing for the Lonazep tournament and, in some apparently lighthearted jousting, Segwarides unhorsed Gareth before, as it seems, joining the merry group in Joyous Garde. (If there are indeed two knights of this name in Malory, the Segwarides who unhorsed Gareth before Joyous Garde would probably be Palomides' brother as distinct from the Segwarides of Cornwall.)

Segwarides was almost certainly a companion of the Round Table, like his brothers Palomides and Safere. He was killed during Lancelot's rescue of the Queen from the stake, which is interesting, since both Palomides and Safere clove to Lancelot's party. [Malory VII, 26; VIII, 13-18, 38-39; X, 16, 60; XX, 8]

SEGWARIDES' WIFE

Before the arrival of La Beale Isoud, Bleoberis de Ganis chose her as the loveliest lady at King Mark's court. She was an early paramour of Tristram's and also attracted the amorous devotion of Mark, but eventually chose to return to her husband. If their reconciliation lasted, she would presumably have become lady of the Isle of Servage when Segwarides became its lord. [Malory VIII, 13-18, 38-39; see Segwarides]

In his excellent novel **Tristram and Isolde: Restoring Palamede**, Erskine names this lady Phenice.

SELISES

Nephew of the King of the Hundred Knights, and "a good man of arms," Sir Selises fought in the Lonazep tournament. He may be identical with the Sir Selises of the Dolorous Tower whom Malory lists among the Round Table knights that tried to heal Sir Urre and who followed Lancelot into exile and was made Earl of Masauke. [Malory X, 67; XIX, 11; XX, 18]

The connection of Selises with the Dolorous Tower is not explained. In the Vulgate, Sir Carados' Dolorous Tower was given to Sir Melians li Gai.

SENEHAUZ†

The paramour of an apparently very minor knight named Blios, Senehauz was rescued by Sir Sagramore, who promptly engendered a daughter on her. The daughter resembled Sagramore more closely than a picture, and was sent to court to be raised by Guenever. Her name does not seem to be given, but she might have been called Senehauz after her mother. [Vulgate VII]

SENTRAILLE DE LUSHON

Sentraille was one of Tristram's knights. After Tristram had escaped the judgement of Mark and Andred by leaping out of a chapel on the sea cliffs down to the rocks below, Sentraille helped Gouvernail and Sir Lambegus pull him up again. Sentraille became a companion of the Round Table. [Malory VIII, 35; XIX, 11]

SERAIDE (Saraide)†

One of the maidens of Viviane, the French Damsel of the Lake, Seraide seems to have held a high place in the Damsel's service. Her grasp of magic, while doubtless far short of Viviane's, Nimue's, or Morgana's, was practical and useful.

At Viviane's instructions, Seraide went to rescue young Lionel and Bors from the court of King Claudas. Claudas resisted giving the children up, and during the fray the two boys mortally wounded Claudas' son Dorin. Seraide, throwing herself between the children and Claudas, received a grievous wound in her own right cheek from the king's sword. Through a magical ruse, however, she did escape with the boys to the Lake, where their cousin Lancelot treated them as equals. Seraide became Sir Lionel's lady in particular and acted as mentor and friend to all four kinsmen — Lionel, Bors, Lancelot, and the British-born Ector de Maris.

After Duke Galeholt's death, Seraide took his sword to Bors. When Lancelot found Galeholt's tomb, it was Seraide who kept him from killing himself in grief and told him that Viviane commanded him to take Galeholt's body to Joyous Garde. [Vulgate III, IV]

Seraphe — see NASCIEN

SAINT SERVANUS†

Young St. Kentigern was put under the discipline of Servanus at the monastery of Culross. [Glennie]

SERVAUSE LE BREUSE

Malory seems to mention this companion of the Round Table only once, among the would-be healers of Sir Urre. The single mention, however, describes an interesting peculiarity:

> Sir Servause le Breuse, that was called a passing strong knight, for as the book saith, the chief Lady of the Lake feasted Sir Lancelot and Servause le Breuse, and when she had feasted them both at sundry times she prayed them to give her a boon. And they granted it her. And then she prayed Sir Servause that he would promise her never to do battle against Sir Launcelot du Lake, and in same wise she prayed Sir Launcelot never to do battle against Sir Servause, and so either promised her. For the French book saith, that Sir Servause had never courage nor lust to do battle against no man, but if it were against giants, and against dragons, and wild beasts. [Malory XIX, 11]

Queen of Sorestan — see QUEEN OF EASTLAND

SORIONDES†

A nephew of Maaglant, this Saxon warrior was involved in the attack on Vandaliors castle. [Vulgate II]

SORNEGRIEU†

A leader of the Sesnes, involved in the attack on Vandaliors castle. [Vulgate II]

DUKE OF THE SOUTH MARCHES

This duke had at least thirteen sons. Gawaine slew seven, for which cause the duke and his remaining six sons were Arthur's sworn enemies. Therefore, when Sir Marhaus arrived with the damsel Été and introduced himself — perhaps a trifle prematurely — as a knight of the Round Table, the duke gave him hospitality for the night but informed him regretfully that on the morn he would have to battle his host and his host's six sons. Marhaus defeated them all and sent them to Arthur's court that Whitsuntide, where they were all reconciled to the King. [Malory IV, 24-25]

Mark Twain makes amusing use of this family and their history in chapters 14, 15, and 19 of **A Connecticut Yankee in King Arthur's Court**.

'Knight With the Strange Beast' — see PELLINORE

ALIESSIN†

Glennie lists him as one of the four great bards of the Arthurian age, the others being Llywarch Hen, Aneurin, and Merlin. (Glennie puts the Arthurian age in the sixth century, while Malory and the Vulgate put it in the fifth.)

"Taliessin is our fullest throat of song," says Arthur in Tennyson's idyll **The Holy Grail**.

TAULAS (Tauleas) AND TAULURD

These two giants were brothers. Taulurd was so large that no horse could carry him. He was a wily fighter who destroyed the lands of Earl Fergus and imprisoned ladies and knights in his own castle. Sir Marhaus killed him by driving him into the water and stoning him to death. Since Fergus later became Tristram's man, I think it probable that Taulurd lived in or near Cornwall. [Malory IV, 25]

Taulas is definitely stated as living in Cornwall. He was a small enough giant to ride a horse. For seven years Taulas kept to his castle for fear of Tristram. One day, hearing that Tristram was dead, he came out to attack Sir Dinant. But Tristram was not dead, only wandering around mad, and at the instigation of nearby herdsmen he came to kill the giant. [Malory IV, 25; IX, 20]

Terican — see TURQUINE

THENEW†

She was the daughter of King Lothus and mother of St. Kentigern. See under Kentigern.

KING THOAS OF IRELAND†

Apparently a Saxon king, Thoas was involved in the attack on Vandaliors castle. He was eventually killed by Gawaine when he tried to invade England with other Saxons. [Vulgate II]

THOMAS THE RHYMER† (Thomas of Erceldoun)

This famous visitor to the land of Faery lived in the thirteenth century. Glennie tells us that many traditions connect him with Arthur, as

> the unwilling, and too quickly vanishing guide of those adventurous spirits who have entered the mysterious Halls beneath the Eildons, and attempted to achieve the re-awakening of Arthur ... only to be cast forth.

The tradition recorded in Malory has Arthur lying not beneath the Eildons, but in Avilion (Glastonbury). Different spatial relationships, however, may hold in Faery than here on the surface.

THE GIANTS OF TINTAGIL

Two unnamed giants took over Tintagil, apparently between the tenure of Gorlois and that of Mark. As a hobby, these giants took up collecting ladies and damsels as their prisoners. Lancelot killed the pesky pair. [Malory VI, 11]

Tirre – see under LAVAINE

TOR (Tor le Fise de Vayshoure; Tor le Fise Aries)

> Forthwithal there came a poor man into the court, and brought with him a fair young man of eighteen years of age riding upon a lean mare ... Anon as he came before the king, he saluted him and said: O King Arthur ... it was told me that at this time of your marriage ye would give any man the gift that he would ask, out except that were unreasonable ... Sir I ask nothing else but that ye will make my son here a knight. It is a great thing thou askest of me, said the king. What is thy name? ... Sir, my name is Aries the cowherd. Whether cometh this of thee or of thy son? said the king. Nay, sir, said Aries, this desire cometh of my son and not of me, for I ... have thirteen sons, and all they will fall to what labour I put them, and will be right glad to do labour, but this child will not labour for me, for anything that my wife or I may do, but always he will be shooting or casting darts, and glad for to see battles and to behold knights, and always day and night he desireth of me to be made a knight. What is thy name? said the king unto the young man. Sir, my name is Tor. The king beheld him fast, and saw he was passingly well-visaged and passingly well made of his years.

Arthur told Aries to fetch the other sons for comparison,

> and all were shaped much like the poor man. But Tor was not like none of them all in shape nor in countenance, for he was much more than any of them. Now, said King Arthur unto the cowherd, where is the sword he shall be made knight withal? It is here, said Tor. Take it out of the sheath, said the king, and require me to make you a knight.

Thus Tor became a knight of Arthur's court promptly for the asking. Only after he was dubbed did Merlin reveal him to be the bastard son of King Pellinore, begotten on the cowherd's wife before her marriage. Coming of such paternal blood, Merlin predicted, Tor would make a fine knight. (Rumors of Tor's birth may have persisted, however, for although he is sometimes surnamed "le Fise de Vayshoure" – "the son of Vayshoure," surely after his mother, he is also sometimes called "le Fise Aries" after the cowherd.)

Tor's original request had also included a place at the Round Table; no bashful lad, Tor. This distinction did not come, however, until after he had proved himself at least twice. The first time was in the quest of the white brachet (see under Nimue). Beginning his maiden adventure, Tor jousted down Sir Felot of Langduk and Sir Petipase of Winchelsea, who had insisted on fighting him, and sent them to court. (Sir Petipase, at least, became one of Arthur's knights and was killed trying to help Mordred and Agravaine corner Lancelot with the Queen.) The dwarf who had served Felot and Petipase requested becoming Tor's dwarf instead, and brought him to a pavillion where he found the white brachet with an unnamed lady. Tor reappropriated the brachet, and was overtaken next day by Abelleus. As they fought for the brachet, a lady of the neighborhood rode up to tell Tor that Abelleus was a villain who had killed her brother before her eyes, "and I kneeled half an hour afore him in the mire for to save my brother's life," wherefore she required Tor to dispose of the scoundrel, which he did, afterwards lodging with the lady and her husband, "a passing fair old knight," who courteously put their house "always at [Tor's] commandment." When Tor returned to court and told his adventures, Arthur – on Merlin's advice – rewarded him with an earldom of lands, although his seat at the Round Table had to wait until after the war with the invading kings of Denmark, Ireland, the Vale, Soleise, and Longtains had left eight vacancies at the Table, which Arthur refilled according to Pellinore's advice. After naming Uriens, Hervise de Revel, the King of the Lake, Galagars, Gawaine, Griflet, and Kay, Pellinore modestly gave Arthur a choice of either Tor or Bagdemagus for the eighth seat.

> But because Sir Tor is my son I may not praise him, but else, an he were not my son, I durst say that of his age there is not in this land a better knight than he is, nor of better conditions and loath to do any wrong, and loath to take any wrong. By my head, said Arthur, he is a passing good knight as any ... for I have seen him proved, but he saith little and he doth much more, for I know none in all this court an he were as well born on his mother's side as he is on your side, that is like him of prowess and of might: and therefore I will have him at this time, and leave Sir Bagdemagus till another time.

Tor makes a brief appearance in the rambling adventures of Sir Tristram. He jousts down Sir Kay in sport, then joins Kay, Tristram, and Brandiles at their lodging, where Tristram sits silent and anonymous while the other three tell "Cornish knight" jokes; on the morrow, Tristram jousts down Brandiles and Tor and snubs Kay before revealing his identity. A little farther on Malory describes a visit of King Mark to Sir Tor's castle, but Tor himself is not in residence at the time and his lieutenant Sir Berluse is the one who grudgingly carries out the duties of host to the unloved king.

Tor was killed during Lancelot's rescue of Guenever from the stake. Tor's half-brothers were Lamorak, Aglovale, Dornar, and Percivale; his known half-sisters Amide and Eleine. [Malory III, 4-5, 9-11; IV, 5; IX, 15; X, 9; XX, 8]

KING TRADELMANS OF NORGALES†

Tradelmans would seem to be the grandson of King Ryons, whom he apparently succeeded. The brother of Tradelmans was Sir Belinans, whose son was Sir Dodinas (Dodynel). [Vulgate II]

Possibly Tradelmans should be identified with Cradelmas.

TRISTRAM (Tristran) OF LYONESSE

The story of Tristran and Isolde has its own vast, rich body of material, and the Tristran cycle often seems independent of, though co-existent with, the Arthurian cycle. Although the Vulgate and other pre-Malory treatments sometimes refer to Arthur and Tristran as contemporaries, Malory's is the earliest version I have yet found to attempt a true integration of the two cycles. Malory's may also remain the best such integration, even though his books of Tristram are perhaps that portion of **Le Morte D'Arthur** where modern readers are likeliest to bog down. (I believe that this may have been Malory's intent – that, in addition to using the Tristran-Isoud-Mark triangle as counterpoint to the Lancelot-Guenever-Arthur one, Malory may have aimed to use the tale of Tristram as a vehicle for showing the disintegration of the original ideals of the Round Table into more or less aimless, wandering, sometimes ridiculous adventures and petty or bitter feuds; be that as it may, Malory himself seems to have wearied of the business and cut it off short well before he got to the actual scene of Tristram's death.)

Hal Foster managed a consistent integration of Tristram into **Prince Valiant** before the time came to kill Tristram off, but the major modern romancers I have read generally seem to concentrate on either Tristram or on Arthur – Tennyson, for instance, uses Tristram in **The Last Tournament**, but does not seem to like him very much; T. H. White seems to use him sparingly and grudgingly; Catherine Christian, although making

Palomides a major character in **The Pendragon,** divorces him from the Tristram affair, which she brushes off with a brief mention as a rather sordid business of very little use to anyone but harpers; Erskine, on the other hand, chose to keep Arthur's court out of his version of **Tristran and Isolde,** even though he had already done a novel about Galahad, Lancelot, and Guenever; and so on.

For the above reasons, and also because I, personally, have a great deal of difficulty trying to generate the interest in Tristran and his cycle that I feel for Arthur and his, I confine the present entry to Malory's version, disregarding all the other and better Tristran romances.

The son of King Meliodas and Queen Elizabeth of Lyonesse, Tristram was born in an unhappy hour — his father had been kidnapped by an amorous enchantress and his mother, giving birth while out searching for her husband, died of exposure. When Tristram was a child, his stepmother tried to poison him so that her own sons would inherit Lyonesse; when she was caught, Tristram showed a forgiving and compassionate nature by pleading for her life. Meliodas granted his request, but, apparently a bit annoyed with his son, sent the boy into France for seven years under the tutorship of Gouvernail, who later became Tristram's loyal and competent squire. It was probably during this period that Tristram attracted the affection of King Faramon's daughter, who gave him a brachet and later died for love; the attachment may have been unsolicited, but I tend to suspect Tristram of some youthful trifling in the art of dalliance — he seems to have been of quite an amorous nature.

> And there was Tristram more than seven years. And then when he well could speak the language, and had learned all that he might learn in that country, then he came home to his father, King Meliodas, again. And so Tristram learned to be an harper passing all other, that there was none such called in no country, and so on harping and on instruments of music he applied him in his youth for to learn.
>
> And after, as he grew in might and strength, he laboured ever in hunting and in hawking, so that never gentleman more ... And ... he began good measures of blowing of beasts of venery, and beasts of chase, and all manner of vermin, and all these terms we have yet of hawking and hunting. And therefore the book of venery, of hawking, and hunting, is called the book of Sir Tristram.

All this in addition to becoming the only fighting man of the time (except Galahad) who could conceivably have been able to beat Lancelot in a fair passage of arms (except during the spiritual adventures of the Grail)! Tristram sounds rather like what later centuries would call "a Renaissance man." And "every estate loved him, where that he went." (Administration, however, does not seem to have been among his many talents; he rarely if ever appears to have returned home to see how his own inheritance of Lyonesse was getting along.)

When Tristram was about eighteen, he fought and mortally wounded Sir Marhaus in a single combat to free his uncle, King Mark of Cornwall, from paying truage to King Anguish of Ireland. Since Marhaus had used a poisoned spear, however, Tristram sickened of his own wounds, until at least, by the advice of a wise woman, Mark sent him into Ireland to be healed Here, under the name Tramtrist, he met, was healed by, and probably began to fall in love with La Beale Isoud, whom he taught to harp. He also seems to have met Palomides for the first time — and not in the friendliest situation — and he developed a friendship with Isoud's father Anguish that survived even Isoud's mother's discovery that Tristram was the man who had killed her brother Marhaus. Tristram and Isoud exchanged rings before he fled Ireland, but on arriving back in Cornwall, Tristram got his father's permission to stay in Mark's court (even though "largely King Melodias and his queen departed of their lands and goods to Sir Tristram"), where he eventually entered a rivalry with Mark for the love of Sir Segwarides' wife. Finally Mark, whose initial love of his nephew had turned to dislike, sent him into Ireland to bring back La Beale Isoud to be queen of Cornwall. On the return voyage, Tristram and Isoud accidentally shared a love potion meant for Isoud and Mark.

The important details of the love of Tristram and La Beale Isoud are given under her name. Eventually banished from Cornwall for ten years, Tristram went to Logris, where he fought at the Castle of Maidens tournament, and was imprisoned for a time, along with Palomides and Dinadan, by one Sir Darras. On his release, he chanced to visit a castle of Morgan le Fay's. She gave him a shield depicting Arthur, Guenever, "and a knight who holdeth them both in bondage," refused to tell him that knight's name, and made him promise to bear the shield at the tournament at the Castle of the Hard Rock. Her lover Sir Hemison, jealous of her attentions to Tristram, pursued the departing champion of Cornwall and was killed.

Tristram distinguished himself at the Hard Rock tournament, smiting down Arthur himself in defence of Morgan's shield. After the tournament, Tristram rode by the stronghold of Breuse Sans Pitie in time to save Palomides from Breuse and his men. Tristram and Palomides separated after setting a day to meet again and settle their old rivalry in a meadow near Camelot. Palomides missed the appointment, but Lancelot happened to ride by Lanceor's and Colombe's tomb, clad all in white and bearing a covered shield; Tristram mistook Lancelot for Palomides, and the two greatest knights and "best lovers" of their generation battled each other as Merlin had prophesied years before that they would beside that tomb. The bout ended in a draw, each champion surrendering to the other on learning his identity, and Lancelot brought Tristram to court, where he was installed as a member of the Round Table, getting Sir Marhaus' old chair.

NAMES

Malory's characters commonly put off name introductions until long after we moderns would do it. Possibly the apparent reluctance of Arthurian characters to ask and give each other their names was an outgrowth of the primitive idea that knowing a man's or woman's name gave you power over him or her. If so, reluctance to give enemies the clue to your name by carrying your own shield for them to recognize might have led to the frequent practice of covering your shield or using an unemblazoned one. Whatever the reason, the shyness of the characters about their names seems to have carried over into the attitudes of the romancers themselves. The romancers, however, are much more conscientious about naming their knights and kings than about naming their ladies, squires, hermits, and so on.

Whereas in our century it is usually good standard style, as a rule, to attach names to most of your characters as quickly as possible, thus giving your readers a handle on them, Chrétian de Troyes introduced most characters without giving their names, so as to arouse readers' curiosity (see Julian Harris' introduction to *Yvain,* New York, 1969, p. 27).

Whereas in reading many novelists, like Fielding, Dickens, and Dostoevsky, we often find ourselves in a sea of names and faced with the task of sorting out the names and making sure we are attaching them to the right characters, in reading the medieval

The rest of Tristram's story as given by Malory can be found under La Beale Isoud. But see also these many entries: Agwisance, Andred, Blamore de Ganis, Bleoberis de Ganis, Bragwaine, Breunor, Eliot, Queen Elizabeth of Lyonesse, King Faramon of France & Daughter, Fergus, Gouvernail, Hemison, Isoud La Blanche Mains, Kehydius, Lambegus, Lady Leech of Cornwall, King Melodias of Lyonesse, Brother Ogrins, Palomides, Persides de Bloise, Sagramore le Desirous, Segwarides, Segwarides' Wife. [Malory II, 8; IV, 28; VII, 35; VIII-X; XII; XIX, 11]

Father: King Meliodas of Lyonesse Mother: Queen Elizabeth Uncle (maternal): King Mark Stepmother's father: Hoel Father-in-law: Hoel Wife: Isoud la Blanche Mains Lover: La Beale Isoud Early lover: Sir Segwarides' Wife Brother-in-law: Kehydius Teacher and squire: Gouvernail Mentor: Brother Ogrins Ally: Dinas Knights and protégés: Fergus, Lambegus, Segwarides, Sentraille de Lushon Squire: Hebes le Renoumes Would-be lover: King Faramon's Daughter	**SIR TRISTRAM'S FAMILY AND RETAINERS**

Tristram's Stepmother — see under MELIODAS OF LYONESSE

TURQUINE (Terican)

While seeking Lancelot and adventures, Sir Ector de Maris asked a forester if there were any of the latter nearby.

> Sir, said the forester ... within this mile, is a strong manor, and well dyked, and by that manor, on the left hand, there is a fair ford for horses to drink of, and over that ford there groweth a fair tree, and thereon hang many fair shields that wielded sometime good knights, and at the hole of the tree hangeth a basin of copper and latten [brass], and strike upon that basin with the butt of thy spear thrice, and soon after that thou shalt hear new tidings, [or] else hast thou the fairest grace that many a year had ever knight that passed through this forest.

Ector thanked the forester and followed his instructions. Forth came Sir Turquine and bade Ector make ready.

Ector began well, striking Turquine such "a great buffet that his horse turned twice about." But Turquine, being a strong knight of great prowess, quickly turned the tables and took Ector prisoner back to his own hall. In honor of Ector's having put up the best fight of any opponent in twelve years, Turquine offered to give him his life in exchange for Ector's promise to remain his prisoner for said life's duration. When Ector refused these terms, Turquine had him stripped and beaten with thorns before throwing him into the deep dungeon with the other prisoners, "three score and four," including some of the Round Table.

Sir Lancelot was guided in his turn to Turquine by a damsel who remarked that she knew of no one else who might conquer the villainous knight. After a battle of two hours, Turquine, much impressed by Lancelot's prowess, asked his name, offering him friendship and the free release of all the prisoners on condition that the stranger was not the one knight whom Turquine hated above all others. Lancelot asked which was the hated knight.

> Faithfully, said Sir Turquine, his name is Sir Launcelot du Lake, for he slew my brother, Sir Carados, at the dolorous tower, that was one of the best knights alive; and therefore ... may I once meet with him, the one of us shall make an end of other, I make mine avow. And for Sir Launcelot's sake I have slain an hundred good knights, and as many I have maimed all utterly that they might never after help themselves, and many have died in prison, and yet have I three score and four.

Lancelot announced who he was. "Ah, said Turquine, Lancelot, thou art unto me most welcome that ever was knight, for we shall never depart till the one of us be dead." It seems almost superfluous to report that Turquine was the one who was left dead. [Malory VI, 2, 7-9]

Somer standardizes Turquine's name as Terican in the Vulgate, where the tale differs in a few details. See also Carados of the Dolorous Tower and, under *Places*, Turquine's Hill.

LBAWES (Ulbause), EARL

This earl of Surluse fought Duke Chaleins of Clarance at Duke Galeholt's tournament, "and either of them smote other down." Ulbawes became a knight of the Round Table. [Malory X, 48; XIX, 11]

ULFIN

Sir Ulfin was a hermit living on the way to Castle Carbonek. Galahad lodged with him one night during the Grail Adventures. Percivale's sister Amide found Galahad here and led him to the ship where Bors and Percival were waiting. [Malory XVII, 1-2]

Ulfin might well be identified with Sir Ulfius.

ULFIUS

The noble knight Sir Ulfius became Uther Pendragon's confidant in the matter of Uther's love for Igraine. It was Ulfius who conceived the idea of fetching Merlin to help the king consummate his desire. When Merlin gave Uther the likeness of Igraine's husband and himself the likeness of Gorlois'

Arthurian romances we face the opposite problem and often learn a great deal about the characters before we know what to call them, besides "the damsel," "the seneschal," and so on. Perhaps the medieval way was no more confusing, after all. Unfortunately, while Chrétien seems fairly conscientious about eventually naming his people, his successors appear to have grown careless, so that by the time we reach the prose Vulgate, numerous characters — not always minor — are never named at all, perhaps through carrying the postponed-naming literary device too far, perhaps through later copyists missing the name when it finally did appear, without benefit of our modern system of capitalization, buried in the text.

It is logical that this system would lead to situations in which a character's name was lost and a later author or scribe would assign a new name. Still later, another reworker of the material might find the character under both names and take him or her for two different characters with similar stories. Meanwhile, other romancers, feeling the need to name some character, were doubtless appropriating names from other major or minor characters, somewhat as Vera Chapman, one of the very best recent Arthurian romancers, has appropriated the name of Bagdemagus — who has become a rather minor character to our century — for the name of a villain who bears virtually no resemblance to the Bagdemagus of the Vulgate. Here I will leave this particular

knight Jordanus, he gave Ulfius the likeness of Sir Brastias, another of the Duke's men. After Duke Gorlois' death became commonly known, Ulfius arranged the treaty and forwarded the marriage between Uther and Igraine.

Some years later, the newly-crowned Arthur made Ulfius his chamberlain. Ulfius served Arthur well during the first rebellion of the kings. The last Malory seems to tell us of Ulfius, at least as an active knight, is when he impeached Igraine of treason for not coming forward to testify to Arthur's identity; this, however, may have been a "staged" rather than a serious accusation. Like many other knights, Ulfius may have retired to a religious life; the similarity of names suggests he should be identified with the hermit Ulfin mentioned in the Grail Adventures. [Malory I, 1-21; XVII, 1]

Ulfius may well have been a companion of the Round Table when Uther had it. The service Malory records Ulfius as doing for Arthur comes before the young king received his father's Table from Leodegrance; Ulfius may have retired or died before Arthur's marriage, but if the old knight did remain long enough in Arthur's court, he would surely have been reinstated or elected to the Round Table.

The "Uncourteous Lady" — see under "CASTLE OF THE UNCOURTEOUS LADY," *Places*

KING URIENS OF GORE

The husband of Morgan le Fay and the father of two sons named Ywaine, Uriens was among the allied kings — probably one of the ringleaders — in the first rebellion against the young Arthur. He fought in the battle of Bedegraine and afterwards hosted his fellow rebels in his city of Sorhaute. He did not join the second rebellion, however; and was reconciled with Arthur, either between the two rebellions or when he came with his wife Morgana to the rich funeral Arthur gave Lot and the other kings who died in battle before Castle Terrabil. On the advice of King Pellinore, Uriens was made a companion of the Round Table after the decisive battle on the Humber against the invading kings of Denmark, Ireland, the Vale, Soleise, and Longtains.

Uriens went hunting with Arthur and Sir Accolon of Gaul on the expedition that led into Morgana's engineered attempt on Arthur's life; but, after the three hunters had fallen asleep aboard the mysterious boat, Uriens woke up next morning in his wife's arms, abed in Camelot. After the failure of her attempt on Arthur's life, Morgan attempted to salvage something by killing her husband, at least, with his sword as he slept, but their son, Ywaine le Blanchemains, prevented her. Although Ywaine promised to keep the secret, on condition his mother try no such thing again, the incident seems to have marked a permanent separation between Uriens and his wife; Morgana shortly thereafter left court and it appears

likely that the royal couple never met again. Uriens remained faithfully with Arthur, being listed among those who attempted to heal Sir Urre. [Malory I, 2, 8, 15, 18; II, 2; IV, 4, 6, 13; XIX, 11]

URRE OF HUNGARY

Urre was a "good knight in the land of Hungary ... and he was an adventurous knight, and in all places where he might hear of any deeds of worship there would he be." In Spain he slew an earl's son, Sir Alphegus, in tournament. But in the fight Urre himself received seven great wounds, three on the head, four on the body and left hand. (Might he have been a left-hander?) Alphegus' mother, a sorceress, enchanted Urre so that his wounds would never heal until searched (probed, or touched) by the best knight of the world. Urre's mother took him in a horse litter, and, with his sister Felelolie and a page to take care of the horses, they searched seven years through "all lands christened" for the best knight of the world, coming at last to Arthur's court. Urre submitted to being handled by every knight of the Round Table then on hand — a hundred and ten of them — before Lancelot returned from an adventure and healed him.

Soon thereafter Urre was made a knight of the Round Table, and his sister married Sir Lavaine, who was elected to the Table at the same time.

> And this Sir Urre would never go from Sir Launcelot, but he and Sir Lavaine awaited evermore upon him; and they were in all the court accounted for good knights, and full desirous in arms; and many noble deeds they did, for they would have no rest, but ever sought adventures.

Urre accompanied Lancelot into exile and was made Earl Estrake. [Malory XIX, 10-13; XX, 18]

UTHER PENDRAGON (Uter Pandragon)

Constans, King of Britain, had three sons: Maines, Pandragon, and Uther. After Constans' death, a number of barons murdered Maines in order to put Constans' seneschal Vortigern on the throne. Pandragon and Uther dispatched Vortigern, and Pandragon became king, but was killed in battle with the Saxons. Uther took the kingship in his turn, adopting his elder brother's name and having Merlin bring the stones of Stonehenge to serve as Pandragon's memorial. [Vulgate II]

Here Malory takes up Uther's story.

> It befell in the days of Uther Pendragon, when he was king of all England, and so reigned, that there was a mighty duke in Cornwall that held war against him long time ... And so by means King Uther sent for this duke, charging him to bring his wife with him, for she was called a fair lady.

It is not clear to me whether Uther's summons was meant, at least ostensibly, to patch up a truce, or whether the war of this paragraph refers to what happens next. Duke Gorlois and

tangle of names and characters — a hopeless or a glorious tangle, depending on how keen you are on scholarly and literary mysteries.

Despite the great number of nameless characters, the romances provide us with an overwhelming number of proper names, most of them very strange-sounding to our ears and twisting to our tongues. The names to be found in the "Who's Who" of the present work reflect a melting-pot of the sources of Arthurian legend and romance. Here are Roman and Classical names: Lucius, Alisander (from Alexander), Colombe, Belleus; names of Hebrew origin: Joseph, Eliazar; Welsh names: Gawaine, Ywaine, Guenevere, Cei (Kay); French names: Brumant l'Or-

guilleus, Floree, Beauvivante; even some solid British names of a more or less modern sound: Ironside. Many of the names, of course, are still in common use today — some, no doubt, as a result of their prominence in Arthurian lore, like Gareth, Lancelot, Gavin, possibly even Arthur, but some, I think, would have remained in use even had there been no popular body of Arthurian lore, like Elaine, Mark, Elizabeth, Hue (Hugh), Edward. (That Kay and Florence are common names today is probably a complete coincidence.) The name of Lancelot's virgin lover, Amable, is not, perhaps, a common name in our generation; and, indeed, I found it only in the appendix to Volume V of the Vulgate — elsewhere she is one of the nameless damsels. But the name

his wife Igraine departed suddenly and secretly when Igraine learned that Uther had amorous intentions on her. By the advice of his privy council, Uther tried summoning them back, and, when they refused, gave Gorloïs plain, fair warning, "and bade him be ready and stuff him and garnish him, for within forty days he would fetch him out of the biggest castle that he hath." This, at least, seems open and honest. But Gorloïs apparently put up a good fight, holding the siege at a standstill. "Then for pure anger and for great love of fair Igraine the king Uther fell sick." (It sounds to me like a fit of pouting impatience.) Uther's knight Ulfius fetched Merlin, who worked his magic to enable Uther to have his way with Igraine, she believing him her husband. That same night Gorloïs was killed in a sortie, after which the barons sued for peace, and Ulfius proposed that Uther wed Igraine. "And anon, like a lusty knight," which he was, Uther assented and, having made an unintentionally dishonest woman of Igraine, proceeded to make an honest one of her, doubtless leaving her very little choice in the matter. It hardly seems farfetched to suppose that Uther had a hand in arranging the marriages of Igraine's daughters also, Margawse to King Lot, Elaine to King Nentres, and Morgan (after a nunnery education) to King Uriens.

Meanwhile, apparently a bit of a joker, Uther was saving up the good news of who was the father of Igraine's next child. She, poor lady, having learned that her first husband was killed before the hour when she had thought he came to her, "waxed daily greater and greater," all the while "marvell[ing] who that might be that lay with her in likeness of her lord" but saying nothing — very likely supposing it to have been a demon, like the one that had fathered Merlin. After about half a year, Uther finally sprang his little surprise, asking her to tell him "by the faith she owed to him," whose child was growing within her. She was "sore abashed," as well she might be — she must have hoped he would accept it as Gorloïs' child, or perhaps his own — and now his question showed he suspected something. But at last, on his promise of loving her better for knowing the truth, she confessed all that she knew. Whereon, having dragged it from her, he graciously revealed his side of the incident, and that he himself, disguised by Merlin, had fathered the child. "Then the queen made great joy when she knew who was the father of her child." (A human seducer, however treacherous, must have seemed preferable to a demon.) Uther did not leave her long to rejoice, however; at the child Arthur's birth, he delivered it unchristened to Merlin, as per the mage's instructions; and, although Uther knew where Merlin was taking the child, he neglected to tell Igraine — it is not recorded that he consulted her at all before taking her son. (And he had burned so with love of her!)

Within two years Uther fell seriously ill. But his enemies were making inroads on his kingdom, so he took Merlin's advice and had himself carried to battle in a horse-litter to St. Albans, where his army met a "great host of the North." Whether inspired by the great deeds of Sir Ulfius and Sir Brastias, or by the presence of their king with the army, Uther's men prevailed. The king returned to London with great rejoicing, but soon fell so sick that he lay speechless for three days and nights. At last Merlin promised the barons he would make the king to speak.

> So on the morn all the barons with Merlin came to-fore the king; then Merlin said aloud unto King Uther, Sir, shall your son Arthur be king after your days ...? Then Uther Pendragon turned him, and said in hearing of them all, I give him God's blessing and mine, and bid him pray for my soul, and righteously and worshipfully that he claim the crown, upon forfeiture of my blessing; and therewith he yielded up the ghost, and then was he interred as longed to a king. Wherefore the queen, fair Igraine, made great sorrow, and all the barons.

I must confess that Igraine's sorrow rather surprises me; perhaps he had turned into a decent husband after all, but it seems to me more likely that she made a public show of mourning, while her private grief was more for being left protectorless in unsettled times and for the knowledge of what he had done with her son having apparently been lost with him than for love of Uther himself. Nevertheless, where his lusts were not concerned, Uther seems to have been a strong and brave king, and, not impossibly, a decent administrator of the public weal. [Malory I, 1-4]

Uwaine – see YWAINE

ADALON†

King Vadalon was brother to the King of Norgales (probably not Ryons) and eventually might have been king of Norgales in his turn [Vulgate IV; see under King Agrippe's Daughter.

A brave but cruel knight named Vadalon received Sir Ector de Maris' seat at the Round Table after Lancelot and his supporters left Arthur [Vulgate VI]. I do not know whether this knight should be identified with the King Vadalon who banded Agrippe's daughter, but I think it not improbable. King Vadalon could also be called "cruel," and, while I have not discovered whether or not Sir Bors encountered King Vadalon during the year he was pledged to carry the shield Agrippe's daughter gave him, or what the outcome of that fight — if it ever took place — might have been, it would as neatly fit the pattern of such events if Bors

seems to have been popular until our own century. It appears, for instance, in Ainsworth's excellent, melodramatic Victorian historical novel **Old Saint Paul's**, set during the London plague and fire of the latter Seventeenth Century, and in other period novels.

There remain a good many especially strange-sounding names, largely from the Vulgate — names which, though from a French source, do not seem quite French. But though a knowledge of modern French can enable a reader to get at least the sense of much of the Vulgate, it must be remembered that there were other dialects in that geographical area besides the one which became modern French. *Langue d'oïl* romancers who transferred their tales from the Breton, *langue d'oc*, and other dialects

would probably have carried the proper names over almost unchanged. Thymadeuc (in the Morbihan), Guenael, Vacandard, Fastrad of Gaviamex, Senanque, Vezelay — these are names that would hardly have sounded out of place among the Arthurian sites and characters in this volume; but I found them in Thomas Merton's book about Cistercian life, **The Waters of Siloe**, and some, at least, must have originated in a French dialect other than the *langue d'oïl*. Alazaïs, Grazide, Vuissane — easily as strange to our eyes and ears as most of the proper names in Malory and the Vulgate, I found in an article about a Fourteenth-century cleric in Occitan-speaking France, totally unrelated to Arthurian studies.

conquered and converted Vadalon and brought him to Arthur as a faithful vassal, eventually to be given a place at the Round Table, as it would if Bors conquered and killed King Vadalon.

KING VAGOR†

Vagor's son, Marabron, charged Sir Lionel with treason. The wife of Marabron's brother had played on Lionel the same sort of trick Potiphar's wife played on Joseph (Genesis 39), forcing Lionel to kill the husband in self-defense. King Vagor held Lionel prisoner in his castle. Lancelot arrived and championed Lionel, fighting Marabron and forcing him to retract the charge. [Vulgate V; see L'Isle Estrange, *Places*]

LADY DE VANCE

All I can find of her is that King Ryons desired to lie with her, which was his undoing; Balin and Balan ambushed him on the way to her and brought him prisoner to Arthur. Ryons had sent twenty of his knights on ahead to "warn" her of his coming, but whether she was willing or not I cannot say. [Malory II, 9]

Vanora — see GUENEVERE

LADY DE VAWSE

All I can find about her is that she held a tournament at which the prize was a rich circlet of gold worth a thousand besants; Sir Marhaus won the prize while adventuring with the damsel Ete (see "Printemps, Été, & Automne"). Lady de Vawse must have lived within two days' ride of the South Marches. [Malory IV, 25]

It is tempting to postulate a scribe's or printer's error somewhere along the line and identify her with Lady de Vance.

VAYSHOURE

I got the name of Aries' wife by process of elimination, since in Malory IX, 15, Sir Tor is called "le Fise de Vayshoure" — the son of Vayshoure.

When Aries the cowherd brought his supposed son Tor to Arthur, the King asked to see Aries' wife.

> Anon the wife was fetched, which was a fair housewife, and there she answered Merlin full womanly, and there she told the king and Merlin that when she was a maid, and went to milk kine, there met with her a stern knight [Pellinore], and half by force he had my maidenhead, and at that time he begat my son Tor, and he took away from me my greyhound that I had that time with me, and said that he would keep the greyhound for my love. Ah, said the cowherd, I weened not this, but I may believe it well, for he [Tor] had never no tatches of me. Sir, said Tor unto Merlin, dishonour not my mother. Sir, said Merlin, it is more for your worship than hurt, for your father is a good man and a king, and he may right well advance you and your mother, for ye were begotten or ever she was wedded. That is truth, said the wife. It is the less grief unto me, said the cowherd. [Malory III, 3]

"VERRINE"

This high-born damsel of Guenever's court was mute until the arrival of Sir Percival, when at last she spoke. Greeting him, she led him to his seat at the left of the Siege Perilous and predicted his future greatness. She also predicted her own death, which took place four days later; she was buried in the cathedral at Cardiff. From the circumstances of the miracle, I assume she had led a holy life. [Malory X, 23; Vulgate V; see also under Percivale]

Vertiger — see VORTIGERN

LA VEUVE DAME DE LA GASTE FOREST SOUTAINE†

According to Vulgate VII, she was the mother of Sir Agloval.

At one time, and in some versions, King Pellinore seems to have been identical with King Pelles/Pellam, the Maimed King, etc. Sommer appears to have been more or less on top of the Maimed King tangle. Since I have tried to follow Malory in differentiating Pellinore and Pellam, I incline to accept "La Veuve Dame ..." as the nearest thing I have yet uncovered to a name for Pellinore's wife and the mother of his sons in wedlock. In Vulgate VII, she appears to be ruling over a number of subjects, and this is not incompatible with the standard tale of Percivale and his mother.

VIVIANE†

The chief French Lady of the Lake — see Lady of the Lake, Nimue, and Nineve.

Viviane's father, Dyonas, was a vavasour of high lineage who long served the Duke of Burgoyne and married the Duke's daughter. The goddess Diane of the Woods, who used to visit Dyonas, promised him that his first child would be coveted by one of the wisest of men. Merlin met Dyonas' daughter Viviane at a fountain when she was twelve years old, and she promised to give him her love when he had taught her his crafts. According to this Vulgate account, Viviane was the woman who imprisoned Merlin.

When Queen Elaine of Benwick left her tiny son Galahad in order to rush to her dying husband, on a hill in sight of their conquered city, Viviane seized the opportunity to take the child. She renamed him Lancelot and raised him in her own rich city, disguised to mundane eyes beneath the appearance of a lake. Hence — "Lancelot of the Lake." Later, Viviane sent one of her chief damsels, Seraide, to rescue Lancelot's cousins Lionel and Bors from King Claudas and bring them, also, to the Lake.

When Lancelot was eighteen, Viviane yielded to his request, coached him in the requirements of knighthood, equipped him, and brought him and his cousins to Arthur's

---

One further point: finding names for characters must have been as common a problem among medieval as among modern storytellers. (That, indeed, may have been another reason why they left so many characters unnamed.) It is entirely possible that some Arthurian names sounded as strange, awkward, contrived, even unsatisfactory to medieval readers — even, perhaps to the very storytellers who had devised them in desperation — as they sound to us.

It seems rather popular in modern Arthurian novels to refer to Arthur's own name as outlandish. Perhaps there is a scholarly basis for this; perhaps it is simply another instance of heightening the sense of difference between eras by referring to a common name in our century as an uncommon name in the past — I have also found the name Thomas so treated. The surprise that characters express in such novels, however — their puzzlement as to where such a name as "Arthur" could have come from — has never convinced me. "Arthur" seems such a logical development from "Uther," and I cannot remember any similar surprise among characters over Uther's name.

court. Viviane continued to act as Lancelot's guardian, through personal visits to Britain and through subordinate damsels whom she sent in her place.

She came to La Roche while Arthur was Camille's prisoner there, and completed the matchmaking between Lancelot and Guenever, counselling the Queen to love Lancelot with all her heart. Viviane then returned home, remarking, "I am anxious not to displease him who loves me, well knowing that a lover can only be happy when the object of his love is near." [Vulgate III, p. 419]

When Sir Bors and Viviane visited each other during Arthur's war with Claudas, Bors invested Viviane's husband with the Chastel del Cor, apparently in France. [Vulgate II-V]

According to the Vulgate, the Damsels of the Lake owed their knowledge of magic — apparently all of it — to Merlin. Tennyson makes Vivien a votary of the old, pagan sun worship. He also makes her definitely evil; but this accords ill with the roles both of Nimue in Malory and Viviane in the Vulgate — moreover, in order to do it, he divorces Vivien from the beneficent Lady of the Lake and makes them two separate characters. Though Viviane has against her the imprisonment of Merlin, the kidnapping of Lancelot (though it may be said to have had good results) and the promotion of the affair between Lancelot and Guenever (but she was not the only go-between in the case) she still seems to be shown in a good light, as a basically beneficent enchantress.

Adopted son: Lancelot
Protégé: Lionel, Sir Bors de Ganis
Cousin: Lunette
Damsels: Rossignol, Seraide
Lover: Merlin

VIVIANE'S FAMILY AND RELATIONS

VORTIGERN† (Vertiger)

Vortigern was seneschal to King Constans of Britain, Arthur's grandfather. After the death of Constans, twelve barons who wanted Vortigern for their king murdered Constans' eldest son, Maines. Vortigern gained the kingship and allied himself to the Saxons. In fear of Constans' remaining sons, Pandragon and Uther, Vortigern tried to build himself a tower, but did not succeed until after the child Merlin had shown him a pair of dragons in a great water beneath the tower's proposed foundations, and made a very unfavorable prophecy about what the dragons symbolized for Vortigern. True to Merlin's prediction, Pandragon and Uther killed Vortigern and burned his tower. [Vulgate II; see Vertiger's Tower, *Places*]

ADE

Sir Wade must have been a great and famous knight in his day, judging from the company in which Dame Lynette puts him, even though this is the one reference I find to Wade in Malory. Rebuking Gareth Beaumains, Lynette says: "wert thou as wight as ever was Wade or Launcelot, Tristram or the good knight Sir Lamorak." [Malory VII, 9]

Wander — see GUENEVERE

QUEEN OF THE WASTE LANDS

While on the Grail Quest, Galahad encountered Lancelot and Percivale in a "waste forest," before the hermitage of a female recluse. When Galahad had unhorsed Lancelot and Percivale, the recluse hailed him, saying, "An yonder two knights had known thee as well as I do they would not have encountered with thee." At this, Galahad departed hastily, lest she reveal his identity. Lancelot also rode off on his own, but Percivale, returning to the hermitess, learned that she was his aunt.

> For some called me sometime the Queen of the Waste Lands, and I was called the queen of most riches in the world; and it pleased me never my riches so much as doth my poverty.

She revealed to Percivale that his mother had died, explained to him certain matters concerning the significance of the Round Table and the Sangreal, and counselled him to find Galahad again, beginning at Goothe castle, "where he hath a cousin-germain, and there may ye be lodged this night" — Goothe must have been in the vicinity of the queen's hermitage. If unsuccessful in getting news of Galahad at Goothe, Percivale was to ride on straight to Carbonek.

Lancelot also, later in the Grail Quest, received sound counsel and advice, as well as dinner, from a recluse. Lancelot's recluse might have been the Queen of the Waste Lands again, or she might have been an entirely different holy woman; she seems to have lived in a deep valley, near a mountain difficult of ascent, with a river in the vicinity — I would hazard a guess that the site might conceivably be somewhere in the Cotswolds, Gloucestershire.

Presumably the Queen of the Waste Lands who comes with Morgana, Nimue, and the Queen of Northgalis to carry Arthur away after the last battle is the same Queen of the Waste Lands who appears in the Grail Adventures. If so, the presence of a Christian mystic and holy woman with two queens who have generally, up to now, been characterized as wicked enchantresses, is very interesting. [Malory XIII, 17; XIV, 1-2; XV, 5-6; XXI, 5-6]

PROPHECIES

According to a hermit's interpretation, one of the visions Gawaine had in Carbonek foretold Gawaine's own death. Gawaine consoled himself (very sensibly, in my opinion) with the reflection that prophecies were uncertain. [Vulgate V]

Merlin's prophecies all apparently came true, though some were notably obscure and thus open to various interpretations, and they must not all have come true during Arthur's own time, for prophecies attributed to the great mage continued to circulate during the historical Middle Ages. [See also *Magical Acts* in the Appendices]

At least some prophecies seem to have been "of God," especially those concerning the Grail. Others, apparently, were discovered through necromancy. The question, of course, is how far a prophecy — even a competent, truthful one — predicts an absolute and unchangeable future and how far it helps create the circumstances it predicts. Personally, I not only question the value of prophecies, but think some of them were mischievous, dangerous, and pernicious. It is a pity that Mordred, when confronted with a devastating prophecy at an impressionable age, did not show his brother Gawaine's healthy skepticism: the end of Arthur's story might have been very different.

From Malory alone, the Queen of the Waste Lands appears to have been Pellam's wife, the couple living apart for greater purity. Tennyson, though skimming over Elaine of Carbonek and giving his own unsympathetic interpretation of Pellam, seems obliquely to second this theory in the Idyll **Balin and Balan**: "Pellam . . . hath pushed aside his faithful wife." The Vulgate, however, makes her the widow of a man killed in an earlier war — possibly King Lambor, Pellam's grandfather. This would make her Percivale's great-great-aunt, and quite a venerable, aged dame. Here too she has a son, Dables (Orabiax, Dyabel, etc.) who goes to Pellam to be knighted. [Vulgate VI]

There may also be some connection or confusion between the Queen of the Waste Lands and la Veuve Dame de la Gaste Forest Soutaine.

ON†, KING

Yon appears to have been a sub-king in Gaul, captured by Bagdemagus during Arthur's war against Claudas. Bagdemagus added Yon's contingent to his own, and Yon himself seems not only to have gone over to Arthur's side, but to have distinguished himself as one of the best leaders on that side. [Vulgate V]

King Yon later turns up in Arthur's court, among the barons. After Lancelot was discovered with Guenever, when Arthur commanded his barons to sentence the Queen without delay, Yon reminded him that it was not the custom to pass any judgments after the hour of Nonne (about mid-afternoon).

Yon was killed in the last battle with Mordred's forces [Vulgate VI].

Might Yon conceivably be identified with Yonec, the title character in one of the works of Marie de France?

Yseult, Ysolde — see ISOUD

YVAINE (Yvonet, Ewain, Uwain, Owain, etc.)

Vulgate VII, p. 240, gives a list of six different knights with this name. The only two I am including here are the sons of King Uriens. His legitimate son, by Queen Morgan, is given under Ywaine. Uriens' son by the wife of his seneschal is given under the variant Yvonet.

YVONET LI AVOUTRES (Uwaine Les Adventurous; Uwaine Les Avoutres, etc.)

King Uriens of Gore had two sons of the same name, Yvonet le Grand by Arthur's half-sister Morgan, and Yvonet li Avoutres by the wife of Uriens' seneschal (Vulgate II). To try to keep things a little less confusing, I have used the more common present-day variant spelling Ywaine for the legitimate son, Le Grand (also called Le Blanchemains, etc.) and reserved the variant Yvonet for Li Avoutres.

Malory uses both brothers, but does not explain their birth history, which may lead to confusion. Both appear together on at least two occasions, once at the tournament at Castle Dangerous and once in company with Sirs Brandiles, Ozana, Agravaine, and Mordred in one of the interminable mix-and-match adventures that largely make up Malory's

books of Tristram. Yvonet, or Uwaine les Avoutres as Malory calls him, was killed by Gawaine, ironically, while they were both on the Grail Quest. Happening to meet, they indulged in a joust, and by misadventure Yvonet/Uwaine was mortally wounded. Gawaine got him to an abbey, where he was unarmed and given the Sacrament.

> Then Gawaine asked him what he was ... I am, said he, of King Arthur's court, and was a fellow of the Round Table, and we were brethren sworn together; and now Sir Gawaine, thou hast slain me, and my name is Uwaine les Avoutres, that sometime was son unto King Uriens, and was in quest of the Sangreal; and now forgive it thee God, for it shall ever be said that the one sworn brother hath slain the other.

[Malory VII, 27+; X, 11; XVI, 2]

YWAINE (Ewain, Owain, Yvain, Yvonet Le Grand, Ewain Le Blanchemains, Uwaine, Le Chevalier Au Lion, etc.)

Ywaine was the son of King Uriens and Queen Morgana of Gore, half-brother to Yvonet li Avoutres (see above), cousin and close friend to Gawaine. He may have come to Arthur's court as early as the funeral of Lot and the other kings of the second rebellion, along with his parents who attended that funeral.

At Camelot, Ywaine found his mother about to slay his sleeping father. He prevented her, exclaiming, "Ah ... men saith that Merlin was begotten of a devil, but I may say an earthly devil bare me." At her pleading, he agreed not to speak of her attempt on condition she did not try it again. She proceeded to leave court, steal the scabbard of Excalibur, and attempt to destroy Arthur by sending him the gift of a poisoned cloak. It would not be surprising if Ywaine felt himself freed of his promise not to reveal her attempt on Urien's life, but the tale seems to imply that he kept the secret, at least for the time; after the poisoned cloak incident, both Morgan's husband and son were suspected of being in her counsel. Arthur quickly dismissed his suspicion against Uriens, but banished Ywaine from court, which must have been hard on the young knight. Gawaine remarked, "Whoso banisheth my cousin-germain shall banish me," and went with Ywaine. They met Sir Marhaus, and shortly thereafter found the damsels Printemps, Été, and Automne in Arroy Forest. Ywaine chose Automne for his guide, saying, "I am the youngest and most weakest [of us three knights] ... therefore I will have the eldest damosel, for she hath seen much, and can best help me when I have need."

Traveling with her, he distinguished himself, winning a tournament near the Welsh marches and gaining back for the Lady of the Rock a barony that Sirs Edward and Hue of the Red Castle had extorted from her. At the end of a twelvemonth, after meeting again with their damsels at the appointed place in Arroy, Ywaine, Gawaine, and Marhaus were found by a messenger of Arthur's. The King must have realized his error in banishing Ywaine almost at once, for he had been seeking his nephews nearly a year. They returned to court, taking Marhaus with them. It may have been at this time that Ywaine was made a member of the Round Table, though Malory only mentions that Marhaus and Pelleas were so honored at the next feast. [Malory I, 2; II, 11; IV, 13, 16-19, 26-28]

Chrétien de Troyes, possibly the father of Arthurian romance as we know it, devoted one of his sprightly poems to Ywaine, basing his tale as it seems on a lost work much like the Welsh **Owen and Lunet**. Chrétien's Yvain is identified as a cousin-germain of Sir Calogrenant (Colgrevance) and as the son of King Urien; but perhaps Uriens and Lot had not yet become identified as brothers-in-law, for Chretien emphasizes Ywaine and Gawaine, Lot's son, as friends rather than as cousins. The temptation is overpowering to insert Ywaine's adventures as described by Chrétien after Ywaine's return to Arthur's court with Gawaine and Marhaus as described by Malory.

Briefly, Chrétien recounts how, while the court was at Cardoile (Carlisle), Ywaine learned from Calogrenant of a marvellous spring in Broceliande Forest: pouring water from this spring onto a nearby rock caused a terrific storm to arise and, after the storm, a knight would appear to chastise the impudent person who had poured the water. (The Golden Bough mentions such a fountain or stream, called Barenton, where "the Breton peasants used to resort when they needed rain.") Ywaine tried his luck at the spring and killed in combat the champion who appeared after the storm. This left the champion's wife, Dame Laudine, the daughter of Duke Laudunet, without a protector for herself, her castle of Landuc, or the spring. Ywaine fell in love with Laudine and, with the assistance of her damsel Lunette, who gave him good advice and a magic ring of invisibility, eventually won her and became guardian of the magic spring in his turn. Now Arthur and his companions, wondering what had become of Ywaine, arrived at the spring, where Arthur poured the water on the rock. When Ywaine appeared, disguised by his armor, Kay took the fight for Arthur and was promptly defeated. There followed a happy reunion and welcome for Arthur, Gawaine, and their party at Landuc castle; but Gawaine persuaded Ywaine that he should spend a year adventuring and tourneying, lest folk say his marriage had made him soft. Laudine let her husband go on condition he return in exactly a year. But he let the months get away from him and stayed away too long, whereon Laudine sent word that she never wanted to see him again. Ywaine went mad with grief and ran amok in the wild forest for a time until a passing damsel recognized him as he lay asleep and healed him with a salve that the fairy Morgue (Morgan) had given her.

Ywaine rescued a lion from a serpent; the grateful lion became his devoted companion. Taking the name "Le Chevalier au Lion," Ywaine embarked on a series of adventures, always fighting for the good, in contrast to his previous year's adventures of tourneying for the mere glory of it. Among other deeds, he rescued Lunette from a false accusation by fighting as her champion in trial by combat. Eventually, still keeping his identity secret, Ywaine showed up at Arthur's court to champion a damsel in a property quarrel with her sister. Unknown to Ywaine, Gawaine was championing the other damsel, so there resulted one of those grand battles, so beloved of the romancers, between two great and evenly-matched knights who are really dear friends or relatives but do not recognize each other in their armor. The fight ended happily: on learning each other's identity, both heroes were healed of their wounds in the infirmary, Arthur gave just judgment in the case of the quarreling sisters, and Ywaine, with his lion, returned to the magic spring and Landuc, where Lunette effected a reconciliation between husband and wife.

Without attempting to summarize Ywaine's adventures as recorded in the Vulgate, we return to Malory. While Tristram, Palomides, and Dinadan were languishing in Sir Darras' prison after the Castle of Maidens tournament, Ywaine le Blanchemains (I have not yet discovered why Malory gives Morgan's son this appellation), seemingly having joined a general search

for Tristram and quite possibly suspecting Mark of further treachery, appeared before Mark's castle and issued a challenge to "all the knights of Cornwall." Only Andred was willing to encounter him, to Andred's immediate unhorsing and wounding. At Mark's insistence, Sir Dinas the Seneschal jousted with Ywaine and was overthrown. Then Sir Gaheris, who happened to be visiting Mark, rode out, but Ywaine recognized his shield and refused to have ado with a brother of the Round Table. As Ywaine rode away, Mark rode after and dealt him a treacherous and serious blow from behind. Fortunately, Sir Kay happened along in time to get Ywaine to the Abbey of the Black Cross to be healed. [Malory IX, 38]

Ywaine fades out of Malory's account after this episode; he is mentioned with his half-brother and namesake [X, 11], and after that, perplexingly, there is little or nothing. Possibly by XVI Malory himself had the Uwaines confused, and considered this Ywaine — rather than his half-brother Les Avoutres — to have been the one who was killed during the Grail Quest and was therefore out of the story. In Vulgate VI we learn that the deaths of Gawaine, his brothers, and Kay, and the rift between Arthur and Lancelot with his supporters, have left Ywaine as Arthur's remaining mainstay. Ywaine is killed by Mordred in the last battle.

Ywaine's coat of arms presumably includes a lion.

A BRIEF BESTIARY

CABAL† (Cavall)

Arthur's dog is not mentioned in Malory, but can be found in pre-Malory sources. Tennyson refers to him in the Idyll **Enid**.

GALTISANT (The Questing Beast)

Pursued first by King Pellinore and later by Sir Palomides (for obscure reasons, since by Pellinore's testimony the beast can be achieved only by himself or one of his close kin), Galtisant is probably the most memorable of the surprisingly few dragon-like creatures in Malory.

Galtisant had a head like a serpent, a body like a leopard, buttocks like a lion, and feet like a hart. From the beast's belly came a noise "like unto the questing of thirty couple hound," which was not heard when Galtisant was drinking — presumably it was heard all the rest of the time. "Questing" seems to refer not to Galtisant's value as an object of pursuit or "quest," but to the noise like that of questing hounds; the pun, however, would hardly have been lost upon the word-intoxicated Middle Ages. [Malory I, 19-20; IX, 12]

Why Pellinore and later Palomides follow Galtisant is extremely unclear, since the beast never is reported as doing any damage, or even as arousing fear in a spectator — only curiosity. Perhaps, as in a fox hunt, the skill of the capture was more important than what you did with the beast once you had it. Or perhaps the idea was to capture it as what we would call today a scientific specimen, or as an exhibit for the King's menagerie. (That Arthur, like later historical kings, kept a menagerie is evidenced by the tale of La Cote Male Tail; see Malory IX,1.) I suspect, however, that T. H. White analyzed the situation perfectly: he had Galtisant chased because Galtisant wants to be chased — the hunt is for affection and attention, not for slaughter; and when Pellinore (White's version of him, not Malory's) retires from the quest for a time to enjoy the luxury of Arthur's court, the Questing Beast actually begins to pine away! Malory neither describes nor alludes to any capture of Galtisant.

"FEUILLEMORTE"†

In the Middle English metrical romance **Sir Gawaine and the Carl of Carlisle**, the Carl gives Sir Kay a very fast, blood-red steed. The reason for the gift is unclear; Kay seems certainly to have done nothing to deserve a gift from his host. Perhaps the steed's temper matches Kay's own. Feuillemorte is my own idea for a name.

GRINGOLET†

Gawaine won his horse Gringolet from Clarions, a leader of the Saxons [Vulgate II]. Gringolet is prominently mentioned in **Sir Gawaine and the Green Knight**.

GRISSELLE†

In the Middle English metrical romance **The Adventures at Tarn Wadling**, this fine gray warhorse is killed from under Sir Gawaine as Gawaine battles Sir Galeron. Though Gawaine is practical enough to call for his black Frisian as a replacement, he mourns for Grisselle as keenly as for a human com-

rade. "Grisselle" might conceivably be a variant of "Gringolet," but I prefer to think of them as two separate steeds.

HUDENT†

At least one dog seems to play a part in most versions of the Tristram tale. Despite the disparity in size and sex, the name of Tristram's large, male hunting hound, Hudent, in Béroul's **Tristran**, might be applied for lack of another name, to the little, unnamed female brachet that King Faramon's daughter sent to Tristram and Tristram gave to La Beale Isoud. Once, when Tristram was carried to Tintagil after a fit of madness, naked and so unkempt as to be unrecognizable, the brachet knew him. [Malory VIII, 5; IX, 21]

PASSE-BREWEL

Tristram's horse [Malory IX, 27].

Questing Beast, The — see GALTISANT

SORREL-HAND†

Sir Ironside's horse [**Sir Gawaine and the Carl of Carlisle**].

Ywaine's Lion† — see under YWAINE

QUESTING AND ERRANTRY

A quest generally lasted only a year and a day, apparently whether accomplished or not. For this we have Gawaine's authority. [Vulgate V, p. 270]

The pattern of errantry seems to have been that you helped whoever first requested it of you, without bothering to investigate which side was more nearly in the right. Unless, of course, one of the parties was a lady, in which case you generally helped her against the male involved. This system could result in the reversal of justice. Once a wronged husband reprimanded Gawaine for the practice of Arthur's knights of taking the woman's part automatically without first hearing both sides [Vulgate V, appendix]. Another time, Gareth, Gaheris, and Agravaine entered a dispute on the right side and were winning it, when Lancelot and Lionel came along, entered on the wrong side without taking time to investigate and weigh the merits of both sides, and won for the wrong side [Vulgate V].

It was considered disgraceful for a knight to ride in a cart, or "chariot." Lancelot turned this into honor as Le Chevaler du Chariot.

For ... because of despite that knights and ladies called him the knight that rode in the chariot like as if he were judged to the gallows, therefore in despite of all them that named him so, he was carried in a chariot a twelvemonth ... [and] he never in a twelvemonth came on horseback. And ... he did that twelvemonth more than forty battles. [Malory XIX, 13; the first trip in a cart had been to Meliagrant's castle to save Guenever after Meliagrant's archers killed Lancelot's horse from ambush.]

Lancelot's quest in a cart may not have been quite so offbeat as it sounds. After a tournament of King Brangoire's, the twelve best knights of the tourney gave "gifts" to Brangoire's daughter, which gifts consisted of extravagant promises of what they were

going to do. The gifts varied from simply silly to needlessly bloodthirsty. The most sensible of the lot was probably the young knight who swore not to joust for a year except with his right leg on the neck of his horse; all he had to do, once he sobered up, was to refrain from jousting at all. One of the worst was he who promised to cut off the heads of all the knights he conquered and send them to the princess. Yet another gallant promised to kiss every damsel he found with a knight; but Lancelot encountered him, defeated him for trying to kiss the damsel Lancelot was escorting, and scolded him for foolishness. [Vulgate IV]

Nevertheless, one sometimes receives the impression that almost anything can be forgiven and overlooked if the perpetrator claims it was done to fulfil a vow or promise, especially one made because of a woman. Sir Ironside, while besieging Castle Dangerous, hanged nearly forty knights by the neck shamefully from trees. But he did it because once he had loved a lady whose brother had been killed by (she said) either Lancelot or Gawaine; she had made Ironside promise by the faith of his knighthood "to labour daily in arms" until he met one of those twain, and to put all he overcame in the meantime to a shameful death. Ironside was not only forgiven, but made a knight of the Round Table. [Malory VII]

In the mischievous Middle English metrical romance **The Avowynge of King Arthur**, Arthur vows to slay a notorious wild boar singlehandedly before the next day. He then commands his companions each to make his own vow. Gawaine vows to keep vigil all night at Tarn Wadling; Kay vows to ride about the woods until day and fight to the death anyone who tries to block his way; Bawdewyn (Baldwin) vows never to be jealous of his wife or any other lady, never to dread death, and to give any comer good hospitality.

II. Places

Introduction

In creating this section, I felt it appropriate to try to locate in the real world as many of the places of the days of Arthur as I could. The efforts have been made in good faith; many of the arguments I used have been included as notes in relevant entries. Such efforts are among the most arcane of literary exercises. The reader may or may not find my logic compelling, but he or she should not understand the result to be an archaeological guide to actual Arthurian artifacts and ruins.

THE ARRANGEMENT

Previous admonitions about unstandardized and variant spellings are in order in this section as well. The choice of a particular spelling may have been made after long consideration of many factors or dictated by simple mellifluosity; in a realm so personal, surely the chronicler may be allowed such gentle influence.

In alphabetizing these notes, such titles or descriptions as "Abbey," "Castle," "Chapel," and "Kingdom" have generally been disregarded; the entry is made by the first distinctive word. In most cases, entries are given as they appear in the text. Names have not been broken by commas in order to set the alphabetized word first, except in the case of the first entry for a particular letter of the alphabet. A "✝" after the entry indicates that the place is not found in Malory. Thus the general arrangement of this section is that of the previous section.

There are however, some general notes and conclusions which may make the reader's going a bit easier.

CASTLES AND CITIES

The distinction between a castle and a city is slight. Malory tells us that Camelot, Astolat, and Dover had castles, and we can assume that most of the rest of the cities listed likewise had their castles. Conversely, a number of references in Malory make it apparent that almost every castle had a town or village around or near it.

Almost every knight seems to have his castle, or to be capable of acquiring one. The lord of any given castle can change. Therefore I have not always given the names of the castellans.

I have tried to include every castle to which Malory gives a proper name, even in passing. I also included some of the castles to which he gives no names, but which seem interesting. I did not try to include every nameless castle held by a nameless or insignificant knight or lady.

Almost all identifications are tentative, except that sometimes I found a castle clearly stated as being in a particular territory. More often, I made an educated guess as to the approximate area of the country by attempting to trace the knights' adventures. Some castles I could not locate even generally.

COURT CITIES

Many modern treatments, especially movies, may give the impression that Arthur held his court only at Camelot and stayed there permanently. This is inaccurate. Like English monarchs of historical times, Arthur made his progresses, keeping his court on the move. Far from amassing material possessions promiscuously, these kings and nobles had to keep their property, at least what they meant to take around for daily use, portable and ready to be constantly packed, transported, unpacked, and repacked by the servants.

By making his progresses, the King was able to hold court and dispense justice all around his kingdom, not simply among those who were able to travel to one particular capital. Also, by moving around, the court would not so totally deplete the food of a given area (although nobles who hosted the courts of such monarchs as Elizabeth I might take years to recover from one courtly visitation).

When Arthur moved his court, did he take along the Round Table? We can assume this table was moved at least twice. Uther Pendragon gave it to King Leodegrance, and Leodegrance gave it back to Uther's son, Arthur, as a wedding present, along with Guenevere. So it was not absolutely immobile. In those days tables were generally boards laid across trestles at meal times, rather than our solid, full-joined pieces of furniture; the Round Table, likewise, may have been a large circular board or several boards which, when laid together across locally-available trestles, formed the circle. Thus, there may have been no problem in moving the Round Table from court city to court city.

Arthur, in Malory X, 68, while attending the tournament at Lonazep castle, sends Kay to check which knights of the Round Table are present at the tournament by reading the names on their seiges, or chairs. (Apparently these names appear only when the knights are near enough to come and take their seats.) By Malory's own identifications, Joyous Garde and therefore the neighboring Lonazep are much too far from Camelot for such a quick and comparatively casual errand between the two places. From this it seems that both the Round Table and its chairs must have been moved around from court to court.

The cities designated court cities are those at which Malory definitely tells us Arthur held his court at least once. I suspect that Arthur also held court at almost any good-sized city in his kingdom. For instance, he apparently had some site near Lonazep castle to set up court; it would be surprising if he did not sometimes hold court at Canterbury.

The length of Arthur's courts might perhaps be gauged by a comment (Vulgate V, 335) that an important court at Camelot, on Whitsunday, when Arthur was planning a large-scale war on King Claudas of France, lasted a whole week, after which the barons went home.

Malory records these court cities: Caerlon, Camelot, Cardiff, Carlisle, Kynke Kenadonne, London, York.

FOREIGN KINGDOMS AND SUB-KINGDOMS

This far from exhaustive list concentrates on the countries named by Malory. The close-at-hand kingdoms and sub-kingdoms include: France [Gaul], with Benwick [or Benoye, or Benoyc, with its city of the same name], Brittany or Little Britain, Burgoyne, Champayne, Guienne; Flanders, with its port city of Barflete; Ireland, with Galway; the Out Isles; and Sarras.

More distant nations mentioned by Malory are: Almaine [Germany], Denmark, the Holy Land, Hungary, Italy, Lombardy, Isle of Longtains [the Shetland Islands?], Rome, Sessoin [Saxony], Spain [Saracens or Moors were here], Tuscany, Vale [the Faeroës Islands], and Wentland [Prussia?].

In Book V, chapter 2, Malory gives a list of the countries to which the Roman Emperor Lucius sent messengers for help in his war against Arthur: Ambage, Arrage, Alexandria, India, Armenia ("whereas the river of Euphrates runneth into Asia"), Africa, Europe the Large, Ertayne and Elamye, Araby, Egypt, Damascus, Damietta and Cayer, Cappadocia, Tarsus, Turkey, Pontus and Pamphylia, Syria and Galatia, Greece, Cyprus, Macedonia, Calabria, Cateland, and Portugal ("with many thousands of Spaniards") — all these being subject to or allied with Rome.

FORESTS

Since Britain was covered with forest in the old days, wherever you move on a map of Arthurian Britain, you will not be far from the nearest forest. Some of the less obviously magical or mystical forests which I found given definite names in Malory or the Vulgate include Arroy, Bedegrain, Bresquehan†, Campacorentin†, Celibe†, Gloevant†, Landoine†, Morris, Roevant†, Sapine†, and Windsor.

RELIGIOUS CENTERS

It can be very hard to distinguish a "Religious Center" from a "Magical Place" or a "Castle."

It is also sometimes hard for me to be sure about whether a given religious center is wholly Christian. I cannot remember finding any Pagan holy places explicitly mentioned by Malory; however, many of the "Christian" or assumedly Christian holy sites were originally Pagan, and it well may be that elements of Paganism were still carrying through in Arthur's time, blending more quietly and peaceably with the Christian than we might have expected.

In a realistic Romano-British setting of the actual Fourth or Fifth centuries, I doubt cathedrals would be much in evidence. In Malory, however, I feel confident they are available. I cannot recall that Malory ever uses the word "cathedral"; but he uses bishops, archbishops, and "great churches." Malory certainly knew St. Paul's cathedral, though he cannily avoids committing himself as to whether or not Arthur knew it [I, 5]. The greatest church of Camelot, St. Stephen's, probably was another cathedral.

Hermits were everywhere. They "held great household, and refreshed people that were in distress" [Malory XVIII, 13]. A favorite form of retirement for a knight appears to have been turning hermit. I suspect that many former knights merely converted their manors into their hermitages. Women, too, became hermits, or "recluses." A lady may have become a recluse even while her husband was still living elsewhere, as wives sometimes entered or were put into convents during the lifetimes of their royal or noble spouses, who were thus enabled to remarry.

Early usage has "convent" meaning a house of either male or female religious. An Abbey would be under the rule of an Abbot or Abbess, a Priory under that of a Prior or Prioress. In an Abbey, the Abbot or Abbess would have a Prior or Prioress under him or her; therefore, a Priory would be a smaller establishment. Sometimes Malory refers to the house of a hermit as a priory, presumably with the hermit as Prior or Prioress. For ready identification, I would suggest using "monastery" for a convent of men and that good old word "nunnery" for one of women.

An "Almery" in Malorian usage is probably either an ambry — a cupboard or storage place in a church or elsewhere — or an almonry — a place where alms were distributed to the poor or where lived the almoner who distributed them for a bishop or prince. (The almoner, I suppose, may not have been a religious official himself, especially if he was a prince's official.)

It seems superfluous to make the next distinction if one knows it already, but many people (including myself in casual speech) use the terms "monk" and "friar" interchangeably. A monk lives in a monastery and stays put; I have even read somewhere that making too many trips abroad can be considered hazardous to his spiritual program. A friar travels around by vocation; itinerant preaching and well-doing is the nature of his calling. Friars were an invention of the later Middle Ages and should not have been around in Arthur's time. I cannot recall that even Malory, who can be quite anachronistic and who lived after the advent of friars, put them into his book anywhere.

Although Vulgate III tells us that regular religious orders were not yet established in Great Britain in Arthur's time, numerous houses would seem to take such names or descriptive phrases as "White Abbey" and "Black Abbey" from the habits of their congregations — habits frequently associated with specific orders, as white for the Dominicans. Malory probably did not trouble himself with the question of whether or not regular orders were established in Arthur's day; moreover, all the religious of a house may well have adopted the same color habit, even before such habits became associated with specific, regular orders.

In this section I have listed or cross-referenced named institutions; institutions that are given a fairly definite location, even if that location is no more than proximity to such-and-such a castle; a few institutions that, although unnamed, play a fairly important role in the action; and some of the more prominent cathedral cities. I have not attempted to include all individual hermitages, even where their location is specified; some of these may be filled in by finding the hermits and recluses in the section of People. Nor have I tried to list the many holy wells and ancient arrangements of standing stones to be found about Arthurian country, although I have given a few examples of these.

I have included a few sites more properly historical than directly related to Malorian and Vulgate romance.

MAGICAL PLACES

I find in Malory no clear cases of transfer into an entire "other world" of faery, such as are encountered, for instance, in old Celtic myth and in such tales as that of True Thomas the Rhymer. The nearest thing to a world of Faery in Malory seems to be "The Lake," which is more fully described in the Vulgate, and which seems to be an illusion masking a city in our own plane rather than a portal into another realm. In the Arthurian romances I have perused, there seems to be but one world for mortals to adventure in, and the faeries and necromancers either co-exist in the mortal world, or conceivably come into it from time to time through ways not open to mere lay mortals. If there is any "secondary world," it is the religious and mystical plane of the Grail adventures, where nothing seems to happen that does not have an allegorical meaning.

Even an otherwise superficially mundane adventure at an apparently mortal castle can have spiritual and allegorical significance in the Adventures of the Grail. I have included cross-references to castles described in the Grail Quest only if such castles seem to have some magical significance or potential significance independently of their Grail context. For example, I include a reference to the "Castle of the Leprous Lady," but not to the Castle of Maidens.

I have included references to castles definitely mentioned as being the stronghold of some necromancer for some period of time. I have not, however, attempted to reference castles if the only hint of occupation by a magic-worker was a name or unspecific reference. Nor have I listed every site at which something magical or mystical occurred, unless the event seemed bound up with or to alter supernaturally the nation of the place itself.

MAJOR KINGDOM DIVISIONS OF GREAT BRITAIN

In Book VII, 26, Malory indicates that the major divisions of Britain were England (or Logres), Wales, Scotland, Cornwall, Ireland, the Out Isles, and Brittany. Later, in VIII, 1, he tells us:

> And at that time King Arthur reigned, and he was whole king of England, Wales, and Scotland, and of many other realms; howbeit there were many kings ... for in Wales were two kings, and in the north were many kings; and in Cornwall and in the west were two kings; also in Ireland were two or three kings, and all were under the obeissance of King Arthur. So was the King of France, and the King of Brittany, and all the lordships unto Rome.

(This was after Arthur's war against and defeat of the Emperor Lucius.)

The difference between a "kingdom" and a "dukedom" seems marginal. We find dukes hobnobbing with kings, apparently as political and military equals; we also find some kings owing homage to other kings, as when King Anguish of Ireland demands tribute from King Mark of Cornwall. We meet kings whose territory seems to consist of a city, as well as kings who appear, like Lerner and Loewe's Pellinore, to have misplaced and even forgotten the names of their kingdoms. "Duke" Galeholt the Haut Prince gives an island to Marsil, who becomes "King" thereof. On the whole, I receive the impression that the principal distinction between a king and a duke lies in the title, and that a dukedom qualifies as a sub-kingdom. Similarly, there probably is not too much social descent to holdings clearly labelled as earldoms. Any knight could become lord of at least one castle and the surrounding territory, and rulers awarded lands and titles to their knights, even though the knights might continue to spend most of their time at court or on quest.

We may perhaps assume, in the lack of other evidence, that a number of Britain's kingdoms and dukedoms might have had pretty much the same boundaries and in many cases the same rulers before Arthur's high kingship as after he came to the throne.

In XXI, 26, speaking of the army Mordred raised against Arthur, Malory lists Kent, Southsex, Surrey, Estsex, Southfolk, and Northfolk. Since these are recognizably the names of modern counties, and since, in consulting a modern map of England, we find we can stick "Duke of" in front of most county names and produce familiar titles of history and romance, I suspect that sub-kingdoms could be formed by following modern county lines. This may not be accurate according to the newer schools of Arthurian realism, but I believe it would be quite compatible with the anachronistic spirit of Malorian romance.

GREAT BRITAIN – SUBKINGDOMS, ALPHABETICALLY

Virtually all castles had villages and territories attached, and sometimes the dividing line between a castle and a sub-kingdom seems rather fine.

Sub-kingdoms are listed alphabetically. Tentative identifications according to place names on modern maps will be found as individual entries. Virtually all identifications are questionable.

The sub-kingdoms are: King Amans' Land, Arroy, Avilion, Benoye, Cambenet, Cameliard, Clarance, the Delectable Isle, Escavalon, Estrangor, the Foreign Land, Garboth, Gore, L'Isle Estrange, the Isles, Leicester, Listeneise, the Long Isles, Lothian, Lyonesse, Malahaut, Nohaut, Norgales, North Marches, Northumberland, Orkney, Orofoise, Pomitain, Roestoc, Isle of Servage, Sorestan, South Marches, Straight Marches, Stranggore, Sugales, Surluse or Sorelois, Taningues, and Tintagil.

II · PLACES

BBLASOURE

All Malory tells us of Abblasoure can be found in XIII, 14:

> And at the last it happened [Galahad] to depart from a place or a castle the which was named Abblasoure; and he had heard no mass, the which he was wont ever to hear or ever he departed out of any castle or place, and kept that for a custom.

Could it be that Galahad heard no mass here because the inhabitants, if any, were Pagan? We are not told Galahad's emotions during his visit. He seems to have gotten along peaceably; this may have been early ecumenism, or he may have found the place deserted, even ruinous.

After leaving Abblasoure, he prayed at a desolate old chapel on a mountain, where a heavenly voice directed him to go to the Castle of Maidens and destroy the wicked customs there.

Rhayader Gwy, in Radnor, Wales, is handy both to mountains and to the Castle of Maidens if Llanidloes is accepted as the latter.

ABERCURNIG†

Glennie states that Abercorn, on the Firth of Forth, "where was anciently a famous monastery," was the Abercurnig of Gildas. By Glennie's map, Abercorn seems about five miles east of Linlithgow on the south bank of the firth.

Castle Adventurous – see CARBONEK

ABBEY OF THE ADVENTUROUS SHIELD (White Abbey)

Sommer seems to call this simply White Abbey, apparently as its proper name, one confusingly generic [Vulgate III, 21].

At this abbey Galahad found his Adventurous Shield. Here the holy Nasciens was either buried or to be buried. This is also, seemingly, the same abbey where there was a tomb from which issued such a noise that those who heard it either almost lost their wits or did lose their strength. The monks thought it was a fiend. Galahad, exorcising it, found on opening the tomb that the body was "a false Christian man." The soul returned, protesting, apparently to Hell, leaving a foul stink, and the monks reburied the body to get it out of the hallowed churchyard. This incident resembles that at the "Abbey of the Burning Tomb," and it is not unlikely that both tales sprang from the same original story, but in the state of the legends today, I would hesitate to recombine them.

The only clue I could find in Malory as to this abbey's whereabouts is that it was about four days from Vagon. That covers quite a territory. Putting Vagon at or near Basingstoke and going strictly by the "minster" or "church" in the name yields possible locations at Kidderminster in Worcestershire, Leominster in Herefordshire, or Church Stratton in Shropshire.

"AGRAVAINE'S HOUSE"†

The Duke of Cambeninc conquered this manor, which was in Bresquehan Forest, and gave it to Sir Agravaine. Later, a damsel carrying a sword led Gawaine to the house. Here numerous knights fought him. They demanded a helmet of his blood for a ransom. Refusing to give it under constraint, Gawaine gave it gladly on learning it was needed to heal a wounded knight. The wounded knight turned out to be his brother Agravaine, although so thin and pale that Gawaine did not recognize him at first.

Some time previously, two damsels had come when Agravaine was asleep, anointed his right leg and left arm with a strange ointment, and then ridden off well-pleased with their revenge. Agravaine's squire had witnessed this, and Agravaine suspected the damsels were sweethearts of knights he had wounded. He could not be healed except by the blood of the two best knights in the world. Gawaine's blood, when rubbed on the wounded leg, healed it. Gawaine later found Lancelot at Duke Galehot's Isle Perdue and sent back a helmet of Lancelot's blood, which healed Agravaine's arm.

One time Gawaine met the daughter of the man from whom the Duke of Cambeninc had conquered this house. She and another damsel were in the company of Agravaine and Mordred. One of the damsels was apparently Agravaine's sweetheart; the other had a younger sister enamoured of Gawaine. [Vulgate III]

Agravain, Tertre† – see DRUAS' HILL

ALENTIVE†

A town apparently in or near Surluse [Vulgate IV].

ALMESBURY

After Arthur's death, Guenever retired to the nunnery at Almesbury, where she became a "nun in white clothes and black," and, as befitted her former rank in the world, Abbess [Malory XXI, 7]. Almesbury is "little more than thirty mile" from Glastonbury [Malory XXI, 11]. It surely must be Amesbury, Wiltshire.

ALPHIN†

This castle is 30 English miles from Camelot [Vulgate VI].

KING AMANS' LAND

Amans, who appears in the Vulgate and is probably to be identified with Malory's King Aniause, took advantage of the war between Arthur, Ryons, and the Sesnes to attack Carmelide (Cameliard). Thus, Amans' land would most likely have bordered Cameliard. Sir Bors later helped Amans' daughter hold her land. Since the area south of Cameliard is Bertilak de Hautdesert's territory, and Bertilak seems to be more or less allied with the powerful Morgana le Fay, I would put King Amans' land north of Cameliard, between about the Mersey River in the south to about the mouth of the Ribble River (at Preston) in the north. Knowing no other name for this territory, I can only call it by that of its king.

ARBRAY

Sir Sadok, flying from Mark's ambush at Tintagil, passed Lyonesse (Liones) castle and continued to Arbray, where he found Sir Dinas, the Seneschal of Cornwall. They gathered the people and stocked the towns and castles of Cornwall. Arbray castle, therefore, appears to have been within the land of Lyonesse. [Malory X, 50]

ARROY

Sirs Marhaus, Gawaine, and Uwaine "came into a great forest, that was named the country and forest of Arroy, and the country of strange adventures," and here they chose for their guides three damsels whom they met at a fountain [Malory IV, 18]. Aside from the intervention of the Damosel of the Lake in Gawaine's adventure, there is not much of the supernatural in the succeeding episodes, as Malory records them.

Gawaine ended up in the middle of the Pelleas and Ettard affair, which may have been near the magical Lake, since Nimue loved Pelleas. Marhaus came to the Duke of the South Marches, while Uwaine rode westward and arrived in Wales. After meeting each other again in Arroy at the close of these adventures, the trio took twelve days to reach Camelot, which may argue quite a distance, or bad roads, or a leisurely trip.

Considering all things, I incline to identify Arroy as Warwickshire, reasonably convenient to Wales, the South Marches, and to Malory's Camelot.

ASTOLAT

Malory identifies this as Guildford, which is in present-day Surrey, south of London [XVIII, 8].

Avalon – see AVILION

AVILION (Isle of Avalon)

This is the place of Arthur's passing. He either died or was taken alive into a magical retreat. I conceive that Avilion must have been a sort of sanctuary: hallowed, neutral ground.

Avilion includes Glastonbury and the territory between the Mendip and the Quantock Hills, Somerset. Malory in his last book seems to confirm this traditional identification. Helen Hill Miller, in **The Realms of Arthur** points out that:

> It is no figurative island. Until recent centuries, the territory between the Mendip and the Quantock Hills, extending far inland from Bristol Channel, was a marsh across which only those who knew secret hidden causeways could travel ... As late as the 19th century the sea broke in ... and spread a brackish flood over miles of flat pasture."

Here, at Glastonbury, Joseph of Arimathea planted his miraculous Flowering Thorn. Later, a number of former knights gathered as hermits around Arthur's grave near Glastonbury.

Avilion may have been simply a geographical territory, difficult of access because of the marshlands. Certainly the place seems to have had normal residents leading normal lives. It must also have been the residence of the mysterious "great lady Lile of Avelion," who appears, from Malory's references to her, to have been a powerful sorceress [II, 1, 4]. I suspect, however, that Lady Lile of Avelion may be an unconscious personification of the island, or "l'i[s]le" of Avilion itself. Arthur may be in a mystical or magical sleep in Avilion, but Malory himself seems more of the opinion that the great king died like any other man.

Nevertheless, Avilion comes across to me as a mystical center of repose, quite possibly Christian grafted onto Pagan with elements of the old creed remaining, and beneficent if a shade melancholy – a "peaceable kingdom" of healing, sanctuary, and permanent, inviolate truce. Or, perhaps, it might have been a gateway to the underworld of the dead.

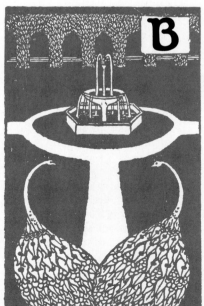

aale† – see KALET

Baillon† – see TANE-BORC

ABBEY OF BEALE ADVENTURE

Arthur founded this abbey fairly early in his reign, on or near the Humber River, at the site of his victory over the five invading kings of Denmark, Ireland, Soleise, the Vale, and the Isle of Longtains [Malory IV, 4]. Judging from the text, it would be a place where the river is crossable on horseback in calm weather [cf. Malory IV, 3]. Perhaps Selby or Cawood?

LA BEALE REGARD

Morgan le Fay was holding this castle, but it was not the one Arthur had given her. She usurped it from an unnamed but lively damsel, the niece of the Earl of Pase. When Morgan imprisoned Sir Alisander le Orphelin here, the Damsel of La Beale Regard helped him escape by writing to her uncle the Earl, asking him to come and destroy La Beale Regard with wild-fire. Alisander afterwards defended the site against all comers and thus met his love, Alice la Beale Pilgrim.

Alisander had started out, on Tristram's advice, for London. Presumably he left from Magouns castle (Arundel). But "by fortune he went by the seaside, and went wrong." At a tournament made by King Carados, he caught the eye of Morgan, who, after a side-battle of Alisander's against one Sir Malgrin, got Alisander into La Beale Regard. [Malory X, 36-38]

Since it is difficult to see how Alisander could miss London and end up in Scotland, I suspect that here Sir Cador of Cornwall is meant as the giver of this tournament, and not King Carados of Scotland.

In southwest Southampton is a town called Beaulieu. "Beautiful place," "beautiful view," La Beale Regard?

BEALE-VALET

This castle seems to be mentioned only once by Malory, as a place where Sirs Palomides and Dinadan spent a night [X, 25]. I would guess it to be somewhere in the southwest. If "Valet" is "valley," the castle might well be in a mountainous region. Exmoor Forest is very up-and-down, and Beale-Valet might be or be near to Ilfracombe, Barnstaple, or South Matton.

BEDEGRAINE

Malory identifies this as Sherwood Forest. So, at least, I interpret "the castle of Bedegraine, that was one of the castles that stand in the forest of Sherwood" [I, 17], coupled with the description in that and surrounding chapters of the battle fought in Bedegraine forest between Arthur with his allies Ban and Bors, and the eleven rebel kings. In a valley in the "forest of Bedegraine," before the battle, Merlin secretly lodged Ban and Bors' host of 10,000 men on horseback, though this may argue more for Merlin's magic than Bedegraine's extent.

BEDEGRAINE CASTLE

Apparently the major one of the castles that stood in Bedegraine (Sherwood) Forest [Malory I, 12, 17]. Inspired by the prominence of the Sheriff of Nottingham in the legends of Robin Hood, I am tempted to identify Bedegraine castle with the city of Nottingham.

La Bele Garde (La Bele Prise) — see DOLOROUS TOWER

BELOE† (Belec, Beloc)

When Arthur returned from France on news of Mordred's rebellion, the party bearing Gawaine's body stopped at Beloe castle. The lady of Beloe grieved for Gawaine as the only man she had ever loved. Upon this, the lord of Beloe, who had never liked Gawaine, killed his wife. For this murder, he was killed in turn by Arthur's knights, who then carried the lady's body with Gawaine's. [Vulgate VI, 358-359]

Mordred had attacked Arthur at Dover, trying to prevent his landing. Beloe must be between Dover and, probably, London or Camelot.

BENOYE

The more famous Benoye, or Benwick, was in France. There seems to have been another Benoye, in Britain — the dukedom of Duke Ansirus the Pilgrim. Ansirus' daughter, Alice La Beale Pilgrim, married Sir Alisander le Orphelin and they retired "into their country of Benoye, and lived there in great joy." [Malory X, 38-39]

Glennie identifies Albany, the area of Scotland roughly between the Firth of Tay to the east and Loch Fyne to the west, possibly with the Firth of Forth as part of its southern boundary, as Benoic. Alice heard of Alisander and journeyed down to see him when he was defending the site of the castle La Beale Regard, which I consider likely to have been somewhere near the southern coast of England. Since Alice's father had the custom of being in Jerusalem every third year, a simple jaunt all the way across Logres might have seemed little enough to her, so Albany remains a strong contender for Benoye.

On the other hand, Benoye might have neighbored La Beale Regard, being perhaps somewhere in Dorsetshire or Wiltshire.

Or Benoye might have been the country, not of Alice's father, but of Alisander's father, Prince Boudwin. Boudwin was the brother of Mark of Cornwall; Mark murdered Boudwin, and Boudwin's wife had charged Alisander to avenge his father. "But, as the book saith, King Mark would never stint till he had slain [Alisander] by treason."

Now it seems likely that Prince Boudwin's principal holdings would have been in or near Cornwall. Had Alisander returned to his father's lands in this part of the country, would he not have attacked Mark first? Also, Malory tells us that Alisander never came to Arthur's court; and it seems that he should have managed that trip, had he remained in southern or south central Logres or in Cornwall, within reach of such major court cities as Camelot, Caerleon, and London. Mark, however, might have contrived to get an assassin up into Scotland. All in all, I prefer Glennie's identification of Albany as the British Benoye.

BENWICK (Benoye, Benoyc)

The kingdom of Lancelot's father, King Ban. In XX, 18, Malory says:

> And so [Lancelot and his party] shipped at Cardiff, and sailed unto Benwick: some men call it Bayonne, and some men call it Beaune, where the wine of Beaune is.

John W. Donaldson identifies Benwick with Burgundy (Burgoyne, Bourgogne). The French Benwick is probably not to be identified with the territory of Benwick to which Alisander le Orphelin and his wife Alice retired.

BIENFAIT MONASTERY†

It was near the forest of Bresquehan, and had the Duke of Cambeninc for its patron [Vulgate III].

BLACK CHAPEL

According to the Vulgate, this is the name of the chapel to which the last of Arthur's knights carried the wounded king after the last battle. It is located somewhere between Salisbury and the sea. Malory's account might lead one to believe that the last knight took Excalibur to the lake from this chapel, and afterwards carried Arthur from here directly to the boat of Morgana and the other queens. The Vulgate, however, specifies that after passing the night at the Black Chapel, Arthur and his last warrior set out in the morning, reaching the sea at noon, and Arthur sent his knight from the seaside to throw Excalibur into the lake on the other side of the hill. Also according to the Vulgate, the last knight later found Arthur's grave at the Black Chapel. This seems to vary from Malory, who apparently makes the chapel near Salisbury distinct from that where Arthur lies buried. [Vulgate VI; Malory XXI, 4-7]

THE BLACK CROSS†

When Josephe and his followers arrived in Britain, Camelot (Kamaalot) was the richest city of the Pagans. The then king, Agrestes, pretended to convert; but, after Josephe left the city, Agrestes martyred twelve of Josephe's relatives. A cross Josephe had erected was stained black with their blood. Agrestes went mad and committed suicide, after which his people called Josephe back. The Black Cross was still standing in the forest of Camelot in Arthur's time. [Vulgate I]

ABBEY OF THE BLACK CROSS

Kay carried Ywaine here to be healed after a treacherous attack by King Mark, and thus it would seem to be in Cornwall, probably in the northern part of the modern county, within easy reach of Tintagil.

CASTEL DE LA BLANCHE ESPINE†

Its lord, Maten, was Arthur's enemy. Lancelot, Bors, Gareth, and Bagdemagus, passing by this fine castle, found a hundred ruffians ill-using Mordred. The four knights rescued their companion. On learning from him that Maten had attacked him simply for belonging to the Round Table, they fired the town, killed Maten, and burned the castle. [Vulgate V]

At this time, Mordred seems to have been an earnest and promising young knight. At least, his villainy had not yet surfaced. Still, it is of course possible that he maligned Maten.

Blanche Espine appears to be on the way from Camelot to the land of the giant Mauduit. Where Mauduit's land was I am not sure, but in non-Arthurian traditions, Cornwall is called a land of giants, and certain Arthurian stories bear this out, although not precluding the possibility that giants inhabited other areas as well.

Warbelow Barrow might be identified with La Blanche Espine.

Between Camelford and Launceston [Cornwall], on Wilsey Downs, is Warbelow Barrow, an ancient fortification of considerable size, in the centre of which is a large mound, popularly called King Arthur's Grave. [Glennie, p. 12]

CASTLE BLANK

Sirs Bliant and Selivant, brothers, kept Sir Lancelot here for a time at their castle, nursing him during a fit of madness [Malory XII, 1-2]. Do not confuse Castle Blank with the castle of Bliant. In earlier versions they might have been the same, but in Malory they are different. Castle Blank might or might not have been near Listeneise.

"Blank" in Malorian names almost certainly means "white" (from the French "blanc"). For Castle Blank I tentatively suggest either Whitehaven on the coast of Cumberland, or Barnard Castle in Durham, near the border of North Riding on the river Tees.

CASTLE OF BLIANT

Do not confuse with Sir Bliant's Castle Blank. The castle of Bliant was one of Pellam's castles, standing on an "island beclosed in iron, with a fair water deep and wide." Pellam gave the castle and island to Lancelot, who had just recovered from a long bout of madness, including a period of nursing at Castle Blank, and who thought he could never go back to Arthur's court. As Le Chevaler Mal Fet, Lancelot held Bliant against all jousters, naming it Joyous Isle and living here with Pellam's daughter Elaine. [Malory XII, 5-7]

Pick out a nice lake in the Lake District and put the Castle of Bliant on it. Alternately, we could bend Malory a little here. Since it looks confusing to have Sir Bliant of Castle Blank and the castle of Bliant so closely connected in this account of Lancelot's madness, the names of the castles might be switched, giving Sirs Bliant and Selivant the castle of Bliant, and Pellam getting Castle Blank. Castle Blank might then be Whitehaven, and the Joyous Isle the shallow peninsula or headland surrounding it.

"FOREST OF THE BOILING WELL"

Sir Lancelot's grandfather, King Lancelot, had a great and honorable love for his cousin's beautiful, saintly wife. The cousin, a duke, misconstrued the relationship. As King Lancelot was on his way home through the perilous forest, he stopped to drink at a fountain. Here his cousin, the duke, ambushed him and cut off his head, which fell into the fountain. The fountain started to boil, and scalded the duke's hands when he tried to remove the head. The duke and his men buried the king near the fountain. As they were entering their castle, a stone fell from the roof and killed them.

King Lancelot's widow erected a tomb. The tomb bled every day in several places, at the hour of the murder. Two lions fought fiercely over a stag near the tomb. They wounded

---

RELATIONS BETWEEN KNIGHTS AND LADIES

Far too much has been written elsewhere on the subject of Courtly Love, how far it was sensual and how far Platonic, for me to attempt to answer the question here. I have, however, culled some relevant passages from Malory:

[The Damsel said] ... almighty Jesu preserve you ... for the curteist knight thou art, and meekest unto all ladies and gentlewomen, that now liveth. But one thing, sir knight, methinketh ye lack, that ye are a knight wifeless, that [y]e will not love some maiden or gentlewoman, for I could never hear say that ever ye loved any of no matter degree, and that is great pity; but it is noised that ye love Queen Guenever, and that she hath been ordained by enchantment that ye shall never love none other but her ... wherefore many in this land, of high estate and low, make great sorrow.

Fair damosel, said Sir Launcelot, I may not warn people to speak of me what it pleaseth them; but for to be a wedded man, I think it not; for then I must couch with her, and leave arms and tournaments, battles, and adventures; and as for to say for to take my pleasaunce with paramours, that will I refuse in principal for dread of God; for knights that be adventurous or lecherous shall not be happy nor fortunate unto the wars, for other they shall be overcome with a simpler knight than they be themselves, other else they shall by unhap and their cursedness slay better men than they be themselves. And so who that useth paramours shall be unhappy, and all thing is unhappy that is about them. [VI, 10]

La Beal Isoud made a letter unto Queen Guenever, complaining her of the untruth of Sir Tristram, and how he had wedded the king's daughter of Brittany. Queen Guenever sent her another letter, and bade her be of good cheer, for she should have joy after sorrow, for Sir Tristram was so noble a knight called that by crafts of sorcery ladies would make such noble men to wed them. But in the end, Queen Guenever said, it

each other grievously, but the drops of blood from the tomb healed them. Henceforth, they guarded the tomb, taking turns to hunt their food. A hermitage, also, was either near this site already or was built nearby in the years between King Lancelot and his more famous grandson.

When Sir Lancelot came to the well, having been directed by his grandfather in a dream, he killed the lions, retrieved his grandfather's head, opened the tomb, and, with the help of the hermit, reburied the body, with the head, at the front of the altar, where King Lancelot's wife was buried. Because Sir Lancelot was not pure, however, the water continued to boil. Only when Galahad arrived did the water cease boiling; the fountain was thereafter called Galahad's Fountain. [Vulgate I and V]

Malory omits the above history, but describes Galahad's coming to the place. Galahad departed from the "Abbey of King Mordrains"

and so came into a perilous forest where he found the well the which boileth with great waves ... And as soon as Galahad set his hand thereto it ceased, so that it brent no more, and the heat departed. For that it brent it was a sign of lechery, the which was that time much used. But that heat might not abide his pure virginity. And this was taken in the country for a miracle. And so ever after was it called Galahad's well. [Malory XVII, 18]

Because Malory's work seems largely a summarization, that Malory recounts Galahad's visit to the boiling well immediately after his visit to Mordrains' abbey does not necessarily mean they are in the same region. The Vulgate tells us that Lancelot lost his way while returning from this forest to Le Tertre Deuee and saw the white stag conducted by four lions. This appears to place the "Forest of the Boiling Well," the castle of Le Tertre Deuee, the abbey of la Petite Aumosne, and possibly King Vagor's Isle Estrange in the general vicinity of Carteloise Forest in southern Scotland.

BOIS EN VAL†

The illusory, magical lake in Benwick, Gaul, at the foot of a hill near Trebes castle. Here the Damsel of the Lake took the young son of King Ban and Queen Elaine and disappeared with him into her lake, where she raised him. Of course, it only looked like a lake to the uninitiate; it was really a rich city.

'Bois en Val' means 'Wood in a Valley.'

BRESQUEHAN†

This forest is near the river Saverne (Severn?). A little river running through Bresquehan formed the boundary between Norgales and Cambenic. [Vulgate II; III, p. 310]

"CASTLE OF BREUSE SAUNCE PITIE"

Searching for Lancelot, Tristam "rode by a forest, and then was he ware of a fair tower by a marsh on that one side, and on that other side a fair meadow." Before the tower Bruese Saunce Pitie and eight of his knights were attacking Palomides, all at once. When Tristram came to the rescue, he drove Breuse and his men into the tower, which suggests this was Breuse's own stronghold. [Malory X, 1-2] The last place Tristram is known to have been before this was the castle of Hard Rock, but he might have come any distance from there to this tower.

Surely the infamous Breuse Saunce Pitie had one or two castles tucked away about the island. I suspect that at least one of them would have been in or on the edge of the Saxon lands, for there is evidence that Breuse was allied with the Saxons on at least one occasion.

BRIESTOC†

Apparently this was in the vicinity of the Dolorous Tower, for the Lady of Briestoc lost all her knights while attempting to rescue Gawaine from Carados [Vulgate IV]. It is possible that Briestoc could be counted as a sub-kingdom, but one can more easily imagine Carados destroying the force of a single castle than that of an entire sub-kingdom.

If Turquine's Hill is accepted as Cadbury, and Carados' Dolorous Tower put somewhere in the middle of modern Devonshire, then Briestoc might be identified with Botreaux. On the other hand, if Botreaux was Briestoc, the lady would have had troublous neighbors at Tintagil — first the giants and later King Mark — too close for her to be that concerned about Carados farther away. Almost due south of Tintagil, about eight miles from the tip of the southern coast of Cornwall, is Brodock, or Brotheck. Norden lists it only as a parish, but the name is at least as close as "Botreaux" to "Briestoc."

BRITTANY (Little Britain)

Also called Armorica in the old days, I assume it was in about the same place but with more territory than the modern province. Brittany, not Great Britain, may well have been the birthplace of Arthurian romance as we know it. France and Brittany almost surely contain such important sites as Broceliande Forest and the Lake in which Lancelot was raised. Sometimes, indeed, the reader of old romances hardly can be sure whether the author had British or Breton places in mind. My putting one Benoye or Benwick in Britain and another in France, and a magical Lake with its Damsel on both sides of the Channel, ultimately may be the result of a fusion or confusion of British and French sites in the original romances.

---

shall be thus, that he shall hate her, and love you better than ever he did to-fore. [VIII, 37]

Then Sir Dinadan told Sir Tristram his name, but Sir Tristram would not tell him his name, wherefore Sir Dinadan was wroth. For such a foolish knight as ye are, said Sir Dinadan, I saw but late this day lying by a well, and he fared as he slept; and there he lay like a fool grinning, and would not speak, and his shield lay by him, and his horse stood by him; and well I wot he was a lover. Ah, fair sir, said Sir Tristram, are ye not a lover? Mary, fie on that craft! said Sir Dinadan. That is evil said, said Sir Tristram, for a knight may never be of prowess but if he be a lover. [X, 55]

And when Sir Launcelot heard [of the death of Elaine of Astolat] he said: ... God knoweth I was never causer of her death by my willing ... but that she was both fair and good, and much I was beholden unto her, but she loved me out of measure. Ye might have shewed her, said the queen, some

bounty and gentleness that might have preserved her life. Madam, said Sir Launcelot, she would none other ways be answered but that she would be my wife, outher else my paramour; and of these two I would not grant her, but I proffered her, for her good love that she shewed me, a thousand pound yearly to her, and to her heirs, and to wed in any manner knight that she could best to love in her heart. For madam, said Sir Launcelot, I love not to be constrained to love; for love must arise of the heart, and not by no constraint. That is truth, said the king, and many knight's love is free in himself, and never will be bounden, for where he is bounden he looseth himself. [XVIII, 20]

For like as herbs and trees bring forth fruit and flourish in May, in like wise every lusty heart that is in any manner a lover, springeth and flourisheth in lusty deeds. For it giveth unto all lovers courage, that lusty month of May ... For then all herbs and trees renew a man and a woman, and likewise

FOREST OF BROCELIANDE†

This is in the Morbihan, next to Cornuailles in Brittany [Glennie, 13]. Here is found the consecrated fountain of Balanton, and here Merlin "drees his weird."

The fountain of Balanton appears to be where Merlin met his lady Viviane, and around which he made to spring up an enchanted Garden of Joy to please her.

"ABBEY OF THE BURNING TOMB"

This white abbey is in the land of Gore. Here both Lancelot and later Galahad found the tomb of King Bagdemagus, slain by Sir Gawaine during the Grail Adventures. [Malory XVII, 17, 18]

Malory, however, not only never describes the actual killing — which is not unusual; Malory has many characters, including Tristram, killed "offstage" — but also resurrects Bagdemagus during Arthur's war with Lancelot, in XX, 19. Sommer failed to find Gawaine's alleged slaying of Bagdemagus actually described in the Vulgate manuscripts, either.

More important than Bagdemagus' tomb, in this same abbey is a burning tomb wherein a soul in torment has been waiting 354 years for Galahad to release him from the punishment he had incurred for sinning against Joseph of Arimathea -- apparently some sort of private purgatory. [Malory XVII, 18; cf. "Abbey of the Adventurous Shield"]

AERLEON (Carlion)

Located on the Usk River above the Severn estuary in Monmouthshire, Wales, this city is sometimes called Caerleon-upon-Usk. By Vulgate III, this was Arthur's favorite city in which to hold court. After Camelot, it is still possibly Arthur's most famous court city. In some romances, indeed, it eclipses Camelot. As a fortress, Malory tells us that it "has a strong tower" [I, 8].

Tertre as Caitis† -- see DRUAS' HILL

CAMBENET

This territory, as far as Malory is concerned, seems to rate mention only in the title of Duke Eustace of Cambenet [I, 14; "Duke Cambines" appears in X, 49].

According to the Vulgate, Cambenic is a rich and prosperous city, and the name of its duke is Escan [Vulgate II]. Cambenic seems to be on or near the Severn river, for when King Lot and his sons helped Duke Escan, they drove the Sesnes into the Severn. A little river running through Bresquehan Forest formed the boundary between Norgales and Cambenic [Vulgate III]. This suggests that Cambenic was the southern half of Shropshire, possibly also including Herefordshire or the northern part thereof.

I assume that Escan is to be identified with Eustace and Cambenic with Cambenet. To save both names, Cambenet might be applied to the whole territory of the dukedom and Cambenic to its principal castle-city.

Cambenic — see under CAMBENET

CAMELIARD (Carmelide)

The Vulgate identifies the kingdom of Arthur's father-in-law, Leodegrance, as the territory between Bedingran (Sherwood Forest) and King Ryons' country (Norgales). Thus, Cameliard would include the eastern half of Cheshire joined to Derbyshire or the western half of Derbyshire, arching above Staffordshire so as not to cut into the territory of Bertilak de Hautdesert and the Green Chapel.

CELIBE† (Seloude, Tibise)

This is the forest through which Galahad follows Percivale's sister to Goothe Castle [Vulgate VI].

CAMELOT

The debate as to where Camelot really was may never be decided. Malory, however, twice clearly identifies it as Winchester [II, 19 and XVIII, 8]. The major church of Camelot is Saint Stephen's, where Arthur and Guenevere were married.

CAMPACORENTIN†

In this forest an unnamed knight, chasing an assailant, came upon two damsels bathing. One of them shot him in the thigh with an arrow which appears to have been magic, for only the best knight in the world could draw it out. The wounded knight went to Arthur's court looking for help; but, since Lancelot was absent, no one could help him. Returning to his

lovers call again to their mind old gentleness and old service, and many kind deeds that were forgotten by negligence. For like as winter rasure doth alway arase and deface green summer, so fareth it by unstable love in man and woman. For in many persons there is no stability; for we may see all day, for a little blast of winter's rasure, anon we shall deface and lay apart true love for little or nought ... this is no wisdom nor stability, but it is feebleness of nature and great disworship, whosomever useth this. Therefore ... let every man of worship flourish his heart in this world, first unto God, and next unto the joy of them that he promised his faith unto; for there was never worshipful man or worshipful woman, but they loved one better than another; and worship in arms may never be foiled, but first reserve the honour to God, and secondly the quarrel must come of thy lady: and such love I call virtuous love.

But nowadays men can not love seven night but they must have all their desires: that love may not endure by rea-

son; for where they be soon accorded and hasty heat, soon it cooleth. ... But the old love was not so; men and women could love together seven years, and no licours lusts were between them, and then was love, truth, and faithfulness: and lo, in likewise was used love in King Arthur's days. ... therefore all ye that be lovers call unto your remembrance the month of May, like as did Queen Guenever, for whom I make here a little mention, that while she lived she was a true lover, and therefore she had a good end. [XVIII, 25]

Passages could be pulled out of Malory to argue that there was no "sensual" love between Lancelot and Guenever; but, on the whole, the bulk of evidence points to a full, carnal affair. Passing on to lesser lovers, extra-marital affairs, whether dignified under the heading of Courtly Love or not, appear to have been common, as evidenced by the tests of the Magic Mantle and Morgan's Drinking Horn (see *Things*). No doubt this was

own castle, he met Lancelot; but since Lancelot was travelling incognito, the wounded knight refused to believe he was good enough to make the attempt. Later, learning that the incognito knight had been Lancelot, the wounded knight set off in his litter to find him again. Eventually he found him at La Fontaine des Deux Sycamors and was delivered of the arrow. Some manuscripts call the forest of the bathing damsels "la forest perilleuse." The wounded knight's own castle was apparently not far from King Vagor's Isle Estrange, which may put it and hence the forest of Campacorentin somewhere in southern Scotland. [Vulgate IV]

CANTERBURY

Although I do not find that Malory states Arthur held court here, it may well have been a court city. Mordred had himself crowned king and apparently held his parliament here, and also retreated here after the battle of Dover. Mordred's alliance with the Saxons works in with an identification of Kent as Saxon (Sessoin) territory. The name may also be applicable to the "Saxon shore" of Britain.

As the seat of the Archbishop, this city is a major Christian religious center. I do not know whether folk were going on pilgrimage to Canterbury in the days of Arthur, before the martyrdom of Thomas à Becket.

CARBONEK (Corbenic, Corbin)

Carbonek was a magical place, the castle where the maimed Fisher-King guarded the Holy Grail until Galahad's coming. It also seems, however, to be a place where more or less normal day-to-day life was possible for the residents, and once Sir Bors de Ganis visited Carbonek without even realizing it was a place of supernatural marvels. On a later visit, having experienced some of the marvels, Bors remarked to King Pellam, "this castle may be named the Castle Adventurous, for here be many strange adventures." [Malory XI, 4]

From portions of the Vulgate, I have the impression that the 'Castle Adventurous' was only that part of Carbonek where the visions and power of the Grail were most immediate. "Adventurous," of course, seems one of those words which could be applied to any place a person felt it appropriate.

In a wide valley before one reached the main castle was another fine castle, where a damsel waited in a scalding bath five years until the best knight in the world came to rescue her. Near her tower a serpent, or dragon, lurked in a tomb. On the tomb was written in gold letters, "Here shall come a leopard of king's blood, and he shall slay this serpent, and this leopard shall engender a lion in this foreign country, the which lion shall pass all other knights." Lancelot lifted the tomb and

the dragon issued out, spitting fire, to give him a long, hard fight before he slew it. The "leopard" of the inscription was, of course, Lancelot; the "lion" Galahad. [Malory XI, 1; Vulgate IV]

During the Grail adventures, Lancelot arrived at Carbonek in the vessel with the body of Amide, after seven months or more of random adventuring on the sea. Finding the back gate to Carbonek guarded by two lions, he drew his sword; but a dwarf (or, according to the Vulgate, a flaming hand) struck him, knocking the weapon from his grasp. The lions threatened, but did not molest him as he passed between them. [Malory XVII, 14; Vulgate VI]

Carbonek would be somewhere in Listeneise, which I have identified with the Lake District. Keswick seems to me a nice choice. It is inland, but not by that many miles; and it seems to be on a lake. Considering the mystic, miraculous nature of the Grail Adventures, a miraculous temporary canal from the sea to accomodate Lancelot's midnight arrival by boat does not seem farfetched. To avoid the necessity of such a tide, however, Whitehaven or Ravenglass might be identified with Carbonek, perhaps moving Bliant castle (or Joyous Isle) to one of the lakes.

CARDICAN

Malory mentions in passing this castle where Sirs Percivale and Aglovale lodged for a brief time while searching for Lancelot [XI, 12]. From the name alone, I assume it to be Cardigan city, at the southwest tip of Cardiganshire, Wales.

CARDIFF

Arthur held court in this city in Glamorganshire, Wales.

CARLISLE (Cardoile)

This is one of the cities wherein Arthur held court. Malory uses both names. For the identification of Cardoile (Caer Lliwelydd, or Cardueil) with Carlisle, see Glennie, cxliv.

CAROHAISE†

Located in Cameliard, this was apparently Leodegran's capital, or at least one of his most important cities [Vulgate II].

CARTELOISE CASTLE

Here Galahad and his companions killed the three incestuous and wicked sons of Earl Hernox, who had raped and murdered their sister and imprisoned their father. After his rescue, Hernox died in Galahad's arms. [Malory XVII, 7-9]

Carteloise castle is in the Marches of Scotland. It would be on the west coast, near the border between Scotland and

---

only to be expected in an age when women were married off for other reasons than their own choice and love; and when, moreover, a lady's husband was liable to be killed in any tournament or chance joust, and a lover or two on the side might provide a reserve husband and protector with the minimum loss of time. We should also remember that, though the women were more likely to receive the censure, they were not always primarily to blame. There was, for instance, the curious request of Sir Bleoberis de Ganis, a knight of the Round Table, who rode into King Mark's court and asked that Mark should give him whatever gift he desired.

When the king heard him ask so, he marvelled of his asking, but because he was a knight of the Round Table, and of a great reknown, King Mark granted him his whole asking. Then, said Sir Bleoberis, I will have the fairest lady in your court that me list to choose. I may not say nay, said King

Mark; now choose at your adventure. And so Sir Bleoberis did choose Sir Segwarides' wife, and took her by the hand, and so went his way with her [on horseback]. [Malory VIII, 15]

It is possible that Bleoberis and other knights in similar episodes in the Vulgate were chiefly interested in winning glory by defeating the men who came after them to rescue the lady; but the business has a suspicious look, especially when such incidents as that concerning Lancelot's cousin Iblis and Sir Gaheris are added. On the other hand, by a sort of triple standard, while an unfaithful wife or hasty maiden might lay herself open to more official censure and marital retribution than an erring husband, there seems also to have been an undercurrent of popular admiration for many such women. Guenever and La Beale Isoud may have risked death for having their lovers, but they also gain the old romancers' sympathy and praise. And, if Pellinore is not

England. Here, where Glennie would be most helpful, he is silent. Port Carlisle might be a fair choice for Carteloise, but it is hard to see how Hernox's sons could have pursued their evil course with such impunity so near one of Arthur's court cities, unless the King had not been there on his progresses for some time. I would place Carteloise somewhere on the Solway Firth. It should probably be not too close to King Pellam's territory of Listeneise; yet we do seem to be in Grail territory, for, after leaving Carteloise castle, Galahad and his companions entered a waste forest where they encountered very holy visions. Perhaps Carteloise could be identified with Workington, Maryport, or Allonby; or, on the Scotland side of the Solway, Kirkendbright, or Southerness.

CARTELOISE FOREST

After leaving Carteloise castle, Galahad and his companions entered a "waste forest." Assuming that this forest would be near the castle, I have called it Carteloise. Here Galahad's party saw the mystical white hart, representing Christ, walking within a guard of four lions, representing the four Evangelists. Others had seen the hart and lions before, but Galahad and his companions appear to have been the first and only folk to follow the animals to a

> valley, and thereby was an hermitage where a good man dwelled, and the hart and the lions entered also. So when they saw all this they turned to the chapel, and saw the good man in a religious weed and in the armour of Our Lord, for he would sing mass of the Holy Ghost: and so they entered in and heard mass. And at the secrets of the mass they three saw the hart become a man, the which marvelled them, and set him upon the altar in a rich siege; and saw the four lions were changed, the one to the form of a man, the other to the form of a lion, and the third to an eagle, and the fourth was changed unto an ox. Then took they their siege where the hart sat, and went out through a glass window, and there was nothing perished nor broken; and they heard a voice say: In such a manner entered the Son of God in the womb of a maid Mary, whose virginity ne was perished ne hurt. And when they heard these words they fell down to the earth and were astonied; and therewith was a great clearness.

When they came to themselves, the holy man expounded the vision, also remarking that he supposed the white hart would be seen no more. [Malory XVII, 9] Although Malory says "they three saw" it, actually there were four, not counting the hermit: Galahad, Percival, Bors, and Percival's sister Amide.

CASTLE OF CASE

Another castle of Pellam's, five miles from Carbonek. Here Dame Brisen caused Lancelot to lie with her.

CHAMPAYNE, Guienne, etc.

After Lancelot breaks with Arthur and goes back across the Channel with his kinsmen and supporters, here is how he parcels out his lands:

> [Lancelot] crowned Sir Lionel, King of France; and Sir Bors [he] crowned him king of all King Claudas' lands; and Sir Ector de Maris ... King of Benwick, and king of all Guienne, that was Sir Launcelot's own land.

He also makes others of his supporters Dukes of Limosin in Guienne, Poictiers, Querne, Sentonge, Provence, Landok, Anjou, and Normandy; and Earls of Perigot, Roerge, Bearn, Comange, Arminak, Estrake, Pardiak, Foise, Masauke, Tursauk, the Launds, Agente, and Surlat. [Malory XX, 18]

Lionses, whom Malory calls "lord of the country of Payarne," and who fights on the side of Arthur, Ban, and Bors, is probably identical with Leonce, the wisest and most loyal man in Gannes according to the Vulgate. [Malory I, 10; Vulgate III] This makes Payarne another French territory.

"FOUNTAIN OF CHANGING COLORS"†

This fountain was located near la Tour Quaree on the Salerne river. I have not been able to locate the Salerne. Once Josephe preached here. The water of the fountain frequently changed color. Josephe explained that the color changes were produced by the approach of sinful and unclean persons; I am unsure whether Josephe himself caused the fountain to take on this attribute, or whether it had already existed and Josephe only explained it.

Josephe caused an inscription to be left here on a stone: "The adventure of the fountain will be achieved by the great lion with the marvellous neckband." The neckband signified obedience; the lion was probably Galahad: I do not know what the "adventure" was, unless this is another version of the Boiling Well.

A wounded knight who heard Josephe preach mistook his comparison of the Trinity to a healing fountain for a reference to the actual fountain at hand. He wanted to drink of it, but every messenger was afraid to bring him a cup of the waters that changed color. The knight appealed to Josephe, who gave him a short lesson in theology. The knight promised to believe in God if He would heal him. Josephe filled a cup at the fountain; the knight drank the water and was healed. [Vulgate V]

CASTLE CHARIOT (Charroie)

According to the Vulgate, this castle was in the marches of Carmelide (Cameliard) and Bedigran, across the territory of

---

scolded by the other characters for engendering Tor "half by force," neither is Tor's mother upbraided for the episode; indeed, there is a hint that she profited by it when Tor was knighted. And surely "it was not then as it is now," for while all this sexual passion was accepted and to some extent sanctioned, purity and virginity were at the same time admired, even in the male — not, as sometimes today, considered the only sexual depravity; chastity was a sign of virtue, not psychological sickness.

Perhaps both views of Courtly Love are correct — it has room for both fleshly and spiritual affairs. Sir Galahad and Percivale's sister Amide exemplify courtly love in its most spiritual aspect, with no fleshly interludes. Lancelot, also, had a strictly Platonic arrangement with the damsel Amable, who, like Elaine of Astolat, fell hopelessly in love with him, but who, unlike Elaine, refused to let it kill her. Instead, she ingeniously proposed that, if she remained a virgin for Lancelot's love, he could love her as a

virgin and his other lady as a paramour, and so love them both without dishonor. The scheme worked admirably. (Malory, however, does not record this affair.)

Whenever a knight succoured, or even met, a lady or damsel, he usually offered to be her true knight forever and in all places. Obviously, such a vow cannot always indicate a courtly love affair.

Dinadan's comments in the third passage cited above are not without reason. There was a curious phenomenon liable to affect any true lover, from Lancelot on down. Sometimes, looking up in the middle of a fight or at another time, and seeing his lady watching him, the knight would go into a sort of trance or stupor, contemplating her beauty and virtue, his love for her, or whatever. In this state, the lover was witless and helpless. Anyone who came along could take his horse's reins and lead him anywhere, push him into the river, and so on. It is fortunate that

King Ryons. King Amans fought to reconquer it while Arthur, Ryons, and the Sesnes were busy with each other. [Vulgate II, VIII]

For a time, at least, Morgana le Fay and her cohorts appear to have used this castle as their base of operations. After Amans' attempt to conquer it, Morgan le Fay and her cohorts found Lancelot asleep and kidnapped him, bringing him to Castle Chariot (called Charroie in the Vulgate). According to Malory's account, which differs in important details from that of the Vulgate, Morgan's companions on this occasion were three — the queens of Northgalis, Eastland, and the Out Isles — and Lancelot was released by King Bagdemagus' daughter, who asked him to help her father at a tournament between him and the King of Northgalis on the "Tuesday next coming." [Malory VI, 3-4]

CLARANCE

Duke Chaleins of Clarance gets a little more mention in Malory than Duke Eustace of Cambenet, generally turning up at tournaments. The most logical territory for Chaleins would be the territory of the historical Dukes of Clarence, whose seat was County Clare, Munster, Ireland, from the 13th century.

CLARENCE†

This city is mentioned in Vulgate II. I assume it to be identical with the holding of the Duke of Clarence in Ireland. Clarence apparently is near another city or castle, Vambieres.

Cole† — see KALET

COLLIBE

During the Grail Adventures, Sir Percivale's sister brings Galahad from a hermitage apparently in the vicinity of Carbonek castle to a ship in which they find Sir Bors and Percivale. Galahad and the damsel pass by a sea called Collibe on the way. [Malory XVII, 1-2]

"CHAPEL OF THE CONJURATION"

After leaving the hermit who had expounded his visions at the "Chapel of the Stony Cross," Sir Lancelot, apparently after less than an afternoon's travel, came to a chapel where an old man was laid out dead, in a shirt of fine white cloth. The old religious man of the place feared that the dead man was damned, because, after being a man of religion for more than a hundred years, he had put off the habit of his order. The living old man, who was probably a priest, put about his own neck a stole (a priestly garment, still required in the 20th century before a priest may administer the sacraments), and, taking up a book, conjured up a fiend to tell him how the dead man had died and where his soul had gone. The priest and Lancelot learned from the fiend that the dead man had left his hermitage by permission, to help his nephew Aguarus win a war against the Earl of Vale. The earl then sent two of his nephews to the hermitage for revenge. They had to burn Auguarus' uncle all night in a fire before they could manage to kill him, and even then, though he died, his body was left whole. The same fiend, coming in the morning, had found the naked body in the fire, removed it, and laid it out in the white shirt. The dead man's soul was in Heaven. [Malory XV, 1-2]

Conlotebre† — see TALEBRE

Corbenic (Corbin) — see CARBONEK

CORNOUAILLE

Distinct from the Cornwall of Great Britain, the French Cornouaille is an area on the southwest coast of Brittany.

CORNWALL

"Old Cornwall" included Devon. Thus Arthurian Cornwall would have consisted of present-day Devon and Cornwall, and the sunken land of Lyonesse (Liones) to the west, of which the Scilly Islands are the touted remains. Sub-kingdoms include Lyonesse, the South Marches, and Tintagil.

CUBELE† (Noble, Tubelle)

A castle in a valley, seemingly some two days' ride from the castle of King Amans' daughter, which is near Cameliard. Sir Bors, arriving here, learned of an impending tournament between the Earl of Plains and the Lady of Hervin's nephew. Malory mentions this castle in XVI, 14; he, however, does not give it a name, and Vulgate VI does — indeed, various manuscripts of the Vulgate give it various names.

CULROSS†

The monastery where St. Kentigern, whom I have reason to believe may have been a nephew of Sir Gawaine, was placed under the discipline of St. Servanus [Glennie, 51].

Culross is on the north bank of the Firth of Forth, five to ten miles west of Charlestown.

this fit never struck Lancelot when he was championing Guenever in trial by combat. A good friend might bring the afflicted party out of his trance by a solid thwack with the flat of a sword, as the Damsel of La Beale Regard once did Sir Alisander; but, on the whole, the thing really must have been enough to make thinkers like Dinadan shy away from becoming lovers. (Percivale, in a similar lover's meditation, nevertheless jousted as well as ever — but Percivale's abstraction was called forth merely by blood and snow that reminded him of his love's complexion, not by the presence of his love herself.)

Once Sir Lamorak met Sir Meliagrant and they promptly started fighting to prove which of their ladies — Margawse or Guenever respectively — was the most beautiful woman in the land. Lancelot came along, rode between them, and asked why two of Arthur's knights were fighting one another. On learning the cause of the quarrel, Lancelot was ready to fight Lamorak himself in defense of Guenever's superior beauty. Lamorak explained, "every man thinketh his own lady fairest." Bleoberis, a neutral party, agreed, saying to Lancelot, "I have a lady, and me thinketh that she is the fairest lady of the world. Were this a great reason that ye should be wroth with me for such language?" Thus they all made up and parted friends, though one wonders why Lamorak and Bleoberis did not speak so reasonably and peaceably when it was a mere matter of Lamorak against Meliagrant. [Malory IX, 13-14] Notice that this is a case in which a knight, Meliagrant, loves as his lady a woman who does not reciprocate; though Meliagrant was later to attempt to force his love by kidnapping Guenever, in this particular quarrel it is possible that Meliagrant is more nearly an example of pure courtly devotion than is Lamorak, who may well already have been enjoying Margawse's favors.

AMAS, CASTLE OF SIR"

Sir Damas was a wicked knight who occupied himself by capturing and imprisoning all the knights in the area lest any of them act as champion of his good brother Sir Ontzlake in an inheritance dispute. Morgana finally caused Arthur to fight Sir Accolon in this dispute. Sir Ontzlake's manor, near the castle of his brother Damas, was two days' journey from Camelot. From the magical aspects of the adventure, it could be anywhere within that radius. [Malory IV, especially 12]

CHASTEL AS DAMES and CHASTEL AS PUCELES†

The 'Castle of Ladies' and 'Castle of Virgins' were located on opposite banks of a river, probably in or near the forest of Carduel (Carlisle). Here, during a tournament between the two castles, Sirs Ector de Maris and Lionel once helped the knights of the Puceles, who were inferior in number, while Lancelot, to balance the influence of his kinsmen, entered on the side of the Dames. Lancelot, however, did not get into the fray until a damsel came by and dropped a hint that he should fight by asking him if she could have his shield, since he obviously had no use for it. [Vulgate IV]

'Chastel as Puceles' is, of course, the equivalent of 'Castle of Maidens,' which may have been a popular name.

DANEBLAISE†

Another of King Leodegran's castle-cities in Cameliard [Vulgate II].

CASTLE DANGEROUS

The castle of Dame Lyonors (or Lionesse) is also called the Castle Perilous. Malory tells of another Castle Perilous, however, one almost certainly different from that of Lyonors.

When Sir Ironside besieged Castle Dangerous, Lynette came to Arthur's court at Caerleon to find a champion for her sister. Lyonors' castle may perhaps be found by attempting to retrace Lynette's return with Gareth Beaumains. After leaving Caerleon, Gareth fights and kills two wicked brothers at a "great river and but one passage." The Severn makes a horseshoe curve at Newnham, below Gloucester, and continues to make little bends between Newnham and Gloucester. Malory's "great river and but one passage" might be somewhere here.

Continuing on, Gareth fights and kills the Black Knight of the Black Laund, that same day, in a valley. Still, apparently, the same day, he defeats the Green Knight (not to be confused with the title character of **Sir Gawaine and the Green Knight**), who lodges him and Lynette for a night and next morning escorts them partway through a forest. This day Gareth defeats the Red Knight by a white tower at the Pass Perilous. I would guess this to be a mountain rather than a river pass, and put it in the Cotswolds, perhaps at Stroud. The Red Knight also lodges them overnight.

The following day Gareth defeats Sir Persant of Inde near a "city rich and fair," which is "seven mile" from Castle Dangerous. Castle Dangerous is later described, in a cry made througout Britain, Ireland, and Brittany, as "beside the Isle of Avilion." Sir Persant's city might be Tetbury or Chippenham, and Castle Dangerous seven miles beyond that, towards Avilion. [Cf. Malory VII, 2-12, 26]

THE DELECTABLE ISLE

Sir Palomides avenges the death of King Hermance of the Red City and the Delectable Isle in Malory's tenth book. Spurn Head peninsula, at the mouth of the Humber river, between Lincolnshire and East Riding, Yorkshire, satisfies Malory's description. (If Glastonbury can be considered an island, so should a peninsula.)

Castle del Trespas† — see TRESPAS, CASTLE DEL

Des Mares† — see MARES

"CHAPEL DESOLATE"

In this desolate chapel, located on a mountain in the vicinity of Abblasoure, Galahad heard a heavenly voice directing him to go to the Castle of Maidens and destroy their wicked customs [Malory XIII, 14].

DEUEE, LE TERTRE†

Sir Clochides loved King Esclamor's daughter, but Esclamor did not love Clochides. So the princess had Clochides take her to a strong castle he built on a hill. Clochides had only one approach to Le Tertre Deuee, and he defended it for twenty years against all comers, imprisoning defeated companions of the Round Table and killing all others. Finally Sir Bors de Ganis defeated and mortally wounded Clochides, but, before dying, Clochides made him promise to keep up the customs. Bors did so. In three months he killed more than sixty knights, and by the time his cousin Lancelot arrived, fourteen members of the Round Table were imprisoned here. Lancelot recognized Bors by his sword, which had once been Duke Galehot's. Then the knights were freed, the customs dropped, everybody reconciled and happy, and I do not know what became of Clochides' princess. Bors knighted his squire Axilles and invested him with the castle. [Vulgate V]

Le Tertre Deuee was in the vicinity of the "Forest of the Boiling Well" and the abbey La Petite Aumosne; possibly also in the vicinity of King Vagor's Isle Estrange. Further on, the Vulgate tells us it was in "the perilous forest," perhaps either Carteloise Forest or an adjacent forest to the east. "The perilous forest" is an appellation belonging to more forests than just one or two.

FONTAINE DES DEUX SYCAMORS†

This book and the nearby castle would seem to have been somewhere in southern Scotland or northern Logres, possibly not far from Carteloise Forest. The brook, or fountain, was defended by two brothers, Sirs Belias and Briadas, sons of Sir Broades, who also had at least one daughter. These two brothers, who wore black armor, were defending the place to demonstrate that they were good enough for the Round Table. Their story had an unhappy ending. Hearing that one of them had unhorsed Gawaine, Lancelot came to encounter them, and ended by killing both them and their father. [Vulgate V]

Cadzow is one possible place in which Fontaine Des Deux Sycamors may be located

Overhanging the brawling Avon [Scotland], and on the skirt of the noble chase which, with its wild cattle and ancient oaks, is all that now remains of that Caledonian Forest, once haunted by Merlin, and which stretched from sea to sea, stands Cadzow Castle [Glennie, p. 84]

THE DEVIL'S ROAD†

A road said to be haunted by devils, where Lancelot heard strange voices but saw nothing [Vulgate IV]. It was somewhere not far from the castle of Gais on the Thames.

DIN DREI†

> Immediately to the south of Melrose ... rise those three summits of the Eildons, the *Tremontium* of the Romans, which Mr. Nash identifies with the Din Drei of Aneurin.... These three summits ... with their various wierdly appurtenants – the Windmill of Killie-law, the Lucken Hare, and Eildon Tree – mark the domes of those vast subterranean Halls, in which all the Arthurian chivalry await, in an enchanted sleep, the bugle-blast of the Adventurer who will call them at length to a new life. [Glennie, p. 60]

If the bend in the Tweed river at Melrose, Roxburgh county, southern Scotland, were considered as three sides of a rectangle, with Selkirk and St. Boswells at roughly the two lower points, Din Drei would not be far from the middle of the imaginary base line. Din Drei is in Rhymer's Glen.

Arthur and all his knights asleep in Scotland seems to be a different tradition from that preserved in Malory and the Vulgate, but perhaps both Din Drei and Avilion lead to the same otherworldly plain, where distances work differently. Even before Arthur's passing, Din Drei and Rhymer's Glen might have been an entrance into a world of Faerie. (See also Ercildoune.)

LA DOLOREUSE CHARTRE†

A small but strong castle near Dolorous (Joyous) Garde. The lord of Dolorouse Chartre was the villainous Sir Brandus des Illes, who was also lord of Dolorous Garde until Lancelot conquered it and made it Joyous Garde. [Vulgate III]

Dolorous Garde – see JOYOUS GARDE

THE DOLOROUS TOWER

The castle of Sir Carados, who collected knights he had defeated and kept them in his dungeons until Lancelot defeated and killed him [Malory VIII, 28]. After Lancelot killed Carados, this castle was renamed La Bele Garde or La Bele Prise, and apparently Sir Melians li Gai and his bride became its lord and lady [Vulgate IV].

I do not think this Sir Carados is to be identified with King Carados or Scotland, nor the Dolorous Tower with Dolorous Garde. Sir Carados and Sir Turquine were brothers, so their holdings reasonably might have been close together. I have some scanty evidence that Turquine's Hill may have been in the southwest, in the region of the South Marches. Carados might have been a spiritual ancestor of the outlaw Doones of Exmoor, with his tower somewhere in the middle of modern Devonshire. A possible identification for the Dolorous Tower is Trematon castle,

> ... a place wherin the former Earles and other chiefe gouernors of *Cornwall* made their abodes ... howsoeuer ... it falleth daylie to ruyne and decaye: The inner buyldinges are fallen downe, only some ragged walls remayne; and in the base courte some Lodginges doe stande, and the Prison. [Norden]

Trematon is near Saltash, where the Tamar flows into the sea on the south coast, near the present-day border between Cornwall and Devon.

DOVER

An important port city, especially for travel between Britain and the Continent. Dover has a good battlefield, Barham Down, nearby. It also boasts Dover castle. Arthur used it for keeping at least one lifetime political prisoner, the duke of a Tuscan town. [Malory V, 12]

DRUAS' HILL† (Le Tertre as Caitis)

Sir Druas defended this hill against all knights who tried to pass over it, killing or wounding them. If Druas was defeated, his dwarf would offer the victor a horn. Blowing this horn would bring Druas' brother, Sornehan.

Sir Agravaine mounted the hill, encountered and killed Druas near a fountain, but – though forewarned – blew the horn when the dwarf offered it. Sornehan was sick at home; but, on hearing the horn, he rose and went out, despite the pleading of his young son not to go. Sornehan defeated Agravaine and would have slain him, but a damsel happened to come by and she asked Sornehan to do her a favor. When he granted it unheard, she asked for Agravaine's life, pointing out that thus Sornehan would save his own life, Agravaine being the brother of the great Gawaine. Sornehan imprisoned Agravaine in the tower on the hill and enclosed the hill with a wall having only one gate, where was a warning that Sornehan would fight whoever mounted the hill. Later Sornehan defeated and imprisoned Gaheris when he tried to cross the hill. Sornehan's niece, whom Gaheris had once saved, succored him and Agravaine secretly.

Gareth finally defeated Sornehan, rescued his brothers, and sent Sornehan as prisoner to the Lady of Roestoc. The hill, hitherto called the *tertre as caitis*, was henceforth called *li tertres Agravaine*. [Vulgate V]

Gareth's sending Sornehan to the Lady of Roestoc suggests a northern site.

DUNDEVENEL† (Dundonald)

A church founded by St. Monenna after Arthur's victories over the Pagans [Glennie, p. 82].

On the west coast of Scotland, on the Firth of Clyde, a few miles north of Ayr, is a small island. A little north of the island is a small, pointed peninsula. A little north of this peninsula is the mouth of the River Irvine. If an isosceles triangle were drawn using the coast from the peninsula to the river's mouth as one side and the Irvine as another side, Dundevenel would be roughly in the middle of the base line between the peninsula and the river's curve, slightly closer to the river.

DUNPELEDUR† (Dunpender Law)

> On Dunpeledur ... as likewise on the three fortified rocks Edinburgh, Stirling, and Dumbarton, at Dundonald, in Ayrshire, and Chilnacase, in Galloway, S. Monenna ... founded a church, and nunnery. These foundations appear to synchronise with the re-establishment of the Christian Church in these districts by Arthur. [Glennie, p. 54]

Glennie goes on to suggest that the 'Castle of Maidens' at Edinburgh takes its name from one of Monenna's nunneries, and that Thenew, daughter of King Lothus and mother of St. Kentigern, was a nun at Dunpeledur.

Dunpeledur is in East Lothian, a few miles south of the River Tyne, apparently a little east of modern Haddington.

astland — see SORESTAN

EDYOPE†

This castle was in the "Waste Forest" — in Wales or in the Waste Lands of Listeneise [Vulgate VII].

ENGLAND (Logres, Logris)

The "country of Logris ... that is for to say the country of England" [Malory XII, 5], excluding Scotland, Wales, and Cornwall. Sub-kingdoms include Arroy, Avilion, Cameliard, The Delectable Isle, King Amans' Land, Leicester, Listeneise, Malahaut, Nohaut, Northumberland, and Roestoc.

CASTLE OF ERCILDOUNE (Rhymer's Tower)†

Here, in the 13th century, lived Thomas the Rhymer, who, according to the ballad of "True Thomas," visited the Queen of Faery in her own land, and who, according to Glennie, became a guide to those adventurers trying to find the sleeping Arthur. Perhaps already in Arthur's day this was a gateway into the otherworld of Faerie.

Glennie puts Rhymer's Tower at present-day Earlston, north of Melrose, Roxburgh county, Scotland, with Rhymer's Glen slanting down below Melrose and including Din Drei.

ESCALON LI TENEBREUX†

This castle had once been called Escalon li Envoisies. But the lord of Escalon had relations with his paramour in the chapel of his castle on Ash Wednesday, where they were found at it by a holy man. From that day, castle and church were enveloped in darkness. Only the churchyard remained light, also giving off a sweet fragrance because of the many holy folk buried there.

Only the knight who succeeded in the adventure of this castle could defeat Sir Carados of the Dolorous Tower. But any knight who entered the cold, dark, malodorous chapel was driven back by a rain of blows from invisible hands.

Fourteen years went by, reapers on the surrounding farms supplying the castle dwellers with food, before Lancelot arrived to make it through the chapel and open the far door, thus bringing back light and freeing the castle from the spell. Henceforth the place was called Escalon li Aaisies. The sight of a certain tomb in the churchyard healed Lancelot's wounds.

From the neighborhood of Escalon li Tenebreux, the only way to the Dolorous Tower, where Lancelot finally defeated Sir Carados and freed Gawaine and other prisoners, went past the chapel of Morgan and through the Val sans Retour. [Vulgate IV]

ESCAVALON (Escaualon)†

According to Sommer, this sub-kingdom is called Kaerlyon, Scatanon, Catonois, or Ycastanon in various manuscripts of the Vulgate. Thus, there is at least a chance that Escavalon is Caerleon and the surrounding territory. The Roman name for Caerleon is Isca, which bears out the theory. I would make Escavalon Monmouthshire.

ESTRANGOR

Malory gives Brandegoris as king of Stranggore [I, 12, 13; XII, 9], while the Vulgate gives Karados as the king of Estrangor [Vulgate II]. Therefore, I cannot bring myself to identify

Estrangor with Stranggore. Carados seems a fairly common name, and the Vulgate's King Karados may be Malory's King Carados of Scotland. Remembering Malory's "many kings in the north," I incline to this view and suggest the peninsula on the north shore of Solway Firth, between Luce Bay and Wigtown Bay, or even the whole area of land between Solway Firth and the Firth of Clyde.

Alternately, Karados might be identified with Malory's Cador of Cornwall, the father of Constantine who became king after Arthur.

L'Estroite Marche† — see under the letter "L"

ALERNE, LA†

A castle in Norgales, belonging to the Duke of Cambenic, but under the immediate control of another castellan or lord [Vulgate III].

Val des Faux Amants† — see VAL SANS RETOUR

LA FONTAINE AUX FEES†

La Fontaine aux Fees was located beneath a sycamore in the forest of Camelot. Here forest dwellers claimed to have seen fairy ladies. [Vulgate IV]

Fontaine des Deux Sycamores — see DEUX SYCAMORS, FONTAINE DES

FLANDERS

Arthur and his host sailed from Sandwich to war against Lucius, landing at Barflete in Flanders [Malory V, 4].

CASTLE DE LA FLECHE†

A well-situated and splendidly-appointed castle a day's ride or less from Windesant [Vulgate IV].

FLOREGA†

Lancelot was six miles from Florega, in the wood of Sapine, when he learned that Meliagaunt's stepsister was to be burned at Florega the next day. That night, on his way to Florega, Lancelot stopped at a house of religion where he found Duke Galeholt's tomb. [Vulgate V] From this I surmise that Sapine wood was in or near Duke Galeholt's favorite kingdom of Surluse. The judgement of Meliagaunt's sister at Florega suggests a location exactly between Surluse and Gore.

THE FOREIGN LAND (La Terre Foraine)

This name applies to a region on the border of Gore. It seems also to apply to Listeneise, since Pelles is identified as king of "the foreign country." [Malory XI, 2] I suspect the name is a descriptive tag rather than a proper name. Maante is the capital [Vulgate I].

"FOUNTAIN OF THE SILVER PIPE"

When Sir Accolon of Gaul awoke after going to sleep on an enchanted ship,

he found himself by a deep well-side, within half a foot, in great peril of death. And there came out of that fountain a pipe of silver, and out of that ... ran water all on high in a stone of marble.

From this fountain a dwarf of Morgana's brought Accolon to Sir Ontzlake's manor by a priory, where Morgana prepared the knight for fighting Arthur. [Malory IV, 8] This fountain, which was apparently near Sir Damas' castle and Ontzlake's manor, seems to have been a "fountain" as we moderns think of fountains, rather than a plain brook or spring in the woodland or elsewhere, which is probably the more common meaning of the word "fountain" in the language of Malory's time.

Turquine's Hill had a fountain suspiciously similar to the one described above [Vulgate V]. This leads me to believe that the two sites were probably the same, at Cadbury.

CASTLE OF FOUR STONES

Sir Balan mentions this [Malory II, 6]. Perhaps it was somewhere mountainous, or near a dolmen or cromlech, and hence got its name. According to Vulgate IV, Meliagaunt's body, after Lancelot killed him, was taken to the Castle of Four Stones. From this it would appear that Four Stones was either Meliagaunt's own castle, or the castle of a friend.

FRANCE (Gaul)

This must have included more or less the area of present-day France, with a few sub-kingdoms unsubjugated or imperfectly subjugated, like Benwick. Malory leaves me confused as to whether France was one small sub-kingdom of Gaul, or vice versa, or whether they were in fact completely interchangeable names. I opt for interchangeability.

The interesting King Claudas may have been trying to bring France under one crown. Malory mentions another French monarch, King Faramon of France, in the story of Tristram; according to Vulgate V, Faramon appears to have been a sort of high king of France during Uther Pendragon's time.

AIHOM (Gohurru)†

The Vulgate says this is the capital of the kingdom of Gore. Gaihom might be identified with the city of Pembroke in present-day Wales.

GAIS†

A castle set on the Thames; Sir Trahans, the castellan, and his sons Melians and Drians, were all surnamed "li Gais," after the castle [Vulgate IV]. Melians apparently became castellan of the Dolorous Tower.

GALAFORT†

The first British castle which Joseph of Arimathea and his followers entered. At Josephe's advice, Duke Ganor, who then held the castle, erected there the Tower of Marvels, where no knight of Arthur's would fail to find a jouster as good as himself. The duke also began a church of the Holy Virgin at Galafort. [Vulgate I]

If Joseph came directly here from the Continent, Galafort would probably be somewhere in the southeast. If he went to Sarras first, and if my identification of Sarras as the Isle of Man is accepted, Galafort would probably be somewhere on the northwest coast.

Galahad's Fountain — see FOREST OF THE BOILING WELL

GALDON CASTLE† (Galadon)

On the Galide river, probably in the part of the country in or around Stranggore [Vulgate].

GALVOIE†

The Lady of Galvoie, the chatelaine, sent a damsel to Arthur's court to request either Lancelot or Gawaine to fight for her. Since both were absent, she settled for Bors.

The Lady's father had rescued Sir Kahenin from captivity. Kahenin had built a castle on an island and given both castle and island to his rescuer. After the deaths of Kahenin and the Lady's father, Kahenin's son Mariales seized the castles. When the Lady arraigned him before King Pellam, Mariales argued that his father had built the castle. Bors came to Pellam's court at Carbonek, defeated — but did not kill — Mariales, and made him restore the castle to the Lady. (It was on this quest that Bors spent two nights at Carbonek without learning of the Adventurous Palace where the Grail was kept.)

The Lady of Galvoie married Gaidon, a knight who was her inferior by birth, but a man of great worth and prowess. He fought for her against Mariales, who was still making trouble. Together with Sir Bors, they were eventually able to patch up peace and friendship with Mariales. [Vulgate V]

I am not sure whether Galvoie is the castle Kahenin built on an island or another castle nearby, but in any case the castle(s) would be in the territory of King Pellam, Listeneise.

GALWAY

As I recall, Malory only mentions Galway as part of a personal name — as, for instance, Sir Galleron of Galway (who, however, is listed among twelve knights, "and all they were of Scotland," either of Gawaine's kin or well-wishers to his family. [Malory XX, 2] There was strong connection between Ireland and Scotland in the early days.

ABBEY OF GANIS

This abbey was near the castle of Ganis.

CASTLE OF GANIS

Malory names Sir Bleoberis de Ganis as its lord [IX, 37]. The abbey of Ganis is nearby. Bleoberis was the godson of King Bors of Gaul, or Gannes, the father of Bors de Ganis. I am not sure whether the "Ganis" of Sir Bors' name refers to this castle, which is apparently in Britain, or to his native land across the Channel.

Carew, in his **Survey of Cornwall**, notes that Cornish residents believe that the local place name Bodrugan is a degeneration of Bors de Ganis. Bodrugan is in about the south center of modern Cornwall, in the division called Powder Hundred, on the east side of Dodman Point.

Garantan† -- see CASTLE OF THE UNCOURTEOUS LADY

GARLOTH

King Nentres of Garloth married Elaine, the sister of Morgana le Fay and Margawse, and half-sister of Arthur. With few clues as to the location of this kingdom, I suggest East Lothian.

GAZEWILTE†

The lord of this castle, Sir Persedes, imprisoned his wife here for five years, until Ector de Maris defeated him and rescued her. I found no clue to the location of this castle.

GLASTONBURY

Here the Archbishop of Canterbury became a hermit after defying Mordred. Here Bedivere, Lancelot, and other knights joined the former Archbishop as hermits at Arthur's grave. All this is at the end of Malory's book, but there must have been enough at Glastonbury already to attract the Archbishop. According to a tradition not found in Malory, Joseph of Arimathea planted a flowering thorn tree here, which bloomed in winter until it was uprooted by Oliver Cromwell. You can still see trees in Glastonbury reputed to be descendants of the original flowering thorn.

All indications point to Glastonbury's having been a Pagan holy place before Christianization. Glastonbury Tor, for instance, is a high, conical hill with an ancient pathway to the top. As part of a ritual, the tor was to be ascended in tiers, the celebrants walking around each tier alternately clockwise or counter-clockwise before climbing to the next.

GLOEVANT† (Gloovent, Glocuen)

A forest, probably in or near Stranggore [Vulgate IV].

GLOUCHEDON†

Gawaine declared he would not have parted with his fresh-won horse Gringalet for this castle [Vulgate II, 343]. From the name, Glouchedon might be Gloucester (Roman name Glevum) or Colchester.

Probably identical with Glouchedon is the castle of Glochedon, the chatelaine of which was a cousin of the Damsel of Hongrefort castle. Hongrefort was in or near the forest of Landoine. Glocedon castle seems to have been near Galdon castle, and probably both would have been within easy reach of Hongrefort.

Gohorru† — see GAIHOM

GOOTHE

The recluse Queen of the Waste Lands told Percivale, who was on the Quest of the Holy Grail, to go to Goothe castle, where Galahad had a cousin-germaine. If he could not find Galahad there, he was to ride on straight to Carbonek. Since she told him he could rest at Goothe "this night," it should have been near her priory. [Malory XIV, 2]

It is possible that Goothe was the castle to which Percivale's sister brought Galahad [Malory XVII, 2]. This would put Goothe in or near Grail territory, not far from Carbonek, and near the sea. The lady of the castle to which Percivale's sister brought Galahad was Percivale's sister's mistress; possibly she was Galahad's cousin-germaine.

GORE (Gorre)

From the Vulgate we learn that this important though apparently small kingdom, the strongest of its size in Great Britain, borders on Sugales and is surrounded by water, the Tembre being its boundary toward Logres. By the dictionary, a gore can be a triangular piece of land, a promontory, or a wedge-shaped portion of a field.

We are almost certainly safe in assuming Sugales to be South Wales. In southwest Wales is a peninsula, the one including the city of Pembroke, which has a city named Tenby near where it connects with the mainland. I would make this peninsula the kingdom of Gore, or Gore could be the whole southwestern tip, comprising more or less the present-day county of Pembroke, with the city of Pembroke as Gaihom.

The Vulgate gives the history of Gore. Uther Pendragon warred against King Urien of Gore, captured him, and threatened to hang him. Urien's nephew Baudemagus (or Bagdemagus) surrendered the land in order to save Urien's life. Urien later reconquered Gore and gave it to Bagdemagus as a reward for his loyalty. After Bagdemagus' coronation, Urien retired into a hermitage. (Possibly this explains his wife Morgana's independent castles and various lovers. Malory, however, has Uriens becoming a knight of the Round Table.) Bagdemagus, in order to repeople his war-wasted kingdom, established the custom of two bridges, the "pont desouz ewe" of one beam, and the "pont despee" of a single plank of steel. Each bridge had a knight guardian; and everyone, knights, ladies, and others, who crossed either bridge was made to swear to stay in Gore until a strong champion arrived who could deliver them. Escades, the guardian of the pont despee, was succeeded by Bagdemagus' son Meleagant, a proud and evil-disposed knight who thought himself as good as Lancelot. Almost needless to say, Lancelot was the champion who eventually delivered the prisoners.

Elsewhere in the Vulgate, it appears that these prisoners were not confined in the territory on the Gore side of the bridge, but also resided in a largish area called the Terre Foraine (Foreign Land) before the bridges were reached. Except that they could not move away until freed by their champion, and that they wore a distinctive type of dress, the prisoners seemed to live comfortably and under no restraint save their parole. The Terre Foraine of Gore would be its marches, or borders.

Despite this seemingly unfriendly custom, Bagdemagus became a companion of the Round Table and one of Arthur's staunchest and most likable allies.

THE GREEN CHAPEL†

Gawaine, arriving at the Green Chapel, and finding it an ancient, hollow barrow or cave, overgrown with clumps of grass, in a steep, craggy valley, considered the possibility that a fiend used it for his devilish devotions — an understandable enough impression, since Gawaine had come here in midwinter to undergo his stroke in the beheading game with the Green Knight.

Helen Hill Miller puts the Green Chapel below Leek Moor, in northern Staffordshire, where the Black Brook and the Dane River converge. Glennie provides an alternate location, placing the Green Chapel on the southern bank of Solway Firth, at about the tip of the small peninsula north of Abbey Holme. I much prefer Miller's identification.

"GUINAS' CASTLE"†

Sir Guinas, seeking to measure Gawaine's strength, erected 12 pavilions near his castle and filled them with knights to dispute the passage to all passing knights. When Gaheris and Sagremor had each unhorsed one of Guinas' knights, Guinas' dwarf told them they were free to proceed, and gave Sagremore a new lance to replace the one he had broken. Here we see that not all knights who guard passages need be bloodthirsty scoundrels, nor all such disputed passages mortally perilous traps. Some of the guardians may be sportsmen, and the disputed passages safe (barring accidents) places to pick up glory.

Gareth eventually conquered Guinas and made him promise to surrender to Gawaine. [Vulgate V]

I found no clue to the location of Guinas' castle. Guinas' sportsmanship suggests a locale in more settled areas, possibly in territory in or near that held by the chivalrous Duke Galehot.

GUINDOEL† (Granidel, Raginel, Gindiel, Guidel)

This castle seems not to have been far from Listeneise, for when Gawaine and Ector separated at the fork in the road beyond the "Chapel of the Conjuration," Gawaine took the right fork and ended at Carbonek, while Ector took the left fork, despite numerous warnings of shame waiting along that road, and ended at Guindoel.

Sir Marigart had once loved Lady Oruale, the rightful chatelaine of Guindoel. When she refused to wed him, and her cousin killed Marigart's brother for insulting her before her people, Marigart invaded the castle by night, killed the cousin, and raped the lady. Declining, now, to marry her, he imprisoned her in a cave guarded by two lions, while he settled down to vanquishing knights (stripping them and having them dragged through the streets) and dishonoring maidens of the village. Marigart may have set up the warnings along the road himself. Four years, forty maidens, and an unknown number of knights later, Ector arrived to kill Marigart, restore Oruale, and offer to be her knight always and everywhere. [Vulgate IV]

ARD ROCK, CASTLE OF THE (Roche Dure)

Tristram "won the tournament of the Castle of Maidens that standeth by the Hard Rock" [Malory X, 7]. From this it appears that the Castle of the Hard Rock either was near to or identical with a Castle of Maidens. Roche Dure or Hard Rock may have been an earlier or an alternative name for it.

CASTEL DE LA HARPE†

This may have been a castle of King Bagdemagus, since Lancelot and Meliagraunt stepsister joined her father here [Vulgate V].

Vulgate VII has the Damoisele a la Harpe, a sister or cousin of Helaes de la Forest Perilleuse. This suggests a location in or near the Forest Perilous. Helaes de la Forest Perilleuse may well be Malory's Hellawes, the sorceress of Castle Nigramous.

HAUTDESERT†

I have assumed that Sir Bercilak, or Bertilak, de Hautdesert, alias the Green Knight of the famous metrical romance, took his surname from the name of his castle. According to **Sir Gawaine and the Green Knight**, the castle is less than two miles from the Green Chapel. Helen Hill Miller puts the Green Chapel at a certain deep ravine below Leek Moor, northern Staffordshire.

CASTLE HEWIN†

Glennie calls this the stronghold of the Grim Baron. It is in Cumberland, perhaps eight miles south of Carlisle, in an area called Inglewood Forest.

The Grim Baron demanded that Arthur bring him the answer to the riddle "What is it that women most desire?" within a year and a day. Arthur got the answer from the Foul Ladye, who demanded — and married — Gawaine as her reward. Although rather famous, (Chaucer has a version of it, for instance) this story is found neither in Malory nor in the Vulgate.

HODDAM† (Hoddelm)

The episcopal seat of St. Kentigern. Hoddam is a few miles north of the mouth of the River Annan, on the north bank of Solway Firth.

Holy Island of St. Cuthbert† — see MEDGAUD

HONGREFORT†

This castle was in or near the forest of Landoine. Its lord left the castle to his two daughters, but their uncle, Galindes, besieged them because the Damsel of Hongrefort refused to marry his seneschal. Sir Bors, brought to the area by the younger sister, defeated four of Galindes' knights, killing two and sending the other two to the Damsel of Hongrefort. One of these two prisoners was the seneschal himself. Very reluctantly he gave his word to deliver himself to the Damsel, and kept it, even though he passed through Galindes' camp on his way to the castle. His fears were fully justified, for the chatelaine, in her haste and rage, had her proposed bridegroom and his companion bound hand and foot and shot from a mangonel into Galindes' camp. Galindes swore to treat any captured enemies in similar fashion. Bors learned of this the next time he went out to fight Galindes' knights on behalf of the Damsel. He finished the fight, defeating fifteen or sixteen men in succession and finally conquering Galindes himself. Bors had to finish this fight with his shield, because at a crucial point Seraide came and tested him by asking for his sword, which he courteously gave her. In displeasure at the chatelaine's treatment of the prisoners, Bors then rode off with Seraide.

The Damsel of Hongrefort, who had been much taken with Bors, left the castle in charge of her sister and rode off with four knights, seven squires, and three other damsels, wearing their garments inside-out and riding horses without manes or tails, to do penance and find Bors. She met Bors again in Gloevant Wood, but did not know him because he was carrying the shield King Agrippe's Daughter had given him. She and her cousin, the Damsel of Glocedon, finally found and recognized him in Roevant Wood, where she obtained his pardon. [Vulgate IV]

IRELAND

Ireland has special importance in the saga of Tristram, and Malory speaks of it, along with Brittany and the Out Isles, as one of the major divisions of Britain. King Anguish of Ireland, La Beale Isoud, and Sir Marhaus are among the Irish characters of the romances. King Anguish long extracted tribute from King Mark of Cornwall.

L'ISLE ESTRANGE† (Lo Leu Estrange, Estrangor)

This is the kingdom and/or castle of King Vagor. The castle was strong, with but one narrow entrance. The name suggests an island or perhaps a valley. The place is probably small, and may be near the "Forest of the Boiling Well." I believe it is probably close to Carteloise forest in southern Scotland.

ISLE PERDUE†

A retreat of Duke Galehot's, this castle was thickly surrounded by woods and located on an island [Vulgate III]. Probably it was in or was near Galehot's favorite country, Surluse.

Do not confuse this Isle Perdue with those described with the entry for the castle of Meliot.

THE ISLES

Pellinore has not forgotten his kingdom in Malory, as he has in the musical **Camelot**. He is King Pellinore of the Isles. Since two of his sons are Percivale and Lamerake of Wales (or, de Galis), his Isles should be in or near Wales. Anglesey and Holyhead islands off the coast of northern Wales answer the description.

AGENT

Malory mentions "a great tournament . . . beside Camelot, at the Castle of Jagent" [X, 8].

LA JOYOUS [Dolorous] GARDE

This stronghold was La Dolorous Garde when Lancelot captured it, became La Joyous Garde while he held it, and turned once more into La Dolorous Garde after his banishment from England.

Vulgate III gives a more complete account than does Malory of Lancelot's actual capture of the castle. The graveyard was full of graves or purported graves of knights who had died or reputedly died fighting the castle's champions. Among the tombstones was a large slab of metal, bedecked with gems, on which was written: "Only he who conquers La Doloreuse Garde will be able to lift this slab, and he will find his name beneath it." When Lancelot lifted the slab, he read: "Here will repose Lancelot of the Lake, the son of King Ban." Thus Lancelot, who had been appropriated in infancy by the French Lady of the Lake, learned his parentage for the first time.

La Dolorous Garde also had a chapel with a door leading to a cave. As Lancelot entered the cave, the earth quaked and a dreadful noise filled the air. Two copper knights holding huge swords struck at him as he entered the next chamber. Here he found a deep and evil-smelling well from which ghastly noise rose, and beyond it was an ugly monster guarding the way with an axe. Lancelot had to break his shield upon the monster, strangle it, and push it into the well. At last a damsel of copper became visible, holding the keys of the enchantments, one large and one small. With the large key Lancelot opened a copper pillar. Terrible noises issued from thirty copper tubes. With the small key Lancelot opened a small coffer, out of which rose a whirlwind. Then at last the enchantments were broken. The obstacles vanished, as did the tombs in the churchyard and the helmets on the wall of knights previously vanquished; and Dolorous Garde became Joyous Garde.

Malory tells us that Joyous Garde had at least three gates [XX, 12]; that Tristram and La Beale Isoud spent some time here as Lancelot's guests [X, 52]; and that the procession bearing Lancelot's body from Glastonbury reached Joyous Garde within fifteen days [XXI, 12]. He further records "Some men say it was Alnwick, and some men say it was Bamborough." [XXI, 12]

Glennie identifies Bamborough with Castle Orgulous and prefers Aberwick, or Berwick on Tweed, for Joyous Garde. I like his placement of Castle Orgulous, but when Malory is more or less definite, as in the case of Joyous Garde, that outweighs Glennie. Therefore I put Joyous Garde at Alnwick, saving Benwick for another site, perhaps the city of Windesan.

Joyous Isle — see CASTLE OF BLIANT

ALEPH†

A castle in Norgales [Vulgate I].

KALET† (Karelet, Baale, Cole)

The castle of Lancelot's friend Count Dagins. Here Lancelot and his party passed the night after rescuing the Queen from the stake. [Vulgate VI, 283]

In Malory, Lancelot and the Queen were surprised together at Carlisle [XX, 2]. Presumably it was there, also, that the Queen was to be burnt, since she had a very hasty trial. The Vulgate version differs widely in important details, but my notes do not include evidence that the locale is changed. Thus, Kalet (not mentioned by Malory) would be within two days' ride of Carlisle in the direction of Joyous Garde, allowing perhaps the maximum time for escaping before stopping to rest. This precludes identification of Kalet with Kaleph, since Kaleph is in Norgales — surely too far, and in the wrong direction.

KARADIGAN†

Apparently the castle of Lysianors, who bore Arthur a son. The exact words are, *chastel de Karadigan que Lysianors la bele demoisele tenoit en sa bailie ou li rois Artus engendra Lohot.* [Vulgate VII, 206]

KYNKE KENADONNE (Kink Kenadon)

Malory tells us it is a city and castle "upon the sands that marched nigh Wales," and that "there is a plentiful country" around it [VII, 1 and VII, 34]. Malory seems to mention this city only in the story of Gareth and Lynette. Not being a Welsh scholar, I can only suggest it be identified with Carnarvon city in present-day Carnarvon county. This sounds like a good old name, and Arthur seems to prefer cities beginning with "C," or at least the hard-"C" sound, for his major courts.

John W. Donaldson tentatively identifies Kynke Kendaon with Kyneton, Radnorshire. Radnor, however, is a landlocked county, and Malory clearly puts this town by the seaside. Several of Donaldson's place identifications strike me as even more questionable than some of my own.

AKE, THE

Here dwelt the Lady (or Damosel) of the Lake, who gave Arthur his sword Excalibur. As Merlin once told Arthur, "within that lake is a rock, and therein is as fair a place as any on earth, and richly beseen." Malory puts the Lake definitely in Britain, apparently somewhere near Carleon. [Malory I, 25] The Vulgate just as clearly puts the Lake in Benoyc, France, and it is where the Damosel of the Lake raised Sir Lancelot from infancy. Hence, there must have been at least two magical Lakes, with one chief Lady of the Lake at a time in each.

Since the Lakes were magical and illusory (although the illusion was apparently quite tangible, even permitting the uninitiated to boat on the water's surface), there is no need to search for real lakes with which to identify them.

LAMBETH

Malory mentions Lambeth in XIX, 4: "Then Sir Launcelot ... took the water at Westminster Bridge, and made his horse to swim over Thames unto Lambeth." I do not know whether in this context Lambeth is a castle, a religious center, or simply a place name for undeveloped real estate.

LAMBOR†

A castle about midway between Camelot and the Humber. Here Arthur stopped with his men for a night on his way from Camelot to Joyous Garde, and reached the Humber on the second day, which is a very fast pace, even on horseback. [Vulgate VI]

"CHAPEL OF THE LANCES"†

An old, dilapidated church in a waste land. On a marble tomb in the churchyard were the words: "Do not enter. Unless you are the wretched knight who has lost the chance of finding the Holy Grail through his luxury, you cannot achieve the adventure of the churchyard." Inside was a burning tomb, with twelve other tombs, each with a lance, surrounding it. When any knight entered, the lances advanced and beat him to unconsciousness.

He would wake to find himself outside again. On the door of the chapel was written: "Only the son of the Dolorous Queen can enter this churchyard without shame." By the Dolorous Queen was meant Elaine of Benwick; the adventure, of course, was for Lancelot.

Going on from this church, one reached a fork in the road. A warning on a stone read: "Do not take the road on the left, for it will bring you to shame." This road led to Guindoel castle. The road on the right led to Carbonek. This puts the chapel between Scotland and Listeneise. [Vulgate IV]

LANDOINE† (Landone)

A forest, probably on the way to Gore [Vulgate IV].

Lands of the Two Marches — see LISTENEISE

LEICESTER†

Mentioned in Vulgate II, this sub-kingdom presumably corresponds to modern Leicestershire.

"CASTLE OF THE LEPROUS LADY"

This castle may have been on the other side of the waste forest near Carteloise castle. The leprous Lady could only be cured by a dish of warm blood from the right arm of a clean virgin who was a king's daughter, and not just any virginal king's daughter at that — they had to find the right one. Accordingly, every maiden damsel who passed by was forced to donate enough of her blood to fill a silver dish. Near the castle was a graveyard full of tombs of damsels who had died by this custom. Twelve of those interred were kings' daughters; all who donated were apparently related in some way to kings. It looks as if the people of the castle interpreted the position of king's daughter rather loosely. Did they also so interpret virginity?

The custom was not always fatal. When Sir Balin and the lady of the slain Sir Herlews le Berbeus arrived at this castle, she survived being bled very nicely, leaving again after a night's rest and "right good cheer."

Sir Percivale's sister Amide finally cured the Leprous Lady, giving her blood of her own free will. Amide died of it, and almost immediately thereafter the vengeance of God destroyed the castle and all its people. [Malory II, 13 and XVII, 9-11]

The "Castle of the Leprous Lady" should not be far from Carteloise castle and forest. It must also be near a river or harbor, since Galahad and his companions put Amide's body into a barge and let it drift to Sarras to meet them there. If Carteloise is put on the north shore of Solway Firth, the Leprous Lady's castle might be located at, say, Annan.

LESTROITE MARCHE†

The lord of Lestroite Marche held it against the King of Norgales, the Duke of Cambeninc, and the King of the Hundred Knights with the latter's seneschal Marganor, putting the castle somewhere in the marches between Norgales and Cambenet; indeed, its name means "the narrow march."

The lord of Lestroite Marche had one child, a daughter, who for some reason could not hold the castle after him. To help defend the castle and try to find his daughter a good husband at the same time, this lord established the custom that any knight who accepted his hospitality must spend half a day defending the castle. Ector de Maris, at that time a Queen's Knight, vanquished Marganor and restored peace to the area, although he cried off from marrying the damsel by pleading that he already had a lady. [Vulgate III]

LEVERZERP† (Loverzeph, Leverzep)

This sounds like a variant of the name Lonazep; but Malory places Lonazep castle near Joyous Garde, while Vulgate III and VII tell us that Leverzerp belonged to the Duke of Cambeninc and place Leverzep on the way from Bedingran to Orofoise. Leverserp and Lonazep must be two different castles.

Near Leverzerp is the Round Mountain, site of a hermitage.

Lindisfarne† – see MEDGAUD

LINTHCAMUS† (Lintheamus)

Here St. Cadoc built a monastery. Since Glennie gives Linthcamus among his Arthurian locales, Cadoc either must have preceded or have been contemporary with Arthur.

Linthcamus is at present-day Cambuslang, near the River Clyde, in the northern part of Lanark county, Scotland.

Liones – see LYONESSE

Liones Castle – see LYONESSE CASTLE

LISTENEISE (Listinoise)

Malory gives Pellam as King of Listeneise and Pelles as King of the Waste Lands; after much consideration I believe Pelles and Pellam to be one and the same. Therefore I feel justified in identifying Listeneise with "The Waste Lands," "The Lands of the Two Marches," and "The Foreign Country" of the Grail Adventures. It is the country of the grail, which the maimed Fisher King keeps at Carbonek (or Corbenic) castle; "three countries" were laid waste by the Dolorous Stroke. Listeneise seems also, however, sometimes to play the role of a more normal country, with Pellam carrying out the usual political functions of a king.

For various reasons, I place Listeneise in the present-day Lake District, which is in Cumberland and Westmoreland counties, due east of the Isle of Man, and includes the Cumbrian Mountains, Windermere, Derwentwater, and Skiddaw Peak. One of my reasons is that Rosemary Sutcliff points out that the Lake land remains unmentioned in the Domesday book, which ends abruptly at the Cumberland fells. (**The Shield Ring**, Author's note.) Remaining unincorporated and Norse-Saxon in Norman England, the Lake District may have acquired an aura of mystery which carried over into Malorian legend. Also, the Isle of Man makes a very handy Sarras.

LONAZEP

This castle, close to Joyous Garde, was the site of a famous tournament [Malory X, 52].

LONDON

Need I comment?

LONDON CATHEDRAL

So in the greatest church of London, whether were Paul's or not the French book maketh no mention, all the estates were long or day in the church for to pray [for the choice of a king]. [Malory I, 5]

"Paul's" would of course be old St. Paul's cathedral.

THE LONG ISLES

Duke Galeholt conquered 30 kingdoms, of which Surluse and the Long Isles seem the most notable. This suggests that the Long Isles may have been close to Surluse. Other evidence, however, points to a Welsh location for Surluse; Holyhead and Anglesey (which are more roundish than long) have already been assigned to King Pellinore on stronger evidence. Islay, Jura, Kintyre, and Arran, in Scotland, certainly answer the description of "long islands," and the fact that they are far distant from Wales may be secondary to a conqueror of Galeholt's caliber.

L'Orguellouse Emprise† – see ORGUELLOUSE EMPRISE

LOTHIAN

The modern place name of Lothian (West, Mid, and East) in Scotland is just south of the Antonine Wall. King Lot, or Loth, of Lothian and Orkney apparently was king of all northern Scotland from the Orkneys to at least some of the area

TIME
Dates
The Arthurian year uses the major feasts of the Christian church as chief reference points. Not all these feasts have been constant, either in date or in importance, through the centuries; indeed, the historical Fifth and Sixth centuries were times of two separate traditions for fixing the date of Easter in the Western church; at one point, the controversy led half of one monarch's court to celebrate Easter while the other half was still in Lenten mourning. I think we may probably assume, however, that to Malory's Arthur, Advent (the beginning of the liturgical year, lasting from about a month before Christmas until Christmas), Christmas, Epiphany, Lent, Easter, Ascension, and Pentecost (Whitsunday) fell about where they fall today in relation to each other and the seasons – Easter and the seasons and feasts counting from its placement (Lent, Ascension, Pentecost) being movable, of course.
Feasts of the saints and even of Mary may be more subject to change than the greater feasts given above. In the Seventeenth century, for instance, St. Joseph's Day fell on March 17; today

March 17 goes to St. Patrick and St. Joseph has been moved to March 19. From various references in the romances, however, I am confident that Assumption fell then when it falls now, and I am also reasonably confident that feasts like All Saints, which appear to have been timed with a view to replacing or Christianizing older Pagan holy days, also remain about where they were in Malory's time. Here, then, are a few modern dates for various feasts of Mary and the saints which may come in handy in finding our place on the Arthurian calendar:

March 25: ANNUNCIATION (Commemorates the angel Gabriel's appearance to Mary. Sometimes called "Lady Day." At one time considered the start of a new year.)

June 24: ST. JOHN THE BAPTIST

July 22: ST. MARY MAGDALEN

August 15: ASSUMPTION (Celebrates the taking of Mary's body into Heaven.)

September 29: ST. MICHAEL THE ARCHANGEL ("Michaelmas")

south of the Antonine Wall. Lot may have been High King of Scotland, with sub-kings under him, before Arthur's advent.

Loverzeph† – see LEVERSERP

LYONESSE (Liones) CASTLE

Sir Sadok passed this castle on his way to Arbray castle, while escaping from Mark's ambushment at Tintagil [Malory X, 50]. I would guess Lyonesse castle to be on the border between the land of Lyonesse and the rest of the Cornish peninsula, and Arbray to be a castle in the heart of Lyonesse.

At the northwest point of Land's End, modern Cornwall, are "the ruynes of an auntiente castle ... vpon a loftie craggie rocke, where yet appeare the ruined walls and forlorne trenches" [Norden]. The site is right for Lyonesse castle.

LYONESSE (Liones)

My edition of Malory spells the land Liones throughout, employing the same spelling as for Dame Liones, Gareth's love. To avoid confusion, I have gone to the more common modern variant spelling Lyonesse for the land, a now-sunken peninsula of which only the Scilly Islands remain.

AANTE†
Capital of Listeneise [Vulgate I].

MADERNE WELL†
North of Penzance, almost half-way to the north Cornish coast, is the parish of St. Maderne,

situate vunder the craggie hills ... nere which is a well called Maderne Well, whose fame in former ages was great; for the supposed vertue of healing, which St. Maderne had therinto infused: And manie votaries made annale pilgrimages vnto it, as they doe euen at this daye vnto the well of St. Winifride, beyounde Chester, in Denbigheshire, wherunto thowsands doe yearly make resort." [Norden]

It is a good guess that these wells had healing powers from Pagan times. The Christian saints, or at least their legends, may even have been invented or modified to Christianize the wells.

There are, of course, far too many such holy wells throughout England to itemize them all, and Maderne, although not specifically connected with Arthurian legend, is included here only as an example. Among powers sometimes connected with such wells is the quality that whichever partner, husband or wife, drinks the water soonest after the marriage ceremony will henceforth have predominance in married life. At Alternun, Cornwall, is a "bowsening pool" wherein mad folk were formerly dowsed to restore their senses. (Let those who laugh compare this remedy with our modern enlightened "shock treatments" for insanity.)

MAGOUNS CASTLE

Malory identifies this as "a castle that is called Magouns, and now it is called Arundel, in Sussex." The constable of Magouns, Sir Bellangere, was cousin to Dame Anglides, who fled here with her infant son, and here remained to raise him. The son was Sir Alisander le Orphelin, and his father, Anglides' husband, was Prince Boudwin, slain by King Mark. [Malory X, 32-34]

CASTLE OF MAIDENS

There may well have been two or more Castles of Maidens, and it or they are not quite like the "Castle Anthrax" which Galahad finds so full of choice damsels in the film **Monty Python and the Holy Grail**.

Perhaps the most notable account in Malory of a Castle of Maidens is that in XIII, 15-16. Seven years before the Grail Quest, Duke Lianour had held this castle. Seven wicked brothers moved in, raped his elder daughter, and murdered him and his son. When the daughter predicted the brothers would all be defeated by one knight, they decided to hold prisoner all knights and ladies who passed by. "And therefore is it called the Maidens' Castle, for they have devoured many maidens." (A "maiden," in older and broader usage, can be a virgin of either sex.) Galahad arrived and defeated all seven brothers in battle, but did not kill them, Fleeing, they ran by chance into Gawaine, Gareth, and Ywaine, who did kill them. The elder sister was dead by now, but the Duke's younger daughter was made mistress of the castle and lands. The spiritual significance (hardly anything happens during the Adventures of the Grail which is not a parable) is that the prisoners represent the good souls that were in prison (Hell or Limbo) before the time of Christ, and the seven brothers represent the seven deadly sins.

November 1: ALL SAINTS

November 11: ST. MARTIN ("Martinmas")

December 26: ST. STEPHEN

Hours of the Day

Arthurian people spoke of what o'clock it was.

... and so the queen lay long in her bed until it was nine of the clock.
Then Sir Meliagrance went to the queen's chamber, and found her ladies there ready clothed. Jesu mercy, said Sir Meliagrance, what aileth you, madam, that ye sleep thus long? [Malory XIX, 6]

Sir, said Sir Bors, I shall do my pain, and or it be seven of the clock I shall wit of such as ye have said before, who will hold with you. [Malory XX, 5]

More common, however, may have been the system of dividing up the day by the liturgical hours of the Church. In practice, the times of reciting these hours is adapted to other demands of monks' and nuns' days, such as field work. Also, the entire period between one "hour" and the next may be referred to by the name of the earlier hour. Here is more or less how the liturgical hours divide the day:

PRIME: 6:00 a.m.

TERCE, or UNDERNE: 9:00 a.m.

SEXT: Noon

NONE: Midafternoon, 2:30 or 3:00 p.m.

VESPERS: Late afternoon or early evening

COMPLINE: Bedtime (I am not sure whether this hour had as yet developed in Arthurian times.)

MATINS AND LAUDS: Frequently recited together. Traditionally, Matins should begin in the middle of the night, a few hours after midnight; in monasteries and convents where the full Office is chanted, Matins and Lauds may go on till dawn in the seasons of longer days. Matins, however, has come to apply in popular parlance to dawn and early morning: "The birds were saying their Matins."

This Castle of Maidens was "a strong castle with deep ditches, and there ran beside it a fair river that hight Severn" [Malory XIII, 15]. It might be near the source of the Severn, at Llanidloes, Montgomeryshire, Wales.

Malory also mentions a Castle of Maidens in IX, 25-35, as the site of an important tournament between the King of North Wales and King Carados of Scotland. This tournament is remembered in X, 58:

> Sir, said Palomides [to Tristram, as they approached Castle Lonazep and saw the tournament set up there], meseemeth that there was as great an ordinance at the Castle of Maidens upon the rock, where ye won the prize.

This may be the same castle as that of XIII, 15-16; the tournament could have been held before the seven wicked brothers moved in. But, by the account of the old religious man who explained its history to Galahad, there would have been no reason to call it the Castle of Maidens before the time of the seven brothers.

Glennie identifies the Castle of Maidens with Edinburgh, speculating that the name may come from a house of nuns (see Dunpeledur). This contradicts both Malory's placement of the stronghold on the Severn and his tale of the seven brothers. If, however, the Castle of Maidens of the tournament is considered to be a different fortress than Duke Lianour's, then Edinburgh could accomodate it nicely, especially with Malory naming Carados of Scotland as one of the tournament's promoters and Glennie mentioning the "fortified rock" of Edinburgh.

John W. Donaldson briefly identifies the Castle of Maidens as "near Dorchester," for no reason that I can see.

See also the Castle of the Hard Rock and the Chastel as Dames.

MALAHAUT† (Malohaut)

According to Vulgate II, the ruler of Malahaut was the King with the Hundred Knights. A town called Le Puis de Malohaut, however, was ruled by the widowed Lady of Malohaut, who became Duke Galeholt's paramour. Perhaps she acted as vice-regent for the King with the Hundred Knights. The location of this sub-kingdom is unknown.

CASTEL DE LA MARCHE†

Since King Brangoire was holding the anniversary of his coronation here, and since the Vulgate's Brangoire is Malory's King Brandegoris of Stranggore, this castle would be on the border of Stranggore [Vulgate IV].

MARCHES

The word signifies borders or border territory. We meet such characters as the Duke of the South Marches, indicating that the Marches could be political entities in themselves. Tentatively, the South Marches might parallel the eastern border of Devon, the Straight Marches follow the eastern border of Wales, and the North Marches extend along the southern border of Scotland.

Marchoise – see MORTAISE

DES MARES†

Kings Ban and Bors stopped here during their visit to Arthur in Britain. The castellan, Agravadain des Vaus (not to be confused with Gawaine's brother, Agravaine), had a beautiful daughter whom Merlin admired and caused to sleep with Ban, resulting in the birth of Lancelot's half-brother, Ector de Maris. [Vulgate II]

Des Mares would probably be near the sea ("mare").

Tower of Marvels† – see under GALAFORT

MEDGAUD† (Lindisfarne)

Site of the Abbey of the Holy Island of St. Cuthbert, Medgaud Island is five or six miles over the sands at low tide, a mile by boat from Bamborough, Glennie's Castle Orgulous.

MEILROS† [Melros]

A monastery, "heretofore noble and eminent," near Rhymer's Glen. About six or eight miles north of Meilros, in Gwaedol (or Wedale), is the Church of St. Mary, where, according to Glennie, were preserved fragments of the image of St. Marry which Arthur brought back from Jerusalem. [Glennie, 60] Meilros is present-day Melrose.

"MELIAGRANCE'S CASTLE"

> Then there was a knight that hight Meligrance, and he was son unto King Bagdemagus, and this knight had at that time a castle of the gift of King Arthur within seven miles of Westminster. [Malory XIX, 1]

Guenevere rode a-Maying with ten unarmed knights and ten ladies in the woods and fields around Westminster. Here Meligrance waylaid them and carried them to his own castle. Later, he trapped Lancelot in his stronghold by causing him to drop "more than ten fathom into a cave full of straw." [Malory XIX, 1-7] Such trapdoors befit the castles of villainous knights.

The Vulgate account of the kidnapping of Guenevere by Meliagaunt is substantially different, longer and more involved, and puts Meliagaunt's castle in his father's kingdom of Gore [Vulgate IV].

See also Castle of Four Stones.

MELIOT

> Within a day or two [after interring twelve kings in St. Sephen's, Camelot] King Arthur was somewhat sick, and he let pitch his pavilion in a meadow ... and saw a knight coming even by him ... [who] passed forth to the castle of Meliot [Malory II, 12].

This knight was Herlews le Berbeus, who was slain by Sir Garlon apparently before he had reached Meliot. Arthur had sent Balin le Savage after Herlews, and Balin's subsequent adventures with Herlews' lady to find Garlon and avenge Herlews' death took them to the "Castle of the Leprous Lady" and to Listeneise. Malory seems to tell us nothing more about Meliot castle by that name. Nevertheless, I would like to identify it with one of a pair of castles where Balin and his brother Balan met their deaths. Malory leaves these fairly important castles unnamed.

One of them was on the mainland and the other on an island, clearly an island in a river. The lady of the mainland castle kept a custom whereby every passing knight had to joust with the knight who defended the island. The knight then defending the island was Balan, in anonymous red armor. Balin, coming to the island with a borrowed shield, kept the custom so vigorously that the two brothers mortally wounded each other in battle before learning one another's identity, and here were buried.

The lady did not know Balin's name to put it on the tomb, but Merlin came along next morning and took care of that detail. He also repommelled Balin's sword, set it in a floating marble block to drift down the river to Camelot at the right time, and left the scabbard "on this side the island" for Galahad, who should win the sword, to find. He also made a bridge of iron and steel only half a foot broad to the island, and only a good and true knight could cross this bridge. Moreover he made a bed to lie upon which brought madness, "yet Launcelot de Lake fordid that bed through his noblesse." [Malory II, 12-19, especially 17-19] I have no idea why Merlin made that bed, nor how Lancelot fordid it, unless the passage refers somehow to one of Lancelot's fits of madness. Balin's sword in its marble block floats down to Camelot for Galahad to draw it at the beginning of the Grail Adventures, and Galahad is already wearing the scabbard, having picked it up on his way to court [XIII, 2-5], but Malory tells us nothing more about bed, bridge, or castle.

In Vulgate V, Gawaine tells of his adventures at the Isles Perdues, where he saw the miraculous bed of Merlin, and also the adventurous sword, by which a hermit predicted that Gawaine's best friend (Lancelot) would kill him through Mordred's fault. On this island was the force of all the enchantment in the world. Here were many damsels, and here the best of knights would find his equal in battle. This has to be where Malory placed the fatal battle of Balin and Balan. The "adventurous sword" must be Balin's Sword, which Galahad apparently sent back to his father Lancelot after the Grail adventures.

Meliot might be the name used for the mainland castle, while the island castle could retain the Vulgate name of Isle Perdues. (Do not confuse with Duke Galehot's castle of Isle Perdue.) Of course, since my grounds for identifying the "castle of Meliot" with this pair of castles is so slight, Meliot might be considered another castle entirely.

In any case we need a site upriver from Camelot for the castle of Balin's death. I suggest the Itchen River.

CASTEL MERLIN†
Despite the name, I found no evidence to connect this stronghold with the great enchanter. Conceivably it may have been connected with the minor King Merlan le Diable, but more likely it was in or near Galehodin's territory (in Norgales?), perhaps being one of Galehodin's own castles. Here Ywaine left Mordred after the tournament at Peningue Castle. [Vulgate V]

"MERLIN'S ROCK"
Probably somewhere in Cornwall, this is where Nimue imprisoned Merlin.

CASTEL DEL MOLIN†
Seemingly a castle of King Marboar's, whose territory was apparently on the way to Estrangore.

Two leagues from Molin was a castle of which Count Thanaguis (Tanaguin, Thangin, Thallagon) was lord. Do not confuse him with Duke Brandelis of Taningues. [Vulgate IV]

"ABBEY OF KING MORDRAINS"
Malory does not make it clear, but from the Vulgate, we know that King Evelake and King Mordrains were the same man,

Evelake being his old name and Mordrains his name as a baptized Christian. He and his brother-in-law, Nacien, were contemporaries of Joseph of Arimathea, with whom they came to Britain. Mordrains lay blind in an abbey for several hundred years, waiting for Galahad to come and restore his sight. After Galahad had done so, Mordrains died happy in his arms. [Malory XVII, 18]

I can find no good clue in Malory as to the whereabouts of this abbey, but from a comparison with Mordrains' and Nacien's adventures at the Isle of Turnance and the Port of Perilous Rock, I would guess it likely to have been somewhere between Arthurian Cornwall and Avilion along the Devon-Somerset border. The Vulgate, however, places the abbey in a wood near Norgales [I, 243-44].

"MORGAN'S CASTLE"
In trying to dovetail Malory's evidence with that of the Vulgate, I am forced to conclude that Morgan le fay had at least two castles. She may well have had even more, here and there about the country.

King Arthur gave Morgan a castle and later regretted his generosity, but never could win it from her again with any kind of siege engine. She sent her knights out by one, two, and three to overthrow Arthur's knights and imprison or at least strip them. This castle appears to have been not too far from Camelot, likely to the south towards Cornwall. [Malory X, 17] Were we to make it, say, Ringwood in southwest Southampton, and make Beaulieu, not far from Ringwood, the castle of La Beale Regard, it would be easy to understand why Morgan would usurp La Beale Regard. "Ringwood," indeed, would not make a bad name for the castle of a sorceress.

According to Vulgate VI, Morgan had a castle near the stronghold of Tauroc, which in turn must have been near Taneborc castle at the entrance of Norgales. Once Arthur and his companions, lost while hunting in the woods around Tauroc, came to this Welsh castle of Morgan's. This was late in Arthur's career, and he was surprised to find his half-sister yet alive — he had presumed her dead, not having heard of her in some years. He found that her castle had silk-covered walls in the courtyard, great splendor and marvelous illumination within, and gold and silver dinner-plate which he could not match even at Camelot.

Morgan had once imprisoned Lancelot in this castle, administering to him a curious powder which made him content to remain with her. He had beguiled two winters and a summer by painting his life's history, including scenes of his love for Guenevere, on the walls of the his room. [Vulgate V] Morgan showed Arthur Lancelot's murals in yet another attempt to convince her brother he was being cuckolded, but he refused to believe it. Aside from this, his visit with here was amicable on both sides, and he invited her to visit court. She replied, however, that she would never return to court until she left her castle to go to Avilion. [Vulgate VI] It sounds as if the castle in the woods near Tauroc was her favorite, and that she had chosen to retire here from the world.

Morgan's Chapel† — see VAL SANS RETOUR

MORRIS
Malory implies that the forest of Morris is in Cornwall, near Tintagil castle. Probably Morris would stretch roughly between Tintagil and Bodmin Moor; possibly it would even take

in Bodmin Moor, accommodating Dozmary Pool as the Perilous Lake of Morris. I have read the statement somewhere that Cornwall has no trees, but that is not quite true; it does have some little wooded areas, and would have had more in Arthurian times. [Malory IX, 39]

MORTAISE (Mortoise, Marchoise, Marcoise, Martorse)

In Malory VII, 24, Mortaise is put in the vicinity of Dame Lyonors' Castle Dangerous, which Gareth and Lynette reach from Caerleon. Here it seems to be a natural body of water, its passage guarded by two rascally knights whom Gareth slew. Later, in the Grail Adventures, Mortaise appears as the water beside which Lancelot was stranded for a time before boarding the ship with Galahad and the body of Percivale's sister, the water near which the Temptress told Percivale she had seen the Red Knight with the white shield, and possibly the water into which Percivale rode the demon horse before reaching the island (of Turnance?). [Malory XVII, 13; XIV, 8; XIV, 5-6]

Vulgate VI gives a fuller description, identifying Mortaise as a lake ("laigue"). After eating bread and water with a recluse, Lancelot passed the night on a high rock, and the next day came to a deep, very beautiful valley between two high rocks, before which lay Mortaise, divided in two parts by a wooded tongue of land. The wood was dense, the water very deep.

To make the Bristol Channel and Severn river the water of Mortaise, and Dundy the Isle of Turnance, should give us room to accommodate all the events Malory describes. The horseshoe bend in the Severn near Newnham might fit the Vulgate's description.

AUNTES

So [the eleven rebel kings] consented together to keep all the marches of Cornwall, of Wales, and of the North. So first, they put King Idres in the City of Nauntes in Britain, with four thousand men of arms, to watch both the water and the land. [Malory I, 18]

Nauntes must have been strategically important, though this seems to be the only time Malory mentions it.

There is, of course, a city named Nantes in Brittany, and Brittany is sometimes called Britain in the old books; nevertheless, the context of the passage suggests that here a city in Great Britain is meant. In present-day Merioneth county, Wales, is a point of land called Cader Idris; it is on the coast, immediately south of the inlet at Barmouth. The name Idris suggests the name of the king delegated to hold the city, making Caer Idris a candidate for "the City of Nauntes in Britain."

Port Neglay† − see POMEGLAY

CASTLE NIGRAMOUS

This was the stronghold of the sorceress Hellawes, and probably located near the Chapel Perilous [Malory VI, 15]. Hellawes probably is to be identified with Helaes de la Forest Perilleuse, who appears in Vulgate VII. Although there may be many Forests Perilous (that seeming as much descriptive phrase

as a proper name), for lack of a better clue Castle Nigramous and the Chapel Perilous could be placed either in the Forest Perilous of Norgales or that of southeast Wales around Dame Lyonors' Castle Dangerous. I would prefer the more southern location, in order to keep Hellawes' sphere of activity separated from Annowre's. Conversely, there might be equal rationale for making Hellawes and Annowre neighbor sorceresses.

Noble† − see CUBELE

NOHAUT†

Nohaut was a castle or a sub-kingdom. Here the Lady of Nohaut was besieged by the King of Northumberland [Vulgate III], suggesting that Nohaut was close to Northumberland.

NORGALES (Northgalis, North Wales)

To accommodate a border between Norgales and Cambenet, I would put the boundary far enough south to include most of Montgomeryshire in Norgales, following the Severn river part way.

Kaleph is a castle in this sub-kingdom. [Vulgate I].

I have not quite been able to work out the relationship and histories of the various named and unnamed kings of Norgales. As a stopgap measure, I have tried at least to gather together those characters who seem connected with this part of the country.

Kings: Agrippe?, Ryons, Tradelmans, Vadalon
Queen of Northgalis
King of Norgales' Daughter and her Handmaid
Lady de Vance? (desired by King Ryons)
Nero (brother of King Ryons)
Galihodin?   **CONNECTED**
Retainer: Phelot   **WITH NORGALES**

NORTHUMBERLAND

The general area we know by the same name.

FOREST OF NORTHUMBERLAND

Here Blaise, Merlin's former teacher, settled down and wrote the chronicles of Merlin's life [Malory I, 17].

RGUELLOUSE EMPRISE, L'†

Duke Galeholt built this castle on a rock washed by a tributary of the Assurne river, which bordered his kingdom of Sorelois. He intended it to be his place of coronation and Arthur's prison, and he never entered it in sorrow without leaving it in joy. After he became Arthur's man, however, Lorguellouse Emprise crumbled to pieces. [Vulgate IV]

CASTLE ORGULOUS

Every knight who passed by this castle was made to joust or else be taken prisoner, or at least lose his horse and harness [Malory IX, 3].

Glennie puts Castle Orgulous at Bamborough, Northumberland, on the east coast, a little south of Holy Island, near Belford but right on the coast, just on the south side of a small, squarish inlet. He gives this description:

Occupying the whole extent of a solitary eminence, it stands among sandy downs, close by the sea, and overlooking a wide plain at the foot of the Cheviots. Nearly opposite the Castle are the Faröe Islands. [p. 64]

Castle Orgulous appears in Malory's story of La Cote Male Taile. If we assume that at the beginning of this tale, in IX, 1, Arthur is holding court at Carlisle or another northern city, I see no reason to reject Glennie's identification, except that Malory gives Bamborough as one of two possible sites for the castle of Joyous Garde.

ORKNEY
I suspect this includes more than just the Orkney Islands — that it includes, in fact, all Scotland south to Lothian.

OROFOISE†
A country *vers Sorelois en la fin du roiaume de Norgales,* which I translate "towards Surluse near the end [tip?] of the kingdom of Norgales" [Vulgate III]. Orofoise would approximate the northern half of Shropshire.

THE OUT ISLES
Somewhat arbitrarily, a good candidate for these are the Outer Hebrides.

ASS DE PERRONS†
This bad pass among sharp rocks was guarded by four knights armed as peasants, one mounted and armed in the usual knightly manner, and yet another mounted and waiting at the other end of the pass. I do not know their motivation; perhaps it was simple brigandage and robbery. No magic seems to be involved. This peril is found on the way to the "pont despee" in the land of Gore. [Vulgate IV]

PELOWNES
A castle by the seaside. Taking Sir Palomides hither, his captors had to pass by Joyous Garde, where Lancelot rescued him. [Malory X, 84-85] Might it be identified with Amble, on the coast of Northumberland, a little south of Alnwick?

PENDRAGON
Bearing the same name as Uther Pendragon, this sounds as if it should have been a more important castle than Malory

otherwise seems to indicate. The lord of Pendragon castle at the time of Sir La Cote Male Taile was Sir Brian de les Isles, "a noble man and a great enemy unto King Arthur," Lancelot vanquished him and freed from his castle thirty of Arthur's knights, including La Cote Male Taile, and forty ladies. Lancelot made La Cote Male Taile lord of Pendragon, with Sir Nerovens de Lile his lieutenant to have rule of the castle under him. [Malory IX, 5-6, 9]

La Cote Male Taile came to Pendragon after leaving Castle Orgulous, for which I incline to accept Glennie's identification of Bamborough.

PENINGUE†
Surrounded by woods and fertile fields, this was one of the castle of Galehodin, the nephew of Duke Galehot. Eventually Galehodin dubbed a wealthy and worthy burger who lived nearby and invested him with the castle. [Vulgate V] Peningue would be in Surluse, or else in Norgales near Surluse.

Pentagoel† — see PINTADOL

Isles Perdue — see ISLE PERDUE; see also MELIOT

CASTLE PERILOUS
Tristram, Gouvernail, Sir Kehydius, and Dame Bragwaine were on their way by boat from Brittany to Cornwall when an extremely "contrarious wind" blew them off course to North Wales, where they came ashore near the Castle Perilous. Tristram went into the forest because "in this forest are many strange adventures, as I heard say." [Malory IX, 10] This would seem to put it near the Forest Perilous of Annowre the sorceress in North Wales [Malory IX, 16]. I would incline to put this Castle Perilous at Dyffryn or Llanbedr, above Barmouth on the coast of Merioneth county. Having blown so far, though, it would not be impossible for Tristram and party to have come ashore even farther along the coast, at, say, Llandudno or Rhyl.

Although I cannot be entirely sure, I do not think this is the same castle as Dame Lyonors' Castle Perilous, otherwise called Castle Dangerous — and not simply because I have already located that Castle Perilous in Wiltshire! For Dame Lyonors' castle, see Castle Dangerous.

THE CHAPEL PERILOUS
Either this was not a Christian chapel, or it had been adapted to her own purposes by the sorceress Hellawes, Lady of the Castle Nigramous, who "ordained" the chapel to entrap Lancelot or Gawaine.

Riding in a deep forest, Lancelot followed a black brachet which was tracking a feute of blood. The brachet led him over an old, feeble bridge into an old manor, where he found the body of Sir Gilbert the Bastard, with his wife grieving for him. Leaving the manor, Lancelot met a damsel he knew, who told him that her brother, Sir Meliot de Logres, had fought and killed Sir Gilbert that day, but been wounded himself. The bleeding could not be staunched, and Meliot could only be saved if his wounds were searched with the sword and a piece of the bloody cloth wrapping the dead knight in the Chapel Perilous. Lancelot proceeded to Chapel Perilous, on the front of which he saw many fair, rich shields hanging upside-down. Thirty armed knights barred his way, grinning and gnashing their teeth at him; but when he resolutely stepped forward, they stood aside and let him pass. In the chapel, by the light of a single dim lamp, he found the body of Sir Gilbert lying covered by a cloth of silk. When Lancelot cut off a little of the cloth, the earth seemed to quake. When he came back outside, the thirty knights threatened his death if he did not lay down Sir Gilbert's sword, which he had picked up in the chapel, along with the cloth. Again Lancelot passed resolutely and safely through their midst. Next he met Hellawes herself, who first threatened his death if he did not lay down the sword, then tried to get him to kiss her once. When he refused, she confessed that either to lay down the sword or to kiss her would have cost him his life. She had been in love with him for seven years, and, despairing of his love, had hoped to have his dead body to kiss and fondle. She had had Sir Gawaine with her once, for awhile, at which time he had fought with Sir Gilbert and cut off his left hand. (Had Hellawes been less lethal with Gawaine than with Lancelot because she did not despair of winning Gawaine's carnal love?) Proceeding from the chapel, Lancelot healed Meliot. Hellawes died. I do not know whether Sir Gilbert was Hellawes' unwilling accomplice or unwitting tool. [Malory VI, 14-15]

The Chapel Perilous would appear to have been in one of the Forests Perilous. See Castle Nigramous and Forest Perilous.

FOREST PERILOUS (Forest Perdue)

In the "Forest Perilous, that was in North Wales" lived Annowre, a sorceress who loved Arthur and enticed him to her castle, later trying to kill him when he would not go to bed with her. The attempt was foiled by Sir Tristram and Nimue, and Arthur slew Annowre. [Malory IX, 16] This seems to be the forest near Castle Perilous, where Tristram had been blown ashore [Malory IX, 10]. Indeed, it is possible that Castle Perilous was Annowre's stronghold.

The Vulgate speaks of a "forest perilleuse" which seems to have been between Castle Chariot and Bedegraine. This is probably another section of Malory's Forest Perilous. Since Castle Perilous and presumably Annowre's section of the woods were near the coast, the forest must have been extensive.

Vulgate II and V give this history of the Forest Perilleuse, also called the Forest Perdue, since those who entered it were lost — temporarily, as things turned out. When Gwenbaus and King Bors were travelling to their brother King Ban at Bedingran, they found many knights and ladies dancing in a fine field in the midst of this forest. Looking on was an elderly knight, who seemed to be in charge, and a very beautiful damsel. Gwenbaus fell in love with the damsel and made up his mind to remain with her. When she wished that the dancing would go on forever, he cast a spell to oblige her, enchanting the place so that the people would go on dancing, and all knights and ladies who loved or had ever loved, on coming by, would forget everything else and join the dancers until the enchantment was broken. After fourteen years, the damsel wearied of dancing and carolling, and Gwenbaus made her a magic chessboard. Eventually Gwenbaus and his damsel both died here, although the enchantment went on.

At length Sir Lancelot came to the field in the forest, where he found thirty rich pavilions. In the center of the field four large pines surrounded a chair on which rested a golden crown, the crown of Lancelot's father, King Ban, who had left it with his brother Gwenbaus. Many knights

and damsels were singing and carolling around the pines. When Lancelot passed the first pavilion, his memory became blank and he joined the revellers; his squire, however, was unaffected and got away. A damsel led Lancelot to the chair and told him he must sit in it and wear the crown to see if he was their deliverer. If he was not, he would have to stay and wait with them. The damsel put the crown on Lancelot's head, saying that it was his father's crown. At that moment, Lancelot saw a statue fall and break. All the carollers recovered their memories. The spell was broken and they were freed.

There appear to have been at least two Forests Perilous, one in North Wales and another probably in southeast Wales (see Nigramous Castle). Indeed, I suspect there may have been a number of Forests Perilous, "Perilous" being the sort of adjective which might have been applied as the speaker saw fit.

THE PERILOUS LAKE

Despite the name, I cannot find that Malory suggests this lake to be magically dangerous. He puts it in the forest of Morris. Dozmary Pool, on a hilltop in Bodmin Moor, was long supposed to be bottomless, which would make it perilous.

The Perilous Lake is rather minor. Malory has nothing much happening here, except that Kay and Gaheris abide at it a while waiting for King Mark [Malory IX, 30].

PORT OF PERILOUS ROCK

I find that Malory mentions this mysterious spot only once, in the Grail Adventures — and in a flashback [XVII, 4]. Nacien, entering a ship at the isle of Turnance, was blown to "another ship where King Mordrains was, which had been tempted full evil with a fiend in the Port of Perilous Rock," all this happening forty years after Christ's Passion. If Turnance is identified with Lundy, then Morte Point, in Devonshire, west of Ilfracombe, might be a good spot for the Port of Perilous Rock, "Morte" suggesting death and therefore peril. I do not know whether the rocks are perilous there today, but even if they are not, they may have been fifteen or twenty centuries ago.

LA PETITE AUMOSNE†

Originally called "li Secors as poures" (Help of the Poor), this abbey, which was rather needy itself, was renamed la Petite Aumosne ('The Little Dole') by King Helisier, a contemporary and convert of Joseph of Arimathea, who quipped that during thirty years of holy wandering, he had received here the smallest hand-out anywhere, though it was all they had to give.

Despite its poverty, La Petite Aumosne was still around in Arthur's time, a source of religious men who could at least give travelling knights the local news.

Petite Aumosne was in the neighborhood of the castle Tertre Deuee and the "Forest of the Boiling Well" and possibly also near King Vagor's Isle Estrange [Vulgate V].

PINTADOL† (Pentagoel)

This castle had fallen into the power of a father and three sons who were all powerful swordsmen. Ywaine defeated them and restored Pintadol to its rightful lord, but my notes do not indicate who this rightful lord was. [Vulgate IV]

Pintadol is probably in the same general part of the country as the Dolorous Tower. I would suggest Pentire Point, across the river's mouth from Padstow, Cornwall. Norden says of Pentyre fort: "a place dowble ditched standing vpon Pentyre hill ..."

CASTLE PLUERE (The Weeping Castle)

Its lord was one Sir Breunor, not to be confused with Sir Breunor le Noir, who is the good La Cote Male Taile.

Here Tristram, Isoud, Governail, and Bragwaine stopped when Tristram was bringing La Beale Isoud back from Ireland to Cornwall for King Mark. They found that Sir Breunor kept this custom: whenever any knight came by with a lady, they had a beauty contest between the newcomer and Breunor's own lady. "An thy lady be fairer than mine," quote Sir Breunor, "with thy sword smite off my lady's head; and if my lady be fairer than thine, with my sword I must strike off her head." Afterwards the two knights would fight, and whichever won would kill the other and keep the castle and surviving lady. When La Beale Isoud proved the fairer, Tristram took Breunor at his word, and, reasoning that the lady was as guilty as her lord, struck off her head. It is a relief to record that Tristram killed Breunor afterwards in the combat, so that Breunor did not go to court and become a companion of the Round Table, as did so many former villains and enemies of Arthur after being defeated by one of Arthur's knights.

Malory makes Breunor the father of "Sir Galahad the haut prince," almost certainly Duke Galehot, who came with the King of the Hundred Knights to avenge his father's death, but dropped the project on learning what a custom Breunor had maintained. Presumably Galehot took the castle and disposed of it as he wished, and the custom almost certainly stopped with Breunor's death. [Malory VIII, 24-27]

There is no reference to any storm that might have blown Tristram off course on this voyage, Therefore, Pluere was probably on the coast of Cornwall or southern Wales. Leaving Ireland from Waterford Harbor would give them less open water to cross, though leaving from Cork Harbor would also have been possible. Wales may be growing overloaded with castles, and I'm not sure I like to put Pluere near Gore and Stranggore. Mark's country, on the other hand, was likely still a bit more wild and less under Arthur's influence. For Pluere, I think I would go for some site around Barnstaple Bay in present-day Devonshire.

POMEGLAY† (Port Nelgay)
A castle near the frontier of Gore [Vulgate IV].

POMITAIN
Duke Galeholt gave this island as a gift to King Marsil of Pomitain [Malory X, 44]. Assuming it was one of the Long Isles, and that the Long Isles were Islay, Jura, Kintyre, and Arran, I would make Arran Pomitain. It might, of course, have been another of Galeholt's conquests entirely.

Chastel as Puceles† — see DAMES, CHASTEL AS, and CASTLE OF MAIDENS

LE PUIS DE MALOHAUT†
From the name, this town has to have been in the sub-kingdom of Malahaut.

ED CASTLE, THE
Sirs Edward and Hue of the Red Castle had extorted a barony from the Lady of the Rock [Malory IV, 26]. This probably was somewhere in the marches of Wales.

THE RED CITY
If King Hermance's Delectable Isle is the Spurn Head peninsula in East Riding, as I think most probable, then the Red City might be Kilnsea.

Rhymer's Glen† and Rhymer's Tower† — see DIN DREI and ERCILDOUNE

LA ROCHE†
Built in the time of Vortigern, this castle was held in Arthur's time by the sorceress Camille. It had a gate near the water (or moat?). This gate closed by enchantment to all strangers, at least during Camille's tenure, and beyond it, the folk of the castle could not be harmed. This did not, however, prevent Lancelot from killing them when he got into the castle; perhaps he entered by another way, or perhaps the ring given him by the French Damsel of the Lake negated Camille's magic. La Roche was located twelve Scottish leagues from Arestueil. Camille was at least half Saxon, and allied with the Saxons. [Vulgate III]

Arestueil was apparently in Scotland, but I have not discovered where. It may be Glennie's Areclutha, the area between the Firth of Clyde and the River Clyde, just below the west end of the Antonine Wall. Possibly, but not necessarily, La Roche is Malory's Castle of the Hard Rock (Roche Dure). There may also be some connection here with Malory's Lady of the Rock (see Red Castle, above), but I doubt it.

For a possible identification of Camille's castle, King's Knot is a possibility:

> ... a singular, flat-surfaced mound within a series of enclosing embankments, which would appear to be of very great antiquity; and where, 'in a sport called "Knights of the Round Table," the Institutions of King Arthur were commemorated,' at least, to the close of the Mediaeval Age. [Glennie, p. 42]

Stirling castle, also called Snowdon castle, King's Knot, or Arthur's Round Table, is at Stirling, near the mouth of the River Forth where it empties into the Firth of Forth.

Roche Dure — see CASTLE OF THE HARD ROCK

ROCHESTER
The Pope charged the Bishop of Rochester to threaten interdict if Arthur did not take Guenever back and make peace with Lancelot [Malory XX, 13]. Rochester is in Kent.

ROESTOC†
Lot and his sons were on their way from Logris back to Arestuel in Scotland when they met 7000 Sesnes leading 700 prisoners on the plains of Roestoc. They battled the Sesnes, at which time Gawaine won his horse Gringolet from King Clarions, though he did not kill Clarions. [Vulgate II] Since it had both plains and a ruling Lady, we are probably safe in assuming Roestoc was a sub-kingdom.

In the sub-county of North Riding, Yorkshire, are the north York moors, which might have been the plains of Roestoc.

ROEVANT†

In this forest the Damsels of Hongrefort and Glocedon caught up with Sir Bors, making it in the same part of the island as Gore and Stranggore. Here, also, the French Damsel of the Lake appointed Bors to be on a certain day. [Vulgate IV]

THE ROUND MOUNTAIN†

Site of a hermitage near Leversep castle.

"CASTLE DE LA ROWSE"

I took the name of the castle from its lord and lady, the Duke and Duchess de la Rowse, enemies of Arthur until Gareth Beaumains conquered the Duke, who subsequently became a companion of the Round Table [Malory VII, 31-35]. The Duke's first name was Ladinas [Malory I, 17]. Their castle would have been near Dame Lyonors' Castle Dangerous.

THE ROYAL MINSTER†

Queen Helayne of Benwick founded this minster and convent in Benwick, France, on the hill where the French Damsel of the Lake had taken the infant Lancelot.

AINT MICHAELS MOUNT

In Brittany, this hill on the tidal flats was once the haunt of a particularly repulsive giant. After slaying him, Arthur commanded Howell to build the famous church of St. Michael's Mount. This was early in Arthur's reign, as he was setting out to conquer the Emperor of Rome. [Malory V, 5]

Do not confuse with St. Michael's Mount, Cornwall, a similar spot east of Penzance on the south Cornish coast.

SALISBURY

The books of the Grail Adventures were kept in this city in present-day Wiltshire. Near here, also, the final battle between Arthur and Mordred took place. [Malory XVII, 23; XXI, 3] Salisbury seems to have had significance as a religious, cultural, and political center. Malory does not say that Arthur ever held court here, but its eems to me likely that he did.

SANDWICH

This Kentish city seems as important a port as Dover in Malory's tales. Here Arthur left for and returned from his war against the Emperor of Rome [V], and from here to Carlisle Lancelot offered to walk barefoot in penance for the war over Guenevere [XX, 16].

SAPINE† (Sarpenic, Sarpetine)

A forest near the castle of Florega. Probably near Sorelois; possibly near Gore. [Vulgate IV]

SARRAS (Soleise?)

Malory seems to mention Soleise only once, listing it with Denmark, Ireland, the Vale, and the Isle of Longtains [IV, 2]. The inclusion of Denmark and Ireland suggests that the other three were also outside the larger British Isle. The kings of these five countries united to war against Arthur, who defeated and killed them beside the Humber River. The Isle of Man is enough outside Great Britain to count as "foreign," and is in a good position for alliance with Ireland; hence, it might make a good Soleise.

The Isle of Man and the Lake District also work very well together as the Sarras and Waste Lands of the Grail adventures. The Quest of Galahad and his companions ended in Sarras, and from Sarras the Grail was taken into Heaven permanently after Galahad's death. Sarras had religious and mystical associations at least from the time of Joseph of Arimathea. Vulgate I tells us that Sarras was the city from which the Saracens take their name. Evalac was the king of the island and city of Sarras when Joseph came and converted him. The island as a whole, however, does not seem to have been fully converted until Galahad's reign — if then. At the time he and his comrades arrived, Sarras was ruled by an unpleasant Pagan king named Estorause, who threw them into prison. This suggests that Sarras was a political entity as well as a mystical place, and that the secular government was unfriendly to Arthur. If Sarras is identified with Soleise, then Estorause must have succeeded the king whom Arthur and his men killed on the banks of the Humber.

SAUVAGE

I have not yet come across the famous Forest Savage, or Sauvage, in my reading of Malory and the Vulgate, except as part of somebody's name: "Sir So-and-so of the Forest Sauvage." I seem to remember that T. H. White put the Forest Sauvage around Sir Ector's castle when Arthur was growing So far I suspect that "Forest Sauvage" simply means "wild woods" and can be applied to any wooded wilderness.

SCOTLAND

A major kingdom, Scotland probably included the territory from Hadrian's Wall northward, with nine sub-kingdoms: Benoye, Estrangor, Garloth, L'Isle Estrange, The Long Isles, Lothian, The North Marches, Orkney, and Pomitain.

ISLE OF SERVAGE

In Book VIII, 37, Malory calls it an isle. In VIII, 38, he calls it also a valley and places it in Wales.

CASTLE OF THE SEVEN SHIELDS† (Seavenshale, Sewing Shields)

Seven Shields was Sir Walter Scott's choice for the name of this, another site beneath which Arthur and his knights are said to lie sleeping.

It is in Northumberland, on or almost on the Wall, apparently on the northernside; Seven Shields is perhaps ten miles west and slightly north of Hexham on the river Tyne.

"Silver Pipe, Fountain of the" — see FOUNTAIN OF THE SILVER PIPE

Sorelois — see SURLUSE

SORESTAN (Eastland)

According to the Vulgate, Sorestan borders Norgales "par evers" Sorelois (Surluse). I do not know whether this means Sorestan was between Sorelois and Norgales, or Sorelois between Sorestan and Norgales, or both Sorelois and Sorestan bordering Norgales; but I think the last is the most likely, and suggest Sorestan be approximately the rest of Chester excluding the peninsula proposed for Surluse.

In Vulgate V, Morgan, Sebile, and the Queen of Sorestan kidnap Lancelot. This seems to be the episode Malory gives in Book VI, 3-4, although Malory has four queens: Morgan and the Queens of Northgalis, Eastland, and the Out Isles. It seems likely that the Queen of Sorestan should be identified with the Queen of Eastland, and, thus, that Malory's Eastland is the Sorestan of the Vulgate.

Malory's Eastland, on the other hand, might for convenience's sake be considered separately from Sorestan. Using this theory, Lincolnshire might be called Eastland. Or the name might be given to the easternmost bulge of the island, including Norfolk, Suffolk, and Essex (which name, of course, derives from "East Sex"). Eastland might, indeed, include all the counties listed as raised by Mordred in Malory XXI, 26: Kent, Southsex, Surrey, Estsex, Southfolk, and Northfolk, which would all be sub-sub-kingdoms.

SORHAUTE

Malory mentions this in I, 18: "a city that hight Sorhaute, the which city was within King Uriens' [land]." This would put it in Gore. The Vulgate, however, seems to put Sorhaute in Sorelois, or Surluse, Duke Galeholt's favorite sub-kingdom [Vulgate IV]. Malory may be mistaken about placing it in Uriens' hands, or he or his immediate source may have confused the name Sorhaute or a variant thereof with Gohorru, the capital of Gore. I would put Sorhaute in Surluse.

SOUTH MARCHES

Almost certainly the marches of Arthurian Cornwall. Putting them east of Avilion would give Cornwall proper more territory and help fill in more of the central region. Or they might simply be the area south of Avilion to the sea, forming a sort of pass from Logres to Cornwall.

THE SPIRITUAL PALACE†

At the Spiritual Palace of Sarras, Christ consecrated Josephe, son of Joseph of Arimathea, as His first bishop (of Britain?). It was for this reason that Galahad and his companions were directed to take the Grail to Sarras. [Vulgate VI]

STONE CIRCLE

If Stonehenge could be called a pre-Christian cathedral, this small antiquity near Land's End might be called a pre-Christian chapel, and is included as an example of such. If you drew a line from Newlyn or Mousehole to St. Just, westernmost Cornwall, the Stone Circle would be in just about the middle of the land thus marked off. I visited this one several years ago. I had a devil of a time finding it — had to go through a cow field or two — and have had a devil of a time relocating what I think to be the same one on my Ordnance Survey map of Land's End. The antiquity had been cleared out during the early part of our century, and apparently not since. The stones, as I recall, were each one about as tall as a person, and the cir-

cle perhaps as large in area as a good-sized living room; it was a very regular circle, in a good state of preservation, much overgrown with weeds and nettles.

STONEHENGE

According to a tradition which I did not find in Malory, but which is recorded in Vulgate II, Merlin brought Stonehenge from Ireland to Salisbury Plain, moving the stones by magic in order to make them a funerary monument for kings slain in battle. This gives us a lovely magical act, but takes away the grandest of the purely Pagan religious centers. I personally would prefer to keep the magical ability of such mighty necromancers as Merlin to move huge stones, but omit its application to Stonehenge, saving the famous place as Britain's major Pagan (whether Druidical or pre-Druidical) religious center.

Examples of the numerous smaller stone antiquities to be found throughout Britain, Brittany, and so on which might be considered pagan 'chapels,' are the Hurlers, the Nine Sisters, the Stone Circle near Land's End, Plouhinec, and many others not included here.

The Druids, of course, are supposed to have used oak groves, which suggests they did not erect many permanent structures. Some of the forests with 'perilous' or 'magical' properties originally may have been Druid holy places. Modern archaeologists believe that Stonehenge far antedates the Druids.

"CHAPEL OF THE STONY CROSS"

After leaving the hermitage of the Queen of the Waste Lands, Lancelot rode at random (Malory does not specify for how long) into a wild forest, where

> at the last he came to a stony cross which departed two ways in waste land; and by the cross was a stone that was of marble, but it was so dark that Sir Launcelot might not wit what it was.

Looking around, he saw an old chapel. The door was "waste and broken," but within the chapel was a fair altar, richly arrayed with cloth of silk and a silver candlestick holding six candles. Lancelot found no way, however, to get inside, so he returned and slept by the cross. In the night, when he was between sleep and waking, he saw a knight borne to the chapel on a litter. The Grail arrived on a silver table and healed the sick knight. Afterwards, concluding that Lancelot must be in some deadly sin because he had slept through the miracle, the newly-healed knight took Lancelot's helm, sword, and horse. Lancelot then heard a voice speaking to him in symbols. Waking, he found a hermitage on a high hill, where the hermit (Nascien?) expounded the vision. [Malory XIII, 17-20]

My guess is that this chapel was either in or near Listeneise. Cross Fell, near the joining of Durham, Cumberland, and Northumberland counties, might be a good place to put it.

STRAIGHT MARCHES

These would seem to be either the marches between Wales and Logres or those between Logres and Scotland. A nice cordon might be made of Staffordshire, Worcestershire, and Herefordshire or a part thereof, between the sub-kingdoms immediately east of Wales and the sub-kingdoms of Arroy (Warwickshire) and Leicester.

STRANGGORE

Identification of Stranggore as the Swansea peninsula to the east of Pembroke, at the western end of Glamorganshire, Wales, is arbitrary but very hand to the kingdom of Gore.

SUGALES†

I find this name in the Vulgate, although not in Malory. It would, of course, simply be southern Wales.

SURLUSE (Sorelois)

At its border is a fair village with a strong bridge guarded by knights who must be defeated if a person would gain admittance [Malory IX, 7]. Vulgate III amplifies this description. Sorelois, or Surluse, was bordered on one side by the sea, and on the other, towards Arthur's realm, by the Assurne river. It was a delightful and fertile country with many rivers and splendid woods. In earlier days it had had many passages; but King Gloier, Duke Galeholt's predecessor, had limited the passages to two, each one barred by a strong tower, a knight, and ten armed sergeants. These bridges were the Pont Norgalois and the Pont Irois. Any knight defeated while trying to cross either bridge had to stay and help guard it. Galeholt, who conquered Gloier and won Sorelois, seemingly maintained these two passages.

I cannot find any Assurne river; perhaps it is too small for my maps. The name of the Pont Norgalois suggests Norgales. In Volume V, the Vulgate says that Sorestan borders Norgales "par devers" Sorelois. There is a longish, squarish peninsula in Cheshire, between the inlets of the rivers Dee and Mersey, which is far and away my personal favorite for Surluse.

ALEBRE† (Zelegebres, Conlotebre, Conlouzebre)

Arthur summoned the barons of Cermelide (Cameliard) to this city when he acknowledged Genievre, alias "the false Guenevere," as his queen [Vulgate IV]. Presumably it would have been in or near Cameliard.

TANEBORC† (Baillon)

A strong castle at the entrance of Norgales, this may have been one of Arthur's own fortresses. It was, at least, a place at which he stayed sometimes, perhaps even a court city. Here, three days after holding court at Cardiff, at a time when he was preparing for war against King Claudas, Arthur received intelligence of Claudas' own preparations across the Channel. At Taneborc, also, Arthur held at least one tournament, after which he and Guenevere spent the night at his castle of Tauroc. [Vulgate V, VI]

TANINGUES† (Tranurgor)

A squire, Helain de Taningues, held a castle in the neighborhood of Taningues. If Taningues is identified as the peninsula at the western end of Sussex, then the castle might be Chichester (Roman name Noviomagus).

TANINGUES (Tranurgor)

This is mentioned in Vulgate IV. By the name, it would seem to be another "Gore" dukedom, with Brandelis as its Duke. But compare with the other Taningues, just above.

Since Sagremor set out from Camelot forest and encountered Duke Brandelis after several other pavilions and adventures, I would guess Taningues to be in the southern part of the island, possibly one of the promontories on the coast of Southampton or Sussex. I propose the peninsula at the southwest end of Sussex between Chichester and Arundel. Since Arundel is Malory's Magouns Castle, the Taningues border would be south of it.

TARN WADLING† (Tarn Wathelyne) in Inglewood Forest

Arthur met the Grim Baron of Castle Hewin here [Glennie, p. 72]. Inglewood is in Cumberland, south of Carlisle.

TAUROC†

This stronghold of Arthur's must have been handy to Taneborc castle, at the entrance to Norgales. Morgan le Fay had a castle in the woods around Tauroc.

"Between Mold and Denbigh is Moel Arthur, an ancient British fort, defended by two ditches of great length" [Glennie, p. 7]. Mold and Denbigh are in Denbigh county, north Wales. I vote to identify Moel Arthur with Tauroc.

Terican's Hill† — see TURQUINE'S HILL

TERRABIL

This was a second castle of the Duke of Tintagil, ten miles from Tintagil. It had "many issues and posterns out." This was where Gorlois was slain the same night Uther begat Arthur on Igraine in the sister-castle of Tintagil. Arthur later battled and defeated the armies of King Ryons' brother Nero and King Lot in the field before Terrabil, where Lot met his death. [Malory I, 1, 3; II, 10]

When I visited Tintagil in the late 1960's, neither the official guide nor anyone else I questioned had ever heard of Terrabil. John W. Donaldson places it near St. Kew, Cornwall, about midway between Camelford and Padstow. This seems more plausible than a few of Donaldson's other place identifications, especially since Mee, in **The King's England: Cornwall** notes prehistoric earthworks and rumors of Arthurian castles. The best clue I have yet found, however, appears in the **Survey of Cornwall**. Carew identifies Terrabil as adjacent to the town of Launceston, and says that it was from the regard of the castle's triple walls that men so named it. The site appears to be a little farther than ten miles from Tintagil — although not, I think above 20 miles, and miles might have been longer in Malory's day, or Arthur's. Having visited the ruins of grand, dour old Launceston castle, I also believe it to be the bones of Terrabil.

La Terre Foraine — see FOREIGN LAND

Tertre as Caitis† — see DRUAS' HILL

Le Tertre Deuee† — see DEUEE, LE TERTRE

TINTAGIL

Naturally, this dukedom comprises the territory around Tintagil castle, possibly including more or less the whole northern half of present-day Cornwall.

TINTAGIL CASTLE

This famous castle on the north coast of Cornwall still bears its name on modern maps. Here Uther Pendragon begat Arthur on Igraine. The castle later was taken over by a pair of wicked giants whom Lancelot finally slew. Still later, it became one of Mark's strongholds. [Malory I, 3; VI, 11; IX, 39]

TOWER OF LONDON

You may have heard that William the Conqueror put this up. Don't believe it! Malory tells us that Guenevere barricaded herself in the Tower of London to escape Mordred, so it had to have been around in Arthur's time. [Malory XXI, 1]

Seriously, there was a tower here at least from Roman times.

Tower of Marvels† — see under GALAFORT

Tranurgor — see TANINGUES

TREBES†

This apparently was the major castle of King Ban, in France. Near Trebes was Bois en Val, site of the "Lake" where the Damsel of the Lake raised Lancelot. [Vulgate III]

Malory identifies Benwick, King Ban's country, as Beaune or Bayonne [XX, 18]. There is a city of Bayonne on the coast at the southwesternmost part of modern France, just north of the Pyrenees. Perhaps eighty miles east of Bayonne is a city called Tarbes. Could Tarbes derive from Trebes?

CASTEL DEL TRESPAS†

Here Ywaine was imprisoned until the rampaging giant Mauduit should come to fight him [Vulgate V]. Probably it was not too far from the Castle de la Blanche Espine.

If Warbelow Barrow were identified with Blanche Espine, then the Castel del Trespas might be Arthur's Hall.

Arthur's Hall is in Cornwall, about midway between Camelford and Bodmin. Glennie mentions it as a "little entrenchment" not far from Camelford. Norden amplifies the description:

> It is a square plott about 60 foote longe and about 35 foote broad, situate on a playne Mountayne, wrowghte some 3 foote into the grounde; and by reason of the depression of the place, ther standeth a stange or Poole of water, the place sett rounde about with flatt stones ...

Camelford is about a third of the way from Tintagil to Launceston, or some three to four miles.

Tubelle† — see CUBELE

TURNANCE

Malory seems to name this site only once, as an island where Nacien spent eight days, some 40 years after Christ's Passion [Malory XVII, 4]. I surmise, however, that it may be the same island where Percivale spent some time during the Grail Adventures [Malory XIV, 6-10]. If so, it is a likely place to experience visions and temptations when one is questing for the Grail. Turnance figures more extensively in the Vulgate account.

I would suggest identifying it with Lundy Island in the Bristol Channel. See also Mortaise and the Port of Perilous Rock, both described in this section.

TURQUINE'S (Terican's) HILL†

Turquine (Terican in the Vulgate) was the brother of Sir Carados, but in the Vulgate it appears that he did not help keep the Dolorous Tower. Instead, he had his own collection point for vanquished opponents on the hill named for him. Near this hill was a fountain running through a silver tube onto a marble slab and thence into a leaden vessel. The fountain was overshadowed by three pines on which hung the shields, helmets, and lances of the knights Terican had conquered. When Sir Ector de Maris arrived, there were sixty shields, including twenty-four belonging to knights of Arthur's. Also near or more likely on the hill was a stronghold where Terican kept his prisoners. After Lancelot killed Terican, Arthur's knights gave the property to one Count del Parc. [Vulgate V]

The fountain with the silver pipe sounds suspiciously similar to that fountain near which Morgana caused Sir Accolon to awake [Malory IV, 8]. See "Fountain of the Silver Pipe." This fountain was near the castle of Sir Damas, which was two days' journey from Camelot — all of which may help to locate Turquine's Hill and his brother's Dolorous Tower.

> Between Castle Cary and Yeovil, on the escarpment of the oolite, abutting on the plain which extends to Ilchester, is Cadbury, 'a hill of a mile compass at the top, four trenches encircling it, and twixt every of them an earthen wall; the content of it, within about twenty acres full of ruins and reliques of old buildings .... In the fourth ditch is a spring called King Arthur's Well. [Glennie, p. 10]

Cadbury is considered a candidate for Camelot, but it sounds to me like a fine site for Turquine's Hill, with King Arthur's Well as the "Fountain of the Silver Pipe." Yeovil appears to be right on the southern border of Somersetshire and Dorsetshire, which might put it in the Arthurian South Marches.

NCOURTEOUS LADY, CASTLE OF THE"

A knight who accepted the hospitality of this castle would do well to keep his sword handy at all times.

> And so Sir Percivale ... came upon a bridge of stone, and there he found a knight that was bound with a chain fast about the waist unto a pillar of stone ... said that knight: I am a knight of the Table Round, and my name is Sir Persides; and thus by adventure I came this way, and here I lodged in this castle at the bridge foot, and therein dwelleth an uncourteous lady; and because she proffered me to be her paramour, and I refused her, she set her men upon me suddenly or ever I might come to my weapon; and thus they bound me, and here I wot well I shall die but if some man of worship break my bands. [Malory XI, 12]

Percivale broke his bonds, despite the efforts of an armed knight who came riding out of the castle onto the bridge to prevent him. He then made the Uncourteous Lady, who stood in the tower watching them, deliver up all of Persides' servants, and threatened to stay around and fordo her evil customs. Deciding, however, that his present business (looking for Lancelot) was more pressing, he left her alone and spent the night at Persides' castle, which must have been nearby.

The castle of the Uncourteous Lady was in the vicinity of Cardican castle.

From Vulgate V, it appears that the name of this castle may be Garantan. The Vulgate account, however, differs enough from Malory's to make me uncertain.

AGON

Vagon is the name of a city, of a castle, and of the old lord thereof. It seems to have been the knights' first stop after leaving Camelot on the Quest of the Holy Grail. [Malory XIII, 8] It might be identified with Alton or with Basingstoke.

LE VAL SANS RETOUR† (Le Val des Faux Amants)

Apparently Morgan's Chapel stood at the entrance to this beautiful valley, located between Escalon li Tenebreux and the Dolorous Tower.

Twenty years before Lancelot defeated Carados of the Dolorous Tower, Morgan le Fay found her faithless lover in this valley with her rival. She spellcast the valley so that no knight could get out, although all other folk could come and go at will. Only a knight who had always been true in love could deliver the trapped knights.

Sir Galeshin's adventures will serve as an example. He came first to a low gate, where he dismounted. He then passed through a large hall to a vault guarded by two pairs of chained dragons, which attacked only knights, and from which Galeshin's sword rebounded as from an anvil. (Perhaps this gate and hall were Morgan's Chapel.) Next he came to a narrow plank spanning a deep water, where two knights knocked him in. Four men rescued him from the water, took his sword, shield, and helmet, and led him in to meet his fellow prisoners, who included three other companions of the Round Table.

Lancelot, coming through on his way to the Dolorous Tower, slew the dragons and crossed the plank through stratagem. Once over, he looked at his ring, which had the power to dispel enchantments, and the plank with its guarding knights vanished. Lancelot then cut down several apparently real defenders, chasing one down the hall stairs, through a garden, over an enchanted stream, through another large hall, and into the pavilion where Morgan lay asleep. Lancelot slew the refugee and apologized to the enchantress for entering her chamber. Thus did Lancelot break the spell and free the prisoners, including Morgan's faithless lover. In return, however, Morgan kidnapped Lancelot while he slept and imprisoned him, although she let him out for awhile on his parole so that he could kill Sir Carados. [Vulgate IV]

VAMBIERES†

A very strong city, apparently near the city or castle of Clarence. [Vulgate]

VANDALIORS†

According to Malory the rebel kings had to leave off warring with Arthur because the Saracens were besieging their castle of Wandesborow. In the Vulgate, however, the rebel kings were called away from their war with Arthur because the Sesnes, or Saxons, were attacking Vandaliors, in Cornwall (Cornuaille).

Vandaliors sounds as if it could be a variant of Wandesborow, which see, and Malory might have confused the Sesnes with the Saracens in this passage. Nevertheless, I would like to consider Wandesborow and Vandaliors as two separate strongholds. Vandaliors I would put on Mount's Bay, Cornwall, either at Penzance or at the Lizard Head. Since Penzance had not in earlier times the prominence it enjoys today, Lizard Head might be better. Just a little north of Lizard Head up the west coast is Goon-goofe, of which Norden tells us:

> A mountayne by the sea side ... [its name] signifying the hill of bloude. There are auntiente markes of martiall actes, as trenches of Defence, and hills of Burialls.

VERTIGER'S (Vortigern's) TOWER†

According to a tradition not found in Malory, this tower kept falling down. Vortigern's astrologers told him that to stand the masonry required the blood of a father child. Vortigern found the young Merlin, who had been engendered by a devil and thus could be considered fatherless, but Merlin saved himself by making explanations and predictions which were found true. According to Merlin's statement, a lake was discovered beneath the tower. There a red dragon (symbolizing Vortigern) and a white dragon (symbolizing Pandragon and Uther, the two sons of King Constans, whom Vortigern had murdered to gain his power) fought to the death. The white dragon killed the red, but soon afterwards died itself. The sons of Constans burned Vortigern's Tower after they killed him.

Clues in the Vulgate led me to believe that Vertiger's Tower was near Winchester. Because of the name, Din Guortigern, mentioned by Nennius and identified by one Mr. Pearson as on the Teviot River, is another contender. [Glennie, p. xxv]

ALES

A major kingdom in legend and history. Monmouthshire is sometimes included in Wales. For purposes of Arthurian romancing, it seems to me that the entire north-south border might be moved east a little, through about the middle of Herford and Shropshire. Sub-kingdoms of Wales include Cambenet, Escavalon, Gore, Isle of Servage, The Isles, Norgales, Orofoise, Sorestan, The Straight Marches (?), Stranggore, Sugales, and Surluse.

WANDESBOROW

The eleven rebel kings had to leave off warring with Arthur for a time after the battle of Bedegraine when they learned that the Saracens had landed and were besieging their castle of Wandesborow [Malory I, 17-18].

The root "Wand," as I recall, means "white." There is a Whitehaven in Cumberland and a Whitby in Yorkshire. Glennie lists a Caer Vandwy and identifies it as Cramond, near Leith, on the Firth of Forth, Scotland. Whitehaven seems too near King Pellam's territory if that is identified with the Lake District. I would prefer to identify Wandesborow with Caer Vandwy.

It may well be, of course, that Wandesborow and Vandaliors, which see, should be considered identical, in which case the Cornish site whould be taken. It does not seem impossible, though, that the rebel kings were simultaneously or coincidentally attacked by two different foreign enemies at two different strongholds.

THE WASTE LANDS
Grail territory. See Listeneise and Carbonek castle.

The Weeping Castle — see CASTLE PLUERE

WESTMINSTER
The name West Minster dates at least from 875 A.D. in a charter of King Offa. Since Malory uses the name, it seems more than fair for us to use it. The monastery was built on Thornêa, a small island formed by outlets of the Tyburn and a ditch. The Thames was the eastern boundary. The monastery already existed at the time of the charter (perhaps on an old Pagan holy site?). Canute or a predecessor established a royal palace here, and Edward the Confessor built a new church and monastery. The town grew up around the religious establishments. In Arthur's England, London would not yet have engulfed Westminster.

White Abbey — see "ABBEY OF THE ADVENTUROUS SHIELD" and "ABBEY OF THE BURNING TOMB"

WINDESAN (Windesant)
When King Idres was put in the city of Nauntes, King Nentes was put into Windesan with 4000 knights to watch by water and by land [Malory I, 18]. Nentres being king of Garloth, the city of Windesan likely was in or was near his own territory, which probably was in the north, possibly East Lothian. For Windesan I suggest Berwick on Tweed. Glennie (who, however, identifies Berwick with Joyous Garde) describes it as:

crowning ... the northern heights at the mouth of the Tweed, looking eastward on the sea, that dashes up to high caverned cliffs, and commanding westward the vale of the beautiful river, here flowing between steep braes, shadowy with trees, or bright with corn and pasture ..." [p. 63]

WINDESORES†
Its lord was Sinados [Vulgate III]. It may be identical with Wandesborow, Vandaliors, or both. Or, perhaps more likely, it may be a variant spelling for Windsor. Norden lists a Windesore which is a mile or two inland from New Quay, on the north coast of Cornwall, "the howse of Mr. Windesore, situate amonge the minerall hills."

WINDSOR
Malory tosses in the name in XVIII, 2. Windsor castle was founded by William I on the site of an earlier fortress.

Windsor Forest is around Windsor Castle. In **The Merry Wives of Windsor**, Shakespeare preserves for facetious perposes the tradition of Herne the Hunter, who haunts this woods; and Ainsworth, in **Windsor Castle**, one of his better historical romances, uses Herne for more genuinely ghostly effects.

ORK
Malory tells us that Arthur held a parliament here [V, 3], sufficient grounds for assuming he also held court at York, the traditional great city of the north. York is inland on the Ouse river, which flows into the Humber.

TOURNAMENTS AND JOUSTING
Tournaments were obviously rough. At that of Winchester, Lancelot

> gave Sir Bors such a buffet that he made him bow his head passing low; and therewithal he raced off his helm, and might have slain him ... and in the same wise he served Sir Ector and Sir Lionel. For as the book saith he might have slain them, but when he saw their visages his heart might not serve him thereto, but left them there. [Malory XVIII, 11]

I should hope his heart might not serve — they were his close kinsmen! Still, it is hardly surprising that we often read in the romances of knights (usually minor characters) having been slain in tournament.

Sometimes tournaments seem to fill the function, more or less, of wars fought between two kings by appointment. A peculiarity of most tournaments, however, seems to have been that a knight could enter on the side that seemed weaker, even against his own sovereign, in order to win greater glory for himself. If, during the melee, it seemed that his chosen side was winning too easily (possibly because of his own efforts), he could honorably change sides. This appears to have been a recognized means of enhancing one's glory as a fighter; the greatest knights of the Round Table indulged in it. (One conjures up visions of football-players-errant, probably mostly backs, travelling around from game to game entering each contest under the above rules of side-choosing and side-changing.)

At one tournament, Lancelot struck Bors saddle and all to the ground. Gawaine, watching this, remarked that Bors was "unhorsed, but not dishonoured" [Vulgate VI, p. 212]. Apparently, if you went down in a joust because your saddle (or presumably — by extension — your horse) failed, you lost no honor. I rather doubt that this rule held true in the failing of lances, for it often seems the usual outcome of a joust that Sir X's lance breaks but Sir Y's lance holds, in which case Sir Y almost automatically bears Sir X to the earth.

Heralds to announce combatants and to cry "Lesses les aler"

("Lessez-les aller" — "Let them go!") and "knights parters of the field" are mentioned in the combat between Lancelot and Meliagrant [Malory XIX, 9]. Though this was a trial by combat, heralds and knights parters must have been found also at tournaments. In this particular combat, the knights parters took off half of Lancelot's armor and bound his left hand behind his back as the conditions upon which Meliagrant agreed to continue the battle — this must have been a rather unusual duty for the knights parters. When Palomides kept his appointment to fight Tristram one time that Tristram failed to appear, the Saracen knight brought with him four knights of Arthur's court and three sergeants-of-arms to "bear record of the battle ... And the one sergeant brought in his helm, the other his spear, the third his sword." [Malory X, 88] Though this was a single combat of the type that may have given rise to the duel of later centuries, sergeants-of-arms would surely also have served at tournaments.

Killing horses in battle seems to have been considered all right in warfare (as, presumably, against Saxons) but it was understandably frowned upon in "friendly" fighting such as that of tournaments. At the Lonazep tournament,

> Sir Palomides rushed unto Sir Launcelot, and thought to have put him to a shame; and with his sword he smote his horse's neck that Sir Launcelot rode upon, and then Sir Launcelot fell to the earth. Then was the cry huge and great: See how Sir Palomides the Saracen hath smitten down Sir Launcelot's horse. Right then were there many knights wroth with Sir Palomides because he had done that deed; therefore many knights held there against that it was unknightly done in a tournament to kill an horse wilfully, but that it had been done in plain battle, life for life. [Malory X, 70]

The incident is perplexing in that Palomides generally seems a more courteous knight. Perhaps, as a Saracen, he retained memories of Arthur's knights slaying horses in plain battle with his own people and did not quite as yet understand the tournament distinction. Or possibly the killing of horses in the lists was prohibited by an unwritten rather than an official rule.

III. Things

Introduction

A GLANCE at the list of Categories of Things on the opposing page will show the scope of this section: a selection of noteworthy weapons and other tools, obstacles, prizes, quest objects, and so on, that entered the lives of Arthurian people. Many of these items are unique, like the Holy Grail; some are types, like Elaine's Sleeve; a few of the notes provide limited observations on the uses of a general class of things, like Rings. The notes are arranged alphabetically under the first distinctive word. For instance, look under "B" for King Ban's Crown. Many of the entry names have been manufactured for the sake of convenience, usually from the name of a prominent user, because the author or compiler often neglected to give such items names of their own. Hence the usefulness of the categories list.

In this section, as in the others, a dagger after the entry name indicates that the thing (or at least that particular name for the thing) is not found in Malory.

Some items may be magical or mystical, but this can be a tricky judgment. Some items may have supernatural properties which my sources did not make apparent. For instance, what about a shield made by Morgan le Fay but which seems to have only natural properties? And what of a thing like the Sign of the Cross, a gesture readily available to anyone — at least to any Christian mortal with a hand — but which has strong power over devils? Some "sorcerous" preparations may depend on mere natural herbs and drugs rather than on what we nowadays consider magic.

This section is not meant as an exhaustive essay in social history, but as a selective supplement. For instance, the note on Gloves gives only a reference to limited ceremonial or symbolic uses, without considering the history, utility, and fashion of gloves as articles of clothing.

CATEGORIES OF THINGS

BOOKS and WRITINGS
Book of the Four Evangelists
Helyes' Book
Book Containing the History of the Grail
Letters in General

COATS OF ARMS
Coats of Arms (main entry,
with following sub-entries:
Arthur
Bagdemagus
Balan
Balin
King Ban
Bedivere
Bors
Breuse Sans Pitie
La Cote Male Taile
Ector de Maris
Epinegris
Galahad
Gareth
Gawaine
The Green Knight
Ironside
Lamorak
Lancelot
Lionel
Mordred
Morgana
Palomides
Pelleas
King Pellinore
Percivale
Persides de Bloise
Priamus
The Queen's Knights
Tristram
Ywaine
Unnamed Welsh Knight

CROWNS
King Ban's Crown
A Crown of Gold

FURNITURE
Merlin's Bed
Perilous Bed

GARMENTS
Prince Boudwin's Doublet and Shirt
Coat (or Kirtle) of the Giant of
St. Michael's Mount
Elaine's Sleeve
Gawaine's Girdle
Gloves in General
The Magic Mantle
Morgan's Mantle
King Ryon's Mantle

THE HOLY GRAIL (Sangreal)
The Holy Grail (Sangreal)
A Holy Herb
Longinus' Spear
A Silver Table

HORNS
Cuckold's Horn
Horn of Elephant's Bone
An Ivory Horn
Morgan's Drinking Horn

MISCELLANEOUS WEAPONS
A Club of Iron
Wild-Fire

RINGS
Rings
Lancelot's Ring
Love Ring(s)
Lyonors' Ring
Morgan's Ring

THE ROUND TABLE
The Round Table
The Siege Perilous
Other Sieges of the Round Table

SHIELDS
The Adventurous Shield
Gawaine's Shield
Guenever's Shield
Maledisant's Shield
Morgan's Shield
Pridwen
Shields
Three Silver Shields

SHIPS
Ships
King Solomon's Ship

SORCEROUS PREPARATIONS
Love Potion
Morgan's Powder
Priamus' Balm
Sleeping Potion
Sorcerous Preparations

SPEARS
Longinus' Spear
(The Spear of Vengeance)
Ron

SWORDS AND SCABBARDS
Balin's Sword
The Broken Sword Wherewith Joseph
was Stricken Through the Thigh
Coreuseuse
King David's Sword (The Sword with
the Strange Girdle) and Scabbard
Excalibur (Caliburn) and Scabbard
Galatine
Gareth's (?) Sword
Percivale's Sword
Priamus' Sword
King Ryons' Sword
Sequence
Swords and Scabbards

OTHER GENERAL
Money
Olive Branches
The Sign of the Cross
Wine

OTHER SPECIFIC
Dragon Banner
A Magic Chessboard
Tristram's Harp

III · THINGS

DVENTUROUS SHIELD, THE

Josephe, son of Joseph of Arimathea, converted King Evelake, giving him the baptismal name Mordrains, and helped him win a war against King Tolleme. The war was won partly with the help of this shield, which had a sweet aroma and of which it was said that it would render its bearer victorious and be the cause of many miracles. At the time of Mordrains' war against Tolleme, the shield bore the figure of Christ on the Cross, and touching this image healed at least one man's battle wound. Thereafter the image disappeared, leaving the shield white as snow. When Josephe lay on his death bed, he marked the shield anew with a cross drawn with the crimson of his nosebleed. He left the shield, so marked, as a token for Mordrains, who was to leave it in his turn in the same abbey where lay Nascien the Hermit, there to await Galahad. [Vulgate I and VI]

Only Galahad could take the Adventurous Shield. Anyone else who tried to bear it away would be killed or maimed within three days. A White Knight, apparently an angel waiting to avenge the shield, struck down and wounded King Bagdemagus two miles from the hermitage when he tried taking it. [Malory XIII, 9-11]

ALIN'S SWORD

An (apparently) wicked damsel wore this sword to Arthur's court, claiming that only a passing good knight of his hands and deeds, one who was without villainy and of gentle blood on both sides, could pull it out and free her of the encumbrance. This is a classic type of test for knightly virtue; but in this case it seems to have been a trap to get Balin to draw the sword and with it slay the damsel's brother, who had killed her sweetheart. Yet, when Balin drew it, she requested it back, saying that if he kept it, it would be the destruction of him and the man he loved most in the world. This prediction came true when Balin and Balan, not knowing each other, gave each other their death wounds in battle.

Merlin put a new pommel on Balin's sword and put it in a block of floating red marble. He also left the scabbard at the castle where Balin was buried, for Galahad to find. [Malory II, 19; see also Meliot, *Places*]

When Galahad arrived in Camelot some years later, he was already wearing the empty scabbard, having apparently picked it up on his way. The sword had just come floating down to Camelot in its block of marble, for the court to marvel at it and read in golden letters on its jewel-decked pommel: "Never shall man take me hence, but only he by whose side I ought to hang, and he shall be the best knight of the world." Lancelot had refused to make the attempt, remarking that whoever tried and failed would receive a grievous wound of that sword. At Arthur's urging, Gawaine reluctantly made the attempt, for which, sure enough, the sword later wounded him. Percivale also made the attempt, but, being almost as pure as Galahad, suffered no retribution from this sword. (However, he did wound himself in the thigh with his own sword in self-penance for having almost been seduced by the fiend.) Galahad, of course, drew the sword. [Malory XIII, 2-5]

Merlin had also predicted that with Balin's Sword Lancelot would slay the man whom he loved best, which was Gawaine. Either there is a confusion here between Lancelot and his son — for it is Galahad who deals Gawaine a grievous, not a mortal, wound with Balin's Sword [Malory XVII, 1] — or else Galahad sent the sword back by Sir Bors to his father Lancelot, who later used it in the fatal combat with Gawaine.

KING BAN'S CROWN

When Gwenbaus decided to stay behind in Britain with his princess in the Forest Perilous (or Forest Perdue), his brother King Ban left his crown with them. Gwenbaus enchanted the forest grove. The crown may not have been magical in itself, but it gained a magical association; the enchantment was not broken until Lancelot came, sat in the chair, and wore the crown. [Vulgate V]

A BOOK CONTAINING THE HISTORY OF THE GRAIL†
Christ Himself wrote this book [Vulgate I].

THE BOOK OF THE FOUR EVANGELISTS (The Gospels)
Oaths were sworn upon this [cf. Malory III, 15]. Possibly any book may be used for swearing oaths upon.

[Lancelot] made bring forth a book [and said] Here we are ten knights that will swear upon a book never to rest one night where we rest another this twelvemonth until that we find Sir Tristram. [Malory IX, 36]

PRINCE BOUDWIN'S DOUBLET AND SHIRT

Boudwin was murdered by his brother, King Mark. Boudwin's widow Anglides kept the bloody garments to give her son Alisander when he grew up and was of an age to think about avenging his father. [Malory X, 32-35]

This is similar to Sir La Cote Mal Taile's wearing the coat in which his father was murdered until he could avenge that deed [Malory IX, 1].

THE BROKEN SWORD WHEREWITH JOSEPH WAS STRICKEN THROUGH THE THIGH

At Mategrant's castle, in Broceliande, the seneschal broke this sword while wounding Joseph of Arimathea in the thigh with it. Joseph miraculously extracted the broken piece of metal from his wound and predicted that the sword would never be joined until the one handled it who would achieve the Grail. The broken sword was held in great honor at Mategrant's castle, at least for a while. [Vulgate I] Later, Sir Eliazer brought it from Mategrant's castle to Carbonek [Vulgate IV].

Malory omits this early history of the sword, but tells how Eliazer, Pellam's son, brought it forth for Galahad and his companions to attempt mending it. After Bors and Percivale tried unsuccessfully, Galahad soldered the broken pieces by simply setting them together with his hands. [Malory XVII, 19]

Kissing this sword would keep whoever kissed it safe from being mortally wounded for the day [Vulgate IV].

LUB OF IRON

After killing the Giant of St. Michael's Mount, Brittany, Arthur kept the giant's iron club as a trophy [Malory V, 5].

COATS OF ARMS

Recognizing knights by their coats of arms was tricky. Tragic as the outcome could be when knights did not carry their own shields, especially in a social milieu where the rule seemed to be to interact first and ask names later, if at all, the practice of bearing somebody else's shield remained popular. A knight might borrow the shield of a friend or help himself to the shield of a defeated foe. Lancelot was especially fond of using an anonymous or a borrowed shield. On one occasion, he saved Kay from attackers, then got up early in the morning, while Kay was still asleep, and took Kay's arms. Kay, riding back to Camelot with Lancelot's shield perforce, arrived unmolested, since knights had already learned better than to meddle with Lancelot; Lancelot, meanwhile, being mistaken for the unpopular Kay, took the chance to leave a trail of unhorsed opponents behind him.

For anonymity, a knight could carry a plain-colored shield (white, black, green, red, and so on), or cover his shield, or even, apparently do both at once! Anonymous shields seem to have been very popular with villainous knights. Where the only thing mentioned about a knight's shield was its color, I usually assumed it was simply the knight's current anonymous shield and did not make a special note of it for this entry. In many cases, the knight's designation – "The Brown Knight Without Pity," "The Black Knight," and so on – tells the color of his shield. Numerous references suggest also that armor was painted, at least sometimes, and not uniformly colored silver or gold as we usually think of it.

Blank shields, usually white but sometimes red (according to Vulgate VI), and presumably any other tincture, were carried by young knights in their first year of knighthood, before they had earned the right to bear a device. Thus, when established knights disguised themselves with blank shields of any color, they would seem to have been disguising their skill and experience as well as their identities. A knight like Lancelot would do this in order to attract more attackers and thus win greater honor; a knight like Breuse Sans Pitie would do it in order to trick potential victims into a false sense of security.

Plain white shields were also used by the Queen's Knights, a sort of secondary company (secondary, that is, to the Round Table) of Arthur's court.

Because it was such common practice to use an anonymous or borrowed shield, knights sometimes resorted to other devices in order to identify themselves. In one tournament, the companions of the Round Table wore round leather badges so as to know each other. Guenever finally insisted Lancelot start wearing her favor in tournaments so that his relatives would know him and not gang up on him as they had done with almost fatal result to the great knight at Winchester.

Miller states that it was Matthew Paris, a St. Albans monk, who first set down a list of Arthurian blazons in the year 1252, and that many such books were made in later years. Unfortunately, I had no access to such a roster. To eke out Malory's scanty information about coats of arms, I have used much later material as source matter in this than in any other section, even citing the opinions of Tennyson and his fairly recent illustrator Robert Ball. The process turned up several blazons for some major knights and none at all for many other important figures; nor are all the devices hereunder described necessarily meant to have been blazoned on the knight's shield. Punning, I think I read somewhere years ago, was popular; thus, for instance, Sir Kay might be given a key on his shield.

I did not attempt to master all heraldic terms, and tried to describe the devices in terms that do not require specialized knowledge for comprehension. Many treatises on heraldry exist to be consulted for deeper knowledge. Nevertheless, a rundown on the tinctures might be useful. I also list how the tinctures are traditionally shown in black-and-white engraver's practice. Color should not be put on color, nor metal on metal, unless the figure is outlined in the opposing tincture. For instance, a red sword should not be put directly on a black field, (both red and black being colors); but if the red sword were outlined in one of the metals, gold or silver, then it could go on the black field.

ARTHUR

According to Geoffrey of Monmouth, he wore a gold helmet with a crest carved in the shape of a dragon, and carried a circular shield called Pridwen, on which was painted a likeness of the Blessed Virgin, "which forced him to be thinking perpetually of her."

> By mid-13th century, however, Arthur's usual blazon consists of three crowns, normally *pale on azure* (silver on blue) but sometimes *or en gules* (gold on red); in late medieval days the number of crowns is raised to thirteen. [Miller, 150-151]

The crowns need not replace the image of the Virgin if, like his nephew Gawaine, Arthur carried the Virgin on the inside of his shield. Miller shows a picture, apparently a miniature from a manuscript in the British Museum, of Arthur with a Virgin and Child on the front of his shield; nevertheless, if he carried her image as a reminder to himself, it would probably make more sense to carry it on the side of the shield facing him and not his foes.

An elongated triangular shield is now usually associated with knights.

BAGDEMAGUS

Lancelot recognized Bagdemagus' pavilion by the golden eagle on top [Vulgate IV].

BALAN

Robert Ball gives him a light-colored shield with a thin line a few inches from the edge running around the shield and a circular boss surrounded by (six?) small dots or studs. This, however, looks suspiciously like an anonymous type of shield — decorated, but not distinctively nor with a blazon.

BALIN

Ball gives him a light-colored shield with a crown across the upper third. According to Tennyson's text, Balin had begged of Guenever "to bear her own crown-royal upon shield" and been granted the favor, thus replacing "this rough beast upon my shield, // Langued gules and tooth'd with grinning savagery." [Balin and Balan]

KING BAN

"Bands of green and thereupon gold" [Malory I, 16].

BEDIVERE

Robert Ball does not show his shield, but on the breast of his light-colored tunic shows three medieval-style flowers or rosettes, with five petals each, light-colored with a small dark leaf between every two petals, the flowers arranged in a triangle pointing downward.

SIR BORS

White with a red lion [Vulgate V]. Tennyson puts a pelican on his casque [The Holy Grail].

BREUSE SANS PITIE

"A shield with a case of red over it" [Malory X, 65]. This sounds like another example of an anonymous shield or shield covering.

LA COTE MAL TAILE

Black, with a white band holding a sword in the middle. Actually, this was the shield brought to court by the damsel Maledisant, who was looking for a knight to fulfill the dead original owner's quest; and it may be a flight of desperation to assume that La Cote Mal Taile kept it as his own device afterwards. [Malory IX, 2]

ECTOR DE MARIS

"A green shield and therein a white lion" [Malory X, 83].

EPINEGRIS

"A bended shield of azure" [Malory X, 65].

GALAHAD

A white shield with a red cross in the midst. This was the Adventurous Shield, which only he could carry. The rest of Galahad's armor was red (cf. Malory XIII, 3).

Robert Ball gives Galahad a light unicorn, rampant, facing to the onlooker's right, on a dark background, the lower tip of the shield separated by a straight horizontal line in order to provide a light background for a small decorative Moline cross. The unicorn would have been the symbol of virginity.

GARETH

During the tournament at Castle Dangerous, early in his career, Gareth uses Lyonors' magic ring to make his armor seem to change color (see Lyonors' Ring). When his dwarf craftily sends Gareth back into the melee after a water break without the ring, Arthur, recognizing the young knight by his hair, remarks, "before he was in so many colours, and now he is in but one colour; that is yellow." Yellow, then, may have been Gareth's usual color. On the other hand, this would have been during Gareth's first year of knighthood, when a knight usually bore blank arms.

Name	Description	How Engraved	DESCRIBING COATS OF ARMS
METALS			
Or	Gold, or yellow	Dots	
Argent	Silver, or white	Left plain in engraving	
COLORS			
Gules	Red (apparently, bright red)	Vertical lines	
Azure	Blue	Horizontal lines	
Sable	Black	Horizontal and vertical lines crossing one another	
Vert, or Sinople	Green	Diagonal lines from dexter to sinister	
Purpure	Purple	Diagonal lines from sinister to dexter	
Sanguine	Murrey-color; i.e., purplish-red or blood-color	Combination of Vert and Purpure	
Tenny	Tawny, i.e., orange-brown or bright chestnut	Diagonal lines sinister to dexter, crossed by others either vertically or horizontally (opinion differs)	
FURS			
Ermine		White with black dots of a distinctive shape	
Vair (squirrel)		Bell- or cup-shaped spaces of two or more tinctures, usually but not necessarily azure and argent	

Many varieties of each fur exist, in various colors; though ermine and vair are the most prominent, they are not necessarily the only furs.

Dexter – right   Sinister – left

GAWAINE

Gold pentangle on gules (red), with an image of the Virgin on the inside of the shield.

Some years ago I had ideas of collecting all the various coats of arms romancers through the ages, down to Howard Pyle and Hal Foster, have assigned Gawaine; where so many knights seem never to be given any coats of arms, Gawaine has a surplus. But perhaps the best plan is to stick with his device as so lovingly and emphatically described in **Sir Gawaine and the Green Knight.**

Vulgate VII, p. 67, gives Gawaine

le lion dor en lescu mi parti le champ dargent & de synople & une bende blanche de besengnis [?] au lion rampant corone.

The description appears again on p. 307, with a little variation:

Un escu mi parti dor & dazur a un lion rampant corone de sinople a une bende blanche de bellic

The only word of which I can make nothing at all is "besengnis," which I take to be an heraldic term referring to the bend. Of the first description I make, "On a field of mixed silver and green [probably a type of vair], a gold lion rampant, crowned, and a white bend." Perhaps "besengnis" places the bend either above or below the lion. Of the second description, "on a field of mixed gold and blue [probably vair with a different color combination], a lion rampant, crowned with green, on [and?] a white bend 'de bellic' " — red (see note on Lancelot's arms, below). Perhaps the bend is two-colored or striped, white above and red beneath.

Leaving Gawaine his gold pentangle on gules, I would suggest, if no other devices appear for his brothers, that the lion rampant in one color combination might be given to Gareth, in another color combination to Agravaine or Gaheris. On the other hand, lions for the Orkney brothers might be dangerous, with so many lions among the devices of Lancelot's kin.

IRONSIDE

Shield: azure with a griffin and fleur-de-lis. Crest: a golden lion. **[Sir Gawaine and the Carl of Carlisle]**

LAMORAK

"A shield of silver and lion's heads" [Malory X, 13-14]. Actually, it is Palomides who appears carrying this shield, but Dinadan pursues the knight bearing said shield under the impression he is Lamorak. Lamorak appears in Malory X, 17 carrying a red shield, and in X, 21 he covers the red shield with leather; but I assume the red shield is for anonymity, and the leather cover for anonymity piled on anonymity.

LANCELOT

After conquering and disenchanting Dolorous/Joyous Garde, his shield was white with a black band [Vulgate III]. I assume that the white shield of his first year of knighthood was given the black device for his great deed.

As Le Chevaler Mal Fet, he used

A shield all of sable, and a queen crowned in the midst, all of silver, and a knight clean armed kneeling afore her [Malory XII, 6].

This lasts a year or three, until Ector de Maris and Percivale find him at the Castle of Bliant and persuade him to return to Arthur's court.

Malory does not give Lancelot a device for more normal times, but Miller says,

sometimes it is a white shield with one, or on occasion three, dark red bands; in one manuscript his shield and horse-trappings bear a heart. [p. 151†]

In Vulgate VI, Lancelot appears on at least one occasion carrying white arms with four *bendes de bellye en lescu*. Sommer explains in a note, *terme de blason, couleur rouge dite aussi gueule.*

Robert Ball, following Tennyson's cue, gives Lancelot three crowned lions rampant, facing to the onlooker's left, dark on a light background, forming a triangle on the shield. "Sir Lancelot's azure lions, crown'd with gold, // Ramp[ant] in the field," as Tennyson puts it. **[Lancelot and Elaine]**

LIONEL

Lancelot's cousin Lionel would almost surely have a lion on his shield.

MORDRED

"A shield of silver and black bends" [Malory X, 12], and "black bended shield" [Malory X, 13]. But see Morgan, just below.

MORGAN

One of Morgan le Fay's knights appears bearing "a shield bended with black and with white" to joust against Sir Lamorak [Malory X, 18]. I say "one of Morgan's knights" because he issues out of her castle; but the description of the shield matches that which Malory has given Mordred to carry only a few chapters earlier, although I find no other indication that the anonymous knight of X, 18 is Mordred. Perhaps the reader is supposed to recognize Mordred by the shield; or perhaps the device is Morgan's and for some reason Mordred had allied himself with her and carried her "livery" for a while.

PALOMIDES

"Indented with white and black" [Malory IX, 36]. Later, Palomides seems to have changed his device:

So then Palomides disguised himself in this manner, in his shield he bare the Questing Beast, and in all his trappings [Malory X, 41].

The Questing Beast had a head like a serpent's, a body like a leopard's, buttocks like a lion's, and feet like a hart's.

PELLEAS

Robert Ball does not show his shield, but on the breast of his light-colored tunic there appears to be a dark swan, facing toward his right shoulder.

KING PELLINORE

"A shield of divers colours" [Malory I, 22].

PERCIVALE

Robert Ball gives him a large crowned lion, rampant, facing the onlooker's left, light on a dark field.

PERSIDES DE BLOISE

"Green shield and therein a lion of gold" [Malory IX, 28].

PRIAMUS

"Three griffins of gold, in sable carbuncle, the chief of silver" [Malory V, 9].

THE QUEEN'S KNIGHTS

When acting in their capacity as Queen's Knights, they carried plain white shields [Malory XIX, 1]

TRISTRAM

"A shield of Cornwall" [Malory IX, 23 and *passim*]. A shield of Cornwall has fifteen circles or balls arranged in a down-pointing triangle like bowling pins or marbles on a

Chinese checkers board, from five balls in the top row to one at the point, pretty well covering the shield as the stars cover the blue on Old Glory. I am not sure of the exact colors, but if my illustration follows traditional engraver's usage, the balls are silver and the field is blue.

Malory also gives Tristram "trappings decorated with crowns" [IX, 23]. The trappings, perhaps, were decorated differently from the shield, for at this point Tristram was carrying his "shield of Cornwall," which he refused to lend Dinadan even temporarily: "I will not depart from my shield for her sake that gave it me," probably Queen Isoud of Cornwall.

> Tristram's lion appears against different colored backgrounds; it is rampant [in at least one source]. In Germany, his animal is a boar. [Miller, p. 152]

Lions seem overpopular on shields. If giving Tristram another than the shield of Cornwall, I would go for the boar.

> ... armour'd all in forest green, whereon
> There tript a hundred tiny silver deer,
> And wearing but a holly-spray for crest,
> With ever-scattering berries, and on shield
> A spear, a harp, a bugle – Tristram ...
> [Tennyson, **Idylls: The Last Tournament**]

Robert Ball does not show his shield, but covers his dark tunic with light-colored stags courant, running towards his right side.

YWAINE

Probably, from the companionable lion whom Chrétian de Troyes gave Ywaine as a friend and protector, Ywaine would have worn a lion on his shield.

AN UNNAMED WELSH KNIGHT

"Green, with a maiden that seemed in it" [Malory XVIII, 23]. Gareth borrowed this shield at a tournament held on Candlemas day.

COREUSEUSE†

King Ban's sword [Vulgate II]. Perhaps it passed down to Lancelot?

THE COAT (Kirtle) OF THE GIANT OF ST. MICHAEL'S MOUNT, BRITTANY

This was decked with gems and embroidered with the beards of fifteen kings whom the giant had vanquished. Arthur kept it, along with the giant's iron club, as a souvenir after killing him. [Malory V, 5]

A CROWN OF GOLD

After being made knight by Galahad, Sir Melias rode into an old forest, where he found a lodge of boughs. Inside this lodge, on a chair, was a subtly-wrought crown of gold. Melias took the crown, and almost at once was accosted by another knight, who fought him for taking what was not his, won back the crown, and left Melias wounded until Galahad came and found him again. [Malory XIII, 13-14] This happens during the Grail adventures. The crown symbolizes worldly pride and covetousness, and may be an illusory temptation rather than an actual physical object.

CUCKOLD'S HORN†

No man who was a cuckold could drink from this horn without spilling the beverage. See under Magic Mantle.

AVID'S SWORD AND SCABBARD, KING

Balin's sword was Galahad's first sword. Galahad's second sword was King David's Sword, which he found on Solomon's Ship, which see.

DRAGON BANNER†

Merlin gave Arthur this banner for his battle against the rebel kings. It was sometimes carried in battle by Sir Kay, sometimes by Merlin himself. On at least one occasion when Merlin was bearing it, the dragon on the banner spat fire and flame; this, however, may have been a specific magical act of Merlin's rather than a property of the banner itself. [Vulgate II]

LAINE'S SLEEVE

In the tournament at Winchester, Lancelot wore the token of Elaine of Astolat, a scarlet sleeve embroidered with pearls. Lancelot did this to insure his incognito, since he was well-known never to have worn anybody's token before. Elaine might have broken her heart for love of him even had he refused to accept her token; but, of course, it caused Guenever much pain, anger, and jealousy when she learned of it. [Malory XVIII, 9-15]

EXCALIBUR (Caliburn) and SCABBARD

Arthur's great sword. Unfortunately, Malory gives two accounts of its origin: as the sword Arthur drew out of the stone and anvil to prove his right to be King, and as the sword Arthur rowed across the Lake to receive from the mysterious arm — which apparently belonged to a damsel of the Lady of the Lake. Unless postulating that between these two events Excalibur was lost (a loss of such magnitude that Malory should have mentioned it), I see no way to reconcile the versions and still keep both swords Excalibur. (John Boorman's film **Excalibur**, however, reconciles the versions deftly.)

In the Vulgate cycle, Arthur gives Excalibur to his favorite nephew, Gawaine, who then consistently uses it throughout. Malory knows nothing of this, but gives Gawaine a sword named Galatine. Galatine might be considered the sword Arthur drew from the stone and then gave to Gawaine when he himself received Excalibur from the Lady of the Lake.

Also according to the Vulgate, Arthur seems to have had a second sword, named Sequence. This might be identified with the sword from the stone. The reason Arthur chose to keep the first sword and give Gawaine the one he had received from the Lady of the Lake might have been to prevent another such incident as Morgana's attempt to kill Arthur by means of a counterfeit Excalibur.

Merlin warned Arthur during the war with the rebel kings that the sword from the stone was not to be drawn until Arthur's moment of greatest need. When Arthur drew it, at the time the battle was going against him, the sword "was so bright in his enemies' eyes, that it gave a light like thirty torches," enabling him to win the battle [Malory I, 9].

After this it seems to have settled down and been merely a tremendously good weapon, not a preternaturally luminous one. Regarding the appropriateness, however, of Gawaine's being given a sword that on at least one occasion shone as brightly as thirty torches — if the sword from the stone is considered as the one Arthur gave him — it is a fairly common theory that Gawaine descends from a solar deity.

In the Vulgate, where Gawaine continues to use Excalibur in the war against Lancelot, Arthur apparently takes it back after Gawaine's death. Here, as in Malory, it is Excalibur that Arthur commands his last knight to throw into the water after the final battle. In the Vulgate account, Arthur regrets that Lancelot cannot have the sword, for Lancelot alone is now worthy of it. [Vulgate VI]

The scabbard of Excalibur, "heavy of gold and precious stones," was, in Merlin's opinion, worth ten of the sword, because as long as a fighter had the scabbard upon him, he would lose no blood, no matter how severely wounded [Malory I, 25; IV, 14]. The importance of the scabbard is an argument for making Excalibur the sword given by the Lady of the Lake, since it is more difficult to account for a scabbard belonging specifically to a sword that appeared sheathed in stone and anvil. Morgana stole this scabbard and threw it into a convenient body of water fairly early in Arthur's career [Malory IV, 14].

ALATINE
Sir Gawaine's sword [Malory V, 6]. See the note for Excalibur, this section.

GARETH'S (?) SWORD
Sir Gringamore, brother of Dames Lyonors and Lynette, gave this, "a noble sword that sometime Sir Gringamore's father won upon an heathen tyrant," to Sir Gareth; or, perhaps, merely lent it for the tournament at Castle Dangerous [Malory VII, 27].

GAWAINE'S GIRDLE†
The wife of Sir Bertilak de Hautdesert pressed Gawaine to accept her sash of green silk, richly embroidered in gold, as a love token, assuring him that it would save its wearer from all injury. Since he had to offer his neck to the Green Knight's axe next day, the promise of a sash that might save him from injury proved too tempting to resist.

Whether the girdle actually had this saving property is in doubt, since while Gawaine wore it the Green Knight did draw blood. Gawaine determined to wear the sash ever afterwards, obliquely across his chest, as a reminder of his failing. The rest of Arthur's court thought he had done rather well and determined to wear similar sashes to honor him. This was the origin of the Order of the Garter. [**Sir Gawaine and the Green Knight**]

GAWAINE'S SHIELD†
According to **Sir Gawaine and the Green Knight**, Gawaine had an image of the Virgin Mary painted on the inside of his shield, to inspire him in battle. Possibly he had taken the idea from his royal uncle's shield, Pridwen.

GIRDLES FOR KING DAVID'S SWORD
See under Solomon's Ship.

GLOVES IN GENERAL
Gloves may be given as pledges and as challenges to trial by combat.

> Hold, said Sir Meliagrance, here is my glove that [Guenever] is traitress unto my lord, King Arthur, and that this night one of the wounded knights lay with her. And I receive your glove, said Sir Lancelot. And so they were sealed with their signets, and delivered unto the ten [wounded] knights. [Malory XIX, 7]

GUENEVERE'S SHIELD†
This shield showed an armed knight and a beautiful lady embracing, but separated by a cleft down the middle, the cleft being wide enough for a person to place one hand through it without touching either side. The French Damsel of the Lake sent the shield to Guenever, to help her in the greatest pain and cause her the greatest joy. The cleft in the shield was to close when the knight had gained the lady's complete love and was a member of Arthur's court. At this time, although he had been dubbed by Arthur and had already pledged his love in person to Guenever, Lancelot was still adventuring around the country.

During the siege of La Roche, the crack was closed. While Arthur was Camille's prisoner in that castle, the French Damsel of the Lake came to counsel Guenever to love Lancelot with all her heart. After the fighting, Lancelot finally became a member of Arthur's court. [Vulgate III]

GUENEVERE'S SLEEVE
Guenever gave Lancelot a sleeve of gold to wear on his helmet at tournaments so that his kinsmen would know him. Lancelot apparently wore it from then on. What else could he do, after not only wearing Elaine of Astolat's sleeve at the tournament of Winchester, but being grievously wounded by his cousin Sir Bors, who did not know him, in that same tourney? All of which had caused Guenever to insist he now take her token [Malory XVIII, 21].

ELYES' BOOK†
This little book could have enabled Helyes of Thoulouse to perform miracles, had he cared to study it. On at least one occasion, he used it to conjure up an apparently demonic apparition to help elucidate a prophecy concerning Duke Galeholt's term of life. None of Galeholt's other clerks had success when they tried to consult this book; perhaps they were not learned enough. [Vulgate IV]

HORN OF ELEPHANT'S BONE
In the best tradition, this great horn hung near Castle Dangerous, ready for knights-errant to blow when they came to fight Sir Ironside [Malory VII, 15].

HORN OF IVORY
This horn bound with gold was used to summon knights to the Castle of Maidens, the one of evil customs. Possibly the horn had some magical or mystical quality, since it could be heard for two miles around. [Malory XIII, 15]

THE HOLY GRAIL (Sangreal)

This is the cup, or possibly, the dish, used by Christ at the Last Supper. Joseph of Arimathea brought the Grail to Britain, where it was put into the keeping of the Fisher Kings, or Rich Fishers, at Carbonek Castle. King Pellam was the last Fisher King to guard it here; when Galahad and his companions achieved the Adventures of the Grail, the sacred vessel moved to Sarras and thence to Heaven.

The Grail fed the worthy, giving each the food he liked best. It also healed wounds. It was not confined to Carbonek, but appeared of itself from time to time and place to place to heal knights [cf. Malory XI, 14 and XIII, 17-20], and once it passed through Arthur's hall at Camelot where the knights were sitting at dinner and fed them, thus touching off the great general Grail Quest.

The Sangreal was not a thing to be used or to be found and brought back. The Vulgate makes it perhaps clearer than does Malory that to seek the Grail was not so much to "see" or to "find" it (it had, after all, been seen; and it was known to reside most of the time at Carbonek) as to behold it clear and unveiled — that is, to learn its meaning. The implication seems to be a quest for mystic or religious enlightenment. Arriving at Carbonek Castle was fairly easy. One time Sir Bors visited there without suspecting he was near a place of great and perilous adventure. But finding Carbonek was no guarantee that the Grail would feed or heal you, or even that you would be let into the castle; Ector de Maris, arriving as his brother Lancelot sat with the castle folk to be fed by the Sangreal, was turned away as unworthy [Malory XVII, 16]; and Lionel, coming just as Galahad and eleven other knights were sitting down to the climactic mysteries, was similarly turned away at the door. To sleep at Carbonek, in the part which Sir Bors named the "Castle Adventurous," could be extremely harrowing, if not downright dangerous; one might see all sorts of visions, including battling beasts, might be grievously wounded by mystical weapons and healed again, after awhile, by the Grail, and so on.

To embark on the Grail Quest, you must confess your sins; you must not take along your lady; and it would not be a bad idea to restrict yourself to a diet of bread and water, maybe wear a hair shirt, and garb yourself in some symbolic outer garment (Sir Bors wore a scarlet coat while on the Quest). You need not be a virgin — Bors achieved the Grail, although he had once trespassed on his virginity — but you must remain celibate while on the Quest. Take heed: if you enter this Quest unworthily, you will return worse than when you set out; this may explain why Lancelot, relapsing into his old sinful affair with Guenever, grew careless about keeping it secret, and why the Round Table seems generally to have gone to pot after the Quest, and why even Bors (after his return to court) did some rather surprising things for a saintly man to do.

Although women are absolutely forbidden to accompany their knights on the Quest, the facts that a maiden damsel was the Grail Bearer at Carbonek and that Percivale's saintly sister, Amide, played a major role in the Adventures, suggest to me that a damsel may undertake the Quest alone, under the same moral conditions as a knight. It is interesting, indeed, that, although Nascien absolutely forbade any knight who went on the Grail Adventures to travel with a woman, the only three knights who achieved the Grail were, in fact, those who travelled at least part of the time with a damsel, Amide. (Vera Chapman, in her excellent modern Arthurian romance **The King's Damosel**, has Lynett achieving the Grail.)

According to Malory, after Galahad's death the Grail was taken up into Heaven and never seen again on earth. Other traditions, however, place it still in England. Some years ago I saw it, or at least a relic believed to be it, on a television documentary; it was a bowl-like wooden cup, olivewood I think, no longer quite whole. I have also found a carving of it on a Cornish church pew, which showed it more the shape of a soup mug than of a goblet, as we usually think of it.

There seems to be an opinion drifting around that the Grail was the mystical uniting force behind Arthur's Round Table. I disagree. Far from powering the Round Table, the Grail seems to have helped destroy it. When all the companions left at once on the Quest, they were of course all unavailable at the same time for a long period. Many of them were killed on the Quest. Those who did come back were all, presumably, worse than when they had left, with the possible exception of Bors (and I have my doubts of him; he seems to have acted as go-between in the affair of Lancelot and Guenevere). Galahad and Percivale, the court's most spiritual knights, had died in the odor of sanctity. It must have taken some time before Arthur could even be sure which knights were definately not returning, so that he could fill up their seats with new members and restore the Table to its full strength.

WOMEN

The Arthurian milieu is predominantly a man's world, yet the picture I draw from Malory and the Vulgate is considerably better for women than most modern interpretations and impressions seem to credit it for being — and I do not mean in regard to chivalrous courtesy (which can so easily degenerate into patronizing) and the Round Table aim of succouring all ladies and damsels. The touchstone is whether the authors treat their female characters as intelligent and responsible adults. I find that Malory is fair to his women in this regard, the Vulgate even fairer. This attitude carries over into the fictional setting, so that women have much more freedom of movement and right to property than we usually think of when we picture the High Middle Ages.

Women, it has been conjectured, made up the bulk of the readership for these romances, and this may account for the place they hold therein as characters. It may also account in part for the rarity with which female characters are given names — perhaps the female readers, or the authors who wrote for them, may have felt it easier for real people to identify with nameless than with named characters.

When the knights of the Leprous Lady wished to bleed Percivale's sister, Percivale protested that "a maid in what[ever] place she cometh is free" [Malory XVII, 10]. This was clearly the ideal rather than the general rule, even in the context of Malory's romance; in the context of the real world of Malory's time it may have been mere wishful thinking, the literary daydreams of female readers. Nevertheless, in the romances themselves, we often meet female characters riding the countryside as freely as knights — sometimes, despite their lack of arms and armor to defend themselves, the ladies even ride with very few attendants. Thus Guenever's cousin Elyzabel sets off with a squire and a dwarf to carry a message from Arthur's court to the French Damsel of the Lake across the Channel — and would probably complete her mission, despite the perils of the road, had it not been for King Claudas' suspicious nature when she stops at his court.

The Damsel of La Beale Regard demonstrates some skill in the donning of armor and use of weapons. Somer remarks in a footnote in Vulgate VIII that a certain passage implies that the ladies traveling with Sir Griflet assist him (to cross a lake, I think). They next appear to give material aid in rescuing a

AN HOLY HERB

> And ... there by the way [King Bagdemagus] found a branch of an holy herb that was the sign of the Sangreal, and no knight found such tokens but he were a good liver [Malory IV, 5].

Strangely, Bagdemagus is unlisted among knights who later achieve the Adventures of the Grail. Gawaine supposedly kills him sometime during the Quest, although the details are fuzzy.

ANCELOT'S RING†

The French Damsel of the Lake, who had raised Lancelot, gave him a last gift before leaving him at Arthur's court to be knighted. She placed on his finger a ring which had the power to break all spells and enchantments. [Vulgate III]

LONGINUS' (Longius') SPEAR (The Spear of Vengeance?)

Balin found this spear in a chamber of King Pellam's castle: "a marvellous spear strangely wrought" standing on a table of clean gold with four silver legs, in a chamber "marvellously well dight and richly, and a bed arrayed with cloth of gold." Since Pellam was pursuing him for killing Garlon, Balin snatched up the spear to defend himself, and dealt Pellam the Dolorous Stroke, at which "three counties" were wasted and most of the castle caved in. Although Balin had not known it, this was the spear with which the centurion Longius (Longinus) smote Our Lord on the cross. [Malory II, 15-16]

It would seem to be as well the same Spear of Vengeance which other knights beheld in the Grail Castle, Carbonek. Sometimes they saw it bleeding; sometimes it came and wounded them when they slept in the Castle Adventurous (cf. Malory XI, 4-5). Galahad healed the Maimed King by anointing him with blood from the spear [Malory XVII, 21].

In XVII, 5, Malory tells us that Pelles was smitten through both thighs with the spear because he dared try to draw David's Sword when he found Solomon's Ship. I suppose that the spear did not come at once of itself, but that some time elapsed before Balin unwittingly administered the punishment of the Dolorous Stroke as described above.

After Galahad's death, the spear was taken to Heaven along with the Grail [Malory XVII, 22].

LOVE POTION

The Queen of Ireland entrusted this, in a little flasket of gold, to Dame Bragwaine and Gouvernail when Tristram came to take the Queen's daughter, La Beale Isoud, to Mark. Bragwaine and Gouvernail were to see that Mark and Isoud drank it on their wedding day; but Tristram and Isoud found it one day on the ship, and, thinking it was simply good wine that Gouvernail and Bragwaine had been keeping for themselves, drank it and loved. [Malory VIII, 24]

LOVE RING†

The Damsel of Lestroite Marche gave this ring to Sir Ector de Maris. It had a stone with the power to make the one who received it love with ever-increasing force the one who gave it. [Vulgate III]

The old nurse of King Brandegoris' daughter had a similar ring, though it is not specified that its power lay in the stone. She gave this ring to Sir Bors de Ganis to compel him to love the princess. [Vulgate IV]

LYONORS' RING

Sir Gareth wished to fight in a tournament without being known.

> Then Dame [Lyonors] said unto Sir Gareth: Sir, I will lend you a ring, but I would pray you as you love me heartily let me have it again when the tournament is done, for that ring increaseth my beauty much more than it is of himself. And the virtue of my ring is that, that is green it will turn to red, and that is red it will turn in likeness to green, and that is blue it will turn in likeness to white, and that is white it will turn in likeness to blue, and so it will do of all manner of colours. Also who that beareth my ring shall lose no blood, and for great love I will give you this ring.

knight, though after he is mounted they then seem to stand back and simply watch. In Vulgate IV, when Lancelot sits down to watch a tournament between the Castle aux Dames and the Castle aux Pucelles, a damsel comes by and asks for his shield, since he obviously has no use for it. The evidence of Sir Griflet's ladies is textually dubious, and that of the damsel asking for Lancelot's shield seems to be a broad hint that he should get into the fight rather than a suggestion that she will if he will not. Nevertheless, the total impression created by these and similar instances is a doubt as to whether the women of the romances were really as unfamiliar with weapons as are the standard "damsels in distress" of our much later tales.

When Arthur and his party chanced upon Morgana's castle in the woods around Tauroc and learned that the porter must speak with his mistress about whether to admit them, Sir Sagramore "wondered that there was no master" [Vulgate VI]. Although we meet an occasional example in the Vulgate of a castle which cannot be inherited by the lord's daughter, we find many more castles and even small countries which appear to be under the governance of ladies rather than knights. In view of this pattern, Sagramore's surprise seems strange. Perhaps the fact that Sagra-more had come from the East had something to do with his surprise.

It was customary for high-born damsels to wait on their parents' guests at table [Vulgate VI]. In the light of the cases of young knights, high court officials, and even of kings serving at table, I interpret the maidens' duty of serving, not as a sign of female subservience, but as a courtly means of finishing their education while including them, to some measure, in society and giving them a chance to hear the guests' news.

The Damsel of Hongrefort bore responsibility for her own actions and for seeking penance and forgiveness. King Agrippe's daughter made a vow and embarked on a quest at least as painful as any knight's. Women appear as skillful surgeons, wise and holy hermitesses, and messengers, as well as highly competent (if evil) enchantresses. They are clever, resourceful, capable of handling livestock and serving as squires. In sum, the women of the medieval romances — whether these were colored by memories of woman's place in old Celtic society or by the wishes of female readers — are very far from the retiring, stay-at-home, rather helpless creatures who appear to have become popular in Victorian retellings.

Gareth wore the ring and his armor appeared now of one color and now of another, which confused combatants and onlookers, although they seemed to realize it was the same knight in all these different colors. "What manner a knight is yonder knight that seemeth in so many divers colors?" asked Tristram. When Gareth rode out for a moment to amend his helm and take a drink, his dwarf contrived to get the ring, wishing, for greater glory, that Gareth be known. Then "King Arthur had marvel what knight he was, for the king saw by his hair that it was the same knight." [Malory VII, 27-29]

MAGIC BOAR'S HEAD

See under Magic Mantle, just below.

MAGIC CHESSBOARD†

Gwenbaus made this for his princess (see Forest Perilous, *Places*). Lancelot later brought it to Guenever. The chessboard had pieces of gold and silver. When anyone began to move the pieces of one side, the opposing pieces would move automatically and soon checkmate the mortal player. The board was to retain this property until the death of the most graceful and best beloved knight, who alone would never be checkmated by it. Guenever, although an expert at chess, lost when she played on this board. Lancelot, however, won, so that the board was finally awarded to him. [Vulgate V]

A precursor to computer chess.

THE MAGIC MANTLE†

Child Ballad number 29, "The Boy and the Mantle," tells of these items:

(1) A magic mantle, which will wrinkle up, change color, or both if any untrue woman wears it. The only woman at Arthur's court who can wear it is Sir Craddocke's wife, and even on her it begins to wrinkle at the toe, until she makes Full Confession: she had kissed Craddocke's mouth once before they were married. (The logical extension of this — that the mantle might have misbehaved on any woman, though she was utterly faithful to one man, if they had had relations before the knot was officially tied — does not seem to have occurred either to the balladeer or to the people in his song.)

(2) A boar's head that could only be carved by the knife of a man who was not a cuckold.

(3) A horn of red gold from which no cuckold could drink without spilling.

Of these items, the mantle definitely has pride of place. Child traces the story through French, German, Scandinavian and other versions dating well back into the Middle Ages. It would have been nice if one of the items had been designed to test the man's faithfulness. But then, this sounds almost like another attempt of Morgan le Fay's to convince Arthur of Guenever's unfaithfulness, and perhaps the drinking horn of the ballad tradition is connected with Malory's tale of the drinking horn Morgan made, from which no faithless wife could drink without spilling.

MALEDISANT'S SHIELD

A great black shield, with a white hand in the midst holding a sword. The damsel Maledisant (later called Beauvivante) brought it to Arthur's court, seeking a knight to fulfill the quest of the shield's dead owner. Sir La Cote Male Taile took the quest. Malory's account leaves the quest unclear. Breuse Saunce Pitie had once taken the shield from Maledisant, and Tristram had regained it for her that time. [Malory IX, 2-9]

MERLIN'S BED

For obscure purposes, Merlin made a bed to lie in which caused madness [Malory II, 19]. Possibly there is some confusion here with the bed in the Castle Adventurous of Carbonek, sleeping on which insured a person visions of more or less peril. See under Meliot, *Places*; see also the Perilous Bed, below.

MONEY

Malory mentions three units of currency: besant or bezant, pence, and pound.

Until the United Kingdom put its money on the decimal system, 12 pence equaled one shilling and 20 shillings equaled one pound. A guinea was one pound plus one shilling. A besant was a Byzantine gold coin which finally varied in value between the English sovereign and half-sovereign, or less. Silver besants were also struck, and were worth between a florin and a shilling. The English florin was issued by Edward III, and was worth six shillings or six and eightpence. The English sovereign was a gold coin minted from the time of Henry VII to that of Charles I, originally worth 22s.6d, but later only ten or eleven shillings.

As for the buying power of these coins, in IV, 25, Malory speaks of a "rich circlet of gold worth a thousand besants" as the prize at a tournament. Speaking of Arthur's body, the former Bishop of Canterbury says:

> But this night ... came a number of ladies, and brought hither a dead corpse, and prayed me to bury him; and here they offered an hundred tapers, and they gave me an hundred besants [Malory XXI, 6].

In XXI, 8, Lancelot returns to Britain after Arthur's passing:

> he made a dole, and all they that would come had as much flesh, fish, wine and ale, and every man and woman had twelve pence, come who would ... And on the morn all the priests and clerks ... were there, and sang mass of Requiem; and there offered first Sir Launcelot, and he offered an hundred pound; and then the seven kings offered forty pound apiece; and also there was a thousand knights, and each of them offered a pound; and the offering dured from morn till night

There are also these entries:

> ... I wot well and can make it good, said Sir Ector [to Sir Lancelot, on finding him in the Joyous Isle], it hath cost my lady, the queen, twenty thousand pound the seeking of you [Malory XI, 9].

> Madam, said Sir Launcelot .... I proffered [Elaine of Astolat], for her good love that she shewed me, a thousand pound yearly to her, and to her heirs [Malory XVIII, 20].

> And so upon the morn [Elaine of Astolat] was interred richly, and Sir Launcelot offered her mass-penny [Malory XVIII, 20].

This seems to be about the extent of Malory's concern with the particulars of money.

MORGAN'S DRINKING HORN

This magical drinking horn, "harnessed with gold," could only be used in safety by ladies who were true to their husbands. If the drinker were false to her husband, all the drink would spill. Morgan le Fay (who could not herself have honestly drunk from it) sent this horn to Arthur in another attempt to publicize Guenever's unfaithfulness, but Sir Lamorak stopped the messenger and made him take it to King Mark instead. Of a hundred ladies of Mark's court, including La Beale Isoud, only four could drink clean. [Malory VIII, 34] To the credit of the men, when the angered King Mark swore to burn Isoud and the other shamed ladies:

> Then the barons gathered them together, and said plainly they would not have those ladies burnt for an horn made by sorcery, that came from as false a sorceress and witch as then was living. For that horn did never good, but caused strife and debate, and always in her days she had been an enemy to all true lovers. So there were many knights made their avow, an ever they met with Morgan le Fay, that they would show her short courtesy. [Malory VIII, 34]

MORGAN'S MANTLE

Morgan le Fay sent a rich mantle, set with precious stones, to Arthur, ostensibly as a peace offering. But Nimue, who was perhaps also acquainted with Greek tragedy, warned Arthur not to wear it or let any of his knights wear it unless Morgan's messenger wore it first. Arthur made the damsel-messenger try it on, and it immediately burned her to coals. [Malory IV, 15-16]

MORGAN'S POWDER†

Morgan tricked Lancelot into her castle. Putting him to sleep with drugged wine, she blew a powder into his nostrils through a silver tube, thus taking away his senses for a time. It seems to have had a curious effect. He did not lose his memory, apparently; for, seeing a man paint the history of Aeneas, Lancelot was inspired to paint his own life around the walls of his room. But he does seem to have been quite content to remain, in effect, Morgan's prisoner for two winters and a summer. At the end of this time, a spring rose, in a garden Morgan had planted outside his window for his enjoyment, suddenly reminded him of Guenevere. So he broke the iron bars of his window, plucked the rose, armed himself, and kept on going, the spell broken. He spared Morgan on this occasion for the sake of her brother Arthur. [Vulgate V]

MORGAN'S RING†

In early days, Guenever gave Morgana a ring which differed from the one Guenever later gave Lancelot only in the engraving on the stone.

Kidnapping Lancelot after he had disenchanted her Val Sans Retour (see in *Places*), Morgan demanded the ring Guenever had given him as a ransom. When he refused, she resorted to drugging him and exchanging rings. He did not notice the difference, and she sent his ring to court with a "confession" and apology purportedly by him, in another effort to uncover Guenever's unfaithfulness to Arthur. Guenever said she had given the ring to Lancelot, but honorably; Arthur said he did not believe Morgan's damsel, but, rather than lose Lancelot, he would let him love the Queen. [Vulgate IV]

MORGAN'S SHIELD

Although it was made by Morgan le Fay, I find no indication that this shield was magical in itself.

The field was goldish, with a king and a queen therein painted, and a knight standing above them, [one foot] upon the king's head, and the other upon the queen's.

Morgan made Tristram carry this shield in the tournament at the Castle of the Hard Rock. The device signified Arthur, Guenever, and Lancelot, although Morgan would not tell Tristram who the painted knight was. [Malory IX, 41]

LIVE BRANCHES

An olive branch was carried as a token that its bearer was an ambassador and messenger, and came in peace [Malory V, 1; XX, 14].

ERCIVALE'S SWORD

In the pommel of Sir Percivale's sword was "a red cross and the sign of the crucifix therein." Apparently this had no special virtue other than reminding Percivale of God. [Malory XIV, 9] Percivale's sword could cut through a chain and be none the worse [Vulgate V; it would be surprising if the other noblest swords did not have this quality also].

Eventually, Percivale received Galahad's sword — apparently Balin's Sword, that Galahad had drawn from the floating block of marble at Camelot, and which he now relinquished because he had acquired King David's Sword. Percivale left his own sword at the hermitage in Carteloise Forest. This would have been the sword with the red cross in the pommel, the one known to be able to cut through chain.

Since Percivale died about a year after Galahad in Sarras, Bors could have brought back Balin's Sword for Lancelot.

A PERILOUS BED†

No knight of Arthur's could rest in this bed without rising in shame. When Gawaine came to the castle in which it was, at the frontier of the Terre Foraine of Gore, he was further told that no one could sleep in this bed without being maimed or killed. Lancelot later stopped here for a night during his pursuit of Guenever and her captor Meliagrant. Lancelot took the risk and slept in the bed. At midnight the house trembled, a whirlwind swept through it, a fiery lance came in the window and advanced toward the bed with such force that it entered half a foot into the ground. Lancelot got up, cut the lance in half with his sword, and went back to bed. [Vulgate IV]

I suspect that this bed should be identified with the one that Malory tells us Merlin made; see Merlin's Bed, this section, and Castle Meliot, *Places*.

PRIAMUS' BALM

When wounds were anointed with this balm and then washed from a vial of the four waters that came out of Paradise, the wounds healed within an hour. This worked for any wound; it was the only way wounds from Priamus' sword could be staunched. [Malory V, 10; see Priamus' Sword, this section]

Lynette may have gotten this balm from Priamus and used it to heal at least one knight of her own. Since her ointment seems to have required no washing with the four waters of Paradise, however, I imagine she had her own magical healing potion.

PRIAMUS' SWORD

Only Sir Priamus' balm could staunch the bleeding of a wound made with his sword. Priamus was a Saracen whom Gawaine encountered in Italy during Arthur's war against Rome; he converted to Christianity and became a knight of the Round Table. [Malory V, especially chapter 10]

PRIDWEN†

Arthur's shield, bearing an image of the Virgin Mary [Geoffrey of Monmouth, as quoted by Miller, p. 150].

INGS

They may be sent from one party to another as tokens of love, distress, identification, and so on, used as signets, and so forth. Rings are perhaps the most useful pieces of jewelry for purposes of communication or of intrigue.

RON†

Arthur's spear, "long, broad in the blade and thirsty for slaughter" [Geoffrey of Monmouth, quoted by Miller, p. 150].

THE ROUND TABLE

Uther Pendragon gave this table to King Leodegran, who in turn gave it, with 100 knights, to Arthur on the occasion of Arthur's marriage to Guenevere. The full complement of the Round table was 150 knights, but presumably this included the Siege Perilous, wherein only Galahad could sit, so that the Table was completely filled only once, briefly. For practical purposes, the full complement would have been 149. Malory remarks in his colophon that "when they were whole together there was ever an hundred and forty," possibly always allowing a few seats for worthy newcomers. At least one modern romancer has considered that Merlin and Queen Guenevere were also allowed to sit in council at the Round Table; conceivably there were 140 seats for knights, with an extra ten for King, Queen, and non-knightly counsellors.

The Table itself seems to have been nonmagical, although it had symbolical significance. According to the Vulgate there were three great tables: the one at which Christ and His apostles ate the Last Supper, the one at which Joseph of Arimathea and his disciples sat when they came to Britain, and the Round Table. The roundness of the Table symbolizes the world. As is fitting to complete this symbol, the Knights of the Round Table come from all parts of Christendom and heathendom [Vulgate VI]. Even baptism may not have been a prerequisite of membership; Sir Palomides seems to have been a companion of the Round Table before his baptism. See also Sieges and Siege Perilous, this section.

KING RYONS' MANTLE

King Ryons of North Wales, like the Giant of St. Michael's Mount, was trimming a mantle with the beards of kings he had conquered. He already had eleven when he sent a message that he wanted Arthur's beard to complete the project. [Malory I, 26] I do not know what became of Ryons' mantle after his defeat.

KING RYONS' SWORD†

This was forged by Vulcan, and had once belonged to Hercules, an ancestor of Ryons. Arthur won it during the battle with Ryons before Leodegran's city of Daneblaise. [Vulgate II]

angreal — see HOLY GRAIL

SEQUENCE†

Apparently yet another sword of Arthur's, which he used only in mortal combat. Lancelot used it in battle before the castle of La Roche, when Arthur was Camille's prisoner there. [Vulgate III]. Could it have been the sword Arthur pulled from stone and anvil?

SHIELDS

You can have all sorts of fun with shields. You can trade them and seem to be somebody else, cover them and get into fights anonymously, or, if you are a damsel, show up at court with one and ask for a knight to finish the dead original owner's quest. You can make veiled innuendoes on shields which you give knights to carry unsuspectingly. Lancelot left his own shield with Elaine of Astolat while he borrowed her brother's, and she nurtured her love for Lancelot while caring for his shield, found out from Gawaine (who recognized the device) the identity of her hero, and eventually died of love. A shield can even be used as an offensive weapon to finish a fight successfully after your sword has been lost or broken. The uses of shields are limited only by imagination.

Not infrequently, knights refer to having received their shields as gifts from their ladies. A young knight bore a blank shield until he had earned the right to a coat of arms.

SHIPS

Magical or mystical ships figure very largely in the Adventures of the Grail. The pattern is that an unmanned ship comes ashore, you find it and get in, and it takes you somewhere, usually to a physical and/or mystical adventure. It can be quite dangerous.

Chief of the holy ships is Solomon's ship. The vessels need not, however, be holy or mystical. In Malory IV, Morgan le Fay apparently sends a similarly mysterious ship to entrap Arthur. The ships not even need be magical. In Malory X, 59, Tristram and Palomides find "a rich vessel hilled over with red silk" in which lies the body of the murdered King Hermance, with a letter in his hand telling his story and asking for an avenger. Here there seems to be no magic, simply human device. Remember also the barget in which, at her own dying request, the body of Elaine of Astolat is placed to go to Camelot; her barge, however, is steered and rowed by a bargeman. [Malory XVIII, 19-20]

At the dying request of Percivale's saintly sister Amide, Galahad and his companions put her body into a barge covered with black silk and set it adrift on the sea, to meet them again in Sarras at the end of the Grail Adventures. Lancelot, finding and entering this ship, "felt the most sweetness that ever he felt, and he was fulfilled with all thing [sic] that he thought on or desired." The Lord fed him as the Israelites were fed with manna, and he stayed with the ship for many months, during which time he was joined for half a year by his son Galahad. Occasionally they left the vessel for a time to adventure on land. About a month after Galahad quit the ship for good, it brought Lancelot to Carbonek, leaving him there to his own Grail visions while it proceeded on to Sarras with Amide's body, which had apparently remained fresh and sweet in the best tradition of saint's bodies. [Malory XVII, 11, 13-14, 21]

THE SIEGES

Sieges — the seats at the Round Table — had a magical property. The name of its proper occupant appeared in letters of gold on the back of each chair, seemingly whenever he was near enough to come in and take his seat. Nevertheless, when a knight was known dead, his successor was chosen by natural means — appointed by the King on the advice of counsellors, or possibly elected. There must have been a waiting list of candidates.

Ideally, companions of the Table should not fight each other, except "for love" or at tournaments. There are, however, numerous instances of Table knights killing their comrades in battle, frequently through the careless but common habit of fighting first, with a strange or a covered shield, and then of identifying yourself to your opponent, or checking to learn his identity, after the damage has been done. There seems also to have been some rivalry, especially in the early days of Arthur's court, between the companions of the Round Table and an auxiliary company of Arthur's warriors known as the Queen's Knights. Also, of course, there was inevitable jealousy and friction between personalities. Lancelot and Gawaine themselves, for instance, were dear friends; but some of their respective followers were capable of vicious bloodshed in the argument which of the two great knights was the greater.

The Knights of the Round Table repeated their vows every Pentecost.

See also under the court cities note at the front of *Places.*

THE SIEGE PERILOUS

If you want to get rid of someone, make him vow to sit in this, the forbidden seat at the Table Round. The Siege Perilous would also be useful to suicide with the maximum dramatic effect. Nobody but Galahad could sit in this chair, and anyone else who tried it was devoured by a column of fire. In the Vulgate, one knight, Sir Brumant l'Orguilleus, came all the way from France to sit in the Siege Perilous. He knew he had made a silly, boastful vow, and wept all the way to the Siege, but a vow was a vow. Lancelot, sitting in the chair next to the Siege Perilous, did not move away when the fire descended, and was not even singed by the holocaust that devoured Brumant.

The Siege Perilous was to be filled by Galahad 454 winters after the Passion of Our Lord [Malory XIII, 2]. This gives us a date for the era of Malory's Arthur.

THE SIGN OF THE CROSS

This, of course, is a gesture rather than a tangible object. It is a prayer made with the right hand. (I imagine the left would do if the right were lost or disabled.) It is natural and available to all — at least to all Christians — yet its effects can be remarkable in the field of mystical temptation. It is readily available and very efficacious in dispelling fiends and breaking diabolic delusions. (See, e.g., Malory XIV, 6, 9; possibly XVI, 12)

THREE SILVER SHIELDS†

These shields were marked with one, two, and three red bands respectively. The French Damsel of the Lake sent them to Lancelot, when he was conquering La Dolorous Garde. The shields were to renew, double, and treble his strength when he used them. [Vulgate III]

A SLEEPING POTION

Morgan le Fay gave Sir Alisander a drink which put him into wakeless slumber for three days and three nights. During this time the enchantress could transport him to the castle La Beale Regard. [Malory X, 37]

A SILVER TABLE

In Carbonek, the Grail rested on a silver table. Sometimes it also traveled on this table [cf. Malory XIII, 18, and XVII, 21].

Spear of Vengeance — see LONGINUS' SPEAR

SOLOMON'S SHIP

When King Solomon learned through a vision that his descendant (Galahad) would be a marvellously good and pure knight, he and his wife made a ship for this descendant to find. The wife, although called an "evil" woman, first advised making this ship and seems to have done most of the planning. The ship was fashioned of the best and most durable wood, covered with rot-proof silk, and stocked with wonderful items:

> King David's Sword.
> A marvellous scabbard for the Sword.
> Girdles of hemp for the Sword and scabbard.
> Three spindles, one white, one red, one green.
> A great rich bed, cover with silk, to hold all the above.
> A purse containing a writ to explain the origin of everything.

The night after the ship was completed, an angel came to sprinkle it with water from a silver vessel and write words on sword hilt and ship. The words written on the ship were:

> Thou man that wilt enter within me, beware that thou be full within the faith, for I ne am but Faith and Belief.

Or, according to another version:

> Thou man, which shall enter into this ship, beware thou be in steadfast belief, for I am Faith, and therefore beware how thou enterest, for an thou fail I shall not help thee.

(Malory gives both versions, one in XVII, 2 and one in XVII, 7).

Solomon beheld the angel in a dream-vision, and on awakening and reading the words on the ship, he himself feared to enter in, and so the vessel was shoved into the sea to move rapidly away of itself.

KING DAVID'S SWORD

Following his wife's advice, Solomon had his father David's sword repommelled with a rich pommel subtly made.

The pommel was of stone, with "all manner of colours that any man might find, and everych of the colours had divers virtues." One scale of the haft was a rib of a serpent "which was conversant in Calidone, and is called the Serpent of the fiend." The virtue of this bone is that the hand that handles it will never be weary nor hurt. The Vulgate names the serpent Papagustes and says its virtue is to guard the bearer from excessive heat. The other scale of the haft was a rib of a fish called Ertanax — Orteniaus in the Vulgate — which lived in the Euphrates. Whoever handled the bones of Ertanax would never be weary, and while handling it, would think only of the task before him at the time; as the Vulgate explains this, he would forget everything except the purpose for which he drew the sword. On the sword were the words:

> Let see who shall assay to draw me out of my sheath, but if he be more hardier than any other; and who that draweth me, wit ye well that he shall never fail of shame of his body, or to be wounded to the death.

Attempting to draw the sword had brought grief to various men through the ages, and Galahad would not have tried it had not Amide assured him the sword was meant for him. Amide gave the name of the sword as The Sword with the Strange Girdles.

THE SCABBARD

It was made of serpent's skin, and written on it in gold and silver were the words:

> He which shall wield me ought to be more harder than any other, if he bear me as truly as me ought to be borne. For the body of him which I ought to hang by, he shall not be shamed in no place while he is girt with this girdle, nor never none be so hardy to do away this girdle; for it ought not be done away but by the hands of a maid, and a maid all the days of her life, both in will and in deed. And if she break her virginity she shall die the most villainous death that ever died any woman.

On the other side, which was red as blood, was written in letters black as coal:

> He that shall praise me most, most shall he find me to blame at a great need; and to whom I should be most debonair shall I be most felon, and that shall be at one time.

This last referred to the adventure of Nacien, some time before Galahad and his companions found the ship. Nacien had drawn the sword to defend himself against a giant, but the sword broke. Later Nacien met his brother-in-law Mordrains, who mended the sword. (So says Malory, but I much suspect that in this passage Malory got the names of Nacien and Mordrains reversed, so that Mordrains was the one who drew the sword, and Nacien the one who mended it.) Amide named this scabbard Mover of Blood "for no man that hath blood in him ne shall never see the one part of the sheath which was made of the Tree of Life." In the Vulgate, the scabbard is named Memory of Blood, which seems to make slightly more sense.

HEMP GIRDLES

Solomon's wife provided hemp girdles because she had no worthy materials to sustain so high a sword. The hemp girdles were to be replaced by a worthy maiden damsel, as mentioned in the writing on the scabbard. When Amide had learned the adventure that was ordained for her, she cut off her hair and wove it, along with golden threads, into a girdle, set with gems and a golden buckle. She carried this girdle with her in a box until her time came to use it for girding David's Sword to Galahad's side.

THE SPINDLES

When Adam and Eve were driven from Paradise, Eve carried along the branch on which the forbidden fruit was hung, and planted it, "for she had no coffer to keep it in." It grew into a tree that remained white as snow as long as Eve remained a virgin, but when God bade Adam "know his wife fleshly as nature required" and they lay together begetting children under this same tree, its wood turned green. (Despite the premium put upon virginity in these legends, the Original Sin in this Medieval version can hardly have been sex!) Later Cain slew Abel under the tree's branches, and its wood became red. When Solomon's wife made a carpenter take enough wood from the tree to make the spindles, the tree bled on being cut. Using the natural colors of the wood, the carpenter was able to fashion a white, a green, and a red spindle.

(How were all three colors preserved? At first glance, it seems as if they should only have been able to make red spindles. Yet once, walking in the woods in winter, I really did find a kind of triple-trunked bush with one slim trunk that looked red, one green, and one whitish, growing from a single base. The likeliest explanation to the problem of the spindles, however, was suggested by my mother: Each time only the outer layer of the tree changed color, and so grew until the next color change, so that the inner rings remained white, the middle green, and the outermost red.)

I do not know why spindles, in preference to anything else, were made from this tree. Perhaps in another version the spindles had something to do with the making of the new girdle by the pure damsel. The Vulgate tells us that they were arranged in, apparently, an "H" shape, the upright spindles white and red, the horizontal one green. [Perhaps symbolizing the "yoke of Christ"?]

THE BED and THE PURSE

They seem purely utilitarian.

[Malory XVII, 2-7; Vulgate VI]

Solomon's would appear to be the same ship that picks up Galahad and his two companions again three days after they leave Carbonek, and takes them to Sarras. This time, when they come on board, they find the Grail, covered with red samite, standing there on its silver table. [Malory XVII, 21]

SWORDS

If a book is not handy to swear an oath upon, a knight can always use the cross formed by the handle of his sword [cf. Malory IX, 39]. I do not know whether such an oath is less binding than one sworn on a book.

ILD-FIRE

Used in military actions to burn ships, castles, and so on [Malory X, 32, 38].

WINE

In Arthur's day, wine was an uncommon beverage in England [Vulgate VI]. This could explain how easy it seems to be to get a person to drink drugged wine.

The wine of Beaune, or Bayonne, France, must have been prized: "some men call it Bayonne, and some men call it Beaune, where the wine of Beaune is" [Malory XX, 18; cf. Benwick in *Places*].

APPENDICES

A Tentative Chronology of Arthur's Reign

In arranging this chronology, I generally gave more weight to the Vulgate than to Malory, since the Vulgate seems to me more internally consistent.

Dates marked *ca.* have been computed. Dates not so marked are known from Malory or from the Vulgate — but I have found only two known dates, 435 A.D. and 454 A.D. Events left undated I theorize to have fallen between the dated events, probably in the approximate order listed. Parenthesized events are in especially tentative placement.

The numbers in brackets give book and chapter of Malory. Events not found in Malory are marked with a dagger; they are from the Vulgate unless otherwise noted.

ca. 410 A.D.

Arthur crowned [I, 7].[1]
First rebellion of British kings [I, 8-18].
(Sagramore arrives in Britain.†)
Alliance with Ban and Bors [I, 8-18].[2]
Merlin meets Viviane, aged 15 [I, 8-18].†
Battle of Bedegraine [I, 8-18].
Arthur engenders Borre (Lohot) on Lyzianor [I, 8-18].
Ban and Bors help Arthur save Leodegran from Ryons [I, 8-18].
Gwenbaus settles down with his princess in Forest Perilleuse.†
Margawse and her sons visit Arthur in Carlion. Arthur engenders Mordred and has nightmare of serpent [I, 19].
Arthur reunited with his mother [I, 21].
Arthur fights Pellinore and gains Excalibur [I, 23-25].
(Mark of Cornwall murders his brother, Prince Boudwin [X, 32-33].)

ca. 413 A.D.

Mordred's birth. The drowning of the May babies. [I, 27]
The death of "Nineve," the first British Lady of the Lake [II].
The final defeat of King Ryons [II].
The second rebellion of British kings, under Lot, and the death of Lot [II].
Lot's sons established at Arthur's court [II].
Balin deals Pellam the Dolorous Stroke [II].
The tale of Balin and Balan [II].
The marriage of Arthur and installation of the Round Table at Arthur's court [III, 1-2].
The first attempt of Genievre to supplant Guenever.†
Pellinore rescues Nimue and brings her to court [III 5, 12-15].
Morgan leaves Arthur's court the first time, meets Merlin in Bedingran and studies with him.†

The invasion of the five kings and the battle at the Humber [IV, 2-4].
Gawaine wins Gringolet.†
Arthur and the surviving kings of the former rebellions, now allied, defeat the Saxons.†
(The affair of **Sir Gawaine and the Green Knight**.†)
Merlin and Nimue visit Ban and Elaine in Benwick [IV, 1].
Nimue becomes chief British Lady of the Lake, imprisons Merlin in Cornwall [IV, 1].
Morgan attempts to kill Arthur and Uriens, and put her lover Accolon and herself on the throne; she permanently leaves Arthur's court when the attempt fails [IV, 6-16].
Claudas defeats Ban and Bors. Viviane appropriates the infant Lancelot. Claudas and one of his men visit Arthur's court as spies for a year.†

ca. 415 A.D.

(Morgan enchants the Val des faux amants.†)
Arthur's first war with Rome. Death of Emperor Lucius in battle. Arthur crowned emperor in Rome. [V][3]
Seraide rescues the young Lionel and Bors from Claudas, brings them to live with Lancelot in the French Lake.†
(Tristram defeats Marhaus and beings his own career [VIII, 4-7].)

ca. 428 A.D.

Viviane brings Lancelot, aged 18, and his cousins to Arthur's court.†
Lancelot wins Dolorous/Joyous Garde.†
Duke Galeholt tries to conquer Arthur.†
Nascien visits Arthur's court, perhaps for the first but not for the last time.†

---

[1] *This date is computed from the following evidence: the Vulgate puts Turquine's capture of Lionel in the 23rd year of Arthur's reign and the return of Lancelot to Arthur's court, after killing Turquine and subsequently spending a year and a half as Morgan's prisoner, is the year 435.*

[2] *According to the Vulgate, Arthur goes to France for a time to help Ban and Bors against Claudas before they cross to Britain to help Arthur win the battle of Bedegraine.*

[3] *Though Malory has Lancelot fighting in this campaign, I had enough trouble trying to fit in such other adventures as the various tournaments and the tale of Gareth Beaumains in the time the Vulgate allows for Lancelot's being with the rest of Arthur's company.*

Lancelot wins Galeholt's allegiance for Arthur.†

Lancelot and Guenever, Galeholt and the Lady of Malohaut, pledge their love at Carduel.†

(The tale of La Cote Male Taile [IX, 1-9].)

Lancelot, still an unattached knight-errant, leaves court again. A search started for him.†

The defeat of Camille and the Saxons at La Roche. Lancelot officially joins Arthur's court, confirms his love with Guenever.†

(The tale of Gareth Beaumains [VII].)

(The murder of Margawse [X, 24].)[4]

(The Surluse tournament [X, 40-49].)[4]

(The murder of Lamorak [X, 54].)[4]

ca. 430 to 432 A.D.

Genievre's second attempt to supplant Guenever succeeds for about two years, during which time Guenever lives with Lancelot in Surluse.†

Carados of the Dolorous Tower captures Gawaine (after the feast celebrating Lancelot's and Guenever's return†).

Lancelot kills Carados, rescues Gawaine [VIII, 28].

On the way to save Gawaine, Lancelot passes through Morgan's Val de faux amants and she persuades him that Guenever no longer loves him; he therefore avoids court and goes mad.†

Deaths of Duke Galeholt and the Lady of Malohaut.†

Meliagrant kidnaps Guenever; Lancelot eventually rescues her [XIX, 1-9].

Bors helps King Agrippe's daughter.†

Bors engenders Helin le Blank on King Brangoire's daughter [cf. XII, 9; XVI, 6].

(The Castle of Maidens tournament [IX, 27-35].)

(The Castle of the Hard Rock tournament [IX, 41-44; X, 1].)

Lancelot follows the damsel Ornagrine to adventure; Mordred, about twenty years old and newly knights, joins the search for Lancelot.†

Guenever sends Elyzabel to France to enlist Viviane's aid in finding Lancelot; Claudas imprisons Elyzabel before she can reach Viviane.†

Lancelot falls sick, meets and is nursed by Amable.†

ca. 433 A.D.

Lionel finds Lancelot; Lionel is captured by Turquine while Lancelot is kidnapped by Morgan and her cohorts [VI, 1-4].

Freed from Morgan's Castle Chariot, Lancelot visits Carbonek, engenders Galahad on Pellam's daughter Elaine [XI, 1-3].

Lancelot frees the knights and ladies in Gwenbaus' Forest Perilleuse.†

Lancelot kills Turquine, frees Lionel and the other prisoners [VI, 7-9].

Morgan captures Lancelot again, holds him two winters and a summer. He paints murals of his life and love.†

(Gawaine and his brothers kill King Pellinore [XI, 10].)

Escaping from Morgan, Lancelot meets Mordred; they travel together until, before the Peningues tournament, Mordred learns the truth of his birth and the prophecy of his future. The turning point of Mordred's career.†

Bors visits Carbonek and its Adventurous Palace [XI, 4-6].

(Alisander le Orphelin marries Alice la Beale Pilgrim [X, 39].)

Lancelot saves Kay and then takes his armor [VI, 11-13].

435 A.D.

Lancelot returns to Arthur's court at Camelot [VI, 18; the date is known from Vulgate V].

Whitsunday: Brumant l'Orgilleus dies in the Siege Perilous.†

(The battle of Lancelot and Tristram; Tristram becomes a knight of the Round Table [X, 5-6].)

(The Lonazep tournament [X, 56-58, 65-80].)

Learning of Elyzabel's imprisonment, Guenever and† Arthur war on and finally defeat Claudas [XI, 6].

Elaine of Carbonek visits Arthur's court for the feast celebrating the victory over Claudas. Lancelot goes mad. [XI, 7-10; XII, 1-3]

ca. 446 or 449 A.D.

Percivale, aged about 15, comes to court [X, 23].

Lancelot is cured of his madness at Carbonek, takes the name Le Chaveler Mal Fet and lives with Elaine two to four years in Joyous Isle [XII, 4-6].

Tristram and La Beale Isoud live at Joyous Garde [XII, 11].[5]

ca. 451 or 454 A.D.

Ector and Percivale find Lancelot and persuade him to return to court. Galahad comes also, and stays in a convent near Camelot [XII, 7-10].[6]

Palomides is baptized [XII, 14].

454 A.D.

Galahad comes to Camelot. The start of the Grail Quest — officially, this would last at least a year, but many knights were gone far longer, and some never returned; Bors must have been gone at least four years [XIII-XVII; the date is known both from Malory and the Vulgate].

(Mark kills Tristram [cf. XIX, 11].)

ca. 461 A.D.

The attempt on Gawaine's life with a poisoned apple is made [XVIII, 1-8].

The Winchester tournament and the Elaine of Astolat affair occur [XVIII, 9-20].[7]

Arthur visits Morgan in her castle, but Lancelot's murals fail to convince him of the affair between Lancelot and Guenever.†

Sir Urre is healed [XIX, 10-13].

Lancelot and Guenever are surprised [XX, 1-8].

Arthur and Gawaine besiege Lancelot in Joyous Garde [XX, 10-13].

Lancelot is banished [XX, 14-18].

Arthur and Gawaine besiege Lancelot in France [XX, 19-22].

The Romans take advantage of the situation and attack Arthur in France. The second war with Rome ends less successfully for Arthur. Kay dies in battle.†

ca. 465 A.D.

The last battle and the passing of Arthur [XXI, 1-6].

---

4 *An alternate dating for these three sequential events would be in the probable interval between Lancelot's return from Joyous Isle and Galahad's arrival in Camelot, ca. 451-454 A.D. Such dating must assume that Malory either invented and embroidered his account in ignorance of Duke Galeholt's death, or had Galeholt confused with his heir and successor.*

5 *"[K]ept not [Tristram] with him La Beale Isoud near three year in Joyous Garde?" [Maolory XX, 6]*

6 *Galahad may have spent up to three years in the holy retreat before coming on to Camelot.*

7 *Arthur remarks just before the Winchester tournament, "this year ye saw not such a noble fellowship together except at Whitsuntide when Galahad departed from the court" [Malory XVIII, 8].*

Just after the Winchester tournament, Gawaine tells Elaine of Astolat (when he sees Lancelot's shield), "I have known that noble knight this four-and-twenty year" [Malory SVIII, 14]. But this would put Lancelot's arrival in Britain in about the year 437 — an impossibility according to the Vulgate account, for the date of 435 for Lancelot's return to court is one of the two definite dates I have found. Either Malory condenses by five to seven years, or Lancelot has only been carrying this particular coat of arms for 24 years, or 24 is used as a common time approximation like a dozen, a score, or the Biblical forty. Perhaps Gawaine is vain enough to knock off a few years from his and Lancelot's true ages.

Magical Acts

In this section, I have not tried to include the making of a number of magical items; these are described instead in the section on *Things*. Nor have I attempted to itemize the various prophecies and disguises of Merlin. Merlin can seemingly appear in any guise from toddler to old beggar, and prophesy anything about anybody, and probably look into everybody's past as well. His prophecies, however, are often mysterious and veiled.

I do not recall that any necromancer except Merlin utters prophecies, not even Morgana or Nimue, who learned necromancy from him. Many holy people expound symbolic happenings and visions and utter prophecies, but these come under the classification of mystical and religious experience rather than of magic as such.

It seems to me that prophecies may do more harm than good. According to the Vulgate, Mordred was doing reasonably well during his first two years of knighthood. Then he met a priest who seized the opportunity to tell him that he was not the son of Lot, but of Arthur; that he was a serpent who would devour his father, that he would do more harm than all his ancestors had done good, and so on, and so on. Mordred's moral disintegration appears to date from this experience. Might things have been different had that priest kept his mouth shut?

It is not always easy to determine whether a given act is really "magical" as we would understand the term, or simply performed with the aid of natural herbs and drugs, persuasion, or other human skill of a high degree.

With the exceptions of Merlin's various disguises and prophecies, the various magical items, and the prophecies and other supernatural deeds that would come under the heading of religious experience, I have tried to give all the specific magical acts performed in the books of Malory, in sufficient detail for as much understanding of the processes and uses of the magic as possible. I have also tried to indicate in the descriptions which acts might have been done with "natural" techniques like drugs. Rather than attempting to classify them, I have given them in the order I found them. Magical Acts numbers 1-21 are taken from Malory; numbers 22-34 are drawn from the Vulgate. No attempt has been made to fit these two sublists into chronological order. For that matter, Malory's work, at least as set up by Caxton, is not always internally consistent in its chronology. It may be of interest, however, to note that, if the mystic Adventures of the Grail are left out of consideration, as here, then most of the forthright magic seems to be found in the earlier adventures.

1. To enable Uther to lie with Igraine, Merlin gave Uther the appearance of Igraine's husband, Uther's knight Ulfius the appearance of the Duke's knight Brastias, and himself the appearance of the Duke's knight Jordanus. This seems a clear-cut case of shape-changing, rather than mere natural disguise. [Malory I, 2]

2. Merlin brought the host of Kings Ban and Bors, ten thousand men on horseback, to Dover and

> northward, the priviest way that could be thought, unto the forest of Bedegraine, and there in a valley he lodged them secretly.
> Then rode Merlin unto Arthur and the two kings, and told them how he had sped; whereof they had great marvel, that man on earth might speed so soon, and go and come. [Malory I, 11]

This might have been no more than excellent generalship and an extremely good horse and knowledge of the roads. Merlin being the author of these deeds, however, it looks more like casting some sort of screen of invisibility over the army, and travelling by supernatural means.

3. Merlin cast a spell on King Pellinore which put him to sleep for three hours. This was at Pellinore's first meeting with Arthur, when Pellinore, learning whom he had just felled in battle, was about to slay Arthur for dread of royal revenge. Merlin thus enabled Arthur to escape without injury to Pellinore, although the sleep was so deep that Arthur at first blamed Merlin for having killed Pellinore. [Malory I, 24]

Under the circumstances, Merlin would hardly have had time to use drugs.

4. Merlin made Arthur invisible to Pellinore and thus prevented a battle. (Pellinore was not yet one of Arthur's friends and advisors.) [Malory I, 25]

5. On the tomb of Lanceor and Colombe, Merlin wrote in letters of gold the names of the two best knights in the world, Lancelot and Tristram, neither of whom had yet appeared, but who would one day fight at this same tomb. [Malory II, 8]

6. Arthur buried the bodies of twelve rebel kings in the Church of Saint Stephen's in Camelot. (These included King Lot, but were not an identical group with the first eleven rebel kings.) Each of their effigies, made of latten (brass) and copper over-gilt with gold, held a wax taper that burned night and day, and above them stood a figure of Arthur holding a drawn sword. Merlin made these effigies "by his subtle craft" and told Arthur that the tapers would burn until Merlin's own death, and that shortly thereafter would come the Adventures of the Grail. [Malory II, 11]

By his "death" Merlin presumably meant his imprisonment; but in fact the Grail adventures would seem to come quite some time after that event. Perhaps the great mage was speaking on a "brevity of human life compared with the age of the world" scale.

7. Sir Garlon went around invisible, killing knights at will. [Malory II, 12-14]

8. Merlin saved Balin after Pellam's castle had fallen on him because of the Dolorous Stroke. Apparently, to do this Merlin had to move a deal of stone by magical means. [Malory II, 16]

9. Merlin "let write" Balin's name and history in letters of gold on his tomb; the lady who had buried Balin had not known his name. [Malory II, 18-19]

10. Because Nimue seems to have acquired a bad reputation for the following deed, which reputation I am not sure she entirely deserves, I give it in Malory's words.

> ... Merlin fell in a dotage on the damosel that King Pellinore brought to court, and she was one of the damosels of the lake, that hight Nimue. But Merlin would let her have no rest, but always he would be with her. And ever she made Merlin good cheer till she had learned of him all manner thing that she desired; and he was assotted upon her, that he might not be from her. So on a time he told King Arthur that he should not dure long, but for all his crafts he should be put in the earth quick. ... Ah, said the king, since ye know of your adventure, purvey for it, and put away by your crafts that misadventure. Nay, said Merlin, it will not be; so he departed from the king. And within a while the Damosel of the Lake departed, and Merlin went with her evermore wheresomever she went. And ofttimes Merlin would have had her privily away by his subtle crafts; then she made him to swear that he should never do none enchantment upon her if he would have his will. And so he sware; so she and Merlin went over the sea unto the land of Benwick [where Merlin prophesied Lancelot's greatness to Lancelot's mother Queen Elaine] .... And so, soon after, the lady and Merlin departed, and by the way Merlin showed her many wonders, and came into Cornwall. And always Merlin lay about the lady to have her maidenhood, and she was ever passing weary of him, and fain would have been delivered of him, for she was afeard of him because he was a devil's son, and she could not beskift him by no mean. And so on a time it happed that Merlin showed to her in a rock whereas was a great wonder, and wrought by enchantment, that went under a great stone. So by her subtle working she made Merlin to go under that stone to let her wit of the marvels there; but she wrought so there for him that he came never out for all the craft he could do. And so she departed and left Merlin. [Malory IV, 1]

11. Arthur, King Uriens, and Sir Accolon were out hunting when they came to the shore and "a little ship, all apparelled with silk ... came right

unto them and landed on the sands." Seeing nobody aboard, the trio got in. Suddenly a hundred torches lit the ship, and 12 fair damsels came out to welcome the men inside, serve them fine supper, and lead them each to separate bedchambers. In the morning Uriens woke up back in Camelot, two days' journey away, in the arms of his wife Morgana (who apparently engineered the episode). Arthur woke up in a dark prison full of woeful knights; to free them and himself, the king had to fight on behalf of the evil Sir Damas against the champion of the good Sir Ontzlake. Accolon woke on the edge of a deep well, and there Morgana's dwarf found him and brought him to Sir Ontzlake's manor to be Ontzlake's champion. [Malory IV, 6-9; see also Fountain of the Silver Pipe, *Places*].

12. Tied in with 11 above, Morgan le Fay counterfeited Excalibur and its scabbard so that she could give the originals to Sir Accolon, her lover. Arthur, fighting Accolon, did not realize the substitution until he found himself bleeding and the false Excalibur breaking in his hands. Nimue, apparently through her magical craft, found out about all this, came to the place, and by enchantments struck Excalibur out of Accolon's hand, Arthur recovering it. Arthur was then able to tear the magic scabbard from Accolon's side and so win the fight. [Malory II, 11; XV, 8-11]

13. Morgana, escaping with forty mounted knights of hers after her attempt to kill Arthur as described above, in numbers 11 and 12,

> rode into a valley where many great stones were, and when she saw she must be overtaken, she shaped herself, horse and man, by enchantment unto a great marble stone.

On this same trip she threw the scabbard of Excalibur into a lake, and later rescued Sir Manassen from a knight who would have drowned him; but both these last were natural acts. [Malory IV, 14-15]

14. Twelve damsels and two knights dwelt in a turret, near a place where Sir Marhaus was staying for at least a time. They were sorceresses and enchantresses who could make a knight, be he never so good of body and full of prowess, "a stark coward to have to better of him." I cannot find out how they did this. [Malory IV, 17-18]

15. Pelleas loved Ettard and Ettard hated Pelleas. Nimue cast Pelleas into an enchanted sleep for two hours, brought Ettard to where he lay, and through her power reversed the affections, so that Ettard died of love for Pelleas while he left her and married Nimue, with whom he lived happily ever after. [Malory IV, 20-23] I could not find whether, while turning Pelleas' love for Ettard into hate, Nimue also used magic to win his affections for herself, or whether she won him by natural means alone. Ever afterward, Nimue kept Pelleas from fighting Lancelot "by her means." This may refer to more magic, or to loving persuasion.

16. Dame Lynette, through her subtle crafts, kept her sister and Sir Gareth honest before their marriage. When Lyonors when down to Gareth, who was sleeping in the hall, Lynette sent a great, grisly knight of her own to attack Gareth in his bed. Lynette's knight wounded Gareth in the thing and Gareth lopped off his opponent's head; but Lynette came in, anointed the head with an ointment, and stuck it back on the neck in the sight of all, healing her knight. Ten days later, Gareth, healing naturally, appointed a night to try it again with Lyonors. When Lynette sent down her knight this time, Gareth not only beheaded him, but hacked the head into a hundred gobbets and threw them out the window into the ditches of the castle. Lynette calmly fetched them up, pieced them together, and restored her knight again. Gareth did not heal this time until Lynette healed him. Apparently, Gareth and Lyonors now decided to wait until they were married. [Malory VII, 22-23, 26]

17. An unnamed lady loved King Meliodas, Tristram's father. One day when he rode hunting, "by an enchantment" he followed a hart to an old castle "and there anon he was taken prisoner by the lady that loved him." Merlin at last rescued him in an unstated way. [Malory VIII, 1-2]

18. Morgan le Fay, developing a passion for Sir Alisander le Orphelin, first inflamed his wounds with one ointment, then healed them with another, apparently to trick him into greater gratitude [Malory X, 37]. This sounds like a simple case of herbal lore.

19. Morgan Fay and the Queen of Northgalis put a damsel into a bath of scalding water, where she remained for five years until Sir Lancelot took her hand and led her out. Other knights had tried, but this was another case where only the best knight would do. [Malory XI, 1]

Although Malory charges the scalding bath to Morgan and her cohort, in the Vulgate the damsel tells those who come to attempt her rescue that she is being punished for sin. Since the tower where she suffers is in or near Carbonek (or Corbin), I incline to the mystical-righteous interpretation and, despite Malory's charge, absolve Morgan and the Queen of Northgalis, except perhaps as instruments of Heaven.

When Gawaine dipped his arm into the water, he thought his hand had been burned off. Only magic or miracle could enable the damsel to survive her long wait in such water.

20. When Lancelot first came to Carbonek, Dame Brisen, who was "one of the greatest enchantresses that was at that time in the world living," was requested by King Pellam to help bring about a coupling between his daughter and the great knight, in order to produce Galahad. Dame Brisen had Lancelot receive "a ring from Queen Guenever like as it had come from her," as a token for a tryst. After arriving at the specified castle and taking those folk for the people normally around the Queen, he accepts a cup full of wine, "and anon as he had drunken that wine he was so assotted and mad that he might make no delay," and bedded Eleine as though she were Guenever.

The wine might have contained a simple aphrodisiac; the mistaking of Elaine's knights for the Queen's and even of Elaine for Guenever might have been accomplished simply through suggestion, darkness and muddling Lancelot's head with wine and herbs. The messenger with the ring like Guenever's is less easy to dismiss. It sounds as if Malory should have told us that Brisen "made one to come to Sir Lancelot [in the likeness of one] that he knew well"; that Brisen, in short, did much the same kind of thing Merlin had done earlier to get Uther into Igraine's bed.

(There is no evidence that Brisen learned any craft from Merlin.)

Later, Elaine and Brisen visited Camelot. Learning by her crafts that Lancelot and the Queen had made a date to spend the night together, Brisen pretended to be Guenever's messenger and brought Lancelot to Elaine's room, next door to the Queen's, where again he slept with Elaine, believing her to be Guenever. When Guenever found them this time, her wrath and jealousy drove him to a fit of madness. This later incident may have been a case of natural intrigue and deceit. [Malory XI, 7-8]

21. Sir Pinel le Savage tried to poison Gawaine with apples, Gawaine's favorite fruit, at a small dinner given by Guenever. But Sir Patrise of Ireland, a cousin of Mador de la Porte, ate an apple first and died. Guenever was accused and Lancelot saved her from execution by fighting Mador; but not until Nimue came and applied her crafts to the problem was the truth of the murder disclosed. [Malory XVIII, 3-8, especially 8]

One wonders why the Damsel of the Lake did not show up earlier and save Guenever the agony of being mistakenly accused. Either Nimue's crafts did not tell her what was going on so quickly as they had in the affair of the false Excalibur (see Magical Act 12), or, perhaps, she was too busy with Pelleas at the moment to check up on the court.

The events of obviously mystical origin — the miracles either of God or of the Devil, which are especially prevalent in the Grail Adventures, would probably be beyond the reach of a simple necromancer, even one as great as Merlin or Morgana. A saintly person who performs such acts does so by the grace and power of God.

Perhaps Malory's most memorable example of the Devil's craft comes in Book XIV, chapters 5 and 6. Sir Percivale, during the Grail Adventures, lost his horse and accepted another from a strange lady. The steed was black and Percivale "marvelled that it was so great and so well apparelled." Trustingly and unthinkingly, Percivale leaped up on its back, and

> within an hour and less [the horse] bare him four days' journey thence, until he came to a rough water the which roared, and his horse would have borne him into it. And when Sir Percivale came

nigh the brim, and saw the water so boistous, he doubted to over-pass it. And then he made a sign of the cross in his forehead. When the fiend felt him so charged he shook off Sir Percivale, and he went into the water crying and roaring, making great sorrow, and it seemed unto him that the water brent.

The devil also takes the shape of a beautiful lady to tempt a knight's chastity, or of a holy man to expound some vision falsely. [Cf. Malory XIV, 8-10; XVI, 11]

MAGICAL ACTS SELECTED FROM THE VULGATE

22. Merlin brought the stones of Stonehenge from Ireland to their present site as a tomb for King Pandragon. (Pandragon was Uther's brother, from whom Uther took his second name. They were both sons of King Constans of England.) [Vulgate II]

23. At first, Merlin was not averse to prophesying in plain language. But a certain foolish baron, trying to catch him up, came to him on three separate occasions to ask "How will I die?" The first time, Merlin told him that he would break his neck; the second time, that he would hang himself; the third time, that he would drown. These seemingly irreconcilable prophecies were all fulfilled when the baron had a freak accident. He was thrown from his horse on the bank of a river in such a way that his neck was broken; the reins were wrapped around his neck, hanging him; and his head and shoulders were under the water of the river.

It was apparently this incident which made Merlin decide to stop prophesying plainly and only prophesy obscurely. [Vulgate II]

24. Disguised as an old man, Merlin brought Gawaine from Camelot to Dover to help Sagramore and his companions, who had landed at Dover only to be beset by the Sesnes. [Vulgate II]

25. Just before battle, Merlin ignited the tents of the rebel barons. [Vulgate II]

26. Arthur was fighting the Sesnes for Leodegran. The porter, apparently not wanting his side to issue forth to fight the foe and perhaps be defeated, refused to open the gate. Merlin opened it by his craft. It reclosed afterwards of itself. Merlin carried Arthur's dragon standard during this battle, and the dragon on the banner spat fire. Towards the end of the battle, Merlin produced first a storm, then a fog to stop the Sesnes. That night, Arthur and his men, still finishing off the foe, were able to see by the fire the dragon standard spat. [Vulgate II]

27. Merlin travelled from Rome to his old master Blaise in Northumberland in 24 hours. [Vulgate II]

28. On first meeting Viviane, Merlin produced a phantom castle, knights and ladies, and an orchard which remained after the other things had vanished. [Vulgate II]

29. Merlin began Viviane's instruction by teaching her how to produce a river. [Vulgate II]

30. While in France helping Kings Ban and Bors against King Claudas, Merlin blew a horn and made a fiery cloud appear in the sky as the signal for battle. [Vulgate II]

31. When Merlin was escorting Ban and Bors back from Britain to their own kingdom, they stopped for a night at the castle Des Mares. Since Ban greatly admired the daughter of the castellan, Sir Agravadain, Merlin cast a spell between her and Ban so that they lay together without any sense of shame. Merlin broke the spell after leading the damsel back to her own room, but she was still left loving Ban (who had a wife back home) better than any other man. The damsel gave birth to a child resembling King Ban. This child was Sir Ector de Maris, Lancelot's half-brother. The incident also resulted, incidentally, in warfare between Sir Agravadain and his daughter's lover.

32. When Seraide went to the court of King Claudas to rescue young Lionel and Bors, she had to give them the appearance of greyhounds. At the same time, two real greyhounds took on the appearance of the boys. When Seraide had gotten the boys safely away and given them back their own appearance, the enchanted greyhounds, which Claudas had imprisoned, also regained their real shapes. [Vulgate III]

33. A clerk of Cologne had found that Duke Galeholt must pass a bridge of 45 planks, which indicated his term of life; but they did not know whether this meant years, months, or days. To find out, Helyes of Thoulouse went alone with Galeholt into the chapel. Helyes got charcoal from the porter of the chapel, closed the door, and drew four groups of 45 lines each on the wall, each group smaller than the preceding one. These groups indicated years, months, weeks, and days. Helyes gave Galeholt the pyx and he himself took the jeweled cross from the altar. Then Helyes read from his book until he was exhausted and feverishly excited. He began to read again, the chapel darkened, and a fearful voice was heard. The two men, each clutching his holy talisman, fell to the floor. The earth quaked, the chapel seemed to turn round, and an arm clothed in an ample sleeve and holding a fiery sword appeared through the closed door. It went straight to Helyes and Galeholt, but could not hurt them becuase of the cross and the pyx. At last the arm went to the wall, effaced 41¼ of the largest marks, and vanished. Thus Helyes understood that the 45 planks were 45 years, the complete sum of Galeholt's life from birth to death, and that the Duke had only three and three-quarters years remaining. Helyes told him, however, that he could prolong his life by keeping his friend Lancelot with him. (But Galeholt refused to take advantage of Lancelot's friendship by abridging his freedom to go where he would.) [Vulgate IV]

Malory records a somewhat reminiscent conjuring up of a demon. [Book XV, 1-2; see Chapel of the Demon, *Places*] The incident in Malory, however, is not only milder and apparently fraught with less danger to the holy man who does the conjuring, but seems more clearly a case of religion than magic. Helyes' summoning of the arm, although it has its religious elements, seems more nearly a case of necromancy.

34. In an effort to make Lancelot forget Guenever, Morgana, with the help of strong drugs, caused him to have strange dreams. She so contrived matters that on awakening he would find himself in the same surroundings he had seen in his dreams, thus convincing him the dreams were real. (This argues a control over someone else's dreams that science fiction hardly dares describe today.) [Vulgate IV]

Character Groupings

SUB-ENTRIES

Bards, Scholars, and Entertainers
Castellans and Chatelaines
Damsels and Ladies
Dwarves
Giants
Holy Folk
Kings
Knights

Knights of the Round Table
Lovers
Non-Britons
Seneschals
Special Cases
Villains
Workers of Magic

In many of the categories, I have used sub-groupings I, II, and III. Sub-group I includes the major figures — the most important of the group. Group III includes those who seem undeniably minor. Group II comprises borderline cases; for instance, characters who are major in one or two episodes only, or who are mainly notable for being related to someone of much greater importance. How "major" a character had to be to get into I or II depends partly on the category; competition was stiffer for Knights than for Kings or Ladies. Characters may appear on more lists than one, but a given character may not get the same importance rating on all lists. In many cases, my ratings might have been slightly different if done on a different day, or under different atmospheric conditions; however, I hope that I have nowhere been

guilty of judging a character as Class I material who belongs in Class III or vice versa.

Arthur and Guenevere are above any such arbitrary rating system.

Bards, Scholars, & Entertainers

Aneurin
Bleise
Dagonet
Eliot
Gildas

Helyes of Thoulouse
Llywarch Hen
Merlin
Taliessin
Thomas the Rhymer[1]

[1] Although he lived much after Arthur's time, Thomas the Rhymer has been connected with legends of the sleeping Arthur.

Castellans & Chatelaines

Most if not all of the important knights had one or more castles and territories of their own, like Lancelot's Joyous Garde — either of their own winning, or their inheritance, or of their lord's bounty in rewarding their services. Since the primary purpose of the list below is to bring together various lesser-known knights, I have tried to give only those actually shown in residence as acting day-to-day administrators of the castles. For instance, neither Sir Tor nor La Cote Male Taile is listed among the castellans below, but their lieutenants Sir Berluse and Sir Nerovens are.

I tried to be more comprehensive with the list of chatelaines, which also includes ladies who appear to rule larger territories than a single castle and its lands. The number of unwed ladies we find to all appearances ruling the daily administration of their castles suggests that the case of the castle of Lestroite Marche, which the lord's daughter was for some reason unable to hold after her father's death, was unusual. Generally speaking, when a chatelaine marries, her husband appears to become the castellan, as in the case of the Lady of Galvoie and Sir Gaidon. The wife, of course, would take the rule again in her husband's absence.

Both lists include names of known castles.

CASTELLANS

Agravadain (Des Mares)
Bellangere (Magouns)
Broades (Castle of La Fontaine des Deux Sycamor)
Lord of Beloe Castle
Berluse (lieutenant of Sir Tor's castle)
Bertilak (Hautdesert)
Bleoberis (Ganis)

Brandus des Illes (Dolorous Garde)
Breunor (Castle Pluere)
Brian of the Isles (Pendragon)
Sir Carados (Dolorous Tower)
Clochides (Le Tertre Deuee)
Damas
Druas (Druas' Hill)
Ector (Arthur's foster-father)

Edward & Hue of the Red Castle
Gaidon (Galvoie)
Galihodin (Peningue)
Geraint
Grim Baron (Castle Hewin)
Guinas
Helain de Taningues
Earl Hernox (Carteloise)
The Maimed Knight?
Marigart (Guindoel)
Maten (Blanche Espine)
Meliagrance (Four Stones?)

Nabon le Noire (Isle of Servage)
Nerovens de Lile (Pendragon, under La Cote Male Taile)
Count del Parc (Turquine's Hill)
Persant of Inde
Persides (Gazewilte)
Plenorius & Brothers (Castle at border of Surluse)
Duke de la Rowse
Segwarides (Isle of Servage)
Selises of the Dolorous Tower?[1]
Sornehan (Druas' Hill)
Turquine (Turquine's Hill)

[1] Presumably, in Malory's version, Lancelot would have given Selises the Dolorous Tower after conquering Carados. In the Vulgate, Sir Melians li Gai becomes lord of the Dolorous Tower after Lancelot wins it.

CHATELAINES

Anglides (Magouns)
Annowre
The Damsel of La Beale Regard
Benigne (Gloucedon)
The Lady of Briestoc
Camille (La Roche)
Ettard
The Lady of Galvoie
Damoisele a la Harpe (Castel de la Harpe?)
Hellawes (Castle Nigramous)
The Damsel of Hongrefort
Lady of the Launds?
The Damsel of Leverzep
Lile of Avelion?

Lyonors (Castle Dangerous)
Lyzianor (Karadigan)
Lore (Branlant)
The Lady of Malohaut
The Lady of the Marches
Morgana le Fay
The Lady of Nohaut
The Countess of Orofoise
Oruale (Guindoel)
The Lady of the Rock
The Lady of Roestoc
The Lady of the Rule?
The "Uncourteous Lady"
Lady de Vawse?

Damsels & Ladies

For more ladies, see Workers of Magic, this appendix. I left most of the female practitioners of magic off this list to avoid too much duplication. There are, however, inconsistencies. For example, Lynette is so widely known as a plain damsel that I included her on both lists. Helaes de la Forest Perilleuse (Damsels, class II), and Hellawes (Workers of Magic, class II), may well be the same woman. So may be Sebille (Damsels, II) and Sebile (Workers of Magic, III).

My impression is that the title "Lady" carries a slightly more

enhanced connotation, as of age, marital status, or authority, than the title "Damsel" (or "Damosel"); but the difference seems so slight that in most cases the terms Lady and Damsel are as good as synonymous. Nimue is called the Lady of the Lake and the Damosel of the Lake interchangeably, and the term Damosel of the Lake persists after her marriage. "Dame" is a term of address and respect for women, the approximate equivalent of "Sir" for men: Dame Guenevere, Dame Laurel, etc.

CLASS I

Amable
Amide
Avenable (Grisandoles)
Beauvivante
Bragwaine
Elaine of Astolat
Elaine of Carbonek
Elyzabel

Ettard
Genievre
Igraine
La Beale Isoud
Isoud la Blanche Mains
Lynette
Margawse

CLASS II

King Agrippe's Daughter
Alice la Beale Pilgrim
King Amans' Daughter
Anglides
"Automne"
King Bagdemagus' Daughter
The Damsel of La Beale Regard
King Brandegoris' Daughter
Queen Elaine of Benwick
Queen Elaine of Garloth (Elaine of Tintagil)
Enid
"Été"
Queen Evaine
Felelolie

Floree
Helaes de la Forest Perilleuse
Sir Herlew's Land (Balin's Lady)
The Damsel of Hongrefort
Laurel
Lile of Avilion
Lore of Carduel
Lyonors
Lyzianor
The Lady of Malohaut
"Malvis"
The Damsel des Marches
Perse
"Printemps"
Ragnell

The Lady of Roestoc
Sebille

Sir Segwarides' Wife
The Queen of the Waste Lands

CLASS III

"Astrigis"
The Lady of Beloe
Benigne
Byanne
The Damoisele de la Blanche Lande
The Lady of Briestoc
"Clarisin"
Colombe
Eleine (Pellinore's Daughter)
Elaine the Peerless
Queen Elizabeth of Lyonesse
The Lady of Galvoie
King Gloier's Daughter
Damoisele à la Harpe
Helain de Taningues' Sister
Heliap
Huntress of Windsor
"Iblis"
Lady of the Launds
Lady Leech of Cornwall
Landoine
Damsel of Lestroite Marche

Damsel of Leverzep
Lore de Branlant
Lunete
Damsel of the Marches
Morgan's Damsel
The Lady of Nohaut
The King of Norgales' Daughter and her Handmaid
The Countess of Orofoise and Sister
Oruale de Guindoel
Duke Rochedon's Daughter
Lady of the Rock
"Rossignol"
Lady of the Rule
Senehauz and Daughter
Thenew
The "Uncourteous Lady"
Lady de Vance
Lady de Vawse
Lady "Verrine"
La Veuve Dame de la Gaste Forest Soutaine

Dwarves

Dwarves appear everywhere, usually as servants. They often seem to fill a role similar to that of squires, but, presumably, with no chance of becoming knights. Occasionally, as in the Vulgate, we read of the daughter or niece of a dwarf becoming the lover of a knight. I theorize that dwarves may have been members of an earlier, conquered race, the folk who are supposed to have gone into the caves and burrows as their land was engulfed by successive waves of Celts, Angles, and so on, the folk who according to one theory became the "fairies" of folklore – Sutcliff's "little dark people." There are also tales, however, of traders called Comprachicos or Comprapequenos who bought children and surgically made them into misshapen dwarves, apparently for resale.

An indication of one dwarf's size is found in Malory VII, 19:

> And then when [Sir Gringamore] saw Sir Beaumains fast asleep, he came stilly stalking behind the dwarf, and plucked him fast under his arm, and so he rode away with him as fast as ever he might unto his own castle.

A dwarf of Morgana's is described as having "a great mouth and a flat nose" [Malory IV, 8]. I wonder if the term "dwarf" might not have become at least partially synonymous with a certain type of servant, so that not all "dwarves" were actually members of a dwarvish race or mutilated children.

Whether a dwarf could serve as a physical bodyguard is doubtful, but dwarves may show considerable intelligence and resourcefulness. Dame Elyzabel once travelled from Britain to Gaul on a fairly dangerous mission with a squire and a dwarf as – seemingly – her only companions.

As an example of master-dwarf relationships, Gareth and his damsel came to a pavilion. The master was gone, but the dwarf was ready to welcome them provisionally on his master's permission. When the master came back, however, he began beating his dwarf for extending even this much courtesy unauthorized. Gareth thrashed the master and made him beg his dwarf's pardon. The dwarf forgave his master on condition he would never lay hands on him again and would bear him no grudge. [Vulgate V]

For all their importance as a class, I do not remember one dwarf who is given a name. The only one I have included in 'People' is Gareth's Dwarf.

Giants

The size of giants varies. The Giant of St. Michael's Mount was probably the biggest, if we take the fact that he split Hoel's wife to the navel while forcing her as indicative of his size – a regular ogre of the "Jack the Giant Killer" tradition. Hargodabrans, the Saxon, was fifteen feet tall. Galapas' size may perhaps be judged by Arthur's remark after cutting off his legs to the knees: "Now art thou better of a size to deal with than thou were." Some giants were small enough to ride horseback, like Nabon le Noire and Taulas. Taulas' brother Taulurd, however, was too big for any horse. Carados of the Dolorous Tower is said to have been "made like a giant"; this may mean simply that he was an especially large man. If it means that he was in every sense a "giant," then the same should be said of his brother Sir Turquine. Lucius' Bodyguard was fifty giants reputedly engendered of fiends. Chances seem good that the giants were or were considered a race apart; the smaller ones at least, though, seem to have been capable of interbreeding with humans. Duke Galeholt was said to be the son of a "beautiful giantess." (Of course, Galeholt is also the reputed son of the wicked

Sir Breunor of Castle Pluere.) There may, perhaps, have been more than one species of giant. It is even possible that at one time the giants had been equated with the Saxons, though I would not care to make too much of that theory at this time. As the Bible says somewhere, "There were giants in the earth in those days ..."

As it happens, all the giants here listed are more or less villains, Hargodabrans probably being the best, since he seems to have been a political foe of Arthur's rather than a dabbler in rapine and murder for the sake of blood. I can conceive, however, of the possibility of a good giant in an Arthurian setting.

I did not include the Green Knight (Bercilak de Hautdesert) among the giants because his size comes from Morgana's enchantment.

Carados of the Dolorous Tower?	Nabon le Noire
Galapas	Giant of St. Michael's Mount (France)
Hargodabrans	Giants of Tintagil
Lucius' Bodyguard	Taulas
Mauduit	Taulurd
Giant of the Mount of Araby	Turquine?

Holy Folk

A question mark after the character's name indicates that we would expect the character to be more holy than secular, but one or two actions cast suspicion on his or her personal holiness. A number of these characters, especially the hermits, recluses, and monastic religious, were previously secular figures, knights, and rulers. Pellam is perhaps the only monarch in Arthur's time to fill the functions of ruler and religious leader simultaneously — he has a unique role as guardian of the Grail.

Joseph and his son Josephe were contemporaries of Christ. They appear in visions in Arthur's time. Mordrains and Nascien were contemporaries of Joseph, whose lives have been miraculously prolonged. Except for Joseph and possibly Dubric, I found no historical saint in the Arthurian romances, although Glennie and Brewer try more or less to tie in David, Kentigern, Monenna, and Thenew with Arthur. I have added these and a few other historical or legendary saints to the list below. Any other saint of the fifth or sixth century, especially one who appeared in the British Isles or Gaul, could of course be added equally well, and even the earlier saints might be included as not unlikely to appear in vision to Arthur's contemporaries. Nor do I see any reason why the Wandering Jew should not appear in Arthur's world. Since the real historical or legendary saints do not appear in the Arthurian romances I examined, I put them in class II, regardless of their importance outside Arthurian tales.

CLASS I

Amide	Bors de Ganis?
Baudwin of Britain[1]	Archbishop of Canterbury

St. Dubric	Nascien (Nacien)
Elaine of Carbonek?	King Pellam?
Galahad	Percivale
Joseph of Arimathea	The Pope
Josephe	The Queen of the Waste Lands
King Mordrains	

CLASS II

Amustans	Gildas?
Bishop Baldwin[1]	St. Kentigern
St. Brandan	St. Monenna
Claudin	St. Patrick
St. Columba	King Pellam's Sister
St. David	The Bishop of Rochester
Queen Elaine of Benwick	St. Servanus
Eliazar of Carbonek	Thenew?
Bishop Eugene	"Verrine"

CLASS III

Adragain	"Iblis"
"Blevine"	Brother Ogrins
Brasias	"Rossignol"
Queen Evaine	Suffragan of Carlisle
Gawaine (Hermit)[2]	Ulfin

[1] Baudwin of Britain and Bishop Baldwin may be the same man; Baudwin seems, however, better known as knight and hermit than as bishop.

[2] Do not confuse with his more famous namesake, Sir Gawaine of the Round Table.

Kings

Including Dukes and a Few Counts

Unless another title is given, "King" is to be understood. I tried to be fairly complete about catching the names of kings, and class III is full of fellows who would have been omitted completely had they been mere knights. Notice, however, that most or all kings are also knights, although, to avoid too much duplication, I have only re-listed among Knights those kings who seem particularly active in their knightly roles. That Arthur is above class I should go without saying.

I have given the names of their holdings or a part of their holdings where known. Many characters are named as kings, but I could never ferret out of what. (Some general areas may be indicated in the appropriate area in 'People.')

This note does not reflect the array of rulers at any one instant in Arthur's time, but is drawn from all periods of his history. Gorlois, for instance, was killed before his birth. Galahad was king of Sarras for a year following the death of Estorause. Some of the rulers, like Hermance, are dead when we first hear of them, but were presumably alive for at least a part of Arthur's reign; others, like Lot, were killed in war against Arthur himself. Possibly Tristram should be named among the kings; but, although he would have inherited Lyonesse from his father Meliodas, and although he is once or thrice called the "lord" of Lyonesse, I find no evidence in Malory that he ever went home to function as king. (Galahad, on the other hand, does seem to have functioned as administrative chief during his brief reign as king of Sarras.)

CLASS I

Agwisance of Ireland (and Scotland?)	Galahad of Sarras
Arthur	Duke Galeholt of Surluse, etc.
Bagdemagus of Gore	(Duke?) Hoel of Brittany
Ban of Benwick	The King of the Hundred Knights (in Malahaut?)
Bors (of Gaul or Gannes)	Karados of Estrangor[1]
Carados of Scotland[1]	Leodegrance of Cameliard
Claudas of Gaul	Lot of Lothian and Orkney

Lucius, Emperor of Rome	Pellinore of the Isles
Mark of Cornwall	Ryons of Northgalis, Ireland, and Many Isles
Mordrains	
Pellam of Listeneise	Uriens of Gore

CLASS II

Amans (or Aniause)	Frolle of Alemaigne
Brandegoris of Stranggore	Duke Gorlois of Tintagil
Duke Chaleins of Clarance	Idres of Cornwall
Clariance of Northumberland	Marhalt of Ireland
Cradelmas[2]	Meliodas of Lyonesse
Duke Eustace of Cambenet	Nentres of Garloth
Estorause of Sarras	King 'Premier Conquis'
Faramon of France	Yon

CLASS III

Alain of Escavalon	Harlon
Agrippe	Hermance of the Red City
Duke Ansirus the Pilgrim	Duke Lianor of the Castle of Maidens
Count Arouz of Flanders	
Arrant of Denmark	Marboar
Astlabor	Marsil of Pomitrain
Bandes	Merlan le Dyable
Belinans of Sorgales	Pannor
Duke Brandelis of Taningues	Pantelion, Master Consul of Rome
Duke Calles	Count Patrides of Flanders
Carbarecotins of Cornoaille (Brittany?)	Pignores
	Duke Ladinas de la Rowse
Clamadon	Duke of the South Marches
Duke Corneus	Thoas of Ireland
King 'Doutre les Marches'	Tradelmans of Norgales[2]
Esclamor	Vadalon
Duke Elise (an uncle of Arthur)	Vagor
Gloier of Surluse	

[1] Carados of Scotland and Karados of Estrangor may be the same man.

[2] It is possible that Cradelmas and Tradelmans are the same man.

Most of the names in class I will, I hope, ring bells instantly. A few, like Bagdemagus, Duke Galeholt, and Lamorak, may be surprises; but they are so important in Malory, the Vulgate, or both that I hope their place in class I will be understood after reading the entries about them. Many class II knights could have been comfortable in class I, such as Blamore, Bleoberis, Pelleas, and Marhaus. Similarly, I put a few knights in III who could have fit nicely into II. Companions of the Round Table are asterisked.

Group III is a mere sampling of minor knights. Some, like Ozanna le Cure Hardy and Yvonet li Avoutres, are borderline cases between II and III. Others are listed for a close relationship to someone more important, or like Marrok and Servause, for traits or adventures I found interesting. May more minor knights will be found under the Villains or Castellans sub-entries, or in the Families and Retainers lists in *People*, etc.

The three most important knights, of course — it is even tempting to put them in a class by themselves, like Arthur or Guenevere — are Gawaine, Lancelot, and Tristram. Gawaine seems to have been in the Arthurian saga longest of the three. He was originally the ideal knight as well as Arthur's favorite nephew. Although Lancelot got into the stories at least as early as the works of Chrétien de Troyes, who has been credited with inventing Arthurian romance as we know it, he is still a comparatively late addition, and undeniably the most spectacularly successful of the later, more artistic and literary creations inserted (like Prince Valiant in our own day) into the cycle. Lancelot supplanted the earlier places both of Gawaine as Arthur's greatest knight and of Mordred as Guenever's lover. Tristram may have developed independently from the Arthurian cycle, into which even today he seems less perfectly grafted than the others; although he became a companion of the Round Table, his story, unlike Lancelot's, could be told without Arthur. Gawaine and Lancelot are each at the heart of a body of relatives and followers. (Gareth, though Gawaine's favorite brother, is more nearly in Lancelot's "camp.") Among their respective kinsmen and adherents there was a certain rivalry as to which was the greater — a rivalry which could grow violent, as when Gawaine's brothers Agravaine and Gaheris slew one of Lancelot's knights at Joyous Gard for calling Lancelot the better knight [Malory X, 55]. In fairness to Gawaine's brothers, be it noted that later, when for awhile Tristram's fame eclipsed Lancelot's, Lancelot's kinsmen "would have slain Sir Tristram because of his fame," causing Lancelot to tell them that he himself would kill any relative who attacked Tristram "with any hurt, shame, or villainy" [Malory X, 88]. Despite this rivalry among their followers, Gawaine and Lancelot were themselves close friends until Lancelot accidentally slew Gawaine's brothers Gareth and Gaheris while rescuing Guenever from the stake. With the deaths of Gareth and Gaheris, the rift between the two groups became a major factor in the downfall of Arthur.

If I were called upon to add four more major knights to make up the mystic number of seven great ones, I would add Kay and Bedivere (Bedwyr) as two who have been at Arthur's side in the legends the longest, then Galahad and Percivale. Or I might substitute Ywaine for Bedivere or Percivale. Other estimates would undoubtedly differ. Sir Tristram's estimation of his contemporaries may be found in Malory IX, 43: Lancelot, Bors, Bleoberis, Blamore, and Gaheris are better than Gawaine, and Lamorak is as good as anyone except Lancelot. (Tristram omits himself for modesty.) Much later, Bors estimates Gareth the best after Lancelot, Tristram, and Lamorak [Malory XVIII, 18]. Lancelot considers Gareth possibly the equal of Tristram or Lamorak [Malory XVIII, 23]. These estimations probably take into account only prowess at arms.

CLASS I

Agravaine*	Kay*
King Bagdemagus*	Lamorak de Galis*
Bedivere*	Lancelot*
Bors de Ganis*	Lionel*
Breuse sans Pitie*	Lucan the Butler*
Dinadan*	Mador de la Porte*
Ector de Maris*	Mordred*
Gaheris*	Palomides*
Galahad*	King Pellinore*
Duke Galeholt*	Percivale*
Gareth (Beaumains)*	Sagramore le Desirous*
Gawaine*	Tristram*
Griflet*	Ywaine*

CLASS II

Accolon of Gaul	Dinas*
Aglovale*	Dodinas le Savage*
Alisander le Orphelin	Dornar*
Andred	Ector (Arthur's foster father)
Balan	Florence*
Balin le Savage	Geraint (or Erec)*
Barant le Apres (The King of the Hundred Knights)*	Gingalin*
Baudwin of Britain *?	Grisandoles (Avenable)
Bertholai	Helin le Blank*
Bertilak de Hautdesert (The Green Knight)	Hervise de Revel*
	Ironside (The Red Knight)*
Blamore de Ganis*	Lovel*
Bleoberis de Ganis*	Marhaus*
Borre*	Meliagrance*
Brastias*?	Oriolz (Ogier?) the Dane
Carados of the Dolorous Tower	Pelleas*
Claudin	Safere*
Colgrevance of Gore*	Segwarides*
Constantine*	Tor*
La Cote Male Taile (Sir Breunor le Noir)*	Turquine (Terican)
	Ulfius*?
	Urre of Hungary*

CLASS III

Bellengerus le Beuse*	Lavaine*
Belleus*	Lionses
Belliance le Orgulous*	The Maimed Knight
Prince Boudwin	Marrok*
Brandiles*	Meliot de Logres*
Bromel la Pleche	Ozanna le Cure Hardy*
Brumant l'Orguilleus	Patrise*
Cador of Cornwall*	Pinel le Savage*
Elias	Pedivere of the Straight Marches
Eliazar of Carbonek	Percard ("The Black Knight")
Epinegris*	Perimones ("The Red Knight")*
Evadeam	Persant of Inde*
Earl Fergus*	Pertolepe ("The Green Knight")*
Galeshin*	Pharien
Galleron of Galway*	Priamus*
Gringamore	Sadok*?
Harry de Fise Lake*	Servause le Breuse*
Hermind (Erminide)*	Yvonet le Avoutres*
Kehydius	

Knights of the Round Table

and Other Folk of Arthur's Court

A question mark after the name of a knight in the Round Table list indicates that he is pretty well established as having been of Arthur's court for at least a time and his known stature or some other evidence suggests he would have been a companion of the Table. The parenthesized word (late) after a companion's name indicates that he only became a member of the Round Table on the eve of Arthur's downfall — Gaheres took Gareth's seat, Helyan Lancelot's, Bellinor that of Bors de Ganis, and Vadalon that of Ector de Maris after the split between Arthur and Lancelot, even though Lancelot, Bors, and Ector were still alive.

These lists do not reflect Arthur's court at any given moment. For instance, Tristram only became a member of the court and companion of the Round Table some time after Marhaus' death at Tristram's own hands. (Tristram took Marhaus' seat.) Even those knights alive at the same time would rarely if ever have all been present at court at once. Knights, Round Table and otherwise, were continually leaving on missions, quests, and other adventures. Lancelot had a habit of going off incognito without telling anyone ahead of time, while some knights, like Tristram, Pelleas, and Galahad, seem to have spent hardly any of their lives at Arthur's court.

The men of the "Other Folk" list are knights unless otherwise labelled. Some may have belonged to the Table. Probably many or most of the Round Table knights created by Arthur were Queen's Knights first. The large number of question marks behind ladies' names reflects the fact that many of these dames were wives or lovers of the knight, which does not necessarily mean that they remained at court. Nimue, for instance, seems to have stayed most of the time at home in her Lake. Margawse appears, from the Vulgate account, to have left her husband Lot when he was rebelling against Arthur, at the same time she was encouraging her sons to join Arthur's side. Lot was killed in battle. On this basis, I put Margawse among the dames of Arthur's court, but do not know how long this may have lasted.

I have not attempted a complete list of all known knights of the Round Table, but only those actually to be found in the 'People' section. Some, however, only appear in the notes for other characters; for instance, the King of the Lake and Sir Galagars are found in the notes for Sir Griflet, Sir Plaine de Force in those for Sir Plenorius. I have left off the titles "King" and "Duke" except where they seemed necessary for identification. The relative importance of these characters is unjudged.

KNIGHTS OF THE ROUND TABLE

Aglovale	Colgrevance
Agravaine	Constantine
Agwisance	La Cote Male Taile (Sir Breunor
Bagdemagus	le Noir)
Baudwin of Britain?	Dinadan
Bedivere	Dinas
Bellengerus le Beuse	Dodinas le Savage
Belleus	Dornar
Belliance le Orgulus	Ector de Maris
Bellinor (late)	Edward of Orkney
Blamore de Ganis	Epinegris
Bleoberis de Ganis	Florence
Borre (Lohot)	Gaheres (late)
Bors de Ganis	Gaheris
Brandiles	Galagars
Brastias?	Galahad
Cador of Cornwall[1]	Duke Galeholt
King Carados of Scotland[1]	Galeshin[2]
Chaleins[2]	Galihodin
Clariance of Northumberland	Galleron

[1] It is possible that Karados of Estrangor is the same man as either Cador of Cornwall or Carados of Scotland.

[2] It is possible that Chaleins and Galeshin are the same man.

Gareth	Mordred
Gawaine	Nentres of Garloth
Geraint (Erec)	Nerovens de Lile
Gingalin	Ozanna le Cure Hardy
Griflet	Palomides
Grummore Grummursum	Patrise
Harry le Fise Lake	Pelleas
Hebes le Renoumes	Pellinore
Helin le Blank	Percivale
Helyan of Ireland (late)	Perimones
Hermind	Persant
Hervise de Revel	Pertolepe
Ironside	Pinel le Savage
Kainus le Strange	Plaine de Force
Karados of Estrangor[1]	Plenorius
Kay	Priamus
King of the Hundred Knights	Sadok?
King of the Lake	Safere
Lambegus	Sagramore
Lamorak	Segwarides?
Lancelot	Sentraille de Lushon
Lavaine	Servause le Breuse
Lionel	Tor
Lovel	Tristram
Lucan the Butler	Ulbawes
Mador de la Porte	Ulfius?
Marhaus	Uriens of Gore
Marrok	Urre of Hungary
Meliagrance	Vadalon (late)
Melias de Lile	Yvonet li Avoutres
Meliot de Logres	Ywaine

OTHER FOLK OF ARTHUR'S COURT: MEN

Accolon of Gaul	Guiomar
Amustans (Arthur's chaplain)	Hue of the Red Castle?
Angis (squire)	Ider
Axilles (squire)	Kanahins (squire)
Bertholai (for a time)	Lanceor
Bromel le Pleche?	Manassen
Dagonet (Arthur's jester)	Melehan?
Damas	Merlin (the great mage)
Dubric (archbishop)	Persides de Bloise?
Eliezer (squire)	Taliessin (bard)
Eugene (bishop)?	Yon

OTHER FOLK OF ARTHUR'S COURT: WOMEN

Beauvivante	Lore of Carduel (the King's
Colombe	Cup-bearer)
Elyzabel	Lynette?
Enid?	Lyonors?
Felelolie	Margawse?
Floree?	Morgan le Fay (for a time)
Genievre (Queen for a time)	Nimue?
Guenever	Perse?
Heliap?	Ragnell
Igraine?	Senehauz
Laudine?	Veraide?
Laurel	"Verrine"

Lovers

This is a rundown on relationships and would-be relationships. It includes notable "passes" on the part of one person or the other, even though the attempted amour was never requited nor consummated. It also includes one-night stands. It may not include all cases of one party, usually the woman, nourishing a crush from afar on some knight, usually Lancelot. It does include marriages and triangles. It is probably incomplete. I have tried to give spouses and paramours in the 'People' section.

AGRAVAINE: Laurel
ALISANDER LE ORPHELIN: Alice la Beale Pilgrim, the Damsel of la Beale Regard?, Morgana
ARTHUR: Annowre, Camille, Genievre, Guenever, Lyzianor, Margawse, Sister of the Countess of Orofoise

BALIN: Sir Herlew's Lady?
BORS DE GANIS: King Brandegoris' Daughter
KING CLAUDAS: Sir Phariance's Wife
LA COTE MALE TAILE: Beauvivante
ECTOR DE MARIS: Damsel of Lestroite Marche, Perse
ELEINE: Miles
ELAINE OF CARBONEK: Bromel la Pleche, Lancelot
EVADEAM: Byanne
GAHERIS: Damoisele de la Blanche Lande, "Clarisin," "Iblis," Lynette
GALAHAD: Amide (platonic)
THE LADY OF GALVOIE: Gaidon de Galvoie
GARETH: Lyonors (Tennyson says Lynette)

GAWAINE: The Lady of Beloe, Sir Brandile's Sister[1], Floree[1], Helaes, Helain de Taningue's Sister, Hellawes, Lore de Branlant, the King of Norgales' Daughter, Ragnell, the Lady of Roestoc?

GUENEVERE: Arthur, Lancelot, Meliagrant

LA BEALE ISOUD: Kehydius, Mark, Palomides, Tristram

LANCELOT: Amable (platonic), Elaine of Astolat, Elaine of Carbonek, Guenevere, Hellawes, the Lady of Malohaut

LANCEOR: Colombe

LAVAINE: Felelolie

KING LEODEGRANCE: Sir Cleodalis' Wife

LIONEL: Seraide

THE LADY OF MALOHAUT: Duke Galeholt, Lancelot

MARGAWSE: Arthur, Lamorak, King Lot

MERLIN: Nimue and/or Viviane

[1] Sir Brandiles' Sister and Floree are probably the same person.

MORGANA LE FAY: Accolon, Guiomar, Hemison, King Uriens

NIMUE: Merlin, Pelleas

PELLEAS: Ettard, Nimue

KING PELLINORE: Lady of the Rule, Vayshoure, La Veuve Dame de la Gaste Forest Soutaine

PERSE: Ector de Maris, Zelotes

PERSIDES OF GAZEWILTE: Elaine the Peerless

EMPEROR OF ROME: Avenable

KING RYONS: Lady de Vance

SAGRAMOR: Heliap, Handmaid of the King of Norgales' Daughter, Senehauz

SENEHAUZ: Blios, Sagramor

TRISTRAM: La Beale Isoud, Isoud la Blanche Mains, Sir Segwarides' Wife

YWAINE: Laudine

Non-Britons

Some of the ladies listed in these groups may, of course, have been brought to the territories in question by their husbands. For instance, Igraine's daughters Margawse, Elaine, and Morgana surely must be called Cornish, but about Igraine herself there is room for doubt.

The Cornish, of course, are Britons; still, in view of the common, frequently-disproved references in Malory to the poor quality of Cornish knights – probably the contemporary equivalent of our "Polish" jokes – it seemed advisable to get the Cornish knights and dames together.

CORNISH

Amant	King Idres
Andred	Igraine
Anglides	Lambegus?
Argius	Lady Leech
Bersules	Margawse
Boudwin	King Mark
Cador	Morgan le Fay
Constantine	Matto le Breune?
Dinas	Meliodas
Elaine of Tintagil	Meraugis de Porlesquez
Elizabeth of Lyonesse	Brother Ogrins
Earl Fergus	Sadok
Gorlois	Sir Segwarides' Wife?
Gouvernail?	Sentraille de Lushon?
Hebes le Renoumes?	Tristram

AREAS OF MODERN-DAY FRANCE

Accolon of Gaul	Earl Grip
Adragain?	Gwenbas
King Ban	Helyes of Thoulouse
King Bors	Hoel
Bors de Ganis	Isoud la Blanche Mains
Brumant l'Orguilleus	Kehydius
Carbarecotins	Lancelot
Chanart	Lionses
King Claudas	Lionel
Claudin	Phariance
Dorin	"Rossignol"
Elaine of Benwick	Seraide
Evaine	Viviane
King Faramon and Daughter	Yon?

IRISH

Agwisance	Lady of the Launds
Bragwaine	Marhalt
Columba	Marhaus
Galleron	Monenna
Helyan	Patrise
La Beale Isoud	Thoas
Lanceor	

SARACENS

Astlabor	Priamus
Corsabrin	Safere
Palomides	Segwarides

SAXONS (SESSIONS)

(Including allies and sympathizers, although living in Britain.)

Aliphansin	Maaglant
Arcaus	Margondes
Breuse sans Pitie (sympathizer?)	Medelant?
Camille	Minadus
Clarions	Oriel
Elias	Ossa Cylellaur
Duke Galeholt?	Pignores (ally)
Gondefle	Soriondes
Guinemans?	Sornigrieu
Hargodabrans	Thoas
Hertant	

OTHER

Count Arouz (Flanders)	Lucius, Emperor of Rome
King Arrant (Denmark)	Melias de Lile (Denmark)
Avenable (Italy?)	King Mordrains
King Estorause (Sarras)	Nascien
Felelolie (Hungary)	Oriolz (Denmark)
King Frolle (Alemaigne)	Pantelion (Rome)
Hontzlake of Wentland?	Sebille (Sarmenie)
Joseph of Arimathea	Sagramore (Constantinople)
Josephe (Arimathea)	Urre (Hungary)

Seneschals

(with their lords)

A seneschal was the household official of a king or noble who administered justice and controlled the domestic arrangements; by extension a seneschal might govern a town, a city, or a province for a great nobleman.

The lord of the seneschal is given in parentheses after the name of the seneschal himself.

Claellus (Pellam)	Bruns de Branlant (Dame Lore de Branlant)
Cleodalis (Leodegran)	
Dinas (Mark)	Marganor (King of the Hundred Knights)
Floemus (Lot?)	
Grisandoles (Emperor of Rome)	Minadoras (Pellam)
Kay (Arthur)	Phariance (Claudas)

Special Cases

OLDER KNIGHTS include knights known to be older, or assumed to be so on reasonable, at the beginning of Arthur's reign. Arthur ruled long enough to that knights young at the beginning of his reign had time to age, seeing sons and possibly even grandsons grow to manhood; no attempt has been made to list "younger knights."

Adragain	Galagars
Agravadain	Hervise de Revel
Baudwin of Britain	King of the Lake
Bercilak de Hautdesert	King Lot
Bertholai	Lionses
Brastias	King Nentres
Breunor of Pluere	Phariance
Cleodalis	Duke of the South Marches
Duke Corneus	Ulfius
Ector (father of Kay)	King Uriens

OLDER LADIES (at the beginning of Arthur's reign):

Anglides?	Igraine
"Automne"	"Ornagrine"?
Brisen?	La Veuve Dame de la Gaste Forest
Elaine of Benwick?	Soutaine?
Evaine?	Queen of the Waste Lands
Elizabeth?	

SEVERAL CENTURIES OLD: King Mordrains, Nascien, Oriolz?

NON-WHITES(?): King Astlabor, Corsabrin, Palomides, Priamus, Safere, Segwarides

A WEREWOLF KNIGHT: Marrok

A LEFT-HANDER?: Urre of Hungary

A KNIGHT WHO SPECIALIZES IN FIGHTING GIANTS, DRAGONS, AND BEASTS RATHER THAN OTHER KNIGHTS: Servause le Breuse

FEMALE KNIGHTS have precedent in romantic literature — Bradamante of the Roland legends, for instance — but the only known female fighter I have found connected with Arthurian romance is Grisandoles, who is shown more as squire and seneschal than warrior, and who is met in Rome during an unwarlike interlude of Merlin's. The other ladies listed below are included because of personal bias, which may have led me to strain my interpretation of the evidence.

Damsel of La Beale Regard	Lore of Carduel
Byanne	Lyzianor
Grisandoles (Avenable)	Sebille
Huntress of Windsor	

Villains

A list of villains is trickier to compile than you might suppose. The following list includes both Arthur's political enemies, like Claudas, and persons who must have been criminally inclined by anybody's standards, like Breuse Sans Pitie. It makes no distinction between persons whose villainy was confined pretty much to the family circle, like Persides of Gazewilte, and persons who attacked folk in general, like Merlan le Dyable. Some villains are listed on the basis of a single incident, others on the basis of a career of infamy.

A great many knights not listed here below are acting as villains when we first meet them — for instance, Sir Ironside. The pattern is that a knight of the Round Table conquers such a man and sends him to Arthur's court, where he reforms and usually becomes a knight of the Round Table himself. Many of the villains on the list below might likewise have reformed if they had not been killed first. Generally, I have tried to keep the reformed villains, like Ironside and Pedivere, off the list of Villains.

Moreover, some of the "good knights, even Lancelot himself, are sometimes guilty of actions much worse than the deeds recorded of some of the folk below. Agravaine and Gaheris could well have fit into the list of villains. A career of evil-doing does not necessarily detract from the respect and admiration that a knight of prowess may win.

Morgana le Fay has to be listed among the villains — for so great a part of Arthur's reign, she is one of his and Guenever's chief antagonists. On the other hand, she is also the chief of the queens who come at the last to bear Arthur off to Avilion, at which time her grief for him seems sincere.

More villains will be found among the giants and the non-Britons portion of this Appendix and in the 'Places' section.

CLASS I

Bertholai	King Mark of Cornwall
Breuse Sans Pitie	Queen Morgan le Fay
Camille	Mordred
Carados of the Dolorous Tower	"Nineve"
King Claudas of Gaul	Turquine
Genievre	

CLASS II

Andred	"Malvis"?
Annowre	Meliagrance
Brandus des Illes	Nabon le Noire
Breunor of Castle Pluere	Queen of Northgalis
Brian of the Isles	Queen of the Out Isles
Queen of Eastland	Pinel
Garlon	King Ryons
Grim Baron of Castle Hewin	Sebille
Hellawes	

CLASS III

Arcaus?	Hontzlake of Westland
Argustus?	Loraine le Savage
Arnold and Gherard le Breuse	Malgrin
Aselaphes (a demon)	Marigart
"Astrigis"	Maten?
Bertelot	Melehan?
Bertolle	Merlan le Dyable
The Brown Knight without Pity	Morgan's Damsel?
Clochides	Nero
Corsabrin	Peris de Forest Savage
Damas	Persides of Gazewilte
Druas	Phelot and Wife
Edward and Hue of the Red Castle	Sornehan
King Estorause of Sarras	The "Uncourteous Lady"
Heliades?	Vadalon?

Workers of Magic

CLASS I — Merlin, Morgana le Fay, Nimue[1], Viviane[1].

CLASS II

Annowre	Gwenbaus	Helyes of Thoulouse?
Bleise	Hellawes	Seraide
Camille	"Nineve"[1]	

CLASS III

Dame Brisen	Lunete?
Byanne?	Lynette (The Damosel Savage)
Queen of Eastland[2]	Queen of Northgalis
The Foul Ladye?	Queen of the Out Isles
Ganieda?	"Ornagrine"?
Garlon?	Sebille
Lile of Avelion?	Queen of Sorestan[2] [1]

[1] Damosel (or Lady) of the Lake.
[2] The Queen of Eastland and the Queen of Sorestan are probably the same woman.

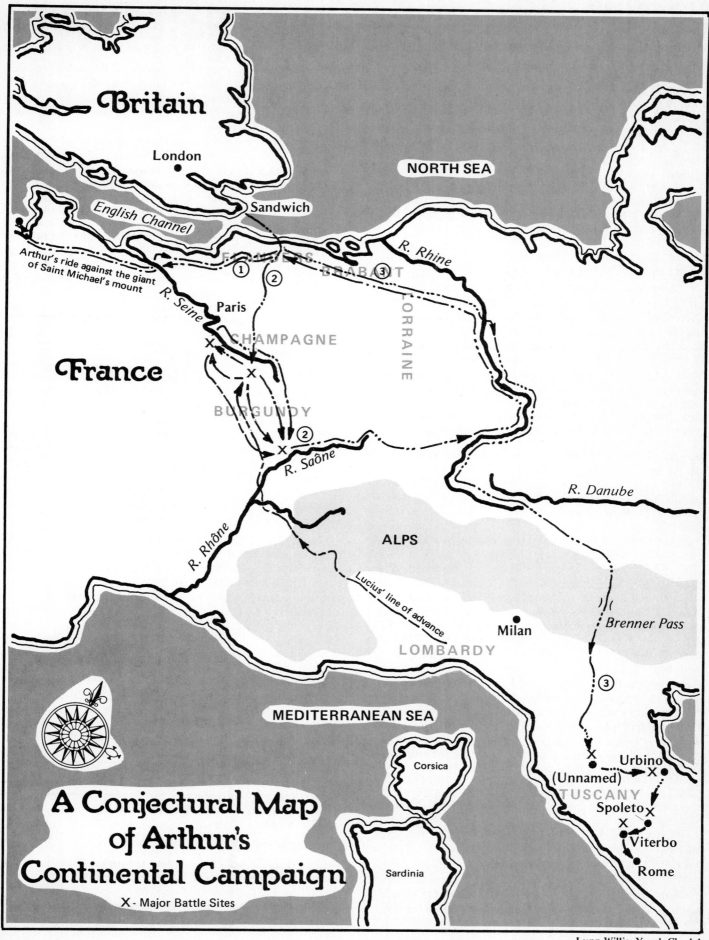

Britain

London

NORTH SEA

English Channel

Sandwich

FLANDERS

R. Rhine

Arthur's ride against the giant of Saint Michael's mount

BRABANT

LORRAINE

① ②

③

R. Seine

Paris

CHAMPAGNE

France

X

X

BURGUNDY

R. Danube

X ②

R. Saône

ALPS

R. Rhône

Lucius' line of advance

Milan

Brenner Pass

LOMBARDY

③

MEDITERRANEAN SEA

Corsica

X

(Unnamed)

Urbino

X

A Conjectural Map
of Arthur's
Continental Campaign

TUSCANY

Spoleto

X

X- Major Battle Sites

Sardinia

Viterbo

Rome

Lynn Willis; Yurek Chodak

Bibliographical Note

I had intended to attempt a longish bibliography of all the titles in my personal Arthurian collection plus a few more for which I have the necessary information. But it seems that every month at least one or two new Arthurian titles are published, besides the older ones that are constantly coming to my attention; so I decided to list here only those volumes that remained constantly at my elbow. The other sources, those I used less frequently, are (I hope) sufficiently identified where cited. Anything like a comprehensive bibliography of Arthurian books and Arthurian-related material would probably be an effort at least as long as the whole of this present book.

Malory, Sir Thomas. **Le Morte D'Arthur; The Book of King Arthur and His Knights of the Round Table.**

There are many editions of this work. My copy has the imprint: New Hyde Park, N.Y.: University Books, c1961; being a one-volume reprint of A.W.Pollard's version as printed in 1920 for the Medici Society. The index is so faulty that I demand it share the blame with me for any mistakes and overlooked references I have made! I do not claim this is the best edition of Malory ever printed, nor even the best presently in print; but it had the great advantage of being the one I had ready to hand, in a personal copy suitable for hard use; and it also has Book and Chapter divisions labelled as originating with Caxton, which facilitates making references.

A superb edition of Malory for the reader who would like to sample the flavor of the original is **Arthur Pendragon of Britain; A Romantic Narrative** by Sir Thomas Malory as edited from **Le Morte D'Arthur** by John W. Donaldson, Illustrated by Andrew Wyeth. New York: G.P. Putnam's Sons [c1943]

Donaldson went on the principle that Malory *would* have edited and improved his work if he had had the chance — so Donaldson attempted to do it for him, cut the length of the book roughly in half, and succeeded admirably in making a coherent narrative of the books of Tristram ... but kept Malory's own language, with a minimum of minor verbal changes (aside from the cuts) everywhere except in the Grail Adventures. I was far from satisfied with the way Donaldson handled the Grail Adventures; the condensing of Tristram's adventures unfortunately cut out most of the episodes where Palomides shows to best advantage and only left those where he shows to worst; and Donaldson's apparent unawareness of the looseness with which terms of relationship were used led him to change Bors de Ganis from Lancelot's cousin to his nephew — with these cautions, I recommend Donaldson's version Very Highly Indeed. I do not recommend Keith Baines' retelling in modern prose, however.

The Vulgate Version of the Arthurian Romances. Edited from manuscripts in the British Museum by H. Oskar Sommer. Washington: The Carnegie Institution of Washington, 1909-1916. 8 v. (Vol. VIII is an index; vol. VII is a fragmentary romance supplementary to rather than continuing the cycle as presented in the first six volumes.)

The text of this is in medieval French, so I do not pretend I combed every page. But Sommer provided what seems to be a pretty complete summary in English glosses on every page of the first six volumes, and even from these the riches of the Vulgate version are obvious. Quotations identified as from the Vulgate are quotations of Sommer's English summary unless otherwise identified or in French. Names drawn from the Vulgate are generally in Sommer's standardizations. The AMS press appears to be making some gesture toward keeping the Vulgate in print at a typically outrageous scholarly price, but I have not yet at the time of revising this handbook been able to obtain the volumes, and have had to depend on the notes made some time ago now, which were done, of necessity, in haste, and may not always be perfectly reliable.

These were my two major sources. The works of Chrétien de Troyes would have been given equal weight with Malory and the Vulgate, but unfortunately as of this time I have been able to obtain only two — **Yvain** and **Perceval** — in a text I can use (**Yvain** in a modern French prose translation and **Perceval** in modern English prose, both more or less satisfactory as far as getting information, but clearly inferior to the medieval French verse original.) I also have **Yvain** and **Cliges** in editions reproducing the original French verse, with German introductions and notes — the German is useless to me, alas. As nearly as I can make out from various sources, the Vulgate version of Meliagrant's kidnapping of Guenever is much closer to Chrétien's **Le Chevalier de la Charette** than is Malory's version.

The introduction and notes to my Dell edition of **Yvain** have been of as much use as the text: **Yvain, ou Le Chevalier au Lion,** [by] Chrétien de Troyes; translated into modern French by André Mary; introduction and notes by Julian Harris. New York: Dell Publishing Co., c1963 (The Laurel Language Library; Germaine Bree, General Editor, French Series).

The Middle English metrical romances constitute a fourth rich source of Arthurian story more or less compatible with Malory and the Vulgate. The most famous and almost certainly the best of these romances is, of course, **Sir Gawaine and the Green Knight**, published in many, many editions, translations both verse and prose, and new versions over the last century or so. My favorite translation is that of John Gardner (in **The Complete Works of the Gawaine-Poet; in a Modern English Version with a Critical Introduction** by John Gardner, Woodcuts by Fritz Kredel. Chicago & London: University of Chicago Press, c1965. Currently available in paperback). A number of other metrical romances are currently available in modern English prose translations in **The Knightly Tales of Sir Gawain**, with introductions and translations by Louis B. Hall (Chicago: Nelson-Hall, c1976). This volume includes **Sir Gawaine and the Carl of Carlisle; The Green Knight** (an alternate version to the famous one mentioned above); **The Adventures at Tarn Wadling; Gologros and Gawain; An Adventure of Sir Gawain; The Avowing of King Arthur, Sir Gawain, Sir Kay, and Baldwin of Britain;** and **The Wedding of Sir Gawain and Dame Ragnell.**

Also constantly at my side was:

Glennie, John S. Stuart. **Arthurian Localities; Their Historical Origin, Chief Country, and Fingalian Relations** ... Edinburgh: Edmonton and Douglas, 1869. vi, 140 p. map.

The chief difficulty in using Glennie was that he wanted to put almost *all* Arthurian sites in southern Scotland and northernmost England. Also, his references to characters are often more tantalizing than enlightening.

After using the Edinburgh edition in a library, I acquired another copy, printed in **Merlin, or The Early History of King Arthur: A Prose Romance (about 1450-1460 A.D.),** edited ... by Henry B. Wheatley; Part [i.e., vol.] III. London: Early English Text Society, ca. 1869; reprinted 1938 by Kegan Paul, Trench, Trübner & Co. for the Society. This printing has the work paginated in lower-case Roman numerals, [xvii] to cxlvi; and the numerals do not coincide with the Arabic pagination of the Edinburgh edition. Where I have cited Glennie with Arabic page numbers, the reference is to the Edinburgh ed. and drawn from my notes; where I have used Roman numerals, the reference is to the EETS publication.

It is popular to slight Alfred, Lord Tennyson's **Idylls of the King** nowadays; but the only faults I find with the **Idylls** are Tennyson's treatment of Guenever and his Victorianizing of Arthurian morality and mores. Otherwise, I think Tennyson's is a lovely version, and I have been not unfavorably impressed with his scholarship. His poem of **Geraint and Enid** appears to be a recognizable version of Chretien's **Erec and Enid,** from what scraps I have been able to find of the latter. My best copy of **Idylls** is the Heritage Press edition of 1939, with illustrations in sepia and white by Robert Ball. The **Idylls** are probably absolutely the latest literary rendition which I would be tempted to use as an "authority" in any case.

For geographical work, I used:

Collier's World Atlas and Gazetteer. New York, P.F. Collier & Son Corp., c1942. Having been the family atlas for as long as I can remember, this shared with the University Books edition of Malory the great advantage of being ever-available.

Norden, John. **A Topographical and Historical Description of Cornwall.** London: Printed by W. Pearson ... 1728. Reprinted 1966 [by] Frank Graham, Newcastle Upon Tyne. Norden probably made his Survey of Cornwall in 1584, according to Graham's preface. The book makes one's mouth water for a description of the rest of Britain in the same style.

I also kept handy, in addition to the Oxford English Dictionary (The Compact Edition, complete text reproduced micrographically. Oxford University Press, 1971) and other dictionaries and standard reference works:

Brewer, E. Cobham. **The Reader's Handbook of Famous Names in Fiction, Allusions, References, Proverbs, Plots, Stories, and Poems.** A new ed., revised throughout and greatly enlarged. Philadelphia: Lippincott, 1899. Republished by Gale Research Company, Detroit, 1966. 2 v.

I confess that I am likelier to get around to reading new Arthurian novels before new books of Arthurian research. My favorite modern literary treatments so far are Rosemary Sutcliff's **Sword at Sunset,** Edison Marshall's **The Pagan King,** Vera Chapman's **Three Damosels** trilogy (**The King's Damosel, The Green Knight, King Arthur's Daughter**), John Erskine's **Tristran and Isolde** (though this one is not really "Arthurian" in that Arthur and his court do not appear), Mark Twain's **A Connecticut Yankee in King Arthur's Court,** Tennyson's **Idylls,** and T.H. White's **The Once and Future King,** which got me hooked on this whole field — if, indeed, Hal Foster's **Prince Valiant** had not already done it. Nor can I close without mentioning the film **Monty Python and the Holy Grail,** which may be to our generation what **Connecticut Yankee** was to Twain's, and which should be seen whenever possible as an antidote to taking the Arthurian legend too seriously. The present work was already in print when I obtained Thomas Berger's 1978 novel **Arthur Rex,** surely one of the grandest Arthurians of our century, although, like rare wine and fine cheese, it may be best savored slowly, in small portions.

The conviction grew greater and greater in me while working on this project, that in style and spirit Hal Foster may be the closest heir to the medieval romancers that our modern era has produced. The comic strip of our day is perhaps the most popular of "literary" mediums, as the presentations of minstrels would have been in the Middle Ages. Foster's technique of making up his own hero and inserting him into the already-existing body of Arthurian material is almost surely what many of the medieval romancers must have done through the centuries; and, had Foster lived before Malory, Val, Aleta, Arn, and others might well have gotten into Malory and thence into the present handbook.

PHYLLIS ANN KARR

has written many recent works of fiction, including *My Lady Quixote, Lady Susan, Frostflower and Thorn, Meadowsong, Perola, The Elopement, Wildraith's Last Battle,* and *Frostflower and Windbourne.* Of special interest to readers of this book is her Arthurian murder mystery, *Idylls of the Queen.* A freelance writer, the authoress lives in northern Wisconsin.